JAVA AND MODERN EUROPE

Ambiguous Encounters

JAVA AND MODERN EUROPE
Ambiguous Encounters

Ann Kumar

LONDON AND NEW YORK

First published in 1997
by Curzon Press

Published 2015 by Routledge
2 Park Square, Milton Park, Abingdon, Oxfordshire OX14 4RN
711 Third Avenue, New York, NY 10017

First issued in paperback 2015

Routledge is an imprint of the Taylor and Francis Group, an informa business

© 1997 Ann Kumar

All rights reserved. No part of this book may be reprinted or reproduced or utilised in any form or by any electronic, mechanical, or other means, now known or hereafter invented, including photocopying and recording, or in any information storage or retrieval system, without permission in writing from the publishers.

British Library Cataloguing in Publication Data
A catalogue record for this book is available from the British Library

Library of Congress in Publication Data
A catalogue record for this book has been requested

ISBN 13: 978-1-138-86314-9 (pbk)
ISBN 13: 978-0-7007-0433-0 (hbk)

Contents

Acknowledgements vi
Abbreviations vii

Introduction 1

Part One: Historical Setting

1 The rise of modern Europe and the Javanese experience 7

Part Two: The Javanese Ancien Régime: Civilization and Society

2 Twilight of the old courts: military princes and guardswomen 47

3 The socialisation of the people: "becoming Javanese" 111

Part Three: The Cancer Within

4 Traditional or modern? Rational-bureaucratic feudalism á la VOC 193

5 Aristocracy and peasantry in the tides of world capitalism: three regions 258

Part Four: Intellectual Transformations

6 New ways of seeing: Ethnicity, history, religion, kingship, society 367

Conclusion: The legacy for Indonesia 430

Bibliography 446
Index 460

Acknowledgements

The author would like to thank Curzon Press for the patience and courtesy they have shown with a difficult manuscript. She is deeply indebted to Ian Proudfoot for the gift of his time and magnificient command of fine detail and large issues. Thanks are also due to John McGlynn for suggesting, and the British Library for granting permission to use, the print used on the cover. B.R. O'G. Anderson and W.G.J. Remmelink generously read and commented upon earlier drafts; errors remaining are the responsibility of the author.

Abbreviations

ARA	Algemeen Rijksarchief, The Hague.
BKI	Bijdragen tot de Taal-, land-, en volkenkunde (published by the KITLV).
CB	Collection Berg, Oriental Collection, Leiden University Library.
KA	Koloniaal Archief, Algemeen Rijksarchief, The Hague.
KITLV	Koninklijk Instituut voor Taal-, Land- en Volkenkunde.
KITLV Or	KITLV Oriental manuscript.
f.	Dutch guilder.
LOr	Leiden Oriental manuscript, from the Leiden University Library.
M 1780	*Memorie van overdracht* of van den Burgh for his successor Johannes Siberg, 1780 (Nederburgh Collection no. 381).
M 1787	*Memorie van overdracht* of Johannes Siberg for his successor Jan Greeve, 18 September 1787 (Nederburgh Collection no. 382).
M 1791	*Memorie van overdracht* of Jan Greeve for his successor P.G. van Overstraten, 1791 (Nederburgh Collection no. 384).
M 1796	*Memorie van overdracht* of Pieter Gerard van Overstraten for his successor Johan Fredrik Baron van Reede tot de Parkeler, 1796 (Nederburgh Collection no. 386).
M 1801	*Memorie van overdracht* of Johan Fredrik Baron van Reede tot de Parkeler for his successor Nic. Engelhard, 1801 (van Alphen – Engelhard Collection nos. 191–2).
NBS	Nederlands Bijbel Genootschap (Netherlands Bible Society) Collection, held at Leiden University Library.

Abbreviations

Rd.	Dutch rijksdaalder, or value see p. 103, note 150.
St.	Dutch stuiver, for value see p. 255, note 48.
TBG	Tijdschrift van het Bataviaasch Genootschap van Kunsten en Wetenschappen.
TNI	Tijdschrift van (also voor: title varies) Nederlandsch Indië.
VOC	Vereenigde Oost-Indische Compagnie (Dutch East-India Company)
VOCOB	VOC Overgekomen Berichten (Repatriated Reports).

Introduction

The "rise of modern Europe" has conventionally been dated in history curricula as somewhere around the period spanned by the French revolution and the Congress of Vienna, though the economic historian K.N. Chaudhuri[1] argues convincingly that the technological breakthrough of the late eighteenth century led to a fundamental structural break between the period before 1750 and that which followed. In this book, my earliest sources are from the 1780s and the latest from the early 1820s, a periodisation chosen becauseof its significance for both European and Javanese history. In Java, this is an inter-bellum period following the prolonged wars of the 17th and 18th centuries, ending in the late 1770s and followed by a period of relative peace – notwithstanding the French and English occupations during the Napoleonic wars – until the savagely fought Java War of 1825–30. It is, in addition, a period in which certain important patterns and trends became entrenched in Javanese societies. And finally, it is a period in which some unique sources can be combined to provide a rich description of both the old and the new in Java – a period of peace between war and turmoil, which allowed the authors whose work is used here to shift their attention from a preoccupation with the exigencies of war to an exploration of what had happened to Java.

I do not intend to deal here with the concept of modernisation in the abstract, or to suggest that modernity is the peculiar property of the West or of any particular place. Nor do I wish to suggest that from this period Europe (or even some favoured European countries) entirely shed its pre-modern characteristics. Western societies retained much of their "traditional" – to set up a rough-and-ready contrast – features even into this century, though Western scholars are less able to perceive the persistence of these in their own societies than in other peoples'. What I do want to suggest is that, building on previous developments, Europe developed from the late 18th century a particular package of characteristics along the whole spectrum between practical and intellectual that both gave it a dynamic capacity for expansion and set the format of what we recognise as the modern world. Because of this development, it posed a serious challenge to large parts of the non-European world. This book presents a case study of Europe's impact on an old (if not in Chinese terms, at least in English ones) and distinctive non-European civilisation. Though it may be that the service owed by a European villager pressed into service in the revolutionary and Napoleonic wars was no less onerous than that owed by a Javanese villager to his local lord, one was an oppressed member of an aggressively expanding system, the other of a defensive and contracting one.

Part One of this book deals with the elements in Europe's strength, technological, political, and intellectual. It also uses Wallerstein's world-systems perspective to provide an economic dimension to this picture of the new world of Europe, and then looks at the important question of the changing place of the Dutch in the new economic order from the seventeenth to the eighteenth century. This is followed by a brief account of the history of the Dutch East-India Company in Java, and its political effects.

Part Two deals with the nature of the Javanese ancien régime, both in court and in provincial circles. Here I introduce a focus on society and civilisation, rather than those staples of Javanese historiography to date, political events and economic statistics. "Society" and "civilisation" have become unfashionable and indeed have almost disappeared as organising concepts in the more sophisticated circles of Western academic discourse of the postmodern era, for better or worse. But they are key concepts in the contemporary Indonesian charter of aspiration, the Panca Sila, and the origins of a focus on society can be traced to the period covered here, while a commitment to what we call "civilisation" is implicit in Javanese discourse much earlier. In addition, even sympathetic "educated laymen" from Europe still make remarks such as "Indonesia had no civilisation before the Dutch came";[2] and other uses of the concept of civilisation, for instance in the analysis of the West's relationship with the Islamic world, also occur in public debate. So I have chosen to pay more attention to these considerations than to staking a claim to being at the forefront of academic fashion.

Introduction

Part Three deals with the overall pattern set by the VOC's changing economic imperatives and with the impact of the successive tides of capitalism on three regional societies of Java.

Part Four deals with the intellectual shifts that took place in this period. It will be argued that these intellectual shifts were less conservative than the socio-economic ones described in Part Three and, though more fragile and vulnerable, were nevertheless far from inconsequential for the future.

Finally, the conclusion attempts to show the significance of these developments for modern Indonesia and the way in which some of the dynamics begun in this period are being played out in the contemporary world.

Both Dutch and Javanese sources have been used for this book. Generally speaking I have not followed the common practice of throwing all these sources into the historian's stewpot, but have tried to maintain the particularity of each: the place and time it deals with, who its author was. It is clear that European sources, despite their ignorance of key areas, have strengths which are not replicated elsewhere: the well-developed and indeed at this time unparalleled European tradition of empirical reportage and the situational characteristic of outsider accounts which by their nature provide comment on things taken for granted by insiders being perhaps the most notable. I differ markedly from former scholars using European sources in believing that the quantitative character of these sources, the basis of their long-established reputation as "reliable", is actually their most suspect characteristic, since it is in the accounting that private interests are most in play: where for instance every Resident is most eager to prove that he is a poor but diligent servant of the Company. Hence I have tried to make more use of the "subjective", descriptive material that they provide – sometimes in asides, sometimes in statements that seem to have been wrung from the writer – than is usually done, believing that this provides extremely valuable insights into demography, the economy, society, and civilization. We find speaking testimony on such subjects as the spread of opium addiction, the prevalence of bands of "rabble" on land and pirates and "smugglers" at sea, and the recurrent theme of population flight. The regional reports also suggest that Javanese society was both more diverse in its socio-economic formations, and more homogeneous – and paradoxically both more Islamic *and* more Javanese – in its culture than has previously been recognised. One or two of these European accounts provide rich perspectives on Javanese culture not duplicated anywhere else, so that we can see for instance that even in the "Islamic" areas of Banten and Gresik the Javanese socio-cultural formation was still very strong and had much in common with what has been seen as the normative heartland of Javanese civilisation, central Java. But despite this affirmation of a very strong, strikingly uniform and enduring Javanese socio-cultural format (still able to contain and subordinate Islamic elements as it had done with Indic ones in a previous age), the explanations I have suggested for what happened in Java over this period are historical, not culturalist.

And the Javanese sources? The Javanese sources make sense of the period, from Javanese points of view. As these viewpoints are plural and different, so is the sense they give us: the wistful dreams of ghostly liberty of the villagers of Pekalongan, oppressed by too much rule; the celebration of aristocratic valour and aesthetics of the guardwoman's diary; the rigour, depth, and sophistication of Yasadipura II's moral re-synthesis for young aspirants to élite leadership; the anger and pain of Yasadipura's other voice and that of the anonymous author of NBS 89, as they confront the military and economic defeat of the Javanese; and finally, the birth from this pain of early intimations of a new non-king-centric social focus, preparing the ground for an intellectual and social revolution, still uncharted, later in the nineteenth century. Without these voices, any structure we may erect in the name of history is a silent shell, empty of human life. With them, one apprehends the magnitude and meaning of Java's ambiguous encounters with modern Europe, their links and breaches with the past, their legacy for the future.

NOTES

1 See Ch. 1 below, p. 7.
2 See the interview with Vincent van Monnikendam in *Tiras*, 20 April 1995.

Part One

HISTORICAL SETTING

1

The rise of modern Europe and the Javanese experience

Java's history is often written without much reference to the outside world, as if Java's fate was solely determined by events – political negotiations, warfare, contracts, and to a lesser extent cultural and ideological factors – taking place in Java.[1] This practice is hardly acceptable even for the early period of the VOC's involvement, and certainly not for the second half of the eighteenth century. The economic historian K.N. Chaudhuri[2] argues convincingly that there was a fundamental structural break between the period before 1750 and that which followed, due mainly to the technological breakthrough of the late eighteenth century. He dates the beginning of European imperialism in the 1750s; and sees the previous eleven centuries, from the rise of Islam in the mid-seventh century, as an entire life-cycle for civilization in general.[3] It is not coincidence that most modern history courses begin somewhere between the French Revolution and the Congress of Vienna: modern Europe was born in this period. Modernity is an abstraction not connected with place or time: it can easily be argued, for instance, that Periclean Greece was more 'modern' than medieval Christendom. Nor is it sensible to reinstate the infamous traditional/modern dichotomy: Western modernity is heavily imbued with the Western tradition: it is just that Western scholars, working from within, do not see this. What is argued here is, simply, that a specific form of modernity crystallised (albeit on the basis of previous developments!) in the West in the late eighteenth century and that this was to pose a great challenge to large areas of the non-Western world – not least, Java.

Historical Setting

THE ADVANCE OF EUROPE

What was the nature of this modern Europe? Braudel's work enables us to give a quick sketch of the most important areas involved in which Europe rose to pre-eminence. He sees the eighteenth century as a time when significant barriers were crossed and major quantitative and qualitative changes ensued, as the following quotations suggest:

> ... the frontier zone between possibility and impossibility barely moved in any significant way, from the fifteenth to the eighteenth century, and then only at a few points.
>
> The right road was reached, and thereafter never abandoned, only during the eighteenth century, and then only by a few privileged countries.
>
> Those who succeeded usually did so ruthlessly at the expense of others. For this advance, though always limited, required an infinite number of victims.[4]

Some of the most significant changes occurred in the following areas:

Demography

Whereas in earlier periods a rise in the number of people had always ended by exceeding the capacity of the society concerned to feed them, and prolonged population rises (e.g. in the West between 1100 and 1350, and 1450 to 1650) were always followed by regressions, the population increase which took place after 1750, as part of the general economic revival in eighteenth century, was not followed by such a regression. China and India probably advanced and regressed in the same rhythm as the West, a synchronism evident in the eighteenth century, with China's extraordinary demographic expansion only beginning after 1680. Other scholars have shown that China's population doubled in the eighteenth century, viewing the effects of this for South-east Asian societies as anything from economically stimulating to cataclysmic. Its effects included a large expansion of trade, as the Chinese demand for South-east Asian products grew, and a very great emigration of Chinese particularly as labourers to many parts of the Nan-yang.[5]

Other areas of Asia did not experience anything like this Chinese population increase. Japan experienced population stagnation from the mid eighteenth century, and the Red River delta area appears to have had a population decline in the eighteenth and early nineteenth century.[6] Braudel describes the "Indian archipelago" and Indochina as really only seed-beds with a few populated regions, compared with the solidly occupied zones of Western Europe, Japan, Korea, and China. Even India was not fully occupied by its mixed civilizations, and Islam was a series of coasts (*sahels*) on the margins of empty spaces, deserts, rivers and seas. A wild animal life existed over vast expanses even at the end of the eighteenth century, and under the human *ancien régime*, there was a correlation between births and deaths with both standing at around 40 per 1000. The balance between births and deaths under this biological *ancien régime* from 1400–1800 was produced by a very high infant mortality, famine, chronic under-nourishment, and virulent epidemics. In the eighteenth century only *part* of Europe began to break free, with life only gaining over death from this time forward.[7]

Technology

Braudel makes the points that technology is always a product of demographic numbers, even if it does not favour all dense populations equally; and that for technological innovations to be implemented, both the technical–scientific and the social–economic context has to be ready for them ("The steam engine was invented a long time before it launched the industrial revolution – or should we say before being launched by it?"[8]). The West experienced its first mechanical revolution in the twelfth and thirteenth centuries, actually a series of slow changes brought about by the increased numbers of wind- and watermills, in which Dutch inventions played an important part. The "preliminaries" of the Industrial Revolution took place in the increasingly active progress of the 1730s and 1740s, following the gradual advance of the fifteenth to eighteenth centuries. Though Braudel is right to note the role of the socio–economic context in launching inventions, it is even more important that by this period – in fact, even earlier – inventions were generally no longer the work of simple working artisans, but of men who were themselves scientists or who depended on the advanced science now developed to a unique level in Europe: Galileo's range tables for artillery are an early example of this phenomenon. So while Braudel is also right to point out that not all areas of technology were equally or best developed in Europe (in metallurgy iron was relatively unimportant before the nineteenth century, with the Chinese more advanced than Europe, which had stagnated in this field after the thirteenth century, until the late success of England after the 1780s[9]). China lacked the systematic and theoretical science which would allow Europe to develop technologically at a speed unprecedented in the history of the world. More will be said about these theoretical advances below.

Ocean navigation and the development of artillery are two areas in which it has long been recognised that the West had developed and maintained a significant lead from the fifteenth century. Braudel comments that the great technological "revolutions" between the fifteenth and eighteenth centuries were artillery, printing,[10] and ocean navigation. He concludes that there was no fundamental technical problem that prevented the Chinese junks or Muslim boats from advancing, and in fact older Arab navigational achievements had enabled Islamic powers to dominate the Old World up to the fifteenth century. Similarly, China and Islam were well endowed with capital.

In 1786, the European fleet stood at 3,372,029 tons, its volume having quintupled in two centuries.[11] Braudel comments that every fleet in every country requires the destruction of enormous expanses of forest, but nevertheless immense forest areas remained outside the clutches of civilization before the nineteenth century.[12] But those in Java did not: as we shall see, the destruction of Java's enormous riches here was already well advanced by the beginning of the eighteenth century.

As far as artillery is concerned, all infantry in Europe at the end of the seventeenth century had rifles and bayonets, but this development had taken two centuries to come about. Military historians have long recognised the essential contribution the introduction of small arms made to modern military discipline, stemming from the fact that the slow re-loading of early hand-held guns left the gunner extremely vulnerable and required perfect coordination with the pikesman. Only rich states were capable of bearing the enormous costs of the new warfare, which eventually eliminated the great independent towns of Europe. The cost of artillery did not end when it had been built and supplied with ammunition: it had also to be maintained and moved. Europe was never short of gunners, arquebusiers or master smelters, some of whom found employment in many other parts of the world. This put Europe in a privileged position vis-à-vis Islam and the Far East, where little innovation was made. Artillery gradually spread everywhere and Braudel remarks that "in the eighteenth century no Malay pirate was without a cannon on board"[13] – a statement which considerably underestimates Malay initiative in this field, since the Portuguese had already encountered widespread use of naval artillery in the sixteenth century.

Monetarization

Braudel remarks that money only comes into being where men need it and can bear its cost. Its flexibility and complexity are functions of the flexibility and complexity of the economy that brings it into being. The importance of this development can be seen in the way medieval Islam towered way above the Old Continent, from the Atlantic to the Pacific, for centuries on end, because no state (Byzantium apart) could compete with its gold and silver money, dinars and dirhems. They were the instruments of its power. All the instruments of credit (bills of exchange, promissory notes, letters of credit, bank notes, cheques) were known to the merchants of Islam, whether Muslim or not.[14] If Europe finally perfected its money, it was because it had to overthrow the domination of the Muslim world.[15] There was an increase in the *scale* of monetary transactions (rather than introduction of new forms) in eighteenth century Europe, by a multiple of twenty or thirty since the sixteenth century – but even in Europe these developments only happened in a few market places, a few nations, a few groups: "what were money and credit if not luxuries in which the majority of men had only a minute share?".[16] Braudel remarks that people can live for a time outside the market economy but they are "condemned men", suffering blows without knowing where they are coming from:[17] in Chapter 6, we shall see from a Javanese source what problems monetisation caused the Javanese. Even in Europe, under the fairly thin skin of the monetary economies, primitive activities continued. Rudimentary economies survived in the heart of Europe, encircled by monetary life which did not destroy them but rather kept them as so many internal colonies within easy reach.[18] By the end of the eighteenth century, the Bank of England was playing a leading role in monetary innovation.[19]

Historical Setting

Braudel sees Japan, Islam, India and China as representing intermediate stages half-way between the primitive economies and Europe, with its more active and complete monetary life.[20] In monetary matters China was more primitive and less sophisticated than India, but its system had much more cohesion and unity. China, unlike India, did not have the rest of the world's cash. He sees Java as still at an elementary stage in its monetary life with its copper coins following the Chinese pattern.[21] However, Blussé has argued that the introduction of monetarization into seventeenth-century rural Java through very low-denomination, low-grade and short-lived coinage spread by Chinese entrepreneurs was actually quite effective, just because the coinage was within the reach of rural peasants.[22] By the period with which we are concerned, a large range of coinage was certainly circulating in Java, but whether this can be equated with an increasingly monetised economy is a question that will arise below in Chapter 5.

Urbanization

The increasing dominance of a particular type of town is seen by Braudel as another uniquely Western development. He writes[23] that, as Weber emphasized, the social structures in both India and China automatically rejected the town and offered it only "refractory, sub-standard material" because society was already frozen in a sort of irreducible system, a previous crystallisation. In India, the caste system divided and broke up every urban community, and the Chinese crisis was resolved in the seventeenth century in such a way as to be against urban freedom. Though dismissing Asian towns as generally "enormous, parasitic, soft and luxurious", Braudel comments that perhaps no site anywhere in the world was more privileged for short and long-distance trade than Canton.[24]

In this view, only the West swung completely over in favour of its towns, and the towns caused the West to advance. though the Japanese town developed along somewhat similar lines. In India official towns were strongly dependent on the prince, and political difficulties, even the prince's whim, uprooted and transplanted capitals, which "wandered like nomads over quite large distances in the course of the centuries".[25] It may be noted that Java also had a succession of different capitals, though within a relatively small area of south central Java, in the seventeeenth and first half of the

The rise of modern Europe and the Javanese experience

eighteenth century, until 1755, when the present towns of Surakarta and Yogyakarta were founded. The towns of the *pasisir* which became VOC factories – Jakarta, Semarang, Surabaya, to name the three largest – had a longer history, as indeed did the coastal *kraton* town of Cirebon. Braudel writes of " . . . the loosely-woven clusters of hamlets in Java, which has remained an 'island of villages up to the present time'": an assessment which understates Java's urban element both historically and in the present.

The distinctive features of western towns (which shared with Islamic towns a confused and irregular form on a large scale, as opposed to the chessboard pattern of the Chinese, Korean, Japanese, and Indian towns) were: unparalleled freedom, great physical change, an urban renaissance linked with a rise in rural vigour from the eleventh century and sustained by a growing money economy, and an invariable link with trade junctions. Certain towns made themselves, for considerable periods, into autonomous, privileged city-states, though they were later absorbed into the nation-state. The 'western miracle' was that in the eternal contest between the towns and the state the town won entirely, at least in Italy, Flanders, and Germany. The Dutch regions of Flanders, Brabant, and Overijssel had a particularly high level of urbanization (as much as 50%) in the eighteenth century.[26]

Braudel describes these towns as the West's first 'fatherlands': their patriotism was for a long time more coherent and conscious than territorial patriotism. The capital towns (pre-eminently London and Paris) represented enormous expenditure, and others had to pay for their luxury. But they produced the modern states, an enormous task requiring an enormous effort, and the national markets, without which the modern state would be a fiction. Added to this was the enormous cultural, intellectual and even revolutionary role of these hothouses. But the price demanded was very high. According to Braudel, this was also true of Batavia, "where precocious Dutch colonialism put forth its most beautiful and already poisonous flowers".[27] In this book a contrary point of view will be argued: that the Dutch establishment centred on Batavia did not produce the modern state, the national consciousness, the modern economy and the modern political culture that arose in the Western capitals.

Science

I have argued above that Braudel underestimates the role of pure science vis–vis practical inventions in his triumphalist view of the rise of Europe. In pure science, the particular period covered by this book seems to have been one of the most productive in Europe's history. The way was led by physics where the groundwork had already been laid by Newton, whose work was confirmed and extended by Laplace, who developed the mechanical view of the world late in the eighteenth century. In the nineteenth century the important disciplines were chemistry and later biology, though the necessity of semen for fertilization, for instance, was proved by Spallanzani as early as 1779. Some "theoretical" work was to have considerable impact on educated men's view of the world: notably the mathematical and astronomical work of Gauss, and Lamarck's work on genetics, which prefigured Darwin's, to which the classificatory systems developed in the eighteenth century by Linnaeus and Jussieu also made an essential contribution. In technology, there were some spectacular indications of future conquests, like Montogolfier balloons. But James Watt's perfecting of the steam engine in the mid 1770s and its application, first to industry (particularly the cotton industry, with the first steam-driven cotton factory set up in Manchester in 1789, and the first steam-driven rolling mill the following year), and later to land and water transport were of more immediate importance. By 1818, the first steamship had crossed the Atlantic. The first telegraph, from Paris to Lille, was inaugurated in 1794; smallpox vaccination was introduced in 1796; and lithography in 1798. The first velocipede was developed in 1779; gas lighting was introduced from mid 1780s (gas street lighting in London in 1807). The metric system was introduced in France in 1795.

Of medical science, Foucault writes[28] that in a quarter of a century, from 1790 to 1817, medical discourse changed more profoundly than since the seventeenth century, probably more than since the Middle Ages, and perhaps even since Greek medicine: a change that revealed new objects (organic lesions, deep sites, tissular alterations, ways and forms of inter-organic diffusion, anatomo–clinical signs and correlations), techniques of observation, of detection of the pathological site, recording; a new perceptual grid, and an almost entirely new descriptive vocabulary; as well as new sets of concepts and nosographical descriptions. Century-old, sometimes age-old categories such as fever or constitution disappeared, and diseases that are perhaps as old as the world, like tuberculosis, were at last isolated and named.

Ways of seeing and describing: quantification and standardisation

But if practical invention was increasingly based on pure science, the latter depended in turn on something else: a habit of mind that had developed in Europe over a long period of time. This was a habit of empiricism, but of an empiricism organised around mensuration and quantification. Rather than deal with this in an abstract way, the point can be clearly illustrated by an early Dutch account of Java itself.

This is the account of François Valentijn, who was born in Dordrecht in 1666 and died in the Hague in 1727. Valentijn studied for the ministry and first saw the Indies in 1685, spending the next nine years in Ambon and Banda, before returning to his native town for the following ten years. In 1705 he went out to the Indies again and was military chaplain on a difficult campaign in east Java. During this second period of residence in the Indies he began to collect material for the great work he had already envisaged on his first sojourn in the Indies, and in 1714, back in the Netherlands, started to write it. In 1724 the first of five huge folio-format volumes[29] appeared, and the publication of the entire work was completed by 1726. It ran to about five thousand pages, lavishly illustrated with plates and maps, its title reflecting the extent of its coverage:[30] *Oud en Nieuw Oost Indien, vervattende een naauwkeurige en uitvoerige verhandelinge van Nederlands mogentheyd in die gewesten, benevens een wydlustige beschryving der Moluccos, Amboina, Banda, Timor, en Solor, Java, en alle de eylanden onder dezelve landbestieringen behoorende; het Nederlands Comptoir op Suratte, en de levens der Groote Mogols; als ook een keurlyke verhandeling van 't wezentlykste, dat men behoort te weten van Choromandel, Pegu, Arracan, Bengale, Mocha, Persien, Malacca, Sumatra, Ceylon, Malabar, Celebes of Macasser, China, Japan, Tayouan of Formosa, Tonkin, Cambodia, Siam, Borneo, Bali, Kaap der Goede Hoop en Mauritius.* (Old and new East Indies, containing an accurate and compendious treatment of Dutch power in these regions, together with a comprehensive description of the Moluccas, Amboina, Banda, Timor, and Solor, Java, and all the islands belonging to the same

Historical Setting

countries; the Dutch factory at Surat, and the lives of the Great Moguls; as also an elegant treatment of the most essential that one should know about Coromandel, Pegu, Arakan, Bengal, Mocha, Persia, Malacca, Sumatra, Ceylon, Malabar, Celebes or Makassar, China, Japan, Taiwan or Formosa, Tonkin, Cambodia, Siam, Borneo, Bali, the Cape of Good Hope, and Mauritius). It is dedicated to Egidius van den Bempden, ex-*burgermeester* of Amsterdam, and the list of subscribers contains over 500 names.

What immediately strikes one about his description of Java is its highly systematic, enumerative, and quantitative character. At the outset he divides Java into 7 sections: the kingdom of Banten; the kingdom of Jakatra; the kingdom of Cirebon; the kingdom of Mataram and its dependencies; the governorship (*landvoogdij*) of Pranaraga, Kaduwang, etc.; the governorship of Surabaya and Pasuruhan and the island of Madura; and the principality of Balambangan. These divisions are premised upon a concept of political rather than natural or geographic boundaries, reflecting a desire to establish "who's in charge here" and to determine the exact line at which one sovereignty passes over to another. After a short statement on the length, breadth, and situation of Java Valentijn takes us through the seven sections one by one. He gives the principal geographical features (mountainous terrain, swampy terrain, coastal cliffs, deserted areas, etc.); notes also every (or so it seems) village and town and the number of its inhabitants, sometimes also recording a significant increase or decrease in population in recent times; states the distances between villages, cities, and other landmarks; and lists the chief items of produce and their means of distribution (e.g. rice and teak, by river). At the end of each section he provides a numerical summary: Banten has (excluding Batavia, dealt with separately) 20 villages and a couple of cities which together contain 8,170 households of an average of 5 people each, thus 40,850 people altogether; Jakatra has 202 villages with 19,390 households totalling 96,950 people; Cirebon has 2 cities, 350 villages, and 63,120 households totalling 305,600 people [sic: correct figure 315,600]; Mataram has 3,616 known villages and an "endless number of unknown" ones, 12 cities and a total of 343,020 households or 1,718, 500 [sic: correct figure 1,715,500] people; the fifth division has 14 cities and 226 villages containing 97,970 households totalling 489, 850 people; the sixth has 5 or 6 cities and 60 villages, containing 41,900 households totalling 209,800 [sic: correct figure 209,500] people, plus the 6 cities, 2,041 villages, 78,350 households = 391,750 people of the island of Madura, making a grand total of 12 cities, 2,101 villages, 120,250 households and 601,250 people {here the total of the two figures is actually correct]; the seventh sector has one city, 12 known and many unknown villages, 50,000 households and 300,000 people.[31]

At the conclusion of this section Valentijn writes: "Thus we find, aggregating everything together, that in the whole of this island of Java there are 38 or 39 principal cities [sic: total given above by Valentijn is 43], 4,496 villages [sic: total listed above is 6,527], and 31,161,250 souls [sic!], of which 31 cities, 3,902 villages and 2,417,850 souls are under the emperor (*keizer*) of Java [i.e. Mataram] from which one can easily measure the power of this prince, though there are numberless other villages and souls besides the abovementioned in his lands. We also see from this description, that there are 5 separate powers on Java, which are not dependent upon one another and each of which is sovereign, of which the soesoehoenan or keizer of Java is the first, the king of Banten the second, the princes of Cirebon the third, the prince of Balambangan the fourth, and the Hon. Company the fifth in rank, though nevertheless the most considerable in weight." Unfortunately for someone who has chosen such a conspicuously quantificative schema, Valentijn's figures are, as the corrected figures given reveal, a dog's breakfast: either he or his publisher must have been very careless indeed. The overall total of 31,161,250 Javanese might be thought to be the sort of simple power-of-ten error that is easily made in numerals, but in fact Valentijn's figures add up to either 3,553,000 or 3,553,300, depending on what option one chooses for the sixth section. Additionally, one must wonder how someone with no access to Javanese records could possibly provide such comprehensive and detailed figures, and question to what extent Valentijn's account respects the actual state of knowledge, and to what extent it represents the enactment of a sort of scholarly ritual, the construction, however artificial, of a product that bore the accepted hallmarks of scholarly discourse. However, though later scholars were increasingly dissatisfied with the extent to which he had lived up to the task he set himself of providing an accurate and quantified account,[32] this does not detract from the power of this ideal as a way of developing in Europe a standardised, verifiable mode of discourse not only in the hard sciences, but also, as here, in the social sciences. Nothing comparable was part of the Javanese tradition, though, as we shall see, a more empirical strain was

Historical Setting

beginning to develop in Javanese intellectual life by the period with which we are concerned.

War, politics, and views of society

In political and social thought a prolific output was produced against a background of warfare of unprecedented scope and duration. The American Declaration of Independence took place in 1776 and the American Revolution in 1777; the Fourth Anglo–Dutch war was fought from 1780–1784. The French Revolution in 1789 began a series of wars in which a man unlucky enough to have been pressed into the navy in England, mother of democracies, might have spent a whole lifetime under a brutal hierarchical discipline.[33] To summarize the major conflicts of these decades, France declared war on Austria, Prussia, and Sardinia, which were regarded as corrupt monarchies, in 1792. 1793 saw the Reign of Terror, the banning of Roman Catholicism, and the Holy Roman Empire's declaration of war on France. From 1793 on the rise of Napoleon carried on the Revolutionary impetus in the French army: in 1797 he was appointed to command the forces for the invasion of England; in 1798 the French captured Rome; in 1799 he was campaigning in Syria and Egypt and in 1800 established himself as First Consul. In the same year the French defeated the Turks and Austrians (at Marengo) and conquered Italy. In 1802 the short-lived Peace of Amiens between Britain and France initiated the only period (of 14 months) between 1793 and 1814 when Britain and France were not at war, which broke out again in 1803. In 1804 Napoleon was proclaimed Emperor. 1805 saw an alliance of Britain, Russia, and Sweden against France. The battles of Ulm and Austerlitz forced Austria to sue for peace but the annihilating victory at Trafalgar confirmed British supremacy at sea. Napoleon became King of Italy and in 1806–7 engineered further military triumphs and the end of the Holy Roman Empire. Louis Napoleon became King of Holland. In 1809 the British commander Wellesley struck a significant blow against the French armies, and Austria was again at war with France, but again had to accept a punitive peace. In the same year Napoleon annexed the papal states. 1810 is often seen as the year of his zenith, before the Wellington victories of 1811–12 and the Moscow campaign of 1812. In 1813 Prussia and Austria again declared war on France, and the French were expelled from the Netherlands. In 1814 Napoleon abdicated, and the Congress of Vienna began. In 1815 came the "100 days" following Napoleon's escape from Elba. Waterloo saw the end of his career.)

Some have represented the French Revolution as the beginning of the modern world in the areas of political and social ideas, contrasting the allotment of political rights according to ascriptive status, under the *ancien régime* with a new order in which all citizens had equal rights (though citizenship and the franchise were still limited, debarring women, for instance), and Government was to be judged by performance, not legitimacy. (It can be argued, however, that not a few of these ideas had been anticipated in the English Revolution.) There was a general Enlightenment rejection of superstition, religious dogma, and established authority such as monarchy. The concept of "community" – an alternative focus to monarchy, a development of significance also to Java as we shall see in Chapter 6 – was first systematically developed by Rousseau. A range of innovative works, published in the last few decades of the eighteenth and first decade of the nineteenth century, many during the generation of war, set the agenda for generations to come in philosophy and political economy. This included the works of Hume, who died in 1776, the year in which Gibbon's *Decline and Fall of the Roman Empire,* and Adam Smith's *The Wealth of Nations* were published. Rousseau and Voltaire both died in 1778; a pale echo of the latter's radical critique of European moral superiority was even heard in distant Batavia.[34] Burke was active from 1770 and Kant from 1770–97. The Encyclopaedia Britannica was first published in 1771. Bentham's works appeared from 1787–1802. Thomas Paine's *Rights of Man* appeared in 1791–2 (followed by Mary Wollstonecraft's *Rights of Women,* in 1792) and his *Age of Reason* in 1794. The "Feast of Reason" was held in St. Eustache church in Paris, 1793. Chateaubriand and Wilberforce were both writing on social, philosophical and religious issues in the 1790s. The Napoleonic civil code was begun in 1800. Malthus' works on population and other issues appeared from 1798–1820; Hegel's works appeared from c. 1807; and Ricardo's from 1809–17.

This was also a period when some of the new social and political ideals that were being expressed were first enacted in law. Measures against slavery began with the banning in 1777 of the import of slaves into the United States, though the complete abolition of slavery in Europe and America proceded very slowly and with significant reverses at times. Legal emancipation of the

Historical Setting

Jews and the right of freedom of worship also date from the last decade of the century (the Inquisition was not abolished in France until 1772). Compulsory education was introduced in France in 1793. Not all social reform originated in the legislating classes: significant pressure from below for reform also occurs at this time, with the first general strike occurring in Hamburg in 1791.

Economic development and the role of the Dutch

Wallerstein's world-systems perspective complements this picture of the new political, social and intellectual world of Europe. In his formulation, the world-system's constituent components are defined as the core, the semiperiphery and the periphery, and

> If there is one thing which distinguishes a world-system perspective from any other, it is its insistence that the unit of analysis is a world-system defined in terms of economic processes and links, and not any units defined in terms of juridical, political, cultural, geological etc. criteria.[35]

Yet despite Wallerstein's objection to the nation-state as the unit of analysis, in effect he has to come to terms with the national factor – most interestingly, for our purposes, the Dutch.[36] The Dutch specialized in the new skills required to run a financial and commercial focus of the world-economy, and the Netherlands were one of the nodal points of European trade from the eleventh to the seventeenth century. It was in the Netherlands alone that a complex national–social revolution occurred in what Wallerstein terms the "second" sixteenth century.[37] The political boundaries that eventuated were the result of geo–military factors: the southern Netherlands was open country where Spanish cavalry could prevail, while the northern part was covered with waterways and other barriers to cavalry movement – in short, ideal guerilla country. In the course of time, the north became Protestant-dominated, the south Catholic. The bourgeoisie of Holland carried through exactly the degree of reform it needed to promote economic expansion and yet feel free from overcentralization. Why did this happen in the Netherlands and not elsewhere? The weakening of Spanish world dominance and conflict between France and England allowed the bourgeoisie of the United Provinces to manoeuvre to maximise its interests. An important point made by Wallerstein which is very evident to the historian of

The rise of modern Europe and the Javanese experience

Java is that the Dutch revolution – unlike the English, French and American – did not serve as a generator of ideological currents. Its importance lay in its economic impact on the European world-economy. The Netherlands Revolution liberated a force that could sustain the world-system as a system over some difficult years of adjustment, until the English (and the French) were ready to take the steps necessary for its definitive consolidation. The Dutch surged forward from being merely a centre of Baltic trade to being a centre of world trade. This illustrates once again the cumulative quality of economic advantage. Because the Dutch had an edge in Baltic trade, they became the staple market for timber. Because they were the staple market for timber, they reduced shipbuilding costs and were technologically innovative. And in turn they were thus still better able to compete in the Baltic trade. Because of this edge, they could finance still further expansion. On this basis Amsterdam became a threefold centre of the European economy: commodity market, shipping centre, and capital market, and it became difficult to say which aspect of her greatness was most substantial, or to dissociate one from dependence on the other two. The special nature of the Dutch enterprise has also been recognized by other historians, not all of them Dutch.[38]

The following theoretical viewpoints on nation formation from Wallerstein are also relevant to developments on Java. Firstly: in a world-economy the first point of political pressure available to groups is the local (national) state structure. Cultural homogenization tends to serve the interests of key groups and pressures build up to create cultural–national identities. This is particularly the case in the advantaged areas of the world-economy, called the core-states. In these states the creation of a strong state machinery coupled with a national culture, a phenomenon often referred to as integration, serves both as a mechanism to protect disparities that have arisen within the world-system and as an ideological mask and justification for the maintenance of these disparities.[39] Secondly: the world-economy develops a pattern where state structures are relatively strong in the core areas and relatively weak in the periphery.[40] Thirdly:

> A state machinery involves a tipping mechanism. There is a point where strength creates more strength. The tax revenue enables the state to have a larger and more efficient civil bureaucracy and army which in turn leads to greater tax

revenue a process that continues in spiral form. The tipping mechanism works in [the] other direction too – weakness leading to greater weakness. In between these two tipping points lies the politics of state-creation. It is in this arena that the skills of particular managerial groups make a difference. And it is because of the two tipping mechanisms that at certain points a small gap in the world-system can very rapidly become a large one.[41]

This is, arguably, the key to the relationship between the Javanese states and the Dutch East India Company.[42]

In this development of European capitalism, the East India Companies played a very special role. As K.N. Chaudhuri puts it,

The VOC, the East India company and the Compagnie des Indes Orientales shared many common institutional features. The principal of joint-stock capital, the national monopoly, and integrated organisation in Asia were innovative elements that were not widespread in European commerce at the time. Was it a historical accident that when the Industrial Revolution changed the technological factors of production, the new system prospered as an economic force on capitalist lines, finding new strength in the evolution of impersonal business firms? The success of Western industrialists in utilising personal or institutional savings through share capital was founded on a type of money market and financial practice that was much older than the technological discoveries of the late eighteenth century. The capital market in Europe developed after 1600 almost in parallel with the growth of trade to Asia and the rising fortunes of the various East India Companies. The most powerful and revolutionary impact of the Companies lay in the public acceptance of the notion that the corporate financial liabilities were someone else's assets. Investment and capital accumulation were at once effected through this mechanism. The capital transactions of the VOC and the East India Company at the height of their commercial activity in the first half of the eighteenth century were comparable to the role played by national institutions such as the Bank of Amsterdam or the Bank of England.[43]

By contrast, succesful Asian merchant firms generally faced serious problems once they grew beyond a certain size:

The rise of modern Europe and the Javanese experience

... the spectre of arbitrary expropriation was never far off from the scene of pre-modern commerce. The vulnerability of merchants to unpredictable shifts in official policy furnished the greatest threat to the continuity of Asian business houses and their uncontrolled growth.

Chaudhuri argues that the pre-industrial capitalism of Asia possessed a remarkable feature. Other factors of production, land and labour, were considered socially divisible; anyone who possessed sufficient purchasing power could buy land and employ labour. But capital utilised in trade and industry remained firmly in the hands of mercantile groups. He argues that the notion that the possession of title to commercial investments yielding permanent income might be better than the direct taxation of merchants does not seem to have suggested itself to Asian rulers, and had it done so this would have led to a move to define such titles and rights under the law.

The VOC particularly, in its seventeenth and early eighteenth century heyday, was truly a remarkable organization, worthy of the role Wallerstein assigns to the Netherlands in the development of the world system. Its capitalisation at foundation (around £530,000 compared with £30,000 for the English East India Company), its phenomenally well-developed and comprehensive accounting system, its extensive political reportage, put it, as far as I am aware, in a class of its own for an institution of that period. Equally, its bureaucratic organization reaching all regional branches and all levels of its organisation, was probably one of the earliest examples of the modern bureaucratic form, often regarded as a post-Napoleonic phenomenon, which is seen by Weberians as the hallmark of modern rationality.

By the second half of the eighteenth century, however, the VOC had not only lost the comparative advantage it had once had over the English, but was slipping rapidly. This decline had been initiated earlier, with the Anglo-French invasion of 1672 that initiated the slow decline of the Netherlands as a global power. Reid points out that it has been calculated that having obtained the highest levels of productivity and per capita income in the world by 1670, Holland's stagnation thereafter endured until 1850, with per capita growth being if anything negative over that long period.[44] This decline was reflected in the Asiatic trade. VOC cargoes arriving in Amsterdam from Asia as a whole rose in volume by 1.7% a year in the 79 years from 1619–21 to 1698–1700. In the following years up to 1778–80, the expansion was much slower (0.1% a year). Nevertheless, the relative importance of the Asian trade increased in the eighteenth century because non-colonial trade fell by about 0.2% a year. By 1780, the Asian trade was about 12.5% of total Dutch trade and Brugmans suggests the Indonesian trade was about half of this. Imports from Indonesia were probably about 3% of Dutch domestic product, and the favourable balance in 1800 represented about 1.7% of Dutch domestic product.[45]

The VOC was always obsessed with the need to clamp down on "illegal" private trade, and this obsession was at its strongest when the threat came from its arch rivals, the English. British private commerce within Asia, known as the "country trade", increased during the first decades of the eighteenth century, particularly with the boom in tea after 1720. With the consolidation of British power in India, from the 1760's on, the country trade expanded dramatically. British captains sought goods attractive to the China market; opium, mostly from India, was one such commodity, as were the sea and forest products of the archipelago. The country traders could offer Indian textiles, opium and guns in exchange for the archipelago's products, and so they were welcome in many ports, if the jealous eye of the VOC could be evaded.[46] A major source of concern for the Company was the rich trade with China, whose commerce with the south seas boomed between 1690 and 1717. This was followed by a brief period of uncertainty before the junk trade with Southeast Asia resumed, to develop towards its late eighteenth century peak, and Chinese merchants appeared ever more frequently in Indonesian ports.[47] The Fourth Anglo-Dutch War (1780–1784) devastated trade connections between the Netherlands and Asia, and had profound effects within Indonesia, weakening Company control and facilitating further penetration by American and British country traders.[48] England emerged from this war as the premier naval, trading, and manufacturing power.[49]

Along with coffee and spices (including pepper), tea was the most important product to appear on the European market before 1795. Whereas their tea trade had been thriving until the outbreak of the Fourth Anglo-Dutch War, the Dutch were now made to feel the supremacy of the English navy and many merchantmen were captured. The China Committee of the Company tried to keep the stagnating trade going by sending ships under a neutral flag; Batavia was pressed to send three or four additional ships to China but as a result of the war and the lack of enough capital from the

Netherlands, had an enormous shortage of goods and money, and could not provide them. In Canton the financial reserve melted away; Americans began trading with China and soon became much more important for the Chinese merchants than the Dutch. There was also internal disagreement within the Company about the importance of the China trade. In addition, the most important commodity that Batavia sent to China was tin, and there was now difficulty with the Sultan of Palembang over the compulsory supplies of this metal, with "smuggling" (i.e. trade in breach of the monopoly arrangement with the VOC) prevalent even after a punitive expedition under van Braam was sent in 1783–4. The English East India Company developed superior tactics, calling on private initiative to make up for the lack of money caused by the shortage of silver in Europe. In addition, English ships and crews were better, as were their charts and new navigation techniques, enabling them to make the voyage more quickly, more comfortably and more safely.[50] Where the Dutch could sometimes bring in 6 or 7 return shipments, the English sent 20 to 30, so that the Dutch relinquished their position as the most important supplier of tea to Europe. After the end of the Fourth Anglo-Dutch War profits fell very rapidly to a level at which it was no longer possible to make any profit and in fact heavy losses were sustained.[51] In 1795 the Batavian Republic was proclaimed and in 1796 the management of the VOC was taken out of the hands of the directors [the Heren XV11] and given to the "Revolutionary Committee concerned with the East Indian Trade and Possessions". In 1798 it was decided that the State should assume all the rights and obligations of the Company and thus take over its 134m guilders in debt.

This brought new policies, implemented by the East India Committee, which functioned until 1800, and the Asiatic Council.[52] After 1795 the shipping component of the Company was dismantled and other means were sought to re-establish a connection with the colonies. Ships sailing under a neutral flag (generally Danish and American ships to Batavia, Swedish and American to China) were used, but this strategy was not very succesful. When it became apparent around 1801–2 that peace would be achieved (as it was with the Peace of Amiens of 27 March 1802, when the Cape of Good Hope was returned to the Netherlands) the Asiatic Council began to make plans for the speedy retrieval of great quantities of products, especially coffee, from Batavia. But with the new outbreak of hostilities in Europe, the

Historical Setting

Dutch found themselves again at war with England in June 1803, and at the end of 1803, the Asiatic Council was forced to admit that of the 65 ships despatched only 3 had been able to complete their journey safely. Chartering American ships proved to be fraught with problems, with the Batavian government not at all interested in supplying them with produce. The strategy of using neutral-flag shipping, which had been a reasonable solution in the Fourth English War, was now extremely risky, because of English strength at sea and readiness to limit the shipping activities of neutral states. The Batavian Republic could make no counter-move, and in Autumn 1803 the Asiatic Council gave up navigation to China. For the new Asiatic Council instituted on May 1 1804, things had come to a head, and it had to be acknowledged that trade with Batavia had been even less succesful than that with Canton. The regular arrival of people and precious metals there stopped, and the High Government itself started selling coffee spices and sugar, in contravention of repeated orders from the Netherlands. Capital and supplies were run down. In 1805 the Asiatic Council finally made the decision to also abandon shipping to Batavia, while the High Government was given control over the products of Java and the Moluccas. For practical reasons the Council decided to cede the shipping ties with the Asian colonies to private enterprise. By the time the decision was made in 1805 to allow Batavia to fend for itself, it was already too late.

Clearly, then, by the end of the eighteenth century the VOC was simply unable to compete in economic or military terms with its chief rivals, the English. It is not enough to say that incompetence and corruption were rife, and that in the midst of its financial crisis, the first Dutch empire in Indonesia "was gently going to sleep".[53] As Jorg and van Eyck van Heslinga have shown, the VOC did attempt, through a number of strategies, to address its problems, but due to long-term developments encompassing Europe's wars and Europe's economy, it was now simply out-gunned, out-sailed, and out-sold. The British occupation of Java from 1811 to 1815 demonstrated that the colonial government that succeeded the VOC had not changed these relativities.

THE JAVANESE STATES

If with the VOC we have the case of an institution which had played a unique role in the development of a certain type of

The rise of modern Europe and the Javanese experience

economy and society at a crucial stage, but which had now well and truly had to cede place to stronger powers, the same can be said about the Javanese state, or rather about the Javanese state in combination with the particular form of social organisation on which it rested. The Javanese states from their beginning were based on wet-rice cultivation, which is generally acknowledged to be a highly dynamic system under which a large volume of additional labour can be absorbed before diminishing returns set in. Through the development of a very efficient wet-rice agriculture and of a society both highly organized and imbued with an ideology as strong and pervasive as that of the Protestant capitalism of the VOC, though very different in content, Java produced an agricultural surplus that could be capitalised upon. This capital went into many other things: the development of metallurgy and weaponry of outstanding quality for their time, and of large armies; and the development of a consciously urbane court civilisation based on an ideology of kingship and of a coherent and unique mythology that are peculiarly Javanese, to name some of the most important. Nothing could be more misleading than to represent Java as a sort of cross-roads for foreign influences which produce the "high civilization" of Java. Javanese civilisation was primarily Javanese, and its export to non-Javanese areas balanced the import of Indian and later Islamic ideas. The export of Javanese civilisation took place, as was to be the case with Western civilisation, partly through force of arms and partly through the sheer éclat and glamour it possessed for those outside it. Java's glamour and power was felt in Bali and Kalimantan, in the Lampungs, in Jambi and Palembang, in the states of the Malay peninsula, in mainland Southeast Asia. Not only were the Javanese raiding as far north as the Tonking delta in the 8th century, their influence on all aspects of Cham culture was far more profound and lasting than can be explained by military raids alone.[54] In 802, Jayavarman II liberated his realm from Javanese dominion and in the eleventh century Khmer inscriptions were erected asking for protection against the Javanese.[55] Java's dominance over the much smaller-scale polities of the Malayo–Indonesian world lasted even beyond the thirteenth century and the heyday of Majapait into the period of Islamic Sultanates such as Demak (and later Banten) and up to the time of Mataram – a name also replicated in the Balinese colonisation of Lombok.

The power and glory of Majapait in the eyes of these polities is nowhere more clearly revealed than in their accounts of embassies sent to Majapait with the aim of out-Javanesing the Javanese.[56] Barbara Andaya's interesting study[57] of the small, localised, culturally distinct groups of the Jambi-Palembang region reveals how in the mid seventeenth century, the ruler of Jambi sought to introduce Javanese culture (already well-established in Palembang) and even passed an edict saying that the people of the interior must lay aside their Malay clothes for Javanese ones if they appeared at court – a suggestive parallel to the Thai royal edicts of modern times decreeing the adoption of Western clothing and hairstyles. The ruler and his nobles had Javanese titles, while wayang, dancing, and gamelan were part of court life, and tourneys on the Javanese model were held every Saturday – not just for entertainment but as an occasion to reward those in favour and humiliate those in disfavour. Attendance by the Dutch and English representatives was compulsory. Other elements of Javanese court culture and state organization which were imported into this region include the *kris* and weapon cult and its association with kingship, the use of the ceremonial *siti inggil* (lit. "high ground"), a small mound of earth or raised platform on which the king sat in audience, and the *sikĕp* system for the mobilization of manpower for military and corvée purposes. In 1641 and 1642, the rulers of Palembang and Jambi successively went to Mataram to pay homage. At this time, these kingdoms, especially Jambi, were dependent on Java for rice because pepper cultivation had become widespread because of its profitability (interestingly, the Hikayat Banjar repeatedly warns against the danger of substituting pepper for rice, the principal mainstay of Javanese kingdoms[58]). For Bali too, as Geertz has eloquently demonstrated, Majapait remained the exemplary kingdom for all subsequent Balinese polities.[59] It is probable that in terms of scale and cultural integration Javanese society early reached a level unattained not only elsewhere in Indonesia but even elsewhere in Southeast Asia. Java enjoyed a long heyday of dominance that no other indigenous civilisation of Southeast Asia has had.

This Javanese expansion overseas took place without what we would see as the normal prerequisite of political unification of the island, though territorial consolidation was an élite goal from the time of Airlangga in the early eleventh century. From the seventeenth century onwards, however, one cannot write for Java the triumphalist history that Braudel has written for the West:

though in the present writer's opinion Braudel underestimates indigenous Asian progress and overstates the role of the West in bringing modernisation to Asia. However, it is true that where the West was expanding territorially, economically, and in the spread of its ideas to the rest of the world, the Javanese state of Mataram was still pursuing the unification of Java, and this concurrently with its unforeseen entanglement with the leading edge of capitalism in the shape of the VOC. From this time on the Javanese elite were losing ground, both in territory, in economic control, and in ability to reach out to the rest of the world on its own terms.

They did not lose without fighting.

JAVANESE, CHINESE AND DUTCH: MILITARY AND ECONOMIC ENCOUNTERS 1628–1755

Within a decade of the VOC's conquest of the settlement that was to become Batavia, the VOC was under attack by the most powerful Javanese kingdom, Mataram.[60] If the Dutch, as represented by the VOC, were much stronger in organisation, resources, and seapower than the Portuguese had been, the Indonesian states that they had to deal with – pre-eminently Mataram on Java and Aceh in Sumatra – were also much stronger than those the Portuguese had faced. Though neither side could have known it, the VOC and Mataram embarked upon a series of military encounters that were to last a century and a half and would exhaust both sides in an epic struggle between two remarkable organisations. Sultan Agung launched two massive attacks, in 1628–29. The Dutch were impressed not only by the size of the armies involved (up to 160,000 men), but by the knowledge of siege-works and artillery (brought overland through terrain considered impassable by the Dutch) among the Javanese. But the Javanese forces did not succeed in their aim of expelling the VOC. After this first fateful encounter there was no further direct attack on the Company, which was, however, increasingly courted by candidates in a series of succession disputes for the throne of Mataram. These were the civil war at the end of the reign of Mangkurat II (1675–81) and the First, Second, and Third Javanese Wars of Succession (1704–8, 1719–23, and 1746–57). The first instalment of what was to be the stupendous price of VOC assistance was the ruler's cession in 1677 of monopolies in the purchase of rice and sugar, the import of textiles and opium, as well as freedom from tolls. These concessions were in lieu of repayment

Historical Setting

of the royal debt to the VOC for its military assistance. The conflict of interest over rice, timber, and indebtedness, which struck at the heart of the Javanese state, was to occur again and again in the eighteenth century. VOC interest in Java had initially little to do with its wider trading interests, merely requiring rice and timber to maintain the strategic post of Batavia. The leader of a mid-seventeenth century embassy to the inland court of Mataram was, however, impressed not only by the magnificent forests of Java, but also by the unbelievable wealth of the island.[61]

Nagtegaal[62] notes of the Company's acquisition of monopolies post 1677 that it could not convert its power into economic success because it was poorly equipped for trade on the north coast, which was predominantly small-scale,[63] and could only overcome this problem by working with Chinese, large numbers of whom settled on the north coast at the end of the seventeenth century and gained an important position in trade. The difficult three-way relationship between Dutch, Chinese, and Javanese, which involved not only economic but also religious conflicts, was to provide one of the major dynamic tensions of Javanese history from the late seventeenth century to the end of the colonial period. The Javanese aristocracy objected to VOC and Chinese economic expansion, particularly the export of lumber, rice, and salt, which had formerly benefited them, and in 1686 this was the major factor in a serious crisis in the relationship between the VOC and Mataram. At this time a Dutch embassy to Mataram was wiped out by the remarkable Balinese condottiere, Surapati, apparently with the connivance of the ruler (Mangkurat II), who allowed Surapati and his men to escape to East Java, there to set up his own principality centred on Pasuruhan. After this the VOC refused to have anything to do with Mataram until 1704, when a succession dispute provided the Company with the opportunity of backing a rebel prince to its advantage. By contract of October 1705 the rebel prince, now Sunan Pakubuwana I, was obliged to reaffirm recognition of Batavia's territory, including Priangan; recognize the Sultanate of Cirebon as a VOC protectorate; cede to the Company the eastern half of Madura; confirm VOC control of Semarang, whence the Company had shifted its coastal headquarters in 1708; grant the VOC the right to construct fortifications anywhere in Java; allow the VOC to purchase as much rice as it desired; confirm the monopolies on opium and textiles ceded in 1677; supply 800 *koyan*[64] (approximately 1300 metric tonnes) of rice per annum, free, for 25 years;

accept a VOC garrison at his court again, and pay for it; and prohibit Javanese from sailing further east than Lombok, further north than Kalimantan or further west than the Lampungs. However draconian these restrictions appear, and however damaging they were to the fabric of the Javanese polity, Java was not, as Ricklefs[65] has remarked, to be conquered for the VOC by pieces of paper.

Subsequent to this settlement and another in 1709, increasing cooperation between the VOC and the new Sunan it had supported developed, with the latter tightening his hold over the coastal Bupati (Dutch "Regents") and backing those who could make most money for him. The VOC was also able to increase its exports, and new cash crops were introduced such as coffee and "dry" indigo.[66] All this led to increased monetarization, and also to an increased need for labour on the part of the VOC, obtained partly through demanding more forced labour from the Bupati and partly through paid labour, both of which the Bupati disliked. The intensification of economic exploitation produced a Javanese reaction, with the Bupati increasingly dissatisfied with the production of lumber imposed on them by the VOC and resentful of the direct purchase of rice by the Dutch and Chinese, because this deprived them of all benefits.

In the 1730s, the VOC exacted the highest ever levels of cash and rice from Mataram, and timber logging, which involved both systematic abuses in the Company's grading and pricing policies and corruption among both Dutch and Javanese officials, remained an enormous burden on the common man and had already produced massive deforestation.[67] By the contract of 1733, the Sunan was obliged to supply 1,000 *koyan* of rice (worth approximately 20,000 *reals*) to service his debts. In the negotations of 1736, the Sunan asked, unsuccessfully, that the Company should purchase rice through his Patih or through the Regents, not through the Company's servants or Chinese. Recent raids on Chinese rice purchasing agents may have had something to do with this request.[68] In the late 1730s there was extortion of money from Chinese tax-farmers by the Sunan's officials.[69] As far as timber was concerned, the Company had been illegally logging the Sunan's forests adjacent to its own Regency of Demak, since the latter's timber was exhausted. Though the Sunan did not know about it, the Regents did.[70] In parallel to the attacks on Chinese rice dealers, this period also saw attacks on the Company's lumberjacks.[71]

Historical Setting

In 1740, Java was once again plunged into war; which this time would be virtually continuous for 17 years. In this case the war began not as a succession crisis but as a conflict between Dutch and Chinese in Batavia. The VOC had made a conscious effort to attract Chinese traders to Batavia, which in the early eighteenth century had a growing Chinese population. Ricklefs[72] estimates that by 1740 there were about 2,500 Chinese inside Batavia's walls, and not less than a total population of 15,000 when one also counts those in the environs, where Chinese-run sugar mills and arak distilleries were a major sources of employment, as also of environmental pollution.[73] He also describes VOC treatment of the Chinese post 1722 as typified by "excessive brutality and corruption". To cut a long and contested story short, Dutch suspicions of a Chinese uprising and Chinese fears that previous executions were to be repeated on a larger scale produced an atmosphere in which Governor-general Valckenier's instructions for a search of Chinese houses seemed to authorize the massacre that followed. (Later in the war, massacre was certainly used as an instrument of policy, not only in Batavia but also in Semarang, for instance.[74]) It should also be noted that prior to 1740 the Chinese houses were scattered through Batavia, providing extra justification for fear and reprisal by the Dutch.[75] There appears to have been not just an ethnic but also a class dimension to this extreme violence. The majority of the Chinese in the countryside around Batavia were poor sugar-mill workers who felt themselves exploited by the well-to-do mill-owners and Chinese urban élite, whose interests the Chinese headmen represented. The first violent acts of Chinese bands had been the looting and burning of sugar mills, whose iron implements and machinery were converted into primitive weapons.[76] After the Chinese had risen in revolt against the Dutch in the aftermath of the 1740 massacre, a court faction convinced the Sunan to ally with the former, though this was not to be the end of anti-Chinese feeling among Javanese. Both the Dutch and the Javanese seem to have shared a common opinion of the Chinese – that they were like women, totally devoid of military qualities. In 1740 the Sunan expressed his surprise that they had had the courage to revolt,[77] and Blussé's Dutch sources frequently refer to the Chinese as cowardly and effeminate.[78]

Some major issues which became apparent during the course of the Perang Cina, the "Chinese War", relate to the role of Islam and the acquisition of legal privileges by the VOC. By this time Islam

The rise of modern Europe and the Javanese experience

appears to have captured the martial, anti-foreign side of the Javanese tradition, as Protestantism expressed hostility to Catholic powers in Tudor England: thus we find the Sunan sending letters to places as far apart as Priangan and Pasuruan appealing to Islam to rally his countrymen against the Dutch (though his appeal was not very successful, since the recipients were well aware that his allies, the Chinese, were equally infidels).[79] Dutch accounts also report "priests" among "the enemy". In 1736 the VOC acquired not only extraterritoriality for its subjects, Dutch and Chinese, but even jurisdiction over certain categories of Javanese, that is, those who lived in the coastal Regencies and who came into conflict with the VOC's subjects. These rights were acquired, as had happened with the purchasing of rice, against the Sunan's wishes and by the time-honoured Company procedure of forcing concessions in practice and later ratifying them legally:[80] the legalistic presentation of the expansion of Dutch rule in colonial scholarship ignores this use of the strategies of forcing concessions in practice before they were legally ratified, and of violence and even massacre. The VOC was also ready to abandon its announced principles such as hereditary succession and punishment of the guilty. If Pakubuwana II was despicably eager to cross the floor, abandoning his Chinese allies and seeking forgiveness from the Company, the latter was willing to receive him, from considerations of pure expediency: they had no-one else better, and since the Sunan would owe his restoration entirely to the Company they would be able to extract better terms from him than from anyone else.[81]

Pakubuwana II paid dearly for his reconciliation with the Company and its support of him against the pro-Chinese party. By contracts of 1743 and, especially, 1746, put through by Governor-General van Imhoff with a view to a more thorough exploitation of Java, he was forced to accept the complete cession of all the coastal Regencies in return for 5,000 *real* per annum, as well as the income from all harbour tolls in return for cancellation of his debts and other obligations to the Company; and also the cession of all interior toll-gates and markets, and import and export duties, including the taxes on birds' nests and tobacco, in return for an annual sum of 9,000 *real*.[82] More important, according to Remmelink, was the Sunan's loss of the power to appoint and dismiss Regents at will, and compel them to appear at court, so that the Regents came to depend on their standing with the Company and their ability to keep at least the appearance of order in their

Regency. "The body politic of Java disintegrated into local units",[83] though eventually Pakubuwana II's successors regained within the core regions some ability to reconstitute the court as a political machine. Pakubuwana II never did: not surprisingly, since the most powerful princes of his court remained in rebellion after he had submitted to the Company's terms. Of these princes, the most important were Mangkubumi and Mas Said (Mangkunegara), whose court, a paradigm of the old military *kraton*, is described in the following chapter. They were not persuaded to surrender until 1755 and 1757, respectively, and at the cost of the partition of Mataram. Mangkubumi became the first Sultan of Yogyakarta, which was with Surakarta, under Sunan Pakubuwana III, twin heir to the old kingdom; Mangkunegara received a much smaller settlement, 4,000 *cacah*, in lien from the Sunan of Surakarta.

JAVA IN THE SECOND HALF OF THE EIGHTEENTH CENTURY

Ricklefs writes of this period:

> There is little doubt that Javanese population grew after the mid-eighteenth century. From 1757 to 1825 the Javanese state at last saw peace, probably the longest period of peace since the fifteenth century, possibly the longest ever.[84]

This statement requires considerable qualification. Firstly, there was not one Javanese state (setting aside the consideration that Ricklefs's "Javanese state", Mataram, was now partitioned up) but four: apart from the fragments of Mataram, there was also the Sultanate of Banten, the Cirebon principalities, and the kingdom or principality of Balambangan. Though Banten was pacified (after the turbulent regency of Ratu Sarifa and the rebellion of Kyai Tapa[85]), by the early 1750s, when it became formally a fief of the VOC, things were very different in the other two regions. Cirebon had been devastated by epidemics throughout the eighteenth century and those of 1773 and 1775 were particularly severe, with 50 inhabitants of the city dying every day.[86] In 1798 began the so-called "Cirebon revolts", in which Chinese penetration down to the village level was a major issue, and peace was not restored until 1819.[87] This was a state that had long been penetrated by both European and Chinese influence, with its legal system re-fashioned to suit Dutch (or, if one prefers, capitalist) procedural norms at least from

The rise of modern Europe and the Javanese experience

the early eighteenth century.[88] The state of Balambangan suffered most horrendously of all, being completely wiped out in a long-drawn-out welter of slaughter when the VOC moved to clear up the unruly "Oosthoek" (Eastern salient) of Java, where the feared and hated English traders were sponsoring "smuggling" in breach of the VOC's monopolies. The situation in Balambangan was further complicated by that state's allegiance to the Balinese state of Mengwi, easternmost Java having for long been a sort of border zone between the domains of the Javanese and Balinese hegemonic states. In the late 1760s the VOC inaugurated a draconian miliary regime in which all rice and provisions were commandeered or burnt, leading to widespread famine. Renewed warfare added a scorched-earth policy to this recipe, leading to the depopulation of the entire region – the only case, as an 1848 observer noted, where a once numerous population was entirely wiped out. Not quite entirely: in 1930 there were still about 180,000 descendants of the old Balambangers, now known as the *wong using*, who were apparently distinguished by their self-respect, honesty, obstinacy, and unwillingness to enter the service of Europeans.[89] After forced settlement of offenders and prostitutes to try to repopulate the region, further devastation followed in 1817 in the form of a sulphur flood, reaching to the sea and wiping out all rice crops and plantations, from the temperamental Mt. Ijen, whose sulphur had provided the VOC with almost the only profit to be drawn from the area. The region was eventually re-populated from the second half of the nineteenth century by a heavy immigration of Central Javanese and Madurese. The government introduced the forced cultivation of coffee, which was a great burden since a single family had to maintain 1000 coffee trees. There was resistance enough to this forced cultivation in the Preanger, but there at least the household unit consisted of an extensive family, while in easternmost Java a smaller nuclear family had to bear the burden. Balinese raids also continued even as late as the second half of the nineteenth century. A temple of the old capital and some of the beautiful statues in a style unique to this region were still to be seen in 1821.[90] When the Governor of the North-East Coast, Nicolaus Engelhard, made a journey through the regions under his authority – the first time any of the Governors had been able to do this since 1784 – His Excellency came to a place which the oldest inhabitants of Banyuwangi told him was Macan Putih, the capital of the last ruler of Balambangan. His grave, much revered by the natives, was still within the walls, but it had been 'managed' for a number of years by the Scriba of Surabaya, Palm, who had dug it up in the misplaced hope of finding goods of value, "and thus ruined an antiquity for which evey inquiring person has respect, and destroyed a tomb so very much respected by the Native".[91] Palm had formerly been a Resident at Surakarta, where his behaviour had made a quite equally unfavourable impression upon native society, in this case at the aristocratic level.[92]

Taking the whole of Java into account, therefore, though Ricklefs[93] may be correct in feeling that population growth increased both in the *pasisir* and in the territories under Surakarta and Yogyakarta (with growth in the *pasisir* most marked, but both areas showing a growth rate of more than 1% per annum), this was certainly not the case elsewhere in Java.

Enough has been said here to indicate the seriousness of the European – and Chinese, in a different way – challenge to Javanese polities and society. A different sort of challenge was posed by the increased penetration of Islam, to which the beginnings of a substantial immigration of Hadramauti Arabs may have contributed. The working-out of this complex relationship between Javanese, the West, the Chinese and Islam is the subject of this book. But first, what was it like, this Javanese court civilisation that formed an exemplary centre for so much of the island world, and this Javanese society with its well-developed socialisation? These are the subjects of the following two chapters.

NOTES

1 This perspective was evident in many of the works of H.J. de Graaf, a historian of the previous generation who was one of the first to focus on the history of Java rather than of the Dutch in Java, but continues to be found in recent works such as Luc Nagtegaal, *Rijdende op een Hollandse Tijger: De noordkust van Java en de VOC 1680–1743*, Proefschrift, Rijksuniversiteit te Utrecht, 1988 and W.G.J. Remmelink, *Emperor Pakubuwana II, Priyayi and Company, and the Chinese War*, Proefschrift, Leiden 1990.
2 K.N. Chaudhuri, *Trade and Civilisation in the Indian Ocean: An Economic History from the Rise of Islam to 1750*, Cambridge U.P. 1985.
3 A different periodization of imperialism is given by Hopkins and Wallerstein, who consider that formal colonial rule by core states over peripheral areas has come in two waves or cycles. The first, centred in the Americas, lasted from the 16th through early 19th century. The

The rise of modern Europe and the Javanese experience

second, centred in Africa, India and Asia, lasted from the late 19th through the mid-20th century: see Terence K. Hopkins and Immanuel Wallerstein, *Processes of the World-System*, vol. 3, *Political Economy of the World-System Annuals*, Sage Publications, Beverly Hills/London, 1980, Ch. 5.: Albert Bergesen, "Cycles of Formal Colonial Rule".

4 Fernand Braudel, trans. Miriam Kochan, *Capitalism and Material Life 1400–1800*, Weidenfeld and Nicolson, London 1967, pp. x–xi.
5 See Alexander Woodside, "Political Theory and Economic Growth in Late Traditional Vietnam", (p. 19) and Carl Trocki, "Chinese Pioneering in Eighteenth Century Southeast Asia" in Reid, A.J.S. ed., *The Last Stand of Asian Autonomies: Responses to Modernity in the Diverse States of Southeast Asia and Korea*, Basingstoke, Macmillan, forthcoming 1997.
6 See Yumio Sakurai, "Abandoned Villages in the Red River Delta in the 18th and Early 19th Century" in Reid, *Last Stand*.
7 Braudel, Chapter 1.
8 Braudel p. 245.
9 p. 278.
10 On the significance of printing in nation building, see Benedict R. O'G. Anderson, *Imagined communities: reflections on the origin and spread of nationalism*, London: Verso, 1983.
11 Braudel p. 265.
12 Braudel p. 268.
13 Braudel p. 295.
14 China also used bank notes from the ninth century A.D. In fact every economy that found itself hard up for metallic currency fairly quickly opened up instruments of credit of its own accord (Braudel p. 359).
15 Braudel p. 329.
16 Braudel p. 372.
17 Braudel p. 326. Braudel also makes the point that after the European impact primitive money (salt, cotton, cowries etc.) was always subject to monstrous and catastrophic inflation, caused by an increase in reserves, and accelerated and even hectic circulation, with a concomitant devaluation in relation to the dominant European money. (p. 332).
18 Braudel p. 333.
19 In 1797 the first copper pennies and pound notes were introduced in Britain: the last gold guinea coins were issued in 1813. In 1798 income tax was introduced as a wartime measure and continued until 1815.
20 Braudel p. 336.
21 Braudel p. 340.
22 Leonard Blussé, "Trojan Horse of Lead: The Picis in Early 17th Century Java", in *Strange company: Chinese Settler, Mestizo Women and the Dutch in VOC Batavia*, VKI 122, Foris Publications, Dordrecht, 1986.
23 Braudel;. pp. 399–440.
24 Braudel p. 388.
25 Braudel p. 412.
26 Braudel p. 376.
27 Braudel p. 424.
28 Michel Foucault, *The Archaeology of Knowledge* and *The Discourse on Language*, trans. A.M. Sheridan Smith, Harper Torchbooks 1972, p. 170.

Historical Setting

29 The third, fourth and fifth volumes are so large that they are bound in two parts.

30 The first volume begins with a rather long (316 pp.) account of Europe's knowledge and penetration of the east, from classical times until the author's day, and then goes on to describe the Moluccas, the Spice Islands which had first drawn the Portuguese and the Dutch into the Indies. The second and third volume describe Ambon, Ceram, Banda, Timor, Celebes, Borneo, Bali, Tonkin, Cambodia, and Siam, but particularly Ambon, where Valentijn spent the major part of his years in the Indies. The second part of Vol. II has an extensive account, with many fine plates, of the shells of the Ambon seas (together with a list, 23 folio pages long, of Dutch "Sea-shell Fanciers"). Vol IV, in two parts, deals mainly with Java, but also has over 150 pages on Surat and the Great Moguls, thirty pages on China, sixty on Taiwan, and an account of Valentijn's first journey out to the Indies and back which runs to over 70 pages. Vol. V Part One describes Coromandel, Pegu, Arakan, Bengal, and Mocha; the Dutch factory in Persia; Persepolis and Malacca (360 pp. so far); the Dutch in Sumatra (46 pp.) and Ceylon (462 pp.); Part Two covers the Dutch on the Malabar coast (48 pp.) Japan (166 pp.), and the Cape of Good Hope (150 pp.) and ends with a few pages on Mauritius.

31 Valentijn does not explain why in this section the household is accounted as comprising six people.

32 The most blistering attack on Valentijn, both as a person and as a scholar, is probably that penned by F. de Haan (*De Preanger-Regentschappen onder het Nederlandsch Bestuur tot 1811*, vol. I, Batavia 1910, pp. 270–80): "As far as his method of work is concerned, he sometimes names his sources, when they are well-known books . . . .; how he obtained the rest of his data he carefully conceals, except where he sees a chance of paying a compliment to one of his patrons." De Haan goes on to give examples of careless copying – and it is, it seems to me, a case of careless copying rather than of careful concealment of his sources, for Valentijn is by no means alone among his contemporaries in his cavalier treatment of his sources, conscientious citation being a development of a later age. He then launches into an extensive attack *ad hominem*, covering everything from Valentijn's fear of sea voyages to the derelictions of duty that eventually lead to his dismissal and repatriation; and concludes: "There we have what appears in the official sources concerning Valentijn. Now that he himself has had the floor on the subject of himself almost alone for two centuries, it is time to hear what others have to say for once. For me it remains a psychological riddle how Valentijn should not have preferred to have remained totally silent in his book about his personal circumstances. It is true, we should then be deprived of the best parts of his work". An annotator of an Austrlian National University library copy of de Haan – perhaps the famous G.P. Rouffaer himself, to whom it previously belonged – who has made a few small corrections to de Haan's own facts, picked up this piece of the characteristic de Haanian sarcasm in a marginal "Hm!!".

33 In addition, the English East India Company military campaigns in

India over this period ran from those of Hastings in the late 1770s to the Mahratta wars. The British occupied the former Dutch possession Ceylon in 1795.
34 In van Hogendorp's Kraspoekol: see Ann Kumar, "Literary Approaches to Slavery and the Indies Enlightenment: Van Hogendorp's Kraspoekol", *Indonesia* 43 (April 1987) pp. 43–65.
35 Hopkins and Wallerstein, 1977: 123.
36 Immanuel Wallerstein, *The Modern World System: Capitalist Agriculture and the Origins of the World Economy in the 16th Century*, Studies in Social Discontinuity, Academic Press, New York/London 1974. Ch. 4, "From Seville to Amsterdam: The Failure of Empire".
37 Wallerstein p. 202.
38 An interesting example is Clark G. Reynolds' view of the 'thalassocracy' as a 'historical force'. Reynolds considers that there have been only 6 thalassocracies in the course of history, i.e. the Minoans (c. 1600–1400 B.C.), ancient Athens (c. 500–400 B.C.), late-Medieval/early Renaissance Venice and Florence (c. A.D. 1200–1500), the modern Netherlands (c. 1600–80), modern Britain (c. 1650–1900), and the contemporary United States (since 1900) [though he seems to have some doubts about the U.S. case later in this chapter]. Each epoch had its own sea, with the development in the 20th century of a single World Ocean. Reynolds also makes a critique of Braudel as erroneously regarding the great maritime empires as being centred in Istanbul, Rome or Madrid, claiming that the Ottoman, Roman and Spanish empires were simply never thalassocratic. By 1650, *two* new thalassocracies had appeared on the scene, i.e. the Netherlands and England. The fact that the period of their greatness overlapped by one generation, c. 1650–80, helps account for the viciousness of the three Anglo-Dutch wars of those years. According to Reynolds there is also a strong relationship between thalassocracy and capitalism. In a thalassocracy or maritime empire economic regulation was not the province of the central government as in continental states, but of an influential association of private entrepreneurs. The economic form of the state was, therefore, capitalist (Reynolds argues that social structure and cultural values are more determinant of business forms and relationships than Marxian economic motivation.) According to this theory, which strongly idealises the thalassocracy vis–vis the land-based polity, the merchant classes of these states promote democracy to be free of feudal oppression. See further Clark G. Reynolds, *History and the Sea: Essays on Maritime Strategies*, University of California Press 1989, esp. pp. 27–44.
39 Wallerstein, p. 349.
40 Wallerstein p. 355.
41 Wallerstein p. 356.
42 The Dutch East India Company is of course not formally a nation, but in its capacity to make war and conclude treaties with states it to all intents and purposes assumed the powers of a nation.
43 Chaudhuri, *Trade and Civilisation* p. 95; p. 213, p. 228.
44 See Anthony Reid, "A New Phase of Commercial Expansion in Southeast Asia, 1760–1850" (p. 3.) in Reid, forthcoming.

Historical Setting

45 Angus Maddison, "Dutch Income in and from Indonesia, 1700–1938" in Angus Maddison and Gé Prince, *Economic Growth in Indonesia, 1820–1940*, VKI 137, Foris, Dordrecht 1989, pp. 15–41.

46 Heather A. Sutherland and David S. Bree, "Quantitative and Qualitative Approaches to the Study of Indonesian Trade: The Case of Makassar" in T. Ibrahim Alfian, H.J. Koesoenanto, Dharmono Hardjowidjono and Djoko Suryo, *Dari Babad dan Hikayat sampai Sejarah Kritis, Kumpulan Karangan dipersembahkan kepada Prof. Dr. Sartono Kartodirdjo*, Gajah Mada University Press 1987, pp. 369–408.

47 Sutherland and Bree pp. 375–6.

48 Sutherland and Bree p. 379. Investment income from foreign bonds also fell, and the reopening of the port of Antwerp brought new competition: see Maddison, "Dutch income", p. 17.

49 p. 67.

50 At the end of the 18th century Dirk van Hogendorp laments that English ships reach Madras from Portsmouth in three months, while the Dutch ones took nine, with unnecessary expense, sickness, and cargo loss: see E. du Perron-de Roos, "Correspondentie van Dirk van Hogendorp met zijn broeder Gisbert Karel", BKI 102 (1943), p. 166.

51 C.J.A. Jorg, *Porcelain and the Dutch China trade*, Nijhoff, The Hague, 1982, pp. 39 f.

52 See E.S. van Eyck van Heslinga, *Van compagnie naar koopvaardij: de scheepvaartverbinding van de Bataafse Republiek met de kolonien in Azie 1795–1806*, Hollandse Historische reeks 9, Amsterdam 1988, pp. 179–84.

53 M.C. Ricklefs, *A History of Modern Indonesia*, Macmillan Asian Histories Series, 1981, pp. 93–4 and 102.

54 See Edward H. Schafer, *The Vermilion Bird: T'ang Images of the South*, California U.P. Berkeley and Los Angeles 1967, pp. 64–78 and Philippe Stern, *L'art du Champa (ancien Annam) et son evolution*, Paris 1942, pp. 109–10. Reference to the Javanese in Cham rituals was still evident to French observers in the colonial period.

55 See Chirapat Prapandvidya, "The Sab Bāk Inscription: Evidence of an Early Vajrayana Buddhist Presence in Thailand", *Journal of the Siam Society* vol. 78, part 2, 1990, pp. 11–14.

56 See J.J. Ras, *Hikajat Bandjar: A Study in Malay Historiography*, Bibliotheca Indonesica (KITLV), The Hague, Nijhoff, 1968 section 6.3, for example, and any account of Hang Tuah's embassy to Majapait in the various versions of the *Sejarah Melayu* or *Hikayat Hang Tuah*.

57 Barbara Watson Andaya, *To Live as Brothers: Southeast Sumatra in the Seventeenth and Eighteenth Centuries*, Honolulu, University of Hawai Press, 1993.

58 See Ras, *Hikajat Bandjar* sections 3.1, 7.2, 39, 14.4, etc.

59 See Clifford Geertz, *Negara: The Theatre State in Nineteenth-Century Bali*, Princeton University Press 1980, especially Chapter 1.

60 Though Mataram was the most powerful Javanese kingdom, and the Javanese kingdoms were the most powerful in Southeast Asia, as Maddison ("Dutch income", p. 16) points out, they were less strong in many ways than the Mughul empire: inland communications were poorer, administrative and military organisation was less developed, and

The rise of modern Europe and the Javanese experience

the economy was less monetised. As a result, the peasantry was probably less oppressed than in India, since the Javanese ruling class lacked the apparatus of extractive mechanisms available to the Mughals.

61 H.J. de Graaf, *De Vijf gezantschapreizen van Rijklof van Goens naar her hof van Mataram 1648–1654*, 's-Gravenhage, Martinus Nijhoff for the Linschoten-Vereeniging, p. 181.
62 Nagtegaal, *Hollandse tijger*, p. 224.
63 This raises another aspect of the VOC's problem in making money out of the concessions granted: the general impoverishment of the population by long-drawn-out warfare: see Ricklefs, *History*, p. 78.
64 The *koyan* varied from place to place but is generally reckoned at 3350 Amsterdam pounds, but 3750 in Mataram and Surabaya.
65 Ricklefs, *History*, p. 83.
66 Prior to this, Java had been a liability (*lastpost*): see M.C.Ricklefs, *War, Culture and Economy in Java 1677–1726: Asian and European Imperialism in the Early Kartasura Period* pp. 150–5 and p. 202. The situation was particularly bad of course in times of warfare on Java, such as the period 1717–23 when VOC income never exceeded 17% of expenses, and averaged less than 10%.
67 Ricklefs, *History*, pp. 85–6; Remmelink pp. 130–3. The forests of Rembang were so heavily felled by c. 1709 that the nearest timber was now 12 days' transport by buffalo inland from the coast, so the forests of Pati, Juwan, Lasem, Tuban, Sidayu and Jipang were declared open to the VOC. (See also Ricklefs, *War, Culture and Economy*, Ch.IX, where it is noted that coastal deforestation was so severe even by 1717 that the Sunan agreed to allow felling of heavy timber further inland in the Kartasura districts.)
68 Remmelink, p. 100.
69 Remmelink, pp. 107–8.
70 Remmelink, p. 110.
71 Remmelink, p. 124.
72 Ricklefs, *History*, p. 87.
73 See Leonard Blussé, "The Story of an Ecological Disaster: The Dutch East India Company and Batavia, (1619–1799)" in *Strange Company* pp. 26–7.
74 See Remmelink p. 128 and p. 148.
75 F. de Haan, *Oud Batavia: gedenkboek uitgegeven door het Bataviaasch Genootschap van Kunsten en Wetenschappen naar aanleiding van het driehonderdjarig bestaan der stad in 1919*, 2 vols, G. Kolff, Batavia 1922, vol. 1, p. 493.
76 Remmelink p. 134. S.a. Blussé, "Batavia 1619–1740: the Rise and Fall of a Chinese Colonial Town", in *Strange Company* pp. 73–96. There is also some evidence of a regional differentiation between the poor and élite Chinese, with the latter, like most Chinese elsewhere in Java, overwhelmingly Fukienese, while the former may have had a major Cantonese component.
77 Remmelink, p. 128.
78 Blussé, *Strange Company*, e.g. p. 78.
79 Remmelink, p. 160.
80 Remmelink, pp. 99–100.

Historical Setting

81 Remmelink, pp. 199–200.
82 Remmelink, p. 202. Some allowances were also paid to the queen, the Patih, and the royal princes.
83 Remmelink, p. 203. Remmelink sees some other indications of innovation in response to new opportunities in the period he covers, for instance the change from manpower to cadastral computation because of the entrepreneurial activities of Javanese aristocrats.
84 M.C. Ricklefs, "Some Statistical Evidence on Javanese Social, Economic and Demographic History in the Later Seventeenth and Eighteenth Centuries", *Modern Asian Studies*, 20/1 (1986) p. 29.
85 A name, with its explicit invocation of Hindu-Javanist religion, that seems strange for the leader of a rebellion in "strongly Islamic" Banten.
86 Paramita R. Abdurachman, *Cerbon*, Sinar Harapan, Jakarta 1982, p. 57.
87 Abdutrachman pp. 59–60.
88 See Mason Claude Hoadley, *Javanese Procedural Law, A History of the Cirebon-Priangan "Jaksa" College, 1706–1735*, Cornell University PhD, University Microfilms 1975. Cirebon is one of the most intellectually challenging of Java's regional cultures, being at once "more Islamic" "more Sinicised" and closer to ancient Majapait traditions of architecture and ritual than the central Javanese principalities.
89 Further on this area see Ann Kumar, "Javanese Historiography in and of the Colonial Period" in Anthony Reid and David Marr eds, *Perception of the Past in Southeast Asia*, Asian Studies Association of Australia 1979, pp. 187–206.
90 See C.G.C. Reinwardt, ed. W.H. de Vriese, *Reis naar het oostelijk gedeelte van den Indischen Archipel in het jaar 1821*, Frederik Muller, Amsterdam 1858, who gives the following account: The temple of Macan Putih lies in the southern district of the Residency, about 6 *palen* [the *paal* was an Indies linear measure of 1506.943 metres] from Banyuwangi, and in a very beautiful and fruitful, nearly flat land, just as Javanese ruins are generally located in the most pleasant and fruitful places. The temple is open from above, but the walls of the square are still in quite good repair. The stones are 14" long, 7" wide and 3.5" thick. They are a soft limestone. The sides of the temple are figured on the outside with a square panel bordered by projecting frames (*uitspringende lijsten*), with the panel as well as the frames ornamented with figures . . . . Many stones have been taken from here. Around the temple at some distance are statues or groups of statues. On the right is a colossal monster, that was certainly 30 feet tall. These statues are made of fired red stone. Many loose stones from such statues lie around. About 22 years ago the temple was in better condition, and the large statues, in front and at the side, namely the crocodile and the other great monster, were still whole. No care is taken of any of this. Resident Harris sent some separate statues to Surabaya. [the last but one instance of the general stripping of the Javanese countryside of its abundant antiquites during the nineteenth century].
91 See ARA, van Alphen collection 2e afdeeling 1900, no. 196, p. 105.
92 On Palm's illegal exactions and other machinations and their contribution to a developing confrontation between the Surakarta aristocracy and the VOC, see Ann Kumar, "Javanese Court Society and Politics in

the Late Eighteenth Century: the record of a Lady Soldier:Part II: Political Developments: the Courts and the Company 1784–1791", *Indonesia* 30 (October 1980), pp. 67–111.
93 Ricklefs, "Statistical Evidence", p. 30. See also Ricklefs, *History*, p. 105, where it is estimated that the population of Surakarta and Yogyakarta grew from c.690,000 – 1,000,000 in 1755 to c. 1,400,000 – 1,600,000 in 1795.

Part Two

THE JAVANESE ANCIEN RÉGIME: CIVILIZATION AND SOCIETY

2

Twilight of the old courts: military princes and guardswomen

The work used here as the central point of reference is a diary:[1] an example of a genre often considered absent from Javanese records, and an example of unusual scope and interest, covering as it does a full decade (1781–91) and being written at the court of Mangkunegara I, one of the major figures of eighteenth-century Javanese history, and one of the last of the old style princes to rise to eminence in the context of a political and military competition for power of the type that was never again to be possible for the Javanese aristocracy.

What is more, the diary was written by a member of a venerable Javanese institution which was also to pass away with the old style of life. She identifies herself in a short introductory note in prose, which forms the first lines of the manuscript itself:

> Attention: the writer is a lady scribe and soldier, bringing to completion the story of the Babad Tutur, in the month of Siyam, on the 22nd day, still in the year Jimawal numbered 1717, in the city of Surakarta.[2]

This passage is followed by the first stanza of (*macapat*) verse, which reads:

> The work then is in Mijil meter; its basis is something else, it follows a different story. Because of the length of the story it was written [in an abridged form in verse??] It was still a [the?] lady scribe who transmitted it[3]

The descriptive material of the diary follows immediately, and there is no further information on the writer either here, at the beginning, or at the end of the manuscript. The small amount of information which is given seems to suggest that the diary in its present form is

The Javanese Ancien Régime: Civilization and Society

a revision of an earlier version, probably an abridgement, since the "length" of the story which formed its basis is given as the reason for (re-) writing. The last entries in the diary are in fact from the first half of the month of Mulud 1718 AJ (November 1791 AD) that is, nearly half a year after the date, Siyam 1717 AJ, given in the opening passage, above. Presumably the authoress of the revised version which we have went on to extend the original text to cover the half-year period which had elapsed since it was written. The revision retained the diary form, for it consistently indicates the day,[4] and, at at least weekly intervals, also the date[5] on which an event took place. There is not an entry, or provision for an entry, on every day, however, and the coverage of the first two years of the decade reported is much less detailed than is the case for the later years. Checked against Dutch archival records, the diarist's dates prove accurate, except for occasional slips. The introductory note describes the work as a continuation of another work, a "Babad Tutur"; I have not been able to identify this manuscript.[6]

It is clearly a matter of regret that the information given on the authorship of the diary should be so tantalizingly brief and cryptic: the authoress is not identified by her name, and it is not even clear whether the women referred to in the introductory note and in the first stanza of verse are one and the same person. Still, it does tell us that the diary represents the work of at least one of the members of a rather special institution, the *prajurit estri* corps of the old Javanese courts.

It was not a personal idiosyncrasy on Mangkunegara I's part to keep such a corps, but a following of old established custom. The female guard of earlier Javanese rulers, the Sultans of Mataram, was remarked upon by the earliest Dutch visitors to the court (during the reign of Sultan Agung) and in the years covered by the diary the future Second Sultan of Yogyakarta also had such a corps, as Ricklefs has noted.[7] Rijklof van Goens, who visited Mataram in the mid-seventeenth century, gives some interesting information on the corps as it existed then.[8] He estimates that it contained about 150 young women altogether, of whom thirty escorted the ruler when he appeared in audience. Ten of them carried the ruler's impedimenta – his water vessel, *sirih* set, tobacco pipe, mat, sun-shade, box of perfumes, and items of clothing for presentation to favoured subjects – while the other twenty, armed with bare pikes and blow-pipes, guarded him on all sides. He says that members of the corps were trained not only in the exercise of weapons but also in dancing, singing, and playing musical instruments; and that, although they were chosen from the most beautiful girls in the kingdom, the ruler seldom took any of them as a concubine, though they were frequently presented to the great nobles of the land as wives. They were counted more fortunate than the concubines, who could never entertain an offer of marriage so long as the ruler lived, and sometimes not even after his death. Van Goens does not describe members of the corps as accomplished in literature, but such accomplishment would not have been easily apparent to a foreign visitor. Valentijn, writing a description of the court of Mataram in the first decade of the eighteenth century, repeats van Goens' description almost word for word, adding, however, that the young women proved "not a little high-spirited and proud" when given as wives, knowing as they did that their husbands would not dare to wrong them for fear of the ruler's wrath.[9]

European travellers give a number of accounts of a somewhat similar institution in seventeenth-century Aceh. The French admiral, Augustin de Beaulieu, who visited Aceh in 1620–21, reported that the Sultan of Aceh had 3,000 women as palace guards. Beaulieu says that they were not generally allowed outside of the palace apartments, nor were men allowed to see them[10] but the Dutchmen who sailed under Admiral Wybrandt van Warwijk in 1603 saw a large royal guard formed of women armed with blowpipes, lances, swords, and shields, and a picture of these women is to be found in the journal of the voyage.[11] On his visit to Aceh in 1637 the Englishman Peter Mundy also saw a guard of women armed with bows and arrows.[12] It is possible that women were employed for guard duties in other Indonesian courts, but the Javanese *prajurit estri*, the most cultivated and privileged group among the hierarchy of ranks which made up the female population of the court, had no peers elsewhere in Indonesia.

It may also be worth remarking that in modern Javanese literature the representation of women in armed combat and on the battlefield occurs much more frequently than one might expect. It is particularly prominent in the Menak epic, with its apparently inexhaustible succession of episodes relating the exploits of the Islamic hero Hamza b. 'Abd al-Muṭṭalib. The Javanese version is based on a Malay version fairly close to the Persian original,[13] but it is very greatly expanded and interpolated, nowhere more so than in the description of the martial exploits of the women characters, which were already striking in the original. Especially remarkable in the Javanese version are the sections devoted to the "Chinese" princess (she is Chinese only in the Malay and Javanese versions) and to the lovely Rengganis[14] The Chinese princess of the Menak story is probably the basis of the simile in the following passage, in which the diarist describes the *prajurit estri* corps on a ceremonial occasion, the reception of a Governor of the northeast coast:

dina kĕmis ing sawal kang sasi	On Thursday, Sawal
tanggal pitu likur wanci asar	the twenty-seventh,[15] in the late afternoon
dĕler sarta kump [ĕ] nine	the Governor[16] and the Company officials
marang ing dalĕmipun	came to the Mangkunegaran.
wau kangjĕng pangran dipati	The Pangeran Dipati[17]
marang laji [loji] amapag	went to the factory[18] to meet
dĕler kang pinĕṭuk	the Governor,
bĕkta prajurit wanodya[19]	taking the guardswomen.
anyuriga ḍuwung cara bali	They wore krises in the Balinese style,
goḍong rere [n] dan epek rere[n]dan	ornamented with gold filigree leaves, in a gold filigree belt.
ting galĕbyar busanane	Their clothes were glittering.
kang lumampah rumuhun	Those who went first
wong nyutrayu ḍarat jĕmparing	were the Nyutrayu corps,[20] on foot carrying bows and arrows
anulya jayengasta	and then the Jayengasta corps,
tan rasukan mungguh [?? illegible]	not properly [?] dressed,
anulya pangran dipatya	and then the Pangeran Dipati,
ginarĕbĕg ingkang prajurit pawestri	ceremonially escorted by the guardswomen,
tan ana papadanya	without peer,
anglir dewa tĕḍak saking langit	like a god descended from heaven,
ginarĕbĕg putri saking cina	attended by princesses from China:
lir mangkana upamane	that is the [only] comparison.
wong sinĕliran pungkur	The picked men went behind
mung punika ingkang tut wuri	– only these brought up the rear,
kang bala kaṭah-kaṭah	for the ordinary soldiers
sadaya tan tumut	were none of them taken along.
prandene wong nononton tembak	Even so the spectators crowded around;
kang busana sruwa kĕncana tulya sri	the all-gold clothing was really beautiful.

Twilight of the old courts

prapta laji [loji] pinapag	They arrived in the factory and were met
tuwan upruk lan sagung upĕsir	by the Resident,[21] and all the officers,
mapan [error for mapag] mring kangjĕng pangran dipatya	coming to meet the Pangeran Dipati.
sami tatabeyan kabeh	They all greeted one another;
dĕler tabeyan lu[ng]guh	the Governor paid his compliments and sat down.
sinasĕgah anginum awis	They were offered *arak*[22] to drink.
kang prajurit wanodya	The guardswomen
sami tata lungguh	sat down in the correct fashion
sinasĕgah num-inuman	and were offered drinks.
nulya upruk nitih reta malbeng puri	Then the Resident went to the palace in a carriage,
manggil anem dipatya	to summon the heir to the throne.[23]
nulya tata kang prajurit esri	Then, correct in their ranks, the lady soldiers
sami ḍarat laji [loji] palataran	descended to the compound of the factory.
tĕdak pangran dipatine	The Pangeran Dipati[24] descended,
lan dĕler suka dulu	and the Governor, delighted at the sight
kang prajurit astri [estri] abaris	of the guardswomen in their lines.
dyan anem dipatine	The heir to the throne
lawan upruk rawuh	and the Resident arrived,
ing laji [loji] sabalanira	at the factory, with the escort.
nulya pangran dipati sĕpuh ngabani	Then the Pangeran Dipati gave the order
mring prajurit wanodya	to the guardswomen.
sarĕng mungĕl drel prajurite estri	The salvos of the guardswomen sounded in unison;
kang ngabani pangeran dipatya	it was the Pangeran Dipati who gave the order.
sĕmbada lawan rakite	They were well-matched and in time
ĕdrel ambal ping tĕlu	as they fired a three-fold salvo.
cingak idab ingkang ningali	The watchers were astonished and amazed,
dĕler goyang kang nala	and the Governor was staggered, and
kacaryan adulu	completely captivated by the sight.
sasampunira mangkana	After this,

The Javanese Ancien Régime: Civilization and Society

nitih kuda prajurite astri [estri] rumiyin	the guardswomen mounted their horses first,
nulya pangran dipatya	followed by the Pangeran Dipati
saha bala pan kondur rumiyin	who withdrew first, with all his armed men,
kantun laji [loji] anem dipatya	leaving the heir to the throne at the factory.

Once home, the corps changed from the gold masculine clothing they had worn for these manoeuvres into plain white women's clothes – and proceeded to archery practice. Later, the Governor came to Mangkunegara's residence where an elaborate entertainment awaited him, and where the *prajurit estri* again displayed their skill with firearms. The diarist comments on this occasion that none of the Company officers had seen anything like them in Surakarta, Yogyakarta, or Semarang.

Since the diarist was herself a *prajurit estri* and takes an unmistakable pride in the different achievements of the Mangkunegaran, her claims to a disciplined skill at arms might be regarded with indulgence. But the Governor, Jan Greeve, for whose benefit this exhibition was made, also wrote a diary of his visit to Surakarta, and the entry for Thursday, July 31, included descriptions of this reception at the Dutch factory and of the later entertainment at Mangkunegara's residence. Of the first, he says that the three-fold salvo was fired

> with such order and accuracy as must cause us to wonder;

and of the second that the women "dragoons"

> once more fired a three-fold salvo from their hand weapons with the utmost accuracy, followed by various firings of some small [artillery] pieces which had been placed to the sides, after which he went to see the Dalem[25] and the house, both fashioned after a very wonderful style of architecture . . .

This was, moreover, a period when skill with firearms was by no means universal among Javanese troops: when Greeve visited Yogyakarta the following month he recorded that the Crown Prince's troops were so unhandy in this respect that they exploded one of their weapons, wounding a European artilleryman.[26]

It may be too that women had a special role at the Javanese courts in the chronicling of court events. A passing reference from

1897 states that at that time it was still the custom at the Surakarta court [presumably the Kasunanan rather than the Mangkunegara] for an old woman (*nyai tuměnggung*) to present to the Sunan the days events set in poetic (*těmbang*) form, and that this material was later written up in a chronicle.[27] The diary used here may represent an intermediate step on the way to a Babad, or court chronicle. As it stands, it resembles others from different milieux in that the reader will find on most pages a miscellanea of information without inherent unity and not in continuous narration, with the exception of certain portions reporting important political developments. Much of what is noted can only be described as odds and ends; and, like the journalists of the future, the diarist displays a particular interest in misadventures, whether major or minor. Those she recorded include kraton fires, some serious;[28] the collapse of kraton buildings, whether in the aftermath of fire or from other causes; brawls in the marketplace; floods; epidemics; and more occasional and striking occurrences such as the most unwelcome pregnancy of an unmarried princess of Pakubuwana III's family,[29] and a ferocious attack on the part of Mangkunegara's peacock, which actually managed to kill a visitor to his residence.[30]

Here a more systematic presentation is attempted, sorting the data contained in the diary into a number of classifications relating to those subjects for which its testimony is especially illuminating, rather than simply presenting them in the chronological order in which they occur. Since the entries are often concise to the point of being impenetrable to an outsider, and the diarist herself makes no attempt to provide either context or a *résumé* of previous developments, this has been supplied from other sources where these are available.

MANGKUNEGARA I (1726–96)[31] AND THE MANGKUNEGARAN KRATON

The diary opens at a late period of Mangkunegara's career – he was approaching sixty – but it testifies to the continuing significance of the pattern and nature of his earlier life. A brief review of this may therefore be useful.

Mangkuněgura was a son of Pangeran Arya Mangkunegara, Pakubuwana II's brother, who was banished to the Cape in 1728. In his youth he was called first Suryakusuma and then Pangeran Prang Wadana. In European accounts, however, he is usually referred to as Mas Said.[32] From very early manhood he was to choose the life of a warrior: though only fourteen when the "Chinese war" broke out in 1740, he was one of the party of the aristocracy who joined the Chinese against the Dutch. He did not surrender with the "Chinese" Sunan (Sunan Kuning or Raden Mas Garendi, who was eventually exiled to Ceylon) in 1743, and remained at large with a number of other princes, insolently close to the capital, Surakarta. Pakubuwana II offered 3,000 *cacah*[33] in Sokawati (Sragen) to whomever could drive Mangkunegara and his associates from their base in that region, a task which the ruler's half-brother Pangeran Arya Mangkubumi undertook. Though Mangkubumi was successful, Pakubuwana's Javanese and Dutch advisers counseled him against fulfilling the promise he had made; and so his half-brother left the court and joined forces with Mangkunegara.[34] This was a formidable alliance: in the field Mangkunegara had acquired exceptional skill in the art of war, and his vivid personality drew men to him;[35] he and Mangkubumi attracted the larger part of élite support away from the ruler who had unwisely allowed Mangkubumi to be publicly humiliated. In the first two years of the war which followed, the VOC, with little help from the wretched ruler it was supporting, made very slight overall progress, despite victories in individual engagements. In 1748 the situation went from bad to worse. The alliance between the two rebel princes was confirmed by the marriage of Mangkunegara to Mangkubumi's eldest daughter. The "fear" and "superstitious reverence" which, according to Dutch contemporaries, they evoked among the common Javanese ensured that large numbers of followers could be enlisted to their cause. On July 28, 1750, Mangkunegara and Pangeran Singasari[36] attacked Surakarta: though the attack was beaten off, twenty-five Dutch troops and a large number of the Javanese auxiliaries were lost.[37] After this, the two princes changed to a tactic of isolating Surakarta. Though the fortunes of war were mixed and the Company's forces inflicted a number of defeats, the situation in Surakarta itself[38] was wretched, with rice and other basic commodities fetching exorbitant prices. At one period, indeed, the Company's governing body considered abandoning the kingdom of Mataram to the enemy forces. But the alliance whose force then seemed irresistible did not hold. In the last months of 1752 there were reports of differences arising between the two princes, a development which might almost have been predicted, since their alliance had been based on Mangkubumi's self-interest rather than on shared principles or objectives, and neither man was of the temperament to contemplate taking second place in whatever settlement would be made. At this juncture the Dutch commandant, von Hohendorff, began to enter into correspondence with Mangkunegara with a view to winning him over; these negotiations were protracted, and though the prince did not break them off neither did he call a halt to the war. On February 10, 1753, the crown prince himself, Pangeran Buminata, fled the capital to join forces with Mangkunegara.[39]

Von Hohendorff now suggested to the Raad van Indië that Mangkunegara might be offered the position of Crown Prince (since Buminata had conveniently forfeited his claims to this), and this proposal was accepted. At the conference of July 28, however, Mangkunegara demanded to be installed not as crown prince but as ruler. He had just defeated Mangkubumi and his forces in an engagement east of Surakarta, and seems to have felt that he was well placed to dictate the terms of peace to the Company, whose prospect of imposing a military solution he absolutely discounted.[40]

Though this confidence in his military superiority and in his ability to attract followers was not unreasonable, the hard line and inflexible demands Mangkunegara pursued in these negotiations seem to show a certain lack of awareness of the danger presented by rivals who were more willing to compromise. He had been told more than once by VOC representatives that there was already a ruler; and he should have realized that the Company was irrevocably committed to maintaining Pakubuwana III, whom it had installed as ruler on his father's death: actual deposition (as opposed to a reduction in his territory or authority) was not to be contemplated. Mangkunegara's insistence on a price higher than the Company felt it could pay opened the way for another, more realistic, claimant, to, in Louw's words, "pluck the fruits of his initiative".[41] When Mangkubumi asked for only half the realm as the price of making peace, the Company saw him as the better prospect. It seems that, after negotiation between the VOC and Mangkubumi were clearly under way, Mangkunegara sent a letter to his former ally, attempting to bring about a reconciliation and suggesting that they should attempt to partition Java between them; but Mangkubumi refused to re-establish relations,[42] and the enmity between the dynasties founded by the two princes was to become a Javanese legend. Warfare between Mangkunegara and Mangkubumi continued in earnest, with both sides suffering heavy losses;

the VOC saw that the best option open to them was to agree to Mangkubumi's demand for half of Mataram; and at the beginning of 1755 the kingdom was formally and finally divided into two.[43]

Despite the fact that the rulers of both the half-kingdoms thus created (the Sunan of Surakarta and the Sultan of Yogyakarta), and the VOC, all directed their military forces towards Mangkunegara's defeat, this was a surprisingly long time in coming. Indeed, he nearly succeeded in burning the new kraton at Yogyakarta[44] and inflicted heavy losses on a Dutch force in the Blora woods, the commander himself, Captain van de Poll,[45] being among the dead. The situation can be described as a stalemate, in which Mangkunegara was unable to prevail against the combined forces standing in the way of his conquest of Java, while these forces could not succeed in overwhelming him. During the continuing negotiations, Mangkunegara now reduced his demands, asking only for equal treatment with Pakubuwana III and Mangkubumi – that is for a division of the kingdom into three, rather than two, parts.[46] Such an arrangement was unacceptable to the two princes who had had the political realism to make a bargain with the VOC earlier; and the Company therefore refused to allow this rearrangement, perhaps calculating that to annoy two princes in order to accommodate one would be an unprofitable move. Eventually, Mangkunegara agreed to submit to Pakubuwana III, becoming a subject of Surakarta in return for a grant from the Sunan of 4,000 *cacah* situated in the Kaduwang, Matesih, and Gunung Kidul regions, and the "high title" of Pangeran Adipati (A) Mangkunegara, Senapati ing Ayuda.[47] He and his followers built the Mangkunegaran kraton in the city of Surakarta itself.

* * *

It is already more than twenty-six years since Mangkunegara laid down his weapons when the diary begins, yet we find in it strong echoes of those mid-century years of war. His court would still have included some who in their youth had chosen to fight by his side, and, even apart from this, something of the character of the period when court and army were on the move seems to have persisted. We see this in the descriptions of the great ritual celebrations of its unity: the tournaments where the Mangkunegaran soldiery competed in horsemanship and other military arts, and the theatrical and dance performances which now, three decades later,

Twilight of the old courts

still re-enacted in dramatic form the victories of past battles.[48] Naturally enough much of the diary focuses on Mangkunegara himself – on his deeds rather than his thoughts (only in moments of acute political crisis do we hear him express his feelings, usually, in these times, of bitterness or resignation) – and especially on his role in maintaining this corporate life. Much of the regular ceremonial of the court, not only in the Mangkunegaran but presumably also in the other Javanese courts, was to honour the ruler himself, most notably the celebrations to mark his birthdays. There were two kinds of birthday, the "big" or annual birthday and the "little" birthday which occurred once every thirty-five days on the occurrence of the particular combination of five-day-week and seven day-week days on which he was born.[49] Mangkunegara himself was a ruler whose personality made a particularly strong impression on those around him. It was he who maintained the court's standards for war (still at this period personally drilling his men), for the arts (he himself instructed his court dancers), and for religion, the third area in which Mangkunegaran unity' expressed itself.

ISLAM

The religious life of the Mangkunegaran occupies a surprisingly large and prominent proportion of the material recorded. We see that Mangkunegara himself, occupied as he was with so many other activities, used to write out the Kuran[50] (and that his cousin's son, the future Pakubuwana IV, asked for, and received one of the copies he had made),[51] as well as the Kitab Turutan and Tasbeh.[52] He was a generous patron of the mosques and of the *kaum* community.[53] Even more striking is his maintenance of *ibadat*, the public observances of Islam. He instructed his people on the correct procedure for performing the prayers, and indeed the whole framework of the diary itself is organized around the periodicity of the weekly *jumungahan*, the observances of Friday prayer. The diarist has kept count of the occasions on which Mangkunegara attended the *jumungahan* in the period covered by the diary: 388 times in all, over about ten-and-a-half Javanese years.

Her descriptions of these *jumungahan* always record certain things: the number of times Mangkunegara had now attended Friday prayer since the time the diary began; the number of worshippers present at the mosque; and the person or persons for

The Javanese Ancien Régime: Civilization and Society

whose spiritual benefit the *slamĕtan* (*siḍĕkah*) given after the mosque service was dedicated (except of course in the fasting month, when the common meal was not partaken of and instead money was distributed as an act of charity).[54] The Friday ritual was, however, sometimes observed with more ceremony than at others. Mangkunegara and his followers frequently kept watch the preceding night, listening to *santri* reciting the Koran or performing the *ḍikir*[55] in unison, as well as enjoying more secular amusements. Translated below are two descriptions, one of a simple and one of a more elaborate *jumungahan*.

malih asalat jumungah	He performed the Friday prayer again,
wus ping satus tigang dasa ngabĕkti	worshipping for the hundred-and-thirty
sasanga ing pujulipun	ninth time,
ing kaliwon jumungah	on Friday-Kliwon[56]
ing rabiyolakir pitu tanggalipun	the seventh of Rabingulakir[57]
tumpĕg tigang dasa sanga	There were thirty-nine *tumpĕng*,[58]
ujude ingkang kanḍuri	and the purpose of the *slamĕtan*
salamĕta pangran dipatya	was the welfare of the Pangeran Dipati
salamĕta putra wayahnya sami	and of all his sons and grandsons
salamĕt sabalanipun	and of all his army.
wong salat gangsal bĕlah	Those at the prayer numbered four hundred and fifty
pujul siji	one . . . .
. . . .	
. . . .	
(100R–101L)	

* * *

. . . .
. . . .
. . . .
. . . .

satĕnipun [sontĕnipun] malĕm jumungah ing dalu	In the evening and through the night before Friday
mĕlek malih ingkang bala	a vigil was kept by the army
kang sĕpuh pangran dipati	of the senior Pangeran Dipati[59]

. . . .
. . . .

Twilight of the old courts

. . . .
. . . .
. . . .

ander munggeng palataran	who circled the courtyard.
jěmparingan dalu sami den-tohi	They placed bets on their skill at archery,
samya ḍikir wadya kaum	while the *kaum* soldiers[60] said the *ḍikir* in unison.
sinḍenan gagamělan	There was singing, and playing of a *gamělan*[61]
gongsa kěnḍang papanganan tengah dalu	of gongs and drums, and there was a meal at midnight.
watěn [wonten] ingkang tatayungan	Some performed a *tayungan*[62]
enjinge asalate malih	In the morning they went to the prayer once again –
wus ping kalih atus salat	it was the two hundred and twenty-fourth time
pujul ping salawe prah angaběkti	the worship had been done,
kaliwon jumungahipun	on Friday-Kliwon
běsar tanggal sawělas	the eleventh of *Běsar*.
salawe prah tumpěng ing siḍěkahipun[64]	There were twenty-four *tumpěng* at the *siḍěkah*[63]
ulam sapi lir kurěban	with the meat of the cow as the sacrifice
salamět pangran dipati	for the welfare of the Pangeran Dipati.
kehnya kang salat ing masjid[64]	The number of those who performed the prayer at the mosque
pan tigang atus sawidak	was three hundred and sixty
pujul papat ingkang asalat masjid	four, performing the prayer at the mosque.

. . . .
. . . .
. . . .
. . . .
. . . .

(166R)

It will be noted that this observance took place on the night of 10th *Běsar*, the date of the Garebeg Besar,[65] which would have been the occasion for a specially festive gathering.

The Javanese Ancien Régime: Civilization and Society

The "dedication" of the *slamětan* following the Friday Prayer varies: Mangkunegara himself is most frequently named, either alone or in combination with his children and grandchildren and/or with his army. The army's welfare is often independently nominated; next in order of frequency come the ancestors.[66] Less frequently the *slamětan* is dedicated to one or more of the following: the different classifications of *nabi* – the six *nabi kalipah* and the 313 chosen *nabi*[67] – the four Companions,[68] and the different classifications of *wali*[69] – the nine *wali*; the "ten *wali* of the north and west" and the "twenty *wali*".[70] Also mentioned specifically are Nabi Kilir and Umar Maya,[71] as well as the Sultan of Pajang and Kyai Ageng Lawiyan.[72] Others occasionally nominated are the cultivators of the soil and the original settlers;[73] the girls of the court and the *priyayi*;[74] or simply "all those performing the prayer".[75]

THE KRATON AS A HOUSEHOLD

Despite this marked commitment to Islam, Mangkunegara was neither ascetic nor puritanical. Indeed, he was frequently in breach of the Kuranic prohibition on the drinking of alcoholic beverages.[76] The diarist records on numerous occasions[77] that he was "drunk" or "very drunk", on one occasion rather charmingly noting that on his return from a celebration he was "not drunk, only rather tired".[78] The following two passages are examples of a number of descriptions of Mangkunegara entertaining his sons and soldiers:

pěpěk děmang tuměnggung	Assembled were all the *děmang* and *tuměnggung*
pra punggawa pra lurah sami	and all the *punggawa* and the *lurah*,[79]
miwah kang para putra	as well as the [Pangeran Adipati's] sons.
sarwi ngaběn sawung	They joined together in cockfighting;
larih anginum adahar	drinks were served and they ate and drank
sisi[n]denan gamělan tur den-si[n]deni	to the accompaniment of *gamělan* music and *sinden* singers.
sadaya wuru panjang	They were all far gone in drink.
kalih rancak gamělan mandapi	There were two sets of *gamělan* on the *mandapa*,[80]
salendro pelog ganti tiněmbang	a *slendro* and a *pelog*,[81] played in turn,
sinelanan susuluke	and alternated with *suluk* songs,
sisinden sarta suluk	[so that there was both] *sinden* and *suluk*.[82]

Twilight of the old courts

wuru kangjĕng pangran dipati	The Pangeran Adipati was drunk.
kang putra pranaraga	His son, the lord of Pranaraga,
datĕng estri jalu	came with his wife,
tumut wuru-wuru panjang	and became very drunk too.
sarawuhnya ngabĕn sawung	After he arrived they began cockfighting,
den-si[n]deni	accompanied by *sinden* singers.
sukan-sukan sadina (133R)	They took their pleasure for the whole day.

* * *

ngabĕn pĕksi nginum wedang	They set birds[83] to fight and drank tea,
wusya wedang nginum awis	after the tea, rice brandy (*arak*):
sami wuru-wuru panjang	they were all far gone in drink.
nginum pangran adipati	The Pangeran Adipati drank too;
anulya dahar larih	and then food and drink was served,
pangran adipati tumut	in which the Pangeran Adipati joined,
tumut nginum dadahar	joined in eating and drinking.
sawusya adahar sami	After they had eaten together
para putra dadu lan pangran dipatya	his sons played dice with the Pangeran Adipati.
punggawa lurah pra dĕmang	The *lurah*, and the *dĕmang*,
rongga tumĕnggung ngabei	*rangga*, *tumĕnggung* and *ngabei*
ingabĕ sawung munggeng ngandapa	set cocks to fight on the *mandapa*;
yen larih salompret muni	they became quiet as soon as the oboes sounded.
putra pangran dipati	The Pangeran Adipati's sons
ngagamĕlan munggeng luhur	played the *gamĕlan* on the platform[84]
pangeran adipatya	and it was the Pangeran Adipati
kang ngĕndang tur	who played the *kĕndang*,[85] accompanied by a
den-si[n]deni	*sinden* singer.
langkung rame pukul gangsal	It was very lively; at five o'clock they stopped
wisan bubar. (222R)	and dispersed.

The diary contains a large amount of interesting material on the structure of Mangkunegara's family and of his household and

The Javanese Ancien Régime: Civilization and Society

army. His own family was very large, as was usual for a Javanese aristocrat. Although the diarist does not record their exact number, it is clear that the kraton housed a considerable population of *sĕlir*. The position of these women requires some further definition. European writers have often translated the term *sĕlir*, an abbreviated form of *sinĕliran* "chosen (ones)", as "concubine" (in Dutch works, *bijzit* or *bijwijf*) while others have seen some such term as "secondary wife" as preferable. Neither usage gives a satisfactory representation of the actual position of the *sĕlir*. It is clear from the diary that it was the practice to marry a *sĕlir* only when she became pregnant: this is recorded on a number of occasions,[86] sometimes involving more than one *sĕlir*. Only then did she become a "wife"[87] and might be divorced after some time if it was necessary for the prince to marry another woman, since his marriages had to be kept within the Muslim limit of four at any one time. On the other hand, the designation "concubine" wrongly suggests that there was a social stigma attached to these women. It is true, however, that their position was not conformant to Islamic law, under which a man may have sexual relationships with only two categories of women: his wives and his slaves. The *sĕlir* of the central Javanese courts were free women to whom the princes were not married. It appears that the rulers of Bantĕn resolved this problem by taking their *sĕlir* only from the villages of royal slaves, that is, those villages which during the period of Islamization had refused to embrace the new religion and had thereupon been declared to be slaves.[88] This does not seem to have occurred in central Java: in fact, according to an 1824 account, the *sĕlir* were chosen from among the daughters of Pangeran and Bupati.[89] The diarist sometimes further defines the *sĕlir* as *abdi sĕlir*. Though use of the word *abdi* (subject, servant, retainer) certainly indicates that their relationship to Mangkukĕgara was seen as one of service rather than of any kind of partnership, it is not the word used for slaves (*buḍak*, or some synonymous term such as *wong dodolan*, "sold man") and is used by the diarist to designate most of those who were in Mangkunegara's service, both female and male.

The diarist does not record the actual number of Mangkunegara's *sĕlir* (or their names: no individual personality emerges) and it is not possible to say whether he kept to the twelve the Sunan restricted himself to in 1824.[90] During the decade of the diary, however, at least fifteen children were born to him. Since thirteen of the fifteen whose births are recorded were boys – a rather unlikely

Twilight of the old courts

sex ratio – it is probable that other, female, children were born whose births were not sufficiently memorable to be noted. Of the fifteen children whose births are recorded, six died very young.[91] There was, of course, a very wide spread in the ages of each generation – Mangkunegara had adult sons and even adult grandsons – and a good deal of overlap between generations, so that the sons born to Mangkunegara in this period were contemporaries of some of his grandsons (such as Raden Mas Saluwat, born to Mangkunegara's son Pangeran Padmanagara and his *garwa padmi* – his wife of equal rank – on 17 Jumadilawal 1713 AJ/March 7, 1787 AD).[92]

Very occasionally, an important event in the life of the young children is mentioned, such as the celebration marking the completion of the first three years of life of one of his daughters;[93] or her circumcision six years later.[94] Once, Mangkunegara had three carbines made as heirlooms for three of his young sons.[95]

Mangkunegara's retainers (*abdi*) figure as prominently in the diary as do his family. They were numerous and their professional tasks varied. As well as those responsible for the more mundane domestic tasks and for waiting and serving, fetching and carrying, there were kris-makers, goldsmiths, grooms, riding-masters, *payung* bearers, and masters of traditional theatre on his payroll.[96] The diarist claims that Mangkunegara liked to make his servants happy,[97] but evidently not all of them were satisfied, and there was certainly an element of compulsion; some *abdi* who tried to decamp were seized and brought back;[98] and from other sources it seems that Mangkunegara was vexed by an exodus of retainers to the Sultan of Mataram's court.[99] By far the most prominent group among Mangkunegara's retainers, at least in the picture of his court presented here, were the soldiery. Mangkunegara's army was large, and it was growing. The diarist records the creation over this period of no less than twenty-four corps of *prajurit*[100] (fighting men). All of these corps had their own names, either denoting martial qualities ("Ferocious Lions") or associated with legendary heroes.[101] The number of men per corps seems to have varied between thirty and forty-four, usually with two *lurah* in charge. In some cases, the *lurah* were blood relations of Mangkunegara.[102]

Mangkunegara clearly spent much time with his army, training them in horsemanship[103] and in the use of traditional and modern weapons.[104] One incentive for the cavalry to learn accuracy in their movements was Mangkunegara's custom of throwing money from a stage to the riders below: those lacking in coordination of eye and hand missed the bonus.[105] He also made every effort to see that his armed forces were well equipped, acquiring larger horses to replace the cavalry's[106] current mounts, and at least trying to acquire the most modern firearms, by soliciting the good offices of Company officials.[107]

It is noteworthy that Mangkunegara had at least three corps of *prajurit* recruited exclusively from the *santri / kaum* community. These were the "Wong Prawira" (forty men under two lurah and two *kabayan*, the "Trunaduta" and the "Suragama" (also apparently forty in number).[108] They are described as *"santri ngiras prajurite"*,[109] *santri* also serving as soldiers, and, as the *bala kaum*, appear in almost all descriptions of the *jumungahan* observances, reciting the Kuran, and performing *ḍikir*.

Although the primary duty of the *prajurit* corps may have been to keep themselves in training and ready for action – which some of them did in fact see during this decade – they also performed non-military tasks, such as planting rice, repairing the buildings of the *kraton*, carrying out irrigation works, and even removing night soil.[110] Court followers in general lent a hand where it was needed; and the *sĕlir* also helped in feathering arrows and painting arrow sheaths.[111] And although they received wages for their work – their military duties, their other labors, their role in maintaining the ceremonial éclat of the kraton – there was little of the modern division between time-bought-by-the-employer and private hours: as we have seen, Mangkunegara and his soldiers not only regularly performed the observances of Islam together. They also took part together in the dances that were a central part of court life. An aristocrat was expected to perform the refined dances depicting Panji, the paragon of Javanese princes, and to cut a good figure in the *bĕksa* or *tayungan*. The Mangkunegaran soldiery frequently gathered for performances of these martial dances. The following passage describes a special celebration, the *kĕnḍuren mulud*, one of the observances held during the month of Mulud in commemoration of the death, as also the birth and life, of the Prophet.[112]

. . . .
. . . .

nulya ing sĕnen kang dina	Then on the day Monday
nĕm likur mulud kang sasi	the 26th of the month of Mulud
pangeran adipati	the Pangeran Dipati's

Twilight of the old courts

kang bala mangan anginum	army took food and drink together;
dĕmang punggawa lurah	the *dĕmang*, *punggawa*, and *lurah*,
lurah lĕbĕt lurah jawi	both inner and outer *lurah*[113]
lan sasabĕt gajihyan miwah kang sawah	and the *sabĕt*,[114] both those who were paid in wages and those holding rice-land,
sarĕng masjid ler	gathered in the north mosque for the Mulud ceremonies.
kaum satus sami ḍikir	A hundred of the kaum recited *ḍikir mulud*[115]
sawusya ḍikir ko[n] dangan	and afterward were invited
tuwuk tur barkat kanḍuri	to eat their fill and gain blessing from the *slamĕtan*.
sarĕng pangran dipati	When the Pangeran Dipati
miyos ningali kang nayub	came from his rooms to see the dancers
kang kasukan manḍapa	and revellers on the *manḍapa*
pinarĕk nginggil ing kursi	he was seated in state on a chair
paringgitan pra sĕlir kaṭah angayap	in the *paringgitan*;[116] all his *sĕlir* attended him.
busana rĕmpĕg sadaya	They were dressed all alike,
babadongan cana sami	wearing white *baḍong*.[117]
pra sĕlir larih sadaya	All the *sĕlir* served drinks,
tarap pra putra lit-alit	along with the young children,
wayah kanan lan keri	the grandchildren of the right and of the left.[118]
atap pra sĕlir ing pungkur	The *sĕlir* sat behind in orderly formation,
ningali kang kasukan	watching the revellers,
bala kasukan manḍapi	the soldiery enjoying themselves on the *manḍapa*.
titinḍihe pangran surya prang wadana	Their leaders were Pangeran Surya Prang Wadana[119]
lan tumĕnggung ing kaḍuwang	and the Tumenggung of Kaduwang.[120]
sadaya tan pĕgat larih	All served drinks without pause,
sarta mangap ḍaḍaran	and opened their mouths wide to eat.
tumut larih kangjĕng gusti	The Pangeran Dipati took a turn at serving the drinks
yen larih salpret [slompret] muni	With the sound of oboes
ingkang amĕdal rumuhun	the first to appear

The Javanese Ancien Régime: Civilization and Society

ingkang baḍaya priya	were the male *baḍaya*.[121]
suka pratama kang gĕnding	The *gĕnding* was "With Highest Rejoicing",[122]
alit-alit pipitu sisi[n] ḍen priya	and the singers were seven small boys
kayuyun ing polahira	charming in their movements,
sarta urmat mriyĕm muni	saluted by the sound of the cannon.
murub muncar kang busana	Their clothing caught the light like the glow of fire.
nulya ringgit munggeng kĕlir	Then as figures on a screen[123] came
alit-alit pawestri	small girl dancers
kang busana abra murub	their clothes a glowing red,
sakawan pelag-pelag	four in number, all extremely beautiful.
ingkang ringgit munggeng kĕlir	These figures on the screen
akĕkĕjĕr anglir parjak [prenjak] tinajenan	fluttered as swiftly as a pair of spurred warblers set to fight.[124]
mandah agĕng adiwasa	If they should be fully grown,
jogede mĕmĕt tulya sri	how captivatingly beautiful would their dancing be!
maksih rare tan sama	For already as children they have no peers:
lir kadi tan ngambah siti	their feet seem not to touch the ground,
kĕbat cukat tarampil	so swift and well-trained they are.
kacaryan sakeh kang dulu	All who saw them were entranced.
wusya nulya kang mĕdal	When they had finished, there appeared
kang baḍaya jalĕr malih	another male *baḍaya*,
pan diradamĕt sisiṇdene priya,[125]	Diradamet whose accompaniment was provided by a male singer.
duk mĕnang prang pranaraga	The victory in battle in Pranaraga[126]
baḍaya ingkang ginĕnding	was portrayed in song and dance,
rakit ing prang kasatriyan	when the knightly warriors joined battle,
pangran dipati jĕmparing	and the Pangeran Dipati loosed his arrows.[127]
susunan mangkubumi	Susunan[128] Mangkubumi
kawon kang bala keh lampus	was defeated, and many of his army killed.
nulya ganti kang mĕdal	Next appeared
pawestri ringgit sarimpi	four female *srimpi*[129] dancers.
kang ginĕnding duk aprang yogya mataram	They sang of the time of the battle of Yogyakarta-Mataram

Twilight of the old courts

duk aprang pangran dipatya	when the Pangeran Dipati fought,
angamuk ngagĕm jĕmparing	attacking fiercely, with bows and arrows.
kang mungsuh mayor walanda	His opponents were a Dutch Major,
kumpni lan bugis bali	the Company troops, the Buginese and Balinese,
wong jawa pra dipati	the Javanese and their Dipati.[130]
prang ngayogya kang arubut	It was the battle for possession of Yogyakarta.[131]
wusya sarimpi nulya	After the *srimpi* dancers,
taledek tiga kang mijil	three dancing women appeared.[132]
kang lĕbĕti rumiyin ingkang ngabĕksa	The first to join in the *bĕksa*[133]
pangran surya prang wadana	was Pangeran Surya Prang Wadana.
sarta kang mariyĕm muni	After the cannon was sounded
nulya tumĕnggung kaḍuwang	then came the Tumĕnggung of Kaḍuwang,
punggawa lurah gumanti	succeeded by the *punggawa* and *lurah*
pra dĕmang ganti-ganti	and the *dĕmang*, turn by turn
ganti lan papatihipun	followed by the Patih[134]
putra ma[n]canagara	and the younger generation from the outlying regions.
pangajĕng majĕgan ganti	The headmen and those holding land in lease followed,
wusya ganti kang para lurah balanjan	and afterwards the *lurah* who were paid money for their upkeep;[135]
kang para raden sakawan	The four Raden,[136]
wong jayengasta sinĕlir	the select Jayengasta corps,
miji nyutrayu kanoman	the Miji, Nyutrayu, and Kanoman corps,[137]
mung sasabĕtira sami	with just the *sabĕt*[138] together,
ganti-ganti lĕbĕti	entered the dance turn by turn.
wusya kandĕg mangan sĕkul	When the dance finished they had a meal of rice,[139]
ko [n]dur pangran dipati	and the Pangeran Dipati retired.

. . . .
. . . .

MONEY

Clearly, the maintenance of such a large establishment must have been expensive. One of the most interesting features of the diary is that it includes a record of much of the monetary expenditures Mangkunegara incurred. With this and information from outside the court we can go some way towards establishing the relationship between Mangkunegara's income and his expenditures, though the data are not always as precise as one would wish.

On the subject of Mangkunegara's income, the diarist gives very little information indeed; and the information available from the records of the VOC is not as useful as that provided for the two major Javanese principalities. This is because at this period the Mangkunegaran was not yet recognised as an independent, hereditary principality, as it was later to be. Mangkunegara, though a mighty subject, was nevertheless still in the service of the Sunan of Surakarta; and there was therefore no separate contract between the Mangkunegaran and the VOC such as bound the Sunan or the Sultan of Yogyakarta.[140] Hartingh's letter of March 29, 1757, reporting the outcome of his talks with Mangkunegara, notes simply that he had promised to obey the Sunan and to appear at court on the days required by custom, and had accepted in return 4,000 *cacah* situated in Gunung Kidul, Matěsih and Kaduwang. He had also requested the "high title" of Pangeran Adipati Mangkunegara.[141] There should have been a charter (*piagěm*) from the Sunan confirming this grant, but this appears to have been lost (as indeed were almost all of the documents regulating the Mangkunegaran's economic relationship with the other principalities or with the Dutch government).[142] According to Rouffaer, Mangkunegara actually received 4081 *cacah*;[143] and in 1772 a conference was held between Pakubuwana III, Mangkunegara, and Governor J. R. van den Burgh, on which occasion Mangkunegara promised to obey faithfully the orders of the Sunan and of the Company; to appear at the Sunan's court whenever required; and not to assemble more followers – especially armed followers – in the kraton or Dutch factory than was allowed according to "old Javanese custom" In return, the Sunan appointed him *wědana* of the districts of "Pandjerlan" (i. e. Panjer) and Pamarden.[144] According to the report of this conference, he already held the *wědana*-ship of Banyumas; at this period the Bupati of Banyumas[145] held the office of *wědana mancanagara kilen*, that is, the official in charge of collecting the tribute payable by the western *mancanagara*. (The lands of the Javanese principalities were classified into two groups: the *nagara agung*, regions immediately adjacent to the capital, in which the appanage lands of princes and office-holders were concentrated; and the *mancanagara*, more distant regions where the land was theoretically the ruler's own property but was managed for him by local governors (the Bupati and their subordinates) who received a percentage of its yield.) The three regions delegated to Mangkunegara by 1772 were of the following sizes, reckoned in *cacah*: Banyumas 2,029 *cacah*; Panjer 1,180 *cacah*; Pamarden 504 *cacah* – thus, a total of 3, 713 *cacah* over and above his original grant.[146]

Calculating a notional income from these lands is, as will become apparent, not entirely straightforward. The Javanese system of landholding and taxation regulations was as complicated as any, and is made unusually inaccessible by the lack of adequate records. We may begin with a statement of the general principles in operation, as set out by Rouffaer.[147] The produce of village land was conceptually divided into five parts. One part was allotted to the *bĕkĕl*, or village head. The remaining four-fifths was equally divided between the cultivator and the monarch – or, as we may prefer to put it, the "state treasury". For it is clear that the two fifths to which the ruler was entitled did not in fact, all accrue to his personal income; and it is in attempting to calculate who shared in this royal two-fifths and in what proportions, that the real difficulty lies.

Rouffaer also gives a formula by which the income from land – which would be, it goes without saying, largely in kind – can be converted into a money figure.[148] In the seventeenth century, one *jung*[149] of land was estimated to produce one Spanish dollar, or *real*,[150] in tax per annum, being the value of the two-fifths due to the ruler. By the period with which we are concerned, however, one *bau* – that is, one quarter of a *jung*[151] – now produced a *real* per annum.[152] Since, for purposes of calculating production and taxation, a *cacah* was equivalent to a *bau*,[153] each *cacah* also produced one *real* per annum for the state treasury. Mangkunegara's lands, therefore, produced 4081 + 3713 *real* in tax per annum.

But to whom did this tax go? Turning again to Rouffaer, we find that different systems for the allocation of taxes allegedly operated in the *nagara agung* and in the *mancanagara*. In the *nagara agung*, where, as we have noted, the appanage lands of princes and office-holders were located, the ruler ceded his entire right to tax to the appanage-holder. In the *mancanagara*, the royal two-fifths (calculable at one *real* per *cacah* per annum) was divided up as follows: one-fifth of this tax to the Bupati; one-fifth to the district heads (*ngabei, děmang*, etc.) and the remaining three-fifths to the ruler.[154]

Mangkunegara's lands lay initially partly in the *nagara agung* and partly in the *mancanagara*. Those in the Matesih and Gunung Kidul areas were in the *nagara agung*; those in Kaduwang, Banyumas, Panjer and Pamarden were in the *mancanagara*. His power to draw tax from these lands should, therefore, have differed between the two categories. In the 1773 land settlement, however, all the latter[155] regions were reclassified as *nagara agung*. According to Rouffaer's systemization, therefore, Mangkunegara should then have been ceded by the ruler the entire right to the tax payable in all his lands, which were now entirely within the *nagara agung* category.

Unfortunately, the evidence of the diary contradicts this formula. In 1788 – well after the reclassification took place – Mangkunegara made a request for an extra 600 *cacah*, or, if this was not possible, to be allowed to hold his existing lands tax-free. Clearly, then, he could not have enjoyed the exclusive right to tax his landholdings at that time, but must have paid a certain proportion to the Sunan. But what proportion? Rouffaer's formula is now clearly inapplicable, but perhaps a rough guide can be obtained by the following reasoning: if Mangkunegara requested either an extra 600 *cacah* (from which the tax revenue would presumably be shared by him and the Sunan in the same proportion as before) or to have the tax due to the Sunan on the earlier 7,794 *cacah* remitted, we may assume that this was a "trade-off", and that the revenue sums involved were roughly equal. (It is unlikely that they would be exactly equivalent: 600 *cacah* looks very much like a "round figure".) Using the following procedure, let A stand for the Sunan's share and B for Mangkunegara's.

$A + B = 1 \quad A = 1 - B$
 A's share of 7794 is
$7794A = 7794(1 - B)$

B's share of 600 is 600B. Since B's share of 600 compensates to B for A's share of 7794, equate the two

$600B = 7794(1 - B)$
$(600 + 7794B) = 7794$
$B = 7794/8394 = 0.93$

Hence, (Mangkunegara's) share is 93%.

Thus, it seems that about 7 percent of the tax revenue of Mangkunegaras lands went to the Sunan. The majority of Mangkunegara's lands [156] had recently been reclassified as *nagara agung*. This reclassification had been greatly to Mangkunegara's economic advantage as the Sunan claimed a much larger proportion of the tax (three-fifths) on *mancanagara* land. The Sunan apparently, however, continued to exact a small proportion of the tax, even though all Mangkunegara's lands were now in the *nagara agung* where, according to Rouffaer, the ruler had ceded his taxing rights to the appanage holder.

We may calculate, then, that 7 percent of the 7,794 *real* produced by these lands went to the Sunan, and a further 20 percent would have gone to pay those of Mangkunegara's *lurah* and other officers who were paid in land.[157] It seems that a *lurah* in Mangkunegara's army might expect to receive about 17 *jung* in lease, plus the loan of a buffalo to work this land.[158] Deducting the Sunan's 7 percent (=546 *real*) and the *lurah*'s 20 percent (=1559 *real*) from the original sum of 7,794 real we arrive at the figure of 5,689 *real* as the sum Mangkunegara himself may be thought to have derived from taxing his landholdings.

One other source of monetary income should be mentioned: it appears that Mangkunegara received a share of the 10, 000 *real* per annum which the Sunan received from the VOC for the lease of the north coast. His share was apparently 400 *real*.[159] Adding this to the income from his lands we arrive at a figure of 6,089 *real* per annum. This income was to be considerably augmented when in the second half of 1790 the VOC granted him an annual allowance of 4, 000 *real*.[160]

This calculation of an "annual cash income" from Mangkunegara's lands is, however, an oversimplification of the actual situation. Since harvests varied from year to year, so too did the money value of the tax levied. One writer notes that a *gaṇḍek* (envoy from the capital) was sent out to the region concerned to make an assessment of the tax due, based on the actual total production, for each harvest. Thus there was considerable variation in the amount of produce coming in, particularly in a period including some years of poor harvests, as was the case in the late 1780s to early 1790s.[162] Secondly, the amount of produce arriving at the capital was divided out in a rather complex fashion, which was probably adjusted according to the perceived needs of the time. An example taken from the diary illustrates the complexities of distribution in the second half of the month of Besar 1717 AJ (August 1791),[163] thirty *amet* [164] of rice arrived from the Mangkunegaran lands and was divided out as follows: to the *abdi balanjan* (that is, those retainers who were paid in cash and kind as opposed to those paid in land); to the Resident; and to the Chinese and small traders (presumably for sale). A few days later more rice (quantity unspecified) arrived and was divided out among Mangkunegara's servants, the Patih and the *wĕdana*, family members,[165] the army, and religious functionaries, namely the *pĕngulu, marbot*,[166] *kĕtib*,[167] and *jamsari*.[168] Again, early in Mulud 1718[169] (late October 1791), one *amet* of rice was delivered to the Resident. At this time Mangkunegara himself and the *prajurit estri* went out to the villages to watch the harvesting. More rice was later given to the Resident and Second Resident, and some to the Sunan and to Mangkunegara's sons in their own districts. Immediately after this distribution was made, however, Mangkunegara had to buy rice from the market: the diarist explains that there was a shortage of rice at this time[170] (perhaps also the reason behind Mangkunegara's despatch of rice to his sons in their appanages). One thousand one hundred and forty *tompo*[171] of rice were bought at a cost of 114 *real*. Half this quantity was distributed among the *dĕmang, lurah, rangga, punggawa* and *tumĕnggung* in Mangkunegara's service and among his sons and grandsons, and the other half was offered in a *slamĕtan*.

We see therefore that the rice was distributed on different bases: to those of Mangkunegara's servants and officers who held no land in lease, as a supplement to their money wages (curiously similar to the system in use for Indonesian bureaucrats today); to the Sunan, in payment of his share of the land's produce; and to the Dutch, Chinese, and traders, for sale. On this occasion, there was not sufficient rice to meet the obligations to retainers and to the Sunan, and to fulfill "contracts" to the Dutch and Chinese for a certain quantity, and Mangkunegara ended up by having to purchase rice in the market.

The yield of the harvest which came in from Sura 1715 (October 1788) had also been insufficient, and rice had to be bought. In a letter of July 1790 Greeve mentions that the rice harvests of the preceding years had been poor, and predicted (the above evidence shows wrongly) that this one would be better.[172]

We can conclude, therefore, that Mangkunegara's income from his lands was subject to considerable fluctuations depending on the size of the harvest in a particular year. Yet his cash commitments were substantial.

Twilight of the old courts

To get some idea of his annual monetary expenditure, we may take the figures given for 1717 AJ (1790/91 AD). He made the following payments:

1. 6 Sapar: wages (amount not specified) paid to newly created *prajurit* corps.[173]
2. 20 Mulud: payment of *anggris* and *ḍuwit* to the value of 1,560 [*real?*][174] (to the *abdi* in general).
3. 24 Mulud: 1,408 *real*[175] (to the soldiery).
4. 28 Mulud: wages (amount unspecified) paid to newly created *prajurit*[176] corps.
5. 17 Rabingulakir. As above, number 4.[177]
6. 7 Jumadilawal. 345 [*real?*] to the *bala kaum*.[178]
7. 12 Arwah. 200 *real* to the soldiers; 6,000 *ḍuwit* to the *lurah*.[179]
8. 11 Sawal. 1,600 [*real*]: half were *real anggris*, half *real batu*,[180] (to the soldiery).
9. 17 Sawal. 1,000 *real* in the form of *ḍuwit* (to the soldiery).[181]
10. 17 Sawal. 300 *real* (to the sons, grandsons and great-grandsons, and to the serving girls).[182]
11. 24 Sawal. 400 *real* and 700 *anggris* (to the *lurah*).[183]
12. 14 Bĕsar. 1,025 *real* (to the soldiery).[184]

Two patterns are apparent in this table: first, the concentration of payments in the months of Mulud and Sawal. Taking the record of the diary as a whole, a pattern of half-yearly payment of salaries is confirmed. The second of these two payments was known as the *gajihing (wulan) Siyam* (Ramadan/fast month salary) but was actually paid in the following month, Sawal. Secondly, it is clear that the wages of the soldiery comprised a very large proportion of the total: in comparison, the amounts received by the other court servants (the *abdi*) and by Mangkunegara's own sons and further descendants, are quite small.

Totalling up the payments for 1717 AJ, we come up against the problem posed by the different currencies in which these are given. Unfortunately, the second half of the eighteenth century was a time of considerable confusion in the monetary situation in Java, when a great number of different types of specie, locally struck or imported from abroad, were in circulation without any well-established mutual relationships.[185]

Secondly, the precise meaning of all of the Javanese terms used by the diarist may need some reconstruction. Most of the payments are specified in *real*, that is, in the Spanish dollars which were for so long the standard unit of exchange on[186] Java and in the neighbouring regions. As noted above, the annual payment made to the Sunan and the Sultan as rent for the *pasisir* and its incomes was made in Spanish dollars (10,000 to each ruler). In some entries the diarist describes the *real* more specifically as "*real batu*", or "*real anggris*". The first term may be taken to indicate the very rough, unfashioned pieces of silver which were provided with a stamp and exported from Spanish America, even as late as the eighteenth century.[187] They were known to the English as "cobs".[188] What exactly the diarist means by *real anggris* is uncertain. According to Crawfurd, this term was used for the Spanish dollar in general, because, in his opinion, it was much used by English traders.[189] It is possible, however, that the diarist uses it for a specific type of Spanish dollar.[190] In any case, the different types of Spanish dollar noted by the diarist were in circulation at equivalent values, and were accepted by her as such (see, for example, entry no. 8).

We find a total of at least 6,633 *real* (Spanish dollars) of different types paid out here; but much more probably a total of 8,538, adding in the two payments (nos. 2 and 6) where the amount is noted but the coinage is apparently not specified. In the present writer's opinion, the diarist uses the word *arta*, which is commonly used to mean money in general, to denote the *real* specifically, and has done so in these two entries. In addition, there is the single payment where the amount is given in *ḍuwit* (6,000). The Java *ḍuwit*, unlike the Dutch coin after which it was named,[191] was accounted at 4 to the *stuiver*, thus 320 to the *real*, so that this amount comes to the quite small sum of 18.75 *real*, bringing the total amount of wages for which the actual amount is recorded to 8,556.75. There remain, however, three entries (nos. 1, 4, and 5) for which neither the amount nor the coinage is recorded. One may suppose that the total wage bill, allowing for these amounts and possible incompleteness in the diarist's records, must have been in the vicinity of 10,000 *real*. It is also worth noting that a majority of the wage payments recorded in the diary seem to have been advances ("*ngĕmping gajih*" – see entries 3, 5, 8, 9, and 10), often at the request of those concerned, so that we may conclude that Mangkunegara's men did not regard their wages as adequate, and the old prince must have been under constant, if respectful, pressure for further payments.

Furthermore, the wage bill was not Mangkunegara's only regular commitment. The diarist records a continuing and considerable

Twilight of the old courts

expenditure on presents, an inescapable requirement of the life of the period, which will be discussed below. He had in addition other expenses which, though not recurrent, might involve very large amounts. In 1787, for instance, he had to pay gold to the value of 3,816 [*real?*] to the Sunan as the *paningsĕt*[192] for his daughter, who was being given in marriage to Mangkunegara's son.

What does this analysis of Mangkunegara's finances reveal? First, a perhaps surprising degree of monetization: wages in cash amounting to c. 10,000 *real*; and other large money payments, such as the gold coins as marriage-payment for the Sunan's daughter. Presumably the means whereby Mangkunegara's income, which would have been for a large part in kind, was converted into cash for his expenditure was via the sale of agricultural produce, principally rice, to Chinese and other buyers.

Second, a rather dangerous balance between income and expenditure. With an income of about 6,000 *real* from his lands, Mangkunegara was paying out about 10,000 *real* per annum on wages, not to speak of the sums required for participating in the obligatory round of present giving described below, and for other expenses unavoidable for a man of his station. Even when he began to receive a further 4,000 *real* per annum from the VOC, this sum would barely have closed the gap between his previous income and his wages bill.

The fact that the largest amounts for wages were paid to the soldiery raises another interesting point. At this period, Mangkunegara was apparently losing more followers to the Sultan than he was attracting to his own kraton. Ricklefs has suggested that the preponderant direction of the movement of courtiers is an indication of which court was "stronger in terms of legitimation".[193] The above analysis suggests that it should perhaps rather be explained in terms of relative economic strength and the ability to meet a large wages bill, which was clearly taxing Mangkunegara's finances to their utmost. Particularly important was the capacity to pay the soldiery – who, as we have seen, received the lion's share of wages – in view of the implications this had for the relative military strength of the rival courts. One should note, however, that Mangkunegara's court was not suffering from a large-scale exodus, that significant numbers of followers (who were subsequently enlisted in the Mangkunegaran military forces) did come over to him from the Sultan's people, and that, as we have seen, a strong *esprit de corps* existed among Mangkunegara's dependents.

The Javanese Ancien Régime: Civilization and Society

Given the unhealthy relationship between his income and expenditure, what could Mangkunegara do? It was not in his power to increase the size of his landholdings and, though he might have tried to obtain for himself a larger share of the tax-bearing capacity of his existing lands, it is questionable how far he could succeed in this. One way of increasing his income was to adapt to new opportunities and changed circumstances by beginning to produce those cash crops which could be sold to the VOC, and this he did. In a letter of 1792, we find him requesting the Company to provide instruction in the cultivation of pepper and indigo, which his men did not then know how to grow.[194] In the nineteenth century, the cultivation and processing of sugar and coffee was a major element in the Mangkunegaran's finances.[195] Another way in which the economic fortunes of Mangkunegara's descendants became dependent upon the colonial government was through the transformation of the highly developed military and equestrian expertise which we have already noted into the institution of the "Mangkunegaran Legion". This was established by Daendels in 1809 as a sort of cavalry reserve for the colonial army, and Raffles subsequently agreed to pay 1,200 *real* per month towards the maintenance of this force, which then consisted of 900 footsoldiers, 200 cavalrymen, and 500 mounted artillerymen. During the course of the nineteenth century, however, the Legion lost its potential serviceability as a real fighting unit, and by 1910 neither the infantry nor the cavalry could be considered fit to see service.[196] Even with these new developments, however, the Mangkunegaran fortunes went through some difficult times in the course of the nineteenth century.[197]

So from the late eighteenth century onwards, the economic viability of the Mangkunegaran became increasingly dependent on its connection with the colonial government, with obvious implications for its political independence. It would be wrong to conclude at once that the same economic forces pushed the two larger principalities in the same direction. They had larger resources than the Mangkunegaran, and a separate investigation is necessary to establish whether these larger resources were a buttress of comparative independence (at least until the series of territorial annexations culminating in the truncation of 1830) or whether they merely produced Mangkunegara's problems on a larger scale. Certainly, it is clear that the Sunan shared some of these problems, in particular the constant difficulty of exerting effective control over his subordinates, with all that this implied for economic strength or weakness. The diarist repeatedly records royal decrees issued by the Sunan and his Patih providing for the chaining, beating, or imprisonment of officers and officials holding land in excess of the amount to which they were entitled,[198] and this suggests that these decrees were not very effective. When the eastern *mancanagara* lands belonging both to Surakarta and to Yogyakarta were annexed by the colonial government in 1830, an investigation was made into the amount of taxation which the two courts had actually drawn from these lands. The figure arrived at represented less than 20 percent of the total revenues of the regions concerned, a notable contrast to the 40 percent which was claimed.[199] This effectively demonstrates, in the economic sphere, how very far theoretical formulations such as those given by Rouffaer may be from actual practice. The diarist does not, however, provide the same detailed information on the Sunan's finances as she gives for the Mangkunegaran, and no more can be said on the subject here.

SURAKARTA SOCIETY: TWO KRATONS AND A VOC GARRISON

The diarist does not concentrate exclusively on the internal affairs of the Mangkunegaran kraton, and the diary gives many fascinating sidelights on the general pattern of life, at least in the ambiance of the courts. The daily round and common task – especially building work in the kraton, and the maintenance of irrigation and water works[200] – are described, as is the ceremonial surrounding special festivities such as royal marriages. On 14 Jumadilakir 1713 AJ (April 3, 1787).[201] Mangkunegara's son, Raden Suryakusuma, married the Sunan's daughter, Raden Ayu Supiyah, a marriage of considerable political importance. Mangkunegara had dedicated two *slamĕtan* to his future daughter-in-law, and Suryakusuma had put away his various *sĕlir* and three children in order to receive the princess "with a pure heart".[202] Two of the children (like their mothers "in a pitiful state")[203] were adopted by Mangkunegara himself, and the third by Pangeran Surya Mataram.[204] The marriage was followed by a number of receptions and on 22 Jumadilakir, cannon salutes from the Mangkunegaran and the senior kraton announced that the consummation of the marriage had now taken place.[205] This cannon salute seems to have been standard ceremonial to mark the consummation of royal marriages, as for instance on the occasion of the marriage of Pakubuwana IV when he was still heir-apparent, where the salute is described as *pratonḍa bĕḍah kuṭa*, "sign that the citadel is breached".[206]

While the rhythm of Mangkunegara's life seems to have been dominated by the observances of the weekly *jumungahan* (Friday prayer), the Sunans appeared as[207] regularly for the *sĕton* as at the mosque. The *sĕton* was a spectacle which usually began with a *watangan* (lance tournament) and ended with a *rampogan sima*, in which the Sunan's men, armed with pikes, formed a square around a tiger, advanced on it together, and killed it.

Very occasionally, *a sima-maesa* (tiger vs. buffalo) fight was held. In view of the symbolism often ascribed to this combat – the tiger representing the Dutch, the buffalo the Javanese[208] – it may be worth noting that the future Pakubuwana IV arranged such a performance for Greeve, the Governor of the northeast coast, while his father lay dying. If this was really a sinister sign of his future attitude towards the Company, it appears to have had no effect on the Governor, who immediately afterwards promised the old Sunan that he would ensure his son's succession.[209]

The royal tigers were also used as a form of execution for rebels and criminals[210] which one might assume was a cruel and certain death, but which in fact was not always fatal. On one occasion two men, accused of entering the kraton without authorization, were set to fight three tigers. Though they were armed only with clubs, and "tired" tigers were exchanged for "fresh" and even "fierce" ones they survived, though wounded, to be exiled, "knowing what life and death were".[211]

The drama of these spectacles was not enjoyed in the Mangkunegaran. When the Sunan held the *rampogan sima*, Mangkunegara usually arranged for cock or quail fighting[212] to be held for his army. This spectacle was greatly valued, not only for the enjoyment it offered, but also because cock and quail fighting were among the *awisan*: the prerogatives of the Sunan and his family, forbidden to anyone else.[213] On two occasions the diarist notes with pride Mangkunegara's exemption from this prohibition, an exemption which was, she claims, obtained for him by the intercession of the "Kumpĕni" (the VOC.[214]). The exemption was perhaps a matter of particular pride because Pakubuwana III otherwise insisted on the rigorous observance of the prohibition on cock fighting, and on one occasion a number of his own followers were imprisoned for a time for infringing it.[215]

Twilight of the old courts

The aristocracy was extremely conscious of the need to maintain the external signs of gradations of rank – a typically aristocratic concern which was in this case somewhat unexpectedly reinforced by the attitude of a structurally nonaristocratic institution, the VOC. Perhaps because, once having committed itself to the maintenance of a certain constellation of Javanese princes, it saw the utility of allowing each star to shine with the appropriate lustre, the Company was punctilious in observing protocol.[216] Invariably, when the Governor of the Northeast Coast visited Surakarta, he, the highest Dutch official present, would place himself by the Sunan, while the Resident accompanied Mangkunegara.[217] Within kraton society a breach of protocol was deeply resented, as when Mangkunegara's sons were seated at a reception given by Pakubuwana IV in a position which did not take account of the fact that they were attending not in their personal capacities but as representatives (*wakil*) of their father.[218]

Outings, presents, and claims

There is little evidence in the diary of anything that can be dignified with the name of European cultural influence emanating from the VOC presence, which consisted of the two Residents and their subordinates and a garrison intended to keep Javanese rulers and princes in line, and hardly displayed an interest in the higher things of Europe. However, the Javanese courts and the Dutch representation to the princely capitals participated in a number of joint functions, and at the period of the diary these seem not to have been the stuffy, formal affairs we know of from the second half of the following century. The musical background provided by both Javanese and Dutch ensembles has already been commented upon;[219] and the last descriptive passage of any length in the diary describes an *al fresco* entertainment, a pleasure trip taken by Pakubuwana IV in company with the Dutch contingent, after his reconciliation with the VOC. This passage falls into two separate parts, with the diarist returning to the subject after a couple of pages recording domestic matters. It seems that she must have received more information about events that had occured during the outing and its aftermath. As a sketch of court life under the young Sunan, it has its own interest and humor, and is reproduced here in full:

The Javanese Ancien Régime: Civilization and Society

akad pon sapar kang sasi	On Sunday-Pon,[220] Sapar[221]
taun je tanggal sadasa	the tenth, in the year Je[222]
prabu sala e[n]jing miyos	the ruler of Sala came out [from his palace]
ameng-ameng acangkrama	to go on a pleasure trip,
měndět ulam bangawan	intending to catch fish in the Sala river
ḍumatěng rantan sang prabu	at the royal fishing-grounds.[223]
pukul pitu angkatira	The time of his departure was seven o'clock.
miyosipun saking puri	He left the palace
tan ngangge urmat sanjata	without the salute of guns:
narendra ical urmate	the king put aside all ceremony
ical wawanguning nata	and regal distinctions.
miyose sasaking pura	He came out of the palace
kori ing pasowan kidul	by the door of the south audience-hall.
tumut sang ratu kancana	The Ratu Kancana[224] went with him.
upruk lan para upěsir	The Resident and all the officers
tumut dragunděr kapalan	went too, the dragoons on horseback.
patih wadana mantrine	The Patih, the *wědana* and *mantri*
pra sěntana estri priya	and the royal relatives, female and male,
lan sagagamanira	with an armed escort,
nitih tanḍu lawan ratu	rode in palanquins, as did the queen.
sang nata nitih turongga	The ruler rode on horseback.
tamtama kapalan sami	The Tamtama[225] corps were all on horseback;
carangan wong prawirengan	a section of the Prawirengan corps,
ḍarat wong kawan dasane	forty men, were on foot,
jajarira tumalatar	beside the men of the Tumalatar,
satus lan wong macanan	a hundred in number, and the Macanan men.
wong nyutra usar ing ngayun	The Nyutra men and the hussars were in front
lampahe mantri wadana	The *mantri* and *wědana* proceeded along,
watěn [wontě] saréng watěn [wontěn] kari	some staying together and some getting left behind;
santana datan atata	the royal relatives did not keep in order
salang tu[n]jang ing lampahe	but went along kicking into each other.
pangeran ing purubaya	Pangeran Purbaya
nusul kantun lampahnya	followed later, for he was left behind

80

Twilight of the old courts

mangkudiningrat tan tumut	Mangkudiningrat did not go along;
tumut santana sadaya	all the [other] royal relatives were there.
jĕng gusti pangran dipati	Our revered Pangeran Dipati
datan tumut acangkrama	was not in the party:
eca aneng dalĕme dewe	he took his pleasure in his own residence.
caosan dalĕm baita	The royal boats were fitted out,
pipitu ginubahan	seven of them, with curtains,
kajang ing papayonipun	palm-leaf walls and roofs.
gamĕlan munggeng baita	There was a set of *gamĕlan* on the boats
sarancak samargi muni	which played as they went along,
sarancak muni ing darat	and another set playing on land.
pangran purubayane	Pangeran Purbaya,
kang sinepa panĕmbahan	who may be compared to a *Panĕmbahan*,[226]
kantun ing puri pisan	was at first left in the palace,
tan dangu [? illegible]	and followed on not long
praptane nusul	afterwards [?].
lĕnguk-lĕnguk pasanggrahan	He sat down to rest in the *pasanggrahan*.[227]
lir pendah sarana sĕkti	As if by magical means
. . . . kahe[228] *pangran purbaya*	was Pangeran Purbaya's . . .
kinĕdep-kĕdepa tyase	His feelings were made clear:
wong salakarta sadaya ja	"All you people of Salakarta[229]
na wani maringwang	be not bold with me!
ingsun kang ju[n]ljung prabu	It was I who raised the ruler;
aja na ingsun pan sirna	without me the king will disappear!"
298L *lampahe sri narapati*	The king proceeded on
sarawuhe pasanggrahan	and when he arrived at the *pasanggrahan*
baris gagaman rakite	the armed escort drew up in their ranks.
mung kadok [kodok] ngorek	Only the *kodok ngorek*[230]
kang ngurmat	gave a ceremonial welcome.
tĕdak sri naranata	The king went down
pinarak pinggir ing banyu	to the edge of the water, escorted
upruk upĕsir sadaya	by the Resident, and all the officers.
lan ratu munggeng ing kursi	The queen sat on a chair.
patih wadana santana	The Patih, wadana, and royal relatives
tarap munggeng ngandap ander	sat in packed rows in the royal presence.

The Javanese Ancien Régime: Civilization and Society

ḍawuh timbalan sang nata	The ruler gave the order:
panjalan mĕnḍĕtana	"Fishing boats, take
ulam ruru[m]pon ing banyu	the fish in the dam out of the water."
sawusya tĕlas kang ulam	When the fish were finished,
tĕḍak nata mring banawi	the ruler went down to the river,
lan upruk lumban baita	and boarded a boat with the Resident
lan para upĕsir kabeh	and all the officers.
sang nata munggeng baita	As the ruler traveled by boat
marang ruru[m]pon ngandap	down to the dam,
sarta gamĕlan tinabuh	the *gamĕlan* was struck.
papatih mantri wadana	The Patih, *mantri*, and *wĕdana*
ḍarat sami ajagani	kept watch on shore,
yen kanḍas gered baita	and if the boat ran aground they pushed it off.
gamĕlan sarta sinḍene	A singer sang with the *gamĕlan*
kasukan lumban bangawan	as they took their pleasure on the river;
ĕnti tyas sukanira	their delight knew no bounds.
gagaman malatar agung	The arm-bearing men were spread out in large numbers,
jajari pinggir bangawan	lining the edge of the river.
buminata mangkubumi	Buminata and Mangkubumi,
rayi nata langkung suka	the younger brothers of the ruler, were greatly delighted.
sarawuh ruru[m]pone	When they arrived at the dam,
pinarak pinggir ing	they were ceremonially escorted along the edge
toya	of the waters.
ruru[m]pon pinĕnḍĕtan	The dam was emptied,
wusya tĕlas ulamipun	and when the fish were finished
nata kondur masanggrahan	the ruler went back into the rest-house.
gamĕlan kang ḍarat muni	The *gamĕlan* on land sounded
mapag watĕn [wontĕn]	to receive them at the
masanggrahan	rest-house,
barung tambur salomprĕte	in concert with drums and oboes.
anulya sang nata ḍahar	Then the ruler was served a meal;
upruk pĕsir sadaya	the Resident and all the officers
sĕntana kang agĕng tumut	and the senior royal relatives joined him,
babangku kursi aḍahar	sitting on benches and chairs.

82

Twilight of the old courts

ḍahar tan pĕgat alarih	As they ate, drinks were served without pause
tan ngangge urmat sanjata	but with no ceremonial salutes.[231]
wusya ḍahar sigra baḍol [boḍol]	When they had finished eating they set out,
ko[n]dur anitih baita	returning by boat.
upruk pĕsir sadaya	The Resident and all the officers
sami anunggang parahu	went by boat,
gagaman lumampah ḍarat	[but] the armed men traveled by land.
sarawuhe batu radin	When they arrived at mBatu Raden
tĕdak saking ing baita	they descended from the boats
nitlh kuda sakondure	and proceeded back by horse,
nata anitih kareta	the ruler traveling in a carriage,
datan urmat sanjata	without ceremonial salutes.
angadaton wanci surup	They came into the palace at sunset,
bala kang ngiring bubaran	and the accompanying army dispersed.

* * *

(299L)
. . . .
. . . .

amangsuli caritane	returning to the story
duk sunan sala acangkrama	of the Sunan of Sala's pleasure trip
mring bangawan rarantan	to the dam on the river:
duk arsa ingangkatipun	when they were about to leave,
kapal dalĕm kinambilan	the royal mount was being saddled
daragĕm ulĕs turanggi	– it was a chestnut horse
pun palugon wastanira	called Battlefield-
dĕlalah budi bĕṭate	and as luck would have it, it was in a temper.
kakapal [error for kakapa] dalĕm wasiyat	The saddle was a royal heirloom
ki rĕmĕng wastanira	called "The Dark One",
tiba tugĕl pĕcah rĕmuk	and it fell, and broke all to pieces.
langkung duka prabu sala	The ruler was greatly angered.
duk wontĕn ing rantan malih	Again, when they were at the dam
wĕlandi angrĕbut dĕgan	some Dutchmen were grabbing at young coconuts,
katiban dĕgan ĕndase	and one was hit on the head as the coconut fell.

The Javanese Ancien Régime: Civilization and Society

walandine kulabakan	The Dutchman fell all of a heap.
malih wong kawan dasa	Also, forty[232] people
kasepak kuda kang baṭuk	were kicked in the head by a horse.
kang nepak kapal barangan	It was the horse of some traveling players,
wasta maesa malati	called Jasmine Buffalo.
kasepak baṭuke pĕcah	[One who][233] was kicked in the head died.
prabu sala sarawuhe	When the ruler of Sala arrived [back]
kapal ginantung ing latar	he hung the horse in the courtyard.
wiwit ga[n]tung salasa	It was hung there from Tuesday
ing jumungah dereng lampus	and by Friday it was still not dead,
tan sinungan ngumbe mangan	[though] it had not been given food or drink.
duk rumiyin anglĕrĕsi	Once, it happened
sĕptu miyos pawatangan	that on a Saturday, when the royal party was leaving for the tournament,
kagĕm dalĕm turanggane	one of the royal horses
pĕṭat ucul kakambilan	broke loose, and threw off its saddle,
pan kalĕbĕt dilalah	seized by an unlucky whim.
umangkat sako[n]duripun	Both leaving and returning
cangkrama tan ngangge urmat	on the pleasure trip were without the ceremonial forms
ical wawangunan narpati	and the regal distinctions disappeared.
pangran purbaya winarna	About Pangeran Purbaya:
marang papatih dĕlinge	he said to the Patih:
sun-dĕnda patih janingrat	"Patih Jayaningrat, I fine you
jaran siji ta sira	one horse,
mulane tan aweh wĕruh	since you did not inform me
duk mangkat nata cangkrama	when the ruler was leaving on the pleasure-trip,
ingsun iki mangkat kari	and my departure was delayed.
purbaya ana ing sala	Purbaya of Sala
kapadakĕn tunggak bae	was made to look like a cast-off!"
ature patih janingrat	Patih Jayaningrat said:
milanipun kawula	"The reason that I

84

Twilight of the old courts

tan kabĕr [kobĕr] ngaturi wĕruh	did not have the opportunity to inform you
bingung kaṭah padamĕlan	[is that] I was distracted by so much work,
tan kabĕr [kobĕr] atur udani	so I had no chance to inform you.
lan angger mongsa kilapa	And, young worthy,[234] how could you be mistaken?
otĕr wong sanagarane	All the people in the city were in a bustle
yen sunan mangkat cangkrama	about the Sunan's pleasure-trip.
pami kula matura	If I had told you,
winastan wong sasar-susur	I would be called a man who does not know the proper thing,
manawi kang paribasan	like the proverb,
ingsun den-wehi udani	'I am given to know
ingsun wus wĕruh piyambak	[what] I already know myself.'
kalingane purbayane	How strange that Purbaya
kaparentah mring janingrat	should be commanded by Jayaningrat!
gĕde kandel janingrat	Great and trusted is Jayaningrat!
kalawan ta malihipun	And moreover,
pangran purbaya neng sala	Pangeran Purbaya of Sala
mangke wus nampni kardi	has now been given authority
barang prakawis ing praja	over all matters of state,
wĕnang macot [mocot] lan agawe	having power to dismiss and to appoint.
janingrat mangke kasimpar	Jayaningrat is now cast aside
lir kadi wong galaḍag	like a serving-man.[235]
yen sampeyan maksa munḍut	If you insist on taking
ḍenḍa kang kapal satunggal	the fine of one horse,
saking barkating narpati	by the beneficence of the king,
janingrat tan kirang kapal	Jayaningrat will not lack a horse,
dinĕnḍa nuhun dukane	craving the king's mercy over this punishment.
malah purbaya kaḍenḍa	In fact Purbaya has been punished,
kantun angkat narendra	by being left behind when the king departed.
neng sala sinĕpuh-sĕpuh	In Sala he is considered so very senior,
kinarya gĕḍig manggala	and has been made the champion.
punapa ta kongsi kari	How could he have been left behind,

The Javanese Ancien Régime: Civilization and Society

wong kinarya panĕmbahan	someone made a Panĕmbahan?
mokal tan mirsa angkate	How could he possibly not hear the departure?
wong sanagara pan mirsa	Everyone in the city heard it."
kendĕl pangran purbaya	Pangeran Purbaya was silent:
kalĕrĕsan sauripun	well-placed was the reply
kiya patih jayaningrat	of Patih Jayaningrat.

One mode in which relationships between the different parties represented in Surakarta were formally expressed was exchanges of presents, which are recorded in great detail throughout the diary. According to the circumstances, they were statements of alliance, requests for advancement from a patron, rewards for services rendered, or efforts to conciliate the loser at the end of a round of political manoeuvres. When a new Resident, Andries Hartsinck, arrived in Surakarta on June 19, 1788, accompanied by his young daughter and by the Resident of Semarang, he presented Mangkunegara with a carbine and gold cloth. Mangkunegara himself gave a diamond ring to each of the two Residents, and to Hartsinck's daughter; and a couple of days later, on the occasion of the Resident's installation, a piece of batik and a Balinese kris to Hartsinck himself and some fragrant oil to his daughter. According to the diarist, Hartsinck was very impressed by the favour done to him, and showed great honour to Mangkunegara.

More was to follow: Mangkunegara's sons, Suryamerjaya and Suryakusuma, now gave Hartsinck a horse, complete with saddle and other accoutrements, and an ornate kris. Two days later, the diarist ingenuously records, the Resident sent a letter to Mangkunegara announcing that Suryamerjaya would be appointed in Wirasaba and Suryakusuma would receive the title of Pangeran. This favour cannot have come unexpectedly, but must have resulted from the "discussions" which the diarist notes that Mangkunegara had been having with the Resident in the preceding days, but whose content is not recorded. Suryamerjaya and another of his brothers immediately called on the Resident to present a gold bowl worth 140 [*real*] and to express the pious hope that the advancements would indeed be made.[236] When Governor Greeve came to Surakarta about a month later, Mangkunegara sent four of his daughters to present a silver and gold tray worth 140 *real* and ten broad and narrow *kain* with 10 headcloths; the sons gave Greeve a horse worth 60 *real* and a gold-ornamented kris

Twilight of the old courts

worth 50 *real*, as well as making various gifts of clothing to those in his entourage.[237]

When the Governor did meet the dying Sunan, the latter asked him to guarantee his son's succession. Greeve agreed, but followed this with a request for the appointment of Suryamĕrjaya to Wirasaba, and elevation of Suryakusuma (whose appanage was in Ponorogo) to the rank of Pangeran. When the Sunan agreed to this, the Governor apparently added, in the diarist's report, "What about T[r]enggalek as well?"[238] Even at this the Sunan did not demur, and this region was added to the appanage of Suryakusuma, who received the title Pangeran Purbanagara.[239] Mangkunegara was then summoned by the Sunan and informed of the lands and rank bestowed on his sons, which he received with appropriate expressions of gratitude. Afterwards he joined the heir apparent on the *maṇḍapa*: the future Pakubuwana IV asked his uncle for a gold bow and arrow, and promised that Suryakusuma's appanage would indeed be increased to include Trenggalek. In the event, Mangkunegara gave him two gold bows, a quiver of arrows, and the saddle and other accoutrements of a horse.

So far, the direction of the present giving may suggest a one-way exchange or even bribery, but the Governor reciprocated Mangkunegara's favor with a return gift of lace clothing, a pair of fine rifles, and six bottles of rosewater, estimated by the diarist to be worth a total of 690 [*real*]. The Dutch on their side also considered present giving as one of the routine expenses of their representation at the courts, and adjusted the value of the gift to the political status of the recipient: see, for example, the entries under "schenkagie" in the accounts of the period.[240] Perhaps there is something symbolic of the increasing technological divergence between the two civilizations in that in these exchanges of presents we find the Dutch requesting the hand-painted arrows and quivers which were a curiosity in their culture, and Mangkunegara and his fellow princes the modern firearms which were unobtainable in theirs.[241]

Was this a Theatre State, as defined by Geertz? Certainly, as we have seen, it had theatre aplenty, but so did the states headed by, for example Henry Grace à Dieu, the Sun King, or Queen Victoria.

But the core of Geertz' definition of the theatre state is that it is one where "Power served pomp, not pomp power", a "to us, strangely reversed relationship between the substance and the trappings of rule".[242] And it is hard to argue on the evidence of this guardswoman's diary that the theatrical element of the Mangkunegaran was not very much pomp in the service of power – military power (as in the dances celebrating past victories), sexual power and virility (so closely associated with military prowess, as the salutes to proclaim that "the citadel was breached" on wedding nights), and financial power (which the salary figures make clear was also linked with military power). This conclusion is strengthened by the fact that all the rest of the diary deals with power plays by the central Javanese aristocracy, particularly Mangkunegara himself, the Sunan of Surakarta and the Sultan of Yogyakarta, by various political and, with the accession of the young Pakubuwana IV, military manoeuvres. I have detailed these political power plays and military mobilisations elsewhere.[243]

But perhaps the whole distinction between states where pomp serves power vs. those where power serves pomp is an untenable one. Is the role played by the, to an outsider, not very different but certainly competing pomps and trappings of the Orthodox and Catholic churches in Eastern Europe merely a cover, an *aling-aling* as the Javanese would say, for power relationships whose "real" substance is something else, or has the symbolism of these trappings actually had a powerful role in determining the focus of conflicting armed forces? Did the Englishmen who died over the decoration of the altar and the ritual surrounding it "really" die because of a power conflict that had nothing to do with their beliefs, or did these beliefs impact powerfully on the structures of English society? – if one may be forgiven for thus baldly and plainly canvassing such dilemmas after a century or more of sophisticated sociological investigation and analysis. The evidence here suggests classic Weberian patrimonialism, rather than a "theatre state".

The court discovers Java

The world of the central Javanese kraton as depicted by the guardwoman seems a very limited one, depicting the centre of the realm and even then only a martial prince, his retainers and his peers and rivals. I should add therefore that there is evidence from other sources that the central Javanese courts were developing an awareness of a larger Javanese world.

The text I shall use is the very large text known as the Major Cěntini which represents a rather late stage of the evolution of its genre. Part of one manuscript of this text was edited by R. Ng, Soeradipoera, R. Wirawangsa and R.M.A. Soerjasoeparta and published by the Bataviaasch Genootschap van Kunsten en Wetenschappen in four volumes between 1912–1915, and a summary of the same text was published in 1933 by Pigeaud.[244] The date of composition is given in the opening lines as 1742 A.J. (1814 A.D.), and the work was commissioned by the Crown Prince of Surakarta. Its authorship is extremely problematic, and it is clear that numerous pre-existing texts of various sorts – not only of the same but of different genres such as *babad*, *primbon*, and *suluk* – have been incorporated in one way or another.[245] This work is only the best-known and most elaborated of a long tradition of works in a genre which has been labelled by Pigeaud "vagrant students' romances containing encyclopaedical passages" (an awkward designation that nevertheless has the virtue of making us pause before pasting a European genre label over them). A Javanese term for these works is *santri lalana*, "wandering scholar". There are very many manuscripts which belong to this classification, most of them of unknown authorship, with boundaries between conceptually separate "works" as we expect to find them in the European tradition greatly blurred by the Javanese practice of continuous revision and silent incorporation of pre-existing material.[246] The core of this classification is formed by the *Jatiswara*, *Cĕntini*, *Madujaya*, *Pujakusuma*, *Dara Murtasiyah*, and *Gatoloco*.[247] The interrelated *Jatiswara* and *Cĕntini* texts span the period from c.1600 to mid 19th century (with an odd example later). In all cases the basic framework is provided by a narrative of the adventures of a "student" (an advanced student, in the sense that scholars call themselves "students") of religious truth who has undertaken extensive travels over Java in search of those who can advance his quest. Moving from one village to another, he debates some crucial aspect of religious knowledge with the religious adepts who offer him hospitality and solicit his opinion. The narration of the hero's adventures is in the third person; it is in verse (*tembang macapat*) and not in prose; and the formal divisions of the text are provided by change of metre, which produces a division into cantos.

A number of different themes are common to the *santri lalana* corpus: separation of the hero from a loved one, who may be father, brother, or wife, the resolution of this theme of separation providing the narrative tension of the text; a series of sexual encounters in which the hero's conduct and its description range from extremely restrained to highly exuberant; and the nature of ultimate knowledge and thaumaturgical power. Despite its apparent "foreignness", there are elements of our own literary landscape in the *Cěntini:* of the heroic-epic theme of the legitimate heir fleeing the capital/kingdom when it is overcome by the enemy, of the picaresque epic, especially the early Spanish type (vide the exploits of the servitors in both cases), and of the philosophical epic, perhaps most notably Tristram Shandy.

The Javanese setting of these works is a setting which becomes progressively elaborated in an interesting and revealing way to the point where it comes to occupy a major part of the text. There seems to be a progression from early, geographically "unlocated" works, set very vaguely in Java but where few if any of the villages and hermitages can be identified with real places and where the hero is not a Javanese but someone from overseas, to later works which describe many places in Java with great specificity. Curiously enough, there is a "coast-to-interior" movement over time in the focus of these texts somewhat analagous to the process of discovery attested in Dutch maps and descriptions: the earliest works of the genre certainly seem to be from *pasisir* centres, notably Cirebon. Why does description of Java (albeit as setting, not subject) appear so late? why is it connected with the itineraries of foreigners coming to Java? Was knowledge of the Javanese landscape previously considerably less panoramic than knowledge of the Java seascape, or is it just that the intellectual tradition of Java was not oriented towards geography? Do the *santri lalana* texts represent a physical or a mental discovery? I believe that both are the case: larger areas of Java were being brought within the purview of the elite, and a shift in the intellectual tradition of Java from a largely a-temporal a-specific, universalistic viewpoint to a more empirical and particular one was also taking place.

The illustrative material I will use here – arbitrarily seizing upon a chunk of this voluminous and inter-related corpus – comes from the beginning of the Major Cěntini. The section discussed here is the first and less reworked and elaborated part, dealing with the adventures of an associate, Ki Cabolang, of the main hero of the *Cěntini*.[248] In a huge text whose bulk makes it difficult to include here, this section comprises 321 cantos of between 10 and 100+ stanzas each, with an average of probably 40–50. Because of the back-and-forth and overlapping of Cabolang's travels, however, to list all the places that he visits might be counter-productive, so I have further limited comment to the itinerary of the first section, a mere 87 cantos.

Twilight of the old courts

The work begins with an account of the political circumstances which led to Cabolang's journey. The story of the hero and his associates is entangled not only in Java's identifiable geography but also in Java's history, specifically the conquest by Mataram of the Islamic "theocracy" of Giri (founded by the *wali* Sunan Giri) in the early seventeenth century. Searching for associates lost in the confusion of war, the eponymous hero (or depending on how one reads the text, anti-hero) Cabolang and his companions visit the following places: the remains of the Hindu-Javanese kingdom of Majapait [fl. 14th-15th centuries] in east Java; the Blitar region and the Hindu-Javanese temple Panataran; the Lodaja and Tuban regions, where they traverse wooded country; Mt. Pandan and the village of Kedaton, where they find very large bones which the head-man explains are the bones of demons slain by Bima; Mt. Gambiralaja, where they see a large phallic image; Bojanagara, where they see a smoking pond; Dander, a village of smiths; Dandangilo, site of a hot spring, Sela, Kasanga, and Grobogan; the remains of the [10th century?] kingdom of Mendang Kamulan; Kradenan; Sela again; Gubug, where they see a fire in the middle of a *sawah* (wet-rice field); Undakan and Prawata; the remains of the Sultanate of Demak [fl. first half 16th century]; the mosque of Demak; Mt. Murya, where they visit the grave of Sunan Murya; Pekalongan and Mt. Panegaran, where they are received by a hermit (*resi*); Mt. Slamet, where they are received by a Shaikh; Mt. Sawal and Mt. Cerme, where they are once again received by hermits; Mt. Tompomas in the Priangan region; the mountains Tunggul, Tangkuban Prau, Burangrang, Wayang, Sanggabuwana in the Krawang area; Mt. Gede and the dwelling of a holy man (*ajar*); Bogor and the remains of the west Javanese Hinduized kingdom of Pajajaran, at the foot of Mt. Salak; Karang; Wanakrama, where they are welcomed to the mosque-school of Sidacerma by the principal teacher (*kyai*); Pasuruhan; the mountainous Malang area, where they visit some temples; the Tengger mountains, a Tengger (Hindu-Javanese) hermitage and holy man; Klakah, the foot of Mt. Lamongan; Kandangan, at the foot of Mt. Smeru in the Lumajang region; Mt. Arga, where they are received by a seer (*wiku*[249]); Mt. Rawung in Banyuwangi; Pekalongan, Sokayasa; Mt. Rawung again, where they are received by a female hermit; Banyuwangi and Mt. Ijen; the remains of the old capital of the Hindu-Javanese kingdom of Blambangan and its temples; Ragajambi, Pekalongan, Sranggi and Sokayasa; the

The Javanese Ancien Régime: Civilization and Society

Hindu temples of the high Dieng plateau; Jalatunda, and Sokayasa again. The section that follows begins with a visit to the holy (Islamic) graves on Mt. Lawet.

Looking back then, what are the features of the Javanese landscape chosen for attention by the author (or authors) of this work? They are firstly, aspects of the natural landscape (woods and springs, caves, mountains, and ravines) and secondly, phenomena of the cultural landscape, especially antiquities, graves, mosque-schools, and hermitages. The mosque-schools are frequently located on the north coast; but the graves and hermitages, which seem in many ways to be the most significant places of pilgrimage, are in the mountains. "Javaneseness" is also celebrated in the text in its voluminous description of all the traditional arts and sciences of the island. The text is heavy with such description, marvellously done: the material on Javanese music, for example, is superbly evocative. For the modern European reader the great barrier to appreciating such material is the fact that as this encycopaedia-ising interest in things Javanese (geography, history, religion, society, arts, civilisation) has developed, the narrative structure of the older *santri lalana* works has been retained, and social and intellectual questions are canvassed as dialogues within the plot, which is not what we expect of encyclopaedias. By comparison, Valentijn for all his personal anecdotal style does objectify and label subjects, such as "Javanese government" or history. And the overall approach, again in contrast to Valentijn, is a non-quantitative one. There is no counting of distances, villages, inhabitants, production, or years. But though the text does not count years or include a section labelled "History of Java", look at the antiquities visited by Cabolang. It is striking that by the end of this first section he has visited the ruins of most of the important Hindu-Javanese kingdoms and of the first Islamic kingdom, the Sultanate of Demak, whose mosque has unique status in Javanese Islam, and also the grave of one of the apostles (*wali*)of Islam on Java, Sunan Murya. It is not only the presence of the Islamic past and the Hinduized past that makes itself felt, but also that of the legendary past: witness the bones of the giants. We can hardly doubt that Cabolang is discovering Javanese society, history, geography and civilisation in a new way and at a new level. If we wish to make a comparison with a European work, it seems to me most useful to adduce, not the great encyclopaedias which were somewhat contemporary, but another 18th century work, Sterne's Tristram

Twilight of the old courts

Shandy, which displays the same encyclopaedic knowledge and philosophical reflection as the *Cěntini* does, albeit on nothing like the same enormous scale.

Both these works in their different ways celebrate Javaneseness. Other views of Javaneseness were becoming tenable, and we shall turn to these in Chapter 6. The following chapter deals with the enormous "reach" of Javaneseness, far beyond the exemplary centre of the courts into the distant provinces, and the socialisation process by which a child – who is by definition, *durung jawa*, "not yer Javanese", becomes Javanese and a member of a society that invested great effort in fitting the peg to the hole.

NOTES

1 The manuscript itself is KITLV Or [Koninklijk Instituut voor Taal-, Land- en Volkenkunde Oriental Ms.] 1 No. 231 of the collection of the Institute at Leiden. It is in book form on Javanese bark paper, and comprises 303 large double pages (that is, when the book is opened only the left page is numbered, so that, according to modern convention, the diary would comprise 606 pages). All references to the diary will cite only the relevant page number, with L or R to signify the left or right side: for example, 311R, 300L.

The number of pages, 202, given in Dr. Th. G. Th. Pigeaud's catalogue, *Literature of Java* (The Hague: Nijhoff, 1968) 2, p. 832, is not correct. The diary manuscript was in a state of disarray when it was presented to Dr. Pigeaud (who later presented it to the Koninklijk Instituut collection) by Mangkunegara VII. Its loose pages were put in order and bound, but the cover-page had suffered considerable wear. This cover-page contains four Javanese- script inscriptions in different hands – none of them that of the body of the manuscript – and one inscription in Arabic script (*pegon*).

Beginning at the top of the page, the first Javanese-script inscription says that the work was written by Bagus Prawiratruna, the scribe of Sergeant Kock ("Sareyan Kok") of "Siti Rawi," (the old name for Ambarawa: see M.C. Ricklefs, *War, Culture and Economy in Java 1677–1726: Asian and European Imperialism in the early Kartasura period*, Asian Studies Association of Australia Southeast Asia Publications Series no. 24, Allen and Unwin, Sydney 1993, p.313 n.5) and also mentions a milkman (*tukang pěrěs*) of Salatiga, whose name (Wiryadirana??) is not fully legible. In addition, it seems unlikely that such a low-ranking officer as a sergeant would have had a "Javanese scribe" assigned to him.

The second Javanese-script inscription, which is upside down, mentions a certain Adiwirya of Semarang (it appears to read: *ngalamat sěrat . . . tura yingkang rama adiwirya ing suměwis*).

The third Javanese-script inscription seems to be just a line of *těmbang* verse with no particular reference to the diary (*lambang raras tansah bronta kingkin*, "harmonious form, endlessly longing," plus a couple of illegible words).

The last Javanese-script inscription apparently names a particular village, now faded out (*punika atur [?] pratelanipun adĕdĕkah [?] eng dusun..*)

The Arabic-script inscription repeats the information contained in the first Javanese-script inscription. Apparently the manuscript has passed through different hands, and the relationship between them is not clear.

2 *pemut kang anĕrat prajurit carik estri/anutugakĕn carita sĕrat babad tutur/ing wulan siyam / tanggal kalih likur / maksih taun jimawal / angganing warsya / 1717 / watĕn [wontĕn] nagari salakĕrta*. Words in square brackets occurring in the Javanese text indicate the standard spelling of words which in the original have either an archaic or an idiosyncratic spelling.

3 *sĕrat lajĕng kang sĕkar pamijil / papanipun seos / urut carita seyos papane / saking panjang carita tinulis / maksih carik estri / kang nĕrat nunurun //*

4 The day of the seven-day week (Sunday to Saturday) is always given, sometimes in combination with the day of the five-day week (Lĕgi or Manis, Paing, Pon, Wage and Kliwon) as in *salasa-manis* (Tuesday-Manis).

5 Because of the importance of the Friday prayer observances, discussed below, the date of the month is given on every Friday for which there is an entry, for example, *dina wage jumungah/tanggal ping nĕm likur bĕsar wulanipun*, Friday-Wage the 26th of the month of Bĕsar. The year is given on the first day of every new year, for example, *nulya di[n] tĕn sĕptu wage salin wulan // tanggal pisan sasi sura / salin jimawal kang warsi / kuda eka syaraningrat*: "then it was the day Saturday-Wage, the first day of the month of Sura. The year changed to Jimawal [the third year of the eight-year *windu* cycle] 'one horse, voice of the ruler' [chronogram for 1717 AJ]. The year is also noted on the occasion of some particularly important event, such as the installation of a new ruler.

6 There are a number of late eighteenth-century Mangkunegaran Babad, but none seems appropriate. The British Library Manuscript No. Add. 12283 (see M. C. Ricklefs and P. Voorhoeve, *Indonesian Manuscripts in Great Britain*, London: Oxford University Press, 1977 p. 45) was written in 1705 AJ (AD 1779) on the occasion of Mangkunegara's 55th birthday, but it describes the wars leading to the partition of Mataram and ends in 1682 AJ (1756–57 AD). Another Mangkunegaran Babad, Add. 12280 though from a later year (1727 AJ/1800 AD) also deals with these wars, breaking off after describing the building of the new *kraton* of Yogyakarta in 1756.

7 Ricklefs, *Jogiakarta*, p. 304, n. 42: apparently the Yogyakarta crown prince's corps was the occasion of "notoriety." See Koloniaal Archief [henceforth KA] 3708, Vereenigde Oost-Indische Compagnie Overgekomen Berichten [henceforth VOCOB I 1789, Semarang to Batavia, August 19, Greeve's diary for August 13.

8 See H. J. de Graaf, ed. *De Vijf gezantschapsreizen van Rijklof van Goens naar het hof van Mataram 1648–1654*, The Hague, Nijhoff, 1956, pp. 25–60.

9 François Valentijn, *Oud en Nieuw Oost-Indiën*, vol. 4, *Beschryving van Groot Djava ofte Java Major*, Dordrecht, Amsterdam: n.p., 1726, pp. 59–60.

Twilight of the old courts

10 See Beaulieu's account in *Navigantium atque Itinerantium Bibliotheca*, ed. John Harris, London: Bennet, 1705, 1, p. 744.
11 *Begin ende Voortgangh, van de Vereenighde Nederlantsche Geoctroyeerde Oost-Indische Compagnie*, vol. 1, *Historishe Verhael Vande Reyse gedaen inde Oost-Indien, met 15 Schepen voor Reeckeninghe vande vereenichde Gheoctroyeerde Oost-lndische Compagnie: Onder het beleydt van den Vroomen ende Manhaften Wybrandt van Waerwijck*, Amsterdam: n.p. [1644] pp. 31–32 of last fascicule.
12 R. C. Temple, ed., *The Travels of Peter Mundy* 1608–1667, 5 vols. Cambridge, Hakluyt Society, 1907–1936, 3, p. 131.
13 The facts of Hamzah's career have been enormously elaborated and expanded in the epics it inspired, which are full of amazing feats and adventures and not always esteemed by educated Muslims. Both Arabic and Persian versions exist, and the Malay and Javanese versions derive from a Persian original: see Ph. S. van Ronkel, *De Roman van Amir Hamza*, Leiden, Brill, 1895, pp. 91–98, 165–66, 176, 184, 245–51.
14 For a synopsis of the Rěngganis story, an original Javanese composition which grew out of the Menak material, see R. M. Ng. Poerbatjaraka, P. Voorhoeve and C. Hooykaas, *Indonesische Handschriften*, Bandung, Nix, 1950, pp. 1–17.
15 The year was 1714 AJ and the date converts to July 31, 1788.
16 The Governors of Java's northeast coast, the most important of the Company's officials so far as the central Javanese courts were concerned, are usually referred to by the diarist as "the Děler," which is derived from Dutch *edelheer*, the title they bore as members of the Governor-General's Council.
17 That is, Mangkunegara, who is nearly always referred to in the diary simply by his title, "Pangeran Dipati."
18 This word is used in its original sense of "An establishment, such as a trading station, where factors or agents reside and transact business for their employers".
19 To be metrically correct, this verse should have two more lines.
20 The Nyutrayu and Jayengasta (see next line) were names of corps in Mangkunegara's armed forces.
21 The V.O.C. (First) Resident at Surakarta is referred to, here and elsewhere in the diary, as the "*upruk*," from Dutch *opperhoofd*, "head" (of mission) the designation generally used in the VOC letters of this period.
22 *Arak* is a strong drink prepared from a base of sugar-cane and glutinous rice.
23 That is, the future Pakubuwana IV, who is referred to here as "the younger Pangeran Dipati," in contradistinction to "the elder Pangeran Dipati," i.e. Mangkunegara.
24 Lit. "the elder Pangeran Dipati."
25 In the Dutch "*dalm*," from Jav. *dalem*, noble or princely residence.
26 See entries of Thursday, July 31, and Wednesday, August 13, in Greeve's diary, which is found under Semarang to Batavia, August 19, in KA 3708, VOCOB 1789.
27 See F.C. de Haan, "Naar Midden Sumatra in 1684", *Tijdschrift voor Indische taal- land- en volkenkunde* 39 (1897), p. 346.

28 See 68, 157–59, 178, 183–84, 198–99. See also the letter of Governor Greeve to Batavia, March 14, 1789, in KA 3754, VOCOB 1790, mentioning a serious fire in the Mangkunegaran. Fire was a constant hazard in the old Indonesian cities and is the major reason for the loss of all old kraton buildings.
29 31R.
30 300L. Even if the Javanese should be read as a plural, this is still a remarkable feat for one or more peacocks. The diarist solemnly concludes that the man must have been a bad character: otherwise, none of the God-fearing Mangkunegaran domestic animals would have harmed him.
31 Mangkunegara celebrated his 59th birthday early in the period covered by the diary, on (Sěptu Wage) 4 Arwah 1709 AJ (23R); so that he was born on 4 Arwah 1650 AJ, which is April 7, 1726. This date is confirmed by another Mangkunegaran manuscript, Add. 12283 (see above n. 10) where the opening passage notes that it was written in Arwah 1705 AJ on the occasion of Mangkunegara's 55th birthday.
32 See, for example, P. J. F. Louw, *De Derde Javaansche Successie Oorlog*, Batavia, Albrecht Rusche, 1889. To avoid inconvenience to the reader, I have used "Mangkunegara" throughout, even at the risk of an occasional anachronism – though it should be noted in this connection that Javanese (as opposed to Dutch) sources claim that this title and dignity were assumed very early, at the end of the Chinese war and certainly before they were "bestowed" by the V.O.C. in 1757. (See, for example, *Babad Petjina* [Semarang: van Dorp, 1874] p. 412.)
33 On the nature and value of the unit *cacah*, see above p. and below p.
34 On the developments which led Mangkubumi to take this step see Ricklefs, *Jogjakarta*, pp. 39–46.
35 Hartingh described him as a small, well-made man whose eyes shone with fire and vivacity. See Louw, *Derde . . . Oorlog*, p. 17.
36 See Louw pp. 18–33, for the developments of these years.
37 Louw, p. 38.
38 Louw, pp. 54–55.
39 Louw, p. 73.
40 Louw, pp. 80–81.
41 Louw, p. 81.
42 Louw, p. 91.
43 On the details of the partition, see Ricklefs, *Jogjakarta*, pp. 61–95.
44 Ricklefs, *Jogjakarta*, p. 91.
45 See J. K. J. de Jonge, *De Opkomst van het Nederlandsch Gezag in Oost-Indie* The Hague, Nijhoff, 1878, 10, p. LXXVII.
46 See Ricklefs, *Jogjakarta*, p. 91.
47 The terms of the settlement with Mangkunegara are to be found in Hartingh's letter of March 29, 1757, reporting the outcome of their talks (KA 2802, VOCOB By 1758).
48 See below pp. 24–25.
49 These are the *tingalan agěng* and the *tingalan alit* (*ngoko* forms *wěton gěde* and *wěton cilik*) noted frequently in the diary. Mangkunegara's *tingalan alit* (small birthday) was on the day Akad-Manis (Sunday-Manis:

according to the system used, Manis, or Lĕgi, is either the first or second day of the five-day week).

50 He also, on occasion, wrote *jimat*, that is, phrases, formulae (usually Arabic) and diagrams written on pieces of paper or cloth and thought to convey special protection. They were carried by soldiers or people engaged in risky undertakings and were specially valued if made by a person who had reached a high level of religious knowledge and practice.

51 117R. On another occasion Mangkunegara assembled 400 *santri* to recite the Kuran for the benefit of the ailing Pakubuwana III, after dreaming that this would cure the Sunan's illness (127R)

52 The Kitab Turutan were schoolbooks for children who had mastered Arab script, and contained simply a small part (at most one *juz*) of the Kuran. See L. W. C. van den Berg, "Het Mohammedaansche Godsdienstonderwijs op Java en Madoera en de daarbij gebruikte Arabische boeken," *Tijdschrift voor Indsche taal-, land- en volkenkunde* (henceforth TBG) 31 (1886) pp. 518–55; esp. p. 519. The Tasbeh is the rosary, with which the names, or eulogies, of Allah are repeated, usually 100 times.

53 See, for example, 115R and 238 for gifts of money, rice, and clothing (*klambi* and *jubah*, the latter a garment worn by mosque officials) to mosques in and around Surakarta. The *kaum* community were Javanese and people of other nationalities especially devoted to Islam, living in the mosque quarter.

54 For example, 150L, 240.

55 *ḍikir* (Ar. dhikr, "reminding oneself", of God): a sort of Islamic litany, of which both the form and the content vary. The *ḍikir* may be said loudly or to oneself; as a solitary exercise or in a group or circle, as here. The content of the *ḍikir* may be simply the name of God (Al-lah) or one of its synonyms, or may include a number of verses of the Kuran. Finally, different techniques (breathing exercises, body movements) may be performed in order to facilitate the inner experience which the *ḍikir* is designed to produce. For a treatment of *ḍikir*, which is of special importance in Muslim religious practice, see G. C. Anawati and Louis Gardet, *Mystique Musulmane*; 2nd ed. Paris, Vrin, 1968, pp. 187–234.

56 Kliwon is the fifth or first day of the five-day week (according to the system used).

57 The fourth of the twelve Muslim (lunar) months.

58 A *tumpĕng* is a cone of rice surrounded by side dishes, prepared for a *slamĕtan* or banquet.

59 Mangkunegara is referred to here as "the senior" Pangeran Dipati because at this period the same title was borne by the Crown Prince of Suiakarta, the future Sunan Pakubuwana IV.

60 On the *kaum* or *santri* component of Mangkunegara's army, see below p.

61 The word "*gamĕlan*" is used by the diarist for any sort of musical ensemble, including an orchestra or ensemble of European instruments. It seems that on specially festive occasions both Javanese and European gamelan played, sometimes overlaid by cannon salutes (see, for example, 265R- 266L for a description of a large party given by Pakubuwana IV to mark the restoration of good relations with the Company).

62 The *tayungan* dance was a dance of ornately-costumed archers: see Th.

Pigeaud, *Javaanse Volksvertoningen*, Batavia, Volkslectuur, 1938, p. 427. In the twentieth century it was performed by a group of courtiers, but in the diary it is performed by the soldiery.

63 The ritual meal after the Friday prayer is referred to either as a *kĕnduri* (from the Persian) or as a *siḍĕkah* (from the Arabic) as in the first passage.

64 The five lines omitted give details of wages paid by Mangkunegara to his soldiers.

65 The Garebeg Besar, one of the three main annual court festivals, celebrates the pilgrimage and Abraham's offering up of Isaac. See J Groneman, *De garĕbĕg's te Ngajogyakarta*, The Hague, Nijhoff, 1895, p. 40.

66 *Luhur sadaya*: see, for example, 167R, 183L, 244L, 251L, 265L.

67 In Sunni tradition the following enumeration of prophets has become accepted (though it is not found in the Kuran): there are 124,000 *nabi* in all, of which 313 have been chosen (in Javanese, *sinĕliran*) to be messengers (*rasul*); the six foremost are Adam, Noah, Abraham, Moses, Jesus, and Muhammad, after whom no more prophets appear. See C. Snouck Hurgronje, *Verspreide Geschriften*, Bonn, Leipzig, Kurt Schroeder, 1923, 1, p. 405.

68 *Sahabat sakawan*: the Companions of the Prophet, who subsequently became the first four caliphs (see, for example, 243L, 263R).

69 See, for example, 154R, 243L, 247R, 263R. The nine *wali* are the apostles of Islam on Java. Javanese lists of these *wali* do not always name the same nine: see Ricklefs *Jogjakarta*, n. 12, pp. 4– 5, for an account of these variations. The lives of some of the *wali* have been described in D. A. Rinkes' series of articles in TBG, 52–55 (1910–13).

70 55L. As the veneration of *wali* (representatives of God or "saints") became more and more widespread in Islam, the idea of a hierarchy (or rather, a number of different hierarchies) of saints also developed. The pinnacle of these hierarchies was usually the "pole" *wali* (the *Ḳuṭb*). The present writer does not know of any system in which there are ten *wali* at each of the cardinal points of the compass, though in some Turkish and Algerian systems one finds a disposition of four "pillar" *wali* at these points; and in other systems one finds also a classification of forty *wali*. On the different *wali* systems, see M. Th. Houtsma, A. J. Wensinck et al., *The Encyclopoedia of Islam*, Leiden, London: Brill/Luzac, 1934, 4, pp. 1109–10.

71 55L. On the cult of Nabi Kilir (Ar. Al-Khaḍir or al-Khiḍr) the "green immortal," and its origins in the Kuran and the Alexander romances, see H. A. R. Gibb and J. H. Kramers, eds. *Shorter Encyclopedia of Islam*, Ithaca: Cornell University Press, 1957, pp. 232– 35. In Java, Nabi Kilir is best known in his role of presiding over the sphere of water. Umar Maya is the most faithful and constant companion of Amir Hamzah in the Hamzah epic, known in Java as the *Menak*.

72 266R. According to Javanese tradition, Pajang has the distinction of being the first Islamic sultanate in central Java. Kyai Agĕng Ngĕnis (father of Ki Pamanahan, the first ruler of Mataram in traditional accounts) was buried at Lawiyan and is presumably the "Kyai Agĕng Lawiyan" honored here. See *Babad Tanah Djawi*, ed. W. L. Olthof, The

Twilight of the old courts

Hague: Nijhoff, 1941, Jav. text p. 46. Another possibility is Pakubuwana II, whose grave is at Lawiyan. See H. J. van Mook, "Koeṭa Geḍe," *Koloniaal Tijdschrift*, 15, p. 359.

73 *Sakehing bumi, cakal-bakal sadaya*: for example, 216R, 253R, 278L.
74 249L, *manggung-katanggung priyayi*. J. F. Gericke and T. Roorda, *Javaansch-Nederlandsch Handwoordenboek*, Amsterdam, Muller, 1901, define the *manggung* as young girls taken into the kraton with a view to their later becoming *sělir* of the ruler. J. W. Winter, in his description of Surakarta in 1824, ranks them as "concubines of the third class" in the court hierarchy. J. W. Winter, "Beknopte beschrijving van het hof Soerakarta in 1824," *Bijdragen tot de taal-, land- en volkenkunde* (henceforth BKl) 54 (1902), p. 52.
75 For example, 243R.
76 There are, of course differing interpretations of the Kuran. In seventeenth-century Aceh, according to an English visitor, alcohol from rice (rather than grapes or fruits) was not considered as prohibited: see Albert Hastings Markham, ed., *The Voyages and Works of John Davis*, London, Hakluyt Society, 1889, p. 151.
77 For example, 98R, 102L, 133R, 161L, 162R, 169L, 264R, etc. Governor Greeve also noted on one occasion that Mangkunegara had excused himself from talks on the grounds that he had drunk too much: see Greeve to Batavia, September 24, 1790 in KA 3833, VOCOB 1792.
78 *Pangran dipati tan wuru/amung ragi kěsěl kewala* (269L).
79 Titles of officers in Mangkunegara's armed forces: *tuměggung* is the most senior, followed by *punggawa, děmang,* and *lurah*.
80 A pavilion (with roof but without enclosing walls) in front of the kraton used for reception of guests and entertainment: modern form *pěṇḍapa*.
81 *Slendro* and *pelog* are the two tone systems of Javanese music.
82 *Sinḍen* usually refers to vocal music (in *těmbang macapat*, the same type of verse in which the diary is written) sung by a female singer in conjunction with dance movements. *Suluk* (also in *těmbang macapat*) are best known as the set pieces sung by the *ḍalang* at prescribed intervals during a *wayang* performance (see, for example, J. Kunst, *Music in Java*, 3rd ed., The Hague, Nijhoff, 1973, 1 pp. 318 ff.), but there are also self-contained songs, not part of a dramatic performance, called *suluk*, which often express religious or philosophical concepts. A number of collections have been published,
83 Female quails (*gěmak*) as well as cocks were used as fighting birds.
84 This refers to the raised inner square stone floor of the open audience hall where the festivities are taking place.
85 The *kěndang*, either alone or together with the *rěbab* (two-stringed bowing lute) guides the tempo of the gamělan, and, because of this function, is "the instrument *par excellence* of the *lurah gěnding*, the leader of the orchestra."(Kunst, *Music of Java*, 1, p. 212.)
86 See, for example, 144L, 202L (more than one *sělir* taken in marriage) 226R.
87 J. W. Winter, writing of the Sunan's court in 1824, says that it was customary for a *sělir* to be married when pregnancy was first clearly evident, at about three months. (Winter, "Beknopte Beschrijving," p. 51.) She would then be known as a *garwa sělir* (*sělir* wife).

The Javanese Ancien Régime: Civilization and Society

88 See Veth, *Java* vol, 1, pp. 356–59, and L. W. C. van den Berg, *Inlandsche Rangen en Titles op Java en Madoera* (Batavia: Landsdrukkerij, 1887), p. 64.
89 Winter, "Beknopte Beschrijving," p. 52.
90 Ibid., p. 52. The Sunan kept other women as *srimpi* and as *manggung*.
91 29L, 351-R, 84L, 140L, 176R, 234R.
92 103L. For this birth, the diarist notes the name of the *wuku*, the patron divinity (Dewa), the bird, and the tree appropriate to the time of birth: see Ch.3. below on the *wuku* system.
93 201L.
94 192R.
95 283R.
96 268L.
97 81R.
98 See also 68R where two Mangkunegaran headmen are dismissed for receiving "Mataram spies," presumably sent to foment trouble and discontent.
99 See Ricklefs, *Jogjakarta*, pp. 232– 34. Ricklefs attributes the trickle of court musicians, artisans, etc., away from Mangkunegara's court to his diminished appeal for elite support in terms of legitimation and status. It would seem however that his economic position must have been the main reason for this phenomenon for, as we shall see below, Mangkunegara's finances were stretched beyond their limit and his followers were continuously asking for advances on their wages. In general, it seems that the flight of retainers from one court to another was for personal reasons (money, love affairs, etc.) and major figures did not change sides for purely political reasons. In December 1783 the Sultan's secretary Setrawiguna, who had been embezzling money, fled from Yogyakarta. He was expected to seek refuge with Mangkunegara but was actually apprehended in Cirĕbon (see Siberg to Batavia, December 20, 1783, KA 3545, VOCOB, 1784)
100 10L, 11R 12R, 15L, 15R, 23L, 26L, 37L, 39R, 40L, 135L, 204L, 209L, 215L, 216L, 238L, 246R, 248R, 258R, 265L, 269L.
101 For instance, "Perang tanḍing," "Wong Prawira," "Menakan,", "Dasamuka," "Dasarata," "Kanoman," "Tanuastra," "Trunasura," "Singakurda," etc.
102 See, for instance, 201R and 204L, where the *lurah* were all grandsons of Mangkunegara. At this time and throughout the nineteenth century, it was common for lesser ranking members of the large families of Javanese princes to be employed in posts of greater or lesser prestige in the kraton.
103 See, for instance, 86L, 103L, l17R, 134R, 144L, etc.
104 See, for instance, 144L.
105 See, for instance, 103L, 169L, 253L, 259L, 265L, 266L, etc.
106 The Kanoman, Miji, and Nyutra or Nyutrayu corps were cavalry corps; see 47L and 137L.
107 On one occasion (186L) the then Resident of Surakarta promised to obtain 200 "Company carbines" for Mangkunegara on his forthcoming trip to Semarang. This was *after* Mangkunegara had lost many firearms

Twilight of the old courts

in a serious fire in the Mangkunegaran complex of buildings. The prudent Governor Greeve, however, decided to postpone the supply of these weapons (in his letter, 140 pair of carbines, 60 rifles with bayonets, and 100 pistols) until after the succession to the throne of the heir to the Sultanate of Mataram (Greeve to Batavia, March 14, I 789, KA 3754) This was a precaution against Mangkunegara's attempting forcibly to obtain this throne for himself. This succession did not in fact take place until April 1792, three years later.

108 See 11R and 15L (the second passage is not completely legible).
109 11R. These companies of *santri* soldiers must have been part of Mangkunegara's formidable armed following during the mid-century wars, for an account of these campaigns mentions on one occasion a "band consisting entirely of priests" under his command. See *Kort Verhaal*, p. 200.
110 208L.
111 144L, 222L.
112 The *kěnduren mulud* is a slametan held, as is clear from the passage quoted, on the 26th of the month, thus some days later than the more public ceremony of the Garebeg Mulud.
113 In Javanese classifications of official position, it was common to divide a given category of official into inner vs. outer, right vs. left, or north vs. south.
114 *sabět*, with a literal meaning of sword, is clearly used by the diarist as the title of a junior military functionary, attached to a *lurah*.
115 The *ḍikir mulud* is a special feature of the Mulud celebrations, involving the recitation of Muhammad's life in verse, with members of the mosque congregation joining in the recital during the refrains and eulogies.
116 The *paringgitan*, "place of the *ringgit*" (i.e., of the wayang) is situated between the *manḍapa* and the royal or princely residence.
117 The *baḍong* is a sort of breast-plate, part of ceremonial court and wayang dress.
118 Grandchildren of the right are descendents through the primary wives, and of the left, descendents of *sělir*.
119 Mangkunegara I's grandson and successor.
120 Probably Mangkunegara's deputy in his appanage lands in Kaḍuwang, and apparently second-in-command of the Mangkunegaran armed forces.
121 The best known court *baḍaya* dance is that performed by a group of nine female dancers, but male dancers also performed dances known by this name. For some information on these dances, see Pigeaud, *Volksvertoningen*, pp. 273 ff.
122 This *gěnḍing* (gamelan melody) does not appear in the list given by Cornets de Groot, nor in Kunst, *Music of Java*, 2. It is probably one of the older and more elaborate *gěnḍing*.
123 This type of dance – of a group of girls or women before a screen – is described by the diarist on a number of occasions, but does not appear to have been noted in European accounts of the different dance forms of the Javanese courts; nor is it known to Dr. Th. G. Th. Pigeaud from

The Javanese Ancien Régime: Civilization and Society

his extensive experience of the present century (personal communication). Nevertheless, the fact that the *krama* word *ringgit* (here translated as "figures") is used both for wayang puppets and for female dancers suggests that it was the screen (*kĕlir*) which was the conceptual link between the live and the inanimate figures whose performance it displayed.

124 *"Lir prenjak tinajenan"*, "like the *prenjak* bird fitted out with spurs" is a literary simile frequently used to describe dancers whose movements are too swift to be pinned down by an adversary.

125 Diradamĕt appears to have been something of a star among the Mangkunegaran dancers: he is mentioned by name also on 146R (depicting the same battle) and 277L.

126 Ponorogo and Madiun, then the two most populous and prosperous districts of Java, were conquered by Mangkunegara in the first half of 1752. In the following year, after his alliance with Mangkubumi had changed to a lasting enmity, the two princes fought several engagements in east Java, and Mangkubumi was decisively defeated (see Louw, *Derde Oorlog*, pp. 57–66; *Kort Verhaal*, pp. 160–206; and de Jonge, *Opkomst*, 10, pp. lxix–lxxi ii). Ponorogo and Madiun were taken by a combined effort of Mangkubumi and the VOC in 1755. After the wars, however, the Mangkunegaran retained a connection with Ponorogo, where Mangkunegara's sons were granted appanage lands by the Sunan of Surakarta.

127 It seems that Mangkunegara was renowned for his skill as an archer.

128 The ruler of Yogyakarta's official title was Sultan, rather than Sunan (that of the rulers of Surakarta).

129 A court dance, usually performed, as here, by four female dancers. Mangkunegara himself instructed his *srimpi* dancers: see, for example, 202.

130 *(A)dipati* (Sanskrit *adhlpati*, commander, ruler) was a title of high-ranking regional commanders. The Javanese referred to are those who by this stage were fighting under Mangkubumi.

131 This would refer to one of two attacks on Mangkubumi's new royal residence made by Mangkunegara's forces (now significantly depleted) in 1756: see *Kort Verhaal*, pp. 219, 228.

132 *Taleḍek* is a general term for dancing girls and women without the same specialization in courtly dance forms as the *baḍaya* and *srimpi* dancers.

133 The *bĕksa* described here involved all the males present in taking a turn to dance with the *taleḍek*. The order of the dance was determined by rank, with each dancer "handing over" to the person immediately junior to him. Hence the dance is begun by Pangeran Surya Prang Wadana, followed by the other commander of the army. See also Ch. 3. p. 137 below.

134 It is interesting to see that Mangkunegara's Patih (the highest ranking "civil" official) takes his turn after the first four ranks of military officers.

135 The diarist classifies the *lurah*, here as elsewhere, by the form of payment they received: *sawah* land, or money wages.

136 This probably refers to the four *lurah* of the Samaputra corps, all

Twilight of the old courts

grandsons of Mangkunegara and bearing the noble title of Raden (see 204L).
137 These were cavalry corps.
138 On the term *sabĕt*, see note 115 above. Because they were the most junior of the military officers, they take their turn last here.
139 That is, rice with the usual accompanying dishes.
140 For the contracts signed during this period by the Sunan and the Sultan, see KITLV H [Hollands: Western language manuscript] 363, *Tractaten gesloten met de zelfbestuurders van Surakarta en Yogya Batavia 1755–1830*. See also volume 5 of F. W. Stapel, *Corpus Diplomaticum Neerlando-Indicum*, BKI 96 (1938) and ibid., vol. 6, The Hague, Nijhoff, 1955.
141 Hartingh to Batavia, March 29, 1757 in KA 2802, VOCOB, 1758.
142 The deeds whereby the Mangkunegaran in 1813 received another 1000 *cacah* [from the Sultan's lands?] and 500 more from the Dutch government in 1830, as well as the documents relating to the rationalization of the Mangkunegaran and Sunanate lands in c. 1903, are all missing. See G. P. Rouffaer, "Vorstenlanden", *Adatrechbundels* 134 (1931) pp. 258–59 and 260.
143 Rouffaer, pp. 240–41.
144 Letter of F. van Straalendorf, P. Boltze, Raden Adipati Sasradiningrat and Adipati Suradimenggala, in van den Burgh to Batavia, August 20, 1772, KA 3256, VOCOB 1773. The reason for the strange form in which the district of Panjer appears here is perhaps that the two districts (which are adjacent) were described in Javanese as "Panjĕr lan Pamarden," that is, "Panjer and Pamarden."
145 Ibid.
146 The figures are taken from the land settlement of 1773: see B. Schrieke, *Indonesian Sociological Studies* 2, The Hague and Bandung, W. van Hoeve, 1952, p. 367, n. 311. Ricklefs, *Jogjakarta*, discussing the meaning of *cacah* in terms of manpower (p. 425 n.), has not noted this increase in the number of *cacah* under Mangkunegara's control.
147 Rouffaer, "Vorstenlanden," pp. 299–311
148 Rouffaer, pp. 301–2.
149 Rouffaer, pp. 301–2.
150 The hard Spanish dollar (*peso duro*) was for long the standard unit of exchange on Java and the surrounding regions, where it was generally known as the *real*, an abbreviation of *real de a ocho*, "eight-real piece." (Other names include Jav. *ringgit; pasmat*, a corruption of the Dutch term *Spaansche mat*; and piaster.) In Europe, it was very close in value to the Dutch *rijksdaalder*: both maintained a value which varied only between £0.22 and £0.23 over the period 1651–1781 (see John J. McCusker, *Money and Exchange in Europe and America 1600–1775: A Handbook*, Williamsburg, University of Carolina Press, 1978, Table 1. 1). In the Indonesian region, however, the Spanish dollar was the preferred currency and always enjoyed an advantage (c. 25–40 percent) over its official value vis-a-vis Dutch monies. (See Robert Chalmers, *A History of Currency in the British Colonies*, London, Eyre & Spottiswoode, (c.) 1893, pp. 281–83, appendix A; John Crawfurd, *A*

Descriptive Dictionary of the Indian Islands and Adjacent Countries, London: Bradbury and Evans, 1856, p. 285; and E. Netscher and J. A. van der Chijs, *De Munten van Nederlandsch Indie,* VBG, 31, 2 [1864].)

151 Strictly speaking, there are five *bau* to a *jung,* but since the one-fifth of a *jung* allotted to the *běkěl* does not produce tax, the Javanese land registers do not take it into account and reckon four *bau* to the *jung.* Rouffaer, "Vorstenlanden," p. 301.

152 Rouffaer attributes this to a decline in value of the Spanish dollar ("Vorstenlanden" p. 303) in central Java. This is contrary to all other evidence (see references in n. 150 above) which indicates that the *real* maintained its value. Rouffaer has probably been confused either by the fact that what was called the *"real"* in Java was actually the piece-of-eight, a *multiple* of the Spanish unit of currency known in Europe as a *real.* Though this latter *real* did indeed decline throughout the eighteenth century, the piece-of-eight was maintained at its old value (by calculating its worth as equivalent to 10 and then 11 *real*); or by the fact that the exchanges in Spain used a "notional" (i e., non-coin) piece-of-eight as a unit of accounting. This notional piece-of-eight (known as the *peso de cambio*) declined in value at the same rate as the (European) *real.* (See McCusker, *Money and Exchange,* pp. 99–100.) It is clear that in Java we have to do with the silver dollar itself and not with the notional accounting money used in Spain. There is no evidence that the silver dollar was accepted at a lesser value: it was certainly not reduced to anywhere near a quarter of its value, which would have had to be the case if its devaluation was the reason for the increase in taxation noted here. It is more likely that we have to do with an increase in taxation pure and simple – itself an interesting phenomenon.

153 On the nature of the equivalence of these terms, see Rouffaer, "Vorstenlanden," p. 301.

154 Rouffaer, p. 304.

155 Rouffaer, p. 240; Schrieke, *Indonesian Sociological Studies,* 2, p. 366 n. 311.

156 I.e., Kaduwang (1,150 *cacah*), Banyumas (2,029c.), Panjěr (1,180c.), and Pamerden (604c.) – a total of 5,212 *cacah* out of the 7,794.

157 See Rouffaer, "Vorstenlanden," p. 304, for the basis of this calculation. In fact, Mangkunegara had difficulty in preventing these men from retaining more than the percentage due to them (see n. 158).

158 102L. Given the traditional saying that one *bau* (one-fifth or one-quarter of a *jung,* according to the method of calculation) of *sawah* land or 2 *bau* of dry land provides a sufficient living for a farmer and his family, 17 *jung* is a very large parcel of land. It seems that Mangkunegara had some difficulty in ensuring that his subordinates paid their share of the tax, since dismissals and replacements among his *lurah* and *děmang* are often recorded, and the reasons, where given, seem usually to be that they have not fulfilled their obligations, are behind in their payments, or have sold (or otherwise "lost") the buffalo loaned to them (see, for example, 154e and 185e).

159 296.

160 It should be noted that Mangkunegara had asked for 4,000 *cacah,*

confirming Rouffaer's calculation that one *cacah* = one *real* in tax revenue.

161 See "Vorstenlanden: Gegevens betreffende bestuur en rechtspraak in het prinsdom Mangkoenagaran (1867–1913)," *Adatrechtbundels*, 25 (1926), p. 79.
162 See below p. 31.
163 289R.
164 The *amet* was the chief unit of measurement for husked rice. Like the *jung* it exhibited considerable variation even within one region. Daendels introduced a standard measure here too, the "government *amet*" of 266–2/3 English pounds (Raffles, *History of Java*, 2, Appendix M.) Previously it might have weighed up to three times this amount.
165 The *santana*, that is, the members of the royal family more distant from the ruler than children and grandchildren.
166 The mosque custodian, responsible for beating the *bĕdug* (great drum) at the times of prayer.
167 Usually a number of *kĕtib* were assigned to assist the *pĕngulu* in his duties.
168 No dictionary lists this word, which the context clearly shows must denote a religious functionary. It does not occur among the titles of religious functionaries in the nineteenth century Mangkunegaran (see "Vorstenlanden: Gegevens," *Adatrechtbundels*, 25 (1926), pp. 75–76 and 91–92). One may tentatively suggest a derivation from Turkish *yeniceri*, "janissary", since military corps modeled on these Turkish ones existed in the Javanese principalities and the Janissary corps had historical connections with religious orders (see, for example, J. Spencer Trimingham, *The Sufi Orders in Islam*, Oxford: Clarendon Press, 1971, pp. 80–81). In the local context, this functionary is very likely to have been associated with "Jamsaren" ("place of the Jamsari") an old-established *pĕsantren* whose clientele was mainly the sons of the Surakarta aristocracy (and which is still in existence).
169 302R-303L.
170 303R (*mila anĕmpur beras/sĕmana kang bĕras awis*).
171 A *tompo* is another measure of rice, also exhibiting considerable local variation in actual weight. In Surakarta usage there were 24 *tompo* to 1 *amet* (see Gericke and Roorda, *Javaansch-Nederlandsch Handwoordenboek*, and Raffles, *History of Java*, 2, Appendix M).
172 See Greeve to Batavia, July 29, 1790 in KA 3802, VOCOB 1791.
173 258R.
174 264L: *Ka[ng]jĕng pangeran adipati gagajih kang abdi-abdi / a[ng]gris kalawan ḍuwit / tĕlas sewu gangsal atus pujul sĕket kang arta* . . . For a discussion of these coins (*anggris* and *ḍuwit*), see below.
175 264: *mulud tanggal salawe prah / kala dina kĕmis manis / kangjĕng pangeran dipatya / paring bala ngĕmping gajih / gagajihe ing be[n]jing / bakda siyam mangke nuhun / prandene pinaringan / sewu arta kang gagajih / pujul kawan atus lawan walung [wolung] reyal / /*
176 265L.
177 269L.
178 269R: *nulya dina kĕmis kang tanggal pipitu / jumadelakir [error for*

The Javanese Ancien Régime: Civilization and Society

jumadilawal] kang wulan // paparing kangjěng pangeran dipati / gajih bala kakauman / dasarambat kalawan dasawani / pijigan panaměngipun / lawan wong dasamuka / dasarata sami ngěmping gajihipun / tigang atus kawan dasa / gangsal ing siyam sapalih

179 277R: *. . . nulya e[n]jingipun di[n]těn akad paing / ing wah tanggal ping rolas // paparing kangjěng pangran dipati / pasumbang pamalěm sangu siyam / mring bala bala[n]jan kabeh / kang arta kalih atus / reyal sami awarni ḍuwit / sarěng paring paněbas / banon be[n]jang katur / lurah bala[n]jan sadaya / tělas něněm ewu ingkang arta ḍuwit / para lurah sadaya // dene sangu paring siyam be[n]jing / sajajare bala[n]jan sadaya / kaum mahas sajajare / kang sabin datan antuk . . .*

180 282L: *salasa inggara [anggara] kasih / sawal tanggal ping sawělas / gagajih wadya balane / jěng gusti pangran dipatya / jajar gajihyan jaba / tělas arta sewu pujul / něm atus sewu pujulnya // sapalih kinarya anggris / sapalih batu kang arta / seos wong ngěmping gajihe / seos gajih wulan běsar / jumadilakir wulan / seos bakda siyam mulud / saking kaṭahe kang bala //*

181 282L: *nulya sěnen manisipun / sawal tanggal ping pitu las // ka[ng]jěng pangeran dipati / gagajih kang bala-bala / bala kang ngěmping gajihe / gajihe mulud ing be[n]jang / sawal nuhun ěmpingan / gajih bebas benjang mulud / nuhun mangke pinaringan // sewu real warni ḍuwit / sarta pujul sangang real / maksih watěn [wontěn] ingkang dereng / ngěmping gajihe mulud / saking kaṭahe kang bala / . . .* The meter (Asmarandana) of the middle verse lacks two lines but the sense seems unimpaired.

182 282R: *sarta sarěng ngěmping gajih / para putra buyut wayah / manggung katanggung sakabeh / gajihe mulud ing be[n]jang / pinaring wulan sawal / tělas arta tigang atus.*

183 282R: *nulya sěnen kang dina / salawe prah tanggalipun / ing sawal pangran dipatya // gajih bala ngěmping gajih / lurah lan sasabětira / lurah lěbět jawi kabeh / ngěmping sawal pinaringan / mulud kang gajih bebas / nora gajih be[n] jang mulud / sakawan atus kang reyal // pujul pitung atus anggris / reyal lan ḍuwit sadaya /*

184 288L: *sarěng gagajih kang bala / sěmana pangran dipati // tělas arta sewu reyal / mapan pujul salawe genya gajih /*

185 The situation was not finally corrected until the introduction in 1854 of a new regulation which brought about a notable improvement.

186 On the value of the Spanish silver dollar, see note 150 above.

187 See Netscher and van der Chijs, *Munten*, pp. 1–2.

188 See Chalmers, *History of Currency*, pp. 390–91.

189 Crawfurd, *Dictionary*, p. 285, sub "money."

190 Different mintings of the Spanish silver dollars carried different devices, for example, the earlier "pillar" dollars, the later "globe" dollars, and still later ones with the Spanish arms. See Chalmers, *History of Currency*, pp. 391–92; William D. Craig, *Coins of the World 1750–1850*, Racine, Whitman, 1966, sections on Spain and the Spanish colonies; and Aldo P. Basso, *Coins, Medals and Tokens of the Philippines*, Menlo Park, Chenby, 1968, p. 19.

191 Netscher and van der Chijs, *Munten*, p. 66. The Dutch *duit* was accounted at 8 to the *stuiver*.

192 The *paningsět* is a present made to the bride when she is the daughter

Twilight of the old courts

of a Pangeran (or, as here, of the Sunan himself) and the groom is of lower rank.

C. F. Winter's article "Instellingen, Gewoonten en Gebruiken der Javanen te Soerakarta," TNl 5, (1843), pp. 459–86, 546–613 and 690–744) describes the *paningsĕt* as comprising a few items of silverware (p. 573) but in the present case it involves a large sum of money (and is termed *arta pamapag*, "money-of-the-meeting", i.e. of the bride). The amount is given (100L-R) as *ardana rĕginira ĕmas sadaya pan pangaji tigang ewu walung [walung] atus nĕm bĕlas*, "riches entirely in gold to the worth of 3816," and, as in other places where the currency is not specified, it seems that the amount is understood to be in *real*. If, however, 3816 gold coins were paid, the sum would be anything from about 1½ to 8½ times greater than 3816 *real*, depending on which gold coinage was involved.

193 Ricklefs, *Jogiakarta*, p. 234.
194 See van Overstraten to Batavia, November 3, 1792, KA 3859, VOCOB, 1793.
195 See Rouffaer, "Vorstenlanden," p. 273.
196 On the Mangkunegaran Legion see S. A. Drijber, "Het Legioen van Mangkoe Negoro," *Indisch Militair Tijdschrift*, 31, 7–12 (1910) pp. 306–11.
197 In the 1880s, government loans to the Mangkunegaran could not be repaid, and Mangkunegara V had to surrender the management of his financial affairs to the colonial government during the 1890s. Financial autonomy was retained thanks to the able management of Mangkunegara VI. (See *Mailrapporten* 1890 no. 578; 1891 nos. 58, 320, 382, and 471; 1893 no. 197; and the *Koloniale Verslagen* for the 1890s sub "Java en Madoera".
198 See, for example, 24R-25L, 30R, 32R.
199 The results of this investigation can be found in P. J. F. Louw and E. S. de Klerck, *De Java-Oorlog van 1825–30*, 6 vols., The Hague: Nijhoff, 1894–1909, 6, p. 168.
200 Notably the Pengging canal, the source of the water supply, which appears to have been a constant source of trouble, needing frequent repairs: see 66L, 96R, lOlL, 127L, 185L.
201 104R.
202 *Eklas kang galih* (100L).
203 *Saklangkung kawlas ayun* (100L).
204 Mangkunegara's grandson.
205 110R.
206 90R.
207 Seton is derived from *sĕptu*, Saturday. In Yogyakarta similar spectacles were held on Mondays, and hence called *sĕnenan*.
208 See Ricklefs, *Jogiakarta*, pp. 274–75, 303–4, 345–46. An alternative explanation, however, sees the buffalo as representative of royal authority and cosmic order, and the tiger of chaos and chthonic forces, or the underworld.
209 157R.
210 For example, 61L, 77L, 213L.
211 272R-273L. The practice of setting criminals to fight tigers continued

into the early years of the nineteenth century, and Raffles (*History of Java*, 1, p. 388) reports that if the man concerned escaped comparatively unscathed this was taken as proof of innocence by ordeal, and he was freed and even sometimes given the position of *mantri*.
212 217. Bets were usually placed on the outcome of these contests: see, for example, 99R, 183.
213 Most accounts of the *awisan* deal exclusively with the items of clothing which were reserved for royal usage: see, for example, Winter, "Beknopte Beschrijving," pp. 77–78, and Rouffaer's notes, pp. 161–64; also Ricklefs, *Jogjakarta*, pp. 163–65. At least at this period, however, the *awisan* were of wider scope.
214 31R: *lan sawarnane kasukan / nagri sala den-awisi amung sawĕwĕngkonira kangjĕng pangeran adipati / kang baton [botĕn] den-awisi kasukan sadayanipun / linilan tan awisan / atas parentah kumpni* / s.a. 101L.
215 94R-95L.
216 It should be recognized, however, that the VOC was equally concerned to regulate the state allowed to its different employees when they appeared in public: see the numerous edicts issued under the heading "Pragt en Praal" in *Realia: Register op de Generale Resolutien van het Kasteel Batavia 1632– 1805*, The Hague: Nijhoff, 1886, 3, pp. 82–83.
217 See, for example, the description of Governor Jan Greeve's visit (156–57 and 251R) where Pakubuwana IV and Greeve travel together in one carriage and Mangkunegara and Resident Johan Fredrik, Baron van Rede tot de Parkeler, in another.
218 267R.
219 See above p.
220 Pon is the third or fourth day of the five-day week, according to the system used.
221 The second (lunar) month of the Muslim year.
222 *Je* is the fourth year of the Javanese eight-year (*windu*) cycle. In this case it was 1718 AJ and the date here is equivalent to October 9, 1791 AD.
223 *Rantan sang prabu*: "rantan" in any possible sense is not listed in any dictionary, but from the context here may be conjectured to mean a place in the river where a pool had been artificially created to draw fish for the ruler's pleasure.
224 The Sunan's third wife. The marriage was arranged for him through the good offices of Greeve, Governor of the Northeast Coast and in charge of the VOC's relations with Surakarta, after Pakubuwana IV abandoned his plan to marry a princess of Yogyakarta. The bride was a daughter of the Tumĕnggung of Pamĕkasan (Madura) and thus a sister of the Sunan's first wife. A third sister was married at the same time to the Sunan's brother Mangkubumi, who had also requested the VOC to find him a wife. According to the diarist, neither marriage was happy, though the Sunan put a better face on things than his brother, and both feared to incur the Company's displeasure by a public breach (287–291; see also Greeve to Batavia, February 28 and May 10, 1791 in HA 3833, VOCOB 1792).
225 The Tamtama, as also the Tumalatar, Macanan, and Nyutra, mentioned below, were all *prajurit* corps of the Sunan's armed forces.

Twilight of the old courts

226 Panembahan, "he who is revered" is a higher title than Pangeran, "Prince," and the diarist sarcastically suggests that it would be appropriate to Purbaya's exalted position in Surakarta. He had been of considerable assistance to the Company in persuading Pakubuwana IV to restore relations with the VOC and in return for these services he had been presented with a ring. He did not write and thank Greeve for this gift: he had apparently expected a more considerable reward, perhaps in the form of title or lands (see Greeve to Batavia, December 13, in KA 3833, VOCOB, 1792). Purbaya was dead by March 1792 (see Governor van Overstraten to Batavia, March 2, 1792, in HA 3859, VOCOB, 1793) and the VOC lost an ally.

227 A temporary shelter or rest-house erected for armies on the move, or for pleasure parties.

228 The first syllable of this line is illegible.

229 The Sunan's capital is usually referred to either by its official name, Surakarta, or by the name of the old village which was its site, Sala (pronunciation and modern spelling Solo). In the diary, however, it is often referred to as Salakarta, a combination of the two forms.

230 The *koḍok ngorek* ("croaking frog") ensemble can be described as a primitive or archaic form of gamelan. It continued to be used at the Javanese courts for certain ceremonial purposes. For a description of the *koḍok ngorek*, see Kunst, *Music in Java*, 1, pp. 260–65, and see Ch.3. on its use in Gresik.

231 From descriptions in the diary it is clear that it was customary for a salute to be fired when a round of drinks was served, both at the ruler's kraton and at the Dutch factory.

232 Sic. Perhaps the forty is an error for some other qualifier of *wong*, "man, person."

233 The Javanese does not make it clear how many, but it is hard to believe that the horse managed to despatch more than one person with a kick in the head.

234 *Angger*: form of address, usually for a younger person of higher rank. Presumably Jayaningrat was older than Pangeran Purbaya.

235 The term used is *wong g(a)laḍag*. The *glaḍag* were a specific classification of workers with the obligation of providing transport for the ruler and his entourage, and other services, in return for which they were exempt from the usual levies. See Soeripto, *Vorstenlandsche Wetboeken*, p. 4.

236 That is, that the V.O.C. would ensure that the Sunan – in whose jurisdiction such appointments strictly speaking fell – duly announced the sons' promotions.

237 150–56.

238 158L *lan Těnggalek awawuh [awuwuh]*.

239 The Sunan officially appointed the brothers on 24 Sawal 1714 AJ (July 28, 1788). The reason for the conferring of the rank of Pangeran on Suryakusuma was that he was married to the Sunan's daughter, who was at the same time given the title of Ratu.

240 As for instance in the volume KA 7035, VOCOB 1789.

241 207R.

242 Clifford Geertz, *Negara: The Theatre State in Nineteenth-Century Bali*, Princeton U.P. 1980, p. 13.
243 Ann Kumar, "Javanese Court Society and Politics in the Late Eighteenth Century: the record of a Lady Soldier: Part II: Political Developments: the Courts and the Company 1784–1791", *Indonesia* 30 (October 1980), pp. 67–111.
244 Th. Pigeaud, *De Serat Tjabolang en de Serat Tjentini: Inhoiudsopgaven*, Verhandeling van het Koninklijk Instituut LXXII/2, Bandoeng, A.C. Nix, 1933.
245 On the Cĕnṭini texts, see T.E. Behrend, "The Serat Cĕnṭini: A checklist of Manuscripts and Preliminary Ordering of Recensions", unpublished paper, A.N.U. 1986. The Cĕnṭini is aptly described by Behrend as voracious in its incorporation of other texts, attributed to the Surakarta court's agressive taking hold of what had been created outside it in a process of literary and cultural hegemonizing (p. 361).
246 For an excellent account both of this genre and of the Javanese literary tradition see T.E. Behrend, *The Serat Jatiswara: Structure and Change in a Javanese Poem 1600–1930*, A.N.U. Ph.D 1987,
247 There is a penumbra of other works which might be considered sufficiently close to this core to be included and of works which share a larger or smaller part of the constituent material: see Behrend, *Serat Jatiswara*, Conclusion.
248 In the summary noted above (note 244), Pigeaud treats the Cabolang material as a separate work, but not everyone would agree with this separation from the Cĕnṭini.
249 Seers, ascetes and holy men and women appear frequently under a number of terms of Indian or Javanese origin: *kyai, resi, ajar, yogi, wiku,* and for women *rara suci*.

3

The socialisation of the people: "becoming Javanese"

RITES OF JAVANESENESS: A VIEW FROM GRESIK

Generally speaking, ethnography was remarkably undeveloped in colonial Java, though there was a late and sparse flowering in the 1920s and 1940s, most strongly represented by the journal *Djawa*. A.D. Cornets de Groot's ethnography of Gresik,[1] however, provides an exceptionally full account of socialisation, social structure, cultural forms and religion, covering most of the systems of shared meaning of such central importance to the Javanese. Though he wrote up his material in 1822–3, he makes reference to the situation as it existed quite some time in the past, and it appears that Raffles used some of his material, on music, for instance.[2] The editor of the published version of Cornets de Groot's ethnographical material notes the correspondence between his information and that provided in Winter's report on early nineteenth century Surakarta;[3] but Cornets de Groots' coverage is fuller on many subjects and, in my opinion, a good deal more interesting than Winter's. It still has rather unexpected limitations: it is surprising, for instance, that for all his decades in Java the author's command of the language did not extend even to getting everyday words right. Of course, Malay was the lingua franca in which Dutchmen communicated with Javanese and knowledge of the latter's native tongue was generally limited to a few words and phrases. I have rearranged the material under headings to make it more accessible, and corrected the Javanese, as far as this was possible: some words defied all attempts at reconstruction. Apart from minor additions of a footnoting nature, I have only made significant additions to the account on three matters, which Cornets de Groot deals with either minimally (housing) or not at all (rites of agriculture and exorcism), because each of these is of great significance. Otherwise, I have chosen not to overlay the account with ethnographic material from elsewhere, but to present it as firmly located in a particular part of Java at a particular time.

RITES OF PASSAGE

We begin with the rites of passage that have always been so important for Javanese. From the tone of the account, it seems likely that Cornets de Groot had gained his knowledge from being an observer at the celebrations of birth, marriage, circumcision, etc., held by the Javanese élite. The ceremonial milestones with which he deals are the following:

The birth of a child. This is greeted with great jubilation, especially among the ruling classes, and announced with a salute of 11 or 12 cannons if it is the descendant of a Bupati, which can only be done with the consent of the current Bupati.[4]

The falling off of the umbilical cord. All the father's adult relatives gather, and the history of Yusup is read, while the baby is held by one of the oldest female relatives. The reading of Yusup's story symbolizes the wish that the child may survive ill-wishers and reach greatness as the Prophet did. This is followed by a rice meal. On this occasion the father gives the child its childhood name,[5] or if the child is the descendant of a Bupati who is still living, he will name it. Usually the first letter of the childhood name will be the same as that of one of the parents.

For the *eight-day ceremony* the father gives another meal of rice, meat, and vegetables, and if the child is a girl her ears are pierced and threaded.

For the *forty-day ceremony* the baby's head is shaved and another meal is given for the relatives.[6]

When the *child reaches seven or eight months*, it is taken to an isolated spot where there are relics of great persons who have lived long lives. This is the first occasion on which the child is allowed to tread the ground. In the case of people of standing, the child is weighed against sweetmeats and money, and the amount used to give a meal at which the wish is expressed that the child may live long and in good fortune.

Circumcision. This is done between the ages of seven and ten, by a Muslim "priest" or someone familiar with the rules of Islam, and preceded and followed by prayers said by priests. The *circumcision*

The socialisation of the people: "becoming Javanese"

of girls takes place between the ages of five and seven, and is done by a Muslim woman, and accompanied by the same prayers as for boys. It results in a small cut and a little bleeding.[7]

The *filing of the teeth* is done between the ages of eleven and sixteen. All senior relatives are present, and the story of Yusup is read. A meal of *nasi goreng* is given. This occasion is considered to mark the transition to adulthood, and subsequently the [male?] child can sign contracts or act as witness.

Marriage is arranged by the parents of both bride and groom and takes place when the boy is *balig*, i.e. 15 or 16; but girls are married at the age of nine, though cohabitation is delayed until they are nubile.[8] If a girl has no father, her oldest male relative takes his place, and if she has none, the *pengulu* as her *wali hakim* gives her in marriage.[9] The father of the groom sends bananas to the bride as a sign that a marriage has been contracted. A lucky day is calculated for the wedding. Eight or ten days beforehand, the bridegroom's father sends one or more buffaloes, their horns decorated with gold or silver, and draped with linen or silk cloth, as well as coconuts, rice, and sweets, and an amount of cash according to his station, a gift known as the *sasrahan nglamar* or *paningsĕt*. For those of small means this consists only of a little money and fruits. Three or four days before the marriage date, the parents on both sides notify their relatives with a gift or sweets, cakes, meat, etc., which is called the *nonjok*. Now the houses of the parents let off cannon salutes, and play the *gamĕlan* in honour of the forthcoming wedding, a festivity called *gantang*. Everyone who is invited to this festivity is obliged to bring a gift, the *buwu* [i.e. *bawah*] or *pasumbang*. This can be money, rice, buffaloes, fruits, or cloth. (These preliminary festivities are omitted by the poorer classes.) The actual marriage is concluded by the *pengulu* [apparently at the Bupati's house for members of his family, otherwise at the "temple", presumably the mosque] between the bridegroom and the father of the bride, after the bridegroom has agreed to pay his wife a piece of gold or silver worth two Spanish dollars. The bridegroom is then dressed in his *dodot*, has his hair decked with flowers, and is set on horseback or in a carriage, accompanied by *mantris, dĕmangs*, pike-bearers and a gamelan. If he is a man of religion, he goes on foot and wears a *jubah* and a *dĕstar*, and is accompanied by other men of religion. On the occasion of this procession, some people give small presents of rice, cloth, etc. to the Bupati. The bridegroom is taken to his home, and a meal called *ruwahan* [*bawahan*] is given. At about 3.30 p.m. the bridegroom is placed in a "Garuda" and taken to the house of the bride, who is also placed in the Garuda [Garuda, the mount of Vishnu and Javanese kings, symbol divine or royal status, to which the bridal pair are assimilated for their wedding day. A twentieth century account describes the groom as riding a horse with a saddle like "a sort of winged boat with a Garuda head"[10] and in the central Javanese court of Yogyakarta the carriage Kyai Garudoyekso is only used for royal accessions.]. A procession to the *alun-alun* in full state takes place, with relatives, officials, pike-bearers, cannon or artillery salutes. At the *alun-alun* the bridegroom must circle three times around, in honour of the Bupati, which is called *bara kĕbayang* or *bayang kuruk* [corruptions of *ambayangkari* or *ambayangkare*, from *bayang*, meaning to carry out this wedding procession]. Then the couple are brought back to the house of the bride, and set on a sort of throne, surrounded by all their female friends and relatives but no men (these are entertaining themselves elsewhere in the house); and they sit there all night until the following afternoon, when the procession to the *alun-alun* is repeated. Then the pair visit their nearest relatives to pay obeisance (*ngujung*) and receive gifts of money or cloth. Afterwards they go to the house of the groom's father and repeat the ceremony here. About midnight the guests leave the young pair to themselves. In former times they were left for up to four or five nights. (In Sidayu, under Madurese influence, the consummation of the marriage takes place on the third night, and two female witnesses pronounce that the girl was a virgin in loud voices, after which a salute is fired and the history of Yusup read. If the bride is found not to be a virgin the groom sends his *kris* to her parents, as a sign of divorce).[11]

Cornets de Groot does not mention the ceremony for the bride on the eve of the wedding, when it was customary for the bride to be adorned by older women and to sit up all night. This goes back to the Old Javanese period, when it was known as the *piḍuḍukan*.[12] Koentjaraningrat reports that the night before the wedding is called the *lĕnggahan midadareni*, when the bride has to remain awake to come into contact with the *Widadari* or moon princess.[13] He says the groom also has to do this. Ponder mentions the preparation of the bride for the wedding by massaging her with a coarse powder called *lalar* and then with a fine powder; also an offering erected the night before the marriage at the sleeping place of the bride to be, which consists of bananas, betel-nut, and two yellow coconuts called *klapa gaḍing*, on one of which is a drawing of Arjuna and on

The socialisation of the people: "becoming Javanese"

the other a drawing of Sumbadra his consort. Here the Hindu Arjuna and Sumbadra, the most popular of the Indic figures because of their resemblance to Panji and his consort, have replaced them on the *klapa gaḍing* (see below p. 386 for a Javanese account of this custom). Ponder also describes a ceremony at which the couple feed each other rice and each holds an egg.[14]

Divorce provisions. A man can divorce his wife without giving any reason by pronouncing the *talak* three times. If he has pronounced it twice, he can withdraw it within three months, but if he has pronounced it three times, the divorce must go through and he cannot re-marry his wife unless she has married someone else in the meantime. After a divorce, the man must pay his wife the debt fixed at the marriage. A woman cannot re-marry before three months are up, but a man can re-marry immediately. After divorce, a woman can choose her own partner, and her parents no longer have the right to force her to marry a person of their choice. This is also the case when a young daughter of the family has happened to have had sex with a man.

A woman can ask the "priest" for a divorce, and if the latter finds her husband has some defect as a man, or has lost his reason, or is not circumcised, or has no means of subsistence, or has not given his wife the *sri kawin*, [bride price] then such a marriage is dissolved and termed *pasah*.

A man who has already four wives and feels compelled to marry a young woman, can divorce one of his wives temporarily with right of re-marriage.

If a man goes on a journey and does not provide maintenance for his wife, the "priest" is obliged to dissolve the marriage. If the man remains absent for four years the woman has the right to re-marry [a period now considerably shortened in the contractual agreement made by Javanese Muslim couples on the occasion of their marriage].

Polygamy: according to the law all wives have a right to their own house and to equal treatment, and if this is not done they have the right to a divorce. In fact the Javanese do not much follow these prescriptions, especially the upper class, where the first wife is of the same rank as her husband and lives in his house (*rumah geḍong*), enjoying many privileges in clothing and maintenance. The other wives have each their own dwelling, and are married when they fall pregnant. [a practice also followed in the central Javanese courts, see Chapter 2 p. 62 above.]

Pregnancy. The Javanese are extremely considerate of pregnant women and give them special treatment. In the first three months they are required to do very little. The young bride, on the day before union with her husband, is specially prepared. In the morning her head is decorated with *pupur* mixed with intoxicating fruits such as *gaḍung* and *kacubung*. This is presented to her in a flower made of paper, to express the wish that the child be beautiful as a flower and her manners intoxicating. The young woman is then washed in water containing flowers and fragrant oils. Afterwards she is dressed and asked to eat a *cĕngkir gaḍing* [young coconut] on one [side?] of which is a picture of Panji Kuda Waneng Pati and on the other Dewi Sekar Taji, Panji's consort, so that her child may be as beautiful.

When she is three months pregnant, the groom's parents give a meal consisting of *nasi goreng* coloured yellow below and white above, symbolizing the union of the male and female in the form of a child.[15] At the seventh month of pregnancy, the parents give a meal called *ngrujaki* at which the hot fruit salad *rujak* is served, signifying the wish that the child be strong in aspect and sweet of face [this ceremony is generally referred to as the *tingkĕban*]. On this occasion the woman wears a *slendang pali*, a silk breastcloth with gold or yellow and green stripes, thought to ease delivery. Also worn in pregnancy is a special *kĕmbĕn* or breastcloth named after a fish that seldom loses its roe, and another one to make the child move as little as possible so the mother does not suffer. After childbirth, the mother has to bathe immediately, and thereafter does nothing at all for 40 days (three months among the upper classes). After the 40 days she can go again to the "temple". At childbirth, her relatives send her some roots of trees, fennel, pluta[16] oil, red onions, and a little bark of the *pulasari* tree. If a boy is born on a Wednesday in a week when the *pasar Pon* falls on Sunday, he is given an ear-ring in his left ear because this day is considered auspicious for females [presumably, to deceive the supernatural world into favouring him].

Women must purify themselves after menstruation and sexual intercourse before entering the "temple".

Sickness and death. The sick are looked after by their closest relatives, so that they are never alone. If a person seems to be nearing death, prayers are said to God and Muhammed so that the last things heard turn the mind to holy things. Priests may be called to recite a part of the Koran called "Jassien" [Yā Sīn, the title of the

The socialisation of the people: "becoming Javanese"

xxxvith *Surah* of the *Koran*, which is usually read to dying persons]. As soon as someone dies he is wrapped in cloth. The corpse is washed for the first time with pure water and placed on a sleeping bench (*bale-bale*) with the head to the east, so that the eyes look westwards, while priests say prayers. It is then washed with *landa* water (water mixed with burnt *padi* stalks) and lemon juice or tamarind water; no oils are used. It is then washed again with pure water and the priest pours holy water over it. Next it is wrapped once, twice, or thrice in white linen: the better off prefer seven times. After this it is laid on a litter with the head to the north. The priests say the requisite prayers, and burial takes place within 24 hours. The funeral procession must be accompanied by all the marks of distinction which the deceased had in life, i.e. pike-bearers, *upacara* (*payung*, *sirih* box, etc.), fine horses, and other insignia of rank. At the graveyard the deceased is buried six foot deep with the head to the north and the face to the west and covered with a teak plank or, failing this, with bamboo. This is filled in with earth on top of which are placed four planks in the shape of a chest without a bottom. Some, especially grandees, later receive stone graves and memorial stones called *pasĕkaran*. Graves always have a different form for men and women: the first have two pointed, and the second two square planks or stones, the height of a foot, facing each other at the two ends of the grave. The priests say their prayers by the grave. In the case of a man they place themselves west of the grave facing east, but for a woman on the east facing west, because a woman should not be seen by men. These prayers are addressed to God and Muhammad and ask forgiveness for the deceased's transgressions in life.

After the burial, a meal called *nusal tanah* [the meal is actually called *surtannah*, the giving of meal *ngĕsur tanah*] is given for those who were present at the burial. Another meal is given after three days, and again on the 7th, 40th, 100th and 1000th days after death. For these occasions rice with meat and a sort of rice-bread called *apĕm* is served.

The native cemeteries are usually located on high and dry ground and are planted with *semloop* [? *sĕmboja*?] and *kĕmuning* trees, which have very fragrant flowers, to dispel any unpleasant odours from rising damp. The Javanese visit their family graves between one and four o'clock on Fridays, and strew them with the branches and flowers of the *sĕlasih* plant as a token of their love [*asih*].

RITES OF EXORCISM

Cornets de Groot's account does not mention one feature of Javanese life that all evidence suggests was both very widespread and ancient, that is, the importance attached to rituals of exorcism and purification. These concepts were brought to bear both at the territorial and at the personal level. At the personal level, there seem to have been three categories of people in need of exorcism, those who had broken a taboo, those whose place in the sibling order of their family was considered inauspicious, under a quite complex system, and those involved in an important rite of passage or significant new beginning. Even today, one can find booklets detailing these rites at unexpected places such as airport bookshops.

A Javanese writer named Inggris[17] writes that among the Javanese, though by no means all of them, there is the belief that whoever drops a *dandang* (a rice pot) or breaks a *gandik* (cylindrical mortar) or a *pipisan* (a pestle) will meet with misfortune. This can be exorcised through *ngruwat*. This is also given for children in the following categories:

1. *bocah ogal-agil*, i.e. an only child
2. *bocah kĕdana-kĕdini*, two siblings, one male and one female
3. *bocah kĕmbang sĕpasang* ["a pair of flowers"], i.e two sisters
4. *bocah ugĕr-ugĕr lawang* ["door posts"], two brothers
5. *bocah pancuran kapit ing sĕndang* ["fountain boy flanked by two springs"], i.e three siblings girl-boy-girl
6. *bocah sĕndang kapit ing pancuran* ["spring girl flanked by fountains"] i.e. a boy-girl-boy combination
7. *bocah pĕndawa*, i.e. 5 brothers
8. *bocah pĕndawa padangan*, 5 sisters
9. *bocah kĕmbar*, twins of whatever sex[18]

In other places *ruwatan* is also given on important occasions like moving house, harvesting rice, births, etc. The *ruwatan* requires an ensemble of life's necessities i.e. agricultural tools (plough, harrow, hoe, rice-knife etc.), carpenter's tools (saw, axe, file, plane, etc), and cooking implements (rice-pot, kettle, pitcher, sieve, pan, etc.). Also frequently included were white cotton, a *kain*, a head-cloth etc.; these things were often given to the person giving the ceremony by family and friends. The child for whom the ceremony is given must be swathed in a piece of white cloth or if not wear fine clothes, and

The socialisation of the people: "becoming Javanese"

sit by the *ḍalang*. Inggris says that in Karangjati the ceremony is held in the daytime as well as at night, but in other places only by day.[19]

Shortly before the *lakon* ends, the *ḍalang* speaks a spell over the child, and at the end of the *ngruwat* the puppet representing Batara Kala is thrown on the roof, and the child must run away fast. Afterwards the equipment and *sajen* (offerings) used in the ceremony were given to the *ḍalang*. However, in Karangjati the equipment was borrowed from fellow villagers, and the *ḍalang* received from the householder giving the ceremony f.34 considered as compensation for the goods (*ḍuwit tĕbasan*) and the *sajen* (a chicken, three *bĕruk*[20] of rice and the sweetmeats called *tukon pasar*). The parents and the child were forbidden to go to bed all night, otherwise the latter would still meet misfortune. The choice of day for the ceremony was left to the father, but if the *ḍalang* was asked to determine it it was usually Anggara-kasih. [Inggris then gives a summary of the *lakon*.]

One of the most active Dutch ethnographers, J.W. van Dapperen, gives the following information on similar rites from Tegal.[21] Here it was only the number of children that was significant, with no account taken of genders. Rites were held for the following:

1. *lare panas*, an only child
2. *kĕḍana-kĕḍini*, two children
3. *ontang-anting*, three children
4. *pĕndawa panturan*, five children
5. *pĕndawa olah-olah*, seven children.

The exorcism was to prevent the mother becoming infertile.

Van Dapperen provides information on the hymns (*kidung*) employed by the *ḍalang*: Koentjaraningrat[22] says there are 23 of these, but van Dapperen only gives about a dozen, e.g.:

Waringin Sungsang, which tells of the all-conquering power of *Batara Kala*, residing in the various parts of his body. Van Dapperen says the title refers to his power to uproot a *waringin*. [The Javanese see an upside-down *waringin* in the nebula of the moon and the *aji waringin sungsang* is a spell to obtain supernatural physical strength.]

Kudangan: a placatory hymn.

Ajale Kala: this deals with the origin of Kala and is intended to bring him back to his original state, that of liquid. Also related is the Kelumpuhan, the spell to paralyze and frighten Kala.

The Javanese Ancien Régime: Civilization and Society

Sari Panggung: a summing-up of all the beautiful things offered to Kala as a substitute for eating the children.

Banyak ḍalang: naming all the means whereby the *ḍalang* makes Kala give up and acknowlege his power.

Sĕmburan pĕnganten: a spell accompanied with blowing and spitting on the children, also used for bridal couples and the mentally ill. It makes all the Kalas afraid.

Konjaya Karna: this makes Kala, who by now is feeling bad, feel a bit better but makes the 40 small Kalas return to their normal places of residence (rivers, yards, wells, parts of the body). Part of this is the *kidung medaha sĕkawan*, saying the letters of the Javanese alphabet, *ha, na, ca, ra,* etc. to guarantee welfare in all four directions.

Tunḍungan buta: a spell to drive away female evil spirits.

Tunḍungan Durga: a spell against this dangerous goddess. As soon as she is driven away and her dangerous influence broken, the *ḍalang* calls forth the kindly Nini Lodaya, the Nyai Lara Kidul, and her relative Nini Sĕntani, the protectress of food and drinking water. these two have been among the onlookers, and the *ḍalang* asks them to come forth.

Prasondohing ḍalang: in this the *ḍalang* calls on God and the Prophet so that the promise that all the Kalas will be driven away will come true.

An appendix has texts of these *kidung*. The first one, in which the *waringin sungsang* occurs, indeed mentions all the parts of the body turning into metal. The *banyak ḍalang* seems to deal with a young man (*kaki kasinoman*) going off to fetch various things, going to Lodaya to fetch *toya wĕning* (pure water) and to Tunjung Bang to fetch the *kĕmbangan cĕmpaka*. He also has to go to the great river (*bĕngawan*) to look at the things thrown in the water and swept along. These are said to be the *banyak ḍalang*. Interestingly enough, this is also the name of the Yogyakarta regalia, suggesting that here too, as in the architectural form of the kraton, court and "folk" religious forms did not diverge but rather conformed to an overarching, peculiarly Javanese format. Clearly, we have here a Hinduized version (see the references to Batara Kala and his demons and to the fearful goddess Durga) of a very ancient system of exorcism that goes back to pre-Hindu times, calling on the indigenous goddesses Nini Lodaya, Nyai Lara Kidul and her relative Nini Sentani for protection, just as in the offerings made to consecrate Javanese houses old divinities like Kaki and Nini

The socialisation of the people: "becoming Javanese"

Among, which are also found in the old Tenggerese pantheon and in the Surakarta court version of the *Cĕntini*, are asked for their blessing. In the literary works and rituals of the courts, in the Tenggerese mountains, and in the villages of the Javanese up to the 20th century, very old gods and goddesses were not forgotten.

RITES OF AGRICULTURE

Cornets de Groot does not cover the cycle of communal *slamĕtan*, as opposed to the cycle of *slamĕtan* that relate to personal and familial transitions or *rites de passage*. Among the former, the community *slamĕtan*, two stand out with particular prominence. They are the harvest festival, the *slamĕtan mĕtik*, and the rite of territorial purification, the *bĕrsih desa*. With regard to the first, the contemporary anthropologist Robert R. Jay gives the following brief but admirably perceptive account:

> The *slametan metik*, the rice harvest slametan, is the largest of all. The guest brings back from it the *sri kawin*, the remains of the food tray – that is to say, almost all of it. This slamĕtan celebrates the marriage of Dewi Sri and Djaka Sudana and as part of its ritual identifies every wife with Dewi Sri and every husband with Djaka Sudana. The *sri kawin* thus becomes spiritually symbolic of the food which a husband gives his wife for her support. Every hearthhold harvesting a plot of rice, even if on only a "thirds" sharecropping basis, holds its own *slamĕtan metik* at the beginning of the harvesting season, to which it invites all husbands in the immediate vicinity. (Unmarried men are not invited.) In this way each wife receives *sri kawin* from the hand of her husband, and husband and wife contribute *sri kawin* through neighbouring husbands to their wives. The villagers treated the occasion with a certain lighthearted mockery, veiling a deep seriousness. The ritual seemed to say something positive about the marriage bond which satisfied them profoundly.[23]

This then, is the origin of the term *sri kawin* in the Javanese marriage rite, which reflects the divine union of Sri and Sadana as well as the royal union of the king and the *widadari* Nawang Wulan.

Jay also mentions[24] the division of labour in rice cultivation, with the earthworking and irrigation and most daily crop tending men's work, but the rice harvesting an almost exclusive preserve of women. (Ponder remarks that the planting of rice must also be done by women:

> Most important of all, it is the Javanese woman's proud privilege to plant out the *bibit* (seedlings) of rice, thus symbolically proclaiming herself the true mother and giver of life to her race. This rule in Java is fixed and absolute. Rice must be planted by women or it will not be fruitful.[25])

Jay also comments that:

> Women handle the rice store. In hearthholds, where the rice is treated traditionally by being stored in a separate chamber at the rear centre of the sleeping section, they do the small daily ritual aimed to keep Bok Sri, the female rice divinity, content.[26]

In fact as another observer has written:[27]

> ... the image of Dewi Sri pervades all layers of society. In the *wiwitan* ceremony in the harvest festival of Central Java, offerings are made to Dewi Sri; the first stalks of rice are cut and tied to make a bride or bridal couple (*mantenan*), which is identified as the goddess herself. This effigy is taken home and placed on a bed in the inner part of the house. Similarly, simple effigies made of rice paste are formed as offerings to sacred *wayang kulit* (shadow play puppets) when these are removed from their storage chests in the *Kraton* Surakarta Hadiningrat (the court of the senior ruler of Java, the Susuhunan of Surakarta), while images of Dewi Sri are incised into the wooden panels of small central rooms considered the heart of village houses in Java. Her association with fertility has a more overt expression in the courtly *loro blonyo* figures ... placed in front of the *kobongan* (ritual marriage bed) in noble houses in Central Java and specifically named Dewi Sri and Dewa Sadana.

SEMANTIC SPACE

The social geography of Gresik

Carnets de Groot relates that in the middle of the *alun-alun* a beautiful leafy tree is planted, called *[waringin] kurung*. This indicates the dwelling-place of a powerful or elevated person.

The socialisation of the people: "becoming Javanese"

When this tree is planted, care is taken to see that it has four branches or arms, which symbolize the four main winds and express the wish that dwellers in the far quarters of the domain may enjoy the same prosperity as those who shelter under the tree. The death of the tree or the loss of its leaves is regarded as an extremely unfavourable sign, and alms are distributed and a meal given with prayers said by priests to avoid disaster. If one of the branches dies, similar precautions are taken with regard to the inhabitants of the corresponding quarter.

Waringin trees are planted by the Bupati in the markets (*waringin suka-sami*, waringin for common pleasure), on the sea-shore (indicating the location of the bandar or Bupati's toll-house) and along the public ways (*waringin sri měnganten*). In former times no strangers were allowed in the Bupati's residence, and to provide a waiting place outside, waringin called *suka jěmbar* were planted.

Cornets de Groot remarks that all inhabitants of good birth prefer to live around the *alun-alun*. The rules governing their location are as follows: the "missigiet" or "temple" [i.e. the mosque] is on the west, facing east. The Bupati's house is to the south or north, with in front of it a *pěndapa* and a small *pěndapa* called a *lenjik*.[28] To the right of the *lenjik* is a gate, outside of which stands a *pěndapa* called *pamagangan*, the place where the retinue of someone visiting the Bupati waits. After this come a gate without doors, called *glediggan* [*glaḍakan*], outside of which one finds a small *paseban* on the right, and on the left the place for the great *gamělan* set used for tourneys. The *glaḍakan* gate, *paseban* and *gamělan* no-one may have except the Bupati, and his likely successor, with the permission of the Susuhunan. These gates are generally not placed directly in front of the house, but in an oblique or sideways direction. If they were placed in a straight line leading to the house, this would be a situation called *naga mamangsa*: *naga* devouring its prey, in which visitors could be eaten by a great *naga*. The proper arrangement is called *naga kapulir*, indicating that the *naga's* head is turned aside. [The *naga* is a prominent motif in the decoration of the houses of the great, on chairs and architectural features, as one can still observe in Java.]

The Jaksa's house is left of the Bupati's and has a *pěndapa lenjik* and two gates; and left again are those of the Kliwon and Nayaka, both of which may have one gate and *pěndapa*. The house of the Bupati's son and likely successor is east of the *alun-alun* and has two gates, a small *paseban*, and a *pěndapa lenjik*. The Aria and Ngabei and remaining sons of the Bupati live in the neighbourhood of the *alun-alun* with one *pĕndapa* and two gates. Inhabitants of other ranks can choose their own location and have a *pĕndapa* but no *lenjik* or two gates. [This is yet another manifestation of the precise differentiation of rank by visible insignia so characteristic of Javanese society.]

The Javanese house

Siting the house

Since Cornets de Groot has already mentioned the system of positioning the door of the house according to a conceptual division of the four sides of the plot into nine sections each, we begin with a full description of this system according to a member of the Javanese aristocracy.[29] Note the systemisation according to the 4/5 and 8/9 enumeration based on the cardinal and sub-cardinal compass points, which occurs in so many spatial and social conceptualizations in Java, for instance in the symbolism of the sheltering banyan tree as described by Cornets de Groot.

I

1. *lawang gĕringan*: much sorrow
2. *lawang sugih tamu*: many visitors
3. *lawang putra*: rich in children
4. *lawang keh siyalane*: many misfortunes
5. *lawang kĕmalingan*: troubled by thieves
6. *lawang oleh arta saking putra*: obtains wealth through his children
7. *lawang budi roso*: strong-willed
8. *lawang antuk dosa saking putra*: the children bring sin (perhaps "disgrace" is a better translation)
9. *lawang mlarat*: brings poverty

II

1. *lawang dosa saking liyan*: suffers evil through others
2. *lawang antuk estri ayu*: obtains a beautiful wife
3. *lawang antuk busana adi*: obtains fine clothes
4. *lawang antuk sampurnaning karya*: achieves perfection in his occupation

The socialisation of the people: "becoming Javanese"

5. *lawang sugih sarama:* much joy
6. *lawang susahan ati:* suffers sorrow
7. *lawang sring tukaran:* quarrelsome
8. *lawang agěng manahe:* generous hearted
9. *lawang kěmalingan:* troubled by thieves

III

1. *lawang antuk anak saking batih:* gets a child from a servant
2. *lawang datan darbe suta:* childless
3. *lawang duka cipta:* bad-tempered
4. *lawang oleh ilmu:* obtains much knowledge
5. *lawang sring kěpaten:* suffers many deaths
6. *lawang ati kěras:* of formidable character
7. *lawang antuk sugih:* becomes rich
8. *lawang cacad mring Ratu:* falls foul of the King
9. *lawang angsal batih katah:* will have many servants

IV

1. *lawang angsal arta karam:* obtains unlawful wealth
2. *lawang angsal garwa ayu:* obtains a beautiful wife
3. *lawang sugih putra:* has many children
4. *lawang měnang ngangkuhi garwa:* able to make his wife respect him
5. *lawang kěmalingan:* troubled by thieves
6. *lawang antuk sugih suka galih:* obtains riches and happiness
7. *lawang běndu:* an aspect bringing great misfortune
8. *lawang antuk arta:* becomes rich
9. *lawang gěringan sědihan:* suffers want and sorrow

There are however other ways of classifying house lots, detailed by a twentieth-century Javanese writer, Sastra Amidjaja of Ngadiluwih, Kediri, who won a competition run by *Djawa* magazine.[30] They are as follows:

1. *gasik*, land that does not become marshy in the rainy season and does not break up in the dry season.
2. *loh*, a fruitful plot with sufficient water and nutrients, good for fruit trees.
3. *jujugan*, an accessible plot, e.g. near a prayer-house, market, station, etc.

4. *rĕja*, a prosperous, blooming place, by the side of a busy road.
5. *ajĕm*: a place in which one feels at home because it is located for example near a ditch or gully with running water.
6. *lĕmpar*, a lot that is spacious and level.

There is also a classification of land according to its slope, which is thought to determine the welfare of the owner. There are 16 types of plot in this classification, named after figures from Hindu-Javanese mythology. A few examples are:

Baṭara-ground or *Siti-Baṭara*. This inclines towards the north. The owner will be favoured by fortune and hence inclined towards charitable works.

Manikmaya-ground or *Siti-Manikmaya*. This inclines towards the east, and brings prosperity, and a happy marriage for husband and wife.

Bĕtari ground or *Siti-Bĕtari*. This inclines towards the south, and its occupier is loved by his neighbours who are always ready to help him.

Sri-Sadana ground or *Siti-Sri-Sadana*. This inclines towards the west and the occupier will be involved in many quarrels with his wife, family, friends and neighbours.

Arjuna Wiwaha ground or *Siti-Arjuna Wiwaha*. This plot is bounded on the north-west by mountains, and on the south by a low-lying plain, and is transversed by a river flowing eastwards. The occupant will go far in life, being promoted if he is a *priyayi*, prospering as a trader, finding treasure if he is a farmer.

Dandang kelangan ground or *Siti Dandang kelangan* [?*ḍandang kalangan?*]. This plot is on a graveyard or surrounded by one. Its occupier will be plagued by sickness and be involved in many police matters, e.g. theft, knavery, etc. He must be content with a lowly station. [Note the strong sense of graveyards as polluting and ill-omened.]

The author mentions however that many Javanese do not take account of these prescriptions in choosing house plots. There is also another system which goes by the smell of the earth. To be avoided are soils that smells of turpentine (*sĕngir*), scorched or smoky (*sangit*) of blood or pus (*arus*), musty or sweaty (*apĕk*), of rotten flesh (*bacin*) of stagnant water (*bangĕr*), unpleasantly alkaline like a bat's nest (*lĕḍis*), or of rice cooked with coconut milk (*gurih*).

The socialisation of the people: "becoming Javanese"

The house itself

Sastra Amidjaja notes that the Javanese house consists of a complex, the *pĕndapa*, *pĕringgitan* or *kampung*, the *griya agĕng*, the *pawon* or *padangan*, and the *gandok*. The *pĕndapa* is a fore-house where guests are received; the *pĕringgitan* or *kampung* is a small house behind the *pĕndapa* and connects it to the *griya agĕng*, and is used for festivities such as wayang. The *pawon* or *padangan*, is a kitchen situated behind the *griya agĕng*, and is sometimes a separate construction in the back yard. If there is an open space by the *griya agĕng*, it can be used for the *gandok*, which is used for receiving people and for storing goods. Or it can be used as a sort of informal "family room". The *griya agĕng* is divided into two sections, the front one, which is bigger, being used as a sitting room and the back divided into three, the *sĕntong kiwa*, *sĕntong tĕngah* (*pajangan* or *kobongan*) and *sĕntong tĕngĕn*. The *sĕntong tĕngah* is also known as the *pasren*. It is the ritual centre of the Javanese house and is discussed further below.

Styles of house: It is the roof shape and construction that defines the Javanese house, and there are quite a number of named, well defined styles. Some of the best known styles are Sinom ("youth"). Joglo, Limasan, Klabang Nyandĕr ("pouncing centipede"), and Kutuk Ngambang ("frog floating").

Walls: These may be wood, in which case the house is called *gĕbyog*, or stone (*griya gĕdong*), or bamboo (*gĕdeg*) – the last very common in village houses. Among woods, teak (*jati*) is most favoured but because of its cost other woods such as *nangka*, *laban*, *sengon* and *wungu*, *klumpit*, *galih* and *mangir* (local preferences differ) are used, and coconut wood is used for wall-plates and rafters.

Types of wood: The favoured teak-wood is sub-classified into *jati sungu*, *jati kunyit* and *jati kapur*. The first is brown, the second yellow and the third is teak of a whitish colour grown on limey soil. There are other types of teak like *jati doreng*, *jati keyong*, *jati kĕmbang*, *jati ri*, *jati landa* and *jati werut*. *Jati gembol* is used for kris sheaths, and is actually a knotty outgrowth of teak wood. The Javanese classify large long-lived trees (*kajĕng taun*) into two divisions, i.e. *kajĕng gamben* the "best wood" and *kajĕng gaben* "spongy, slightly weathered". The first has a hard heart, and does not split. The second generally has no heart. Wood which is prone to split

The Javanese Ancien Régime: Civilization and Society

(*wĕlonan*) must be avoided, as must wood from a graveyard or a holy tree, and *sungsang* wood which is said to have its bark in the heart of the wood. *Oyod-mimang*, the roots of the *waringin* or similar growth, is considered to have supernatural power: it is worn for protection against danger, and hung above the door (or buried below it) to prevent theft.

Roofing: materials used are *alang-alang, renbuyuk, Sĕlang*, coconut leaves, *aren* fibres, zinc, tiles, or planks. A house roofed with *alang-alang* is called *griya atĕp*, one with planks *sirap*, one with aren *ijuk*, and one with zinc *griya seng*.

The heart of the Javanese house: the pasren, place of Sri

The *pasren* is the place where one pays homage to Sri (from whose name the word is derived), who brings livelihood and fortune and is the goddess of rice. She is honoured in statues where she is either sitting or standing and holding a *gantang*[31] of rice. She is conceived of as living in heaven (*kahyangan*) but descends from time to time to the *pasren*. The *pasren* has other names,[32] i.e.

1. *pĕtanen*, "place of the farmer". In some villages it is the custom that after harvest to put or hang four *gantang* of padi at the corner of the upper part of the pillars of the *pasren* and to put several *untingan* (*gantang*) of *padi* seed in front of the *pĕtanen*.
2. *krobongan*, so called because the upper parts of the four pillars are draped (*dikĕrobongi, dipajang, disĕlubungi*) with beautiful cloth such as *cinḍe* or silk. Also the bottom part around the sleeping platform (*blabag*) where the pillow and mattress are put is draped with beautiful cloth. In Yogyakarta and Surakarta what is called *krobongan* is the circumcision enclosure, and it is draped with white cloth.
3. *sĕnṭong tĕngah*. The traditional Javanese house is usually divided into the *sĕnṭong kiwa, sĕnṭong tĕngah*, and *sĕnṭong tĕngĕn*. The right and left ones are used for goods or for sleeping, the middle one for meditation or for making offerings to Dewi Sri or the ancestors.

Pĕtanen is a village word; the most refined term is *pasren*, used by educated people, while the term *sĕnṭong tĕngah* has lower-class associations.

The socialisation of the people: "becoming Javanese"

A fully equipped *pasren* has the following furnishings:

1. four *guling* (large pillows) piled up on the mattress.
2. four ordinary pillows, two to the left and two to the right of the mattress.
3. on the ceiling (*pyan*) pleated *cinḍe* or silk,
4. a curtain, half open, at the front, held with a silk or wood curtain clip in the form of a Garuda, Vishnu's vehicle.

It contains the following objects for making offerings:

1. a pair of *klĕmuk*, which is a small *kĕlĕnṭing* or *buyung* (water-pot) made of *gĕrabah* and with a lid. These are placed on a base (*bancik*) formed by a wooden flower-pot. The *kĕlĕnṭing* are placed in front of the *pasren* on the left and right.
2. a pair of brass bowls (*bokor*)
3. a pair of water-pitchers (*kĕnḍi*) of earthenware on a base formed by a brass pot
4. two chandeliers or hanging-lamps [*robyong*] placed in front of the *pasren* on the left and right.
5. a standard oil lamp [*ajug-ajug*] placed between these two hanging oil lamps
6. a pair of spittoons

Plus the following materials for the same purpose:

1. the so-called *kĕmbang tĕlon* ("three flowers"): rose, jasmine, and *kenanga*.
2. incense
3. water which is put in the *kĕnḍi*.
4. yellow rice, or white rice which is put in the *klemuk*. Some is also put in the brass *bokor*.
5. a small brazier and a *sapit* [pair of tongs] for burning the incense.

According to Yusuf, there is no great uniformity about the names given to these things, or in the way they are used, e.g. some people put rice in the *bokor*, others flowers. Some people use a *bango tulak* serviette beneath the lid of the *pĕdaringan/klemuk*.

The *pasren* also contains two highly significant statues or figurines, known as the *loro blonyo*. *Loro* means two, *blonyo* means rubbed with *lulur* (a yellow powder. The statues are of wood or clay and are placed in front of the *pasren*. These symbolize the couple whom Dewi Sri will bless. The head-dress of the male varies: sometimes it is the *ikĕt sinṭingan*, at other times the *songkok* (*kuluk*).

The Javanese Ancien Régime: Civilization and Society

The first goes back to the period before the *blangkon* was invented and was used by all classes. It can be seen on a pair of *loro blonyo* at the Jakarta Museum while the pair at the Sono Budoyo, Yogyakarta, wear the *kuluk* as a sign of their aristocratic dignity.[33]

As noted above, in the traditional Javanese house the *pasren* is flanked by the *sĕntong kiwa* and *sĕntong tĕngĕn*. The *pĕringgitan* is mainly found in houses of the better-off. The *gĕbyog / patang aring* is a wall which if it has a curtain or is closed prevents the *pasren* from being seen from the *pendopo*. It is usually made of teak and ornamented with reliefs of beautiful floral or tendril motifs: there are local variations and the Jepara and Kudus *patang aring* are particularly renowned for their beauty. Usually the *patang aring* is separate from the *pasren* but sometimes it is joined on to it, as in the Arosbaya *patang aring* in the Sonobudoyo Museum. The room in which the *pasren* is situated may be ornamented with pictures of dead ancestors to the left and right of the *pasren*, and often contains an object called the *ploncon* which is for *pusaka* lances, krisses, pennants, and *payung* of state.

Yusuf says that the *pasren* is particularly associated with the *daerah kejawen* (as opposed to *pesisiran*), defined as Banyumas, Kedu, Yogyalarta, Surakarta, Madiun, Malang and Kediri, but notes that there are also houses with *pasren* in Demak, Kudus, and Japara.

The centrality of Sri's shrine to the ordinary Javanese house is fully reflected in the ruler's palace. Behrend[34] writes that the single most important building in the *kraton* complex lay just to the west of the ceremonial axis at the centre of the *pelataran*. This was the *dalĕm prabasuyasa*, the ritual heart of the palace. Though the ruler did not live there, it housed the *pusaka*, and within its several rooms, an ornamental bed (i.e. a *pasren/krobongan*) and *loro blonyo* representing Sri and Sadana; the eternal flame of Ki Agung Sela; the *sekar wijaya kusuma*, which would bloom as long as the king possessed the *wahyu*; the regalia (*ampilan dalem*: heirloom weapons, ornamental betel sets and standards carried behind the ruler) and the symbols of state, the *upacara* (in Surakarta, eight figures cast in precious metals and embellished with rare stones and gems, i.e. a cock, a crowned *naga*, a goose, a roe deer, a garuda, two elephants and a bull). The Javanese author Mangunwijaya also remarks on the centrality of the *pĕtanen*, as he calls it, to the palace, claiming that all Javanese rulers were farmers.[35]

An unsigned handout from the Yogya kraton provides the information that the relative rank of the husband and wife of the

The socialisation of the people: "becoming Javanese"

house is also encoded in the *pasren*: if the man of the house is of a higher rank than his wife, the male statue is to the right of the female one.

The *klĕmuk* are described as the symbol of the food store, because inside them are stored the products of the earth such as rice, maize, soya bean, *botor* and *gude*. These grains are covered with cloth in the pattern *sawat, bango tulak* or *gadung mlaṭi*. One of the oil lamps must burn constantly, like Ki Ageng Sela's lamp in the Prabasuyasa of the kraton, above.[36] A bride receives from her parents a special chest which contains traditional medicines and is kept at the back of the *krobongan*.[37] In the evening before Friday and on Selasa Kliwon incense is burnt and offerings made, as also on important occasions for the inhabitants of the house e.g. birthdays and ancestors' birthdays.

Occupying the house: the cosmically auspicious moment

To calculate this, the Javanese used a system called *bincilan*, said to be of Majapait origin and therefore sometimes called Majapaitan. The choice of a good day is considered very important for avoiding misfortune. Good days are: the birthday of the builder of the house or his wife or child; the birthday of Mohamad, or of a ruler from whom the house-builder has received favours; or a day on which the builder of the house has had very good fortune. Much to be avoided are the so-called Na'as days, i.e. the Javanese New Year, the 10th of Asyura, the 27th of Rejeb and the 1st of Puwasa, unlucky days for Muslims. The 7-day/5-day week combinations on which these dates fall in a given year are also to be avoided throughout that year. Also to be avoided is *naas*[38]-*tiyang sĕpuh*, the day of death of the parents or grandparents of the couple; and *pupak-pusĕr* (*naas jĕjĕr* or *naas-pancĕr*), the day on which the umbilical cord of the house-builder fell off; and the day of any catastrophe such as flood or war (*naas nĕgari*). There are five basic *bincil-Majapaitan*, i.e.

1. *Sri:* a good time for building a rice barn
2. *Wrĕdi:* the time for building an animal pen
3. *Naga:* the time for building a kitchen
4. *Kancana:* lucky for building the *griya-agĕng*
5. *Saloko:* for building the *pĕnḍapa*

To relate these five to an actual day, the numerical values [*nĕptu*] of the days of the 5-day (*pasaran*) and of the 7-day week are added together, and the number obtained is then counted through the series from Sri to Saloko more than once if necessary.

Offerings. These consist of: *sěkul kěbuli*, rice cooked with coconut milk; *sěkul golong*, spherical rice, *tumpěng*, rice in a cone, *apěm*, a rice-flour pancake, and also five different sorts of porridge, i.e. *jěnang makuṭa*, porridge prepared with sugar, *jěnang abrit* or red porridge, white porridge, porridge of fine bran; *běkatul* porridge or *jěnang baro-baro* (which includes *sěkul-megonun* and *sěkul-pěnakan*, rice in nuggets rolled in a leaf), plus cooked vegetables or *janganan*. *Sěkul kěbuli*, rice cooked with coconut milk, is to obtain Muhamad's blessing. *Sěkul golong*, is in honour of the guardian spirits of the land; *sěkul tumpěng* is in honour of all the Prophets from Adam to Muhamad; *apěm* is in honour of the dead and their descendants; *jěnang baro-baro* is in honour of brothers, sisters, and parents still alive. The five different sorts of porridge are in honour of the placenta. *Jenang makuṭa*, also called *sěngkala*, is in honour of the good spirits Kaki Among and Nini Among otherwise known as Sang Marmarti or Mahamarti, who watch over small children (*měmětri*, "to hold in honour", is a corruption of this name).[39] The white porridge is in honour of the waters that break just before childbirth. The black or sometime blue porridge is in honour of the afterbirth. The pink porridge is in honour of the umbilical cord, and the red for the blood, so that the intention of the five different coloured porridge is to ask help of the five things that come into the world with the child.

There is another system of offerings which distinguishes four types i.e. *sambung-tuwuh*, *siram-tuwuh*, *sajen* and *cok bakal*. All four should be offered (which is expensive) for the construction of the *griya agěng*; for the *pěndapa sajen* can be omitted; for an outbuilding or kitchen *siram-tuwuh* and *sajen* are appropriate; for an animal house, only *cok bakal*; and for a rice-barn, the last three.

Sambung-tuwuh consists of *bango-tulak* cloths (to be put on the posts); flags of fine cloth in *cinḍe* (a flowered silk cloth worn by bridegrooms and princes); *plangi*,[40] and *tuwuh-watu* (sort of grey linen with white or light blue border); reed stems (*těbu mangli*); sheaves of rice (*Sri kuning*); green sweet coconuts (if not available, then old dry ones) (*klapa ijěm, klapa lěgi*); a bunch of bananas ripened on the tree (*pisang suluhan*), preferably *pisang Sri* or *pisang raja*. These offerings are affixed to prescribed parts of the house, and left with the owner. Note that the *bango tulak* pattern of cloth is perhaps the most sacred of Javanese textiles, recurring in many sacral contexts, such as weddings and the ceremony for the child's first step onto the ground. It takes its name from the stork (*bango*), a bird which seems to be associated with the moon-princess deity, Nawang Wulan.

Siram-tuwuh, or *kěmbang sětaman*, is water with fragrant flowers, and must be buried in the middle of the floor.

Sajen consists of cooked rice, *kěmiri* nuts, *kěluwak*, the fruit of the *pucung* tree, which like *kěmiri* is used as a spice [the unprepared *pucung* fruit is poisonous]; coconut meat; two bunches of *pisang raja*; coconut sugar; eggs; Spanish pepper; *lawe wěnang*, i.e. rough threads used as a charm against evil spirits in epidemics; and other spices.

Cok bakal is *takirs*, i.e. bunches of bananas made into a basket shape and containing a *kěmiri*, a *kěluwak*, two different sorts of onion, a small quantity of salt, a bit of *badeg* (a strong drink made from *tape-kětan*) and rice yeast (*ragi*).

Occupation of the house. This is subject to the same considerations re favorable days as building it, so that houses often remain unoccupied for long periods after they are built. It is also necessary to take account of the so-called *naga-dina, naas-tanggal* and *naga-taun* or *jati-ngarang*. Jati Ngarang is the name of a dragon whose tail is attached to the navel of the earth and which turns towards a different direction every three months: it is very dangerous to proceed into that direction. In Syawal, Sela and Besar he is in the north; in Sura, Sapar and Mulud in the east; in Rabingulakir, Jumadilawal and Jumadilakir he is in the south, and in Rejeb, Ruwah and Siam in the west. One must avoid these directions at these times when going into a new house [This belief is also mentioned by Raffles[41] in his treatment of Javanese astronomy]. On moving in, a slametan is given, generally in the evening or night, and the owner, his wife, and a couple of other people stay up all that night.

* * *

Thus Javanese domestic architecture, though neither durable in European terms nor datable, nevertheless, like the genes of a family or race, enduringly re-manifests its complex and typical forms though the individual carriers last no more than a generation, and transmits semantic systems of profound meaning for society. As we have seen, house construction is shaped by the requirements of a number of originally separate systems, some empirical, some religious, observed in practice to varying degrees. In form and symbolism, however, its fundamentals have remained constant over many centuries, in the courts[42] as in the villages, and of deep significance at all levels of society.

From Cornets de Groot's account we see that even planting the garden was not a purely utilitarian and/or aesthetic activity. He says that there are many sorts of bananas, some considered lucky and some unlucky for the householder, based on word-play associating the name of the banana with a word denoting good or bad fortune. The most favoured of all bananas was the *pisang raja*, the king or royal banana. The author tells us that the very pleasant grapes called *nganger* (*anggur*) are not planted because the word *nganger* (*nganggur*) means to Javanese of rank, end of service, [dismissal] and to Javanese of low rank, falling foul of authority. Supernatural forces around the house also required attention, with various ways of propitiating the devil, whose favourite spots included graveyards, cross-roads, river-mouths, and brooks, and getting him to release thieves from his influence and to return stolen goods. To ward off burglary etc. many Javanese put the head of a tiger or crocodile over the house entrance; also stunted coconuts (*apa-apa*) or bits of *alang-alang* are used – these are called *tulak* or *cegah* [i.e. prophylactics or preventatives].

CEREMONIAL AND SUMPTUARY RULES

Games and amusements. The tourney or *sěnen* was an occasion for those of high birth and senior and junior Mantri to put on their *dodot* [large cloth wrapped around the lower half of the torso on ceremonial occasions] and, instead of the usual headcloth, a *kuluk* and a sort of gold-mounted cap, as well as a cummerbund or *epek* of gold lace and trousers, the attire worn for weddings. The Bupati and his family were distinguished by their *sodor* (tourney lance) with flowers and large decorations, and by the gold-mounted saddlery their horses wore; the Mantris were only allowed simple saddlery. The *gamělan sěnen* was played on Mondays at about 7 a.m., in the *alun-alun*, to announce the tourney, and again at about 3.30 p.m. if it was to take place in the afternoon.

Prescriptions re ceremonial. The authority to prescribe these originally lay with the Susuhunan of Kartasura and was subsequently taken over by the colonial government.

The socialisation of the people: "becoming Javanese"

A Bupati was allowed 1 *payung bawat*, [ceremonial sunshade], 1 ordinary *payung*, a *kandaga* (box), 3 *panurung* (pikes), 1 *epok* (box) for *sirih*, 1 *lante* [ceremonial mat] 1 *gĕnder* [one of the metallophones] or "*sermambu*" [?], 1 *kĕndi* (long-necked water pitcher), 4 pikes of state, 1 other pike, 1 spittoon (*paidon*), 1 kettle [kettle-drum?], 1 *sodor* (tourney lance with [pennant]), 4 fine horses;

The Patih, son or brother of a Bupati and the Ngabeis had 1 *payung* (if agreed by the Bupati), 1 *epok*, 1 mat, 2 *awinans* (servants [specifically, those who follow a member of the nobility carrying the insignia of rank]);

The senior Mantri, Jaksa and Rangga had 1 *payung*, 1 *epok*, 1 mat. The junior Mantri and Demang had 1 *epok* and 1 mat.

When the *gamĕlan sĕnen* had been beaten for the third time, all participants gathered on horseback, in order of battle. When the gamelan played the tune "lagandjoor" [??] the procession began, and, with the gamelan still playing circled the *alun-alun* thrice. If the Bupati headed the procession, everyone else had to hold their lance upright, though this was optional for him. Afterwards the Bupati or the next most senior person present gave the command to begin. The contest consisted of duels with the object of unseating the other party. The one who parried the attacks of his opponents with most dexterity was acclaimed the best of the tourney, a great honour. After everyone had shown his talent, the procession again made its three-fold circle, and then the cavaliers ranked themselves behind the Bupati, who used the occasion to make reports and issue orders. After this the games were sometimes, especially at New Year and other ceremonial occasions, continued on foot.[43]

Krisses. Every Javanese had two or more krisses and pikes. These were of different types, and a kris worn for everyday purposes could not be used on an occasion of state. The same was true of pikes, which were principally used at night.

GAMES, AMUSEMENTS, THEATRE

In *Puasa* and in the west monsoon there were wrestling games and a game called *jaguran*. The first was held by moonlight and involved two wrestlers. *Jaguran* was a children's game held in the day-time, also one-on-one.

Other games included *wayang* of various types, *ronggeng*, and *terbang*, as well as songs in the *kawi* and modern language, which the author lists. Games of chance included dominos, chess, *macanan* ["tiger game", a sort of draught or siege game], *cuke* (draughts) and *dakon*, played by women.

Wayang

Cornets de Groot says that there were two sorts, *wayang purwa* and *wayang gĕdog*, using puppets of buffalo leather and beautifully gilded and painted. Javanese of rank had performances twice weekly. For the *wayang purwa*, the stories were of Watu Gunung, Arjuna Wijaya, Bima Suci, Bomantaka, Pendawa Jaya and Parikesit [all stories from the Indic repertoire except for the Watu Gunung myth, on which see below]; for the *wayang gĕdog* they were "Dandang Welis, Kudanarawangsa, angrene, angron akoong, magatkoong, prijembada, prowelas maroe, moerdaningkoong, Djaja koesoema, kalmendang dadang dewa and wahoe djaja" [all bastardised forms of the names of different stories from the Panji epics]. The *topeng*, or masquerades, was played by masked men, and the stories were the same as those of *wayang gĕdog*. The *wayang krucil* were wooden puppets.

Tandak or ronggeng. Cornets de Groot says that this is a dance by one or more young women, accompanied by song and gamelan, on the occasion of marriages, circumcisions, changes of name and other celebrations, for a small payment. These women were usually of the poorest classes or reduced to this profession because of bad character. They lived together in groups of two or more or boarded with someone who provided food and clothes for 2/5 of the *ronggeng*'s earnings; she had to give another fifth to the gamelan owner and a fifth to the musicians, so that she retained only one fifth for herself.[46] There were different sorts of *ronggeng* performances, to wit *tandak*, "laedraek or badut" [*ludruk*[47]] and *andong*. The *tandak* was the simplest; it was usually performed for the native heads and accompanied by the compositions *"laras"* and *"gandung"* [*gending*].[48] On these occasions all the men present took a turn dancing, called *maju* or *bĕksa*, when the women sang the style *"ngudang"* [*ngidung*]. The male handed the dancer over to the one who follows him in rank; each was obliged to give the *ronggeng* some money. *Ludruk or badut* was a dance with two harlequins or clowns, one dressed in women's clothing, both of whom had to learn witty stories and add all sorts of mime. The *tandak bĕbarang* was a troop of wandering players with gamelan. The *tandak andong*

The socialisation of the people: "becoming Javanese"

was a troop that played at night in public places. Everyone had the right to dance with the woman of his choice and to choose the tune; afterwards the woman embraced the man, gave him some *sirih*, and received some *stuivers* in payment.

The *tĕrbang* or *rabana* presented Arab histories called "*rengonis, praloe raro* and *baktie djamal*" [i.e. Rengganis, Prabu Lara and Bakti Jamal, all characters from the Amir Hamzah or Menak romance] to the accompaniment of the tambourine. This performance was often given by poor, crippled or blind persons, who went around the kampongs accompanied by a gamelan consisting only of *kellaak* [*kĕṭuk?*], *kĕnong, kĕnḍang, gambang* and *rabab*. These histories were performed on the occasion of weddings by priests or in public places. The music was principally used in *puasa*, to the accompaniment of reading prayers. Some poor priests or other people also sent their children around on Thursdays with tambourine music to read prayers for money.

Cornets de Groot goes on to describe cock-fights, reeve (Javanese *burung gĕmak*) fights, cricket fights, and *lawanan ayam*, for which one chose young birds with long feathers and thus best able to fly: the winner was the one that flew furthest.

Games of Chance. The Javanese were very fond of these, and had, with Chinese cards, i.e.*karta [kartu] cina, lima Sampi* and *lowak*, also the games *pedek, kĕcik, adu klapa, adu kĕmiri gandring, gimĕr, gangsal ganĕp, cĕplek, lobang, kĕmpyang, dadu,* and *bentangan*.

pedek was a game involving throwing *sawo* stones; the one whose stone breaks loses.

kecik was a game for four persons involving *sawo* stones; three of them chose a number from one to four and the fourth player counted out a handful of the *sawo* stones into groups of four. The winner was the one who had the same number as the stones which were left over.

adu klapa was a game played by two players each with a coconut; they banged them together, the loser being the one whose coconut broke. *Adu kĕmiri gandring* was a similar game involving throwing two *kĕmiri* fruits against one another.

gimĕr was a simple heads-and-tails throwing game.

in *gangsal ganĕp* one threw eight copper *duits* [copper coins of small value] against an object; an even number [staying on the object?] won, an uneven one lost.

in *cĕplek* one placed two copper *duits* with holes on top of each other with the head sides touching. Then one threw them on the ground, and if they both had either heads or tails, one won.

lobang was a game involving trying to throw *duits* into a hole from a certain distance; if one was not successful, they were arranged in a circle around the hole and one tried to hit the first, thus winning; otherwise one paid a penalty.

dadu was a game played with two dice, for money placed in two cups; particular numbers on the dice won the money in one or in both cups.

bentangan was a game involving putting *sawu* stones in a pile on a small elevated object and trying to knock some off by throwing, so that an uneven number remained.

Music

Cornets de Groot lists the following types of *gamĕlan* as in use in the Residency:

1. The *gamĕlan salendro*. This was considered the preferred *gamĕlan* for all grand occasions. In Gresik Residency it consisted of the following instruments: *rĕbab, gĕnder, gambang kayu, suling, bonang, saron babon, pĕnĕrus, dĕmung, kĕnong, gong, kĕmpul, kĕncer, kĕndang* and *ketuk*.
2. The *gamĕlan mĕntaram* or *pelog miring* had larger instruments with a heavier tone. Added to it were the following instruments: *bĕdug, puksur, bĕnde, bonang pĕnĕrus, saron bonang* and *kĕmpyang*; the *gĕnder* was not used in the *pelog* set. The *gamĕlan salendro* was used to accompany *wayang purwa*, and the *gamĕlan pelog* or *mĕntaram* for the *wayang gĕdog* and *krucil*.
3. The *gamĕlan surabayan* or *surapringgan* was like the *gamĕlan mĕntaram*, but the instruments were smaller and the *bĕdug, rĕbab, gĕnder, pĕnĕrus, saron bonang* and *dĕmung* were not used.
4. In the *gamĕlan kodok ngorek* the *bonang* had 15 notes [instead of 10] and the *puksur* was very much like a triangle. The *rĕbab, gĕnder, gambang, suling, kĕndang, saron, ketek, dĕmung* and *kĕncer* were not used. This *gamĕlan* was considered the oldest and was used for ceremonial processions, festal days or meals, and never to accompany *wayang*.
5. The *gamĕlan cara bali* or *wangsul* did not have the *rĕbab, gĕnder, gambang, saron* and *dĕmung*; otherwise its instruments were the

The socialisation of the people: "becoming Javanese"

same as in the *salendro*, except that they were as large as the *pelog* ones.
6. The *gamĕlan sĕkaten* was like the *pelog*, except that its instruments were even larger and heavier of tone. It was exclusive to the ruler and seldom used except for great occasions, and the eight days of the Mulud celebration.
7. The *gamĕlan sĕnen* was used for state and war processions and for the tourney, and constituted the idiosyncratic war-music of the country. At the courts [but not in Gresik?], besides the usual instruments, an unusual sort of gong and trumpets, were added, and the instruments were all of larger size as in the *gamĕlan koḍok ngorek*.
8. The *gamĕlan sĕrunen* consisted only of a *sĕlompret*, a sort of trumpet, *kĕnḍang*, *kĕnong*, and *kĕmpul*, was mostly used for marriage processions and festivities of the common people, and was found in all villages.

Appendix III gives a list of gamelan melodies (named) in use for the different types of *gamĕlan*. The relative numbers are:

Sĕnen and *Koḍok ngorek*: 2 (the same for both)
Cara Bali: 6
Bonang Rentong (said to be used by Bupatis and other grandees[49]): 13
Salendro: 68 (for the wayang)
Mĕntaraman: 25 for *wayang gĕḍog*, 15 for amusement
Pelog: 13 for the use of Bupatis and other grandees
Surabayan: 11
Sĕlompre [*sĕrunen*]: 3

SEMANTIC TIME: THE CALENDAR

Cornets de Groot gives the following account of the calendar as used in early nineteenth century Gresik. The day is divided "in the Buddhist way" (*wawayahan*) into ten parts:

1. 5–6 a.m. is *biyar raina* (note: ms. *pajar raina*), indicating that the fast starts at 5 a.m.
2. 6–7 a.m. *schajur*, sunrise [the derivation of this word is unclear].
3. 7–10 a.m., *rame pasar*.
4. 10–11 a.m. *wisan gawe*, time to rest.

The Javanese Ancien Régime: Civilization and Society

5. 11–12, *lingsir wetan*, i.e the sun begins to incline westwards.
6. 12–1, *těngange*.
7. 1–3 p.m., *lingsir kulon*, indicating the sun is already in the west.
8. 4–5p.m., *asar*.
9. 5–5.30 p.m., *tunggang gunung*, indicating the sun descending behind the mountains.
10. 5.30–6 p.m., *saput bumi* or *surup srěngěnge*, indicating that the sun has set but it is not yet dark.

The night is divided into seven parts:

1. 6 to 6.30 p.m., *sore*, indicating that it is dark.
2. 6.30 to 8.30 p.m., *sirěp lare*, time for children to rest.
3. 8.30 to 11.30 p.m., *sirěp wong*, time for adults to rest.
4. 11.30 to 12.00 p.m., *těngah wěngi*, midnight.
5. 12.00 to 3.00 a.m., *lingsir wěngi*, past midnight.
6. 3 to 4.30 a.m., *kluruk ayam*, cock-crow.
7. 4.30 to 5.00 a.m., *běḍug telu*, time to wake.

[Note the Islamic influence in *schajur, asar* and *běḍug telu*.]
These times are grouped into five main ones, as follows:

1. from *schajur* to *rame pasar* is under Batara Guru (who is lucky).
2. from *rame pasar* to *lingsir wetan* is under Batara Wisnu (neither lucky nor unlucky).
3. from *lingsir wetan* to *těngange* is under Batara Brama (exceptionally unlucky).
4. from *těngange* to *lingsir kulon* is under Dewi Sri (lucky).
5. from *lingsir kulon* to *saput bumi* is under Batara Kala (most unlucky of all).

[Raffles gives a much simpler system,[50] ie.:

Day-time:

1. 6–8 a.m., *esuk*.
2. 8 a.m. till noon, *těngange*.
3. noon till 1 p.m., *běḍug*.
4. 1–3 p.m., *lingsir kulon*.
5. 3–6 p.m., *asar*.

Night-time:

1. 6–8 p.m., *sore*.
2. 8–11 p.m., *sirap wong*.

The socialisation of the people: "becoming Javanese"

3. midnight till 1 a.m., *těngah wěngi*.
4. 1–3 a.m., *lingsir wěngi*.
5. 3 a.m. till daylight, *bangun*.

Jasper, writing about the Tenggerese gives the following information:[51]

– the Muslim Javanese divide the day into 6 periods, i.e. *wisan gawe* (from 6–10 a.m.), *těngah dina* (10 a.m.–2 p.m.), *asar* (2–6 p.m.) *ngisa wěngi* (6–10 p.m.) *těngah wěngi* (10 p.m.–6 a.m.) and *lingsir wěngi* (2–6 a.m.).
– the Tenggerese have the old system of 2 times 5 or 10 divisions. These are for night-time: *sore* (6–8 p.m.), *sirěp wong* (8–11 p.m.), *těngah wěngi* (11 p.m.–1 a.m.), *bangun* (3–6 a.m.); and during the day: *esuk* (6–8 a.m.) *isan gawe* (8–11 a.m.), *běḍug* (11 a.m.–1 p.m.), *lingsir* (1–3 p.m.) and *sore* (3–6 p.m.). And this old division into 5 is called *sad* (6)!

But it will be noted that in Jasper's account *sore* occurs in both the day and night divisions for times that run into each other, i.e. 3–6 p.m. and 6–8 p.m].

However, Cornets de Groot says that Javanese who know something about Islam, mostly the priesthood, use a different system, in which the day is divided into 5 chief *waktus* which are dedicated to some of the Prophets. The chief *waktus* are sub-divided into minor waktus:

1. *subuh*, from 5 to 12 a.m. [elsewhere: 12.30], dedicated to Adam, and sub-divided into 5 smaller periods of unequal times
2. *luhur* from 12.30 to 3.30 p.m, dedicated to Ibrahim.
3. *asar* from 3.30 to 6 p.m., dedicated to Yunus.
4. *mahrib* from 6 to 7 p.m., dedicated to Ngisa.
5. *yssah* i.e. *Ngisa* from 7 p.m. to 5 a.m., named after *sembayang ngisa*, dedicated to Musa.

[The 5 main divisions follow the 5 daily prayers, i.e. Arabic ṣubḥ, źuhr, 'aṣr, maghrib and 'ishā'. The times for these are actually set not by the clock but by the position of the sun, which of course does not change very much by clock time so close to the equator. I am not sure what the sub divisions of the first prayer period are.]

Cornets de Groot says that the proper Javanese or Buddhist calendar, which was once in general use and now is used by the less enlightened, and in particular in the interior, is as follows:

The Javanese Ancien Régime: Civilization and Society

The Hindu-Javanese months (*mangsa*)

Cornets de Groot says that these are governed by the sun [whereas some Western scholars, notably Damais have treated them as lunar months]. He says that the civilized Javanese have a sun-dial; however, they believe the sun does not have a fixed course and when things don't seem to work out as they should, they add to or subtract from the *mangsas*. At the end of *kapat*, two days are omitted[?] and at the end of *kawolu* they do not count three days when the sun is at its zenith and gives no shadow[??]. The *mangsa* are:

Kasa, when the fruits are ripe, (around August).

Karo, when low water holds up the fish catch.

Katiga, the time for changing the teak leaves for salt making (October).

Kapat, the turning of the east monsoon, when the fields are prepared for earth-fruits. and crops, and fishing begins again (November).

Kalima, the rainy season and the time of new growth; also the time for sowing and planting earth-fruits (December).

Kanem, the time when the west wind blows and the seed-padi for the *sawah* is sown (January).

Kapitu, the time of heavy rain and wind, of the planting of the *sawah* and the gathering of fruits and crops (February).

Kawolu, the time to harvest various earth-fruits (March).

Kasanga, the time of the turning of the monsoon and for harvesting the rice from the *tegal* or dry fields.

Kasapuluh, a time of little rain and heavy east winds; the rice called *jitek* is harvested in this month (May).

Desta, the time for the sawah harvest; fruit trees bloom and salt-making begins (June).

Sada, the time of the coldest nights (July).

Year cycles

Cornets de Groot gives a 7-year cycle where the year is classified according to which day of the 7-day Hindu week falls on the first day, as follows. If the year begins on

Dite (Sunday) it is called *Dite Murcita* or *klabang kala jengking* and has a centipede as its sign. Heavy rain followed by light rain can be expected.

The socialisation of the people: "becoming Javanese"

Soma (Monday), the year is called *Soma Werjit[a]* or *cacing*, and has a worm as its representation. It is characterised by intermittent moderate rain.

Anggara (Tuesday), the year is called *Anggara Katto* or *yuyu* and has a crab as its sign; its characteristic is heavy rain.

Buda (Wednesday), the year is called *Buda Maesa* or *Kebo* and has a buffalo as its sign; its characteristic is alternating heavy rain.

Respati (Thursday), the year is called *Respati Mintuna* or *Mimi* and represented by the *mimi* fish; its characteristic weather is moderate rain.

Sukra (Friday), the year is called *Sukra Mangkara* or *urang*, and has a shrimp as its sign; characteristic, alternating heavy and light rain.

Tumpak (Saturday), the year is called *Tumpak Menda* and has the sheep as its sign; characteristic, intermittent rain.

If *Dite* comes again immediately following Dite Murcita, the year is called Dite Luwing and characterised by first light, then heavy rain.

This 7-year cycle is given in a variant form by Raffles:

Sunday	Klabong	centipede
Monday	Wichitra	worm
Tuesday	Mintuna	a species of fish
Wednesday	Was	scorpion
Thursday	Maisaba	buffalo
Friday	Mangkara	prawn
Saturday	Menda	goat

The 8-year windu cycle

The years are as follows:

Karal: characterised by treachery and lies, the ruler has grief with his officials, but his subjects are happy and rich; money is easy to come by, the world is bright and lively; the old are subjugated; rain crushes the field crops.

Koro: wars will certainly occur, there is much danger, insecurity, and flattery; the ruler will be perplexed and inactive, and his subordinates are guided by money given to them, so that much deceit plagues the earth.

Setra: a serious war will occur, with heavy casualties and widespread destruction, and the ruler will be driven out.

Kěrta: everything is good and well-regulated, subject and ruler both prosper, though many people die of sickness, and means of livelihood are expensive and many people filled with hate. Laziness causes much evil; others display their virtues without shame.

Pěrniti: all negotiations and dealings succeed; the ruler is fortunate, his orders are carefully carried out. The people are rewarded in superabundance for their work and the whole land is fruitful and the crops blessed.

Pěrnila: the people refuse to perform their services for the ruler, and many of the great are insubordinate and rebellious; there are many robbers and evil-doers. This year is particularly known for deceit, and the roads are unsafe. The Ajars and Pandita come from the mountains; the caves break and the valleys split.

The usual system of numbering the windus by Arabic letters in Javanised form (*Alip, Ehe, Jimawal, Je, Dal, Be, Wawu and Jimakir*) is not given here. However it is used on the next page in the author's table of the Muslim calendar. In this account, the days of the Muslim week, the months of the Muslim year and the years of the 8-year cycle, as well as the days of the *pasaran* week, all have *naptus* or numerical values.

These *naptus* [also: *něptu*] have two functions:

1. They allow the calculation of the first day of any month, e.g. if one wishes to calculate the first day of the month Muharam of the year Alip one adds the *naptu* of Muharam (7) and of Alip (1), which is 8; and then counts from Wednesday (*Rěbo*) up to 8, which is again Wednesday, and that will be the first day. One always counts from Wednesday.
2. By adding the *naptus* of the 5-day-week (*pasaran*) and 7-day-week days together, one can find out if that particular day is favourable for various purposes. The days of the *pasaran* week are *Pon* (*naptu* 7), *Wage* (*naptu* 6), *Kliwon* (*naptu* 8), *Lěgi* (*naptu* 5) and *Paing* (*naptu* 9). For choosing the propitious days for everyday activities and special occasions, special wooden or palm-leaf diviners containing all the necessary information are used.

The Watu Gunung story and the *Wukus*

The version of this founding myth given by Cornets de Groot is much fuller and more elaborated than the Babad Tanah Jawi account. It runs as follows:

The socialisation of the people: "becoming Javanese"

There were two gods, the elder named Basa Endara and his sister Dewi Basa Endari; they loved each other and since they could not live together in heaven, descended to earth, where they lived on *Gunung Alit* (Small Mountain) and had two daughters, the elder Dewi Sinta and the younger Dewi Landep. When they were grown, their parents returned to heaven, and they lived in poverty and asceticism. There was a Pandita named Arsi Gana, son of Batara Termuru and grandson of Sang Yang Arsi Narada; he went down to earth to avoid being married, but when he did this he had a dream of the two sisters and fell in love with them. They did not want to marry him because of his advanced age, but he prevailed, although they refused to sleep with him. By supernatural means he or Batara Guru himself impregnated Dewi Sinta, who gave birth to a boy named Watu Gunung, who had no navel and a hard cranium. He grew amazingly fast, and one day when he had again asked his mother for rice, she hit him on the head with the rice-spoon. He went off in search of rice, and came to a place called Měndang Kamolan where he forced the inhabitants to give him rice. He then went to a place in a wood, named Sela Gringsing, where he became a Maharaja.

There was a ruler of Tunggala called Maharaja Brama Raja, who handed over the kingdom to his son Raden Citra Baga and went to do asceticism on Mt. Sela-krendra, taking the name Bagawan Arsi Tama; he heard about the beautiful sisters living on Mt. Landep, Dewi Dara and Dewi Dari, who had refused many Pandita, and decided to try himself. They refused him, and retreated to Giling Wesi ["iron rod"], followed by Arsi Tama. Watu Gunung had a dream that he would get two Widadari as wives; on asking for an explanation of this dream, he was told of Dewi Dara and Dewi Dari. After an involved three-way conflict between Watu Gunung, Arsi Tama and the ruler of Giling Wesi, Watu Gunung triumphed and became ruler of Giling Wesi; he married the two Dewis, though he was cursed by the former ruler of Giling Wesi to die the same violent death as he had. After a year Dewi Dara had twin sons named Raden Wukir and Raden Kurantil, after another year twins named Talu and Gumbreg; two more named Wari Galit and Wari Gagung [i.e. Wariga alit and Wariga gung]; two more named Julung Pujud and Pahang, two named Kuru Wĕlut and Marakeh, two named Tambir and Medangkungan; two named Maktal and Wuye; two named Manail and Prang Bakat, two named Bala and Wugu, two named Wayang and Kulawu; and finally a son named Dukut, making a total of 27 sons; thus totalling, with Watu Gunung and his two wives, 30 persons.

Watu Gunung was enterprising and undertook to build an iron city; he was warned by a voice from heaven to offer the proper prayers to Batara Guru and to do asceticism, after which he built the iron city in less than seven years. He subsequently became more and more conceited and populated the city with 40 men resembling the gods and 40 maids like the *Widadaris*, claiming that it was like the palace of Batara Guru.

Now it transpired that Dewi Dara dicovered the scar on Watu Gunung's head and realised that she had married her own son, for Dewi Dara and Dewi Dari were actually no other than the Dewi Sinta and Dewi Landep. To extricate themselves from this shameful situation they made a plan to get Watu Gunung to ask the gods to give him Dewi Sekandi as wife (at the time he asked, Batara Guru and Batara Wisnu were disputing which of them she should marry). Watu Gunung sent his son Prang Bakat to heaven with a letter, containing two riddles to be solved. Batara Wisnu solved them. A heavy battle followed, with many casualties on both sides, but the gods could not kill Watu Gunung because he was invulnerable. A certain Semar Petruk [Semar and his son Petruk are two powerful indigenous gods who play an important role in *wayang lakon*] sent an envoy named Wilawuk to find out his weak point. Wilawuk changed himself into a snake and contacted Dewi Dara and Dewi Dari, who managed to worm out of Watu Gunung the information that he could be killed by cutting off his arms and legs, and that his body should be put on a *pĕḍati* (cart) on an Anggara Kasih, i.e. Tuesday/Kliwon,[52] at the hour when the sun stands above the earth.

As a result of their betrayal Watu Gunung and all his sons were killed; but then Dewi Dara and Dewi Dari began to weep and wail, and since they were of heavenly birth this had the power to create a great noise and flood in heaven. Batara Guru sent the god Sang Yang Arsi Narada to ask what they wanted,

The socialisation of the people: "becoming Javanese"

and at their request Watu Gunung and all his sons were taken to heaven with them: first Dewi Sinta and Dewi Landĕp, then the 27 sons in order of age, and finally Watu Gunung.

This myth is clearly a Hinduized version of an indigenous Javanese myth, presumably a creation myth. Note that Watu Gunung is ruler of Giling Wesi and, as a person who is invulnerable and threatening to the gods, he builds an iron city inhabited by god-like people. A shorter version is found in the opening passage of the *Babad Tanah Jawi*, and a slightly different version in Raffles' *History of Java*. It is the basis of the divinatory *wuku* calendar, which shows the same partly Hinduized character. The version of this calendar given by Cornets de Groot follows. It corresponds very closely to the one still in use in Java today, as represented in the Javanese almanacs, those inexpensive and unpretentious paperback volumes that provide a fairly comprehensive guide to the practice of *agama Jawi*, Javanese religion, and Javanese socialisation. Where different or additional information is given in the almanac, this is indicated in square brackets. It will be seen that each *wuku* is presided over by a combination of the following signs: a god, a tree (invariably), a bird, a foot, often with water, a house, and a pennant (*umbul-umbul*: a flag indicating rank, e.g. military). These, in combination, establish the characteristics of this week and thereby predict the character and fortune of those born in it.

The 30 week (*wuku*) calendar

Wuku and characteristics	Significance
1. *Sinta*	a beautiful, sorrowful woman.
God: Yang Yama Dipati	holds a pennant in his hand, is lord of the dead.
Tree: *kendayakan*	this tree is very leafy and means: providing shadow, protecting.
Bird: crow	that is, when old, retains the appearance of youth, like a crow; prudent (it is said that the crow gives omens).
Feet in the water	signifies heavy rain.
House in front	means that a person born in this *wuku* displays his wealth and is open-handed.
[Pennant held above the head	prospers greatly. In summary,[53] a child born in this *wuku* is feared, prudent, great

147

The Javanese Ancien Régime: Civilization and Society

	in under-takings, long young, of pious works, but poor.]
2. *Landĕp*	in this *wuku* many beautiful women die and much rain falls.
God: Yang Maha Dewa	a handsome, courageous god.
Tree: *kenḍayakan*	sheltering.
Bird: *alah [atat] kĕmbang*	as this bird is rare, it signifies the love of the ruler.
House in front	spreading out on display all one's riches or abilities.
Back foot in the water	there is rain in the last part of this *wuku*. Therefore a child born in this *wuku* is a protector of his fellow men, a favourite of rulers, mild, with a severe appearance but actually goodhearted. This *wuku* is harmful for fish, so, to catch large fish, choose this *wuku*.
3. *Wukir*	mountain-dweller.
God: Maha Yakti	holy or pious god.
Tree: *nagasari*	beautiful and fragrant.
Bird: *manyar*	this bird sings incessantly, the sign for a talkative person.
[Feet set to climb the mountain	always tries to rule others].
House in front	to make kindness felt.
Pot with water beneath	heavy rain and hospitality. Therefore a child born in this *wuku* is pious, kind/good, beloved, talkative, open-handed and hospitable. This *wuku* is ruinous for wild animals, so it is good for e.g. catching a tiger. It also has much rain.
4. *Kurantil*	backward in manners, unmannerly.
God: Batara Angsoar[Langsur]	undergoes many difficulties.
Tree: *tangan [ingas]*	active, industrious.
Bird: *mlinḍit [slinḍitan]*	upside down, signifying to act wrongly (this bird often hangs head down).
House in front, on its side	gives everything away, very gentle, wasteful, purse upside down.
Water on the left	sets aside good things.
Pennant behind	has persisting difficulties. Therefore a child born in this *wuku* is always accompanied by difficulties, is wasteful, always

The socialisation of the people: "becoming Javanese"

| | does things the wrong way, avoids good things, is always behindhand and has no end to his troubles. |

5. *Tolu*
God: Batara Bayu
Tree: *wali kukuh [branjangan]*
Bird: *branjangan*
House in front
Pennant behind

luck begins towards the end.
the court calmly giving orders.
steadfast.
wakeful at night.
generous, wasteful.
lucky later on. Therefore a child born in this *wuku* is lucky only in old age, is wakeful at night, is careful and pious; if he practices fasting, finds fortune; is steadfast, enterprising, respected and well-grounded. This *wuku* is bad for all creatures, but good for plants.

6. *Gumbrĕg*
God: Batara Candra [Cakra]
Tree: *wandara [waringin]*
Bird: wood-hen [=*ayam alas*]
House in front [to the left]
Left foot in the water

has much influence on fellow men.
handsome and upright.
provides kindly shelter to mankind.
favourite of the ruler.
generous.
warm in front, cold behind. Therefore a child born in this *wuku* is sweet of speech, upright, a source of protection, loved by the great, generous; of severe appearance, but actually goodhearted. This *wuku* is bad for giants. There are moderate winds.

7. *Wariga alit*
God: Yang Asmara
Tree: *sulastri*
Bird: *kapoḍang*
A *caṇḍi* (funerary temple) in front

beautiful, like Venus.
fragrant.
solitary.
melancholy. A child born in this *wuku* is beautiful, but fickle; is solitary, shy, or melancholy. This *wuku* is bad for troops.

8. *Wariga gung*
God: Panca Resmi [Batara Maharsi]
Tree: *cĕmara*
Bird: *beṭet (parikit)*

a house in front *and* behind
pennant behind

difficult to satisfy.
sweet of speech.

gives no shadow (shelter).
thieving [almanac says aggressive and good at finding food].
division of possessions.
lucky later on. A child born in this *wuku*

149

has many difficult wishes, is sweet of speech, often unlucky for his nearest, can seek good fortune and accumulate money; in his old age he finds luck. This *wuku* is bad for small fishes and is very hot.

9. *Julung Wangi* — compassionate.
God: Batara Sambu — a good kinsman.
Tree: *cĕmpaka* — fragrant and beloved.
Bird: *kaṭilang* [*kuṭilang*] — favourite of the great.
Pennant on the shoulder — spreading his treasures on display.
Pot with water in front — generous. A child born in this *wuku* is respected and loved, is indulgent, knows how to make friends and is sweet of speech; when he goes into service, he is loved and trusted by his master; he does however flaunt his fortune, and is liberal, but in order to be seen so. This *wuku* is bad for wild animals, but good for plants.

10. *Sungsang* — choleric.
God: Batara Gana — has an elephant's trunk, signifying strength.
Tree: *tangan* — trouble.
Bird: *luri* [*nori*] — has a function/service. [very extravagant, unhappy, not straight-forward]
House behind, upside down — prodigal, the housekeeping upside down. A child born in this *wuku* is no master of his heart's desires, but conscientious and industrious; he is however prodigal, liberal, and not inclined to show displeasure. This *wuku* is bad for youth and hot.

11. *Galungan* — unlucky.
God: Yang Kama Jaya — handsome.
Tree: *tangan* — trouble.
Bird: *biḍu* (silent) — choleric, turbulent.
Water on the lap [in copper vat] — A quiet way of life [self-indulgent, unable to save, small income]. A child born in this *wuku* is unlucky, handsome, but undergoes many difficulties; is turbulent and set on his comfort. This *wuku* is bad for all plants, like bamboo, rattan, etc., and also very dangerous for all humans and tigers.

The socialisation of the people: "becoming Javanese"

12. *Kuningan* close-fisted, money-hungry.
God: Batara Indra independent.
Tree: *wijaya kusuma* enterprising.
Bird: [*urang-urangan* quick in everything he does, moody, given to feeling shame].

House behind and closed close-fisted. A child born in this *wuku* is shameless, proud, solitary and close-fisted. This *wuku* is bad for all trees.

13. *Langkir*
God: Batara Kala cruel.
Tree: *cĕmara* [*-sol*] and *ingas* repels others, does not get along with anyone.
Bird: fighting cock [=*gĕmak*] wild. A child born in this *wuku* is brave, cruel, unsympathetic, enterprising and grim, but can do good by undertaking fasting. This *wuku* is bad for old people and good for children. It is very hot.

14. *Maṇḍasiya*
God: Batara Brama magnanimous, choleric.
Tree: tamarind [=*asĕm*] cool or beloved.
Bird: *hatak bowang* [*plaṭak bawang*] firm, steadfast
House behind, closed [in front] secretive, close-fisted. Therefore a child born in this *wuku* is choleric, but beloved, steadfast but sharp and close-fisted. This *wuku* is bad for medium-sized fishes and accompanied by pleasant winds.

15. *Julung Pujud*
God: Yang Luratna [Gurĕtna] silent.
Tree: *nipa* [*rĕmbujuk*] useful.
Bird: *prit cowang* believable.
[House facing a mountain has great ambitions to command, but is lazy and others surpass him.

Pot with water behind The outcome of his orders are loving[? his wishes are discovered later]. Therefore a child born in this *wuku* is patient and will not show his anger; is loved by the great, good-hearted and truth-speaking, and patient in command. This *wuku* has no house, so he can keep no money, and is indifferent to it. This *wuku* is bad for profits and many animals fall sick.

The Javanese Ancien Régime: Civilization and Society

16. *Pahang*
God: Batara Tantra
[holding up weapons
Tree: *kĕṇḍayakan*
Bird: *cocak*
[House on its back

Left in the water[sic] [water in a pot]

few relatives
proud.
on the alert, speaks hastily, fault-finding].
sheltering.
speaks with intelligence
very extravagant, not attached to worldly goods]
cool in his orders. A child born in this *wuku* has few relatives, is lonely, proud, but protected; speaks much, but falsely, commands severely, but without outcome. This *wuku* is hot and bad for birds.

17. *Kuru wĕlut*
God: Batara Wisnu, armed [with *cakra*]
Tree: *parijata*
Bird: *sesepahan*
[House in front

bellicose

beautiful
careful, swift.
displays his wealth, open-handed but not compliant, not to be taken lightly]. Therefore a child born in this *wuku* is brave and bellicose, knows how to bring men into good order, perseveres with fasting; his commands are hot-tempered in the beginning, but without outcome; he has no regard for profit. This *wuku* is bad for *kapas* [kapok] and similar plants and is also very hot.

18. *Mrakeh*
God: Batara Bok Wĕrang [Surenggana]
Tree: *tanguli [trĕngguli]*
Bird: see below.
Pennant reversed
House in front [held high]

his desire unfulfilled.

has inedible fruits.

easily attains prosperity.
shows the love of the gods. A child born in this *wuku* cannot attain his goal, is at enmity with his family, asks no-one's advice and is self-willed; his fortune must [however] come and he displays the kindnesses of the gods to everyone. There is no bird, since he cannot go far without meeting with an accident/mishap. He is

152

The socialisation of the people: "becoming Javanese"

                    the flower of the audience-hall (*paseban*). This *wuku* is bad for wild animals and for bamboo and is very hot.

19. *Tambir*
God: Batara Siwa
Tree: *upas* (poison tree)
Bird: *prenjak*
House above

half blue and half red.
not protecting.
speaks of its own choice.
rich. [almanac says three houses all closed, i.e. self-seeking and acquisitive but cannot become rich, only has just sufficient]. A child born in this *wuku* is threatening, unapproachable, proud of his treasures, can twist himself [? *zich verdraaijen*], is jealous and choleric. This *wuku* is harmful to mankind and is itself a sickness.

20. *Měndangkungan*
God: Batara Basuki
Tree: *plasa*
Bird: *pělung*
Water behind
[House above

humble.
lucky and pious.
wild wood.
lover of water.
later on one discovers a stratagem.
elevates worldly goods, receives the lord's favour, is careful of money. A child born in this *wuku* is humble, good, kind-hearted and pious; he sequesters himself for religion, and is pure whenever he conducts himself virtuously; he is solitary, and only later on does one discover his stratagem. This *wuku* is harmful for crocodiles and similar animals and is also very hot.

21. *Maktal*
God: Batara Sakri
Tree: *nagasari*
Bird: wood-hen [=*ayam alas*]
House lying on a *kěndil*[54]
Pennant on the house

brings the world's goods.
beautiful and fragrant.
favourite of the great.
i.e. rests on riches.
rich. Therefore a child born in this *wuku* is the ancestor of great office-holders, is a favourite of his lord, has abundance, is generally loved, is rich but inconstant. This *wuku* is harmful for wild animals and is very hot and windless.

The Javanese Ancien Régime: Civilization and Society

22. *Wuye*
God: Iyang Kuwera

Tree: *tal*
Bird: *kapoḍang [gogik]*
House in front, upside down

sorrow. The god stands with a bare *kris* in his hand, signifying sharp-witted.
long-lived.
jealous.
open-handed. A child born in this *wuku* is sorrowful, lives long, is jealous, solitary and greedy, sharp-witted, open-handed, sympathetic, but careless of himself This *wuku* is bad for birds, but good for planting.

23. *Manail*
God: Tritra Gatra
Tree: *tĕgaran*

Bird: *sasĕpahan*
Water behind [in a pot]

upright.
useless, without a function [i.e. is not granted a position at court, unlike the child born in the *wuku* Bala, see below].
careful and strong.
his stratagem is concealed. Therfore a child born in this *wuku* is upright and has no [official] employment; his stratagem is discovered later on; he takes offence at everything, and thinks over everything; he is treacherous. This *wuku* is bad for crops.

24. *Prang bakat*
God: Batara Bisma
Tree: *kalapa* [coconut]
Bird: *urang-urangan*
[right] foot in the water

haughty.
abundance.
swift, but timid.
the orders later become cruel {his way of commanding is cool in the beginning, heated later]. A child born in this *wuku* is not false, but haughty, rich and swift, and cruel in his orders. This *wuku* is harmful for all large trees.

25. *Bala*
God: Batari Durga
Tree: *cĕmara*
Bird: wood-hen [=*ayam alas*]
House in front

troops.[55]
angry.
does not give shelter.
favourite of the great.
making use of one's treasures. Therefore a child born in this *wuku* is given to anger,

The socialisation of the people: "becoming Javanese"

poor, bad, loquacious, but the favourite of princes; he puts his riches on show. This *wuku* is bad for Paṇḍitas.

26. *Wugeo [= Wuku or Wugu]*
God: Yang Singa Jalma
Tree: *wuni*
Bird: *kapodang*
House behind, closed

proud.
wants everything.
jealous.
very close-fisted. Therefore a child born in this *wuku* is proud and idle, on his guard, greedy and makes little use of what he desired, is very secretive and in the highest degree close-fisted. This *wuku* is bad for the dangerous fishes, and much rain falls.

27. *Wayang*
God: Dewi Sri
[a bared *kris*

Tree: *cĕmpaka*
Bird: wood-hen [=*ayam alas*]
Pot with water in front

rich.
sharp and on the alert; orders are easy at first, hard later]
beloved.
favourite of kings
open-handed. Therefore a child born in this *wuku* is rich in everything, the favourite of the great and loved by all; open-handed. This *wuku* is unfavourable for the envoys of the king and for sowing and planting [this seems strange, since Sri is the patron goddess of rice]. There are also many fires.

28. *Kulawu*
God: Kajang [?] Sadana
Tree: *siwalan [tal]*
Bird: *luri [nori]*
House in front
[sitting in water at the edge of a bathing-place
Sharp weapons behind

grey.
abundance.
long-lived.
favourite of rulers.
abundance of everything.
i.e. always cool and calm in giving orders.]
later on his heart is known. Therefore a child born in this *wuku* is rich, steadfast, lives long, is the favourite of kings, is handsome and has abundance of everything. His personal qualities are known

155

The Javanese Ancien Régime: Civilization and Society

	later in life. This *wuku* is bad for anyone who has two wives. "Thick weather" (*dikke lucht*).
29. *Dukut*	
God: Batara Sakri	very fond of postponement.
Tree: *paṇḍan [-wangi]*	sharp of speech.
Bird: wood-hen [=*ayam alas*]	favourite of kings.
Unsheathed *kris* in front	brave in the handling of weapons.
House behind	close-fisted. Therefore a child born in this *wuku* is negligent, sharp of speech, brave, close-fisted, the favourite of kings, beloved and rich. This *wuku* is bad for Panditas. There is rain and good crops.
30. *Watu Gunung*	
Gods: Nagagini and Antaboga	love.
Tree: *wijaya kusuma*	handsome.
Bird: *gunggek [gogik]*	solitary.
A large funerary temple (*caṇḍi*) in front	sadness. Therefore a child born in this *wuku* is amorous by nature, handsome, solitary, likes fasting and is sorrowful, This *wuku* is bad for all comers. There is much heavy rain.

The almanac version of the *wuku* system is also more elaborated in the following aspects: each *wuku* has a particular danger inherent in it, e.g. being bitten by a snake, wounded with a weapon, etc., which can be averted by performing a *slamĕtan* with specified offerings and making a money offering. These are all noted in detail. Also noted is information about a monster called Jabung Kala who watches over the *wuku* and rotates in a circle synchronically with the *wuku* weeks, changing position every seven days. His position is important i.a. for generals, who should orientate their battle lines so as not to get across him. Ricklefs[56] notes of the *wuku* system that *wukus* appear in Old Javanese inscriptions from the early tenth century AD., and that the 210-day cycle (of 30 seven-day weeks, each of which begins with Sunday (Ahad, Rĕdite) and ends with Saturday (Sĕtu, Tumpak)) still constitutes an indigenous year in Bali, though in Java it has not had the status of a year at least since the appearance of the first dated Old Javanese inscriptions, which use the Indian Śaka year. Nevertheless, *wukus* are often given as an element in dates. *Wuku* Sinta begins upon Sunday-Paing-Tungle in the seven-, five-, and six-day weeks. This

The socialisation of the people: "becoming Javanese"

sets the combination of days upon which each of the *wukus* begins, so that *wuku* Landĕp always begins on Sunday-Wage-Ariyang, *wuku* Wukir on Sunday-Lĕgi-Wurukung, and so on.

Ricklefs also gives an account of a further refinement of the *wuku* system: the thirty *wukus* are again subdivided into five groups of six *wukus* each (*wukus* 1–6, 7–12, 13–18, 19–24, and 25–30); this system is called *ringkĕl ing wuku*. Within each of these groups there are six *ringkĕls* (just as there are six days in the *paringkĕlan* week), but now each *ringkĕl* is not a day but a week of seven days. Five of the six *ringkĕl ing wuku* have the same names as the days of the six-day week, but here Jalma is the first, whereas in the six-day week Tungle (Goḍong) is the first. One of the *ringkĕl ing wuku* has a different name, and just to compound confusion its name is Wuku. Thus the *ringkel* Wuku means the fifth *ringkĕl ing wuku*, which is the same as *wukus* Tolu, Galungan, Kuruwĕlut, Mĕnahil, or Dhukut (the fifth, eleventh, seventeenth, twenty-third, and twenty-ninth *wukus*). The names of the *ringkĕl ing wuku* are as follows:

1. Jalma (*wukus* 1, 7, 13, 19, 25)
2. Sato (*wukus* 2, 8, 14, 20, 26)
3. Iwak (*wukus* 3, 9, 15, 21, 27)
4. Manuk (wukus 4, 10, 16, 22, 28)
5. Wuku (*wukus* 5, 11, 17, 23, 29)
6. Goḍong (*wukus* 6, 12, 18, 24, 30)

Within each 210-day cycle, therefore, the *wukus* give thirty sets of seven days[57] beginning on the same day of the seven-day week (Sunday), and the *ringkĕl ing wuku* gives five sets of six weeks (of seven days each) beginning on the same days of the six-and seven-day weeks (Sunday-Tungle).[58] What is interesting here is that the names of five of the six *ringkel ing wuku* mean, in order: humans, animals, fish, birds, and leaves. This, taken in conjunction with the Watu Gunung story, suggests that this was originally the Javanese creation myth, and certainly more work could be done on this subject. Particularly interesting is the portrayal of Watu Gunung as constructing a city of *iron*, and being strong enough to challenge the gods, which suggests an iron-age myth.

Zerubavel[59] calls the Javanese *wuku* calendar "the most remarkable week-calendar ever invented", and the most intricate.[60] He notes that the entire calendar "year" essentially consists of 210 unique types of calendar days, each of which is defined in accordance with its relative positions within the nine weekly cycles of from two to ten days. However, since 210 = 5 by 6 by 7, the 210 types of calendar days can actually be produced by the interaction among only three of those cycles, the five, six and seven day weeks, and all traditional holidays are celebrated once every 210 days and defined in terms of this combination of days. The festival Galungan, for example, is celebrated on Boda-Klion-Ariang. The distinctive names of the thirty *wuku* weeks are the result of a calendrical practice found elsewhere only in Bahai and Central American calendars, and remind us that this is essentially a week calendar and the 35-day "month" produced by the interaction of the seven and five day weeks is not a month in our sense, being unrelated to the lunar (or solar) cycle. Unlike the Central American week calendar, the *wuku* calendar is not integrated into a larger calendrical system approximating the actual solar year (though the Śaka year was used, the *wuku* cycle was not integrated into it). "Being based entirely on weekly cycles created by human beings, the Indonesian week-calendar is a rare example of an exclusively artificial time-reckoning system that is totally disregardful of nature and its rhythms. It is essentially a calendar where neither the seasons nor the lunar phases play any role whatsoever. As such, it is probably the most remarkable calendar ever invented, a unique manifestation of the workings of the rational human mind as well as of humans' capability of living in accordance with entirely artificial rhythms which they create."[61] This "unnatural" character unrelated to the seasons and agriculture squares with the preoccupation the *wuku* calendar seems to show in the significance of its symbols with gaining official position and the favour of the ruler, suggesting that it was originally designed for those in the immediate service of the ruler, rather than the population at large, who would presumably have had more interest in the changing of monsoons and seasons for agricultural purposes.

A good deal more could be said about the finer points of the *wuku* divinatory system and the range of variations found, but sufficient has been said to indicate its complexity, and its fundamental Javaneseness, surviving the introduction of Hindu presiding deities, who are not the same in all versions.[62] It seems to be connected to what must be an indigenous creation myth cum iron-age myth sufficiently enduring and important to be the first story of the Babad Tanah Jawi, the official history of the kings of Java compiled in the court of Mataram, last of the great kingdoms.

The socialisation of the people: "becoming Javanese"

MYTHOLOGY: A WELL-POPULATED PANTHEON, JAVANESE AND HINDU

The pantheon

Cornets de Groot begins by saying that statues, graves, temples, etc are considered by the Javanese to be the work of persons who have, through fasting, acquired an elevated state: a reference to the Javanese concept of *tapa* which figures so prominently in the writing of Yasadipura II (see Ch.6). He also describes the visits and offerings made to these places in times of sickness and other trials, still a common practice in Java today. He goes on to say that not many people are knowledgeable about antiquities and fables, but some of the old stories of the gods are still known in this Residency, and he has recorded them as being not without worth.

He gives both a taxonomic and a chronological account of the cosmology. For the first, he says the *Dewas* and *Widadaris* are divided by the *Boedoes* [i.e. Budas, Javanese who have not yet converted to Islam] into nine classes. There are 46 of the former and 42 of the latter. The rank order is: the ruler of all the *Dewas*, and his brother, the Patih; 19 *Dewas* classified as "Natasanga" who live in Suralaya; then 13 *Dewas* who do not live in the kingdom of the gods but hold sway over worldly affairs; then 5 *Dewas* who have power over earth and water; then 7 Dewas who are wholly of the earth and separated from the kingdom of the gods [the Sanskrit names of all these gods are given]; then 12 *Widadaris* "from the story of Setami"; then 8 Widadaris belonging to the kingdom of the gods; then 14 who came down to earth; then 4 *Widadaris* in the *Sapta Patala*, the seventh level of the earth, and 4 on the bottom of the waters. The chronological account of the birth of the gods and their actions is like that given in the *Babad Tanah Jawi* wherein Islamic figures (Adam and Eve, Nabi Sis, and a personification of the divine light, Nurcahya) appear first, before Hindu-Javanese gods like Sang Hyang Wenang, Sang Hyang Tunggal or Wisesa; and the main actor, Batara Guru or Sang Yang Giri Nata, who is to be the ruler of all the gods, comes on the scene rather late in the piece. His 15 names are listed.

The names of the *Widadaris* are as follows:

A. those who occur in the story "sestamini" [??] and live in the kingdom of the gods: Ling-ling Mendana, Mayang Sari, Nawang

Wulan, Nawang Sih, Nawang Kain, Sukasih, Suwarti, Selastri, Suwiskar, Warsiki, Wardati and Madati.

B. Those given to Arjuna as reward for his fighting Dewa Ditia Kawaca. They are said to have been 40 in number but only 7 names are known, i.e.: Supraba, Tilutama, Dersa Nala, Praba Sini, Sri, Tunjung Biru, Gagar Mayang, and Ratih (the last taken by the god of love Kama as consort).

C. *Widadaris* who descended to earth: Dewi Sri, reborn first as Citra Wati, then as Sinta and Sěmbadra; Dewi Bandan Dari, married to Dasa Muka, Hendradi, Dewi Tara and Dewi Tari, married to Raja Subali; Dewi Rauwati, reborn as Dewi Ragu and married to Dasa Rata; Dewi Lasmadari who married Dasa Rata but was abducted by Dasa Muka; Tampa Uni, reborn as Dewi Srinadi; Basu Endari, who returned to heaven after giving birth to the twins Sinta and Landep [see the Watu Gunung story, above]; Dewi Uma who was at first the beautiful wife of Batara Guru but was subsequently cursed by him when pregnant and gave birth to Batara Kala; Dewi Indra Narum, who married Dasa Muka; Dewi Kumalaram, who married Indrajit; and Dewi Budru Bumi, who married Eka Laya.

D. *Widadaris* living in Sapta Patala: Dewi Prawi, who married Batara Kresna, Dewi Naga Gini, who married Sena, Dewi Srenggeni Wati, who married Nakula, and Dewi Naga Wati, who married Sadewa.

E. *Widadaris* living on the bottom of the waters: Dewi Gangga Wati, who married Prabu Dasa Muka;. Dewi Ganggi Hara, who married Gatut Kaca, Dewi Wantnu Hara, who married Arjuna, and Dewi Wiratna.

These *Widadaris* are of central importance in indigenous Javanese mythology, especially Nawang Wulan and Nawang Sih, royal consorts and patron goddesses of rice, and Dewi Sri, another form of the rice goddess. In numerous parts of Java there were ritual games, called *sintren* and *lais*, designed to call down the Widadari or to transform a young girl into one. Maurenbrecher notes performances in Tegal and Banyumas and describes in detail one in Cirebon which had apparently a more antique character.[63] *Sintren* was and is also performed in Pekalongan.[64] Maurenbrecher says that performances could only take place by moonlight in the west monsoon after the planting-out of the padi harvest. A woman served as the *panjak* (or *ḍalang*) of *sintren*, and a man as the *malim* of

The socialisation of the people: "becoming Javanese"

lais. The onlookers used to pay a small contribution. For *sintren*, only a non-nubile girl (*prawan kĕncur* or *sunṭi*) could act, and only a boy of the same age (*jaka kumalakala*) as *lais*. It is preferred to train a daughter or son of a former performer, and practice can only be held once every 4 or 5 days, otherwise it will lead to psychological disturbance. The *panjak* requests the *widadari* to descend into the *sintren* by singing the following:[65]

1. *turua sintren, sintrene widadari nĕmu kĕmbang ayon-ayonan, kĕmbange widadari, widadari tumuruna, ngranjing ing awakira*; and then: 2. *encek kawongane ngĕlontong, alimbung sana, wis ngĕlontong, alimbung sana, wis ngĕlontong alimbung sana* (sleep, *sintren*; the *sintren* of the *widadari* has found flowers, to adorn herself, flowers of the *widadari*; descend, *widadari*, enter the body destined for you, see, the body is already empty, the place is free). This corresponds closely with the words by which in the Nini Towong game, a very well known girls' game, the *Widadari* is invited to enter into the doll.

For *lais* a *hajat* is made by the *malim* on *malam jumuah* (eve of Friday) at which specified dishes must be offered. It is offered to the Widadari, Buyut Ki Kuwu, Ki Mas, Ki Tuhan, Ki Bekel, Ki Klowo, Ki Ori, Ki Ngabei and Ki Limas. Two couplets are sung, the first addressed to the Widadari as in *sintren*, the second not intelligible to Maurenbrecher. *Lais* appears to be more Islamicised.

Viewing the cosmology as a whole, one can only be amazed at the incredible richness and prolixity of the pantheon, part Javanese, part Hindu, part Islamic – and all this in Gresik, in the very heartland of Javanese Islam.

ISLAM

Observance of Islam is slight, according to the author. The *sahadat* or *doewa kaliwa* [i.e. *doa kalimah*] is performed at home after 6 p.m., rarely in the temple (Cornets de Groot explains that this, the confession of faith, is a prayer acknowledging the one God and his prophet Mohammed). The *sĕmbayang* at the set times is carried out by only a few. The author describes the process of bathing and putting on clean clothes untouched by dogs, pigs, or strong drinks – the latter are, however, widely enjoyed [as we have seen in the previous chapters, this was also the case in the "strongly Islamic" Mangku-negaran court]. He says that before visiting the "temple" they take a little water (kept in a *kula* or water-tank) called *banyu wulu* to purify

The Javanese Ancien Régime: Civilization and Society

the hands, crown of the head, ears, and feet. They say *salam* before entering, and face west for the prayers. The Imam wears a long very wide white *kĕbaya* called a *kĕbaya jubah*, and a headcloth called sorban [*sĕrban*] or doster [*dĕstar*], as well as a wrap and a rosary [*tasbih*], made of more than a hundred corals. All clothes made of silk are considered sacreligious. Fasting is done from 5 a.m. until sunset, principally in the fast month, whose start is determined by the sight of the moon, so that there are variations between districts. Most Javanese of all classes observe this fast. Those who are prevented from doing so by reason of age or sickness give 60 *kati* of rice called *samut* (which means "what can lie in both hands") to the needy for some days [this passage is not very clear]. If someone is prevented for some good reason from fasting one or more days, they make it up at another time of the year. Travellers and nursing women do not fast; some of them do so at another time of the year. The first day after the breaking of the fast all the fasters spend in religious observances. In Sawal there are six days for fasting, the 2nd to the 8th [i.e. the six days following *Idu'l Fitr*] (Cornets de Groot says that this is based on the calculation that one has to fast one day in ten, and these six days are for the remaining 63 of the year). There are two fast days in the month of the Haj, named "poeasa tarwia" and "anpat" as a sort of penalty for those who cannot make the pilgrimage. [cf. Snouck Hurgronje:

> On the 10th day of this month the great sacrificial feast in connection with the Hajj is celebrated in the valley of Muna (the ancient Mina), which lies to the east of Mekka . . . The two preceding days are also regarded as specially eligible for voluntary fasts. Those who are performing the hajj, however, do not usually fast, as this cannot be required of them in view of the fatigues of their journey. It is a very popular view in Java, that the feast-day of this month derives its significance from this identical fast. And yet there are but few in Java, who submit to what is there called the antarwiyah and ngarpah, the fast on the days of tarwiyah and 'arafah, i.e. the 8th and 9th of this month.[66]

In this respect as in others then, Gresik can be regarded as an exceptionally orthoprax Muslim area.]

The *sembajang trawie* and *witro* are said very loud on the nights of the fast [these are extra prayers said in the fast month after the fifth daily prayer].

The socialisation of the people: "becoming Javanese"

In case of lack of rain, the priests and heads go to the inland, without ceremony, and say prayers in the fields.

For earthquakes they give *sĕdĕkahs*, and for eclipses of the sun and moon special prayers are said. The author gives a list of the prophetic meaning of an earthquake in each of the twelve months of the Islamic calendar, e.g. in Mocharam an earthquake in the daytime means war, and one at night means many calamities because of the dearness of rice and other means of livelihood. In all cases (i.e. any earthquake in any month by day or by night) it is an ill omen. He then gives a parallel list for eclipses of the sun, which is also without exception an ill omen.

The residency's "clergy"[67]

This consisted of, in descending order of rank:

– 8 Pangulus, two at Gresik, of which the one in the capital was the Head Pangulu and chief of all the "priests" with the exception of two Princes spiritual, who were not under the Head Pangulu, and who both lived in the division *(afdeeling)* of Sidayu. Their titles were Pangeran Gandakusuma at Drajat and Pangeran Ardikusuma [Adikusuma?] at Sendang. Their chief purpose was to tend the holy graves. The second Pangulu of Gresik lived on Mt. Giri and looked after the graves of the Susuhunans and Panembahans of Giri.

– Next were the Katibs [Kĕṭib], 27 at Gresik, 7 at Lamongan, 26 at Sidayu. They were charged with collecting information about important marriages and about divorces, which they brought to the Pangulu, who made a decision. At the Friday prayer one of the most learned Katibs stood behind the Pangulu as he read the Koran, prompting him if he faltered. Every day a Katib must be in the mosque to perform marriages, for which permission has previously been obtained from the Pangulu. Written permission was necessary for those who had divorced and were re-marrying. The Bupatis and their families, however, were married by the Pangulu, who also acted as *wali hakim* for older people or orphans. The Katibs changed shifts at the mosque every 24 hours, and were obliged to keep it in a good and clean state.

– Next in rank were the "Kaijhaijangs"[??], two at Gresik, one at the capital and one at Mt. Giri, two at Lamongan and four at Sidayu (two with the *Pangulu* and one each with the two Princes). These

The Javanese Ancien Régime: Civilization and Society

were responsible for the upkeep of the temple, the proper changing of the watches, and for notifying the Pangulu when the native heads were pleased to carry out their devotions. All spiritual persons had to be notified when it was *pasamuan* [congregation], "which is always on Friday", when they must carry out their devotions in the church/temple or, if sick, send a note to the *Pangulu*.

– Next were the Marbots: 55 at Gresik, 15 at Lamongan. They cleaned the temple and collected the *jakat* from the villages.

– Next were the Modins: 252 at Gresik, 113 at Lamongan, 201 at Sidayu, of whom there had always to be at least one or two in the temple to say the prayers for those who came there, to act as witnesses, and to beat the *bĕḍug* [great drum] announcing the times for prayer (i.e. *Subuh* at 4 a.m., *Luhur* at noon, *Asar* at 3.30 p.m., *Mahrib* at 6 p.m., *Isa* at 7 p.m.), and also at mid-night and to signal the fasts and other high days. The Pangulu himself announced the fast etc. to persons of high rank. They were also in charge of washing and winding corpses.

– Cornets de Groot goes on to say that there was "a group of clergy called *Santri*." They took no part in the service at the temple, but they belonged among the priests because they were entrusted with the education of the youth, for which they received an annual reward in rice, called *jakat*, from the parents, and also a part, at the pleasure of the Pangulu, in the *pitrah badan*. [the annual contribution of rice made by members of the mosque contribution at the end of the fast month, for the specified purpose of allowing the poor to celebrate the breaking of the fast, a major Muslim festival]. There were also clergy called "Alim" [Arabic "learned", more familiar in Indonesia in its plural form *ulama*, the learned men of Islam], who were those who were far advanced in reading the Arabic of the Koran. Many of them journeyed to other islands to teach the reading and writing of Arabic, and religious treatises. They lived mostly by making copies of religious works and Korans, which they sold for considerable prices.

The income of the clergy

This consisted of:

1. A government salary
2. The different sorts of *jakat*, i.e.

The socialisation of the people: "becoming Javanese"

a. *jakat padi*, one tenth of the harvest; those whose harvest was less than 300 bundles (*gedengs*) were exempt. In former times this was collected by the Kaṭibs, but now it was voluntary and all the Javanese avoided it.
b. *jakat mas*: those who had seven Spanish dollars in gold were supposed to pay half a Spanish dollar, but very few did.
c. *jakat arta*: one guilder of every forty, also paid by very few.
d. *jakat banda*: a tax of one in 40 guilders on trade goods; this was paid by some Arabs, but few Javanese.
e. *jakat kewan*: of every 30 livestock, one should be given to the clergy for festivals.
f. *jakat anak*: every father who has 25 children should give one to the clergy; these children were then bought back by the parents at a moderate price.

It should be said that these provisions as listed by Cornets de Groot follow Islamic law very closely. The first corresponds to the provisions of Islamic law for a *zakat* of 1/10th on fruits of the earth, the second to the *zakat* upon gold, except that in Islamic law it is not a fixed percentage and 1/7th is rather high, the third, *jakat arta* or money *zakat*, to the *zakat* of 1/40th on silver above 200 *dirham*, the fourth to the *zakat* of 2.5% i.e. 1/40th on articles of merchandise valued at more than 200 *dirham*, the fifth to the *zakat* of one calf for every 30 cattle.[68] There is also provision for *zakat* on camels, horses, sheep and goats in Islamic law but I do not know of any canonical justification for the tax of one child in 25 or a redemption payment. Was this a form of extortion, or a Javanese joke? It can hardly have affected many people.

3. The *pitrah badan*, a per head gift of 5 *kaṭi* of rice, *kacang*, or other earth fruits from those who could afford it. Some also gave money.
4. The *slawat kawin*, for marriages. Javanese of rank gave money to all the priests present, of whom there might be hundreds. The common man paid from a guilder to four *stuivers* to the Pangulu, who divided it out.
5. The *slawat sunat*, for the one who performs the circumcision: not more than a guilder to a quarter-guilder.
6. The *slawat orang mati* for prayers, burial, and purification of the corpse, as for marriage.
7. The *slawat orang mati* for saying the prayers 40 days after the death – a smaller sum.

The Javanese Ancien Régime: Civilization and Society

8. The *slawat amil*, the eleventh penny of the worth of all goods divided up at divorce or death.
9. The *slawat mulud*, in honour of the birth of Muhamad. On the 12th of the month the Bupatis gave money and food, followed by lesser officials in order of rank. The Arabs made gifts virtually daily.
10. The *slawat tadarus*, an amount according to the means of those giving sĕḍĕkahs [slamĕtans] for the saying of prayers.
11. The *slawat slamatan*, given to the priests for blessing petitions, or journeys, or praying for rain or success, or providing *jimats* (amulets), for which some Javanese paid considerable sums.
12. The *slawat tugĕl kuncung*, for saying prayers for children who have reached the age of 9 to 15, at the time when hair from the crown was cut.[69] This [no. 12 alone?] goes mostly to the Santris, only the prominent Javanese ask the Pangulu or Modins.

The clergy also earned money from the *tatah* or *papar untu* (tooth filing) which took place at puberty, and according to Cornets de Groot was repeated a number of times by some well-off people e.g. at marriages and other ceremonies.

Religious meals

The priests had "religious meals" every month, as follows:

Muharam or *Sura*: in honour of the ascension of Isa,[70] a meal of *bubur suro* [Sura porridge] was given.

Sapar: a meal of red *bubur* to commemorate Muhamad's hiding himself in a cave to escape his enemies [when he was leaving Mecca].

Rabingulawal: a meal of *nasi kĕbuli* to commemorate Muhamad's emergence from his cave.

Rabingulakir: a meal of rice to commemorate Umar's death sentence on his son.[71]

Jumadilawal: a meal of rice as reconciliation re the despatch of the ruler Osman by those who would not obey him.[72]

Jumadilakir: a meal of rice in commemoration of the murder of the ruler Ali by his groom.[73]

Rejep [*Rejeb*]: a meal of red or white *bubur* in commemoration of the death of Hasan through his enemies.[74]

The socialisation of the people: "becoming Javanese"

Saban or *Ruwah*: in this month Jenal Abidin[75] gave a meal named *ruwah* in memory of his father Husain, and in imitation of this a meal of rice was given.

Ramelan or *Puwasa*: in this month Nabi Adam came from heaven to earth, so that on the nights of the 21, 23, 25, 27, and 29th of the month a meal of rice and sweets was given.[76]

Sawal: a feast of rice or sweets was given to commemorate Noah's coming out of the ark.

Dulkangidah: in this month Musa underwent a trial from God for claiming to be wiser than all other men.[77]

Dulkijah: a meal of *kuban sapi* [note says perhaps *kebon sapi*; but maybe *korban sapi*] to commemorate Ibrahim's willingness to sacrifice his son.

The Javanese can hold these feast-days themselves, but if they do not do so then they must give an offering of rice or food to the clergy.

Most of these festivals do seem to correspond to important events in Muslim theology or history, though there are some errors, which seem likely to be due to Cornets de Groots' small knowledge of Javanese, let alone Arabic. What is surprising about the list however is that it seems to have a rather Shi'ite character, with three of the religious meals commemorating Hasan, Husain, and Ali, unexpected in Java, which is part of the Sunni Muslim world.[78]

What is very striking here is that the Islamic religious tradition was obviously as comprehensively and carefully observed as the Javanese one, at least by part of the community.

THE STATE OF THE PEOPLE[79]

Cornets de Groot gives some interesting information on demographic trends. He says that 25 to 30 years ago [from 1823] the population was declining, because of the very thin population in the interior Regencies of Lamongan and Sidayu; here there were many untended fields which by the time of Cornets de Groot's writing were nearly all under cultivation in Lamongan, and partly so in Sidayu. In Lamongan the population had increased by a half, and in Sidayu by a third. This was due to three factors: peaceful conditions, in which the people of these regions have always lived, vaccination, and in-migration of Solorese and Madurese. The scarcity of rice and oppressive subjugation practised in Madura caused an annual emigration, formerly to Lamongan and now to Sidayu.

Cornets de Groots says that Gresik Regency, favorably situated on the sea for trade and fishing, has always been well populated, and the population is visibly growing by the year, with the formation of new villages and hamlets. [In the section on opium (see below) Cornets de Groot gives the population in 1823 as 220,000.] The European population is also increasing: from 1789 there has been a significant increase, now by more than half (this is in Gresik: in Sidayu there are only a few of European descent, and in Lamongan none). The author suggests measures for further increase: abolition of tolls and other grievances, and provision of buffaloes and tools, which people often lack. He notes that in times of harvest failure or other difficulties many people go to Surabaya to earn a living as artisans, but says they always return in better times.

Household life was very simple, with furniture "provided by nature". Cornets de Groots says that the Javanese' love of his children amounts to worship, though he is not strongly attached to his wife. Old age was greatly revered. At sunrise the family rises and bathes in the nearest river or stream, which is repeated three times a day. Then they eat a tasty breakfast in one of the warungs [food stalls]. The women immediately depart for the rice-fields or pasars, and the diligent man to his work, after sending their children for education to a man of religion. At 11 a.m. they re-group at home and enjoy a very simple meal of rice, fish or a little buffalo meat and vegetables, prepared by the oldest woman of the household. Then the household rests until 1 or 3 p.m., after which the women go to work again until 6 p.m. After the evening meal the men have little to do – as is the case with some even during the day – but many women do handwork until late in the evening.

It is noteworthy that he also says that most children die before the age of 14. Those who survive this period live to be 48 or 50, and few reach 60.

Sicknesses

Cornets de Groot says that endemic sicknesses are skin, eye, and stomach complaints and consumption.[80] Among the first is *buduk*, a sort of leprosy which is incurable and contagious, so that sufferers are made to live separately. Among the incurable sicknesses are

The socialisation of the people: "becoming Javanese"

counted consumption and *busung*, which is a sort of "waterziekte" [dropsy?]. Stomach complaints are *lessapanangan* [? *lesu panganan*, hungry-from-eating?], *sur* [cholera] and *kĕmandang* [? this word means "echo"], which carry many off and are accompanied by severe pain, but the timely application of warming medicine has good results. Headache, swellings, and congestion are the most common complaints and few Javanese are free of them for a number of days on end. Then there is venereal disease and hot fevers; in the last many become insanely angry, called *mata gĕlap*. The sickness which kills most children is called *sarap* [? this word means "underlay", "breakfast", or perhaps more likely, "nerves"]. In former times many were killed by the pox, but this has become rare since the vaccine (The scourge of smallpox will be noted again by the Dutch authors of reports on Banten and Pekalongan in Chapter Five.) Cornets de Groots says that this is carefully carried out throughout the Residency, and the demonstration effect has been such that the inhabitants bring their children of their own volition. The number vaccinated has risen from 671 in 1816 (of which 526 were succesful) to 4,301 in 1820 (3,261 succesful). The total number of succesful vaccinations over these years was 10,584. (Carey[81] claims that smallpox had only reached epidemic proportions in the more sparsely populated areas of Java such as the eastern outlying provinces, like Madiun and Kediri, of the central Javanese principalities and in the Priangan, where 20% of those affected by the 1780 epidemic are said to have died. Smallpox was known as *lara bocah*, or "children's disease", indicating an old-established disease, since such diseases predominantly affect young children. The vaccination program described by Cornets de Groot began in 1804; Carey says the numbers vaccinated were insignificant before the Java War but this does not seem to have been the case in Gresik.)

Mentality and morality

Cornets de Groot begins this section[82] with a paragraph characterising the people as peaceful but simple. A few, he says, show unexpected mental abilities, considering that they have to acquire everything through their own powers of observation, and virtually without education. The people of the coast have acquired more knowledge and are sometimes disobedient and disrespectful. Little knowledge is to be expected of the upper classes in general. The mass of the population know little of Islam, are brought up in

The Javanese Ancien Régime: Civilization and Society

superstition, and easily led into misdemeanours and immorality, without however being really bad. There is a great number of priests, and it is seldom that two of them teach the same thing. The people of the coast, through association with foreigners, have had their morals corrupted, while those of the interior maintain the old simplicity [this seems to be a faint echo of the frequent claims in Dutch reports that the Chinese tend to greatly deprave the Javanese from their former state of natural grace]. Not much can be said, in his opinion, for the marriage bond among the Javanese. Polygamy notwithstanding, there is much infidelity and they are ready to break even the loose tie that marriage is in this society for any reason, such as sickness. [This is a theme repeated over and over again by nineteenth century observers: for a compendium of judgements, see Boomgaard.[83] Though divorce was certainly particularly easy in Javanese society,[84] on the larger question of public morality it should be noted that most of these observers are contrasting Javanese *practice* with European *ideals*.] Cornets de Groot says that this is unfortunately rather encouraged than discouraged by the priests, out of lust for money.

The use of opium was not very great, despite the fact that Grissee was visited by many seafarers and had a population of fully 222,000 souls. Consumption rose from 4 chests [the standard measure for opium] in 1815 to 6.5 in 1820.

At another place,[85] Cornets de Groot has more to say about the Javanese character: a passion for gambling, polygamy and lovelessness are the worst faults, even among the chiefs. However they are good of nature, though they do little to carry out the rules of their religion, and are generally envious, and great lovers of show and amusement. They are of quiet nature, and one seldom encounters falsehood or treachery. However their revenge, especially in the interior parts, knows no limits. He goes on to say that the oft remarked-upon laziness and stupidity of the Javanese is due to his circumstances, and if given the opportunity, there is actually little they could not achieve in the way of skills.

Native ranks, titles, and offices

There had been an important change in nomenclature in this Residency around 1820. Prior to this, the system had been as follows:

The socialisation of the people: "becoming Javanese"

The original Arabic "priests" who ruled Gresik took the title Susuhunan in 1481, on Mt. Giri. This was changed to *Panembahan* in 1626 and then to *Pangeran* up till 1752, when the Sultan of Demak [this cannot be right, the Sultanate of Demak was much earlier] instituted a more regulated system and installed a *Bupati* with the title *Tumenggung*, later *Adipati*, but known to the natives as *Bupati*.

Titles of birth: these were *Raden, Mas,* and *Kyai*. The author says that when these titles do not go with an office they make little effect on the population and there are some places in the Residency where one finds no-one but *Radens*, all of the lowest class.

Titles of office: these were *Raden Adipati, Mas Pati, Kyai Pati* (note: these three are probably titles of the same person, and in the last two should be *Patih*, not *Pati*), *Raden Tuměnggung, Raden Patih jawi, Mantri ageng, Raden Patih lěbět, Raden Arya, Raden Ngabei, Raden Niyaka, Raden Rangga, Jaksa, Kaliwon ageng* or *Lurah kaliwon, Wadana, Kěnduruwan, Děmang* or *Mantri alit, Tali waro, Kajiněman, Kaliwon alit, Paněkar, Pětinggi, Běbau, Kabayan* – the last three constituting the village government.

The *Patih Jawi* was immediately subordinate to the *Bupati* and considered the second person in the Regency.

Mantri ageng was not a specific position: all officials beneath the *Patih Jawi*, down to the *Děmang* were called *Mantri Ageng*, and those below the *Děmang, Mantri Alit*. Only the *Mantri Ageng* could use the *songsong ageng* [great ceremonial sunshade].

The *Patih Lěbět* had authority over all matters within the *dalem*, but not outside it.

The *Raden Aria* was the adult brother of the Bupati and had the same sort of authority as the *Patih Jawi*, though he was subordinate to the latter.

The *Ngabei* was immediately subordinate to the *Patih Jawi*.

The *Niyaka* was a judge or member of the Bupati's council: without him no sentence could be passed.

The *Rangga* was the commander in time of war.

The *Jaksa* was the prosecutor of all misdeeds, pronounced sentence in civil matters, brought criminal matters to the notice of the Patih Jawi, received his orders for pursuing miscreants, and was thus subordinate to him.

The *Kaliwon* was the messenger of the *Bupati*, and was also charged with the provision of *kulis* and *baturs*. He looked after strangers, when the *Patih Jawi* had given authority for this. Cornets de Groot says that the word *Kaliwon* means "unifier". [The title

The Javanese Ancien Régime: Civilization and Society

Kaliwon of *Kliwon* is usually regarded as derived from *kalih ewon*, i.e. 2000, because it traditionally carried an endowment of 2000 *bau* for the official who held this appointment. This official later carried the title of *bupati anom* at the court of Surakarta.[86] "Kliwon" is also one of the days of the 5-day week and in the correspondence between these days and the four compass points and center which is part of the Javanese tradition, *kliwon* is aligned with the centre. This may be the origin of Cornets de Groot's translation of "unifier".]

The *Wĕdana* was charged with gathering the incomes of the *Bupati*, and so had a vast number of *desas* over which he had government, and from which he drew rice. He had particular responsibility for agriculture, seeing that things were planted at the proper times, that the dams and waterworks were in good order, and referring serious matters to the Patih Jawi (the author notes that the title *Wĕdana* means "face", like the Malay *muka*).

The *Kanḍuruwan* was the emissary of the Bupati, and was obliged to know the whole Regency.

Dĕmang was a title given to all very old *Mantri alit*; they were always in the neighbourhood of the *Bupati*, and gave advice on household matters or other small things.

The *Tali waro* received all complaints in matters concerning the *Jaksa*, and notified the latter of them.

The *Kajinĕman* was a police officer, under the command of the *Jaksa*, who helped in investigations and also acted as executioner. (the author says the word means "strong as six persons", which seems a fanciful etymology)

The *Kaliwon Alit* was the servant of the *Kaliwon Agĕng*.

The *Panĕkar* was the emissary of the *Wĕdana*.

Village government

The *Pĕtinggi* was the village head, the *Bĕbau* (in a few places called *Carik* or *Juru Tulis*) his scribe and stand-in where necessary and the *Kabayan* the one who carried out all orders and replaced the *Pĕtinggi* if the *Bĕbau* did not have the necessary talent. He could be recognised by the cane he carried. All owners of villages were called *Lurah*.[87]

Cornets de Groot claims that the *Kamituwas* were found in most villages in very substantial numbers. They had authority over ten inhabitants, whether these were farmers or had other professions. They regulated the division of the fields at the discretion of the

The socialisation of the people: "becoming Javanese"

Pĕtinggi and all things carried out by the people were entrusted to them; they watched over, in a word, their interests and had a say in the settlement of disputes. They also collected the land rent and were answerable for this to the *Pĕtinggi*. The word *Kamituwa* was said to mean, "the oldest of ten persons, over whom he has authority". In some villages they had the title of *Kĕpala*, and in this case there was only one of them who, when the *Pĕtinggi* was absent, took upon himself the immediate government. When there were a number of *Kamituwas* and no *Bĕbau* or *Kabayan* in the village, then the oldest *Kamituwa* took on the village government.

The inhabitants called *Kraman* were generally the oldest inhabitants, and had therefore acquired the right to land. The *Orang Kraman* were divided into three classes. The *Kraman Tuwa* had, by way of privilege, the largest and now mostly the best lands, and were also somewhat exempt from the general work duties and had a lighter load. Then followed the *Kraman Tĕngah*, who, however, were not found in all villages, and the *Kraman Nom*, the least wealthy and youngest farmers. [The use of the term *kraman* to signify nuclear villagers is very old, going back at least to the thirteenth century, when it was used in the old form of *karaman*, referring to the *rama desa*, or village fathers.[88] Interestingly enough, in modern Javanese the word has acquired another meaning, that of a rebel.]

The *Orang Angguran* are those who have no *sawah* or *tĕgal* fields as their share, and spend their days in idleness (the meaning of *angguran*) or very light work.

The *Pĕrjaka* are the unmarried who are under the separate authority of a head named *Lurah Kanoman*.

All public works like repairing bridges, roads, etc., were mostly carried out by the farmers and very seldom by the *Orang angguran*, who also contributed very seldom to public feasts or meals given to the priests, and seem to be a sort of lower class, most of whom were in service with or dependent on the *Orang Kraman*.

[Note the very elaborate hierarchy of ranks, a feature not just of élite but also of Javanese village life, and the distinction between core landholders and those seen as transitory and dependent, which, though the terminology differs, occurs in so many regions.[89]]

The Javanese Ancien Régime: Civilization and Society

The burdens of the common man

Cornets de Groot says that here too there have been important changes recently.

Under the rule of the rulers and Bupatis, the obligations of the *orang kraman* were as follows: working in the Bupati's house, in the stable, kitchen, etc., carrying pikes, serving in the house, playing the gamelan, cleaning the house, building and maintaining houses for the *Bupati* and other native heads and their children, laying out gardens, and building roads, dams, rivers and bridges. Those who had no rice-fields, such as artisans, traders, or those who had no fixed income, or paid no tax, were only called to work on special occasions, but paid by way of compensation a very considerable house tax, from 5 to 8 guilders, as well as a yearly tax of *f*.2.15, called *petik grabak [petek* and *grabag*: see Chapter 4 Part 3 on these taxes] and, under the name of *wang pelawang*, 7.5 *stuivers*, as well as six skeins of yarn, and 6 *kati* of coconut rope, which was levied on all households without exception. Every farmer was obliged for every *jung* of *sawah* land that had proved succesful to give the Bupati 7.5 *pikul* of rice, 75 bundles of padi and 5 bundles of padi under the name *jujon* (for the Bupati's horses [see also Chapter 4, Part 3, on Pekalongan]); and further one out of every ten calves that he got from his animals yearly, under the name *welasan*.

For festivals, marriages, circumcisions etc. held by the Bupati the common man was obliged to make a present, consisting usually of rice, buffalo, cows, capons, eggs, money, fish, or coconuts. For the Bupati's written permission for a marriage, it was necessary to pay f.2 in copper money, plus two strong threads, 10 *kati* of rice, two hens and four coconuts, and also a *slawat* payment to the chief priests of f.1 to f.7.5. The farmer was also obliged to give 30 out of 300 bundles of padi to the clergy, which was very strictly maintained [see above].

The Bupatis were obliged to go to Semarang annually for the hire of their salt [pans?]. They took a retinue of more than 400 men, without counting the serving people, pike-bearers, soldiers, musicians, and lesser servants, the Mantri Ageng and his family, making a dozen people, plus his retinue of 12 to 20 people; then the Mantri Alit, Demang, Kajineman, about 20 in number, each accompanied by 4 to 6 people, altogether about 700 men. There were also about 150 horses and 25–30 litters. All this was extorted from the common man, proportionate to the number of members of

The socialisation of the people: "becoming Javanese"

the household. The hirers of fish ponds did not have to provide men, but paid journey money, 2–5 Spanish dollars per head, according to the size of their ponds. The Bupatis also took one large or two small *pancalangs*, to carry the rice and gamelans. The sailors were men of the Regency who were experienced seamen, and were paid nothing. If there were 40 sailors in the Regency 20 had to man the ships and the other 20 pay from 3 to 5 Spanish dollars for the journey. The Mantri Ageng and Mantri Alit all took their retinues from their districts, and of 15 men, 10 would be taken along and the other 5 paid 4–6 Spanish dollars each. Cornets de Groot gives a list of the presents the Bupatis took to the Dutch administrative centre of Semarang (mainly fans and textiles), with a total value 1237.20 Spanish dollars: the great expense of present-giving has already been noted in Chapter Two and occurs again in the regional reports used in Chapter Five.

The burdens on the common man at the time of writing were: the land rent on lands with or without buildings, coffee gardens, *sirih* gardens, fish ponds and *nipah* woods, and the levies on the markets, goods, fish catch, passages and ferries; also the construction and upkeep of bridges, roads and rivers [sic], waterworks, dams and sheds. They must also maintain the clergy, but these days the common man was only subject to the *pitrah badan*, the *jakat padi*, the *slawat sunat*, and the *slawat orang mati*: all the rest was at the pleasure of the giver, and most Javanese have withdrawn the other contributions [in other words, colonial rule removed the secular arm of power enforcing religious obligations, as was the case with the British in Burma, when disorder in the Buddhist *sangha* resulted from the abrogation of the sovereign's power to punish offenders].

The government's share in the *sawah* harvest was half for the first grade [of land], 2/5 for the second, 1/3 for the third. For the *tĕgal* it was 2/5th for the first grade, 1/3 for the second, and 1/4 for the third. This was from the net income, after a fifth of the harvest had been distributed to all those who helped gather it. The Government's share of *sirih* and *nipah* gardens was also up to half. The monetary worth was fixed by the average market price in the district.

Education

There was no teaching of the Javanese language in the Residency, though there were people who could do it. The Arabic language was taught to young people from the age of two years. [This situation, where education involved teaching Arabic but not the vernacular, also obtained in the Malay world at this time.[90]] Only about one Javanese in a hundred could read and write. The sons of Bupatis and other respectable Javanese could all read and write, being taught by the Mantri Ageng, and many of them can even write good Malay in Dutch characters.

THE OVERALL PICTURE

A number of salient and striking features emerge from Cornets de Groot's picture of Gresik. We have here a society in which the socialisation of its members through a series of well-defined *rites de passage* conforms very closely to what we know, from Winter's account, of central Javanese society at the same period, and also with what we know of twentieth century Java (with a couple of obvious differences, such as the discontinuation of tooth filing). A well-defined pattern emerges, which is the same even in Gresik, in the heartland of Javanese Islam, an area which one could also describe as "*santri*" and orthoprax.[91] And in this pattern of *rites de passage*, the place of Islam is also the same over space and time, that is, it is limited to a significantly circumscribed place, principally in the rituals for circumcision and death: the first can only be an Islamic ritual, the second is an area of ritual pollution for the Javanese and one which they have apparently been happy to relinquish to Islam, unlike the marriage ceremony, which is in a way the central ritual of Javanese society and remains unmistakeably *Javanese*. So it seems that the nature of the accommodation which this self-conscious society had seemingly decided to make with Islam had already been rather firmly established, so that places like Gresik were both "very Islamic" and "very Javanese" in that members of society were socialised through the same core Javanese rituals as were Javanese in less Islamic areas, while at the same time at least some people observed Islam with a punctilious and well-informed regard for prescriptions going well beyond the five pillars and the common observances.

We also see a society with an inescapable preoccupation with hierarchy and status, which is exactly and carefully defined and publicly marked at both the élite and the village level – again, a preoccupation not limited to this area, as nearly every chapter in this book attests. Finally, we see a society with a remarkably well

The socialisation of the people: "becoming Javanese"

developed culture, both a high culture and a popular one, again with very strong continuities over space and time, including both the central Javanese courts of the time and also classical Java (witness, for instance, the continuing appreciation of literature and songs in *kawi*). The Hindu-Javanese legacy is of course also strikingly evident in the pantheon of deities and in the mythology. Beyond that again, the oldest founding myth of Java, that of Watu Gunung, is also present in a highly elaborated form, as are the theatrical presentations of Java's most "darling hero", Panji.

This must change our picture both of the *pasisir* and of Java as a whole. The *pasisir* is usually regarded as definitely provincial, not participating in the rich culture of central Java and, on the other hand, more influenced by Arabs and Chinese. These influences (in the case of Gresik overwhelmingly the former, though in places like Cirebon very much of the latter) are present, but they are by no means dominant. Perhaps much of this richness was lost from the regions in the later impoverishment of Java and could only be preserved in attenuated form at the courts?

As for our picture of Java as a whole, it is I think time to recognize that Javanese society and civilization is far more elegantly integrated and all-of-a-piece, older, more elaborated and substantial, more proselytizing, more urbanized, and above all more consistent over geographical space and over huge reaches of time than anyone has so far been willing to admit. Western scholars have generally not found it worthwhile to take these social structures and this civilization seriously, and it is usually treated as one example of a reductionist picture of "Southeast Asian" society, religion, and culture or on the other hand as a society and civilization that owes its high culture to Indian influence and at the popular level is characterised by a motley collection of highly localised folk beliefs.[92] It seems to me that the fundamentals, the very enduring fundamentals, of both the great and little tradition are firmly, systematically, and consistently Javanese. If it now appears a disparate collection of bits and pieces, this is due to, firstly, our immense ignorance: we simply have not read enough to pick up on enough pieces of the jigsaw, and have not thought enough about how they fit together; and secondly, the disintegrative pressures of historical developments since the seventeenth century – devastating and continuing warfare, social dislocation, and increasing impoverishment. Taking this position is not a denial of regional variation or of change over time under the pressure of many and varied contingencies – this will be elaborated in the following chapters – it is an affirmation that we can no more ignore the enormously enduring social and cultural structures and preferences of Java than we could for, let us say, China or Japan.

JAVANESE AND NON-JAVANESE: THE MINORITIES

The tolerance of the Javanese has often been commented upon, a tolerance related to a syncretic and relativistic outlook, and with reason.[93] Yet it has as often been assumed, wrongly, that this is an open-ended, free-floating, amorphous syncretism. In fact the Javanese synthesis has been a firmly defined one, and clear priorities have led to a selective and exclusive attitude to external elements, absorbing some and rejecting others. That not *any* synthesis of indigenous, Indianised and Islamic components entitles one to be regarded as "Javanese" is very clearly demonstrated by attitudes to culturally-defined, non-Javanese minorities. Some of these – notably the Kalang, Pinggir, and Gajah Mati – have lived among the Javanese for many centuries without losing their separate identity, despite their small numbers and what seem to an outsider relatively minor differences from the majority population.

S. Soehari's article on the Pinggir reveals how this separation operated from the Javanese side.[94] Accounts of the origin of the Pinggir say they were brought from Balambangan after Sultan Agung's conquest in the early seventeenth century. From these captives he created the corps called the Prajurit Balambangan (later split into two, the Suratětana and the Jayatětana), who were also used as guinea-pigs (*coban*) for new weapons (if the man died, the weapon was fit for use in battle). The women were used as wet-nurses for royal children, being famous for their bluish milk, described as "*satěngah wulung*" (semi-indigo); but also performed some polluting tasks euphemistically called *jamban* or bathroom services. When they married they used a *wali hakim* (assigned to them by the Naib when they identified themselves as Pinggir), as opposed to one of the woman's male relatives acting as *wali*, and the number of *talaks* was reduced from three to two. These particular provisions seem to be those that Islam makes for slaves. In an edict (*Angger Agěng*) issued by the Patih of Surakarta on Sunday 3 Besar Wawu 1747 i.e. 4 October 1818 it is further laid down that when there is a difference between man and wife, among the Kalangs the man shall be given preference, but among the

The socialisation of the people: "becoming Javanese"

Pinggir or Gajah Mati the woman shall be given preference. The Kalangs were treated as a both culturally and occupationally distinct group, sharing certain religious observances with the Tenggerese and also engaging in occupations apparently disfavoured by the Javanese majority.[95]

Java's most heavily studied minority, one that has lived in isolation from the Javanese majority and that has exercised an obvious fascination both for Westerners and for the Javanese, is the Tenggerese of the Pasuruhan/Lumajang/Probolinggo region. The most recent study of the Tenggerese describes them as "Hindu Javanese"[96] yet Commandant Adriaan van Rijck, who was Commandant at Pasuruhan from 1768 to 1790 and played an important role in developing the cultivation of the European vegetables for which the area became known, describes them as Mohammedans[97] who were very negligent about circumcision, marriage and burial rules. In other words, he placed them rather low on the scale of Muslim orthopraxy, but did not see an absolute cultural divide between them and the Javanese majority. It is quite clear that there were indeed Islamic elements in their culture in the nineteenth century at least and many of their other usages, beliefs, and legends they share with the Javanese.[98] These include the religious significance of the garment called Antakusuma, worn by Javanese kings and originally the robe of the *widadari* Nawang Wulan who brought eternal rice; a calendar which uses the *wuku* system, the divisions of the day and the *naptu* system as described by Cornets de Groot, with minor variations[99] and a version of the Aji Saka legend which incorporates some recognition of Islam as of equal validity with Javanese culture.[100] Javanese accounts, however, describe the Tenggerese as belonging to 6 sects which are clearly differentiated from Javanese religion. The Javanese, like Western observers, were also very struck by the use of dolls (*petro*) which are burnt in the Tenggerese death ritual, a custom shared with the *Kalang ngobong* ("burning Kalang") who are considered most fully Kalang.

The Kalangs have had a definite connotation of an outcast group[101] and have specialised in occupations – wood-cutting, carrying, copper-working, the making of rattan brooms, and leatherworking in particular – which were evidently looked down upon by real Javanese. Up until 1762, when they were placed under the jurisdiction of the Regent in whose Regency they lived, they had always had their own heads.[102] They appear at one time to have lived something of a wandering life. The Kalang are also known for legends of origin which attribute their genesis to the union of a princess and a dog that picked up her weaving shuttle, or to a pig.[103] Some writers have seen many non-Javanese elements in the Kalang, while others have said they have no racial characteristics that distinguish them from the Javanese majority but are simply a group of social outcasts. It is possible that Kalang is a contraction of the Javanese word *kĕpalang*, "excluded, shut out". In relatively modern times they have been described as *tiang Hindu mambĕt*, "stinking Hindus" but it is obvious that their pariah status does not derive from their non-adherence to Islam but goes back to a much earlier period.

In short, the Javanese have clearly excluded certain minorities, none more notably than the Kalang, but also groups used at the court for special service, on cultural and occupational grounds over a long period: which is not to say that some of the minorities, particularly perhaps the Tenggerese, have not chosen to distinguish themselves from a Javanese Other.

* * *

In the richness, variety, and nature of its cultural forms, as well as in the pervading emphasis on rank, status, and military prowess as demonstrated in the *fêtes galants* of the tourney, "provincial" Gresik bears a surprising remembrance to the central Javanese courts. Thus we see in Java the contradiction in our terms of a civilisation without cities of the size and dominance found in Europe. Javanese society was not, in comparative terms, characterised by a tendency to centralisation in one or two dominant cities, but replicative, given to the hiving-off of villages by what Christie has called fission and the provincial replication of kratons. As Christie has pointed out of much earlier Javanese states, "There is a tendency in academic literature for rural communities to be equated with isolation, ignorance, and poverty, and for economic systems not served by an orderly placement of greater and lesser urban centers to be equated with inefficiency and inelasticity. Neither of these truisms seems to be supported by the early Javanese data. States of early Java were demographically dispersed, but by no means inefficient in their handling of flows of goods and information."[104] Despite the lack of large urban nodes of the scale that we in the West equate with progress, this tightly-knit and remarkably all-of-a-

The socialisation of the people: "becoming Javanese"

piece (by pre-industrial standards) social web was somehow integrated and "civilized", even in the provinces. There is a great consistency in the Javanese socio-cultural formation over both space and time, a Javanese commonality between capital and province, aristocrat and villager.

* * *

Reflecting on this in its way exceptionally comprehensive ethnography, one can readily emphasize with the sense of entry to a rich new world that comes through in some Orientalist writing of this period: as an example, who more appropriate than "Oriental" Jones, founder of the British Royal Asiatic Society and initiator of much of subsequent British scholarship on this new world? Jones wrote of an Asia that was fertile in human genius and the nurse of sciences and delightful arts.[105] Who could deny that Javanese society as depicted here was not only enormously inventive and replete with "delightful arts" but in itself a highly evolved and refined work of art? or that it provided a rich and stimulating environment for the aesthetic and intellectual faculties, and gave Javanese a sense of belonging and shared values? It would also be unfair to suggest that it did these things better than many of the social environments in which we now live by the maintenance of "tradition", and to set up a contrast with the Europe of that time. It is true that we see in the society described here many "traditional" elements, but it should be remembered that these were *also* strongly present in Europe, even post-revolutionary Europe, as for example the structuring of human time and life according to a calendar based on a religious myth, or the pervasiveness of social hierarchy. And to present "tradition" in Java as essentially unchanging, only increasingly elaborated, is also manifestly unfair. This is nowhere clearer than in the accomodation of Islam, a recent arrival relative to the antiquity of a distinctively Javanese pattern of religious and social life, within the pattern, both at court and in the provinces. Where there *does* seem to be a tenable contrast with Europe relates to the unique European investment in education, particularly in scientific and empirical education, going back at least to Galileo's time. In the field of practical technology, Java had remained essentially dependent on the superb agricultural apparatus and the metalworking and other practical skills developed millenia before. Of theoretical science there was no sign. However, there seems to have been a shy emergence of empirical perspectives on the world from within the Javanese intelligentsia, and some of the works in which this can be seen will be discussed in Chapter Six. Before that, it is necessary to fill out this survey of Javanese society by reviewing the ways in which Java's progressive incorporation into the world system, via the agency of the VOC and its successor government, had impacted and continued to impact upon society generally, and on a number of different regional societies and economies more specifically. This is the subject of the next two chapters.

NOTES

1 This is a manuscript by by A.D.Cornets de Groot which is now held in the collection of the Koninklijk Insitituut voor Taal- Land- en Volkenkunde, Leiden, H. no.379. It is also published (somewhat abbreviated) under the title "Bijdrage tot de kennis van de zeden en gewoonten der Javanen" in TNI 1852, Part II, pp. 257–80, 346–67, 493–418, and 423–432 (the last pages being notes by Rouffaer); and TNI 1853 Part I, pp. 81–103, which is a separate text, a report written in response to a government questionnaire sent to the Resident. In the published version the author is referred to as Resident of Gresik at the time of writing, but in fact he did not become Resident until 1825: in the period 1817–1825 the Resident was Wijnand de Groot: see J. Hageman Jcz., "Namen de gewestelijke Europesche Gezaghebbers, enz., op Java en Madura", TBG XIII (1864) pp. 227–265 (p. 251).
2 See "Aanteekeningen", TNI 1852/II, p. 423.
3 See C.F. Winter Sr., "Javaansche Overleveringen", *BKI* LV (1903), pp. 403–441
4 On the Bupati of Gresik, see R.A.A. Kromodjojo Adinegoro, "Begraafplaatsen der Oude Bupatien van Grisee voor, tijdens en na Compagnies Tijd", *Djawa* 5, 1925, pp. 253–7. In 1803 they apparently had a battalion of native soldiers under their command (p. 255).
5 See further Koentjaraningrat, *Javanese Culture*, Institute of Southeast Asian Studies, Singapore, O.U.P. 1989, p. 355.
6 H.W. Ponder, *Javanese Panorama: A further account of the world's richest island with some intimate pictures of life among the people of its lesser known regions*, London n.d. [written at beginning of Second World War?] p. 54 says that the birth ceremonies are firstly, the *sĕpasaran* ["one 5-day week"}, kept up for six days after the birth, and the *selapanan*, thirty -five days after the birth. According to Koentjaraningrat, *Javanese Culture*, p. 357, the first has now been combined with a Muslim ceremony on the seventh day after the birth. Both Koentjaraningrat and Ponder state that the next ceremony is on the 35th, not the 40th, day after birth, a significant occasion in that it is the child's *wĕton*, the birth-day consisting of the combination of the day of the 5-day week and day of the 7-day week on which the child was born, which is very important

The socialisation of the people: "becoming Javanese"

for predicting his or her character and fate. See also Ch.2 p. 57 above on the celebration of this birthday in later life.

7 In Indonesia and Malaysia a milder form of circumcision for Muslim wonen is practised, involving making an incision in the clitoral hood.
8 Marriage ages seem to have been the same in other regions of Java: see Peter Carey, "Waiting for the Just King: the Agrarian World of South-Central Java from Giyanti (1755) to the Java War (1825–30)", *Modern Asian Studies* 20/1 (1986) p. 102, who says men were married at around 16 years and women at 13–14
9 The Javanese distinguish between the *wali* (legal guardians) by blood relationship (*wali nasab* or *wali bapa*) and the *wali hakim* for those who have no blood relation available: see further C. Snouck Hurgronje, trans. A.W.S. O'Sullivan, *The Acehnese*, vol. I, E.J. Brill, Leyden, 1906, p. 330ff.
10 Ponder, *Javanese Panorama*, p. 43.
11 Ponder p. 42 f.
12 Helen Creese, unpublished manuscript.
13 Koentjaraningrat p. 130. This may also be reflected in the "moon necklace" which is part of the wedding attire of brides and grooms: see *Sieraden en lichaamsversiering uit Indonesia*, Volkenkundig Museum Nusantara, Delft 1984, pp. 58–9 and 106.
14 Ponder, *Panorama*, p. 50.
15 In Java, the male and female principles which combine in reproduction are conceptualised as red and white.
16 I have been unable to identify this as either a Javanese or a Latin plant-name.
17 Inggris, "Het roewatanfeest in de desa Karangdjati in Bagelen", *Djawa* 3, 1923, pp. 45–50.
18 Koentjaraningrat, *Javanese Culture* p. 377 expands this list to 14 categories.
19 Koentjaraningrat, *Javanese Culture* p. 378 says it is a day-time ceremony unlike other wayang.
20 A *běruk* is a unit of measurement of about two-thirds to three-quarters of a coconut shell.
21 J.W. van Dapperen, "Het Tegalsche Ruwat (Het Verlossen, bezweren van kwade invloeden)", *Djawa* 3, 1923, pp. 223–30.
22 Koentjaraningrat *Javanese Culture* pp. 377–8.
23 Robert R. Jay, *Javanese Villagers: Social Relations in Rural Modjokuto*, MIT Press 1969, p. 214.
24 Jay p. 43.
25 Ponder, *Panorama*, p, 125.
26 Jay, *Javanese Villagers*, p. 43.
27 Helen Jessup, *Court Arts of Indonesia*, p. 59
28 This word is not listed in standard dictionaries; it may be a regional usage.
29 P.A. Koesoemo Joedo, "Het Javaansche Voorerf", *Djawa* 4, 1924.
30 "Het bouwen van Javaansche huizen", *Djawa* 4, 1924, pp. 105–117.
31 A *gantang* is a measure of rice that varies from region to region, being about 10 kaṭi in central Java and 5 kaṭi in east Java: a standard kaṭi is about 0.62 kilograms.

The Javanese Ancien Régime: Civilization and Society

32 Achmad Yusuf, "Pasren dalam rumah adat Jawa", Jakarta Museum 1982.
33 Two different pairs of aristocratic *loro blonyo* can be seen in Jessup, *Court Arts*, p. 29 and p. 58.
34 T.E. Behrend, "Kraton, Taman, Mesjid: A Brief Survey and Bibliographic Review of Islamic Antiquities in Java", *Indonesia Circle* 35, November 1984, pp. 29–55 (see p. 34 on the Prabasuyasa).
35 Y.B. Mangunwijaya, trans. Thomas M. Hunter, *The Weaverbirds*, Lontar, Jakarta 1991.
36 p. 350.
37 See S. Tirtakusuma, "Tumplek Punjen", *Djawa* 2 89f.
38 The word *naas* is derived from Arabic *naûs*, inauspicious, unlucky, of things and stars, but I am not sure that the particular set of unlucky days named here is Islamic.
39 See J. E. Jasper, "Tengger en de Tenggereezen", *Djawa* 7 (1927) p. 31 ff. Among a very large number of gods Jasper lists gods associated with particular places, and mostly bearing the title Sunan; a group of water gods associated with springs and waterfalls; and a group of guardian gods who watch over the earth and the sky, the body, qualities, and particular occasions. These divinities bear the title Among, which means to watch over: thus marriages are watched over by Kaki and Nini Among Panggih, while Kaki and Nini Among Tuwuh, watch over growing things. There are also Kaki and Nini Among Suka (for pleasure), Kaki and Nini Among Raga (who watch over the body: this name also occurs as that of the central figure of the Centini), Kaki and Nini Among Sugih (for wealth) and Kaki and Nini Among Teguh (for steadfastness) and Kaki and Nini Among Tětěp (for constancy).
40 *Plangi* are rainbow resist-dye textiles in which small areas are bound off by cord or palm strip that reserves them from the dye. Patterns are generally built up from small circular forms.
41 Raffles, *History of Java*, vol. I p. 478f.
42 See Jessup, *Court Arts*, p. 124 on the remarkable survival of the indigenous architectural format in the courts despite sixteen hundred years of Buddhist, Hindu, Islamic, Chinese and European cultural influence.
43 On the survival of equestrian pride in Java into the mid-twentieth century, see Ponder p. 62, describing a gathering of village headmen at the Wedana's house: "Usually they ride up on ponies, which are noticeably well fed and groomed. The well-to-do Javanese countryman is a keen horseman and takes great pride in his mount, especially if it be a kore, a pony trained to a smart "amble" pace. These are rare, and command very high prices. A prettier sight in its way than these native councillors cantering or "ambling" down the village street under the great overarching trees, with the dappled sunshine striking now and then on a pony's glossy flank or on the polished hilt of a kris, it would be hard to find."
44 P.J. Veth, *Java*, vol. p. 454–8 and p. 55.
45 *Javanese Panorama* p. 27 ff. Ponder also notes that at an old-fashioned wayang, the dalang and men sit on one side, the women on the other, seeing only the shadows.

The socialisation of the people: "becoming Javanese"

46 In the Principalities and other parts of Java it seems to have been the custom for the *ronggeng* dancers, also called *taledek*, to live in a separate kampung under their own head, called *lurah taledek*: see Th. Pigeaud, *Javaanse volksvertoningen: bijdrage tot de beschrijving van land en volk*, Batavia, Volkslectuur, 1938, #37, and Peter Boomgaard, *Children of the Colonial State: Population Growth and Economic Development in Java 1795–1880*, Amsterdam, Free University Press, 1989, p. 162

47 *Ludruk* is a particular specialty of the north coast: see Pigeaud, *Javaanse Volksvertoningen*, p. 322 #318. In Surabaya it has evolved into a sort of popular theatre in the form of melodrama with social commentary, in which however the elements of travesty and clowning are still present: see James L. Peacock, *Rites of Modernization: Symbolic and Social Aspects of Indonesian Proletarian Drama*, University of Chicago Press 1968.

48 In fact *laras* is not a particular composition, but means "tuning" generally, and "gĕnḍing" is the generic term for "a gamelan composition".

49 The full gamelan is sometimes called *gamelan bonangan* to distinguish it from the *gamĕlan klĕnenga*n, a small ensemble without *bonangs*. I think the *gamĕlan bonang rentong* may be the gamelan mentioned by Jaap Kunst (*Music in Java: Its History, Its Theory, and Its Technique*, The Hague, Nijhoff, Third Edition, 1973, vol. I p. 155) as specifically designed for use in processions, with the *bonang rancakan* carried on a pole between two men.

50 Thomas Stamford Raffles, *History of Java*, Vol. 1, London, Black, Parbury and Allen 1817, pp. 530–1.

51 J.E. Jasper, "Tengger en Tenggerezen" Hoofdstuk III, *Djawa* 7 (1927), pp. 229–30.

52 In court and village, Anggara-Kasih is the most sacred day of the thirty-five day Javanese month, being dedicated to the goddess of greatest power (the rice goddess, and in later times, Nyai Loro Kidul, the sea goddess).

53 In the almanac, the summaries are expressed in a so-called *candra*, three to four words of an allusive and metaphorical character, e.g. the *candra* for those born in the *wuku* Wukir is "a beautiful mountain seen from a distance", meaning someone who seems refined and looks pleasing from a distance, but when approached is dangerous because he has a difficult nature.

54 A large metal pot for cooking rice.

55 *Bala* in Javanese means not only troops but also, presumably by extension and in view of the military character of the Javanese court, subjects, more particularly those in the direct service of the ruler. So there is an inherent logic in the proposition that a child born in the *wuku* Bala is the favourite of princes.

56 M.C. Ricklefs, *Modern Javanese Historical Tradition: A Study of an Original Kartasura Chronicle and Related Materials*, SOAS, London 1978, p. 226

57 Rouffaer claims the *wuku* week formerly had 10 days

58 There is another system, the *mangsa wuku*, which gives six sets of thirty-five days beginning on the same days of the five-and seven-day weeks (Sunday-Paing) within the 210 day cycle: see Ricklefs p. 226.

The Javanese Ancien Régime: Civilization and Society

59 Eviatar Zerubavel, *The Seven Day Circle: The History and Meaning of the Week*, University of Chicago Press 1989 (original edition, The Free Press 1985), pp. 55–9.
60 Zerubavel p. 55.
61 Zerubavel pp. 58–9.
62 Raffles, *History of Java* vol. 1 p. 476 has a list of the *wuku* and their presiding deities, differing somewhat from the Cornets de Groot and almanac versions. In the last there are even some Islamic elements.
63 E.W. Maurenbrecher, "Sintren en Lais in Cheribon", *Djawa* 20 (1940) pp. 119–121. *Sintren* is apparently still performed in the village of Pananjung in the Pangandaran area of west Java.
64 See below p. 350.
65 Instruments used to accompany the song are 2 *buyungs* (earthen waterpots), 1 bamboo gong and 2 *bumbungs* (bamboo cookers). The *buyungs* are played on the opening with *ilirs* (bamboo fans) as *kĕndangs*. The *gong* and *bumbungs* are struck with sticks and the last is also beaten on the ground with both hands.
66 Snouck Hurgronje, *The Acehnese*, vol. I p. 242.
67 The word used is Dutch *geestelijkheid*.
68 See Thomas Patrick Hughes, *A Dictionary of Islam, being a Cyclopaedia of the Doctrines, Rites, Ceremonies and Customs, together with the Technical and Theological Terms of the Muhammadan Religion*, London, W.H. Allen n.d. (originally written c.1886), p. 699f.
69 This refers to the custom of ceremonially cutting some hairs to about a thumb's-length on the forehead of young women on the occasion of their marriage or alternatively of their circumcision. The hair is taken from the place where as young children they had a *kuncung*, that is, the forelock of hair grown long while the rest of the hair is cut extremely short. In twentieth-century Java, the *kuncung* seems to have been worn by male children only (personal communication, Dr. Supomo Suryohudoyo).
70 This cannot be right, since Muslims do not recognize the divinity of Jesus (Isa). Perhaps Isrā', the ascension of Muhammad, is meant.
71 The caliph Umar is said to have scourged a son to death for drunkenness and immorality.
72 This caliph was murdered on 18 Dhu'l-Hijjah, A.H. 35.
73 Ali was murdered by the Kharijite ibn Muttam (see Philip K.Hitti, *History of the Arabs from the Earliest Times to the Present*, London, Macmillan, 7th edition, 1961 p. 182) but in Ramadan A.H. 41 (A.D. 661). I do not know a source that states this man was his groom.
74 Hasan died c. 669, probably poisoned by a jealous ex-wife in league with one of his enemies: see Hitti p. 190.
75 Jenal Abidin (Zayn al-'Abidīn) is another name for 'Alī, who survived the battle of Karbalā' and became the fourth Shi'ite Imam.
76 The fast month is the month in which the Koran was taken from the divine throne to the heaven of this world. The last odd-numbered dates of the month are possibilities for the celebration of this event, the Night of Destiny (*laylatu'l-qadr*) but it has nothing to do with the Prophet Adam (personal communication, A.H. Johns).

The socialisation of the people: "becoming Javanese"

77 Moses was sent by God to the Green Prophet, Nabi Kidir, to find out his error and the event is described in Koran *surah* 18: 60–82.(personal communication, A.H. Johns)
78 I owe this insight to A.H. Johns (personal communication).
79 Information on population and the following sections is taken from a separate report entitled *Staat der bevolking* written in 1823, see note on first page, TNI 1853.
80 In an account of the Jakatra and Priangan lands ("Beschriyving van het Koningryk Jaccatra", VBG 1 pp. 19–41) the most prevalent illnesses are said to be dysentery (*afgang*), which is usually fatal, and skin diseases. In 1750 a plague called *bobik* carried away many people.
81 Carey, "Just King", pp. 106–7.
82 See TNI 15/2 (1853) p. 81.
83 Boomgaard, *Children*, Ch.8.
84 Carey, "Waiting for the Just King", p. 102 quotes a source from the second decade of the nineteenth century reporting cases of Javanese who had married as many as ten or twelve times.
85 See TNI 15/2 (1853) p. 103.
86 R. Soemantri Hardjodibroto, "De wijzingen der gebruiken en gewoonten aan het Solosche hof", *Djawa* 11, 1931, pp. 159–170.
87 This is followed by an account of the ranks and titles currently [i.e. in 1823] in use, which I have omitted. Under the revised system, there seem to be more officials (some for new functions e.g. the *tukang cacar*, or vaccinator, who were mostly "priests") and quite a number of officials were no longer reimbursed with a piece of land, *palungguh*.
88 See Th. G. The. Pigeaud, *Java in the Fourteenth Century*, vol. IV, p. 301.
89 *Bumi* and *numpang* in Priangan, *sikĕp* and *batur* or *kuli* in central Java, etc.
90 See Abdullah bin Abdul Kadir, trans. A.H. Hill, *The Hikayat Abdullah*, Oxford U.P., Kuala Lumpur and Singapore etc. 1970, p. 42.
91 See, for example, the strict and detailed observation of the Muslim fasts and the different types of *zakat*, p. 165 above.
92 It hardly seems worthwhile to include Brandes' weak and bloodless characterization in his famous "10 points", which have nothing to say of the enormously elaborated social and cultural forms we find throughout Java's history.
93 The best-known treatment is Benedict R.O'G. Anderson, *Mythology and the Tolerance of the Javanese*, Cornell Modern Indonesia Project Monograph Series 1965.
94 "Pinggir", *Djawa*. 9 Parts 4–5, 1929, pp. 160–8
95 On the Kalang, see Friedrich Seltmann, *Die Kalang: Ein Volksgruppe auf Java und ihre Stamm-Mythe: Ein Beitrag zur Kulturgeschichte Javas*, Stuttgart, Franz Steiner, 1987; and Guillot,
96 Robert W. Hefner, *Hindu Javanese: Tengger Tradition and Islam*, Princeton U.P. 1985.
97 Published in VBG VII, 1814
98 See J.E. Jasper, "Tengger en de Tenggereezen", *Djawa* 6 (1926) pp. 185–92 and 7 (1927) pp. 23–37, 217–237 and 291–304.
99 According to Jasper, they use an older division of the day and night into

5 periods, whereas the Muslim Javanese divide it into six periods: See Jasper, *Djawa* VII pp. 229-30.
100 Hefner, *Hindu Javanese*, Ch.6. The legend as reported by Jasper (*Djawa* 7 p. 291f), however, could be interpreted as an explanation of the Tenggerese choice *not* to embrace Islam.
101 See T. Altona, "Over den Oorsprong der Kalangs" TBG LXII (1923) pp. 515-547, comparing them with the Hindu outcast group, the *caṇḍāla*.
102 Ir. W. Zwart, "De Kalangs als houtkappers in dienst der Compagnie" TBG LXXIX (1939) pp. 252-261 (p. 260).
103 See Altona, "Oorsprong" and E. Ketjen, "Bijdrage tot de geschiedenis der Kalangs op Java", TBG XXVIII (1883) pp. 185-200.
104 Jan Wisseman Christie, "States Without Cities: Demographic Trends in Early Java", *Indonesia* 52 (Oct. 1991) p. 36.
105 See Garland Cannon, *The Life and Mind of Oriental Jones: Sir William Jones, the Father of Modern Linguistics*, Cambridge U.P. 1990, p. 199.

Cornets de Groot's sketches from a wedding procession of the Bupati class

The sketches do not fully convey the sheer size of this wedding procession, since Cornets de Groot has generally sketched only one pair belonging to a particular category (human, equine, vehicular, weaponry, etc) to represent a more numerous group. Thus in the first illustration the top two human figures represent a group of 12, and the pikes drawn behind the lower figures represent a group of 100. The two pairs of *gunungan* at the top of sketch 5 also represent a group of 24.

Some of the main features are:

– the number of different types of gamelan and other musical ensembles, i.e. a "Bali-style" gamelan in sketch 3, the archaic and sacral *gamelan koḍok ngorek* in sketch 5, a *gamelan salendro* in sketch 6, a *gamelan Mataram* and a *gamelan Surabayan* in sketch 8, and a smaller ensemble, the so-called trumpet gamelan, in the first sketch.

– the number of figures representing the creatures of the jungle and untamed nature, e.g. the four children dressed as monkeys (by the application of cotton fluff) and the larger monkey figures below them in sketch 2 and also in sketch 3. This category also includes the crocodile, tiger, and elephant on wheels in sketch 4, and the small and large *gĕndruwo* figures in the first sketch and on horse-back at the bottom of the second sketch. *Gĕndruwo* (also *gandarwa, gandarwo,* and *gĕndrowo*) though the word is derived from the Sanskrit term for the musicians and singers of Indra's heaven, was generally used in Java to mean a garden or wood ghost of male sex and sometimes colossal size that wanders in the woods awaiting incarnation. This representation of the creatures of the wild may mirror the symbolism of the *alas-alasan* ("creature of the forest") motif of the special *dodot* worn by bride and groom.

– the wedding carriage (sketch 7), in the form of Garuda, the vehicle of Vishnu and Javanese kings:.

The socialisation of the people: "becoming Javanese"

The Javanese Ancien Régime: Civilization and Society

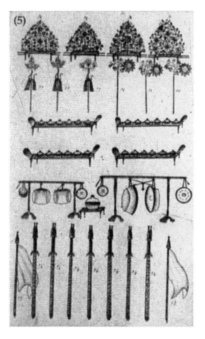

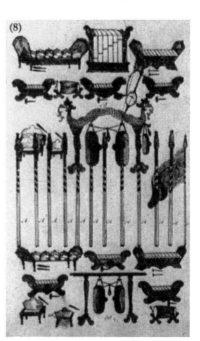

Part Three

THE CANCER WITHIN

4

Traditional or modern? Rational-bureaucratic feudalism à la VOC

As we have seen, the Dutch East India Company came from a Europe that in the late eighteenth century was producing unparalleled innovation in political organisation and thought, urban dominance, military techniques, intellectual life, science and technology. It had been at the leading edge of the development of capitalism. And we are accustomed to think of the West as bringing more centralised and modern forms of organisation to its colonies. But on Java none of these innovations were introduced. The VOC did establish new cities, where European art and architecture was indeed introduced, but they were not seedbeds of modern social and political ideas. Batavia was by VOC intent not a Javanese city or part of the Javanese body politic: it was considered politically necessary to keep Javanese outside the city as far as possible. After 1740, when a separate quarter for the Chinese was established, the possibility of an ethnically diverse urban *community*, as opposed to a congeries of ethnic *kampung*, receded further. Even if the life of the Dutch gathered in and around the VOC had been more open to Javanese, it was hardly an example of bourgeois liberalism. As Wertheim has said, "The East India Company's monopoly system made the existence of a free Dutch bourgeoisie . . . impossible. The fact that the centre of government was the Governor-General's and not the town-hall, where the sheriff and aldermen had their seat, was not without symbolic significance. The administration was not democratic (as in towns in Holland) but autocratic."[1] One lone reformer who, under the influence of the enlightened philosophy of Voltaire, complained about the moral and intellectual morbidity of the city received very rough treatment indeed.[2]

The Company impacted upon the lives of most Javanese in ways that had nothing to do with urban life or modernity. It had destroyed, partitioned, and weakened the pre-existing Javanese states, thus nullifying the enormous social investment that had been made in their creation and precluding the possibility of reform from within them. It replaced them with a political and social structure that was if anything more regressive, a loose ramshackle union of regional rulers who may be compared with the satraps and nomarchs of ancient Persia and Egypt, based on primitive economic and military mechanisms. Like the Javanese states that had preceded it, the VOC state was prebendial in character: the Company's own employees were more like prebendaries than salaried officials, operating within a system in which office generated profit, sometimes enormous profit as we shall see in the next chapter, for the office-holder. In its interaction with the Javanese élite, this state actually created in some areas, generally the most inaccessible, such as the difficult mountainous terrain of Priangan, what could be described as feudal lords in hereditary possession. Like the vassals of feudal Europe, the Javanese Bupati and Tumenggung (Dutch "Regents") as well as the princes, Sunans, and Sultans, owed allegiance to their overlord (the VOC) by a fixed contract, which stipulated their tribute and most importantly their military obligations in case of war. This fealty was confirmed by the swearing of an oath of allegiance.[3] Regents subordinate to the Governor of the North-east Coast – except the Madurese – were obliged to leave a representative at the VOC's head office at Semarang.[4] Within their jurisdictions however they held undivided power, (military, legal, executive and spiritual), providing their obligations to the overlord were fulfilled. In the case of the more powerful Regents and Princes, we also see a parallel to sub-infeudation and the "sub-fief" in which the original feudatory/fief-holder in turn delegates authority in a defined area to a junior in the hierarchy in return for similar obligations. Since the VOC had acquired its authority over different parts of Java at different times and with different conditions, the tributary state that resulted was, as is usual with such states, a congeries of jurisdictions and differing relationships.

THE OVERALL PICTURE

This overall picture does not leap from the VOC sources, but has to be assembled piecemeal, for instance from the reports, known as

Traditional or modern?

Memorieën, written by the departing Governors of the largest administrative unit of Java, the North-east Coast, for the benefit of their successors. These and other similar reports are essentially the tribute lists of the VOC's feudal state. The reports from the North-East coast, which as we shall see also covered other areas, are as follows:

Memorie van overdracht of van den Burgh for his successor Johannes Siberg, 1780 (Nederburgh Collection no. 381) [henceforth M1780].

Memorie van overdracht of Johannes Siberg for his successor Jan Greeve, 18 September 1787 (Nederburgh Collection no. 382) [M1787].

Memorie van overdracht of Jan Greeve for his successor P.G. van Overstraten, 1791 (Nederburgh Collection no. 384) [M1791].

Memorie van overdracht of Pieter Gerard van Overstraten for his successor Johan Fredrik Baron van Reede tot de Parkeler, 1796 (Nederburgh Collection no. 386) [M1796].

Memorie van overdracht of Johan Fredrik Baron van Reede tot de Parkeler for his successor Nic. Engelhard, 1801 (van Alphen – Engelhard Collection 2nd section, 1900, nos. 191-2) [M1801].

Though these reports are voluminous (they may be over 600 pages, though some are shorter) they are not exhaustive and so they have been supplemented where necessary by material from other archival sources, either dealing with general subjects such as rice cultivation or with a local focus, and from secondary studies. Senior VOC officials were preoccupied with delivering the goods, literally. Other aspects of Javanese society are only noted insofar as they bear on this task. In addition, a major responsibility for the Governors of the Northeast Coast was the European community: its housing, public buildings, church affairs, and the operation of institutions such as the Council of Justice, Land Council, Orphanage College of Trustees, Poor-relief Board, Almshouse, Church Council, and Naval School. The affairs of the European community therefore bulk much larger in their reports than those of the Javanese majority, especially of the "ordinary" Javanese. The Governors of the Northeast Coast are in fact only marginal witnesses to Javanese society, living on its fringe. Their sources of even basic information were shaky:

Van Overstraten, for instance, had students of the marine school at Semarang begin the work of making accurate maps of the Company's territories (M1796 #180). In his letters Dirk van Hogendorp complains that there is not a single Dutch map of the

Indies which is just passable, while the French and English have superb maps.[5] Travel seems to have been regarded as a rare and difficult thing: a diary of a journey made by Governor Engelhard in 1802[6] makes it clear that this was the first time since 1784 (when it had been undertaken by Siberg, Governor-General in 1802) that a Governor had been able to make such an extensive tour of inspection. Greeve had been prevented from doing so by a politico-military crisis in the central Javanese principalities involving Mangkunegara 1, and though van Overstraten had inspected the western *pasisir* in 1792 his projected tour of the eastern *pasisir* in 1793 was cancelled when the Napoleonic wars broke out. Nor is this the only source that suggests that many VOC officials had never seen most of the territory over which they had jurisdiction: Dirk van Hogendorp claims that his precursor as Gezaghebber of the Oosthoek did not even know the district of Surabaya itself, much less the whole Oosthoek; he never went two leagues' distance from his headquarters in the city of Surabaya, and was absolutely ignorant of the size of his district, its population, the quality of the soil, and its revenues.[7] Even at the lower level of Resident, where we would expect more local knowledge, there are some surprises. J.L. Umbgrove's 1795 report on Cirebon, made at the request of S.C. Nederburgh (Nederburgh 371, ARA)[8] begins with an eloquent apologia for the shortcomings of this report which has echoes of many literary apologiae, both European and Javanese.[9] He goes on to say that he has based his report mainly on what the indigo makers, who had travelled through the regions concerned, had to tell him. The body of the report is basically a topographical account with touches of the pastorale, though it does attempt to provide information, unlike some other comparable reports, on the inhabitants and their activities.

The standardised format of the *Memorieën* is often followed in a perfunctory way, a notable exception being van Overstraten, whose energy and forwardness burst through the format in his voluminous report. However, by a close examination of the *Memorieën* and regional reports and a collation of usually passing references one can put together some information on a number of important subjects.

Javanese labour: the unaccounted input

The first item is an absence. Alongside the export produce which the VOC siphoned from Java, the labour of its Javanese subjects formed a major input into its business. This is mentioned here and there in passing, but never computed. Usually corvée obligations were an inseparable concomitant of land-holding, and the burden of corvée had increased in the areas under VOC control after about 1780.[10] So heavy was it that there is even reference to the development of a preference for non-agricultural occupations such as fishing, carrying, navigation, etc. in some areas.[11] Forced labour was the universal substitute for money payment. In many places there was competition between the Company and the Javanese élite for labour: a report from Yogyakarta[12] describes the Sultan's attempts to limit the Company's demand for labour for indigo and pepper production. The amount of labour required can be inferred from the Resident's statement that the whole population of Bagalen, including women and children, would be required to pick the pepper harvest. This and other such statements are juxtaposed with exhortations to the author's successor that the Javanese Regents should be prevented from making excessive demands on the common people, revealing the constant struggle for control of labour carried on between the Company and the Javanese elite. The 1806 report on rice cultivation also reveals the extensive demands for labour not related to rice cultivation that were made on the population (work in warehouses, and hospitals, on cruising vessels, loading and unloading ships, serving in unpaid militia, work at indigo factories, transporting the VOC's goods overland, maintaining roads, bridges and buildings, on coffee and pepper plantations, spinning cotton thread etc.)[13] It seems that in the areas under the VOC labour demands were so heavy as to produce a shift to communal landownership.[14]

Apart from the work involved in the growing and transport of produce, the Javanese were also required for VOC military constructions, and to make up levies of soldiers and sailors. During the period from 1780 (i.e. the beginning of the Fourth Anglo-Dutch War) these military needs increased substantially.[15] Javanese labour is also mentioned in connection with the shipment of produce: Javanese were used because of lack of other manpower, but the work was abhorrent to them and they deserted (M1791 #165). Van Overstraten states that he took care to engage only volunteers, and to take measures to reduce the numbers who died or were lost in Batavia in the shipping (rafting) of timber there. Javanese sailors were cheaper and better than Chinese ones, who could not be induced to climb (M1796 #241–8).

The Cancer Within

Despite all this, during this period there was a strong response on the part of the Javanese peasantry to the opportunity to profit from cash crops, notably cotton, indigo, and tobacco. This capacity to respond to market opportunities was to persist up until the terrible poverty, and in some areas famine, of the 1840s, when the ever-larger demands on peasant labour finally wiped out the time available for independent cash-cropping.

Travel and security

This was forbidden without a special pass; and the sending of personal letters also prohibited (M1796 #183). This and the forcible direction of "idlers" into agriculture underlines the intention to fix the Javanese as serfs in the VOC's tributary state, but in practice the Company was not able to control all travel – indeed, whole blocs of population sometimes left their villages, and there are quite frequent mentions of "rabble", obviously bands outside the control of any jurisdiction, attacking particular areas, both along the coast and in central Java, where they were known as *kecu* bands.

Money

There had been a process of increasing monetization of the economy of rural Java from at least the early seventeenth century, with the introduction of the small-value lead *picis* by itinerant Chinese.[16] This was by no means complete by the late eighteenth century, though at this period it was hastened by an increasing tendency to require that the land-rent (*pajěg*) be paid in cash. But there was a severe shortage of coinage. In 1780 van den Burgh noted that inland trade was mostly conducted with *duits*, and that there was a great scarcity of other coinage, especially in the Eastern Salient. He attributed this chiefly to the situation in the overseas trade, in which Javanese products were fetching low prices, from the Palembang traders selling pepper and tin, for instance, resulting in a negative balance which the Company had to pay in Spanish silver dollars. The trade with Batavia represented a further drain on Java's currency reserves, since what Batavia took from Java fetched only half the price of the opium, cloth, silk, manufactures, lace, Chinese wares etc. which Java purchased from Batavia. In addition, much of the gold and silver which the Company brought in found its way into the treasure chests of the princes or was melted down.

Traditional or modern?

Finally, he estimated the yearly supply of silver to be below Rd. 23,000, which he thought would have been less than the Java Chinese repatriated to China in specie. In 1787–8 quantities of *picis* were imported from Japan: these circulated almost solely in the vicinity of Semarang. Elsewhere, the increasing shortage of coinage led to an increase in the use of papers of credit (M1791 #178). In 1801 van Reede tot de Parkeler notes that tin farthings had been introduced but counterfeiting had resulted. The Japanese copper pieces of 1 and 2 *stuivers* were being melted down by the Javanese and Chinese because of the shortage of copper. There was also a shortage of paper money (M1801 #432–8). In the next chapter, we will look in more detail at the role of money in the economy of Priangan.

Chinese entrepreneurs

Serious economic effects of Chinese penetration of the economy are canvassed as early as 1780 (M1780 #101). Van den Burgh remarks that the Chinese are both necessary for the development of agriculture and trade because of their diligence and industry, and dangerous for Java because of their increasing numbers and their practice, now widespread, of renting *negeri* from Regents [which was, of course, a practice the Dutch themselves used]. This practice was seen as pandering to the indolence of Regents, especially of those who were indifferent to the extortion and oppression[17] practised by the Chinese upon those under then, and their practice of exhausting fields and woods as long as they could make a profit. Furthermore, in Demak and other rice areas Chinese were storing up rice not only from their own lands but also from neighbouring *negeri* so that the Regents were obliged to buy rice in the open market at high prices from those they had leased land to. Van den Burgh therefore stipulated that the rent of rice-producing *negeri* could not be paid outright with cash, as had been the common arrangement, but should be paid immediately after the harvest with rice, reckoned at Rd. 13–1/3 per *koyan*, or in case of default a 150% penalty, an arrangement that would always work out to the advantage of the Regents whether the harvests were good or bad, since they received from the Company the price of Rd. 15 per *koyan* of rice for their contingents, and which should help them to make prompt deliveries. From Siberg onward a policy was followed of preventing the Regents from renting villages and *negeri* to the

The Cancer Within

Chinese. Customs (*shahbanderijen*) were nearly all in the hands of the Chinese, who thereby became independent of the Regents.

Chinese control of tax-farming, in particular, magnified Chinese commercial advantages and widened the gulf between Chinese and indigenous traders. There is already evidence both of anti-Chinese feeling and of the Chinese being seen as hand-in-glove with the Dutch. This last comes from both Dutch and Javanese sources. In the diary used in Chapter Two, in which Mangkunegara 1 is said to have dreamed that all the houses of the Dutch and Chinese were burnt down one night. This was at a time when he was having discussions with the young Sunan Pakubuwana IV about "standing firm" with him in opposition to the Dutch, though no agreement had yet been reached.[18] In 1801 the existence of many toll-gates in the Eastern Salient, in inland Java and in the Company's territory is noted. Van Reede tot de Parkeler comments that these tolls are operated by the Regents and Chinese against the orders of the Company and oppress small trade in the inland (M1801 #391). There were also tolls in other areas such as Madura and Tuban, where they inhibited trade, but nothing was done about this impediment to a more integrated economy and in fact the tolls subsequently grew apace and the hardship and resentment caused was a major factor in the outbreak of the Java War.

Chinese enterprises were of course affected by general economic conditions. In 1780 the annual profit to the Company from the customs was 143662.5 Rd., and the profit to the various Regents 3637.5 Rd. (M1780 #123). From 1787 on there are reports of remission of contracted payments as the trade situation worsened (e.g. M1791 #171, remission to the Kapitan Cina of payments for the customs in 1796 this man, who was also involved in the import and export of rice, was granted a further remission of unpaid rent). In 1796, when trade was at a virtual standstill, van Overstraten commented that it was amazing that the lease prices remained so high in such depressed times, when most of the leaseholders had suffered enormously. Leaseholders in Semarang, Tegal, Joana and Rembang were between 5500 Rd. and over 70,000 Rd. in arrears, though van Overstraten was confident of quite a lot of this money coming in (M1796 #249–54).

There is also a recurrent theme in Dutch sources of the need to restrict the growth of the Chinese community on the grounds of the threat this could pose – the Company had not forgotten the Chinese revolt of 1740 and the war that followed – and a view of the Chinese

Traditional or modern?

as corruptors of the Javanese (e.g. M1796 #184). The Chinese were the chief distributors of opium, whose growing use is deplored as a growing cancer in many regional reports. Thus, the relationship with the Chinese community, seen on the one hand as making an invaluable economic contribution and on the other as oppressive, extortionate, bad husbandmen of their resources and moral corruptors of the natives, was a highly ambiguous one. Van Ysseldijk's 1793 report[19] on Yogyakarta remarks that the Chinese leaseholders were generally hated on account of their oppression of the natives, and it had been necessary to levy a fine of 200 *real* (an enormous sum, of which van Ysseldijk got one half and the Sultan the other) on every Chinese found murdered on the road, to be paid by the surrounding villages if no culprit was identified. Here we may note Lieberman's comment that Chinese control of tax-farming, which seems to have spread from Java to Thailand and Cambodia in the eighteenth century, was a major factor in widening the gulf between Chinese and indigenous traders in the region.[20] Ambiguity is also found in judgments on the Javanese: it is not infrequently said that they are generally wasteful, which is why they are poor, and that the Regents are arbitrary and ignorant and misuse the common people (M1796 #177, 178). Yet elsewhere a Romantic attitude appears in which the Javanese are seen as possessed of an inborn simplicity that should be preserved from corruption.[21]

Learning Javanese

M1801 #567 makes reference to van Overstraten's suggestion to train four or five young men in the Javanese language. Three (P.A. van Ijsseldijk, Matthys Lumaas and W.V. Duijnhooven) were already fully competent, and it was considered necessary always to have in training the full number as proposed, in case some were lost through death or transfers. It seems they were trained on the coast as well as in Surakarta and Yogyakarta. It was very rare for a VOC official to know Javanese. A twentieth-century Dutch writer remarks that at the end of the eighteenth and early nineteenth century both in the Netherlands and the Indies, linguistic competence was at a very low point, in contrast to the energy and intelligence in the field of knowledge of language, land, and people shown by English officials, especially Raffles. The deeply nationalist J.C. Baud spoke with sharp regret of the "shameful incompetence of our officials" in contrast to the English. In addition, the serious study of fields such as geography, language, and ethnography was substantially begun by men like Raffles, Marsden, and Leijden.[22] The Cornets de Groot ethnography used in the previous chapter is a notable exception to this generalisation.

Local custom

Van Overstraten, who appears to have been a Governor of exceptional energy and initiative, felt it necessary to make an investigation of the norms of local government in order to prevent the Regents exceeding them to extort more from the common man (and thereby encourage settlement in the regions under Company rule), but had only got as far as a survey of Semarang. He claimed that every Regency, nay every district and village, differed from its neighbour (M1796 #178).

Political reportage and "popish" plots

The Governors' reports include an extensive account of personal relationships among the Javanese élite across the island. This virtually never rises to any level general or analytical enough to suggest any developments related to political ideology, though there does seem to have been a growth of "popery" a term used to indicate the presence of Muslim teachers with large followings, in Surakarta and Sumenep (see M1801 #14–5 and #241–2).

Defence

This was a major preoccupation of the Governors of the North-east Coast and is canvassed in all their reports. They were responsible both for making preparations for the eventuality of an attack by a hostile European power (first the French, then the British), and for the defence of the coast against pirates. Piracy was a major problem which van Overstraten inherited from Greeve, with pirates coming from as far away as Borneo, Magindanau and Balangingi (M1787 #108).[23] This was part of a general "boom" in piracy in island Southeast Asia between 1780 and 1820.[24] However, a Resident of Yogyakarta reports that piracy is a result of the oppression of the ordinary people,[25] suggesting a more local origin for much of the problem. Van Overstraten had great difficulty in addressing it within the very limited resources the Company would provide and eventually decided on a strategy in which the Company would build the boats (15 galleys of differing sizes), the Regents would provide the sailors, and the costs would be defrayed by contributions from the Regents, the Chinese community and the Company's officials. At the end of his term of office 10 galleys had been constructed (M1796 #312). Much of his report is concerned with his plan for the defence of the coast and for a retreat into the interior if necessary. In 1791 the standing military forces under the Governor of Java were set at a total of 3367 men, 200 cavalry, 2881 infantry, and 286 artillery. Of these, all the cavalry, 1300 of the infantry and 150 of the artillery made up the garrisons at Semarang, at the central Javanese courts, and at Surabaya, Banyuwangi, Pasuruhan etc.; while the remaining 1400 infantry and 150 artillery formed a reserve corps for use as necessary. In times of war, it was laid down, every company of 100 men on garrison duty should be augmented by another 25 men, and the reserve force of 1500 men should be doubled. This planned augmentation was contingent upon the arrival of the Hartoch van Württemberg's regiment. However, not only was part of this regiment siphoned off to Malacca, as had been planned: another part was sent directly from the Cape of Good Hope to Ceylon, and one more company was posted to Ambon, where they went over to the English when the latter attacked, and took part in the subsequent English attack on Banda. This left van Overstraten with only three companies of these not strikingly reliable reinforcements (M1796 #312, #304) and at one stage he was required to send 150 European soldiers to Batavia to fight in Banda and elsewhere. (M1796 #338). He had also begun to form a militia of Javanese supplied by the Regents (M1796 #317–32).

By 1801, the military situation was still worse. Van Reede tot de Parkeler's report notes van Overstraten's 1795 statement that the number of European military on the north coast could not possibly be reduced, and adds that since that time the number *had* decreased, due both to mortality and to the requisitioning of men to the capital. The part of the Württemberg regiment stationed on the north coast was to be permitted to recruit native soldiers to make up its depleted ranks, and the native militia – still described as "to be formed" – was to be made subordinate to it (M1801 #506–9). By this time too piracy had greatly increased, but very little progress had been made towards carrying out van Overstraten's 1792 plan to create a substantial naval force. In theory the

Company's north coast establishment should have maintained a fleet of 15 galleys (3 large, 80 feet in length, and 12 medium, 66 feet in length) in addition to the contribution of the coastal Bupati. This latter had initially comprised 2 *pancalangs* and 26 *praus* from the Bupati of the Brebes-Tuban stretch, 2 *pancalangs* and 18 *praus* from the Bupati of the Eastern Salient, plus 2 vessels from Pamekasan, but the supply of this shipping was commuted in favour of an annual levy of 330 Javanese sailors and payment of Rd. 10050. In fact, however, the Company was well below establishment: it seems that the maximum attained was 4 large and 11 medium vessels, of which 1 large and 1 medium had been sent on an expedition to Ternate and 1 medium on an expedition to Banjarmasin; 2 large and 2 medium had been captured by the French and English; 2 medium vessels had been captured by pirates; and 2 medium vessels had been condemned. This left only 1 large and 3 medium vessels on the north coast stations. The Regents on the other hand had not come up with either the sailors or the money payment. Furthermore, it was considered too dangerous to send out against pirates what ships were available, given the presence of English shipping. A task that could not be avoided was escorting the wood-fleets of Tegal and Batang to the capital, an operation which seems to have stretched the Company's naval capacity to the maximum. The main centres of pirate vessels were the Batang point in the west, or the "Devil's cliff" in the central coast, and Anyer-Anyer point in the east. These vessels were generally able to evade capture through their capacity to row against the wind (M1801 #525–30). The Company was boxed in on land, unable to act either against the "smuggling" trade that breached her theoretical monopoly or against outright piracy. Her military arrangements – resting on the requisition of men and local ships from her Javanese vassals – were as primitive as her economic and political arangements.

JAVA'S TRIBUTE

As remarked above, the reports of the Governors and their subordinates were essentially tribute lists, arranged region by region. The VOC wrote and quantified more, but it was essentially maintaining a system of feudal tributes. Furthermore, many of its figures represent ideals rather than realities, since the amount set could not be collected: this is at least often noted, however. But the power of setting up this web of figures, tables, and reportage

Traditional or modern?

binding Java should not be underestimated. It set a goal, which, however poorly approximated in the present, could be pursued with growing effectiveness by those running the VOC's successor state in the future.

The administrative divisions of the VOC state were generally based upon pre-existing political sub-units, though some new ones had been created. Administratively, Java was divided into the following categories: A. The lands under more direct VOC rule, comprising I. The lands under the so-called "Governor and Director of Java's North-east coast" and II. The VOC's West Javanese possessions; and B. The areas with a semi-independent, but still regulated and tributary, status, that is the old Sultanate of Banten and the Central Javanese principalities, heirs to the former kingdom of Mataram.

A. AREAS UNDER MORE DIRECT DUTCH RULE

I. THE DOMAIN OF THE GOVERNOR AND DIRECTOR OF JAVA'S NORTH-EAST COAST

These Governors were the most powerful territorial officials on Java, and the post was often an indication that the man who held it would be the next Governor-General of the VOC's Indonesian possessions. They had authority over an area larger than we would understand from the term "north-east coast",[26] since although one extremity of the area was indeed the north-easternmost point of the coast, it extended on the other side as far west as Brebes. The Governors also had jurisdiction over Madura (which was more indirectly ruled than the coastal areas) and were expected to keep an eye on developments in the central Javanese principalities as well.

The area under the Governors of the Northeast Coast had a population of 1,495,908 Javanese in 1795, according to van Overstraten's survey of the lands under his jurisdiction (excluding Bawean, Ulujami, Besuki and Panarukan), the first somewhat reliable census of population made (M1796 #179).

Authority over this area and its people was divided into six VOC offices or *Kantors*, i.e. the Eastern Salient (Dutch *Oosthoek*), and the Rembang, Japara, Semarang, Pekalongan and Tegal offices (listed from east to west). These offices each had jurisdiction over a number of Regencies, under Bupati, as follows:

1. The Eastern Salient office

This was under an official called a Gezaghebber, reflecting the military occupation of the recently conquered Eastern Salient. He resided at Surabaya and had jurisdiction over two regions, Besuki and Panarukan, which were leased to a Chinese leaseholder, and over the Regencies of East Balambangan (Banyuwangi), West Balambangan (divided into Lamajang and Banger, Jember and Adirogo, Prajekan, Sentong and Sabrang), Pasuruhan, Malang, Bangil, Porong, Surabaya, Gresik, Lamongan and Sidayu. The Gezaghebber was also responsible for Madura, divided into three principalities, Sumenep, Pamekasan and Bangkalan, which had a large measure of independence.

2. The Rembang office

This had jurisdiction over the Regencies of Tuban, Lasem, Rembang, Panjangkungan, and Palo.

3. The Japara office

This had jurisdiction over the Regencies of Juwana, Pati (including also Glonggong), Cengkalsewu, Japara, and Kudus.

4. The Semarang head office

This was the headquarters of the Governor of the Northeast Coast, who administered the Regencies of Demak, Semarang, Kendal, and Kaliwungu. Semarang also had jurisdiction over Adilangu, which was the hereditary fief of the priest-princes who bore the title Pangeran Wijil, or Sunan Kadilangu, and were descendants of the *wali* Sunan Lepen.

5. The Pekalongan office

This had jurisdiction over the Regencies of Batang, Pekalongan, and Wiradesa. It also included the district of Ulujami, which was leased to a Chinese leaseholder.

6. The Tegal office

This had jurisdiction over the Regencies of Pamalang, Tegal, and Brebes.

In the following, we look at the above administrative divisions under the Governor of the Northeast Coast in more detail.

Traditional or modern?

1. The Eastern Salient (Oosthoek)

Historical background

This area, from Pasuruhan eastwards, was ceded to the Company by the contract of 11 November 1741, ratified 11 November 1743. The Surabaya region (divided into two parts, Gresik, and Lamongan with Sidayu) was also administered as part of the Eastern Salient, and the port town of Surabaya was the headquarters of the administrator of the Eastern Salient, who bore the title Gezaghebber. The first holder of this office was appointed in 1742; the last (now with the title Landdrost instead of Gezaghebber) Arnold Goldbach, in 1811. In 1795 the famous Dirk van Hogendorp was appointed to the position, and it was held from 1798–1808 by Frederik Jacob Rothenbuhler, who wrote some of the best descriptions of Java's coastal areas during his time there. Otherwise, the European establishment was small, about 7 civilians and 13 military officers, at the forts at Surabaya, Banyuwangi, Panarukan, Pasuruhan and Gresik. Though it had been officially ceded to the VOC by the Sunan of Mataram, the area resisted Dutch rule for longer and at greater cost than any other part of Java. The nature of this resistance – the "raiding parties", "murders" and "piracies" of bandits, outlaws, and pirates as they are termed in the Dutch reports – surely deserves further investigation, though it is outside our scope here. The VOC's military campaigns did not begin until 1767, when Surapati's grandson Melayukusuma was driven out of Malang. Balambangan and Besuki were next, followed by the southern regions between Malang and Banyuwangi. In 1770 a redoubt was built at Puger, and in 1771 one on the island Nusa Baron. The conquered areas, then well populated, were divided into five Regencies: Banyuwangi, Lamajang, Besuki, Panarukan and Prabalingga (Banger). In the same year an uprising in Balambangan wiped out the VOC garrison of 60 men. Subsequently about a hundred leaders of the rebellion were lured onto Dutch ships under false promises by the Commandant, Hendrik Schophofft, and were beheaded there. Batavia declared all the inhabitants there slaves, and sent troops who, in the six years of warfare that followed, virtually depopulated the land: an estimated population of 80–100,000 fell to 5–8,000. According to Boomgaard, population density was probably higher in the time of Majapait (fourteenth century) than in 1800.[27] Even after this time the position of the Dutch military occupation remained insecure. 1777 saw the conquest of the island of Nusa Baron, where Balinese, Makassarese and Mandarese together held sway over about 2000 Balambangers, who were returned by the Company to various places on the mainland, and the island rendered as far as possible uninhabitable (M1780 #88[28]). However, the island was subsequently occupied by Mandarese sea-raiders in league with Balinese princes and with the *běkěl* of Nusa Baron itself. Many Balambangers fled to Bali, Panarukan, Puger and Besuki during this period of hunger and death: in 1806 the Captain Lieutenant and Commander at Banyuwangi was still requesting that he be empowered to forcibly return them to their native soil[29] in order to bring under cultivation the plentiful land lying idle due to lack of manpower. In 1790 the Commandant at Pasuruhan, Major van Rijk, depopulated the whole coast and so thoroughly devastated it that there was scarcely a trace of human habitation to be seen in an area once populous and blooming.[30]

Later on there was immigration from Madura, where all land suitable for rice growing had been taken up and there was a shortage of rice. Immigration from other areas of Java was inhibited by the fear of military service contingent upon entering an area under the Company. Anyone found "idling" here was forced to grow rice, albeit with the provision of a span of buffalo, a major capital investment. Even this was a somewhat uncertain gift, however, since cattle stocks were continually depleted by the need to provision the numerous warships and Company ships making port.[31] It is in the light of these conditionss that we must read the data on this region at the turn of the century.

Another characteristic of the Eastern Salient during this period was the very strong Chinese element in the *élite*. This element was largely composed of the descendants of a single man, Han Hin Song, who at around the time of the massacres of Chinese following the 1740 uprising converted to Islam and married the daughter of a Javanese Regent. Three of their sons were brought up as Chinese and two as Muslims. This family were not only leaseholders (and after the changes instituted by Daendels and Raffles, landowners) but also Regents. This situation lasted through the period we are concerned with up till 1818, when there was a complete purge of the Sino-Javanese Regents and officials on the basis of trumped-up charges instigated by a conspiracy of Javanese and Dutchmen.[32]

Traditional or modern?

The leased regions of the Eastern Salient: Panarukan and Besuki

These districts, which suffered greatly in the conquest of Balambangan, were afterwards leased to Han Boey Ko for Rd. 1875 and 10 *koyan*[33] of rice per annum. When he died in 1778 his son Han Tjampit, Chinese Captain of Surabaya, paid Rd. 1250 and 10 *koyan* of rice for Besuki and Rd. 625 for Panarukan (the former, which had good rice land that attracted settlers, was much more flourishing than the latter: M1780 #86, M 1787 #95). This sum was raised again in 1794 to Rd. 6210 (M1796 #159) when van Overstraten commented that the prosperity of Besuki under Chinese management fully corroborated Governor van den Burgh's assessment (M1780 #86) that a Chinese as leaseholder can do more than a Javanese as Regent. One of the innovations of the Chinese in this area was to do away with a large number of intermediate officials, establishing direct contact between their overseers and the village. The rent was later raised to Rd. 9000 by Daendels, always with the obligation to deliver 10 *koyan* of rice. The leaseholder bought these lands in 1810, but they were repurchased by the government in 1813. There was a fortification (consisting in 1789 of a wood and bamboo building surrounded by palisades) with a small garrison (22 men in 1780, later only about a dozen) close to the shore in Panarukan to cover the north side of west Balambangan, and a cruising *prau mayang* (a sort of middle-sized Javanese fishing boat) to patrol the seas. Later, plans to set up an indigo factory and to introduce pepper cultivation were made (M1801 #272).

Prabalingga (Banger)

This area, estimated at 1000 *cacah* (wet rice farms[34]) in 1796, was under the Regent of Lamajang, who after 1784 had to supply from it 8 *koyan* of rice and 8 (M1780 #85: 6) *pikul* of wax (to Lamajang) free, and 2 *pikul* of cotton thread, for payment (prior to 1784 there were no deliveries, because of the disturbed situation) (M1787 #93–4; M1791 #115; M1796 #158). In 1799 the rice contingent was increased from 8 *pikul* to 40 *koyan*, suggesting that rice cultivation was picking up (M1801 #260).

The Cancer Within

The Eastern Salient proper

East Balambangan (Banyuwangi)

This was the largest of the Balambangan Regencies but also the wildest and most sparsely populated. In 1773 it was placed under Tumenggung Wiraguna, described as the former chief minister of the last ruler of Balambangan, Pangeran Patih. Wiraguna's sister was Pangeran Patih's widow, who subsequently married the Panembahan of Madura, but then asked the Company to be allowed to return to Balambangan. Van den Burgh advised that she never be allowed to do so. Wiraguna himself married a daughter of the Panembahan of Madura who died in 1770, and it was hoped that her prestige would attract Madurese settlers. The Regent's residence (*dalĕm*) was established at Banyuwangi, and a lesser one at Kali Buntu, described as the least unhealthy sites in an unhealthy region, and well located to keep an eye on the straits and traffic to and from Bali. A couple of *pancalang* (a sort of local trading ship) and two built-up *prau mayang* provided a small cruising fleet. Two *bentengs* (fortifications), whose wooden buildings and palisades were soon devastated by white ants, housed 114 men under Lieutenant Pieter Mierop. Until 1786 no deliveries were required, except for some payment for the lease of the birds' nest collection, part of which was allotted to the Regent for his upkeep. The region had some wax, cardamom, pearls and *tripang* but the *sapan* wood was exhausted (M1780 #89–90). In 1787 the Regency delivered 40 *koyan* of rice free, and as much indigo as could be produced, at Rd. 83–1/3 per *pikul* for the Regent and a supplement, withdrawn by 1791, of Rd. 16–2/3 per *pikul* for the producers. In 1791 the Regency was apparently still under-populated (a problem addressed by using it as a place of banishment) and under-developed, though coffee and pepper had been planted, but by 1796 it is described as flourishing, with "beautiful rice-fields and the most luxurious coffee and pepper plantations" (M1787 #102; M1791 #124; M1796 #167). Nevertheless, in 1806 a report on rice cultivation says that there was still a lot of land used as rice fields before the Balambangan War which had now become a wild and sometimes impenetrable wilderness.[35] Production of birds' nests was leased to a Chinese for 850 Spanish dollars per annum of which Rd. 250 went to the Regent as a *douceur* [the standard term in the Company's accounts for the sort of payments which fall somewhere between a

Traditional or modern?

commission and a bribe]. Van Overstraten would have liked to raise the price but was prevented from doing so by the "unfortunate times". Sea-raiders sometimes harvested the nests first (M1787 #101). In 1792 a soldier of the occupying force was charged with indigo making. The shipping toll was held by another Chinese, at 350 Spanish dollars per annum. In the VOC classification, this region was a military commandment, from 1800 held by the *Vaandrig*[36] Johan Cezar van Wikkerman.

West Balambangan

This Regency comprised the districts Prajekan, Sentong, Jember (Adiraga) and Sabrang, each of which had its own head until 1779, when Tumenggung Prawiradingrat (a son of the Regent of Pasuruhan, much praised by the Company for his loyalty and diligence: M1780 #91) was installed as Regent. On his death, little improvement having taken place in the productivity of the region, van Overstraten installed the Rangga of Besuki, Suraadiwikrama, describing him as a well-to-do man of demonstrated ability, only wanting the Regency for the title of Tumenggung. In 1780 there was a military detachment of 56 men at Puger but the location was found to be very unhealthy and it was redeployed to Batu Ulu (M1780 #91). Two *pancalang* and a built-up *prau mayang* constituted the naval force. The deliveries instituted in 1784 were as follows:

Prajekan: 2 *pikul* of long pepper and 2 *pikul* of wax, free.
Sentong: half a *pikul* of wax, free.
Jember: one *pikul* of wax, free.
Sabrang: one *pikul* of wax, free, and one *pikul* of cotton thread, for payment. (M1787 #99; M1796 #162).

Expeditionary parties were periodically sent to the south coast to drive off sea-raiders. In 1790 the Mandarese Captain Buton was entrusted with the gathering of birds' nests (M1791 #119, M1796 #161-3), which he did succesfully for a time before being suspected of piracy and killed by a Dutch expedition sent from Pasuruhan to arrest him. Van Overstraten comments that this episode showed the dangers of using foreigners and leased the birds' nest cliffs to the Regent of West Balambangan for two years at an annual payment of 400 Rd (M1796 #163).

Lamajang

The first Regent was Tumenggung Jayanagara. Lamajang had a military detachment of at most two dozen men housed within a fortification of earth walls and "living palisades" (M1780 #79). It was immediately subordinate to the Commandant of Pasuruhan and to it the posts at Puger, Klatak (West Balambangan), Nusa Baron and Sempu were in turn subordinate. By 1792 all of these posts except Klatak were evacuated.

Pasuruhan and Porong

Pasuruhan had been a frontier region during the Balambangan campaigns and had suffered greatly from the coming and going of armed forces and from the requisitioning of men as porters and soldiers (M1780 #79). For this reason it was excused for three years, ending in 1781, from supplying its notional contingent of 60 *koyan* of rice, free. Its Regent, Adipati Nitidiningrat, had distinguished himself by loyal service to the Company in the wars. The Commander in 1780 was Lieutenant A. van Rijck, and in 1796 Lieut. J. Coert (M1787 #89; M1796 #153). Porong, under the Regent of Pasuruhan from 1771, is noted in 1780 as having a delivery of 70 *koyan* of rice, free, but was like Pasuruhan excused from this for three years because of the devastation of the wars (M1780 #81). Its remaining obligations were 3 *pikul* of cotton thread, for payment; and Rd. 42.5 in Kalang money[37] and Rd. 48.75 in capitation tax. In 1787 and 1796 it was apparently delivering 10 *koyan* of rice (M1787 #90; M1791 #111; M1796 #154). In 1801 the combined rice delivery of Pasuruhan and Porong was raised to 110 *koyan* of rice. At this time a forest was being logged to establish rice-fields. Two indigo factories had been set up but were not required to make deliveries. An initial 20,000 pepper trees were to be planted, and 10–12,000 annually thereafter (M1801 #251). In 1806 there was still plenty of suitable land available for rice cultivation.[38]

Malang and Ngantang

Malang was the area of the old kingdom of Singasari, and was later called Supit Urang. In 1780 van den Burgh reported that the area, more or less under Company rule since 1767, was very poorly populated after the wars, and that since all deliveries had to be

Traditional or modern?

brought over high mountains and deep valleys along steep bad roads to Pasuruhan, it was unreasonable to expect rice deliveries. Malang had been (like Pasuruhan, Porong, Antang, Banger and Bangil) released from its previous obligation to deliver 10 *koyan* of rice for three years till 1781 and van den Burgh recommended that it continued to be exempt from rice deliveries (M1780 #82). The Regent of Malang, Kertanegara, paid Rd. 87.5 capitation tax, raised to 100 rd. in 1801. By 1801 the rice delivery was 8 *koyan*. From 1791 he delivered 3 *pikul* of cotton thread, increased to 4 *pikul* in 1801 when 10 *pikul* of spun or twisted *gumuti* thread (for rope-making) were also required (M1801 #254). In 1780 and 1787 van den Burgh and Siberg state that Ngantang really belongs to the Sunan but that he tacitly waived his right to it (M 1780 #84, M1787 #92). In 1788 however the Sunan asked for it back, in vain (M1791 #112), and would have petitioned van Overstraten for its return had the latter not prevented him: van Overstraten also advised his successor to continually act as if it belonged to the Company (M1796 #157). In 1794 Kertanegara was retired at his own request and the Company then allocated Malang and Ngantang to the Regency of Bangil for 6 years initially, with the prospect of permanent incorporation if the Regent developed them as well as he had Bangil (he had also to pay Kartanegara Rd. 250 annually in maintainance until the latter's death in 1796: M1796 #155). There was an army post at Malang with a very small garrison (18 men under a Sergeant in 1780, housed in a *benteng* with living palisades and earthen walls and wood and bamboo buildings).

Bangil

A small Regency, one of those excused from rice deliveries until 1781 on the grounds of the extraordinary burden of the Balambangan campaigns (M1780 #78). In 1787 through 1796 the Regency paid Rd. 45 in Kalang money and delivered 10 *koyan* of rice free, plus 2 *pikul* of cotton threads for payment. The Regent from 1780 to 1796 is named as Ingabei Suraadiwija. Siberg remarked that if his title was upgraded to Tumenggung, as was warranted by the size of the Regency, Bangil could be expected to supply 20 *koyan* of rice (M1787 #88), and this was done in 1787 (M1791 #109; M1796 #152). Because of his good performance, the districts of Malang and Ngantang were added to his Regency. In 1801 the rice delivery was raised to 35 *koyan* (M1801 #247) and by 1806 there was no more unused land suitable to rice cultivation.[39]

The Cancer Within

Surabaya and dependencies

The Regency of Surabaya is described in 1780 as only partly recovered to its old grandeur after the recent troubles: deaths, the Balambangan wars, a decline in shipping and trade, and bad harvests. For these reasons it could no longer be considered as a counterbalance to Madurese strength (M1780 #66). Estimated at 7000 *cacah* in 1796, its annual delivery of produce was 1000 *koyan* of rice (less in times of harvest failures), free; 800 cans of petroleum, free; 8 *pikul* of cotton thread (raised to 10 in 1791 [M1791 #93], though it is not clear that this amount was being delivered in 1796 [M1796 #139]), for payment, and Rd. 141.5 iin Kalang money. The Gezaghebber also had to deliver 16 *pikul* (22 from 1791, at least in theory) of cotton thread, for payment. Surabaya had two Regent families, the *kasepuhan* (Raden Tumenggung Panji Jayengrana in 1780, Tumenggung Panji Cakranegara over the period 1787 to 1796) and the *kanoman* (Tumenggung Jayadirana – who had marriage connections with the ruling families of Madura, Pasuruhan, and Semarang – over the same period). There was considerable rivalry between them (M1780 #365; M1787 #73; M1791 #91; M1796 #139). Surabaya in 1787 was said to be recovering from its decline (M1787 #73). The city of Surabaya was the head office for the Eastern Salient: it was the residence not only of the Gezaghebber but also of the Commander of the Militia and of the Residents of Gresik, Sumenep, and Bangkalan.

Gresik

Estimated at 3200 *cacah* in 1796, Gresik had a delivery of Rd. 487.5 and 160 *koyan* of rice, for payment, as also 6 *pikul* of cotton thread (from 1790, 6 *pikul* extra with Sidayu and Lamongan) (M1787 #71; M1791 #91; M1796 #138). It had two Regents, who were related to one another (M1780 #64). In 1799 the quantities were increased to 180 *koyan* of rice and 10 *pikul* of cotton thread for both Regents but the attempt to run an indigo factory was abandoned (M1801 #210). The Resident (B. W. Fokkens in 1780, A. Schwencke in 1787, P.C.W. Mossel from 1794) also had to deliver 25 *pikul* of cotton thread annually. Gresik also produced one or two shiploads of timber from 1782, wood which came from the lands of the central Javanese rulers along the Solo river. This was an area of very heavy logging that also supplied 500–600 logs to the quotas of Tuban. There were

Traditional or modern?

two Regents, Tumenggungs Arjanagara and Bratanagara, appointed in 1787, over the period 1787 to 1796. In 1780 this formerly flourishing port – which had the unique privilege of being allowed to issue passes to vessels engaged in private trade – was already in decline due to the general shut-down of trade and the multiplication of tolls on the Solo river run by Chinese appointed by the central Javanese rulers, a situation which continued through the 1780s and 1790s (M1780 #65; M1787 #71–2; M1796 #138).

Lamongan

Estimated in 1796 at 1000 *cacah*, Lamongan had a delivery of Rd. 162.24 in *cacah* money, plus 250 *koyan* of rice (increased from 1802 by 15–20 *koyan*) and 3 *pikul* of cotton thread, for payment (M1780 #64; M1787 #70; M1791 #90; M1796 #137; M1801 #204). The Regent in 1787 was Tumenggung Jayadirja, an outsider from Japara, as was his predecessor. Van Overstraten comments that the Regency had suffered from the appointment of these foreign Regents who did not provide much supervision. In 1795 Jayadirja asked to be replaced because of his age and eye trouble and he was succeeded by a brother of the late First Regent of Surabaya, a "particularly capable and active Javan" with the title Tumenggung Candranegara. An indigo factory was set up at this time (M1796 #137).

Sidayu

Estimated in 1796 at 2500 *cacah* (M1796 #136), Sidayu was the most westerly Regency of the Eastern Salient, reserved for a son of the Panembahan of Madura by the 1743 contract, and administered under the Residency of Gresik. Its delivery was Rd. 325 as *cacah* money and 200 *koyan* of rice and 6 *pikul* of cotton thread for payment, raised to 220 *koyan* and 10 *pikul* in 1801. The Regent over the period 1780 through 1796 is named as Tumenggung Suradiningrat, described by van Overstraten as extravagant, wasteful, and "very much addicted to the Popes" (M1780 #62; M1787 #69; M1796 #136, M1801 #199).

The three Regencies above, Gresik, Lamongan and Sidayu, had all reached a halt in the extension of rice cultivation by the early nineteenth century, given that the remaining land was stony, infertile, or without adequate water.[40]

Eastern Salient Summary. In all, this area of c. 12733 sq. *palen*,[41] brought in for the Company 3040 Spanish dollars (f. 7752) 3215.25 *rijksdaalders* (f. 6173), 1208 -2/3 *koyan* of rice, 12.5 *pikul* of wax, 2 *pikul* of long pepper, 800 cans of petroleum, besides the profit on the rice, cotton thread, birds' nests and indigo purchased at minimal prices. Out of this, their officials and soldiers had to be paid. The flotilla of 18 *prau mayang* and 2 *pancalang* was provided by the Regents but its upkeep cost f. 13.664 for the whole coast, of which the Eastern Salient's share was f5466.

Madura

The eastern half of the island was ceded to the VOC by Pakubuwana I in 1705, and the remainder by Pakubuwana II in 1743, a cession that led to the revolt of Cakradiningrat IV, prince of Bangkalan.[42] The island was divided into Sumenep, Pamekasan, and Bangkalan. It was Company policy that Sumenep should be strong enough to counterbalance "Madura" (i.e. Bangkalan, to which area the term Madura is restricted in documents of this period), just as the Madurese princedoms as a whole were employed to counterbalance the Javanese ones. The Madurese rulers had an important role in providing military support for the Company, and under the succeeding colonial government this role was formalised in the creation in 1831 of the *barisan* corps.[43]

Madura was very different from Java in ecology and agriculture. It is notoriously dry and infertile and *sawah* were relatively unimportant. *Tegal* ricefields and maize-growing predominated. Madura was perpetually short of arable land and of rice[44] and the Madurese were more ready to emigrate from their island to the Eastern Salient, for example, than most Javanese were.

Sumenep

Sumenep's geographical remoteness allowed its ruler, Pangeran Natakusuma, said to have been of "common priestly origin", to "plot" with parties in Sulawesi, Borneo, and Bali to his advantage, and van den Burgh describes him as "bold on account of his riches" (M1780 #75). The former wealth of Sumenep's ruling class is still attested by the impressive architecture of the period, with its interesting admixture of Chinese and European influences, the former particularly evident in the mosque. Direct rule by the colonial government was finally introduced in 1883.

Traditional or modern?

Estimated in 1796 at 5000 *cacah* Sumenep's delivery was 80 *koyan* of green *kacang*,[45] 17,500 cans of coconut oil, and 25 *pikul* of cotton thread, free; 10 *pikul* of cotton thread, 30 *koyan* of green *kacang* and 3750 cans of coconut oil, for payment as required; and Rd. 2000 for the salt-making at Pingir Papas. In 1784 a tribute of Rd. 10,000 was added, but this was abolished in 1790 because of objections raised, on condition that the ruler pay 40,000 Rd. in 3–4 years, which he did by August 1794 (M1787 #84; M1791 #104; M1796 #148). In 1801 the *kacang* delivery was changed to a total of 80 *koyan* at Rd. 40 per *koyan* and provision was made for extra coconut oil and cotton to be bought in good years (M1801 #242).

From 1772 the prince of Sumenep had jurisdiction over a number of islands – Solombo, Kangean, Sapudi, Sapanjang, Rahas, Gili Ginting, Telangu and nearly twenty smaller ones – lying to the east, southeast and northeast, which he had received in exchange for Prabalingga, his reward for the part he had taken in the Balambangan campaign of 1767. He had to build and maintain a fortress there (M1787 #85–7). His possession of these islands was taken into account in the calculation of tax-farm payments, in 1792 12,180 *real*. Van Overstraten was of the opinion that it would not be advisable to lease these islands to a Chinese, as suggested by Greeve, believing that the Prince and, through him, the Company could derive considerably more income from these islands if they were more efficiently managed. The islands were visited by Makassans collecting *tripang* and because of their remoteness were an obvious rendezvous for "smugglers", the VOC term for those carrying on trade without Company permits. Further action was postponed until the arrival of peace (see M1796 #150). The Residents over this period were P.H. Schelkes, and J.M. van Bronckhorst (M1796 #151).

Pamekasan

This was estimated in 1796 at 600 *cacah*, [M1796 #147] but Hageman[46] gives what seems a much larger population [if we accept that the *cacah* is a unit of population[47]] i.e. 15,000 inhabitants, living in 150 villages, in a small area of territory that bisected the island from north to south. This region had belonged to Sumenep before its separation and the installation of its own Regent in 1745. The Regent from 1780 through 1796 is named as Raden Tumenggung Cakradiningrat, the sole surviving descendant of the old

Sumenep ruling line, and married to a Bangkalan princess, half-sister of the Panembahan. Direct rule by the colonial government was introduced in 1858.

Its annual delivery was 30 *koyan* of green *kacang*, 7500 cans of coconut oil and 12 *pikul* of cotton thread, free, and 2 *pikul* of cotton thread against payment. (M1780 #73; M1787 #83; M1791 #103; M1796 #147.)

Bangkalan

Bangkalan, or "Madura", as it was called, comprised the districts of Arosbaya, Baliga and Sampang. Though the prince of Bangkalan, Panembahan Adipati Cakradiningrat VII, had a close relationship with the Company, Bangkalan itself remained very much an uncharted *terra incognita* until well into the second half of the nineteenth century. Direct rule was introduced in 1885. Many soldiers from Bangkalan died in the Balambangan wars and others served in Makassar so that in 1780 the population had decreased (M1780 #69–70).

Bangkalan was estimated at 8000 *cacah* in 1796, and supplied annually 4000 Spanish dollars for the maritime tolls, 12000 cans of coconut oil and 60 *koyan* of green *kacang*, free (after 1801 at Rd. 40 per *koyan*), 2000 cans of coconut oil for 6 *stuivers*[48] the can, and 30 *pikul* of cotton thread for payment (an extra 8 *pikul* when conditions allowed being agreed upon in 1789). The prince of Bangkalan had also to maintain a fort with a garrison of 22 men and a few sailors and to pay for the upkeep of members of his family whose relationship with the Company had not stood the test of time and who were now in exile in Ceylon and Semarang. By 1796 he was seriously behind in his payments for these exiles, and van Overstraten arranged some remission. He had been severely criticised in 1787 for his patronage of Muslim "popes", especially a "fanatic" called Mahmud, removed in 1782 by Siberg. Siberg even recommended the prince's dismissal, but van Overstraten reiterates van den Burgh's assessment that he was a gentle good-natured man, friendly to Europeans if a little too weak for the tough Madurans, though he noted the influence of a new, Javanese, advisor who "cannot be watched too closely" (M1787 #75–82; M1791 #95–102; M1796 #140–6, M1801 #237). The European official in charge of Bangkalan was a Commander until van Overstraten recommended the installation of a Resident (Hendrik van Ligten).

Traditional or modern?

Bawean

This island of about 20,000 people (M1801 #188 8–10,000) was under its own head, sometimes bearing the title of Pangeran (prince), and sometimes of Tumenggung, a lower noble title with military connotations. In 1780 van den Burgh reports that this ruler connived at smuggling to Lasem and Tuban and himself sent ships clandestinely to Johore and Riau (M1780 #60). In 1782 the Company entered into an agreement with the then ruler for the suppression of "piracy and smuggling", and installed a military post (4 Europeans and 21 Indonesians) on the island. Administratively, Bawean was not under the authority of the Gezaghebber of the Eastern Salient at Surabaya, but under the Governor of the North-east Coast at Semarang. From 1787 Bawean delivered 2500 cans of coconut oil at 5 *stuivers*, and from 1790 3 *pikul* of cotton thread, for payment. However, cotton growing did not do well. The tax-farm amounted to 1300 Spanish dollars annually, since the island was the centre of considerable trade.

2. *The Rembang Office*

The annual deliveries were as follows:

Rembang

This was estimated in 1796 at 650 *cacah*. The Regent in 1780 was Secadiwirya and the Resident W. A. Palm; the Regent from 1787 through 1796 was Ingabei Sumadipura; the Resident in 1787 was A. Hartsinck, and in 1796 G. van Massari. The delivery in 1787 was Rd. 86.25 in capitation tax and 2 *pikul* of cotton thread for payment; in 1796 it was Rd. 135 and 5 *pikul* of cotton. At times the Resident also apparently supplied 4 *pikul* of cotton (M1780 #54; M1787 #59; M1791 #81; M1796 #129). Rembang had a small fort and also a shipyard – it had an easy roads and a fine river – but as at Joana the Company had virtually stopped commissioning ships there in the 1790s and in 1801 it is reported that the reduction in shipbuilding, the greatest source of income for the people, had resulted in further depopulation (M1801 #169). There was a separate administration for the forest districts (*blandong*) of Trembulan, Waru, Kasirman and Mondoteko, which were not administered by the Regents but by four *mantri* or "boschloerahs",[49] as they are called in the Dutch sources, appointed by the Governor. The *blandongs* supplied 2000 logs annually for the usual payment and extra wood for shipbuilding at 50% more than the normal price. From 1780, when heavy logging had left little of the Rembang forests, this wood actually came from Blora (which was itself subsequently largely deforested by 1796), in the Sunan's territory, or from Lasem and Tuban. In 1796 van Overstraten approved higher rates of payment because the wood had to be brought from so far away (M1780 #56; M1787 #60–1; M1791 #82; M1796 #130). In 1799 the contingent had to be reduced from 2000 to 1500 logs since no replanting had been carried out. Van Reede tot de Parkeler suggested that the *mantri* in charge of the forests be paid a salary to attach them more strongly to the Company's interests (M1801 #170).

Palo and Pajangkungan

These two areas were each under a separate head until 1790, Palo supplying one *pikul* of cotton thread and Pajangkungan 2 *pikul* of cotton thread and Rd. 48.75 in capitation tax (M1787 #57–8). A general flight of population led to the impoverishment of Palo and Pajangkungan, which were for this reason incorporated into Rembang and their contingent abolished (M1796 #128).

Lasem

Estimated in 1796 at 2000 *cacah*, Lasem had to deliver 6 *pikul* of cotton thread and 600 logs to Rembang, for payment, plus one *pancalang* of 11–12 fathoms length with a Dutch rudder, and Rd. 192.5 in capitation tax. Here again, van Overstraten introduced an indigo factory. The Regent over the period 1774 to 1796 is named as Tumenggung Suradipura, a son-in-law of the Regent of Demak (M1780 #58; M1787 #63; M1791 #85; M1796 #132).

Tuban

Estimated in 1796 at 3000 *cacah*, Tuban had to deliver 1000 logs, 60 *koyan* of rice and 6 *pikul* of cotton thread for payment, plus Rd. 325 in capitation tax. Van Overstraten introduced an indigo factory but in 1801 it was still not in production. In 1801 the logging was stopped and an extra 70 *koyan* of rice required in substitution. The Regent over the period 1773 to the end of the century was

Traditional or modern?

Tumenggung Purbanagara, another son-in-law of the Regent of Demak (M1787 #59; M1787 #64; M1791 86; M1796 #133; M1801 #187).

Rembang summary. One vessel of about 70 feet length, free, and Rd. 737.25 (f. 1415.52), plus the profit on the logs, rice, cotton thread etc. purchased at minimal prices made up the annual profit from this region of c. 1200 sq. *palen*.

3. The Japara Office

The contingents were as follows:

Japara

Estimated at 5000 *cacah* in 1796 (M1796 #122), Japara had two Regents (Tumenggungs Citrasuma and Reksapraja in 1780 and 1787: M1780 #46). It supplied 120 *koyan* of rice, 20 *pikul* of cotton thread (in 1780 and 1801 a further 12 *pikul* from the Resident is added), at least 20 *pikul* of indigo, and 2000 logs, all at minimal prices, plus Rd. 812.5 in capitation tax. The quota of logs was reduced by 500 in October 1794 due to the bad state of the forests, a reduction continued in 1798 for a further 5 years (M1787 # 50; M1791 #74; M1796 #122; M1801 #154). In 1801 it was noted that the area, being mountainous, did not have enough rice fields to feed its inhabitants in normal times, relying on imports from Grobogan, and had recently been affected by bad harvests which slowed down deliveries.

The city of Japara had long been a commercial centre for both the Dutch and the English. It had a fort, still occupied by a couple of dozen soldiers but almost derelict at the end of the eighteenth century, and a water-driven sawmill which converted the logs of Japara and Kudus into planks. This saw-mill belonged to the Resident, who had to provide Batavia with an annual shipment of 40–50,000 planks, plus 12 *pikul* of cotton thread. Dirk van Hogendorp held this position from 1792 until his appointment as Gezaghebber of the Eastern Salient in 1794.

Kudus

A "small but fruitful" Regency (M1780 #47) estimated at 2000 *cacah* in 1796, Kudus supplied 500 logs, 12 *pikul* of cotton thread and about 10 *pikul* of indigo at low prices, plus Rd. 325 in capitation tax. The Regent from 1778 through 1796 was Raden Tumenggung Suradiningrat, a Madurese by birth and with family connections to the Sunan (M1780 #46; M1787 #51; M1796 #123). He is described as diligent and suitable, with the result that Kudus was better populated than Japara.

Pati

Estimated at 300 *cacah* in 1796, Pati was supposed to supply 900 logs, 400 *koyan* of rice, and 18 *pikul* of indigo (which was however seldom delivered) for low prices, plus Rd. 393.25 in capitation tax and Rd. 325 in Kalang money. Due to "continual meagre harvests", however, the full contingent of rice had not been delivered for the last 10 years of the century (M1801 #157). Pati had two Regents (Raden Tumenggungs Aria Megatsari and Mangkukusuma in 1780, the latter being a son of the Regent of Demak, Suradiningrat, and married to a daughter of Pangeran Mangkunagara; and Raden Tumenggung Aria Natapraja and Mangkukusuma in 1787: the first was replaced by Tumenggung Megatsari, Mangkukusuma's father, by 1791, M1780 #48; M1787 #52; M1791 #76; M1796 #124).

Glonggong (administered under Pati)

This was under a Kalang or forest headman (*bosch hoofd*). The delivery consisted of 15 *koyan* of rice, Rd. 195 plus a further Rd. 50 for two villages previously under Japara (M1787 #52; M1796 #125).

Cengkalsewu

This was a small poorly populated area – an estimated 500 *cacah* in 1796 – that delivered 75 *koyan* of rice, 2 *pikul* of cotton thread, and Rd. 31.25 in capitation tax. The Regent from 1780 through 1796 is named as Ingabei Panji Singasari, son of the first Regent of Demak and brother of the second Regent of Pati. The area is described in the Governor's reports as in the first line of attacks by "evil rabble": it was completely plundered three or four times in van den Burgh's period of office and the situation does not seem to have improved through the 1780s and 1790s (M1780 349; M1787 #53; M1791 #77). In 1796 van Overstraten reported that the region was not really capable of supplying 74 *koyan* of rice annually, and it would be better to introduce a delivery of castor oil to compensate the Company for the loss of the rice. Since, however, times were difficult, he recommended that the quota should remain as it was until the arrival of peace (M1796 #126), a sentiment echoed in 1801 by van Reede tot de Parkeler, who attributed the low population to the proximity of the Vorstenlanden, which attracted population away from the area (M1801 #159).

Juwana

Estimated at 1000 *cacah* in 1796, Juwana had to supply a delivery of 300 logs, 140 *koyan* of rice and 4 *pikul* of cotton thread, at low prices, plus Rd. 137.5 in capitation tax. The Regent was Tumenggung Sumawikrama in 1787; he was deposed in 1792 for fathering a child on his sister and replaced by Raden Tirtakusuma. The Resident (M.L. Gaaswijck in 1787; followed by B.J. van Nieuwkerken alias Nijvenheim and P.H. Schelkes) had to deliver a minimum of 4 *pikul* of cotton thread and grew coffee, pepper and indigo. Juwana had a fort that also served as a warehouse, and, after 1778, a shipyard as big as that at Rembang, though the Company was having very few ships built by the 1790s. The harbour was good and the river broad and deep, which attracted small trade from the uplands. Due to bad harvest and poor supervision Juwana had deteriorated for some years in the first half of the 1790s but by 1796 it was recovering rapidly. (M1787 #54–56; M1791 #78; M1796 #127). In 1801, however, it was behind in its rice contingent (M1801 #162).

Japara summary. This region of c.1400 sq. *palen* paid Rd. 2074.75 (f4149.50) in tax, plus the profit on the products delivered at a low price.

4. The Semarang Head Office

Semarang

Semarang itself had few ricefields and no great teak woods, and was estimated in 1796 at 2950 *cacah*. The Regents generally bore the title of Adipati Suradimanggala: a young Regent succeeded his uncle in 1791 (M1791 #68). They delivered annually 224 logs, 40 *koyan* of rice and 12 *pikul* of cotton thread, at low prices (M1787 #43). For his rights to the districts of Torbaya, Gumelo, Kaligawe, Grogol, Tanjung Item, Ambarawa and Urut Dalem he paid the rather small sum of Rd. 1000 Kalang money annually, a sum that was considered too low but which was apparently difficult to increase. Van Overstraten introduced pepper and cardamom, and set up an indigo factory (M1796 #118). He remarks that Semarang was unable to grow enough rice to feed its population and had to import it from Demak. In 1801 when Governor van Reede tot de Parkeler felt that the pepper, cardamom and indigo cultivation constituted a further burden on a Regent with many problems (including an inefficient administration) and few resources, the deliveries of indigo and logs were abolished (M1801 #146).

The city of Semarang was a key military centre, with its stores and barracks, cavalry (about 50 men under 3 officers), infantry (480 men under 10 officers), the Württemberger regiment of nearly 600 men (from 1792), the militia (*krijgsmacht*) of 204 cavalry and 1413 infantry, and fleet of 8 vessels. Though the number of Company officials was not more than a dozen, including the Governor of the North-east coast, Semarang had some of the institutions and amenities of Batavia: a Protestant ministry, a police council, a council of justice and *landraad* (court for natives), institutions for the protection of the poor and orphans, a *proveniershuis*[50] for invalided military personnel, and a marine training school. The city itself was irregularly laid out and crowded, and in-migration was discouraged, especially of foreign Asians whose trade, it was feared, led to the export of capital. In Semarang the Dutch once again followed the policy of separating the different ethnic groups into their own kampungs, and appointing a head for each of them. Van Overstraten laid down that the son of a Malay or Buginese must follow his father's nationality, and allotted a piece of land between Semarang and Kaligawe to the Peranakan Chinese, who till then had lived scattered throughout the city (M1796 #115). A similar development had taken place earlier in Batavia, with dispersed Chinese settlement being replaced with a designated Chinese area after the uprising and massacre of Chinese in 1740. There had been a Chinese arak distillery in Semarang, but it was closed down before 1780 to protect the Batavian production. Governors van den Burgh and van Reede tot de Parkeler proposed over the period 1780 to 1799 that the Chinese be allowed to operate it again but this request was refused.[51] The Governors pointed out the loss of income to the municipality and the fact that arak was considered indispensable by the common Europeans and had

Traditional or modern?

become scarce and unprecedently costly during the English blockade of Batavia (M1780 #37–40; M1796 #116; M1801 #143–4). The city's population continued to increase rapidly, causing a housing shortage in the last two decades of the century and pressure on food supplies, nine-tenths of which were imported from Demak. There was a huge fire in the Malay-Makassarese kampong in 1800 which convinced people of the need to construct stone houses. By this time, however, there were very few prosperous citizens, since trade had been destroyed by the war and by the introduction of restrictions in 1778 which had badly affected the trade of Malays and Makassarese with Semarang. The drying-out of the river bank had also had a deleterious effect on small-scale local trade (M1780 #38–40; M1801 #139).

Demak

This Regency was estimated at 6000 *cacah* in 1796 (M1796 #119). The two regents (Adipati Suradiningrat and Tumenggung Yudanagara in 1787; Raden Tumenggung Prawiradiningrat and Wiryadiningrat in 1796) had to deliver a yearly quota of 1000 logs, 1000 *koyan* of rice and 4 *pikul* of cotton thread for low prices. A watch was kept on the estuary to ensure that the Chinese exported no rice or logs before this quota was filled. The capitation tax was Rd. 475. The area was famous for its fertile *sawah*, but also for vagabonds, robbers, and pirate bands of up to 200 men. It bordered on Grobogan and other lands of the central Javanese princes where lawless elements hung out in the mountains and woods (M1780 #44; M1787 #47–8; M1801 #149). In Demak too van Overstraten began indigo-making, having each Regent set up a factory, but these were abandoned in 1798 and the deliveries of cotton thread raised by 5 *pikul* for each Regent (M1796 #120; M1801 #152).

Adilangu

This small area was the hereditary fief of the priest-princes who bore the title Pangeran Wijil or Sunan Kadilangu and were also related to the famous rebel Pangeran Rangga The incumbent in 1780 was also personal physician to the Sunan (M1780 #45). From 1775 Adilangu supplied 6 *koyan* of rice for a small payment (M1787 #49; M1787 #73; M1796 #121).

Kendal

Estimated in 1796 at 1500 *cacah*, Kendal had to deliver to Semarang 336 logs, 100 *koyan* of rice and 2 *pikul* of cotton thread, plus a capitation tax of Rd. 205 and Kalang money of Rd. 300 (M1780 #35). In 1801 a delivery of 336 logs from the Kaliwungu forests was also required (M1801 #132). Kendal was another very fertile area. Indigo making was introduced c. 1795 by van Overstraten but initial results were not very good and van Overstraten did not expect an annual production of more than 4 to 5 *pikul*; production in 1797 actually amounted to 831 lbs., but sank to 162 lbs. in 1800 (M1801 #132). The Regent over the period 1787 to 1796 was Tumenggung Sumanagara. (M1787 #36; M1796 110).

Kaliwungu

This was an area where no more rice was grown than was sufficient for local consumption. Its annual delivery consisted of 440 logs and 16 *pikul* of cotton thread, for a small payment, and Rd. 218.75 in capitation tax. Indigo making was introduced c. 1795. The Regent in 1787 was Tumenggung Sumadiwirya, but he was subsequently deported for murder of the inhabitants. His successor, Raden Tumenggung Natadiningrat, was also found unsuitable, and replaced by Sumadiwirya's younger brother, with the title Mas Tumenggung Adinagara (M1787 #37; M1796 #112).

Semarang summary. This region of 2300 sq. *palen* yielded Rd. 2198.75 (f. 4397.60) annually in capitation tax, plus the profit on products delivered and sold.

5. *The Pekalongan Office*

The annual deliveries were as follows:

Batang

Estimated in 1796 at 2000 *cacah* (M1796 #108), Batang is described in 1780 as ruined by war, death and two bad Regents, necessitating a reduction of its rice contingent to the tune of 40–50 *koyan* out of 125, which van den Burgh recommended should be continued for at least 12 years and which was confirmed later. In addition to the aftermath of war, the area, though fertile, had a terrain which was mostly woods and mountains, and made rice growing difficult. Even in the valleys floods could wash away the young rice and a prolonged drought often followed the flood, so the area was a poor one. To compensate for the loss of rice production, Siberg recommended the introduction of indigo in 1787, leading to an annual delivery of between 6 and 10 *pikul*, along with 2 *pikul* of cotton thread at low prices, and Rd. 333.8 in capitation tax (M1789 #34; M1787 #35). Batang had supplied 320 logs from the forests of Weliri until the woods of the area became exhausted, and logging was stopped for 10 years in 1780 and in 1790 for 15 years. The forests were surveyed again in 1801 when it was found that it was still not possible to resume logging (M1801 #131). At this time 100 *cacah* were transferred from Pekalongan to Batang to try to redress the depopulation and decay of the latter. As a result of this transfer Batang's contingent was raised to Rd. 473.8 in capitation tax, 125 *koyan* of rice, 2–60/125 *pikul* of cotton thread, 390 logs and 11 *pikul* of indigo. The Regent over the period 1787 to 1796 was Tumenggung Wiryanagara; he was accused by the retiring Governor Johan Fredrik van Reede tot de Parkeler of "bad management" (M1801 #129).

Pekalongan

Pekalongan was the largest Regency west of Semarang, a heavily populated area (estimated at 7000 *cacah*: M1780 #33; M1796 #106) sometimes under one and sometimes under two Regents. There was a small fort with 16 soldiers. Its deliveries were 350 *koyan* of rice, 6 *pikul* of indigo, 4 *pikul* of cotton thread from the Regent and 4 from the Resident, all at low prices, and 480 logs (subsequently abolished until 1805 because of over-logging) plus Rd. 1225 in capitation tax and Rd. 500 in Kalang money until 1800 when 1000 *cacah* was separated off and transferred to Batang. The amounts required from Pekalongan were then reduced to 300 *koyan* of rice, 3 – 65/125 *pikul* of cotton thread, 5 *pikul* of indigo, 410 logs when logging should resume, 1085 rd. capitation tax and Rd. 500 Kalang money, plus 5 *baturs* (coolies) and a horse for delivering letters. Pekalongan had several interesting features. Under Mataram the Jayaningrat (later Jayadiningrat) Regent family, who were Chinese traders in origin, had become established there. Jayaningrat I was an ambitious man who became the head of all the Regents of the western *pasisir*, and also took part in political intrigue at the Mataram court. His son Jayaningrat II was a son-in-law of the Patih, Danureja.[52] Later Regents of Pekalongan with the title Jayaningrat, however, were descended in the male line from a son of Adipati Natakusuma, a high official at the Sunan's court and from the earlier *peranakan* Chinese Regents through the female line.[53] In 1779 another Regent of Pekalongan, Sumanegara, who was from Semarang and had previously risked his life in the Company's service when taking the field against the rabble who had over-run most of Demak, again showed himself a man of action by having the other Regent of Pekalongan murdered. He was subsequently condemned by the Semarang Council of Justice to be tethered to a stake and burnt by "small fire" until dead, a sentence carried out in 1790, when his whole family were exiled to Balambangan (M1780 #33; M 1787 #34). In 1796 the Regent Raden Adipati Jayadiningrat was criticised for being very "addicted to popes" (M1796 #106), "popes" and "priests" being the pejorative terms used in Dutch documents to refer to Muslim scholars and teachers. The Resident of Pekalongan from 1794 was Frederik Jacob Rothenbuhler, who was previously Resident of Tegal (1785–7) and Batang before being appointed Gezaghebber of the Eastern Salient, and has left much written material on the north coast. His account of Pekalongan in 1798 will be used in Chapter 4.

Wiradesa

This Regency was estimated in 1796 at 1500 *cacah*. Deliveries were 100 *koyan* of rice, 12 *pikul* of indigo (seldom delivered) and 2 *pikul* of cotton thread at low prices, plus Rd. 278.75 as capitation tax. The Regent in 1780 and 1787 was Tumenggung Jayadiwirya and in 1796 Tumenggung Jayengrana (M1780 #32; M1787 #33; M1796 #105).

Ulujami

A small densely populated (no *cacah* figure is given) and fertile area, Ulujami was leased to the Captain of the Chinese at Semarang, Tan Lekko, in 1771 for his lifetime at the price of Rd. 3750, plus 300 *koyan* of rice at Rd. 15 and 100 more at Rd. 20 when required. The cash component was raised to Rd. 5000 for his successor Tan Jok. Van den Burgh and Siberg comment that if Ulujami were under a Regent it would not produce much because of its size, which was smaller than Wiradesa, whereas leased to a Chinese it now contributed as much as one of the largest Regencies (M1780 #31; M1787 #32). Van Overstraten comments that the productivity of the area is in great part due to the fair treatment enjoyed by the common people and their exemption from corvée service. Though fertile, the area was subject to floods and should, therefore, be in the hands of someone who could always supply another lot of seed padi, which a well-to-do Chinese was much better able to do this than a Javanese (M1796 #104). This alerts us to one reason for the superior economic performance of the Chinese, the evident fact that they were better capitalised, with larger resources in cash as opposed to produce.

At another juncture (M1787 #110) Siberg comments on the Regents' tendency to lease areas to Chinese and the subsequent increase in Chinese settlement, which he was attempting to stop by telling the Regents that if they worked harder they could enjoy the same profits as were then enjoyed by the Chinese. The Regents, however, remained convinced that they derived more money from leasing to the Chinese than they could otherwise extract from their lands (M1787 #110).

Pekalongan summary. Pekalongan paid Rd. 7336.75 (c. f. 14672) plus the profit on products delivered, and the tax-farms, from an area of 4–500 sq. *palen*.

6. The Tegal Office

Pamalang

This was a fertile Regency suited to rice but sparsely populated (estimated at 2000 *cacah* in 1796: M1796 #101) that delivered 250 *koyan* of rice, 7 *pikul* of indigo, and 6 *pikul* of cotton thread, for a small payment, plus Rd. 308.36 in capitation tax. The young Regent, Tumenggung Jayanegara, who succeeded his father in 1789 at the age of 13, was noted as remiss in the supply of these requisitions. Logging had been carried out for 35 years until it was stopped in 1777, apparently because the Company did not need light wood. Siberg recommended the resumption of logging in 1787 (M1780 #30; M1787 #31), a proposal that was opposed by the Resident. It had been resumed at an annual quota of 500 teak logs by 1791 (M1791 #56), which led to a drop in population due to the heaviness of the work and transportation. In 1796 an investigation into the state of the forests was recommended (M1796 #102) and in 1801–2 logging was stopped because Pamalang was so "decayed and depopulated" (M1801 #123).

Tegal

The population of this Regency was estimated in 1796 at 4800 *cacah* (M1796 #99). Its three Regents (from 1782: they had 1800, 1500 and 1500 *cacah* respectively) delivered annually 700 *koyan* of rice and 13 *pikul* of cotton thread for a small payment, plus Rd. 771.42 in *cacahgeld* (*cacah* money, a poll tax, also called *grabag*, paid by some or all households, with local variations). Tegal had a small fort, with 18 soldiers. The Residents oversaw the making of indigo, the cultivation of coffee and pepper, the delivery of cotton thread, and the local trade with neighbouring Banyumas, Dayeuhluhur, Panjulang etc., which supplied cardamom, long pepper and cubeb.[54] The 1780 and 1787 reports complain that this trade was not flourishing (M1780 #29; M1787 #30). The reports of 1780 –1796 also describe the career of the Regent of Tegal Raden Tumenggung Panji Cakranagara, who after his pilgrimage to Mecca changed his name to Raden Haji "Sigaar", asked permission to engage in private trade and became "too wild". He subsequently fled to Bali where he was protected by the Gusti of Karangasem until the latter's death in 1789, when he was handed over to the Company and exiled to the Cape of Good Hope (M1791 #125–7; M1796 #170). Trade is described in 1796 as "all but destroyed" by the wars with the French and then the English; and in 1801 as at a total standstill (M1801 #120). J.L. Umbgrove was Resident in 1787 and Th. van Teylingen in 1796.

Brebes

This is the first area – moving from east to west – with a Sundanese population. Brebes was scantily populated, estimated at 1500 *cacah* in 1796 (M1796 #98). Annual delivery was 500 logs, 50 *koyan* of rice, 5 *pikul* of indigo and 5 *pikul* of cotton thread at low prices, plus Rd. 243.36 as capitation tax. The Regent over period 1787 to 1796 was Puspanegara. (M1780 #28; M1787 #29; M1791 #52; M1796 #98). In 1801 Brebes is noted as carrying a debt of Rd. 2500 (M1801 #119).

Traditional or modern?

Tegal summary. The annual contribution of this area of c. 1900 sq. *palen* was Rd. 1324 (f. 2648) plus the profits on products delivered, and some taxes on the small amount of trade that existed.

II. WEST JAVA: THE CIREBON AND BATAVIA OFFICES[55]

1. The Cirebon office

Cirebon Residency (with an area c. 4800 sq. *palen*) comprised the small semi-independent principality of Gebang, along the Losari river; Indramayu, Galuh, Limbangan and Sukapura, under Regents; and Segala erang and Cininga, which the Sultan Anom, one of the two main Cirebon Sultans, leased to the Company in 1799 for 20 years. The population – all Sundanese except for some Javanese in Indramayu – was estimated at 305,600 in 1705 but in 1754, 1778 and 1795 at only 90,000. Cirebon was a region where European and Chinese influence had both been heavy for over a century. By the middle of the eighteenth century, Chinese had leased much of the land in the interior from the rulers and this was a major factor in the long series of uprisings from 1798–1819. For VOC officials, Cirebon was a profitable and coveted post – the "nose of the salmon", as it was called.

According to Umbgrove's 1797 report,[56] the total contingent of indigo and cotton thread was 68 *pikul* and 163 *pikul* respectively, paid for at the rate of 78–1/8 or Rd. 62.5 per *pikul* for the two qualities of indigo, and between 18.1 and Rd. 41.1 per *pikul* for the four qualities of cotton. In fact, however, this total was more of an ambition than anything else: the two Sultans, for instance, actually supplied scarcely half of their quota of 11.25 *pikul* each of first-class indigo. The other products supplied were as follows:

Coffee: as much as could be grown at Rd. 4.5 per *pikul* up to 120,000 *pikul* with an increment of Rd. .5 per *pikul* above that amount. Coffee grew very well in the Mt. Talaga area, which was governed by four princes subordinate to the Kasepuhan *kraton* (one of the two main Cirebon princely houses). They supplied three quarters of the coffee from this area and the local Chinese the remaining quarter.

Pepper: an insignificant quantity at Rd. 6 per pikul.

Cardamom: formerly paid at f. 50 per 100 lb, price subsequently reduced to Rd. 16 per *pikul*, which led to a drop in supply.

Rice: c.100 *koyan* at Rd. 16 per *koyan* of 3400 lb as well as the straw sacks at f. 500 the hundred *pees* ("twists"); and 500 *koyan* at Rd. 25 per *koyan* of which Rd. 2.5 was accounted as shipping losses (a small quantity, not more than 16–25 *koyan*, from Gebang at Rd. 16 per *koyan*). The rice of Mt. Talaga was mainly in Chinese hands.

Sugar: 400 *pikul*; changed on 2 June to 5000 *pikul* powder sugar (Umbgrove report illegible).

Kacang: Cirebon could seldom deliver as much as was required, and it seems that the delivery was abolished and the field left to private trade.

Pinang and salt: these were no longer required in Umbgrove's time.

Umbgrove also laments the effects of Chinese penetration. He accuses them of cruel and inhuman treatment of the Javanese of the mountains and distant areas and claims that they had used "fire and sword" to deliver their rice contingent before this was abolished. The Chinese were also involved in the making of *picis*, ran a gambling-house at Indramayu, and ran the opium trade, which another late eighteenth century report describes as a growing cancer for the impoverished cultivators of the region, draining more money than all the sale of exports could provide.[57]

2. The Batavia Office

This office had jurisdiction over the city itself, over the so-called *ommelanden* (Batavian Environs) and the Preanger (Priangan) lands.

Priangan

In February 1677 the eastward limit of the Company's jurisdiction was set at the river Krawang; but in October of that year Amangkurat I, in recognition of the Company's military help in his accession to the throne, agreed to extend the boundary to the Panarukan river, a request refused on the earlier occasion. This was confirmed by treaty with Pakubuwana I in 1705. This area included the districts Bandung, Batulayang, Parakan-muncang, Sumedang, Cianjur, Jampang-ilir and Jampang-ulu, Ciblagong, Cikalong, Cilingsi, Bogor, Wanayasa, Adiarsa, Pagaden, Ciasem, Pamanukan, and Krawang, apart from Cirebon itself and the *ommelanden* (Environs) of Batavia. In 1706 they were put under the authority of a Pangeran Aria of Cirebon, in recognition of Cirebon's former jurisdiction over Bandung, Parakan-muncang, Sumedang, Ciasem, Pamanukan and Pagaden. Later they were withdrawn from any Cirebon authority and assigned to Batavia, under the name of the "Batavian Preanger Regencies" (in contradistinction to Galuh, Limbangan, and Sukapura, the Cirebon Preanger).

The whole of Priangan was administered by a single European official, whose title was *Gekommitteerde tot en over de zaken van den inlander* (Delegate for Native Affairs), of whom more will be said in the following chapter. There was otherwise virtually no European presence here, apart from the Commandant of Fort Philippina at Bogor, and half a dozen planters at Bogor, Cianjur, and Cipanas.

The Production of Priangan crops

Prices: Pepper brought Rd. 8 per 125 lb; indigo 30 *stuivers* of 4 *duits* per lb for first quality, and 24 for second quality, with poorer qualities provided free; cotton thread Rd. 35 per *pikul* of 125 lb for first quality, Rd. 24 for second quality, Rd. 18 for third and Rd. 10 for fourth (sale prices in the Netherlands were 3–400% higher); cardamom Rd. 26.2 per *pikul* of 132 lb before 1789 after which the price was raised to Rd. 31.12, but reduced to Rd. 16 in 1793; and curcuma (turmeric) Rd. 5 per 150 lb. The products were paid for by advances in cash or goods (opium, textiles, etc.), transmitted to the producers through the Regents. Transport of crops to the Company's warehouses was at the cost of the producers. The advances paid out, at interest, by the *Gekommitteerde tot en over de zaken van den inlander* generally amounted to between Rd. 200–250,000, but fell considerably below that figure in the 1790s. In 1793 the total amount paid by the Company for 67,237 *pikul* (of 148 lb) of coffee was Rd. 403,434, which included payments to officials and Rd. 117,169 to the Regents. In fact by this time the Regents were deeply in debt to the Company: a debt which had risen from Rd. 140,000 in 1753 to Rd. 128,890 for the four districts of Sumedang, Krawang, Adiarsa and Pamanukan alone in 1793. The Regents had many other expenses: provision of horses, maintenance of warehouses, roads and canals,

The Cancer Within

douceurs, rents, annual homage payments, etc. etc. Finally, the common man: he received about Rd. 2–2.5 per *pikul* of coffee beans, i.e. an average of 240 *duits* per 148 lb, delivered to a warehouse which might be 15 *palen* distant. These 240 *duits* were however generally in goods of Dutch manufacture, consisting of textiles and peddlers' goods, despite prohibitions, at least on paper, of this practice. Nederburgh raised the price to 285 *duit* per lb.[58]

The situation in 1794–5 was as follows: statistics for this area exhibit more detail, reflecting the longer history of VOC penetration under the "Priangan System" (*Preanger stelsel*).

Ciasem

This comprised 64 villages inhabited by 3040 people, who from 270,784 coffee trees produced in 1793 376 *pikul* and in 1795 252 *pikul* of coffee beans at Rd. 6 or together Rd. 2259 gross and Rd. 704 net, plus half a *pikul* of cotton thread. 600 coconut palms and 2000 pepper plants were said to be planted here.

Pamanukan and Pagaden

These two districts were under one Regent, and together comprised 66 villages with 4951 people. They produced 511 *pikul* of coffee in 1793, and 466 *pikul* in 1796, from 238,645 coffee trees. They also produced 2 *pikul* of cotton thread. There were an estimated 8–900 coconut palms and 5000 pepper plants.

Adiarsa

This district had 54 villages, and a population of 1280. 92,500 coffee trees produced 130 *pikul* coffee in 1793 and 138 *pikul* in 1795. The district also produced half a *pikul* of cotton thread.

Krawang

This district was under one Regent with Wanayasa. It comprised 199 villages, with a population of 16,048. 1,140,500 coffee trees produced 1727 *pikul* of coffee in 1793 and 1590 *pikul* in 1795. Coconut palms were estimated at 4900, pepper plants at 61,500, and buffaloes at 719.

Traditional or modern?

Summary of the above 4 districts. This area of 2323 sq. *palen* had 383 villages with 25,319 inhabitants. Its 1,679,420 coffee trees produced 2744 *pikul* of coffee in 1793 and 2446 *pikul* in 1795 and it also supplied 2.5 *pikul* of cotton thread. There were 2100 coconut palms, 68,500 pepper plants and 744 buffaloes.

Parakan-muncang

This district comprised 767 villages and 42,926 people. It had 5,530,000 coffee trees which produced 7064 *pikul* of coffee in 1793 and 2446 *pikul* in 1795, as well as 34.5 *pikul* of cotton thread and 14.75 *pikul* of indigo. The Regency had an estimated 15,300 coconut palms, 24,000 cardamom plants and 89,000 pepper plants, 6160 buffaloes and 960 oxen. There were also 390 "priests".

Batu-layang

This was a district of 318 villages and 1509 people. 1,692,000 coffee trees produced 3685 *pikul* of coffee in 1793 and 3700 *pikul* in 1795. There were an estimated 1300 coconut palms, 1600 buffaloes and 360 oxen.

Sumedang

This was a district of 402 villages and 18,066 inhabitants. 1,240,000 coffee trees produced 5300 *pikul* of coffee (at 148 lb each) in 1793 and 5538 *pikul* in 1795; besides 30 *pikul* of cotton thread and 7 *pikul* of indigo. There were an estimated 6,300 coconut palms, 42,000 cardamom plants and 66,000 pepper plants, 6690 buffaloes, 580 oxen and 960 horses.

Bandung

This was a district of 646 villages and 34,400 people. 4,462,000 coffee trees produced 10,294 *pikul* of coffee in 1793 and 10,618 *pikul* in 1795; besides 23 *pikul* of cotton thread, 5 *pikul* of indigo and 620 *pikul* of turmeric. There were an estimated 6014 coconut palms, 25,000 pepper plants, 4240 buffaloes and 250 oxen.

Cianjur

With Jampang Ilir and Jampang Ulu Cianjur made up a Regency of 1975 villages and 44,721 people. There were 7,402,000 coffee trees, 43,000 coconut palms, 4000 buffaloes, 500 carts and 50 oxen. Coffee production was accounted together with Bogor's: 29,960 *pikul* in 1789, 34,188 *pikul* in 1790, 45,220 *pikul* in 1792, 38,150 *pikul* in 1793, and 34,799 *pikul* in 1795; besides 15.2 *pikul* of cardamom.

Summary of the above 5 districts. An area of c. 8768 sq. *palen*, populated in 1795 by 141,612 people in 4108 villages, produced in 1795 67,970 *pikul* of coffee (64,493 in 1793), 89 *pikul* of cotton thread, 27 *pikul* of indigo, 620 *pikul* of turmeric and 17.2 *pikul* of cardamom.

Bogor (Buitenzorg)

Boomgaard[59] comments that Buitenzorg was in the unique position of being both a private estate and a Regency. Before 1750 it was almost empty because of the many wars that had been fought in the area. But after it was given to the Governor-General as a private estate,[60] it quickly became populated. As the Governor-General could not administer the estate himself he rented it out to the Regent of Kampung Baru. Later on Buitenzorg and Kampung Baru were more or less merged into one Regency, with the leaseholder as Regent. This Regent, like most in Priangan, was heavily indebted to the Company because the expenses incurred in coffee cultivation were greater than the monetary profits. A large part of his income consisted of the *cuke*, one-tenth of the rice produced by his subjects, and the rice from his own "crown lands", concentrated around the capital. His domain lands were tilled by subjects exempted from coffee cultivation duties. He was also entitled to a percentage of all "religious" taxes: *jakat*, *pitrah*, and marriage fees. There was not always a clear-cut division between the duties of the secular and religious officials. Muslim dignitaries were employed as vaccinators against small-pox [a rather swift application in the Indies of a new European discovery, as in Gresik – see ch. 3, p. 169 above] and overseers of irrigation works, etc. They came from the same background as the secular officials. Nor was there a sharp line between aristocrats in the lower echelons and those who were eligible for the position of Regent, as would increasingly be the case later in the nineteenth century.

Traditional or modern?

Buitenzorg was not as commercialized as the Batavian Environs, and the only cash crop grown was coffee, cultivated with corvée labour as in the Priangan but also sometimes as a free peasant crop – apparently a sound commercial proposition, because it attracted wage labourers from as far as the central Javanese Principalities. Transport of coffee from the central warehouse in the town of Buitenzorg to Batavia was undertaken by a class of independent cart-drivers and small Javanese entrepreneurs. In the capital, the market was farmed out to a Chinese, always called the Potia, who monopolized the trade in opium, salt, and palm-sugar, and who earned an additional income from gambling and cock-fighting. The rent he paid for one year (1799) was Rd. 10,000 silver. Like the *warungs* in the Batavian Environs, the pasar attracted all sorts of criminals.

According to Hageman,[61] the statistics for Bogor were as follows: it had a population of 19,854 people in 91 villages, within an area of c. 1940 sq. *palen*. There were 1,306,000 coffee trees, 10,400 coconut palms, 30,000 cardamom plants, 2300 buffaloes and 450 carts. The Regent of Bogor supplied to the Company all the coffee grown in the Regency: in 1793 this was 3843 *pikul* from the villagers and 1758 *pikul* from coffee plantations; the price was Rd. 6 (note that in 1711 it had been Rd. 20) per pikul of 148 lb, but the costs of production were high and it was estimated that his profit was only Rd. 1 and 36 *stuivers* per *pikul*.

The Jakatra Lands

These lands formed a strip running between the north and south coast and bounded by Banten on the west and Cirebon on the east: J.P. Coen proclaimed that they had been conquered by the Company on the morning of 30 May 1619. This area included Cianjur and Bogor (see above) and the following areas:

Tangerang with Grinding

On the west of Batavia, running along the boundary with Banten, to which they formerly belonged, these lands made up a Regency under a Javanese Regent who paid the Company Rd. 800 per annum as rent and had an income of nearly Rd. 3000 in sub-rent and bazaar tax. He delivered 551.5 *pikul* of coffee in 1793 (down to 392 in 1795) for which he was paid at Rd. 6 per 148–150 lb, a total of

The Cancer Within

Rd. 3309 Of this sum not less that Rd. 2494 was costs – payments to officials from the Director-general down – and the remaining Rd. 814 was retained for payment of the rent. The Regent was also responsible for maintaining the post to and from Banten, for the upkeep of roads and bridges, and for the supply of 396 cans of oil to the watch at Batavia. He also had to supply a *prau* for the Company post at Tangeran, as well as being subject to a number of other exactions. Apart from this, he was free of supervision in his Regency.

The population of this area was estimated at 10476 people in 152 villages; it contained one million coffee trees, 1838 coconut palms, 13000 cardamom plants and 2500 pepper plants. Coffee deliveries were paid at Rd. 2.30 per *pikul* of 148 lb on receipt at Tangerang.

Pondok Gede, Ciseroa and Cipanas

These areas were under the control of planters, and produced between c. 1200 and c. 2000 *pikul* of coffee annually. The planters received a salary plus Rd. 4.5 per 148 lb of coffee; the producers Rd. 3–2/3 per 148 lb.

The Batavian Environs (Ommelanden)

These were officially ruled by the *Kollegie van Heemraden* (College of Reeves) at Batavia, but were in reality under very mixed administration: sold, leased, gifted or allotted against services. The areas Ciblagong, Kampong Baru, Kedong Badak, Cilubut, Jatinegara, Citrap, Cipamingkus, Cikalang, Klapa Nunggal, Cilingsi and Cisuru, south and east of the city, were under Regents or other Javanese administrators. The Company lands of Sadeng, Kuripan, and Janglapa lay more to the south-west. Near to the city lands were leased to native officers and commandants. Siringsing, Depok, Materman, Cikias, Cigoncen, Cilubut, Jatinegara, Cipamingkis, Kampung Baru and a part of Tangerang were sold to private owners (Dutch, Chinese, and a few Javanese) after 1745, with certain obligations to the Company. Hageman lists 91 in 1790,[63] on all sides of the city and stretching out to Banten, about two dozen of them being valued at over Rd. 20,000. Those located in the south were largely deforested *gaga* wilderness; the lands lying south of Tangeran along the west bank of the Cidani were considered populous (with a predominantly Chinese population) and prosperous, though deforested.

Traditional or modern?

Boomgaard compares the private estates (*particuliere landerijen*) to the Latin America hacienda and the medieval European manor. They varied in size from small to very large, the inhabitants were sedentary peasants with various forms of tenantry, and they had a demesne or owner-operated area with cash crops, worked with corvée or wage labour. The peasants paid rent (or tax) either instead of corvée labour or on top of it. In the case of the private estates the commercial crop was often sugar, grown by wage-workers (*bujang*) hired for a year. The *bujangs* also operated the sugar-mill. The peasantry paid a tithe (one tenth) of their staple crop, rice, the so-called *cuke*. They had to perform corvée once a week: probably confined to the upkeep of roads and bridges and perhaps some transportation. However, whatever the official regulation, there were instances of landowners squeezing the peasantry dry: in 1795 11/16th of the rice crop is reported as the average tax. From 1790 onwards robbery, murder and the use of opium assumed alarming proportions. To cope with this, landowners were permitted to have private jails. Focal points of trouble were the *warung*, for which every landowner could get a licence, and which they usually sub-let to a Chinese for 100 times the original fee. The *warung* were combinations of shops, opium-dens, gambling-houses, brothels, and cockfighting arenas. Here the *bujang*s got into debt, and Chinese *warung*-keepers were often murdered (as were landowners and overseers). Robber bands, from a few men to a few hundred, were endemic.

Very high, speculative, land prices obtained in the Ommelanden and were connected with the ever increasing insecurity, because the only way to recoup the heavy outlay was for the new owner to increase the *cuke* and the corvee labour, thereby creating a still larger landless proletariat, potential recruits for gangs.

Products included some coffee, pepper, indigo, rice, cotton thread and ginger. This was the only area where sugar was milled, but there was a decline in output at the end of the century. In 1767 there were 82 sugar mills, producing about 13 million pounds of sugar, but this had declined to 48 in 1785. Sugar production, with its heavy demand for wood for the fires, stripped the land of trees, so that the areas west and south of Batavia were virtually deforested.[64]

The Company also levied taxes on the sale of land and on markets, and had rights to corvee service. The population of the Batavian Environs was estimated in 1795 at 101,000, though the boundaries of city, suburbs, Batavian Environs and Regencies were hazy.[65] In 1778 there were 60 brick kilns, 34 tile works, 18 lime kilns and 7 potteries, run by Chinese, Malays, Javanese or Sundanese, or by Europeans using slave labour. There were a number or military posts in the Batavian Environs: close in east of the city the forts Ancol, De Ketting, De Vijfhoek and Wilgenburg, and further out Fort Tanjung-pura, on the Citarum near Krawang; to the west the forts Angkee, De Fluit, De Qual, and Tangeran, in the place of that name on the Cidani river, the border with Banten; to the south of the city were Meester Cornelis, Rijswijk, Jakatra, De Waterplaats, and Noordwijk. Most of these fortifications were of crude construction.

B. SEMI-INDEPENDENT SULTANATES, KINGDOMS, AND PRINCIPALITIES

The Sultanate of Banten

After the deposition of Sultan Ageng in 1682 as a result of VOC intervention, Banten's rulers were forced to abandon their formerly independent stance as a trading centre to conform with Dutch requirements; seventy years later, as a consequence of help received to suppress the Kyai Tapa rebellion of 1750–2, Banten formally became a fief of the Company. (It was annexed by Daendels in 1808, after which the Sultans became figureheads, and the last Sultan was exiled to Surabaya in 1832.)[66] The Sultanate extended over about 3900 sq. *palen* on Java, and had had tributary claims on regions outside Java: the Lampungs, Silebar, Indragiri and Palembang on Sumatra, and Landak and Sukadana on Kalimantan. By the end of the eighteenth century these claims, except for the Lampungs, were no longer enforced. Banten's population, a mixture of Javanese and Sundanese with some Malay and Sumatran elements, was estimated at 30,000 men able to bear arms: the total population would probably have been at least four and probably six times that number, but was unevenly distributed, since much of south Banten was little more than wilderness. North Banten was the location of the appanage and hereditary lands of members of the royal family and the Sultan's officials. The Company maintained a military commandment at the capital, and there were Company outposts at Anyer and Cerita on the straits, but the interior of Banten was almost unknown to Europeans.

Traditional or modern?

Up to 1780 Banten was in a reasonably flourishing state and supplied the Company with up to 6 million pounds of pepper annually, at a price of between 10 and 12 guilders per hundred pound. After this time, however, the European wars imposed a great strain on Banten in supplying the Company's demands for fortification works and military levies. The English established themselves in the Lampungs and captured the greater part of the pepper trade. Banten will be considered in more detail in the following chapter.

The "Vorstenlanden" or Princely Lands

In 1749 on his death bed Pakubuwana II ceded his whole kingdom to the VOC, and thereby the whole of "Java proper" as it was termed.

The Vorstenlanden comprised all the lands along the south coast of middle Java, from Mt. Kawi in the east to the Cidonan in the west, held in fief by the Sunan of Surakarta and the Sultan of Yogyakarta, whose lands were inter-twined in a complex manner. To the Sunan belonged Panaraga, Kutekmanek, Jagaraga, Srengat, Blitar, Kediri, Trenggalek, Pace, Caruban and Ngawi in the east, Purbalingga, Ngayah, Banyumas, Rema and Jatinegara in the west, and parts of Pajang, Mataram, Kedu, Bagelen and Sukawati. To the Sultan belonged Magetan, Madiun, Tulung, Ngrawa, Berbek, Gunung Kidul and the remainder of Pajang, Mataram, Kedu, Bagelen and Sukawati.[67] These lands were governed by the rulers' subordinate officials of greater and lesser rank. This was an area of c. 15,889 sq. *palen*, with a population estimated at 1.5 million. It was the seat of the princely courts of Surakarta and Yogyakarta, and the smaller Mangkunegaran. The central or core area (*nagara gung*) was an area of princely appanages. This area supported a rapidly growing population in the late eighteenth and early nineteenth centuries, thanks to the peace that prevailed and the extension of rice cultivation (it was thus a considerable contrast to other areas of Java such as the Eastern Salient, Banten and Cirebon). The extension of rice cultivation took place by opening new land (after the peace of 1755) and the provision of irrigation. However, the decades 1790–1810 appear to have produced a particularly large number of poor harvests.[68] There was greater insecurity, with endemic robbery and violence, and therefore less expansion of agricultural production, in the outlying regions. In general, Carey sees the late eighteenth century as a sort of golden age for the

The Cancer Within

central Javanese land-owning peasants (*sikĕp*), who were prosperous and enjoyed the freedom to choose the crops most suitable to local soils, unlike the Javanese who lived under VOC rule on the coast. In central Java important cash crops were tobacco (in Kedu), indigo (in the Mataram region) and Javanese long-staple cotton[69] which were interplanted with rice, and traded extensively, especially with the north coast. The cotton was also made into piece goods.[70] Not all developments boded well for the central Javanese peasantry, however, with the increasing introduction by appanage holders, from the late eighteenth century, of tax farming through agents known as *dĕmang* or *mantri desa*, in place of the far less onerous system of using village tax collectors (*bĕkĕl*) as their direct agents.

The VOC had a monopoly of the supply of textiles and opium, and the right to purchase at low prices approximately the following:

5000 *koyan* of rice at f. 24 (80 *duits* per 125 Amsterdam pound); 100,000 pounds of pepper at f. 9.12 per 100 pounds; all the salt at f. 14.8 per *koyan*.; all the indigo at f. 1.10 per pound; *kacang* at f. 38.8 per *koyan* of 3500 pounds; cotton thread at 6 to 15 *stuiver* per pound; and cardamom at a similarly low price.

The Company had a military post at both Surakarta and Yogyakarta. The one at Surakarta was manned by 132 infantry and 75 cavalry (M1780 #24: the total establishment of the Company, including military, was 233 at Surakarta and 124 at Yogyakarta). There were also small military posts on the road between the two princely capitals and on the road to Semarang. (M1780, #24: the Company's forts were the *Ontmoeting* at Unaran, the *Herstelder* at Salatiga, and the *Veldwagter* at Boyalali).

Mataram was the most powerful of the Javanese kingdoms that the VOC had encountered, and the one whose submission they were least certain of. It was also in some senses the intellectual heart of Java, and we shall return to that aspect in Chapter 6.

* * *

JAVA'S TRIBUTE: A TALLY OF PRODUCE

In 1780 Governor van den Burgh noted (M1780 #102) that most of Java's exportable produce was from the Company's own lands. Though the central Javanese Principalities and other areas produced cotton thread of the coarsest sort, round and long pepper and cubeb, and some cardamom, these were far less important than the deliveries of the coastal Regents. The deliveries of this produce were made at Mulud – the most important of the Javanese Islamic festivals on which members of the aristocracy had traditionally appeared at court to pay homage to their ruler – to the designated Company centre. Apart from the head office at Semarang, other offices like Tegal were also collection points for certain areas.

The most important deliveries were:

Rice. In 1795 the delivery was 5524 *koyans*, of which 1148 were without payment, and the rest at minimal prices (4076 at f. 29.14, 300 at f. 36, 100 at f. 48). The common price of rice was between f. 36–53 per *koyan* in the years 1772–76 and between f. 96 and f. 108 a *koyan* in the years 1796–1801. In 1796 van Overstraten made the following comments on rice cultivation:

> though rice is a very uncertain crop, Java is fortunate in that local conditions vary so dramatically that there is never an overall crop failure; planting of rice has increased, but there is still so much uncultivated land that no matter how large Java's population becomes one need not fear that enough rice could not be produced; and women contribute most to rice-growing, the men doing no more than preparing the irrigation channels and ploughing and sowing the fields (M1796 #188).

However, local shortages are noted from the 1780s on (the devastation of the Eastern Salient by warfare had long-lasting effects on rice cultivation, and see above sub Pati, Cengkalsewu, Juwana and Batang) and the second half of the 1790s were times of rice shortages. By 1801 when the delivery had increased to 5751 *koyan* (1245 without payment, 4506 at Rd. 15 per *koyan*), this had become apparent. On the coast the price of rice had risen due to an increase in the supply of money, although its circulation was still minimal due to transport difficulties and a shortage of credit. In the Vorstenlanden an abundance of rice was grown, to the extent that there were often not enough people to harvest it. In places at a considerable distance from the courts, rice could sometimes be bought as cheaply as Rd. 5 per *koyan*. Transport however was extremely difficult and expensive, up to three times the price of the rice itself. This difficulty of transporting bulky goods (commercial crops such as coffee as well as rice, requiring enormous inputs of labour and time from the peasantry in both cases) over a very poor infrastructure of roads was a very significant feature of the Javanese economy. When there was a small harvest in the hills little rice was sent to the coast, and even with a good harvest transport overland was a serious problem (M1801 #322 and 325), which exacerbated the effects of a local crop failure. Transport of rice to Batavia was increasingly costly and the Company had to resort to impounding the boats of owners who did not want them used to transport this rice (M1801 #398).

Coffee. This product had been in decline after 1736. In the Vorstenlanden it was planted only for local consumption, and trees elsewhere were destroyed. In 1787 we find Siberg informing his successor Greeve that.cultivation was forbidden except for local consumption (M1787 #123). Next year, however, the Company decided to allow 20,000 *pikul* at 135 lb per annum to be grown, which it would purchase at Rd. 4.5 (M1791 #152). In 1792 Greeve raised the amount to 40,000 *pikul*s per annum, a target that was not reached in 1796 although over 1.5 million of the 5 million trees planted had been destroyed on the Company's orders, to prevent over-production (M1796 #214). Van Overstraten remarks that Javanese coffee was not inferior to that of Jakatra although coffee buffs preferred the Cirebon variety (M1796 #214). In 1801 the amount set was still 40,000 *pikul*. (M1801 #354–5) but the amount actually delivered is missing. This was still a small amount compared to the amounts coming in from Cirebon and Priangan (see above), whose deliveries were five or six times as much. In the table of production/export figures supplied by Boomgaard, coffee is shown as doubling between 1791 and 1795.[71] In the early 19th century, and up to 1860 production of Javanese coffee increased steeply.[72]

Sugar. Cultivation was restricted to protect the interests of planters and millers in the Batavian Environs. In 1801 there were 18 sugar mills in the Japara-Kudus region, 8 in Joana-Pati, 3 in Pekalongan-Batang, 2 in the Eastern Salient as well as some smaller Chinese ones. The millers were angry at their exclusion from the manufacture of *arak* and *tjiouw* for the benefit of the Batavian industry, and claimed that they were obliged to sell syrup at a very low price or throw it away. Great quantities of sugar were piling up in Joana, Japara and Pekalongan which the Company had no prospect of trading even at cost price (M1801 #368–77). Though in

Traditional or modern?

Boomgaard's table of export/production figures, sugar doubles in the period 1796–1800, this was only a return to levels of the late 1770s.

Cotton thread The total delivery was 350 *pikuls*, rising to 371 in 1796, of which 39 (67 in 1796) were without payment and 311 (304 in 1796) at a graded scale of prices ranging from Rd. 15 to 45. In 1787 Siberg remarked that since cotton thread was in so much demand in the Netherlands he had made every effort to secure a supply, but some of the Chinese lease-holders preferred to pay the fine applicable for non-delivery of their quota (M1787 #114; M1796 #192). In 1796 van Overstraten wrote that this product "is no less wanted in the fatherland, than it is burdensome for the natives to deliver it": the absence of the women spinning cotton for a week in the *dalems* of the Regents was apparently widely resented (M1796 #191). Premiums paid for cotton over and above the required delivery did not have much effect, apparently because only the Regents and not the growers benefited. Not much success was achieved in obtaining seed from Coromandel, and as a fall-back Makassarese seed was used in preference to Javanese (M1787 #115; M1796 #194). By 1801 the delivery had been increased to 379 *pikul*, of which 40 were without payment, with a price rise of 25% for the remainder, and the average annual amount delivered had risen from 422 to 473 *pikul* (M1801 #322 and 331 and tables at end).

Javanese garments. When demand declined at the end of the century the weavers were forced to sell at a lower price. They were not keen to re-enter the business when the Company renewed its demand and asked for a greater quantity than before. Van Reede tot de Parkeler recommended a price rise but this was not considered necessary by the First Resident and leaseholder. (M1801 #339). However, there was an indigenous textile industry that responded well to high market prices, and this continued to exist until 1840-5 when it was killed by declining prosperity and lack of time.[73]

Cubeb ("tail pepper") and long pepper. These were products from the central Javanese principalities: the Sunan and Sultan were each contracted to supply 5000 lb of each (M1787 #125) but actually delivered only between a half and a fifth of this amount (M1796 #226).

Indigo. In 1787 it was grown in Pekalongan, Wiradesa, Pamalang, Brebes, Japara, Kudus and Pati, which supplied 7255 lb, and planting had begun three years previously in Banyuwangi, at an initial premium of Rd. 16–2/3 per *pikul*, leading to a production here of 142 lb in 1790. It was an unpopular crop (M1787 #120, MR 1791 #147). Van Overstraten pushed indigo making hard, introducing 34 new factories and persuading the central Javanese rulers to allocate land to indigo: production was 381 *pikul* over 5 years (M1796 #201–210). In 1801 11 of the 34 indigo factories in the coastal region had been destroyed, and production was down slightly over 1795 (see tables at end of M1796 and M1801). The significant effects of indigo cultivation in Pekalongan are discussed in the following chapter.

Coconut oil. This was supplied from the Eastern Salient, which in 1796 delivered 37,000 cans without payment and 6500 cans (M1801 #322: 2500 cans) at 6 *stuivers* per can.

Petroleum. 800 cans at f. 0.4.15 (M1801 #322: without payment).

Logging. 9300 square-cut logs were delivered, at minimal prices. Serious deforestation of the *pasisir* had been underway from the early eighteenth century. The annual harvest of teak was reduced in 1780 from 106,000 square-cut logs per annum to 9800 because the Regents of Pekalongan and Batang had been excused for some years from delivering their 800 logs (M1780 #105). Van Overstraten attributes the exhausted state of many of the forests to, apart from the Company's demands, extensive private logging by the Residents, who had transcended the Regents' authority in this area, and poor management and re-afforestation due to the enormous demands on the time of the loggers.[74] As on many another subject, he remarks that this will have to change when times improve (M1796 #190). Boomgaard[75] makes the important point that deforestation adversely affected irrigation (and therefore agriculture), as most irrigation systems depended upon the water supply of rivers originating in the wooded mountainous hinterlands.

(Black/round) pepper. In the first half of the 1790s the cultivation of this product was still at an early stage in both central Java and along the north coast. In 1796 none of the central Javanese pepper had yet been delivered to the Company and the coastal production amounted to about 300 *pikul* annually, which posed considerable

problems of storage since the war made it impossible to ship it out. Some land in the Semarang-Kaliwungu region was granted to private individuals on the condition that they grow pepper there. The price paid was Rd. 7 per *pikul* (M1796 #215–225). By 1801 there had been a great extension of the cultivation of round pepper and a yearly increase in the amount delivered, which rose from 272 *pikul* annually in the period covered by the 1796 report to 1005 in that covered by the 1801 report (M1801 #357 and tables at end of M1796 and M1801).

Salt. The Company received its salt from the lease-holder at Paradesi. Salt was at one time a major item of private trade, but this declined very much due to the shortage of money and the development of local salt making in places like Madura (M1796 #228).

Sapan wood and sandalwood. The former came from Pasuruhan (where the supply was exhausted by 1791), Banyuwangi, Bima, and Bali; van Overstraten experimented with the planting of the latter on Java (M1791 #162; M1796 #230–1).

Sulphur. The principal deliveries of this product were from Mt. Merapi over the period 1789–94, collected by the Commander of Banyuwangi (M1791 #164; M1796 #233). The price in 1801 was Rd. 6 per 100 lb and 25% overweight including transport costs (M1801 #384). The actual production of sulphur fell by two-thirds between the periods of the 1796 and 1801 reports (see tables at end of M1796 and M1801).

Saltpetre. In 1795 Dirk van Hogendorp established a saltpetre factory at Surabaya at his own expense, and this produced good quality saltpetre, for which the Company had hitherto been dependent on the English production at Bengal (M1796 #234). In 1801 van Reede tot de Parkeler proposed a delivery from the factory of 200 *pikul* unrefined at Rd. 8 per *pikul* of 125 lb to replace delivery of the refined product at Rd. 12 per *pikul* (M1801 #385).

Tobacco. This was an item of private trade. Considerable amounts of good quality tobacco had once been produced but a rapid decline took place in the 1790s (M1796 #237).

Green kacang from Madura. This was an intermittent delivery sometimes replaced by a cash levy in lieu (M1801 #327).

The Cancer Within

Other products. These included birds' nests, a trade in the hands of the Sunan and Sultan who sub-leased as a monopoly to Chinese traders (M1801 #382), wax and cardamom (Siberg in 1787 and van Overstraten in 1796 report a slow start: M1787 #122; M1796 #213 and by 1801 production was down to one fifth of the 1796 figures: see tables at end of M1801), mustard, tamarind, coriander and cassia (cinnamon). Rope fibres were introduced in 1785 and made into rope in Surabaya. In 1801 the Eastern Salient delivered 1100 *pikul* for payment and this was considered a burden on the inhabitants (M1801 #340–1).

A post 1795 boom?

As Boomgaard points out,[76] one of the major characteristics of the Company's system was that under the monopoly policy the Gentlemen XVII (the directors of the Company in Holland) periodically set the required quantity of each product and what should be paid for it in accordance with market conditions. This resulted in a stop-go cycle in the production of cash crops for foreign markets. Short periods of growth alternated with phases of decline, because prices were lowered and/or quantities to be accepted were reduced. The principal victims of this policy in Java were sugar and coffee, an annual plantation crop and a perennial peasant crop respectively. Lesser victims were cotton, indigo, and pepper, the first two annual peasant crops, the latter a perennial one. The reductions of quantities and prices as applied to perennial peasant crops were an especially heavy burden for the peasantry, because of the time-lag between planting and harvesting. Often an order to plant more coffee trees was followed after some years by a price reduction or even an order to extirpate a number of trees just when the new trees began to bear fruit, wiping out large investments of time and energy.

In his recent book, Boomgaard describes the post-1795 situation as follows: an important change in economic policy took place when, in 1795, the European war made regular communication between Holland and Batavia impossible. Batavia decided to sell its products to foreigners, and other ships (American, British, Danish) and other markets (British India, China, the United States) took over the role of the VOC and Holland. Boomgaard writes:

Traditional or modern?

Batavia was no longer subject to the cyclical changes in the production decisions of the Gentlemen XVII, and it could sell its products to the highest bidder. This change in economic policy could hardly have occurred at a more propitious moment. For a number of unrelated reasons both production and prices of coffee and sugar had started to rise after 1790, mainly as a result of the slave rebellion of 1791 in St. Domingue, by far the most important production area of both coffee and sugar at that moment. Production of coffee in Java had been increasing since 1789, because a zealous Commissioner of Native Affairs had started to expand coffee cultivation in the Priangan since 1785. This had been reinforced by an urgent request of the Gentlemen XVII in 1788 for more return cargo, especially coffee, in order to generate more profits for the ailing Company. In the same year coffee planting in the Pasisir area was stimulated, while in 1792 this order was repeated for the Principalities. Sugar production received a stimulus in 1793, when the sugar millers were permitted to dispose of the produce exceeding their quota as they saw fit. Until then the sugar trade had been a VOC monopoly. The VOC sugar price was increased several times. The benefit of these measures fell largely to the Pasisir sugar millers, who were less hampered by shortages of firewood and labour than their colleagues from the traditional production area, the Environs of Batavia [see above on the ecological disaster in this area]. It is, therefore, not surprising to find more technological innovation (water mills, metal cylinders) in the Pasisir area than in the Environs. From 1790 onwards the production of cotton (yarn), indigo and pepper was also encouraged, and probably for the same reasons (more return cargo for the Company).

This combination of a new commercial policy, increasing production and high prices is said to have resulted in an agricultural boom between 1795 and 1810, largely ignored in the literature.[77]

In another article, however, Boomgaard presents material that considerably qualifies this sanguine picture.[78] Although in his conclusion[79] he does state that between 1775 and 1875 two "agricultural revolutions" can be distinguished, i.e. the 1795–1810 period; and the first two decades under the Cultivation System,

1830–50, both periods being characterised by a boom in export crops and stagnant or even decreasing food production per capita and per unit of land, elsewhere in the article he seem less confident that the earlier period was in fact a "boom". Thus he speaks of "stop-go cycles 1775–1830" and "slow and interrupted growth" [between 1790 and 1820].[80] Also though he attempts to generalize across sugar and coffee, the figures he gives[81] show the two products as following quite different trends over this period, and production figures are not distinguished from export figures, so that the extent to which previous stockpiles were involved is not clear.[82] The difference between coffee and sugar, which did not take off until after 1830, is confirmed by Reid.[83]

The sources used by me do not provide evidence for growth on a scale which we could call a "boom". Those relating to the north coast, which as Boomgaard points out was the new growth centre for export crops, suggest that the establishment of these crops encountered quite a few hitches in this period. Making a comparison between the 1796 and 1801 reports[84] we find that indigo was down slightly; cardamom down to 1/5th; round pepper was up considerably (1005 over 272 *pikul* annually) and tail and long pepper had been introduced; sulphur was down 2/3; and cotton was up (473 over 422 annually). Semarang was said to be depressed (see above p. 225), and the trade of Tegal destroyed throughout this period. There was a pile-up of sugar at Joana, Japara and Pekalongan warehouses in 1801; and a decline in tobacco. However, private trade by Chinese was threatening VOC quotas. The 1806, report on rice says that the new pepper and coffee plantations set up in Semarang, the Pasuruhan districts and Banyuwangi had failed because unsuitable land had been chosen.[85] Another document from 1806, the *Diary of the journey made to the comptoirs east of Semarang, Japara, Joana, Rembang, as well as the island of Madura, and including the Oosthoek to Banjoewangie and from there back to Semarang, by Nicolaus Engelhard, First Councillor and elected Director General of Batavian India, furthermore Governor and Director of Java's North East Coast, in 1802, kept by the first sworn clerk of police, Johan Hendrik Kistler*,[86] also deals with the very bad beginning made with coffee and pepper cultivation. Rothenbuhler's report on Surabaya, dated 31 August 1808[87] states that when he had arrived coffee had already been planted, but within a few years it was obvious that the trees were not doing well. He made a new start in what he considered to be more suitable soil. All in all, the picture

Traditional or modern?

seems to be one of a very patchy recovery from depressed conditions, with a distinctly shaky start in the new initiatives on the north coast, rather than a "boom".

But if the period was not a boom, it might well be called an agricultural revolution (at least for parts of Java, notably the coast) in the sense that it involved a very difficult transition to a cash-crop agriculture governed by the demands of the overseas market, as mediated by the Company, to the detriment of food production. At this period there was still an ability among the peasantry to respond to market opportunities, e.g. by the increased production of cotton. By the time of the Cultivation System, however, things were very different: commercial peasant crops, such as cotton, indigo, and tobacco, almost disappeared, due to lack of time and land, during the period 1830–50, particularly in the 1840s, a decade of widespread hardship that drastically crippled the Javanese peasantry's ability to take initiatives in response to market opportunities.

Boomgaard[88] contests on good evidence Burger's earlier picture of subsistence agriculture, self-sufficient villages, an undifferentiated mass of peasants, no wage labour, no trade or markets to speak of, hardly any money, and virtually untouched by Western influence. However, the VOC's decline from an internationally competitive trading company to an impoverished suzerain of a conglomeration of fiefs was not conducive to the continuation, let alone the expansion, of individual enterprise, inter-regional trade, an increasingly monetized economy, industrialization,[89] and the other developments that flow from these. As we have seen, the Javanese were discouraged from becoming an increasingly urbanised population – they were in fact often forcibly returned to the cultivation of their land – and the characteristic division of Dutch colonial cities, Semarang like Batavia, into ethnic kampung militated against them becoming the "fatherlands" of the nation-state Braudel discerns in European cities.[90] This remained the case until other developments made the idea of an Indies/Indonesian rather than a Javanese fatherland conceivable.

As a forerunner of the Cultivation System, which was more efficient but essentially organised on the same principles, this period is of crucial importance: it was indeed a case of back to the future. The Cultivation System when it came was doubly regressive, re-instituting the arrangements described here which were already backward-looking in their time. However, Javanese

The Cancer Within

society was not an undifferentiated format of wet-rice peasantry supporting a theatre-state Indic *nagara*. It exhibited considerably socio-economic diversity, and these regional formations and the way in which they became involved with the VOC at different times and with different results have been given insufficient attention. It is to this that we turn in the next chapter.

NOTES

1 W.F. Wertheim, *Indonesian Society in Transition*, W. van Hoeve, The Hague, 1964, p. 172.
2 See Ann Kumar, "Literary Approaches to Slavery and the Indies Enlightenment: van Hogendorp's Kraspoekol", *Indonesia* 43 (April 1987), pp. 43–65 on Willem van Hogendorp's critique and its fate.
3 Memorie of Pieter Gerard van Overstraten for his successor Johan Fredrik Baron van Reede tot de Parkeler, 1796 (Collection Nederburgh 386, Algemeen Rijksarchief) (M1796) #176.
4 Memorie of Johannes Siberg for his successor Jan Greeve, 18 September 1787 (Collection Nederburgh 382, Algemeen Rijksarchief, The Hague) (M1787) #108.
5 E. du Perron-de Roos, "Correspondentie van Dirk van Hogendorp met zijn broeder Gijsbert Karel", *BKI* 102 (1943), p. 166.
6 ARA, van Alphen collection 2e afdeeling 1900, no.196.
7 E. du Perron-de Roos, "Correspondentie van Dirk van Hogendorp met zijn broeder Gijsbert Karel", *BKI* 102 (1943), pp. 125–273, letter of 4 October 1794, p. 175.
8 J.L. Umbgrove was the son-in-law of Governor-General Alting. Before his posting to the lucrative Residency of Cirebon, where his father-in-law liked to place a family connection, he was Resident of Tegal: see F. de Haan, *Priangan*, vol. 3 #1839.
9 "Hoe onvoldoende ik in mijn gewenscht voornemen geslaagd ben, zal uijt het ondervolgende blijken, en ik zoude tot in de ziel beschaamd geraaken, bij aldien ik geene gegronde reedenen, voor deese mislukking Produceeren konden.

Het behaage Uw HoogEd: dan gratieuselijk in aanmerking te neemen, dat alle aangewende Pogingen en navorschingen, om onder de oude Archiven en Papieren, Eenige beschrijvingen of Landkaarten van de Cheribonsche Landen in't generaal, of van de 3. Preanger Landen onder deese Residentie Sorteerende in't bijsonder te vinden vrugtloos geweest zijn; En daar het mij door des Nootlottige en Creticque tijds omstandigheeden veroorzaakt, niet heeft moogen gebeurenm, om de aan mijn bestier toevertrouw de Landen te door Reijsen en in Oculaire Inspectie te gaan nemen, zoo droeg ik niet meer dan Eene oppervlakkige en gansch onvoldoende kennis van dezelve, dat op niets anders dan lossen discoerssen steunde, waarop doorgaans weijnig of in 't geheel geen staat te maaken is." (p. 2). Note i.a. the

Traditional or modern?

10 Boomgaard, *Children*, p. 51.
11 *Reflections by several people*, answer to Qn. 2. in "New Set of Questions", p. 42, referring to the Eastern Salient, where shortage of manpower was particularly severe.
12 Wouter Hendrik van Ysseldijk, *Short Sketch of the Sultan's Javanese Court*, ARA, Collection Nederburgh 989, #68–70.
13 *Reflections by several people*.
14 On regional variations in land ownership, see further Boomgaard, *Children*, pp. 16–20, and 50–59, and Carey, "Agrarian World" pp. 84–5, and *Reflections by several people* on the Eastern Salient.
15 See also Boomgaard, *Children*, p. 51.
16 See Blussé, *Strange Company*. ch.III, "Trojan Horse of Lead: the Picis in Early 17th Century Java".
17 See below p. 228 sub Ulujami however for an example where the prosperity of the area is related to the fairer treatment the Chinese leaseholder gave the population. See also below p. 209 sub Panarukan and Basuki and Ulujami, where it is remarked that a Chinese leaseholder can do more than a Regent and that the Chinese are better placed to provide the seed paddy [being better capitalised] than the regents.
18 199R-200L: *rěbo wage ing siyam kang sasi / taun alip ing dalu nupěna / pagriyan walandi kabeh / lawan pacinan iku / sami kobar* [kobor] *katingal wěngi / lan kobar* [kobor] *kapurbayan / pangi*[m]*pening dalu / sarěng sang prabu taruna / rěmbag kěncěng panggah saliring prakawis / nanging dereng mupakat //*
19 Wouter Hendrik van Ysseldijk, *Short Sketch of the Sultan's Javanese Court*. Anno 1793, #54–7.
20 See Victor Lieberman, "Some Thoughts on Mainland-Archipelagic Patterns during the 'Last Stand of the Indigenous States', c. 1750–1850", in A.J.S. Reid, forthcoming, p. 23.
21 *Reflections by Several People*, pp. 7–10.
22 H. Kraemer, "Het Instituut voor de Javaansche Taal te Soerakarta: Bijdrage tot de geschiedenis van de studie van het Javaansch", *Djawa* 12/6 (Dec. 1932), pp. 261–2.
23 See also *Reflections by Several People*, p. 4 on the continuing problem of piracy in east Java.
24 See Trocki, "Chinese Pioneering".
25 Van Ysseldijk, *Short Sketch* #53.
26 Even the use of the term "Java" in Dutch sources of this period does not conform to modern usage in that the term "Java proper" is used to refer to 1. the "northeast coast" (actually comprising more than we would understand by that term, as explained above); and 2. Mataram. Thus it excludes Batavia, West Java and other areas.
27 Boomgaard, *Children*, p. 74. In the 19th century the agricultural potential of the Eastern Salient reasserted itself in the highest rice-yields on Java. But since the relative dryness of the area requires irrigation, in times of warfare the breakdown of irrigation systems would have added famine to the other causes of death.

28 Van den Burgh here expresses the wish that the then Gezaghebber of the Oosthoek, Hendrik Breton, had accepted the submission of the ruler of Balambangan, Pangeran Patih, when it was offered in 1763, which would have saved much bloodshed. The same sentiment on Pangeran Patih's side – the retaliation he had expected from his Balinese overlord came when he was summoned to Mengwi and murdered – is echoed by the writer of a Javanese Babad dealing with these events: see Ann Kumar, "Javanese Historiography in and of the Colonial Period: A Case Study" in Anthony Reid and David Marr eds, *Perceptions of the Past in Southeast Asia*, ASAA Southeast Asia Publications Series no. 4, Heinemann 1979, pp. 194–5.

29 *Reflections by several people*, attachment in the form of an extract from of letter by Johan Cesar van Wikkerman.

30 See Hageman, "Overzigt", p. 279.

31 *Reflections by several people* answers to questions 4 and 9 (ms. 22–4 and 30–32) in first set of questions and Wikkerman attachment, answer to question 6 in second set of questions (ms. 63).

32 See Heather Sutherland, "Notes on Java's Regent Families", Part One, *Indonesia* 16 October 1973, pp. 145–6.

33 The *koyan* varied from place to place but is generally reckoned at 3350 Amsterdam pounds, but 3750 in Mataram and Surabaya.

34 The term *cacah* – a numerator – seems originally to have been used to designate a unit of land, specifically rice-land. In later usage it came to designate the number of cultivators and their dependants (anywhere between 3 and 30 people) who could be maintained on a particular area of *sawah*: see Peter Carey, " 'Just King'", p. 68. It was sometimes used in this period as a rough guide to population numbers, but would obviously totally leave out of the picture all those people not directly holding these units of rice-land. The term can also be used as synonymous with *sikĕp* to refer to the head of the household himself (in the 19th century the terms *kuli* and *gogol* are also used for the household head): see Boomgaard, *Children*, p. 61. For further information on the *cacah*, see following chapter, section on Pekalongan.

35 *Reflections by several people*, answer to Question 2 in first set of questions (ms. 16).

36 Vaandrig is a military rank (lit. "standard bearer") below the officer cadre but above the rank and file and non-commissioned officers.

37 The Kalang were a separate, more or less outcast group who carried out some tasks such as woodcutting and leatherworking which were not performed by real Javanese. Because of their role in woodcutting, the Company had made an effort to detach them from Javanese jurisdiction and bring them under its own, though this was resisted by the rulers of Mataram, with an attempt in 1679 to prevent the Kalang supplying wood to the Company. In 1705 the Company achieved jurisdiction over the Kalang, and henceforth had the right to collect the poll tax the Kalang paid. Up until 1762 the Kalang were under their own separate heads but after this date they were under the Regent of the Regency in which they lived (see Ir. W. Zwart, "De Kalangs als houtkappers in dienst der Compagnie", TBG LXXIX, 1939, pp. 252–61). See also Chapter

Traditional or modern?

    3, Part 2 above on the Kalang. There was also a poll tax on slaves (M1796 #256).
38 *Reflections by several people*, answer to Question 1 in first set of questions, ms. 11–13.
39 *Reflections by several people*, answer to Question 1 in first set of questions, ms. 11–13.
40 *Reflections by several people*, answer to Question 1 in first set of questions, ms. 11–13.
41 The *paal* was an Indies linear measure of 1506.943 metres.
42 For a brief summary of the VOC's relationship with Madura, see Ann Kumar, *Diary of a Javanese Muslim: Religion, Politics and the Pesantren 1883–1886*, Faculty of Asian Studies Monographs, New Series no. 7, Australian National University, Canberrsa 1985, pp. 30 ff.
43 See Kumar, *Diary*, p. 31–2.
44 Due to the monopoly on land holding by the Regents and lesser heads, it was very difficult for the common man to obtain *sawah*: see *Reflections by several people*, answer to Question 1 in "New Set of Questions", p. 36 and report on Sumenep by the Resident, J. Diensbach, dated 26 February 1806 in same report.
45 *kacang ijo* (Malay *kacang hijau*), a very cheap and common item of diet used to make a sort of gruel.
46 Hageman, "Overzigt", p. 289.
47 See note 12 above.
48 In VOC book-keeping, there were 48 *stuivers* of 4 *duiten* to the Rijksdaalder of 2.50 guilders (the Dutch *stuiver* had 8 *duiten*).
49 "Forest lurahs [head-men]".
50 That is, an institution run by the church.
51 On the Chinese role in making arak in Batavia and its social use there, see Ann Kumar, "A Swedish View of Batavia in 1783–4: Hornstedt's Letters", *Archipel* 37 (1989) pp. 247–82.
52 On this family see Remmelink, pp. 19, 25, 34, 36–7, 39–40, 51–2, 57, 65, 79, 85, 99, 111, 118, 120, 123–4, 136, 140, 155, 215, 217, 224, 226, 231, 235, 238, and 265–6.
53 Remmelink, pp. 169, 177, 185.
54 These were high country products. Cubeb (*piper cubeb*), also known as tail pepper, was originally from the Spice Islands. It was used both for flavouring food and as an aphrodisiac in China and the archipelago and is a source of medicinal cubeb camphor.
55 This area is not included in the reports of the Governors of the North-East Coast. The following section is therefore based on archival sources dealing only with this area, and the work of Boomgaard, Blussé, and Hageman (J. Hageman, JCz "Geschied- en aardrijkskundig overzigt van Java, op het einde der achttiende eeuw, TBG IX, 1860, pp. 261–419).
56 HRB 1000, Algemeen Rijksarchief, The Hague, p. 16.
57 HRB 1001.
58 See Hageman, "Overzigt", pp. 353–5.
59 Peter Boomgaard, "Buitenzorg in 1805", *Modern Asian Studies* 20/1 (1986) pp. 33–58.
60 It was ceded to Governor-General van Imhoff in 1745, and subsequently

The Cancer Within

sold to succeeding Governors-General in private transaction until 1780 when the Batavian government made it an ex officio possession of the office (still subject to a gratification payable to the outgoing Governor-General). The income from land rent and other sources was about Rd. 11,000 annually: see Hageman, "Overzigt" pp. 350–1.

61 Hageman, "Overzigt" pp. 349–50.
62 rood: Dutch *roede*, a linear measure, of which there were a number of different ones (Dutch, Amsterdam, etc.). The one in use in the Indies however seems to have been the Rhenish rood (*Rijnlandsche roede*) of 12 Rhenish feet, making 3.767 metres.
63 Hageman, "Overzigt" pp. 364–70.
64 Hageman, "Overzigt", p. 360, and Blussé, "The Story of an Ecological Disaster", in *Strange Company*, pp. 15–34.
65 Hageman, "Overzigt", p. 364.
66 See Sartono Kartodirdjo, *The Peasants' Revolt of Banten in 1888*, VKI 50, 1966, pp. 73–4.
67 On the division of the princely lands in the land settlements of 1755–6, 1768, 1770, and 1773–4, see M.C. Ricklefs, *Jogjakarta under Sultan Mangkubumi 1749–1792: A History of the Division of Java*, London Oriental Series no. 30 (School of Oriental and African Studies), Oxford University Press 1974, pp. 71–2, 89, 144–5, 157–63.
68 Carey, "Agrarian World", pp. 59–137 (see pp. 89, 105, 113.)
69 According to Boomgaard (*Children*, p. 94) Javanese cotton (*kapas jawa, gossypium arboreum*) was a short-staple variety. However, as he says, the taxonomy of "old" Java cottons is not well advanced.
70 Carey, "Agrarian World", pp. 86–93.
71 Peter Boomgaard, "Java's Agricultural Production 1775–1875" in Angus Maddison and Gé Prince eds, *Economic Growth in Indonesia, 1820–1940*, VKI 137, Foris, Dordrecht, 1989, table p. 119.
72 See Anthony Reid, "A New Phase of Commercial Expansion in Southeast Asia, 1760–1850" (p. 19), in Reid, *Last Stand*.
73 Boomgaard, "Production", p. 115.
74 Dirk van Hogendorp remarks that the inhabitants are paid so little for the wood that they have no interest in maintaining the forests: see E. du Perron-de roos, "Correspondentie van Dirk van Hogendorp met zijn broeder Gisbert Karel", *BKI* 102 (1943), pp. 125–273.
75 Boomgaard, *Children*, p. 76.
76 Boomgaard, *Children*, pp. 29–31.
77 Boomgaard also points out that between 1795 and 1820, the north coast became much more important relative to West Java as a coffee and sugar growing area.
78 Boomgaard, "Agricultural Production".
79 Boomgaard, "Agricultural Production", p. 117. s.a. p. 116 re a "cash crop boom" between 1795 and 1810.
80 p. 101.
81 see table p. 119.
82 Boomgaard describes sugar as "less satisfactory" (p. 98) though his tables show it doing better than coffee over this period, both in absolute and in per capita increase.

Traditional or modern?

83 Reid, "Commercial Expansion" (p. 18).
84 MR 1796 and MR 1801, tables at end of reports.
85 *Reflections by several people*, p. 2.
86 ARA, van Alphen collection 2e afdeeling 1900, no. 196.
87 India Office, Mackenzie Private Collection no.3, pp. 37–71.
88 Boomgaard, *Children*, pp. 119–20.
89 Boomgaard, *Children*, p. 119–20 quotes an 1820 survey as revealing the existence of a certain number of factories producing soap, candles, rope, oil, textiles, brick, pottery, etc. in the early 19th century.
90 See Ch. 2. p. 13 above.

5

Aristocracy and peasantry in the tides of world capitalism: three regions

BANTEN: FROM TRADE CENTRE TO BACKWATER.

When we think of Javanese society, we generally think of an immensely fertile wet-rice society, inland and "centripetal" in Hildred Geertz's classification,[1] and when we speak of the Javanese state we generally let the state of Mataram stand for the whole. But there have been other Javanese societies and states. The example taken here is of a region which was far from fertile but was the seat of a powerful Sultanate, centred on the coast and oriented towards the sea, whose economic greatness was dependent on trade. It was poorly equipped for agriculture, with a preponderance of infertile soils unlike the famous black soils of central Java, and with inadequate irrigation. The most fertile area was the mountainous area covering Pandeglang regency and the Ciomas district of Serang regency, while south Banten was particularly infertile and sparsely populated.[2] The contrast with other areas of Java is underlined by the fact that Banten was the only area of Java where slash-and-burn (swidden) agriculture, typical of the less developed areas of the outer islands, is still practised today, along with wet rice (*sawah*) and dry rice (*gaga* or *tipar*).[3] Banten's soils, and those of its colony the Lampungs, were more suitable for pepper, which was a major item of trade and, as Braudel has pointed out, a commodity of particular significance in developing a more highly capitalized economy.[4] Banten, like Aceh, had made a determined bid for dominance in the pepper trade. Under its greatest Sultan, Sultan Ageng,[5] Banten had received English, French, Danish and other traders, and with their help had built up a large fleet of ocean-going ships. He had been at war with the VOC three times, but the Company was finally able to overthrow him by supporting the

Aristocracy and peasantry in the tides of world capitalism

rebellion of his son, Sultan Aji.[6] The latter accepted the status of a VOC protectorate in 1684 as the price of the Company's military assistance in his rebellion against his father, and this effectively ended Banten's independent trade. In 1808 Banten would be annexed by the Netherlands under an act of Daendels though a Sultan remained as nominal ruler until 1832, when the last vestiges of the monarchy were abolished.

At the end of the eighteenth century, in terms of the VOC's classification of its regional branches, Banten was not a Residency but, like the Eastern Salient (Oosthoek), a military Commandery. The VOC establishment was centred around Fort Speelwijk, named after Governor-General Speelman, who began its construction in 1683. Its situation on the river a short distance from the shore behind muddy flats meant that it could not be approached by ships but only by a landing, which it could withstand given sufficient men, ammunition and provisions. The official establishment for the Commandery of Banten was 372 men, of which 22 were political officers, 327 military and 23 sailors; but usually only two-thirds of this number were in place.

A member of this VOC establishment, Jonkheer Jan de Rovere van Breugel began his career in the service of the VOC as a Fiscaal and was subsequently promoted to Secunde and Administrateur of the Banten comptoir. After seven years' service in which he had been weakened by continuing sicknesses, he returned to the Netherlands for family reasons in 1788. He wrote two long memoranda on Banten in about 1787: the *Beschrijving van Bantam en de Lampongs* (Description of Banten and the Lampungs) and the *Bedenkingen van den staat van Bantam* (Reflections on the State of Banten). Somewhat abridged versions of both documents are published in the *BKI* of 1856.[7] The (unsigned) introduction says that these papers were intended to be published by the Bataviaasch Genootschap but that Governor-General Alting had advised the author against this on the grounds that they revealed more than one of the VOC's secrets. In the *Beschrijving*[8] he argues that Banten's proximity to Batavia allowed men to be brought up from there in times of emergency, and that it should be downgraded from a Commandery with 372 men to a Residency or *Opperhoofdij* with 185 men in order to reduce the Company's financial losses from the post, since " . . . the poverty of the King precludes him from starting anything". The Company also had posts comprising a corporal and two common soldiers at Anyer, Cerita and Cikoning, whose task was to keep a watchful eye on shipping and report to Banten. There were also small posts (of not more than 20 men) in the Lampungs at Tulang Bawang and Lampung Samanka.

The realm

The only area for which de Rovere van Breugel supplies population figures is the coast between the Tangeran river and Prinseneiland, where he estimates 45,000 people lived in 84 *negeri*. The remainder were mostly hamlets of 10–20 dwellings. In all these villages the houses were of bamboo but the larger ones had "Mahometan temples" of stone, with tiled roofs. The interior was mostly mountains, and most of the pepper was grown here. The population was "about the same as that of the coasts", and the people came down weekly to sell their produce. The south coast was a very different area: though it was counted as part of Banten, the population of this remote area were actually subject to no authority, according to de Rovere van Breugel. The Sunda Strait islands belonging to Banten were mostly uninhabited and covered by impenetrable forests. The Thousand Islands were leased by the Sultan to the Company, which sub-leased them to Chinese who quarried coral for lime ovens. They were often used as a hiding-place for Mandarese smugglers and pirates who sometimes made the voyage between Banten and Batavia very unsafe. Krakatau, Pulau Besi and the Keijsers- and Princen-eiland, were inhabited by a few people in miserable huts, and used to produce a reasonable amount of pepper, but no longer did so. The forests of Krakatau, Princen-eiland, Pulau Lagondi and other islands could have been a valuable source of heavy timber, but transport was very difficult.

The bight of Banten, notwithstanding the marshy shores of the east and south and the reefs of the west, provided an excellent anchorage, even under the highest winds, thanks to the sheltering formation provided by its islands. These were all uninhabited except for Pulau Panjang, ceded to the Company in 1733, where about 100 Malays and Buginese grew bananas for the Banten market. The Commander had a lime kiln there where 3–4,000 baskets of lime was fired annually. Kapok, tail pepper and *benkudu* (which was used to produce a red dye) grew there in the wild, and the island was well situated for the establishment of a supply station for Dutch shipping. Only the lack of drinking water, which had to be brought from Banten, prevented further development.

Aristocracy and peasantry in the tides of world capitalism

The Hollandse Kerkhof, the island closest to the river of Banten and the anchorage for Dutch shipping, also had a shipyard for the repairing of the Sultan's ships.

The capital, Banten

This had once been enclosed by walls and bulwarks, but these had been completely destroyed in the preceding warfare The fortifications were never re-built, but new houses were set up on the same site as the old city "and the quantity of these is the reason that one still designates it a city". It was situated between the Karangantu river and the Kali Gede (Great River), both very shallow, so that vessels deeper than four feet could not enter them and even light vessels had to wait till the tide was at high springs. The situation had become worse in recent years with the buildup of the river bed: five years previously the Company's lighters, five to six feet deep, had been able to pass upriver. The tides were very irregular, which de Rovere van Breugel felt was probably because of the outflow of waters from the Banka straits against the hook of Banten and the varying effects of these on tides in the bight: some years' work needed to be put in to mapping the coastal waters. The river water, though it tasted fresh, was muddy and, with the amount of refuse that was thrown in it, very unhealthy to drink. De Rovere van Breugel sees this as the cause of the high mortality among the European military – 24 out of 100 – in the past thirty years.

The houses of the Bantenese were mostly of bamboo, a few in wooden frames, and roofed with *atap*. Some officers of state, like the chief minister and "priest" and a few others, had stone houses, but most of these belonged to the king and were only lent to their inhabitants. The Chinese had two *kampungs* of stone houses, one at Karangantu, the other close to the Company fortress along the Kali Gede. Also at Karangantu, opposite the Sultan's castle, was a Moorish quarter, with some houses of bamboo and others of stone.

The ruler's castle[9] was an irregular square with four points or bastions, and a half-moon, equipped with 58 pieces of artillery, most of them ineffective, and all of them ill-provided with carriages and ramparts. Around the bastions and by the gate were the buildings housing the VOC garrison. Inside the fortress were buildings housing the king and his household, all women: no men are allowed to spend the night there on pain of death. Three double walls separated the royal residence from the perimeter of the fort, and the interior, being forbidden to outsiders, de Rovere van Breugel could not describe except to say that in the midst of irregularly placed buildings were a number of baths, whose water was refreshed from the aqueduct from the king's pleasure-ground (Tasik Ardi), which brought it from the mountains. This aqueduct was built in 1701 and ran under the walls of the fort and out the other side to the river. (Despite a contractual agreement with the VOC to build a similar aqueduct for the Company's Fort Speelwijk neither the reigning Sultan, Abul Nazar Muhamad, or his predecessor had ever made a beginning on this beneficial project). Tasik Ardi itself, one and a half hours' journey inland, was a square, stone, two-storey building on an artificial island, surrounded by moats 20 *roods* [i.e. about 75 metres] wide. There was once a bridge, but this was not renewed when it became ruinous and access was thenceforth by a small flat-bottomed boat rowed by women. Around the moats was a thick hedge of *patah tulang*, and there was a watch at the entry: admission required a special dispensation of the ruler. The Sultan had begun to construct a pleasure-garden and stone house within the ruins called Kota Rubuh, of which only the exceptionally thick walls remained. Lack of materials and rice for the labourers (the ruler was, it will be remembered, extremely poor) had brought this project to a standstill.[10]

There were three markets in Banten: Karang Antu, Tumanggung, and the new market. These, however, were declining "from day to day, and no longer resemble what they have been" just as Banten, once so illustrious, no longer merited the name of city.[11]

On the other side of the river was the office of the King's *shahbandar*, the inn, the residence of the inspectors of the boom, and some small food stalls. From the *shahbandar*'s office a lane led to the garden of the Fiscal, separated from the river by the Company stables, south of which lay the newly-established garden of the administrator. Some distance from the fort, on the south side, were the King's pepper warehouses, and further still a street where Chinese and Malays lived in stone houses, at the end of which the Javanese *negeri* began.

The aristocracy[12]

The gloom with which de Rovere van Breugel surveys the present state of the city is repeated in his description of its inhabitants. The Sultan, Abul Nazar Muhamad, is described as much under the

Aristocracy and peasantry in the tides of world capitalism

influence of the foreign popes who had gained great influence in Banten and particularly at the court. Formerly the ruler, who was very cognizant of the power of the Company and respectful towards it, had substantially adapted himself to the European style in clothes and in his household, but now he had wholly altered. His poverty compelled him to undertake all sorts of makeshift measures to alleviate it. He was severe towards his servants, and with reason, fearing that some of the great men of the realm criticised him to the Company. In recent years he had gone through many phases: a lover of pomp and state, he had spent much money on fine buildings, furniture, and clothes; collecting dogs, and then turtle-doves; desirious of knowing every woman in the realm; then withdrawing sated from all his desires to spend whole nights in prayer. His unimaginable extravagance had produced such debts that he had even stooped to selling off in public various pieces of furniture and other goods, nay even some of his own clothes, an unbecoming expedient which the Commander should have prevented. Nevertheless De Rovere van Breugel saw his character as fundamentally benevolent, magnanimous and noble, traits which would emerge strongly if he had better counsel: under the influence of someone he respected (and who could moderate his blind religious fervour), he would set aside his jealous maintenance of his rights in favour of magnanimity. The aristocracy were dependent on the ruler, who strongly discouraged them from associating with Europeans The aristocrats were in general poor, their principal possessions consisting in some diamonds, gold and silver. Some had pepper gardens and/or rice-fields. Tenure of office was usually co-terminous with the reign of one ruler, and few could pass on any wealth to their children. For the most part they were contented with a convenient dwelling, a pleasure-boat, a riding hack and some beautiful women. The overseer of the ruler's pepper warehouses, Kyai Aria Astradinata, was the son of a Chinese bricklayer who had himself circumcised [i.e. converted to Islam] and became rich by completing many important buildings and bridges for the king. The son was appointed overseer of the pepper warehouses on the understanding that this position would be hereditary in the family. Pangeran Raja Kusuma, uncle of the king, was a virtuous man, though said to be rather avaricious. He was old and decrepit, and spent most of his time in religious observances and daily lamentation of the decay of his fatherland.

De Rovere van Breugel does not note one feature of the Banten aristocracy that distinguished them from their central Javanese counterparts, that is, the existence of large landholdings in the hands of the nobility. The aristocracy were given land grants (as opposed to rights to part of the proceeds of land, as was the case in Mataram) rather than prebends recoverable by the ruler at will. Boomgaard describes these lands as "something between hereditary fiefs and allodial properties".[13] They were often grants to undeveloped land which was subsequently opened up either by professional land-reclaimers (*malim*) or by peasants who afterwards became share-croppers. Though this system was abolished in 1810, these landholdings retained in their name (*sawah carik, sawah kaprabon* or *sawah turunan*) an indication of their origin.[14]

De Rovere van Breugel notes that the King of Banten rarely gave his relatives any lasting power or office. Under treaty with the VOC no member of the royal family might hold the office of "Rijxbestierder" [Patih], and all holders of this office had to swear an oath of loyalty to the Governor-General and Council as well as to the ruler, though de Rovere van Breugel says the last two had not done so. Other influential officials were the two presidents of the great council, one in charge of administration and justice and the other in charge of pepper cultivation; a secretary; and a number of "Pangauwas"[*Punggawas*, barons], some of whom achieved much influence before being returned to the dust from which the King had lifted them – as in the case of the Chief Minister who had been dismissed and again restored to office and favour. Other officials were the overseer of the King's pepper warehouses, and two royal customs officers, one at the boom of Speelwijk and one at Karang Antu.

In de Rovere van Breugel's description of the royal family and officials, twice as many princes have Sanskrit-derived names as have Arabic-derived ones; the latter are also more common among officials, except of course religious officials.

Sources of income of the ruler. These were:

1. His largest source of income, profits from the pepper trade. The ruler purchased pepper at 7–9 Spanish dollars per *bahar* (375 Amsterdam pounds[15]), and sold it to the Company at 15 Spanish dollars. In addition old-established usage allowed him 11% of all the pepper delivered to him, and the actual amount levied was closer to 20% acording to de Rovere van Breugel.

Aristocracy and peasantry in the tides of world capitalism

2. The income from the revenue farms (*pachten*), estimated to bring in 30,000 Spanish dollars annually.
3. A tithe on rice production, which he usually contracted out for a fixed payment of padi: at the time of writing raised from 4,000 to 18,800 *sangga*.[16]
4. His other incomes were hard to determine, but de Rovere van Breugel comments that one can still see that he was very well off, and were he not so spendthrift and wasteful could maintain himself and make an annual payment against his enormous debts. In the Bedenkingen[17] he remarks that the ruler is extremely poor, due to his enormous debts. These were made up of the Company's expenses incurred in the suppression of the 1752 rebellion, which came to 502,095.10 guilders, and some earlier debts, the total to be paid off at the rate of 25,000 *real* per year for 25 years, though this annual payment had to be reduced first to 18,875 real and then to 12,000 real plus 3,125 *real* for the two garrisons in the Lampungs. Due to further borrowings, the ruler's debts had risen to a million guilders (369,725 *real*) by 1783. De Rovere van Breugel says that the ruler constantly sought postponement of his payments, and was spendthrift to boot, so that the Company could not get 32,400 guilders (12,000 *real*) annually on a sum of one million guilders.

The ruler's annual income over the years 1765 to 1778 inclusive is given by de Rovere van Breugel as 81,000 Spanish *real*, i.e. 68,587.5 *real* from pepper sales to the Company (an average of 9145 *bahar* per annum at a price of 15 *real* of which half went to the ruler) plus 12,412.5 *real* from the revenue farms, leasing of lands and sugar mills, etc.:[18] this apparently leaves out of consideration his profit from the rice tithe. [By way of comparison, the Sunan of Mataram in the early 1730s had an annual income of at least 100,000 *real*;[19] and in 1808 the Sultan of Yogyakarta had an income of 170,000 *real*, of which his expenses came to 73,000 *real*, and he spent some on gold and jewels, leaving savings of 80,000 *real*.[20]

The people

Villages

In the villages, the houses were situated at random, with no overall plan. Most villages possessed an open, rectangular building constructed of bamboo and raised some feet from the ground which served as the meeting house, "where the Prince's orders were announced", and the council chamber. The remaining houses, again of bamboo, were nearly all built directly on the ground.

Household effects consisted of some tools for the man, a spinning wheel or loom for the woman, and a few mats and cushions in the sleeping-apartment, plus two or three bowls and many plates, their kitchen equipment, and a wooden tray for *sirih* and *pinang*.

The heads of the *negeri* had, in addition, two or three chairs and a small table in their houses, but made little use of them. The very richest – principally those who lived in the city – embellished their houses with chairs, tables, and benches, some also with one or two mirrors and hanging lamps, in the European fashion, while their sleeping apartments were hung with fine chintz or silk curtains, and contained a couple of dozen long cushions of silver or even gold material – purely for show, for the cushions in daily use were just as grimy and oil-smeared as those of the meanest slaves. In the women's sleeping apartments in such houses there were lavish dressing-tables formed of five varnished and gilded chests of graded size, the largest on the bottom, and the smallest serving as a betel box [sets of chests like this, often with metal inlay in a Middle Eastern or Indian geometric style, were probably commonly used by the upper classes of Java, and specimens may be seen in the musea in Cirebon, for instance].

Food

The most common food was buffalo and goat meat, poultry and all sorts of fish. All their food was prepared without salt. The inhabitants of the uplands contented themselves with vegetables, poultry and rice, with goat and buffalo only on special occasions. Fruit was extremely varied and plentiful:[21] it was exported to Batavia as well as consumed locally. Vegetables were similarly varied and plentiful.

Clothing[22]

The clothing of the Bantenese – that is, of the great – consisted of long trousers over which they draped a folded "coast-cloth" [from the Coromandel coast?] fastened around the waist with a girdle, usually of gold, while on the [upper] body they wore a vest or shirt of white linen, and over this again a jacket of chintz, velvet, or gold stuff. On their head they wore a cap of gold cloth lined with linen, flat or pointed above, covering the skull but allowing some hair to fall down. When thus attired they also wore jewelled rings and a gold or "sawassen" [?*suasa*, gold with a large admixture of a special alloy to improve its appearance and quality?] cover for the sheath of their *kris*; some wore embroidered mules, but that was generally a prerogative of the royal family.

Those of small estate contented themselves with a handkerchief on the head, short trousers, and a common garment on the naked [upper] body, over which they wore a chintz or gingham *kebaya*.

The clothing of the women also varied according to rank, at least when in public, for in the privacy of their houses they wore just a single covering of the lower body, and a piece of linen under the arms, which was in fact all the clothing the common women ever wore. [In other words, the women of Banten wore the style of dress once common in Bali and central Java, but now reserved for ritual occasions. This dress was in former times also worn in west Java, and some early photographs also show women with bare breasts, like Balinese women before Independence.] Those of standing wore gold armbands, diamond rings, real and diamond flowers in their hair, jewels in their ears, and gold necklaces. They also wore garments of fine coast linen, or red silk worked with gold flowers, called "Sonkits" [*songket*. cloth with supplementary weft patterning. *kain songket* are the silk and metallic cloths of Palembang]. They held a handkerchief in their hand, with a gold or "sawassen" chain with a little box of the same metal at the end, for betel. Their breasts were covered with fine coastal Cacambans [*kemben*, breast-cloth], the ends hanging down over their shoulders. Their bodies were anointed with all kinds of fragrant salves, and their faces with a sort of "varnish" to make their complexions whiter than their natural state.

Weapons[23]

These were the kris, and for the mountain people the "common *parang*" with a horn haft, used both as tool and weapon. Their other weapons were pikes, one or two of which were carried behind the officials of state when they went out in public. They also had *sumpitans* or blowpipes, which they used with great accuracy, small cannons, matchlocks and blunderbusses, all these weapons being used on their boats in defence against pirates. Some of the nobles had collections of all sorts of weapons kept in a special armory.

Temperament and life-style[24]

By nature the Bantenese were as proud as any of the native races, according to de Rovere van Breugel – and lazy, allowing their women to do all the work of the household. The great spent their time eating and drinking, chewing betel, and going out on horseback. They lived from the income of their lands in the form of a yearly tribute. Trade was left to a lesser sort of person, called *Orang Dagang*, or traders, who sold their wares either at the market or in itinerant trade. A few of them had ships with which they conducted trade, personally or through agents, to the Lampungs and other places. Two or three equipped ships for the voyage to Java's [north] coast.

The common people lived from the work of their hands and were "not much better than slaves". They collected the products of the uplands, and did all sorts of coolie work. In the uplands they worked in farming and pepper culture. The coastal people worked as fishermen or in the sea trade.

De Rovere van Breugel comments on the Bantenese habit of washing two or three times daily, and on the extent of opium smoking among the men. The population was generally well-inclined to Europeans and respectful of the Company, but the ruler forbad any association.

Marriage[25]

Children were generally betrothed at the age of eight to ten years, but remained in their parents' homes, and the betrothal could still be broken off, though in that case the girl's parents lost the payment they had made. If a man had a child of outstanding beauty or virtue, he sometimes bought a son- or daughter-in-law for a money payment, choosing someone he considered worthy of such a paragon.

The marriage feast was held at the home of the bride, and the guests all brought a present, usually of fruit or other food. Towards evening the bridegroom, having prepared himself through prayer, set out in state for the bride's house (usually by water) accompanied by all his friends and with stately music. On arrival he was met by a relative of the bride, or if he was of higher rank, by his father-in-law himself, and invited in to take his place beside his intended, on a raised sitting-place with gold and silver cushions behind and hung with fine linen or silk curtains and strewn all over with flowers. There the bridal couple were blessed by the "Priests or Elders", and subsequently given a little cooked rice by a married woman who had lived in harmony with her husband for many years. Twenty to fifty women sat around them on the floor. They were given a cup of tea and a little betel, which they did not keep in the mouth for long. Two children fanned them with a beautiful fan. In other apartments the guests enjoyed betel, tea and comfits, followed by a hot meal, which they ate seated on mats, in order of rank. The bridal couple ate separately, and without saying a word to one another. There was always music and dance, which continued far into the night, after which the groom returned home in the same way as he came.

This ceremony was repeated three times at the house of the bride and thereafter three times at the house of the groom – the six days were not always consecutive, it being usual to have a couple of days rest between the festivities. After this the bridegroom took his bride home, where according to de Rovere van Breugel she was completely subject to his wishes, though there were some who stood up for certain conditions [perhaps a reference to the automatic divorce that the woman can claim should her husband fail to fulfil certain conditions set down in the Javanese wedding ceremony]. Men were allowed by their religion to marry as many women as they liked, but were usually contented with one or two, each in a separate dwelling, where they were cared for by female slaves, some of which were the man's concubines. Of these, only the most dear were raised to the status of wife. Divorce was very easy: once a man repaid the *mas kawin* [bride price] to his wife he was free to send her back to her parents.

Laws

De Rovere van Breugel notes that the Bantenese were said to have a law book but for the most part the natural laws of all nations were followed: blood was repaid with blood, theft with imprisonment or slavery, which was also the penalty for non-payment of debts. He claims that the judges were inconsistent and partial, and injustice was rampant. No-one might be condemned to death without the approval of the king, who in matters not touching himself consulted with the "High Priest"; in matters such as seduction of his concubines he exercised his right of summary execution, and was accountable to no-one.

Religion [26]

According to de Rovere van Breugel, the Bantenese were Muslims, but the inhabitants of the mountains and of the Lampungs professed a mixture of Mahometan and heathen belief, mixed with the "most stupid superstitions", being Muslims only in that they were circumcised. Their temple, called a *massigit*, was a square building entered by wading through a pond, which had steps going down into it and up again into the mosque. Inside, they were completely without ornamentation; there was a sort of pulpit or elevated seat against the wall in the middle, from which the priest, now standing and now sitting, conducted the service, which consisted of reading some verses from the Koran, and the saying of prayers, to which the congregation always responded: Amen.

When someone died, a great number of priests was called to commit him to earth with ceremony. The corpse was washed and wound in white linen. Then it was put on a *bali-bali* or bamboo bench, around which sat ten or twelve priests, reading the Koran, praying and singing by turns. The corpse was then taken to the graveyard followed by some of the priests and a number of the close relatives. It was put in the grave on one side, with the face bare and the nose against the ground. The head was supported by some balls of earth, the face towards the west. While the priests made their prayers and blessings, the grave was closed and strewn with flowers. On the third, seventh and fourteenth day after the death a meal was held and flowers strewn on the grave. The priests were once again present to say prayers. Those present each took home some food, and the priests received an honorarium. Some people also commemorated the hundredth and thousandth day of the death and visited the grave every Friday. Others were content to tidy the grave once yearly on the occasion of the fast, and particularly on its last day, when the grave was strewn with flowers. Banten was full of holy graves. Most of the islands in the Sunda strait had holy graves where many people came to make offerings when they were about to begin some undertaking. In the bay of Banten there was a coastal *negeri* named Boja Nagara where there was a famous holy grave on top of a high mountain. It was customary to make a pilgrimage there, stopping halfway at another such grave on an island.

Banten's products[27]

De Rovere van Breugel. gives the following information on Banten's products:

Pepper. This was the principal product, and was mostly grown in west Banten, in the uplands, and most importantly in the Lampungs. The trees on which the pepper vines grew were called *dadap*. They were planted six to seven feet apart and each supports a single pepper vine. Each vine produced a half pound to a pound annually, or more. Some pepper gardens were owned by the great men of Banten who lived in the capital; others were owned by private citizens, some of whom lived on the estate. Supervision was in the hands of *mandors*, who had to ensure that every inhabitant [of the uplands] over the age of sixteen maintained 500 trees. If this had actually been done Banten would have produced 3.5 million pound of pepper annually, whereas in fact the annual total was less than a fifth of that amount. The average annual delivery was about 9000 *bahar*, with a high in 1724 of 19,000 *bahar* and diminishing production in the last five years, with a total of 28,930 *bahar* or 5500 *bahar* per annum. Of the 45,000 people in the uplands ten or twelve thousand could be employed in pepper cultivation but only 5000 were currently employed. Furthermore while 500 trees could have produced a *bahar* of pepper annually, at present they yielded less than half that amount. (According to a calculation made in 1763, 1000 trees could produce 10 *bahar* annually, though according to information given to Commandeur Meijbaum, in Tulang Bawang 2500 and in Samanka 1500 pepper plants were needed to produce 10 *bahar*. De Rovere van Breugel. was not sure whether the Lampung *bahar* was a larger measure.[28]) The salary of the mandors was half a Spanish real for every *bahar* delivered and they also derived profit from selling clothing, opium salt and pottery to the planters, all at anything up to double the market price. Trade in pepper was a royal monopoly. White pepper was also produced, by soaking the best corms in lime water for a couple of days to soften them and then drying them again. Because of the losses involved in making black pepper into white, the price paid was twice as high (thirty as against fifteen Spanish *real* per *bahar*).

In 1683 it was estimated by the ambassadors of the ruler of Banten that Banten could produce 1200 *bahar* annually, the Lampungs 2000 *bahar*, and Tulang Bawang, (which in de Rovere van Breugel's's time delivered only 50–200 *bahar*; p. 148, 30–100 *bahar*), also 2000 *bahar*. Sillebar, which subsequently seceded from Banten and was occupied by the English, was said to have a capacity of 24000 *pikul* [8000 *bahar*] per annum. Such large quantities were never delivered to the Company, but there had certainly been more delivered in former times than in De Rovere van Breugel's time, which he attributes to a lack of a sufficient labour-force and to the small payment which growers in the uplands received. In the five years 1767/8–1771/2 over 1100 *bahar* per annum were delivered. A table[29] shows that the Lampung deliveries had gone down from 7734 in 1780 to 3438 in 1786. However, de Rovere van Breugel says that much of the pepper of the Lampungs was being sold to the Mandarese and English, who paid a better price.

In early 1787 de Rovere van Breugel sent Assistant C.H. Cramer to make a proper investigation of pepper cultivation in the uplands – as opposed to a pleasure trip well rewarded by bribes from the planters for not reporting the true state of the pepper plantations (De Rovere van Breugel offered to make up the amount of bribes offered from his own purse). De Rovere van Breugel kept a signed duplicate of this report for himself, calculating that the Commandeur of Banten would keep it from the Raad and Hooge Regeering, and quotes from it here. It vividly reveals the over-stretched lines of command and information in the Company's pepper operations. Due to the state of the roads, it was physically very difficult for Cramer to actually visit the pepper plantations, and the local population made the most of this circumstance to prevent him from seeing the true state of affairs. He persisted, however, and saw enough to say that the plantations were in a much worse state than had previously been reported, and all those involved in pepper growing complained that they were either not paid at all, or paid with clothing and goods reckoned at extremely high prices. Pepper plantations in the west were in an even worse state than those in the south and south-east, though the area was better suited to pepper growing. Pasir Uri was in the same sad state, with the same complaints from the population over the lack of payment. In some places it was clear that the work of pepper growing had only been started on the approach of Cramer's party. He found a decrease over the reported totals for the previous year of 48,000 pepper plants and 171 planters in the east, and about 112,000 plants in the west. There were also many uncultivated lands and unemployed men who could grow pepper on them. When the party came to the Jakatra border they found a flourishing and unconcealed illicit trade in all sorts of goods. The report also includes some suggestive details about particular localities. At Bankalot, the first village past Ceram, Cramer found three *mandors* [overseers] preparing to flee the area with the greatest part of the population: the first and second *mandors* had been ordered by their overlord, Kyai Aria Wiryakusuma, to deliver 1000 *sangga* of padi each, and the third 60 *sangga*. In the nearby kampong of Kawung Sawang, the *mandor* Ratu Bagus Pangulu alias Rangeen had recently been released from three months in irons by his overlord Pangeran Suramenggala, who had taken his store of 100 *sangga* of padi. [perhaps evidence of the conflicting demands of the VOC and Banten aristocracy]

Coffee. This grew as well in Banten as anywhere on Java, but the inhabitants were forbidden to grow more than was needed for local consumption.

Indigo. This was also mostly for local consumption. The Bantenese had a great aversion to the new method of delivery, in dry pieces. De Rovere van Breugel recommends that its preparation be encouraged by offering high prices for an initial period.

Sugar. In 1755 four sugar mills were set up, at Karang Kerang, Tanjong Kait, Ketapang, and Salmurang Sumur, or Kramat. The first two were reduced to one, and all were in a poor condition, The Chinese rented them from the Sultan, and delivered the sugar to the Company in Batavia, apart from a few hundred *pikuls* which were consumed locally.

Pinang. This product was sold at a better price in Banten than anywhere else in Java. The best quality was grown in the region of Ceringin and the neighbouring uplands, where it grew in superabundance. Millions of pounds were transported annually to Batavia and Semarang, besides what was dried and cut into four pieces to be sold by weight. Most of the latter was bought from the lease-holder by the Chinese of Batavia to load their junks.

Coconuts. These too grew in abundance in the Ceringin region. Much coconut oil was made here, and some of it was taken by clandestine routes by sea through the uplands to Batavia. (it sometimes sold for as little as 14 *duits* per can in Ceringin whereas the Batavia price was 12 *stuivers*. The ruler of Banten placed a heavy tax on it, however.) The outer husk of the coconut, which was put to various uses elsewhere, was here thrown away, but the inner hard shell was used for making spoons and bowls, which were sold in the market. *Tuak* was also made in Banten.

Sandalwood. It was said that much of this wood grows in the mountains, but very little was cut and sold, due, according to de Rovere van Breugel, to the laziness of the Bantenese. The little that was cut cost a *real* per *pikul*, and was taken by the Chinese junks to Batavia where it sold for Rd. 3.

Kayu soga. This was used to produce a brown dye for batik and fish nets: about 1000 *pikul* was transported to Batavia annually.

Sintok, puasari and katten. These were trees whose bark was used for medicine and dyes: small quantities were traded to other parts.

Pandang and pucuk. These were used for mats, bags, and sails: they were also taken by the Chinese junks. Nipa palm which grew along the coast, principally in east Banten, was also used for mats but only for local consumption: it was dearer than what was sold at Onrust and Batavia.

Rice. This grew in superabundance, though some years ago the King had to buy a few hundred *koyan* from the Company at Rd. 30 per *koyan*, something that would not be necessary in future.

Cotton. Most of this came from the Lampungs, but it was not enough to supply Banten's needs, and the King was permitted to purchase 144,000 strings (elsewhere: 155,000 strings) from Batavia or Semarang annually, a right he leased to a Chinese for 1500–2000 *real* per annum. This cotton was then made into clothing by the latter's employees and sold at a high mark-up. De Rovere van Breugel recommended that the Company enter directly into this trade and reduce the mark-ups to a reasonable level. The Bantenese women also spun and wove cotton and made garments from it which were sold in Batavia. They were generally not equal in quality to the Makassarese and Buginese products, shrinking a great deal when washed, but there were some of finer quality which were much sought after and sold at a very high price.

Buffaloes. The inhabitants of the uplands sold these to people from the Jakatra region. Their fat, hide, and horns etc. were also items of trade with the junks.

All trade was in the hands of a few individuals who had a monopoly which they purchased for an annual payment to the King, and all profits left the region.

Pottery. All sorts of pottery for the kitchen were made here, as were flower-pots and columns: if one desired a new design, one could have it made by supplying a sketch.[30] There were also brickworks, but the uncertain demand held back their development.

Coral. This was brought from Ceringin, Anyer, Pulau Limas and the Thousand Islands, and a great quantity of whitewash was exported to the capital annually. Pulau Panjang alone could produce 10,000 sacks of mortar annually.

Salt. There were salt pans in the bay of Banten, for local consumption and to supply the Lampungs.

Kapok. Large amounts were grown in the uplands. 2000 *pikul* could be supplied annually, but at the moment only 100 *pikul* was required by the capital, for the hospitals. Cleaned kapok sold for Rd. 5 or more per *pikul*.

Rattan. Most of this was brought from the Lampungs, though a very long variety used for the standing rigging on native boats was grown locally.

Bamboo. This grew in superabundance in the Pontang uplands, which supplied the whole of Banten with this commodity used for so many different purposes.

The Cancer Within

Other small items (goods made out of horn, copper, lead and iron; herring; rope) were not of much significance.

Pearls were said to be found around Princen-eiland.

Products and fruits of the Lampungs[31]

Pepper and cotton. These grew here in greater abundance than in Banten; and much of Banten's rattan was brought from here (see above) and some was exported to China. Rice was grown in the Lampungs, but only enough for local consumption.

The coastal waters both of the Lampungs and of Banten itself were rich in fish, and shrimps and other fishes were used to make *těrasi*. In olden times, says de Rovere van Breugel, it was common for 60 *praus* to set out together from Banten to Batavia, to supply the common people with fish in the season when it was scarce there. Nowadays however if 60 *praus* were to leave Banten there would not be many left there.

Birds nests. There were three different qualities. The first quality were found in the bay of Samanka and were snow-white and as good as the Riau nests. Trade in these was a royal monopoly, but there was also smugglers' trade. Trade in the second and third qualities was strictly forbidden, but the Chinese bought them up and in small parties took them to Batavia either by sea or overland through the mountains. De Rovere van Breugel estimates that perhaps two to three *pikul* of the extra-white quality and six to seven of the other two were exported yearly, though it was not possible to get accurate figures. There was also a very poor quality of nests, black and full of dirt, which could be purchased for Rd. 20–25 per *pikul* locally and fetch up to Rd. 100 in Batavia: some Chinese claimed that they had greater invigorating properties than the white ones, and they fetched very high prices in certain places in China.

Agar-agar and tripang. The latter was caught by hand along the Lampung coast of the Sunda straits and even more in the waters of Princen-eiland, cooked alive in large iron pots, gutted and dried. These products were much prized by the Chinese and when their junks departed were bought up by the *pikul*.

Gold-dust.[32] This was found in Lampung Tulang Bawang. Most of it was bought by the Palembangers – who were engaged in smuggling and slave raiding from the uplands – in exchange for opium and other goods, a trade which the small garrison could not prevent. A little gold was exported to Batavia, for a 50% profit after the King's levy was paid. Ivory was readily obtainable but because of the superstitious fear of the Bantenese and Lampungers of carrying it in their boats, it too was mostly sold to the Palembangers.

Damar. There were two sorts, simple *damar* and *damar kaca*, which was finer and found mostly in the Lampungs. The latter was most sought after in Java for batik making, and sold for four to eight *real* per *pikul*, whereas it could be bought in the Lampungs for only one to two *real*. De Rovere van Breugel estimates that 1000 *pikul* of *damar kaca* and 4–5000 *pikul* of the ordinary sort could be traded annually, though a mere 100 *pikul* of the first and 2–300 *pikul* of the second was actually marketed.

Trade in all these items was carried on only by the inhabitants of the coast, whose land was unfit for growing pepper, so this trade did not adversely effect its cultivation.

The eastern side of the Lampung coast produced sulphur. Superstition, says de Rovere van Breugel, prevents its exploitation: the first people who tried to dig it were affected by serious and even mortal sickness.

Throughout the whole section on produce, there is a sense of decay, decline, and under-production.

Imports

These included all sorts of Chinese goods, except silk; Javanese garments; all sorts of native dried herbs and medicines; *bankudu* root (used to dye thread red), salted eggs, onions, *jarak* and *kacang* oil; light wooden items, iron, steel, and sheet copper (for *sirih* containers and other copper goods which were then exported); coastal [i.e. Coromandel?] goods and Bengal linen cloth, the trade in which the Company had abandoned for some years because of the poor traffic; Javanese and Chinese tobacco, ginger; and other goods of which less and less was imported every year, as the land became more and more depopulated and the monopolistic nature of the trade caused prices to be so exorbitant that the common people became more and more frugal in their consumption.

The Cancer Within

Opium[33]

In the capital the sale of opium was a royal monopoly leased to the Lieutenant of the Chinese for a monthly payment of 300 *real*. The Lieutenant was obliged to buy his opium from the Societijt in Batavia. There was, however, considerable smuggling of opium into the uplands, mostly by Chinese from the border areas of Jakatra, bringing opium smuggled from Tangerang, a trade facilitated by the much improved routes over the mountains between Jakatra and Banten in recent years. This opium sold in the uplands was cheaper than that marketed in the capital. Opium was also traded in the Lampungs by the Mandarese, on their return voyages from Benkulen. Their opium and textiles were exchanged for birds' nests, ivory, and sometimes also for pepper. Finally, the Chinese sugar-mills between Batavia and Banten purchased opium from Onrust and the surrounding islands, or directly from the English. In De Rovere van Breugel's description of the princes of the realm[34] five, or about one third, are said to be opium addicts.

Smuggling and piracy[35]

The Mandarese were the most active in smuggling. Their voyages, despite all prohibitions against them, had been taking place uninterrupted for a long time, both through the Straits of Sunda and along the south coast of Java. Some of the vessels visited Bankaulu, but most travelled along the west coast of Sumatra and the islands along this coast up to Aceh, whence they returned with slaves, gold, birds' nests, tripangs, and turtle meat. Those who made land at Padang or Bengkulen mostly brought opium, textiles and camphor, and according to de Rovere van Breugel these were the only ones who could actually be considered smugglers, the others, though they sailed without Company passes, being only small traders who could not do much harm to the Company. He suggests that the most economical way of cutting down on illicit trade would be to institute a system of rewarding informers with the goods of any vessels they report for being engaged in this trade.

As in many other regions at this period, piracy was an endemic problem. De Rovere van Breugel recommends that the Company do more to raise the standards of Banten's fleet, for instance by supplying gunpowder, since these vessels were the most effective against pirates, whose light, amply sailed craft could always escape

European rigged ships. Raising the operating standards of the Banten fleet would do much, he says, to reduce the incidence of piracy. Piracy had formerly been rampant in the Lampungs, with the pirates carrying off coastal dwellers to be sold as slaves for pepper cultivation. With the decline of piracy, pepper cultivation had also declined. Piracy had by no means been eliminated, however, either in the Lampungs or in the bay of Banten. De Rovere van Breugel had seen a number of expeditions sent out against pirate ships, always too late and using unarmed and unwilling men taken off the street, which could have been succesful if better organised. The ruler's fleet consisted of one large *panjajap* [a sort of barge or sloop] manned by 40 men and armed with swivel guns, matchlocks, and pikes; a small *panjajap* manned by 30 men and similarly armed; and 12 fishing boats of 12–16 oars, manned by a crew of twenty, armed with swivel-guns and matchlocks and reinforced like the pirates' praus; thus a total of 14 vessels and 310 men. Only the two *panjajap* were maintained from the ruler's revenues, since he could not afford to keep the rest, which were the responsibility of different members of the aristocracy. This fleet was divided into two halves, one of which was sent to cruise for a three month period while the other remained in Banten under the obligation to be ready for deployment on six hours' notice. Any booty taken on these cruises was divided up among the crew: for each pirate handed in for trial the commander received Rd. 30. and the common sailors 10 rd; for every enemy killed in battle the Company paid Rd. 5. The owners of the vessels were responsible for seeing that they were properly maintained and ready for action, under established regulations which de Rovere van Breugel says were in fact hardly in force.

De Rovere van Breugel's conclusion concerning the present state of Banten and plan for reform

The Creator, he says, has richly supplied Banten with everything necessary for a flourishing kingdom; but the Asiatic Mode of Government to which it was subjected prevented the execution of all good undertakings, through the absence of a just oversight. The pitiable inhabitants would be benefited by a more moderate government which would strive to populate the kingdom and encourage trade and the free arts and sciences. When we compare Banten at the time when Europeans first came to the Indies with the impoverished present we are astonished at the unfathomable ways of the Almighty God who makes men rich and reduces them to nothing again at will. The greatest trading-place in the east has become the habitance of the wretched: in the midst of all nature's plenty the Bantener lives like another Tantalus, unable to satisfy his hunger and thirst. How blessed in after generations would be the name of those who restored so many thousands of souls, if not to former glories, at least to a happier state than the present one.

De Rovere van Breugel here introduces the theme of a land that has fallen on bad times that is repeated again and again by both Dutch and Javanese writers in this period. The picture contains recurring elements – depopulation, loss of trade (with, in Banten's case, also an exodus of the Chinese population), lack of capital, indebtedness, addiction to opium (a commodity which had been forbidden by Sultan Ageng in Banten's heyday), piracy. It also like other accounts comments on the extent of the "smuggling" trade of varied origins, Mandarese, English, and Chinese (the last two in cahoots in the smuggling of opium), which at this time had made Java a leaking sieve as far as the VOC's alleged monopoly was concerned. His account reveals classic signs of under-capitalisation both as regards the Sultan and as regards the Company. It reveals too a picture of peculation at all stages among both Dutch and Javanese along the very long line of communication that stretched between Batavia and the Bantenese pepper grower, a line that the VOC simply could not maintain as an effective conduit. Finally, it suggests that Banten, which had led the way on the capitalist road (albeit of a Colbertian French rather than Dutch or English model) was now if anything not only in a state of decline but being demonetized, with payment to cultivators made in goods sold at grossly inflated prices, an abuse that will be seen again below in the section on Priangan.

In his reform plan, De Rovere van Breugel begins with an analysis of Banten's history in the seventeenth and eighteenth centuries, ending with the rebellion against Ratu Sarifa which was, he says, the moment when the Company should have introduced much-needed reforms into Banten's system of government, dividing the Sultanate into eight to twelve Regencies and setting up a superordinate Landraad. The old fort of Banten, now called De Diamant, could have been demolished and replaced by a number of smaller forts in the Regencies. Pepper cultivation too could have been devolved to the Regency level, thus abolishing the ruler's exorbitant "overweight" rights and raising revenue without placing an intolerable burden on the mass of the population. Banten would thus have been transformed from a liability (*lastpost*) to a place at least able to cover its costs by paying an annual tribute totalling 400 *bahar* of pepper, counting the production of the Lampungs [sic: this figure must surely be an error given that the annual deliveries in Banten's present decayed state were averaging 900 *bahar*]. This would have involved a much lighter burden than was presently carried by the population, who were obliged to perform corvée service at the village level and usually for the ruler too, in a situation where no-one dared to appear rich, lest he be robbed, and there were scarcely ten Bantenese who were engaged in trade of any significance; and where the land was depopulated from day to day, a situation which had been going on for 20 to 30 years. De Rovere van Breugel suggests that the Company send an Opperhoofd to Banten to stay for a long period and work together with the ruler and gain his trust. This Opperhoofd must be someone who could command the respect of his own subordinates, not one who treats them capriciously, as was all too common at present. The program of reform which this Opperhoofd should set in train with the ruler's cooperation was as follows:

1. The revenue-farm taxes (*pachten*). The extraordinary ones should be reduced by half and the small ones, which affected the common people more, should be abolished altogether. Import and export taxes should be fixed at 8%, and taxes on internal trade at 4%, except for the right to cut wood and the tax on sugar-mills. This measure would encourage trade and bring back the Chinese, who in the last six to eight years had left Banten with their families, especially if they were allowed to take up the many lands now uncultivated and make them productive as they were doing in Jakatra. They should be particularly encouraged into pepper cultivation in the uplands. The extent of Chinese out-migration could be seen in Karang Antu, once a substantial Chinese settlement, but where four-fifths of the houses were now unoccupied. In 1779/80 the capitation tax payment indicated a population of 8–900 both here and in Tanara, while now there were only 200 in both places, and still more were leaving for economic reasons.

The ruler was also advised to waive his right as owner of all land to evict people from their homes and to allow free hereditary possession, totally unknown at present. (The ruler's ownership of all land had been a jealously guarded right, and the Company had had difficulty in obtaining a free title to the land on which their buildings stood). He should permit free association between Bantenese and Europeans, which the present ruler more than any of his predecessors had discouraged, so that the Bantenese had a greater fear and indifference to Europeans than any other inhabitants of Java. The Commander of Banten, apart from his contacts with the Patih, chief priest and chief customs official and two or three members of the royal family, would be only partially familiar with perhaps four nobles of the realm. The ruler should allow the settlement of foreigners [Asians] and permit everyone to engage in trade provided they channelled it to the capital and paid taxes on it.

2. Vaccination against smallpox (the so-called children's disease, Dutch *kinderziekte*). This disease caused indescribable devastation, with whole villages fleeing on hearing that there was an outbreak, and the ruler and his officials should set the example by vaccinating their own children.
3. Advancement of the population. Everyone should be free to own horses and carriages whether for pleasure or for agriculture – something which the ruler did not allow. (The current Commander, Gollenesse, was the first VOC official to be exempted from this prohibition, and no other Company employees were allowed this inexpensive recreation in a generally unhealthy and cheerless post). Anyone should be allowed to employ Bantenese, men or women, without fearing that they will be taken away by the nobles under pretext of contravening a prohibition, and made into slaves or sent to the Lampungs as a penal measure.
4. The common European in Company service. At the moment these were liable to go out on illicit nocturnal excursions to Javanese settlements and even to climb the ruler's *dalem*, all at peril of their lives and with deleterious consequences to their health, already undermined by the insufficient and bad quality food they receive. These men should be allowed to take local wives and set up a house where they would be permitted to spend some of their time in domestic repose, making them better watchmen when on duty. [In 1, 3, and 4 de Rovere van Breugel's suggestions for reform indicate the existence of a deliberately-maintained social distance between the ruler's subjects and the Company's employees based on religion or nationalism or the confluence of both.[36]]

5. Silting-up of the river. A serious problem, since in six years De Rovere van Breugel had seen the river lose three feet in depth. He proposes that vessels anchoring in the river for any length of time be taxed to pay for the work of digging out the bed back to an adequate depth. This would also render the water more drinkable and remove the unhealthy effects of shallow and marshy places along the river. The fish-ponds and fish-drying sites along the river were also unhealthy and should be moved out of this area.
6. Burial of the dead. The Company's dead were buried only ten roods from the fortress and were a source of infection. The ruler was requested to provide another site (a number are suggested).
7. Introduction of consistent and fair laws.
8. Encouragement of marriage. Tax remission should be instituted for families as they had more children, and divorce, now frequent, should be discouraged by a financial penalty for both parties.

Banten in later years

As an Appendix to De Rovere van Breugel's *Beschrijving van Bantam in 1787* is printed J.H. van Heekeren's diary (covering the period 26 August to 19 September) of the investiture of the last Sultan of Banten in 1802.[37] The ceremonial shows a characteristic mix of Javanese, Dutch, and Chinese rituals. There were military processions,[38] refreshments consisting of *"morgenwijn, thee en gebak"* (morning-wine,[39] tea and cakes) were served;[40] there were ten toasts with 9 to 21 gun salutes;[41] signing and sealing of an act of investiture was part of the procedures;[42] there was a ceremonial crowning of the Sultan[43] and a military procession;[44] passing mention is made of the Sultan's visit to the "temple" (mosque) in his state coach[45] followed by a formal meal at the coronation house, with more toasts and a 30 gun salute to wish the new Sultan a prosperous reign. Next there was a *bĕḏaya* dance, the great religious performance signifying the ruler's union with the divine forces guaranteeing plenitude to his realm.[46] Then there were Chinese fireworks, and presents (timepieces, gold and silver) were given.[47] The Sultan gave in return a "present" of 2000 *real* to be shared among the military who accompanied the embassy. Finally there was a *wayang orang* performance and more toasts with 13 to 21 gun salutes (The Sultan and Ratu Latifa only received 16, Zijne Hoog

Edelheid – the Governor General – and the heeren Raad van Indie – his Council – 21), native dancing, and Chinese instrumental music.[48]

The editor of this journal remarks[49] that only six years later the castle "de Diamant", where in September 1802 Heer van Ijsseldijk gave the sign for the drinking of so many " little glasses of friendship", was the setting of a treacherous murder: the Dutch Commander Dupuy and a number of other Europeans were murdered on the order of the Sultan, when they were in the palace in the course of their duties [an indication if ever there was one that a situation of social distance had progressed to one of desperate hatred]. From that moment, he asserts, the lot of the Banten dynasty was decided.

Had de Rovere van Breugel been able to see a century or a century and a half into the future, he would have found it a depressing denial of his vision for a more prosperous Banten. The region essentially remained a subsistence monoculture throughout the colonial period, with little grown except rice (in the three types of systems noted above[50]). Though all the main crops of the Cultivation System (sugar, indigo, and coffee) were introduced in Banten, only the last succeeded – though greatly resented by the peasantry, who found they derived more profit from rice – and the overall rate of participation in the System was well below the Javanese average. Again unlike the rest of Java, there was no development of commercial or industrial centres or of plantation agriculture. The region suffered from poor access, unlike the north coast which benefited from Daendels' great trunk road. It had other classic hallmarks of backwardness: a very low degree of urbanization even by Javanese standards, a high percentage of the population migrating to neighbouring areas for low-paid labouring jobs (as pepper growers in the Lampungs and as labourers in Batavia and on the private estates in its region). Its depressed appearance is noted by an official who wrote in 1920, "almost nowhere (in Java) does one see more disorderly villages, dirtier houses and more neglected fields".[51]

Banten also had a reputation among Dutch officials not just as an economically unrewarding area but as a notoriously difficult one: "Banten bantahan", combative Banten, as it was called. Banten had a large aristocracy of whom many were not coopted into the colonial bureaucracy. Regents and other *priyayi* were routinely brought in from outside, and were, therefore, less than popular in

Aristocracy and peasantry in the tides of world capitalism

Banten: indeed, among good Bantenese Muslims anyone who worked with the Dutch in this way was considered ridiculous and reprehensible.[52] Banten retained a strong sense of nationalism, an identity which was for many Bantenese still centred on the abolished Sultanate, a focus of numerous small-scale rebellions in the nineteenth century, and of the somewhat more serious rebellion of 1888.[53] In the twentieth century, an explosive mixture of Islam and Marxism led to Banten's becoming one of the two loci of the 1926 "communist revolt".

If Banten was a constant source of exasperation and worse to the colonial government for its perpetual readiness to rebel, it seems paradoxically to have had an exceptional ability to engage the Dutch conscience. It has distinction of being the setting of no less than two of the very few Dutch literary works written to express a sense of guilt at the morality of Dutch actions in the Indies. These are Onno Zwier van Haren's tragedy, *Agon Sulthan van Bantham*,[54] which is based on the downfall of Sultan Ageng because of Dutch support for his perfidious son; and the much more famous colonial novel by "Multatuli", *Max Havelaar*, which focuses on the impotence of a well-intentioned Dutch official – a moral heir to de Rovere van Breugel perhaps – to achieve any support at all for reforming a system that condemned the region to perpetual poverty and backwardness. Perhaps the Bantenese, a nation of sea-going traders espousing a puritanical version of their religion and with a strong, xenophobic nationalism, were sufficiently like the Dutch to cross that barrier of the sympathetic imagination which otherwise seems to have been so strong in the colonial Indies.

THE OLD PRIANGAN-SYSTEM: THE BUSINESS OF FORCED LABOUR

In pre-colonial times the Priangan area had been more decentralised, politically and culturally, than the central Javanese principalities or Banten. Its strong local lords, members of the *menak* class, the equivalent of the central and east Javanese *priyayi*, were substantially independent of Mataram despite a tributary relationship. In 1677 the Sunan of Mataram had ceded his rights over Cirebon and Priangan to the VOC. Under the VOC, the Priangan Regencies, unlike the Batavian Environs (*Ommelanden*), still retained much of the traditional administrative structure, though the Regents were now tributary to the VOC instead of to Mataram.

Regents could be dismissed, as happened in 1802 both to the Regent of Parakanmuncang and the Regent of Batulayang, who was addicted to liquor and opium. Generally however, the position of these Regents, especially those in the more economically important Regencies, was very strong. Priangan was governed by Regents drawn from an inter-related complex of very old families, of which the Sumedang, Galuh and Cianjur lines were particularly important. The Sumedang Regents' pre-eminent role as representatives of Mataram was reflected in their title: they were usually Pangeran (Prince) or sometimes even Pangeran Adipati (the title of the Crown Prince in the central Javanese kingdoms) or even Panembahan, which implies quite exceptional political or spiritual authority. Apart from a period between 1773 and 1791, when Sumedang was under Regents of the Parakanmuncang family, there was an unbroken line of succession in Sumedang for over 350 years.[55] Regencies consisted of several *cutaks* or districts, headed by a *kepala cutak* or *umbul*. There were no private estates.[56]

The source used here, *Reflections on the Jaccatran and Preanger Regencies, and on the question of whether more profit for the Company can be drawn from them than is now the case*,[57] is a somewhat dense and opaque report by the leading conservative S.C. Nederburgh dealing with the Preanger Regencies of Bandung, Batulayang, Parakanmuncang, Sumedang, Krawang, Wanayasa, Adiarsa, Ciasem, Pamanukan, Pagaden (the last two under one Regent); as well as Cianjur and Jampang (under one Regent) and Tangeran and Grinding, which belonged to the so-called Jakatra lands or Batavian Uplands.[58]

Nederburgh begins with the remark that, among all the territorial possessions which the Company has in the Indies, there are none which have brought such profit during the last few years as these provinces on Java. However, some people were of the opinion that the Company could draw much more profit by reducing the cost price of the products which the Regents supplied yearly to the Company especially the coffee, or by altering the financial arrangements with the Regents or the Delegate for Native Affairs, or by selling some parts of the territory of these provinces to private individuals. In May 1794 Nederburgh went to Cianjur with this in mind, but was not there long enough to get all the necessary information and was unable to return in the good monsoon of 1795 and 1796. To achieve his aim, he had to use more roundabout methods. He claims that, although many speak of the Regencies, very few know facts and useful information, and he sets out to supply these. He begins with a rather confused account of the relationship of the jurisdictions of the Company, the Sunan of Mataram and the rulers of Cirebon in this area: the latter had formerly ruled Bandung, Parakanmuncang, Sumedang, Ciasem, Pamanukan and Pagaden. Sumedang and Parakanmuncang were under Batavia from 1730 until 1758, when they were returned to Cirebon, but were reclaimed by Batavia in 1765. The rest of the report covers much difficult ground on the way to Nederburgh's conclusion about ways to increase the Company's profits. In order to provide some signposts to the reader, I have supplied headings and have shortened numerous passages.

The inhabitants

[By way of background, the following may be helpful. The peasants of this region cultivated rice, maize, sweet potatoes for subsistence, and also peanuts, palma christi, and cotton for oil and textiles. They paid *cuke* to the Regent, and in addition had to perform corvée labour, mostly for coffee cultivation. These services were calculated per *cacah* – which Boomgaard defines as the extended family of a well-to-do peasant, including *bujangs* and *numpangs* who were not necessarily related to him. A *cacah* had to plant, maintain and harvest between 500 and 1000 coffee trees. A large number of the Regent's relatives and employees were exempted. The burden varied greatly from district to district, and in the period under consideration entire villages or even districts were abandoned by their population, a phenomenon which Nederburgh admits below. Transportation costs were prohibitive, but salt and mats did travel as far as Batavia for sale. Tobacco, cotton, peanuts, palma christi, palm-sugar processing and handicrafts like spinning and weaving were partly for domestic consumption. There seems to have been hardly any wage-labour.

The area was very thinly populated, and a large part of the population led nomadic lives, subsisting upon slash-and-burn cultivation and the collection of roots and other forest produce. In the mountains of southern districts lived the so-called "bird people", dwelling in hovels constructed in trees, who were probably hunters and gatherers. Large tracts of wilderness were reserved for hunting, a favourite pastime of the Regents, and there were many tiger and rhinoceros.[59]]

Nederburgh explains that those who live on the Preanger lands are divided into two lineages, the *Bumis* and the *Numpangs*.[60] The *Bumis* are the "descendants of the land",[61] giving them of old the duty of carrying out all the country's services for the Regents and lesser Heads. It is they who have to plant the coffee and pepper, and it is up to them to supply most of the contingents of indigo and cotton threads for nothing, to transport it to the city and deliver it to the Company's warehouses. From this it can be deduced that they are in general very poor because, continually kept busy at their compulsory labour, they scarcely have any time left to earn their own living. This explains their inclination to leave one Regency for another when they are tormented too much, to escape the oppressive burdens imposed upon them. From the beginning the Hoge Regering kept a vigilant eye on this and pressed the Regents to recover their deserting subjects.

The *Numpangs* comprise all the other natives who have settled in the Regencies for a certain period of time, including *Bumis* who move to Regencies neighbouring the one in which they were born because their life had been made unbearable there, going against the Javans' inborn desire for their place of birth.

In former times the Regents exonerated the *Numpangs* from all services and compulsory cultivation. Their unforced work consisted of breeding cattle and planting paddy or growing other products as they saw fit. They paid certain contingents from the former, and a tenth of the latter [the *cuke*] to the Regents, who therefore profited from the number of *Numpangs* in their Regencies. This explains why the Regents were favourably inclined to them. As they were treated the best, they chose to stay. By staying for a long time they were usually treated almost as *Bumis*.

It was only after 1785, when coffee cultivation was seriously continued, that the number of *Bumis* was judged insufficient for the extra deliveries, and the obligation to plant coffee also fell on the *Numpangs*. Each family, irrespective of whether they were *Bumis* or *Numpangs*, was then assigned a certain number of trees, and obliged to supply their crop to the Company. In some Regencies the *Numpangs* participated in the supply of indigo and cotton thread as the number of *Bumis* was too small, although in no way to the same extent as the latter.

Nederburgh says that the *Numpangs* have to be treated very carefully, because they are less attached to particular places. They have no difficulty in moving to another Regency at the slightest bad treatment by a Regent or even just to find a better opportunity for planting *sawah* fields, leaving their home, coffee gardens and often their wife and children when these do not want to follow them.

This indifference has, however, been somewhat restrained, since the orders of the Hoge Regering of 18 September 1739 were put into effect against the natives' deserting from one Regency to another, applying to both the *Bumis* and *Numpangs* without distinction. *Numpangs* who deserted were picked up and returned to where they came from. All Regents received a general order not to keep deserting *Numpangs* or *Bumis*. This law had to be strictly observed to prevent the deterioration of the coffee culture in some Regencies and the depopulation of those districts which were unsuited to the establishment of *sawahs*. [Here again we see the VOC's policy of fixing the population to the soil, returning them by force if necessary, as in the Eastern Salient.[62]]

However, the obligation to plant coffee did not come into force directly at the arrival of a *Numpang* in a Regency, and in the Regencies of Bandung and Cianjur he was excused from it and from all other obligatory deliveries during the first three years, in order to give him the opportunity to establish himself and lay out a *sawah* or *tipar* field. During this time he also did not give 1/10th [of his crop, the *cuke*] to the Regent so that he could retain something for buying a buffalo, plough and other tools. The time limit was more arbitrary in other Regencies and, to a large extent, depended on whether many young trees had been planted and whether the newcomer could buy a buffalo and a plough. After this period of time had passed he was registered as being a resident of the Regency and was obliged to lay out his coffee garden and to be employed in the service of the Regent. Nederburgh concludes that when something was eventually done about the extortion by the Regents and lesser Heads and all oppression averted, and when the natives obtained payment for the products they delivered to the Regent, the population of the Preanger lands would increase rather than decrease.

Nederburgh says that the native is lazy, indolent and unsuited to any work which he did not judge to be unavoidably necessary for his maintenance. This was principally the planting of paddy, which Nederburgh says was not only the natural food of this country but also very easy to cultivate because once it had been planted the native only had to watch that it is provided with sufficient water. Also, when the paddy began to ripen, he had to watch out for the birds. This was done in a manner which was very suited to his lazy nature: in the middle of the field he places a small covered house on four bamboo sticks where he can lie with some small necessities beside him. The house is called a *ranggon*.[63] Ropes stretch over the paddy-fields and dried banana or other leaves are fastened to these. At the edge of the field the ropes are fastened to trees or stakes and supported in between by other stakes with the *ranggon* forming the middle-point. All the native has to do is to move the rope to frighten a bird away. Javans who have learnt to do handwork, like making mats, baskets or native straw or cane hats can easily do that as well if they are not too lazy. Most natives whose paddy-fields were quite far from home stayed in these *ranggon* for whole days and nights, provided only with what they need for their sustenance. This consisted only of dry rice, salt and *dinding* (dried and salted buffalo, horse, hartbeest or tiger meat). Before being eaten this was put on the fire for a short time. Nederburgh comments that the Javan is very skilful at making a fire by rubbing together two pieces of bamboo, which is to be found everywhere in the forest. The rice is put into a banana leaf which is suited to the quantity and then pushed into a green bamboo which is cut to the right size. It is closed at the top with the leaf so that no steam can pass through. This bamboo is placed on the fire until the rice is cooked in the moisture of the bamboo which the fire forces inwards. Rice which is cooked in this way is somewhat oily and tastes very good. The Javans boiled water in the same way. Those who stayed in the field for a long time were visited by their wife and children, who sometimes stayed there for a night.

The *gaga* or *tipar* [unirrigated rice-field] took even less trouble to grow. This rice was cultivated at the time of year when there is the greatest rainfall. After it had been sown it needed no further care other than chasing away the birds when it started to ripen. On the other hand, this culture, which was totally dependant on the rains, was subject to many bad harvests and was usually grown by the poorest class among the natives, and also when there was a shortage of *sawahs*.

Generally speaking, the harvesting of the rice caused no trouble. When the paddy was ripe, wife and children went to the fields to cut and harvest it, about which the natives were uncommonly helpful. It often happened that those who had either planted no paddy or whose crop had failed, would help others to cut the paddy for the pleasure of the 1/5th part of what they cut, which they immediately receive *in natura* and take home.

Aristocracy and peasantry in the tides of world capitalism

The clothing needed by the native was limited to a dress (*kleedje*) for himself and his wife, a pair of pants and a cloth they wrapped around their heads: for the rest they went naked. The children of both sexes wore no clothes at all until they were 8 or 9. The cloth for these clothes was made by the women in all villages. They planted the *kapas* themselves and worked it into thread. Their weaving machines were very simple and easy, but only suited to make linen of a certain size for their clothes.

Nederburgh says that what we understand by luxury was still unknown in the Regencies unless one wanted to include the use of opium.[64] But here the common man used little (high-class natives abstained totally), which can be gauged from the scantiness of its consumption, amounting to rather less than 35–45 cases per year in all the Regencies classified under Batavia.

Nederburgh claims that native games are extremely simple. [However, another un-named author of an account of this area from about the same time[65] gives a much richer picture of games and amusements: which apparently included *pantun, topeng, barongan*, cock-, quail- and sword-fighting, as well as board games.]

Nederburgh goes on to say that this simplicity is only true of the Javans who live in the mountains, because those who live on private estates are so carried away and spoilt by the fertile discoveries of the Chinese and Europeans in entertainment, debauchery and dissipation that, when a shortage of money prevents them from giving full reign to their extreme inclinations, they find it no imposition to steal from their fellows or even to commit murder in order to acquire it. Therefore a close watch is kept that the mountainous Javans are kept to their simple way of life and that they are given no occasion for dissipation and debauchery. To this purpose it is especially necessary to watch carefully that no Chinese is given free admission to the Regents' lands, whatever the pretext, because once this shall have taken place, these blessed places would quickly become prey to their insatiable profiteering and be irredeemably spoilt.

Products and profits

The main products were rice, tobacco, coffee, pepper, cotton thread, indigo, cardamom and curcuma.

Rice was for the sustenance of the natives and was only cultivated in such quantities as to satisfy this demand. The cost of transporting rice made it difficult to do so profitably. **Tobacco**, on the other hand, could support these expenses and quite an extensive trade was carried on to the lowlands and Batavia. It was also consumed locally in the Preanger lands.

The remaining products were all delivered to the Company itself. The question to be answered was, how to achieve greater profits for the Company?

The VOC's coffee deliveries

Among the products of the Jakatran and Preanger Regencies the coffee beans earned most. Coffee was brought to Batavia in 1697 and 1698 by the then Governor, General Zwaardecroon, from the Malabar coast. Under his government, hard work was put in to produce it for the first time in 1718.

The planting and intensification of the cultivation during recent years was due to the Company, which accepted the whole quantity which was harvested each year. On 4 February 1752 the High Government resolved that the Regents would together have to deliver 10 *pikul* of pepper with every 100 *pikul* of coffee, but that level could not be sustained and [the order] was retracted on 21 May 1756.

The coffee and other products from the **Regencies of Cianjur and Buitenzorg,** dealt with first as being the largest, were delivered to the Buitenzorg warehouse by the common man who was paid directly by the post-holder of Fort Philippina. The coffee price was Rd. 4^{68} per mountain *pikul* of 222 pounds, which came to Rd. 2⅔ for a *pikul* of 148 pounds, the weight shipped off to the Company's warehouses. The nurserymen of Pondokgede, Ciseroa and Cipannas enjoyed Rd. 4½ for each *pikul* of 148 pounds for the coffee they collected. These deliveries from all three nurserymen were not appreciable, amounting in 1792 to 2036 *pikul*; in 1793 to 2424 *pikul*; in 1794 to 1758 *pikul*; in 1795 to 1493 *pikul*, making a total of 7335 *pikul*, on average 1467 *pikul* per year over 5 years.

The transportation of the coffee, both to the warehouse at Buitenzorg and from Buitenzorg to Batavia, was totally at the expense of the Regent. Nederburgh lists the expenses incurred for every Regency. Here that for Cianjur and Buitenzorg is given as a specimen of the accounting system, while for the remaining Regencies only the bottom line is noted:

For the sacks of each *pikul* of 148 pounds
to which the mountain *pikul* was reduced
at transport..*stuivers*[69] 6:-:
For the freight casks for the transportation
to Batavia or actually to Kampung
Gunung, for each *pikul*...14:-:
To the overseers, clerk and workers in
the warehouse at Buitenzorg and Kampung
Gunung and the *prau* wages from the
warehouse in Kampung Gunung to the
Company's warehouses... 4:-:
The *douceur* for the Commander of Buitenzorg
in which the overseers of Cianjur shared
half since 1793... 6:-:
The *douceur* for the Heads of Cutaks...................................8:-:
for the Delegate for Native Affairs 24:-:
Total for every transported *pikul*..62:-:
making Rd. 3:46 with what the common man was paid on delivery.

The common man delivered the products from Bandung and Batulayang Regencies to the warehouse on the Cikao, which was situated on the Citarum, 7–8 hours above the field entrenchment Tanjungpura.

The Regent of Bandung received the coffee from the common man at its own weight, at 270 pounds the hill *pikul*. He paid Rd. 4 or 2:10$\frac{2}{3}$ for a *pikul* of 150 pounds just as he transported it to the Company's warehouses. His expenses per *pikul* came to 62 *stuivers*, which together with the payment to the common man adds up to a total cost of Rd. 3:24$\frac{2}{3}$.

The Regent of Batulayang received the coffee from the common man at 225 pounds the hill *pikul* and paid Rd. 3$\frac{1}{2}$ or 2$\frac{1}{3}$ for it, i.e. one transport *pikul* of 150 pounds. The expenses were the same as for Bandung, i.e. Rd. 1:4, so that one *pikul* of coffee from Batulayang weighing 150 pound comes to Rd. 3$\frac{5}{8}$.

The coffee from **Parakanmuncang and Sumedang Regencies** was delivered by the common man to the Gintong warehouse, also on the Citarum situated 5–6 hours above Tanjungpura.

It was received by the Regent of Parakanmuncang at 226 pounds the mountain or hill *pikul* and paid at Rd. 4 or Rd. 2:31$\frac{1}{2}$ for a *pikul* weighing 150 pounds. Expenses came to 56 *stuivers* per *pikul*, making a total cost of Rd3:39$\frac{1}{2}$.

The Regent of Sumedang received the coffee from the common man at 250 pounds the hill *pikul* and paid Rd. 4 or Rd. 2:20 for a transport *pikul* of 150 pounds. The expenses were the same as for Parakanmuncang, Rd. 1:8, which made, with the payment to the natives, Rd. 3:28.

In **Krawang and Wanayasa Regencies** the common man delivered the coffee to the warehouse on Babakan in the main *negeri* just above Tanjungpura at 150 pounds the *pikul*, and received Rd. 2.5 for it from the Regent, who delivered the *pikul* at 147 pounds to the Company's warehouses. Expenses were 48 *stuivers* per *pikul*, adding up to a total cost of Rd. 3:22.

The Regent of Adiarsa received his coffee from the common man in the main *negeri*, just above Krawang, at 160 pounds the *pikul*, for which he paid Rd. $2\frac{2}{3}$ or Rd. $2\frac{1}{2}$ for a Company *pikul* weighing 150 pounds, to which he reduced it for shipment to Batavia. The expenses were the same as those of Krawang and with the payment for the natives amounts to Rd. $3\frac{1}{2}$.

The Regent of Ciasem received the coffee from the common man in the main *negeri* at Rd. $2\frac{1}{2}$ for 180 pounds, which was the weight he ships to the Company's warehouses for Rd. 2:4.

The coffee from the **Pamanukan and Pagaden Regencies** was delivered in the same way. They were situated at the greatest distance and the transportation took place in large vessels over the sea which was all paid for by the Regent. Nederburgh says that he was not able to get a precise account. For 25–30 years the products were picked up from these Regencies (which were, however, not of great importance) with the Company's vessels and brought to Batavia.

The Regent of Tangerang paid Rd. 4 to the common man, who delivered the coffee to the main *negeri* (just above the Company's post) up to 226 pounds the *pikul*. This brought his expenses to Rd. 2:30 for a *pikul* of 148 pounds which was how he transported it to Batavia. Adding the usual transport expenses and payment to subordinate heads and the Delegate @ 24 *stuivers* per Batavian pikul, the total cost was Rd. 3:27 per *pikul*.

All the coffee, without exception, was received by the Company at 146 lbs the *pikul* which was paid at Rd. 6. The *pikul*'s excess weight at transportation served to compensate for spillages on the way. Of the difference in weight (being 147, 148 or 149 pounds) no other reason was given than that the coffee from some Regencies was given to less spillage than others, on account of greater proximity and facility in transportation and the use of gunny-bags instead of straw sacks. However, the poverty of the Regent also seemed to be the reason that the transport *pikul* for Krawang had been paid at 147 pounds since 1777. This delivery was also not of great importance.

In most Regencies the coffee was weighed in at delivery on the Company's scales and dishes, but with the Regents' stone weight, which was equalised with the Company's weight. The High Government ordered that the Company's weight had to be used but it appeared that it has not yet been possible to overcome the Regents' special attachment to their own weights. These were used throughout all Regencies and the people trusted them. This was not regarded as a problem, as long as the overseers carefully checked it in the warehouse every now and then against the Company's metal weight. Nederburgh remarks that intentional deception could also be the case with the Company's as well as the Regents' weight, and there were numerous examples of this.

The difference in the payment for the coffee in the various Regencies at delivery by the common man was to be ascribed to the manner of payment and the extra expenses which fell on the coffee from the eastern Regencies on account of their great distance and the difficulty in transportation over arduous and extensive mountains which sometimes took two months and longer. The transportation of coffee along the Citarum was also difficult and dangerous and no year passed without boats turning over. As the coffee *praus* lay very low in the water they were very exposed to the sea which spoilt the coffee. The Company coffee would not accept coffee contaminated with sea water.

The Regents of Bandung, Parakanmuncang, Batulayang and Sumedang received most of the coffee in the main *negeris* since their subjects were mostly too poor to acquire beasts of burden for transportation. Some freight journeys took up to 40 days, and a beast of burden or buffalo could not carry much more than 100 lbs in one go, aside from the rice which the driver needed for himself on the journey. From this it could be seen how great an imposition the trouble and costs of transportation was for the common man. The Regents could not stay as far and as long from home as was necessary to receive all the deliveries at a certain place, as these did not take place all at the one time. Therefore, they kept a number of beasts of burden in their *negeris*, which they bred only for that purpose, and with which they transported the coffee at their expense to the transportation places on the Gintong and Cikao, but for which they charged the common man in freight wages, at rates varying between Rd. 1:12 to Rd. 1:36 per *pikul* of 225–270 pounds.

Nederburgh comments that at first glance one might think that this system, which was very hard on the common man, was in need of improvement. But precise information has taught him, he says, that it can't be any different, and that the coffee supply from the Regencies would deteriorate markedly if any changes were made.

Other deliveries to the VOC

Pepper. The cultivation of this crop had not been very succesful. The Delegate for Native Affairs has recently made another test by laying out four gardens containing about 450,000 trees and, to give more impetus to this work, he freed the natives from planting coffee and all other country services. But up to Nederburgh's time the quantity of pepper delivered each year to the Company remained insignificant.

Cotton thread and indigo were compulsory deliveries and each Regency had a certain set contingent which was, however, seldom completely delivered.

The payment for indigo was first grade at 30 *stuivers* the pound, and second grade at 24 *stuivers*. 13 and 14 *stuivers* had formerly been paid for the third and fourth grades but for some time these grades were delivered to the Company for nothing as rejects, as they had little value.

The payment for the cotton threads was Class B: Rd. 35, C: Rd. 24, D: Rd. 18 and E: Rd. 10 for 125 pounds. There was no A classification for Jakatran cotton threads, though Nederburgh comments that from prices recently realised in sales at Hoorn one could see that the local cotton was just as worthy of this classification as that of Japara [which was famous for its cotton]. But because a re-classification could lead to the Regents wanting a price increase, he considered it best to leave things as they were.

The contingents of both these articles were:

Indigo
Bandung and Batulayang 10:-
Parakanmuncang 15:-
Sumedang 7:-

Aristocracy and peasantry in the tides of world capitalism

Ciasem .... ¼:-
Pamanukan and Pagaden .... ½:-
total *pikul*.. 32¾ :-

Cotton thread
Bandung and Batulayang .... *pikul* 35:-
Parakanmuncang..35:-
Sumedang..25:-
Krawang, Adiarsa and Wanayasa..15:-
Ciasem 1:-
Pamanukan and Pagaden 2:-
total *pikul*.. 113:-

Actual deliveries to the Company in 1794 were however much less.

According to the size of the population of each Regency there was the following obligation for the natives to contribute to the Regents' contingents: *Bumis* – 1½ or 1 *kati*[70] thread and 1 or ¾ *kati* indigo; *Numpangs* – ½ *kati* thread and ½ or ¼ *kati* indigo. The common man had the option of supplying this *in natura*, but since the cultivation was very difficult in most Regencies and subject to yearly crop failures which made the supply even more of a burden for the poor mountain Javan, most of them prefered to give the Regent the following payment: *Bumis* – Rd. 2 for one *kati* indigo and Rd. 1 for one *kati* thread. Should the supply still be insufficient, the shortage was divided proportionally among the *Numpangs* and supplied by them.

The Regents then bought the indigo in the Cirebon lands where it grew profitably along the southern and northern beaches. They paid one *ducatoon* per *kati* or 100 ducatoons per *pikul* which almost absorbed all of their inconsiderable profit from this product.

The cotton thread was largely cultivated by the lesser Heads of the districts in each Regency and delivered to the Regents. But if there was not enough the remainder was bought in the Cirebon districts.

The Regents had their subjects deliver both these articles for nothing, the only exception being that the Regent of Krawang paid the common man Rd. 4–8 and the Regents of Ciasem and Pamanukan Rd. 4½ for each *pikul* (125 lb) of thread and indigo. What the Company paid them was therefore pure profit for most Regents and largely profit for the others.

The Regents of Cianjur and Buitenzorg supplied neither indigo nor cotton thread to the Company. Buitenzorg had not been burdened with contingents for about 50 years, being a private land. The Regency of Cianjur always used to have to deliver 35 *pikul* of indigo and 15 *pikul* of cotton thread but was exempted on special consideration following the decision by the High Government on 13 October 1789. It was given the obligation to participate in 5 years time in the supply of 5000 *pikul* of coffee above the quantity it was already taxed with, or being burdened with the supply of indigo and cotton thread. Nederburgh goes on to say that this extra amount of 5000 *pikul* would be a very insignificant burden compared with the oppressive burden of the deliveries of indigo and cotton thread. He also says this arrangement was a favour to the Regent and implies that certain Company officials had financially benefited.[71] ("This and other similar examples show clearly to what lengths former servants who were employed in the government of the Regencies were able to increase their income, which was already very considerable, all due to the insatiable thirst for money.")

He goes on to say that the exemption from the indigo and cotton thread deliveries brought no comfort at all to the common natives who remained nonetheless under the obligation to contribute the same amount in money as they used to i.e. Rd .5 per household. As a result it had been necessary to instruct the Regent of Cianjur emphatically to cease imposing this burden. It only brought in Rd. 3000–4000 per year but was nonetheless an oppressive burden on the common Javan.

[This is followed by a long and complicated paragraph exonerating the present Commissar Guitard from any suspicion of being responsible for this arrangment.]

In 1793 and 1794 the harvest of **cardamom** was determined at 5000–6000 lbs, from Jakatra, Semarang and Cirebon, which was a barely appreciable amount. Its price had always fluctuated, in response to a lack of it in Europe, and it was decided to intensify its cultivation. However, arbitrary changes in the price paid to the disadvantage of the Regents had apparently had a bad effect (Nederburgh remarks that such actions diminish trust in and affection for the Company). This could have been spared especially in this case as the profit which resulted was not even Rd. 600 over the whole delivery, which was very little, and the Regents got no profit from it at all because the common man was paid for the cardamom at the same price as the Company paid.

Aristocracy and peasantry in the tides of world capitalism

Curcuma. The yearly supply was determined by the demand. The largest amount was 800 *pikul* collected by the Regent of Bandung. The Company paid Rd. 5 for each *pikul* of 150 pounds. This carried the extra burden of transport expenses etc. which cost the Regent ca Rd. 3.

The system of cash advances

The Regents of the Eastern Regencies (Bandung, Batulayang, Parakanmuncang, Sumedang, Krawang, Wanayasa, Adiarsa, Ciasem, Pamanukan and Pagaden) received an advance in January from the Delegate for Native Affairs when they left for the Regency. It was one third or half of the money they believed they would need for that year. When reaching their Regency they made a general estimate of all districts, settling how much each district could supply, according to the number and state of the trees. In about April they sent their messengers to Batavia to get the rest of the money for the payment. Should this be insufficient, which happened when the harvest exceeded the rough calculation, the Regents made a further demand, sending messengers again. Should they have received too much so that their delivery was short, this was discovered at the close of the delivery when making the account. This took place each year in the presence of special delegates, i.e. the Head Cashier and other officials.

When the Regents had received the money they summoned the Heads from all the Districts and paid them in the presence of a European overseer, each according to the amount of coffee he undertook to deliver. These Heads shared it with the common man in their districts and each common man delivered to his Head at harvest the amount of coffee for which he had received money. This coffee was then brought to the Regent's warehouse, either by the deliverers or by the Heads, after a certain transportation wage had been deducted. The warehouse was in the main *negeri* or in the *negeri* whence direct transportation to Batavia took place.

Nederburgh says that he offers no opinion on this manner of payment in former years. However, he had seen for some years how pleased the Regents were to receive the money and had found no cause for presuming that it would not reach the common man. To counter all abuses in this matter and especially, to prevent this money being spent on goods, the present Delegate had, since 1792, introduced a system whereby the monies were properly sealed up in cases which were sent off to the Regents. The keys to the cases were given in person to the overseers, or sent over. One could also have no doubt that fraud surrounding the payment of the common man would be discovered at once due to the most disastrous results it would inevitably have on the delivery of the coffee. If there was a considerable reduction in the supply, and this was not the result of an exceptionally bad harvest, one could be sure that there was something wrong with the payment.

Nederburgh says that as a result of precise investigation into the procedure of the present Delegate, he had found that the Delegate had always transferred these remittances to the Regents purely in cash (in a mixture of currenices including ducatoons, Spanish reals, 'paijement' and farthings (*duiten*[72])), in no way involving himself in trade, except for sending off a case of opium to the Regents every now and then. However, this was never mixed with the money related to the coffee, but put onto separate IOU's. He could not give such firm reassurances that the Regents had all been equally scrupulous in this. In some cases misuses had crept in, so that they paid their subjects partly with trade wares instead of cash. However, that was not as disadvantageous as one might imagine, since the Regents were provided with goods which the middle-class of the natives needed most, i.e. cloth, porcelain, iron objects etc. and which they could not come by in any other way in the Regency other than at great cost. The Regents and lesser Heads who took such goods from the Regents in payment could nonetheless commit much misuse if it were not for the Delegate whose job it was to watch this carefully. It would be extremely difficult to avert, or even to discover abuses, when the business itself was allowed. The respect of the ordinary Javan for his Regent was such that if the Regent had paid him in trade wares but had told him to deny this should he be questioned, he would certainly not disclose it. This attitude of the common man would always be a reason why much extortion by the Regents and lesser Heads remained hidden. The Javan would rather leave his home than accuse his Head of crimes. His total subjection to the latter was a matter of religion to him.

Aside from this advance on the harvest in the Eastern Regencies, the Regents also generally took from the Delegates at the start of the year a sum of Rd. 60–70,000 in paper money for their maintenance and to buy necessities. In June a start was made in the repayment for the coffee by sending cash to the Commander of Buitenzorg, usually Rd. 25–30,000. This was continued, according to the demand, until the delivery ceases. The whole amount came to at least Rd. 200,000 a year. In sending off this money the same precautions were used as mentioned above.

Finally, the Delegate also advanced the Regents Rd. 15–20,000 cash paid during the last 6 months of the year in small sums. This was for expenses incurred in the transport of the products.

The cash needed for the advances on the harvest in the Eastern Regencies and on the payment of the coffee from Buitenzorg was provided in various instalments from the Company's pay-office on exchange of paper, on the order of the Director-General, to the Delegate. The latter enjoyed an interest of ¾ % per month or .75% from the Regents on this money as well as on other advances he gave them. It was reckoned over the time they had enjoyed it or from when the remittances for payment had taken place. Nederburgh notes briefly that in former times gross abuses had also taken place in this matter.

The Regents' profits on the coffee

In 1794, 67864½ *pikul* were delivered. The contribution of each Regency was as follows:

Cianjur and Jampang, classified under Adipati Wiratanudatar, along with the Regent of Buitenzorg, Aria Rangga Gede, delivered 38150 *pikul* coffee beans of 148 lbs at Rd. 6 per *pikul*, receiving from the Company Rd. 228,900. Once again, expenses had to be deducted and once again, these are given in great detail for every Regency. Here I give the Cianjur and Jampang list as an example and as before, only the bottom line for the other Regencies.

Expenses deducted.
32548 *pikul* coffee delivered by the
common man from Cianjur Regency, paid at
Rd. 2⅔ per *pikul* .... Rd. 86794:32
3843½ *pikul* coffee from Buitenzorg.............................. 10249:16
1758½ *pikul* coffee delivered by the
nurserymen paid at Rd. 4½ per *pikul* 7913:12
Interest on capital, advances on
payment of the coffee... 4597:-
Sacks for transportation
at 6 *stuivers* per *pikul*... 4768:36

Wages for transportation to Batavia at
14 *stuivers* per *pikul*.. 11127:4
Wages for the *praus* from Gunung to the
Company's warehouse at 1 stuiver per *pikul*..................... 794:38
Wages on the Gunung warehouse at ½ st. per *pikul*............ 397:19
'Coolies' wages in the Buitenzorg warehouse
at ½ *stuiver* per *pikul* 397:19
Expenses of the overseer and clerks in
the Regents' warehouse at Buitenzorg and
in Gunung at 4 *stuivers* per *pikul* 3179:8
Dues to the Delegate from the coffee at Rd. ½ per *pikul*... 19075:-
Allowance to the Commander or post-holder
of Buitenzorg for the payment of the
coffee, at 3 *stuivers* per *pikul*...2384:18
Overseers of Cianjur at 3 *stuivers* per *pikul* 2384:18
Heads of the districts at 8 *stuivers* per *pikul* 6358:16
Yearly salary for the overseer, Smith of Cianjur 1000:-
Yearly salary for the overseer Voogd of Cianjur 800:-
idem for the nurseryman of Cipanas 1000:-
idem for the nurseryman of Cisarua............................... 750:-
idem for the nurseryman of Pondokgede 750:-
Payment of the office of the Director-General,
for providing the coffee ordinances 210:-
Payment to the First Merchant for making up
the ordinances.. 120:-
½% of Rd. 228,900 to the Cashier for the
coffee money received.. 1144:24
Maintenance of the road to Kampung
Gunung, Jakatra and Sontar 600:-
Renting land in Buitenzorg and Dermaga
to the Governor-General..3500:-
Total .... Rd. 170295:20
Remainder for the profit of the Regents
of Cianjur and Buitenzorg .... Rd. 58604:28:-

The Regent of Bandung, Adipati Wiranatakusuma,
delivered 1029½ *pikul* coffee beans for which he
received at Rd. 6, 6 per weighing 150lbs .... Rd. 61767:-

Expenses deducted
Total in Rd..39212:15
The Regent therefore retained Rd. 22553:33.

Aristocracy and peasantry in the tides of world capitalism

The Regent of Batulayang, Tumenggung Rangga
Adikusuma, sent 3685 *pikul* coffee beans, receiving from
the Company at Rd. 6 per *pikul*.............................. Rd. 22110:–

Expenses deducted
Total in Rd... 14840:1
What remains for the Regent .... Rd. 7269:38

The Regent of Parakanmuncang Adipati Surianatakusuma
delivered 7064–½ *pikul* coffee, and was paid Rd. 6 per *pikul*

Expenses deducted
Total in Rd... 29795:33¼
The Regent retains Rd... 12591:14¼

The Regent of Sumedang Tumenggung Suranagara
sent 5300 *pikul* coffee beans for which he received at
Rd. 6 per *pikul*... Rd. 42387:-

Expenses deducted
Total in Rd... 20777:42
This left the Regent with Rd. 11022:6, of which he enjoyed for his maintenance Rd. 3000. His expenses during his stay in Batavia amounted to Rd. 1042:35 and the remainder was deducted from the debt of Rd. 76122:46 and was one year's interest on that capital.

The Regent of Krawang Adipati Singasari Penatayuda delivered from his Regency and Wanayasa 1727½ *pikul* coffee at Rd. 6 per *pikul*, receiving for it Rd. 10365.
He also received Rd. 6600 for renting a forest. Of this the Regent enjoyed Rd. 2000 for his maintenance. His expenses in Batavia amounted to Rd. 410:31 and the remainder was deducted from his arrears of Rd. 32900, and was one year's interest on that capital.

Expenses deducted
Total in Rixdollars 7330:44
The Regent retained Rd. 3034:4.

The Regent of Adiarsa Aria Surengrana delivered 130 *pikul* at Rd. 6 per *pikul* for which he received Rd. 780

Expenses deducted
Total in Rd... 521:6
The Regent retained Rd. 258:42:.

The Cancer Within

To this must be added Rd. 478:24 transferred from the account of Krawang in interest to reduce the arrears of this Regent, following the resolution of the High Government of 17 December 1793. Rd. 130:19 was for the maintenance of the Regent, on account of the same arrears to the Delegate, being Rd. 9156:17½, Rd. 194:45 and Rd. 412:2.

The Regent of Ciasem Aria Kartayuda delivered 376½ *pikul* coffee at Rd. 6 per *pikul*..Rd. 2259:-

Expenses deducted
Total in Rd..1553:23
Leaving the Regent in profits Rd.. 705:25
The same Regent administered the Regencies Pamanukan and Pagaden which delivered 511 *pikul* coffee at Rd. 6 per *pikul* Rd. 3066.

Expenses deducted
Total in Rd..1936:38:
What remained for the Regent was Rd. 1129:10: of which Rd. 360 served for his maintenance in Batavia, and Rd. 390:33 was deducted from his arrears to the Commissar-in-office of Rd. 10626:15, Rd. 478:9 being one year's interest on the capital [?passage not clear].

The Regent of Tangerang and Grinding Aria Sutadilaga delivered 551½ *pikul* coffee at Rd. 6 per *pikul*, therefore receiving Rd. 3309.
Expenses deducted
Total in Rd...2494:26½
Leaving the Regent with Rd. 814:21½

The Regents' other profits

The Regent of Cianjur was exempted from the obligatory delivery of indigo and cotton thread in 1789 but nonetheless kept on enjoying for a long time the tax of half a Rixdollar per household. If this has not yet ceased it should be abolished immediately. Aside from this he also has an income of Rd. 3–400 in dues for marking buffalo in his Regency, and another Rd. 3–400 for the crossing of the Citarum at Biabang, for supplying his subjects with passes when they leave the Regency, and for the renting of the homes lived in by the Eastern traders in the main *negeri*.

This Regent generally had some overweights on the coffee between receiving it from the common man and transporting it to Batavia. In 1794 this profit came to Rd. 1912 but he did not share in the profit, distributing it yearly among the overseers, clerks, workers etc. according to a voluntary arrangement.

In 1794 this was as follows:
To the overseer of Cianjur Smith .... Rd. 150
To the overseer of Cianjur de Voogd 100
To nurseryman Weeber 300
To nurseryman Matz 250
To the overseer of Buitenzorg Pradehand 500
To the former nurseryman of Tjipanas Joost Geyber 120
To the clerk of the post-holder Roode 400
To the workers at the warehouse 922
Total Rd 1912

This Regent was not involved in trade. He bought 6–8 cases of opium a year from the Delegate and distributed it to various people.

The Regent of Bandung also did not trade except in opium and, as the consumption in that Regency was only 5–6 cases yearly, the profits could not be great. In general all trade in hill necessities in the Regency occurred through the Heads of the districts, the priests and the Orientals who were spread throughout the land.

On the contribution which the common man made for the supply of indigo and cotton, after deducting the cost price he retained Rd. 6–700 per year.

Lastly, he rented his department's houses in the Cikao district at Rd. 500 per year. Roughly calculated, his income, outside that from the coffee, was calculated at Rd. 4000 per annum.

The Regent of Batulayang conducted no trade. His profit from the common man's supply of indigo and cotton amounted annually to Rd. 2–300. His share of renting houses in the Cikao district amounts to Rd. 100. Together, excluding some minor presents (such as cattle and cloth) from subordinates his profits came to Rd. 4–500.

The Regents of Parakanmuncang and Sumedang had no profits at all, neither in trade nor rent, nor in money contributions for the supply of indigo and cotton. They did not have the common man supply their contingents of these articles, so that their income, other than from coffee, consisted only in what they received from the pay-office for the indigo and cotton. The *warung* in the Regency of Sumedang was rented for Rd. 300 per year, but this profit was enjoyed by the book-keeper and overseer of the coffee plantations in the Regency.

The Cancer Within

The Regent of Krawang had no income other than the rent of his forest and fishing for which he received Rd. 7500 annually. From this Rd. 900 had to be deducted as annual payment to the *Heemraden*[73] for the fishery so that the pure profit amounted to Rd. 6600 annually. Some other minor sources of income brought in Rd. 200 a year. He did not engage in trade. The income from 4 *warungs* set up in the Regency came to Rd. 160 in rent which he gave to the overseer of the coffee plantations as an extra *douceur*. The remainder of the supply of 4 100/125 *pikul* of cotton amounted to little or nothing. His income could be reckoned at under Rd. 7000 and it was used to pay off his debt.

The Regencies of Adiarsa, Ciasem, Pamanukan and Pagaden are left out of consideration as the Regents were very poor and scarcely able to continue as Regents and support their families. Along with all the other Regents they had 1/10th of the paddy but they had to give some of this to the Heads of lesser districts for their maintenance so that little remained. Cianjur was an extensive Regency, nonetheless the share which the Regent received from the paddy harvest in the whole Regency did not amount to 400 hill *caing* of 50 bundles, which came to about 100 Heemraden *caing*.[74]

The Aria of Tangerang and the Grinding had a yearly income from padi and the renting of ground for *kacang* gardens amounting to Rd. 3247, from which the rent paid to the Company (Rd. 800) and other expenses totalling 1680 Rd. had to be subtracted, leaving the Aria Rd. 1567. The Aria also conducted trade in all kinds of articles from the town and hills, but it was difficult to know how much he profited from this as it depended on his own industry and bore no direct relation to him as Regent, since in this respect he was equal to any other private individual as trade there was permitted to all.

The Regents' other expenses

Here we give, as before, a complete list for the first Regent and the sum total only for the remainder.

The Regent of Cianjur:
To the Aria or second-in-command of the Regency,
annually in cash .... Rd. 5000
Purchase of 78 horses for the lesser Heads
both in the Regency and in the Cutaks, used
in the coffee plantations at Rd. 14 each 1072

Aristocracy and peasantry in the tides of world capitalism

Clothing etc. for 78 Heads at Rd. 7 each 546
Purchase of tools needed in weighing the
coffee and processing it.. 150
Expenses for the maintenance of the roads for
the transport of coffee and maintenance of the
big bridge between Pondok Gede and Cisarua
which usually had to be renewed every 3–4 years,
if it has not been washed away before that......................... 400
Repairs to and maintenance of the coffee
warehouses on Buitenzorg and in
Kampung Gunung... 500
Expenses for the yearly attendance in Batavia
with family and following, including a gift
of Rd. 4–5000 for the Delegate and expenses
to the office, amounting to Rd. 600 8000
Interest on Rd. 24000, his and the Aria of
Buitenzorg's debt to the Company, at 6% per
year, coming to Rd. 1440, of which his
share was ¾ 1080
Interest on a capital of Rd. 20000, the value
of 3 warehouses on Buitenzorg, 2 warehouses
in Kampung Punung, the purchase of 3
medium Company scales with the same metal
weights, and the construction of some wooden
buildings serving as resting places,
at 6% per year.. 1200
Extra douceurs for both overseers 1800
Yearly maintenance of the Aria, or
second-in-command of the Regency,
banished to Ceylon.. 305:2
Total Rd..20053:2

The Regent of Bandung:
Total expenses in Rd. 5130

The Regent of Batulayang:
Total expenses in Rd. 1460

The Regent of Parakanmuncang:
Total Expenses in Rd... 2540

The Regent of Sumedang:
Total Expenses in Rd... 1708

The Cancer Within

The Regent of Krawang:
Total Expenses in Rd... 1075

The Regent of Ciasem, who was also at the time administrator of Pamanukan and Pagadeen, as well as **The Regent of Adiarsa** had insignificant expenses which were left out of consideration.

The Aria of Tangerang:
Total Rd.. 1062

(this included various accidental expenses for all committees of the *Heemraden*[75] etc., namely provision for the servants and slaves, paddy for the horses etc. .... 250)

Aside from this, every now and then the Regents had extra expenses eg in 1793 the improvement to the Trunang River to facilitate the transport of coffee, work contracted by the *Heemraden*[76] worth Rd. 573:40, to which the following contributed:

Bandung... Rd. 150
Batulayang 100
Parakanmuncang... 150
Sumedang 73:40
Krawang 100
.... Rd. 573:40

In that year the Regent of Tangerang had to contribute Rd. 1064 towards work in Pajangkangan. In 1795 the Eastern Regents were again made to deliver 70 horses to the Company. It would not be difficult to find more such expenses. While each was small, they were as a whole a burden on the Regents.

The income of the Delegate for Native Affairs aside from that derived from the supply of the products

Nederburgh remarks that since it was decided not long ago that this matter should be looked into he did not think that he should go into this in great detail. Up till now he had had no reason to doubt the present Delegate's income account. Any income enjoyed by the Delegate aside from what had already been made known could only arise from bad practices and unjustified extortion. If, contrary to his reasonable expectations, it was found that this still took place,

Nederburgh's suggestions as to how the Company might draw more profit from these Regencies

Nederburgh remarks that coffee is the only product from these Regencies which is a source of welfare, enabling the common man to earn a *stuiver* in cash, albeit through hard work and for a meagre reward. The income of the Regents and Delegate are just sufficient. No other new means of finding finance for the Company can be thought of other than reducing the price paid for the coffee, either directly, or through indirect methods.

The price of the coffee which was delivered to the Company from these Regencies had not been constant. Following the resolution of the High Government in 1711, it was set at 10 light or 8 heavy *stuivers* the pound. In 1716 a price rise was allowed but this was not followed up. In 1726 the price was reduced by half and set at 4 *stuivers*, i.e. for a *pikul* of 125 pounds at least Rd. 10. Governor Zwaardecroon complained about this and at his request, the decision was reversed. In 1730 the price was reduced due to the greater increase in the cultivation than desired by the Company. The coffee from the Regencies fetched Rd. 6 per *pikul* and that from private individuals Rd. 7. As this was not thought to be a sufficiently low price to counteract the expansion, the coffee plantations in the Regencies classified under Batavia and Cirebon were reduced by half and the price for coffee from private land made the same as that from the Regencies i.e. Rd. 6 per *pikul*. In 1736 the High Government even went so far as to reduce the price per *pikul* by another half Rixdollar, to Rd. 5½. In 1740 the supply of coffee for the whole of Jakatra was set at 20,000 *pikul* and in 1747 at 24,000 *pikul*.

Meanwhile the cultivation of coffee had received such a shock from the uncertainty regarding the price and other arbitrary decisions which had been taken, that the "serious insistence" on an increase in supply at Rd. 5½ per *pikul* had no appreciable effect. Although the supply of hill products like coffee, pepper, indigo and cotton threads had for some years increased considerably in quantity and quality, due to constant watchfulness and work, except for the crop failures which sometimes caused a smaller harvest, in spite of all the trouble and effort, it has not yet been possible to satisfy the goals of the Government. One factor was undoubtedly that the pepper would not thrive in the hills, and another that the reduced payment for the coffee now greatly disadvantaged suppliers. The Delegate had brought forward several times how the respective Regents had complained about this, showing how the small profits they made from the coffee were necessarily lost each year to the indigo, thread and pepper requirements. He suggested that the price of the coffee be Rd. 6 again and pepper be Rd. 6½ instead of Rd. 6 for as long as necessary to get a considerable store of it, in order to cheer up the poor Javans as much as possible and encourage them.

In 1752 and 1754 the supply of pepper was withdrawn in proportion to the coffee and the price of the coffee kept at Rd. 6 per *pikul* of 128 pounds. Really, with over-weight, they were 146–150 lbs. Of the Rd. 6 per *pikul*, Rd. ½ or 24 *stuivers* was deducted as a means of existence for the Delegate.

In 1777 the Governer-General proposed that the price of the coffee beans be reduced again, setting it at Rd. 5½ per *pikul* but the High Government decided to keep it at Rd. 6 (except for Sumedang and Parakanmuncang). The reason was that most Regents had onerous debts which had risen to the enormous total of Rd. 450,000. The interest on this, estimated at Rd. 50,000 at least, the Regents could never pay, their debts rising daily to such an extent that they were unable to pay the common man for his products. The likely result was a depopulation of the lands and deterioration of the cultivation.

The Regents of Sumedang and Parakanmuncang used to deliver their coffee to Cirebon but following a resolution in 1729 were paid only Rd. 4½ per *pikul*. In 1730 the price was raised to Rd. 5 but in 1766 returned to Rd. 4½. In 1771 the Regents were given the choice of delivering their coffee at this price to Cirebon or to Batavia. They chose Batavia. In 1771 the price was increased to Rd. 5½ and in 1790 it was finally agreed to set the price of the coffee from these Regencies at Rd. 6, the same as all other Regencies classified under Batavia.

The experience of the damaging consequences of an ill-advised price reduction led to the decision not to seek a new and greater immoderate profit which would be extremely dangerous in the execution, leaving one open to losing the solid profit enjoyed at the present.

Nederburgh now addresses the question: How far *may* and *can* one go without harming the rules of justice or endangering the Company's important interests?

Aristocracy and peasantry in the tides of world capitalism

He begins with the following excursus on the situation: It is probable that the fore-fathers of the present Regents put themselves freely and uncoerced under the protection of the Company. Otherwise, these lands were ceded to the Company by the Susuhunan of Mataram. In neither case can the Company lay claim to such arbitrary authority over these natives that it may force them to work the land and till it like slaves, in the sweat of their brow, solely for its use and profit and to have to deliver the products at such cheap prices as it (the Company) decides to pay, thinking of its own interests. If it is only the patron and protector, it is on the contrary obliged to save them from oppression. If it is the lawful sovereign in the strictest sense then it must govern according to the eternal rules of reason, grounded on the duties and relations between governments and subjects, which do not suffer that the latter are abused and crushed with an iron sceptre by the former.

But it is not only obliged to do so: its own interests also compel it to this course. From the beginning it has wisely understood that these lands, however they came into its power, were not suited to be governed by the Company itself, but that they had to stay under its open supervision under the rule of the original Heads of the people, following their ancestral laws and customs, enjoying the pleasure of the profits of trade which the land's products, delivered at reasonable prices to the Company, could put into their treasury. This must remain its system if it does not want to see these blessed places, like most of the lands of the out-stations as far as the mountains, become a stage for chaos, robbery and murder. There must be the industrious and hearty co-operation of the Regents and lesser Heads and "furious" (*woest*) work done by the ordinary natives for it [the Company] to enjoy these profits.

There is no doubt that the ordinary Javan only needs a sign from his Regent to completely neglect his coffee garden. At present he enjoys reasonable payment in cultivating it with his (for him) bitter labour, but with such a nature and life-style as described above, he can easily find everything he needs presented to him, for little effort on his part, by nature. He has no idea of pleasures which he could buy beyond what he has. He also has no desire to earn money by labour. Therefore it can surprise no one that the compulsory cultivation is the most difficult thing he can be forced to do. It makes him despondent even to think of it, while on the other hand the encouragement consists only of a payment which is really very scanty. It is often not sufficient to make good the transport costs. If the Regents, European overseers and lesser Heads did not make use of the most serious and emphatic means to oblige the Javans to plant, the Company would harvest little coffee. For this reason one need never be afraid of a delivery which is larger than desired.

Nederburgh's major conclusion is that it is principally the interests of the Regents and lesser Heads which must be bound to those of the Company through the pleasure of profits. To some extent these can compensate for the loss of many pleasures which they used to enjoy. These were simpler and more in accordance with their life-style. With the expansion of the cultivations they had to say farewell to their hobbies and amusements like stock-breeding, fishing and hunting. They saw the power which they were accustomed to exercise decline because each native was now bound to compulsory work and, consequently, no longer able to be at the service of their Regents as before. However, they put up with these sacrifices and, with the most praiseworthy industry, co-operated with the Company's desire for expansion of the cultivation, spurred on by the prospect of the profits which would also flow in their direction. Therefore, to reduce their small profits would only serve to make the Company contemptible in the eyes of the whole world and hated forever by the natives [of the ruling classes].

From what has been said about the income of the Regents and especially their profits from the coffee, it is apparent that these are not so great as one would superficially imagine. Aside from the Regents of Cianjur, Buitzenzorg and Bandung the rest cannot even be said to enjoy a plentiful existence. The profit on the coffee per *pikul* comes to no more than:

Cianjur and Buitenzorg	Rd. 1:36
Bandung	2:8
Parakanmuncang	1:36
Batulayang	2:36
Sumedang	2:4
Krawang	1:36
Ciasem	1:41
Pamanukan and Pagaden	2:15
Adiarsa	2:-
Tangerang	1:21

However, on the other hand it is true that the state of the Regents' income is much more advantageous than it was for many years, when they were oppressed with heavy debts and delivered fewer

Aristocracy and peasantry in the tides of world capitalism

products. Nederburgh believes that on the grounds of reason one can and should make use of this situation to effectuate a more profitable arrangement for the Company's interests.

Nederburgh vehemently rejects the idea of reducing the Regents to the position of salaried officials, which would humiliate them before neighbouring princes, and remarks: "I do not have to mention what fatal consequences these perceptions could have, especially at a time when it is no longer possible to conceal the Company's impotence from the natives, who can see a mighty enemy appear along these coasts every moment. And this is not even to mention the harmful effect which would result for the cultivation of the products, should the Regents be angered by such improper and unstatesmanlike measures. I maintain that there is no way to keep the cultivation going and to promote it, without the goodwill and co-operation of the Regents. From the moment the Company considered itself obliged to put into effect means of oppression and violence in these remote and extensive places, it would lose the considerable profits which it draws from them now."

Grounds for a new arrangement to seek greater profit for the Company can only be searched for in the resolution of the High Government in Dec. 1777. At that time the situation with the Regents was quite wretched, almost hopeless, due to slack management and all kinds of extortion. In 1763 their debts were Rd. 140,000. Subsequently they grew to such an extent that in 1777 Gov-Gen. de Klerk declared that the debts had risen to Rd. 450,000, computing in the Rd. 50,000 annual interest.

The High Government took the decision that, so that the Delegate did not rashly harm or oppress the natives, 9% interest per year was to be paid on the money owed to him by the natives [i.e. the Regents] in the hills, and he would get 24 *stuivers* of each *pikul* coffee, pepper etc. delivered, but it was forbidden for him ever to interfere with the natives' [Regents'] finances.

The Regents were advised that the overweights on the products would stay in their favour and that they must deliver the coffee direct to the Company's warehouses without it passing in revue through the Delegate. Further, the money would now be paid to themselves by the pay-office after the products had been weighed without any interference from the Delegate.

Since then various Regents had completely absolved their debts, including the interest on them, and the rest had reduced them, so that the whole amount came to Rd. 139,242:46 in Dec. 1795:

The Cancer Within

Regent of Cianjur to the Company .... Rd. 24,000
Regent of Sumedang to the Company .... Rd. 14,000
Regent of Sumedang to the Delegate .... Rd. 56,820
Total debt of Regent of Sumedang .... Rd. 70,820
Regent of Krawang to the Delegate .... Rd. 25,449:46
Regent of Adiarsa to the Delegate .... Rd. 8,736
Regent of Pamanukan to the Delegate .... Rd. 10,237

However, the debt of the Regent of Cianjur can scarcely be reckoned here as he has long been capable of repaying it whenever he desired, but it had been decided to let it rest, for political reasons.

The thing which saved the Regents from the almost hopeless situation of 1777 was the decision of the High Government *that the overweights of the products stayed in their favour.* Therefore Nederburgh believes that a further reasonable agreement could now be made regarding the overweights to the advantage of the Company. This would not have many harmful consequences and would be practical . . . For the Regents who have caught up with their arrears there would be an increase to 160 pounds to the *pikul.* [i.e. an increase of 14 lb per *pikul* on the 146 lb *pikul* previously received by the Company and paid at Rd. 6]. Of course, this had not been the same weight as the *pikul* sent off by the various Regents, which was anything from one to several pounds heavier to compensate for alleged spillage along the way: see above.[77] This would also apply to the other Regents as soon as they got out of debt.

Then when the administrators were also obliged to account for 140 lbs per *pikul* instead of 125 lbs as at present, for the coffee which they would receive at the above-mentioned weight, the Company would make a profit of Rd. 64,800 on a delivery of 100,800 present-day *pikul* of 125 lbs. For Cianjur and the Regencies which had paid off their debts it would amount to about Rd. 56,000.

However, this matter should be introduced carefully, not only to avoid as much as possible the unpleasant sensation which this always provokes in the Regents, but also to prevent the great increase in weight becoming a grievance for the natives. Nederburgh says he would consider making use of the situation to make uniform the payment to the common man and the weight at which the coffee was delivered to the Regents in all the Eastern Regencies e.g. Rd. 4 the hill *pikul* of 260 or 270 lbs, and seriously recommends the use of Dutch scales, both in the main *negeris* and Cikao in the

Gintong. These measures would help to bring to light the frauds and extortions and to counteract them.

[Here follows a long excursus on the question of the supply of gunny-sacks. It seems that the supply of sacks had been, like many other matters, in the capacious hands of the Delegate for Native Affairs, and he had been drawing up his accounts to conceal the profit he made. Nederburgh concludes that if the Company undertook to purchase these sacks in Bengal and supply them directly, they could make a profit of about Rd. 12,500 per year: see table below].

Nederburgh states that the transportation money (14 *stuivers* per *pikul*) to Batavia and the prau wages of the coffee from the Eastern Regencies could not be reduced. It was already very difficult to get hold of the necessary carts and praus. These tasks were laborious and often unpleasant so that those carrying them out should not be rewarded scantily, all the more because then one could demand of them that they carry out their duty faithfully and have no part in devious methods and extortion. They had more opportunity for this because they were at a greater distance and not in sight.

Only 4 *stuivers* per *pikul* used to be included for the Cutak Heads, but this amount was fixed at a time when the delivery from Cianjur and Buitenzorg only came to 12–13,000 *pikul*. Its increase to at least 50,000 *pikul* had not only made the appointment of more Heads necessary but also meant that the distribution must be more than before. As a result, for some time the Regents had made a distribution of Rd. $\frac{1}{6}$ per *pikul* instead of Rd. $\frac{1}{12}$, as it was delivered to the Company's warehouse, or Rd. $\frac{1}{4}$ per hill *pikul*, which came to $1\frac{1}{2}$ Batavian *pikul*, distributed as follows:

To the Heads of each district per hill *pikul*	St. 5:-
To the Camat or 2nd overseer	1:-
To the Panlukar or messengers	2:-
To the clerks	1½:
To the Company's overseers	2:-
Total	St 11½:

The remaining ½ *stuiver* was divided among the 5 delegates, one in each district in the Regency, whose job it was to survey the plantations each day.

The other Regents also provided 8 *stuivers* per *pikul* for the Cutak Heads etc. but these were divided in quite a different way, according to the different constitution of the regions. Nederburgh says that in truth, these people really need that small pleasure when one takes into account how attentively they have to watch the plantations and the trouble they have to go to in order to keep the Javans at work, so that a reduction here was also unthinkable.

The *douceur* of 24 *stuivers* per *pikul* [see above] is lawfully allowed to the Delegate and included in his income, says Nederburgh. But, he says, the Company would be able to make a profit of more than Rd. 21,000 on a delivery of 90,000 *pikul* of 140 pounds, on which the harvest for the following one was calculated, if it paid the ordinary advances directly from its pay-office, at an interest rate of 0.75% per month, which was now enjoyed by the Delegate. [In other words, by taking away from the Delegate his position as a moneylender at interest, a considerable reduction of his income in favour of the Company's would be effected.]

[This is followed by considerable detail re the physical delivery of the money, which was to be packed, as was current practice, in closed sealed cases when given to the Regents or their messengers, and the keys given to the overseers with a prohibition to open the cases except in their presence, with the aim of stopping this money from being spent on trade [goods] etc. Nederburgh also details the accounting practices which should be followed to prevent any confusion.]

Finally, would the Company profit from the sale of some pieces of land? Nederburgh does not believe so but promises to address this question later.

The total extra profits which these measures would produce are estimated as follows:

1. on the increase of the weight of each *pikul* of coffee delivered to it by the Regents, 14 lbs for a delivery of 90,000 *pikul* .... Rd. 56,000*
2. on the delivery of the sacks on an equivalent yearly delivery in the second and subsequent years 12,500
3. on the advances of cash on the crop and for the payment of coffee, at an interest of 9% per year 21,000
Total Rd.. 89,500

*this will grow to Rd. 64,800 as explained above

Batavia 23 November 1796.

Aristocracy and peasantry in the tides of world capitalism

* * *

To sum up, Nederburgh proposes to make more money for the Company out of the Priangan deliveries, primarily coffee, by a) increasing the size of the *pikul* to be delivered by the Regents, bringing an end to the arrangement whereby the "overweights", i.e. the difference between the weight of the *pikul* received by them and the weight of the *pikul* they had to supply to the Company, remained their profit (it seems curious that although Nederburgh feels that a price reduction would cause too much resentment among the Regents to be politically possible, he is happy to suggest an increase in the size of the *pikul* which would have exactly the same effect.); and b) taking away from the Delegate for Native Affairs his right to 0.75% monthly interest on the money advances paid to the suppliers and leaving him only his *douceur* of 24 *stuivers* per *pikul*, as well as cutting him out of the profits of the gunny sack trade.

What does this report tell us about the economy and society of Priangan?

First, it does not really achieve its stated aims. On the Regents' incomes, for instance, too many factors remain unaccounted for, such as what they did with the advances paid to them. The Regents appear to be getting nothing out of the system, but this may not have been the case if their other income was fully known. Also, Nederburgh spends some time accounting the profits from such customary levies as the 3–yearly bull branding, but these must have been trifles compared with 10% of the rice crop (the *cuke*) which they received and which does not enter the accounts. In addition the system was so ramshackle in its operation, being a congeries of highly various local arrangements which could not be effectively supervised, and which left so many opportunities for peculation and concealment that the accounting of it was, if not entirely notional, certainly not a transcript of economic realities.

However, the report does tell us other things. It is hard to miss the over-riding importance of political considerations, as in the case of the Regent of Cianjur, said to be well able to repay his debt but not pressed by the Company because of his political importance. Nederburgh remarks that this was "a time when it is no longer possible to conceal the Company's impotence from the natives, who can see a mighty enemy appear along these coasts every moment". If, as seems wholly unlikely, the Javanese had not realised like the

The Cancer Within

Malays that "where there is sovereignty, there is gold", they must have had many occasions to learn this under the Dutch. It is noteworthy that when Nederburgh talks about the rights of the Company's subjects not to have oppression and violence practised upon them, it is the Regents he is talking about, not the common man. Oppression was the constant norm for the latter, who would be apprehended and returned to the cultivation of coffee, as against the preferred crop of rice, as if choice of location and occupation were a criminal act. Though noting that the system was hard on the common man, Nederburgh feels that things could not be any different, and is clearly anxious not to find any evidence of malpractice on the part of the Regents and to a lesser extent the Delegate for Native Affairs (who could, after all, be replaced) if he could help it. His is the voice of the conservative, not the reformer, even a mild one like de Rovere van Breugel.

On the question of the degree of monetization of society, Boomgaard writes that "A society where the Regents could ask from every recently established household (not yet forced to cultivate coffee) an annual payment of 36 *stuivers* had to be rather monetized." However he notes that in 1796 Batavia had introduced a new copper coin, the *bonk*, which was rejected because of its appearance and the fact that it weighed less than the 4–*duit stuiver*, its token value. If peasants were forced to accept *bonken*, they immediately exchanged them for salt to use for barter in their home village. In 1808 it was reported that they were now accepted and used for copper utensils. The *duit* introduced in 1730 had never encountered resistance, nor had silver, except for small transactions. All this seems to support the impression I have from the above report that "monetization" in this society meant something different from our usual perceptions of the role of money. In Priangan at this time, money seems almost to have been itself a trade good, with a large number of varieties shipped in at a certain period every year.

The lack of standardisation and articulation of the economy is also reflected in the number of different local weights in use.

The question of payment to the cultivator in over-valued trade goods rather than in cash has already appeared in Part One of this chapter, on Banten. Nederburgh says that there is no evidence of this (just as he found no evidence that the Delegate for Native Affairs was increasing *his* income by unauthorised means) and that that even if it *had* been done it would have been a means of making goods desired by the middle classes available to them more easily

Aristocracy and peasantry in the tides of world capitalism

and cheaply than was otherwise the case. Boomgaard however notes that it became the custom for the Company to pay the planter directly when he delivered his harvest at the government warehouse.[78]

Again despite its shortcomings, the report gives a useful perspective on why existing Javanese élites did not become entrepreneurial. The Bupati of Priangan were not experienced in this field, and the VOC, if it did not exert a hawk-like vigilance, certainly had a better overview of the economic scene than they did. Thus we see the Company acting in such a way as to prevent the Regents ever building up capital reserves, as for instance by raising the stipulated weight per *pikul* as soon as the Regents cleared their debts.

It is interesting to note that in the Priangan "priests" (presumably *kyai* and *ulama* attached to the *pesantren*) were important in trade. Though there were no Chinese here, we find another example of the involvement of *santri* in trade that placed them in competition with Chinese elsewhere in Java.

* * *

In the inacessible mountain valleys of Priangan, unlike in Banten, there was little tradition of extensive mercantile activities. Incorporation into the Company's economic enterprises involved a rude shock to both aristocracy and peasants. The sufferings of the latter are noted but considered unavoidable by Nederburgh. The Regents had, as he remarks, to give up many of their old simple pleasures such as stock-breeding, fishing and hunting to participate in the Company's economic system and found the transition to a money economy a rocky road of debt. In the long run however they survived this transition rather well compared to their counterparts elsewhere in Java. The Priangan Regent families went on to enjoy a uniquely high position, compared with their counterparts elsewhere in Java, until the end of the colonial period. The following description gives an idea of the mestizo magnificence of the major Regents:

> After wandering down this road for a few minutes, one arrives at the *alun-alun*, a large grassed plain, which is planted with beautiful waringins [banyans], and has in the centre a stone *pendopo*, [pavilion] raised ten to twelve feet above the ground. On the western edge stands, a little to the side in a

place apart, the beautiful mosque built in 1850 at the government's cost. On the south side, behind a white wall, rises up the Regent's *dalem*, one of the largest and most beautiful in Java. An oblong ancillary building, consisting of a large ante-room with glass windows, a number of rooms furnished in European style and an open rear room looking onto a beautiful pond inhabited by *guramis* and other fine fish, is wholly fitted out for the reception of prominent Europeans. The Regent who died in 1874, Raden Adipati Wira Nata Kusuma, was famous for his hospitality and courtesy, and many a European official and traveller can tell of the glittering reception he received in the *dalem* at Bandung, at which the eastern splendour of the diamond-sparkling clothes in which the Regent appeared, and the attendants who dragged themselves behind him on their knees with his staff and krisses, his betel-box and cuspidor, were well-nigh the only things to remind the visitor that he was in the abode of an Asiatic prince. The Regent was a great lover of horses, and had not a few in his well-filled stables, resplendent with Arab, Persian, and Bima steeds Not seldom did he entertain his guests with the dancing of his richly-clad *bedajas* [female court dancers], while on festive occasions the *alun-alun* was the theatre of all sorts of games and popular amusements. Besides the *senenans* or tournaments, mention deserves to be made of a sort of ballet performed on a mat by dolls about half a foot high dressed in European style, and operated by a hidden mechanism, whose leaps and somersaults parodied the European art of the dance to the amazement of the onlookers. One also often saw the *debus* or *gedebus*, an exhibition of so-called invulnerability led by *hajis* or *santris* (mosque students), which consists of some initiates calling on the Prophet and Sheikh Abdulkadir Jaelani and to the accompaniment of savage gestures and dancing apparently stabbing themselves with sharp iron bodkins, without, however – presumably because a hidden spring makes the point go back in – suffering any injury"[79] (There follows an account of the salaries paid to the different Regents of this region, and the huge amounts they received as percentages of coffee deliveries).

Under the *Preangerstelsel* (Priangan system) the Dutch continued to exploit the coffee gardens of the Sundanese mountains in the old

Aristocracy and peasantry in the tides of world capitalism

VOC style. Since forced cultivation was continued, the nineteenth-century reforms brought in elsewhere did not apply to Priangan and the development of individual economic activity was inhibited. Just as the Cultivation System resulted in an overall strengthening of the Regent's position in all the areas where it operated, so its prolongation in Priangan helped to perpetuate the local Regents great prestige and their ability to live in the grand style at a period when this was no longer possible elsewhere. Even after the abolition of the *Preangerstelsel* in 1871, percentages from coffee production gave the Priangan Regent a high income (in the late nineteenth century some earned 20,000 guilder annually compared to a Javanese average of 12,000) while the legacy of their earlier freedom and special privileges was apparent in their dominance of local society. As Sutherland remarks,[80] both the exploitative and paternalistic aspect of the Regent-peasantry relationship were well developed in Priangan, and the strength of ties was such that early twentieth century Dutch observers spoke of a special tradition of *ngawula* – the loyal and absolute service owed by the subject to his lord – in Priangan. A central Javanese version of the ideal of Service is given below in Chapter 6.

These ties between lord and subject and the relative cushioning of Priangan society from the disruptive and modernizing influence that affected other parts of Java through the nineteenth and twentieth centuries were factors in the outbreak and intractability of the Darul Islam rebellion in this part of Java. Jackson and Moeliono's explanation of the Darul Islam movement centres on the fact that Sundanese society remained very much on the traditional side of the traditional-modern dichotomy.[81] Yet in a sense this only serves to displace the question to one that asks what was the particular shape of tradition in this society. A satisfactory answer must await an investigation of nineteenth century Javanese Islam in its social and intellectual aspects, surely one of the largest lacunae of our present state of knowledge.

NEW INITIATIVES AT PEKALONGAN: FORCED LABOUR AND TAXES

F.J. Rothenbuhler's report on Pekalongan[82] not only takes us into a different region but also down to a different level of Javanese society. It was one of a number of regional reports written for S.C. Nederburgh, the conservative Commissioner-General of 1791–5 who was responsible for many of the fact-gathering reports of the 1790s[83] and for continuing the VOC's conservative policies after its demise. Rothenbuhler had a distinguished career in the colonial bureaucracy, rising to the position of Gezaghebber of the Oosthoek, and wrote a number of useful reports on the *pasisir*. At the time of the report used here, he lived in Pekalongan, a fortified comptoir (the fort was built in 1753) with a small European contingent (a bookkeeper, a forester, a surgeon, a sergeant, 2 corporals, a drummer, 12 privates, a gunner and a sailor, apart from 13 private citizens concerned with trade). Under him were three Regencies – Pekalongan, Batang, and Wiradesa – and the leased district of Ulujami. Pekalongan and Batang were sizeable Regencies, though the latter was for the most part mountain, marsh, and wasteland, with only a small populated area. According to Rothenbuhler, both the great-grandfather of the current Regent of Pekalongan and the first Regent of Batang were *peranakan* Chinese, that is Chinese who had embraced Islam.[84] Wiradesa was a much smaller area which had previously been attached variously to Batang, Tegal, or Brebes. Ulujami had been carved out of Pekalongan by the VOC and leased to Chinese: the current leaseholder was the Captain of Chinese at Semarang. Though small, Wiradesa was very fertile, and the leaseholder also rented two of the best districts of Pekalongan and Wiradesa, viz. Kalang and Seragi.

Products and profits

Rothenbuhler deals primarily with the collection of the produce of the region on behalf of the VOC, the taxation and corvée levied upon the population, and the relation of landholding to these last and to social differentiation. It thereby gives a perspective on Javanese society not found in either of the previous reports, which deal only superficially and in passing with those outside the aristocracy. Rothenbuhler's list of the VOC's contingents of the four regions[85] differs somewhat from that given in the Governors' reports over the period 1787–96. Ulujami was evidently now supplying cotton thread and indigo as well as rice. Rothenbuhler gives some interesting information on the way these three products were collected for the contingents, as follows.

Rice: Every "jonk" or *jung* of sawah was taxed at the rate of 8–10 "takkers". These units of measurement require some explanation.

Aristocracy and peasantry in the tides of world capitalism

The *jung* was evidently, at this period, a unit based on the productivity of the land rather than its actual size: it seems that a *jung* in the mountains was much larger than a *jung* in the fertile lowlands. Even in the lowlands there was great variation, since the *jung* of Wiradesa was larger than that of Pekalongan, and those of Batang were larger still. In all areas the *jung* was accounted as a parcel of land 280 rods long by 20 wide, but the length of the rod differed from place to place.[86] Apparently, this had not always been the case: the rod had once been a uniform measure equal, according to some, to 60 Chinese *picis* laid in a row or, according to others, the length of the pole of the state *payung* of a certain Javanese prince.[87] Until 1793, 67 "takkers" were supplied to make up one *koyan* [a variable measure generally reckoned at c. 3375 Amsterdam pounds] but after that time only 60 were required.[88] However, the actual amount of rice levied was varied by the Regent's subordinates in the light of the actual harvest. Rothenbuhler claims that the estates given to the Javanese were of such a size as to take into account the rice tax, that no hardship was involved, and that any change or reduction in the tax would only result in the profits at present enjoyed by the Resident – which, he claims, were almost the only ones he had in this area – going to the Regents, who already had enough profits. [Nearly all the reports by Residents written at this time stress the poor returns they got from their position, but one need not feel too sorry for Rothenbuhler at least: subsequent to holding the post of Gezaghebber, we find him bidding against a Chinese leaseholder for the lease of the district of Probolinggo for the sum of a million rixdollars,[89] so it is evident that he had managed to save something. However, there seems to have been a decrease in the a mount of money repatriated by VOC employees after 1790.[90]] A different arrangement for the collection of rice operated in Ulujami and in the other areas – Kalang in Pekalongan and Seragi in Wiradesa – leased by the Chinese leaseholder. According to Rothenbuhler, all the rice-fields here were the property of the leaseholder (with the exception of a very few given to village heads for their maintenance) who hired labour from nearby villages, paying them a small share of the harvest. After filling his contingent to the VOC, the leaseholder used the rest of the harvest for private trade.

Cotton: In the Regencies, this was obtained by a levy on each household of one or two strings per year. The leaseholder of

Ulujami acquired his quota of cotton through purchase, as did the Resident his own contingent.[91]

Indigo: In Rothenbuhler's time, the number of indigo factories in the area under his jurisdiction was four, but had subsequently increased to six. The people who worked in these factories had to be supplied by the Regents and the leaseholder of Ulujami. The Regents' people were paid by the allocation of rice-fields for their maintenance; those sent by the leaseholders were paid in cash.[92]

Rothenbuhler also reports that a start had been made with pepper and coffee cultivation, and very small amounts were supplied to the Company for the payment fixed. He had recently heard from Semarang that some sugar would be required at a fixed price in future. There were two private sugar mills in the region, one in Pekalongan and the other in Batang.[93]

Logging: No timber was supplied to the Company after 1781, due to the exhaustion of the forests. Since existing forests were 10–12 hours' journey away, at the border of Kendal and in the mountains, and timber had to be brought downriver by raft, the labourers had to spend months away from their families in very hard conditions in forests uninhabited except by wild animals. Also, many buffaloes were lost. To address the problem of timber supply, Rothenbuhler began replanting the Waleri wilderness, which was close to the sea, with young teak trees. Criminals in chain gangs provided labour, the Regents got the iron for the chains at cost price from the Company and supplied rice themselves, the Captain of the Chinese at Semarang provided salt, and Rothenbuhler now and then gave a little *sirih* money.[94]

The Regents' incomes

From the collection and delivery of this produce Rothenbuhler and the Regents derived much of their income. The three Regents' income and expenditure is given in the report as follows:

Pekalongan

Income:
Rental of *desas*, *dukuhs*, and rice-fields........................ Rd.   9000
Poll-tax (*wang petek*) from Javanese freed from corvée . Rd.   500
Tax on the sale of opium, buffalo hides, etc................ Rd.   400

Aristocracy and peasantry in the tides of world capitalism

Profit on the rice contingent on a good harvest	Rd.	400
Profit on indigo supplied to the VOC	Rd.	700
Ditto on cotton	Rd.	100
Profit from other unspecified sources	Rd.	500
Total:	Rd.	11,600

Expenditure:

Capitation tax	Rd.	980
Ditto for Kalangs	Rd.	400
Agio [premium] for the receiver of the domeins of above monies	Rd.	28
New Year's money for the Governor	Rd.	184
Yearly gift to the Governor's valets	Rd.	34
Money paid to Land Council	Rd.	108.5
Panaiban or marriage money for the fiscal of the Land Council	Rd.	35
Yearly allowance for the woodsman so long as logging is discontinued	Rd.	84.5
Cost of *praus* and crews for the Karwelaan timber raft to Batavia	Rd.	225
Cost and maintenance of vessels used as cruisers, plus their armament and ammunition	Rd.	335
Cost of indigo seed and linen for the sieves	Rd.	90
Cost of maintaining the *gladak*[95] as well as the ceded ricefields	Rd.	336
Maintenance of *prajurits* [soldiers] as well as the above-mentioned ricefields	Rd.	510
Travel money for *baturs* sent to work in Semarang	Rd.	650
Cost of 12 *koyan* Mulud rice for the Governor @ Rd. 20 per *koyan*	Rd.	240
Maintenance of Regent's household and other expenses	Rd.	2000
Total:	Rd.	6240

Batang

Income:

Rent from *desas, pasars*, and ricefields	Rd.	2472
Capitation tax for Javanese freed from corvée	Rd.	250
Tax on the sale of opium and buffalo hides	Rd.	30
Profit on indigo supplied to the VOC	Rd.	100
Ditto on cotton thread	Rd.	40

Ditto on rice on a good harvest................................. Rd. 50
Gifts in kind to the Regent .... Rd. 200
Total:.. Rd. 3142

Expenditure:
Capitation tax paid to the VOC.................................. Rd. 266
Agio payable to receiver of domeins.......................... Rd. 5
New Year's gift to the Governor .... Rd. 40
Annual gift to the Governor's orderlies .... Rd. 17
Money payable to Land Council .... Rd. 31
Panaiban or marriage money payable to the fiscal of the
Land Council.. Rd. 10
Yearly allowance for the woodsman.......................... Rd. 24
Cost of indigo seed and linen for the sieves [?]........... Rd. 35
Cost of one *prau* per annum plus the crew of the
Karwelaan timber raft.. Rd. 56
Maintenance of a cruiser, crew, and armament .... Rd. 84
Cost of the *gladak* .... Rd. 129
Money for the *baturs* in Semarang............................. Rd. 225
Cost of the *prajurits*, excluding ricefields................... Rd. 190
4 *koyan* of rice for the Governor, @ Rd. 20 per *koyan*.... Rd. 80
Maintenance of Regent's household and other
expenses.. Rd. 1500
Total .... Rd. 2692

Wiradesa

Income:
Rent from *desas*, *pasars*, and ricefields .... Rd. 1675
Capitation tax of Javanese freed from corvée............. Rd. 425
Tax on the sale of opium and buffalo hides................ Rd. 17
Profit on the supply of indigo to the VOC.................. Rd. 333
Ditto on cotton thread.. Rd. 56
Ditto on rice on a good harvest.................................. Rd. 300
Other articles in kind... Rd. 150
Total:... Rd. 2956

Expenditure:
The *cacah* money which has to be
paid yearly to the Company .... Rd. 223
Agio due to the receiver of the domeins .... Rd. 7
New year's obligation to the Governor...................... Rd. 30

Aristocracy and peasantry in the tides of world capitalism

Gift to the Governor's orderlies	Rd.	17
Yearly contribution to the Land Council	Rd.	23.25
Panaiban or marriage money of the inhabitants	Rd.	7.25
Yearly allowance for the woodman	Rd.	18
Cost of the necessary indigo seed and linen for sieves	Rd.	40.5
Cost of a prau with the crew for the Karwelaan timber-raft, yearly	Rd.	56
Maintenance of a cruiser, with the necessary crew, ammunition etc.	Rd.	84
Cost of the *gladak*	Rd.	124
Cost of the *baturs* working in Semarang, excluding rice-fields	Rd.	150
Cost of the *prajurits* or soldiers, excluding the rice-fields	Rd.	80
Cost of 3 *koyan* of rice which the Regent is obliged to supply to the Governor each year at Rd. 20 per *koyan*	Rd.	60
The amount the Regent needs for his own household and some other expenses	Rd.	1000
Total	Rd.	1920

Comparison of the Regents Incomes: The Regent of Pekalongan had an income of Rd.11,600 and expenses of Rd. 6240, leaving a profit of Rd. 5360; the Regent of Batang had an income of Rd. 3142 and expenses of Rd. 2692, leaving a profit of Rd. 450; and the Regent of Wiradesa had an income of Rd. 2956 and expenses of Rd. 1920, leaving a profit of Rd. 1036.

Population, the labour force and payment for labour

In his listing of the contingents Rothenbuhler notes a reduction in the amount of capitation tax or *cacahgeld* – from Rd. 1225 to 980 (and from Rd. 500 to 400 for the Kalangs) in the case of Pekalongan; from Rd. 333:8 to Rd. 266$\frac{8}{15}$ for Batang; and from Rd. 278.75 to 223 for Wiradesa. In 1796 a survey had been made of the population of the three Regencies which produced the following figures:

Regency total	Villages	Men	Women	Children	Pop.
Pekalongan	1055	17545	20936	31549	70030
Batang	360	6741	8278	13646	28665
Wiradesa	225	5222	5979	8616	19817
Totals	1640	29508	35193	53811	118512

Rothenbuhler remarks that since the survey was made many people had left the region due to a long succession of bad harvests, but would very likely return. The figures given in this census should be compared with those from a population census made in 1802 for the Governor of the North-east Coast, Nicolaus Engelhard.[96] Rothenbuhler gives almost the same population figure for Wiradesa as the 1802 census (19,817 compared to 19,812), but considerably lower figures for Pekalongan (70,030 compared to 100,007) and Batang (28,665 compared to 38,046). The number of villages in each Regency is also considerably higher in the 1802 figures: nearly 100 more in Pekalongan, 60 more in Batang, 65 in Wiradesa. Furthermore, Rothenbuhler remarks that since the survey was made many people had left the region due to a succession of bad harvests. Even if all those who left because of the bad harvest returned within a year of Rothenbuhler's writing, this would mean that the population of the Pekalongan-Batang-Wiradesa region increased by a third in three years, an annual rate of increase that would imply very heavy in-migration from somewhere else. Alternatively, there is a large margin of error in one or both sets of figures. On population distribution, Knight[97] notes that separate majority of cultivators lived in very small clusters of population scattered widely across the countryside: the "typical" big Javanese village was uncommon in Pekalongan, in contrast to both the neighbouring *pasisir* Residencies to the east and west.

Rothenbuhler describes below the special treatment given to those in outlying districts and the "mountain people" to keep them satisfied, and it should be noted that the entire mountain range between the *pasisir* and the central Javanese heartland was covered with forests and probably contained more tigers, rhinoceroses and wild boars than people.[98] This was always a potential refuge for those fleeing from the excessive labour demands of the pasisir, and an eyrie for the "rabble" that periodically swept down on the more law-abiding lands of the coast, as reports on Demak from this period attest.

Very significantly, Rothenbuhler also saw a far more serious and less localized population problem: over the "whole of Java" one saw the remains of human habitation and of land laid out as *sawah* in the middle of what were now uninhabited forests and wildernesses. What, he asks, could be the cause of this phenomenon? The often-given explanation in terms of the "gruesome events of the previous Javan wars and the ravages of the plague which followed" was not,

Aristocracy and peasantry in the tides of world capitalism

he thought, sufficient in itself. He considered two other scourges particularly responsible: smallpox, and the Javanese way of treating it which involved washing and rubbing so that the pernicious substances were drawn in with fatal results; and the consumption of opium. Both factors are also noted in de Rovere van Breugel's account of Banten, particularly the fear which a smallpox epidemic evoked in the population.

Corvée labour

As far as the VOC was concerned, the labour demands upon this population, which the Regents were obliged to supply along with their contingents, had been as follows:

Pekalongan
34 *baturs* [coolies] apart from their headmen, for the fort and warehouses
4 *prau mayang* as cruisers to counteract the pirates
4 *prau mayang* for daily use at the fort
4 horses for the delivery of letters

Batang
15 *baturs*, as well as their headmen, for the warehouses
1 *prau mayang* as a cruiser
1 *prau mayang* for use at the fort
4 horses for delivering letters

Wiradesa
12 *baturs*, as well as their headmen, for the fort
1 *prau mayang* as cruiser against pirates
1 *prau mayang* for use at the fort
2 horses for delivering letters

This adds up to a total of 61 men from the three Regencies. But Rothenbuhler then goes on to say that "since circumstances have changed a lot since the setting up of the contracts, and new needs have continually arisen it is self-evident that the corvées can no longer be what they were". So the Regents have now also delivered for many years the following:

Pekalongan
1. *For the fort*:
96 *baturs* [coolies] working in the warehouses and for some officials
63 *baturs* loading ships

The Cancer Within

6 artisans
2 messengers[99]

2. *For paseban [field of audience, tourney-field] or Regency duties:*
23 *baturs* to carry the goods of arriving and departing Company officials
30 *baturs* for special circumstances
(100 *baturs* for logging when this was in train)
5 *baturs* for work in the Waleri wilderness
5 *baturs* to guard the prisoners of the Regency
2 *baturs* in the *gladak* where provision is made for official travellers
6 *baturs* keeping watch at the flag-poles on the beach[100]

3. *For the three indigo factories:*
3 *děmangs* or overseers
6 *umbul* s [village officials in charge of the coolies on duty]
20 *lurahs*[101]
260 *baturs*
5 coppersmiths

4. *For the military:*
50 gunners
150 musketeers
120 bowmen
60 spear-bearers
170 pikesmen

5. *For Semarang:*
272 *baturs* for the barracks, the batteries and other works
2 *mantri anom* [junior *mantri* in charge of commercial crops]
4 *baturs* of the *mantri anom*[102]

Batang

1. *For the fort:*
26 *baturs* in the warehouses
24 *baturs* for loading the ships and other work
2 artisans when required[103]

2. *For paseban or Regency duties:*
20 *baturs* to transport the goods of Company officials
10 armed and mounted men to protect the postillions on their way to Semarang
4 *baturs* at the crossing of the Batang river
6 *baturs* at the Roban crossing

330

Aristocracy and peasantry in the tides of world capitalism

8 *baturs* at the Kali Urang crossing
3 *baturs* at the flag-poles
5 *baturs* to guard the roads in the Waleri wilderness
(40 *baturs* for felling trees when logging is in train)
3 log keepers[104]

3. *For the manufacture of indigo*:
2 *dĕmangs* or overseers
1 *bebau* or sub-overseer
16 *lurahs* and lesser heads
153 *baturs*
2 coppersmiths

4. *For the military*:
40 musketeers
40 bowmen
60 pikesmen

5. *For Semarang*:
89 *baturs* for the batteries and other works
1 *mantri anom*
2 *baturs* for the *mantri anom*[105]

Wiradesa

1. *For the fort*:
24 *baturs* in the warehouses
12 *baturs* for loading ships and other duties
1 artisan when required[108]

2. *For paseban or Regency duties*:
8 *baturs* to carry the goods of travelling VOC officials
3 *baturs* to assist the salt-seller
4 *baturs* at the flag-poles
3 *baturs* who watch over the alarm-block[107]

3. *For the manufacture of indigo*:
1 *dĕmang* or overseer
9 *lurahs*
160 *baturs*
3 coppersmiths[108]

4. *For the military*:
30 musketeers

40 bowmen
55 pikesmen

5. *For Semarang*:
50 *baturs* working at the batteries
1 *mantri anom*
2 *baturs* of the *mantri anom*[109]

Rothenbuhler adds the following comments on these lists: the same people do not keep working, but are replaced from time to time by others, with the exception of the soldiers and the indigo workers, who work close to home. The number of people working in Semarang is not constant, but varies according to demand, as is also true of those on *paseban* or *gladak* duty, with many more than the above figures being required at times. If the number of *baturs* needed at Batang and Wiradesa is more than 30 ("30 head", as Rothenbuhler says), the extra contingent, or part of it, has to be supplied by Pekalongan, which has a larger population and whose people do not have so far to travel.

It will immediately be seen that this is a staggering escalation in the amount of labour extracted by the VOC, from 61 men to over two and a half thousand, i.e more than a forty-fold increase, exclusive of those who were required when logging was in train.

Furthermore, these lists do *not* include the corvée work carried out for the Regents and their families, which Rothenbuhler describes as "very considerable", though variable. Ulujami was completely free of corvées and did not have to send any labourers to Semarang or the Pekalongan comptoir.

Recompense for labour

As may be expected, payment for work, whether for the Regents or for the Company, was in the form of land. Rothenbuhler gives the following table of landholdings among different classes of employees. He has given the total landholding of all employees in that particular category: the unit of measurement is the *jung*.

Pekalongan Regency, landholdings in jung
The Patih 90
70 *mantris* 616
64 "priests", including the chief priest 63
4 *kabayans* [village official, factotum] 14

Aristocracy and peasantry in the tides of world capitalism

39 *umbuls* [village officials in charge
of the coolies on duty] 117
75 *lurahs* 112

Workers at the fort:
192 *baturs* in the warehouses.. 125
126 ditto loading ships... 36
12 artisans when needed 11

Workers on Regency duties:
46 *baturs* at the *paseban* 42
60 ditto as needed 15
10 ditto at Labuan 5
10 ditto at the alarm-block... 10
4 ditto at the *gladak* 4
1 head of the *gladak* 2
12 men at the flag-poles 12

Indigo workers:
3 *děmangs*.. 26
6 *umbuls* [village officials in charge of the coolies on duty].... 18
20 *lurahs* 30
260 *baturs*.. 90
5 coppersmiths.. 5

The military:
50 artillery-men... 25
150 musketeers 143
120 archers... 120
60 assegai bearers 18
170 pikesmen 168

Workers at Semarang:
544 *baturs*... 544
2 *mantri anom* 27
8 *baturs* for the *mantri anom* 8
4 *děmangs* for the cruisers 34
88 sailors 44

The Regent's own servants:
4 *mantris*.. 34
8 *palangkungs* or lesser heads 26
5 *kabayans* 7

333

26 lurahs 40
80 garden boys..35
71 grooms..65
34 in the kitchen[110] 31
30 household servants..25
36 musicians..45
14 *wayang* and *topeng* performers 15
31 clerks and artisans...51
20 cattlemen...18
Batang Regency, landholdings in jung
The Patih..25
34 *mantri* 111
1 *pangulu* and 16 lesser "priests" and functionaries 13
10 *kabayans* 5
14 *ulus-ulus* [irrigation officials]..3.5
10 *lurahs* 10

Workers at the fort:
52 *baturs* in the warehouses 5
48 ditto for loading ships 12
4 artisans.. 1

Workers on Regency duty:
40 *baturs*..15
20 armed men with their horses..15
36 *baturs* at the 3 crossings 2
6 ditto at the flag-poles 2
12 ditto for guarding the roads 2
6 at the signal-block... 3

Indigo workers:
2 *děmangs* 4
1 *bebau* 1
16 *lurahs* 6
153 *baturs* 30
2 coppersmiths.. 2

The military:
50 musketeers 31
40 bowmen.. 10.5
60 pikesmen..30

334

Aristocracy and peasantry in the tides of world capitalism

Workers at Semarang:
178 *baturs* on different tasks... 89
1 *mantri anom* 4
4 *baturs* 2
1 *děmang* or headman of a cruiser.................................. 3
22 *baturs* of the above.. 18

The Regent's own servants:
1 *mantri* 6
6 *lurahs* 6
12 gardening boys 2.5
37 boy grooms... 14
20 kitchen servants 8
26 household servants.. 10
25 musicians 15
15 clerks and artisans... 4.5
10 cattlemen... 5

Wiradesa Regency, landholdings in jung
The Patih... 40
32 *mantris* 259
The *pangulu* and 20 lesser "priests".......................... 15.5
8 *umbuls* [village officials in charge of the coolies on duty].... 32
14 *lurahs* 42
6 *kabayan* 16

Workers at the fort:
48 *baturs* 48
24 ditto for other contingencies 6
2 artisans 2

Workers on Regency duty:
16 *baturs* 16
6 ditto at Bebah.. 1.5
8 ditto at the flag-poles 6
6 ditto at the signal-block 6

Indigo workers:
1 *děmang*.. 8
9 *lurahs* 16
160 *baturs*... 70
3 coppersmiths.. 1.5

The military:
30 musketeers	35
40 archers	13
55 pikesmen	50

Workers at Semarang:
108 *baturs*	48
1 *mantri anom*	8
4 *baturs* of the above	2
1 headman of the cruiser	3
22 *baturs* of the above	22

The Regent's own servants:
2 *mantri*	11
4 *lurahs*	8
10 garden boys	3
22 boy grooms	16
13 kitchen servants	9
10 household servants	7
14 clerks and artisans	17.5
29 musicians	20

Corvée, landholding, and taxation

Here it in necessary to clarify two terms used for units of measurement, the *jung* and the *cacah*. The meaning of the term *cacah* has been a matter of different interpretations among historians. Rothenbuhler gives the following explanation,[111] based, he says, on "guesswork" and "inadequate reports". *Cacah*, he explains, is actually no more than a numerator. But in the sense in which he is interested, i.e. the *cacah karya*, or "work *cacah*" it means an estate (*landerij*) allotted for the maintenance of Javanese in service. For without such maintenance no-one had any obligations beyond paying some capitation tax each year, and now and then doing some *kampung* duty which consisted only of improving the roads, deepening the rivers, etc. Among those who were involved in other labours, the reward was proportional to the heaviness of the task. Some *baturs* had two or even three *cacahs*, while others had only three-quarters or a half. (Another very striking differential is that between ordinary workers, *baturs*, and officials in the amount of land allocated: the Patih of Batang for instance had 90 *jung* for

Aristocracy and peasantry in the tides of world capitalism

himself while 192 *baturs* working at the warehouses only had 125 *jung* between them.) When there was a shortage of land, money payments were made but this was not popular as it slipped too quickly through the fingers. People preferred to work their lands themselves, using their products themselves, storing or selling them. They could also trade with the communal estates or commons. These usually consisted exclusively of rice-fields, at least in districts where there was no shortage of these. In these cases half a *jung* of rice-fields made up one *cacah*, and a whole *jung* two *cacahs*. But in places where there was a scarcity of rice-fields, like Batang, a *cacah* consisted of only a small amount of rice-field and the rest was *gaga* fields, orchards, bamboo, etc.

This interpretation of the *cacah* as a way of counting parcels of agricultural land, of quite variable size from one region to another, confirms the interpretation given by van Niel in his article on land rights in Java.[112]

In the official accounting, Pekalongan is reckoned at 7000 *cacah*, Batang at 2000, Wiradesa at 1500, and Ulujami at 1000 (totalling 11500). However, Rothenbuhler estimates the actual situation as follows:

Pekalongan	3693 *jung*	7499 *cacah*
Batang	584 *jung*	2065 *cacah*
Wiradesa	1293 *jung*	1749 *cacah*
Ulujami (old figures)	500 *jung*	1000 *cacah*
Totals:	6070 *jung*	12313 *cacah*

Rothenbuhler cautions against regarding the increase in the number of *cacah* as indicative of an increase in the area under rice or otherwise in cultivation: the reverse, he says, is actually the case, with a considerable fall in the export of rice from the region. In a somewhat unclear passage he suggests that the *cacah* had been tampered with [i.e. reduced in size] because of the way in which labour obligations were always linked with this unit of measurement. Only in Wiradesa was it the case that new land had been brought under cultivation, with the drainage of swamp land. This land, however, could only support a rice crop once every two or three years.

Taxation

Rothenbuhler appears to divide the working population of the Residency into two basic categories, *baturs* and "free" inhabitants, the first of which had a number of subdivisions. It is clear that he uses *batur* as synonymous with the more widely known term *sikĕp*, though according to Boomgaard *batur* almost always meant a corvée labourer.[113] Boomgaard distinguishes four subdivisions of *sikĕp*[114] (i.e. *batur* in Rothenbuhler's account) and this was the case in Pekalongan, but not in Batang and Wiradesa, where there were only one or two groups. Also, the way in which Rothenbuhler distinguishes the four groups, on the basis of the nature of the work assigned to them, is different from the criterion used by Boomgaard, their position in the village hierarchy, and Rothenbuhler's top two groups were subject to corvée, whereas Boomgaard's are not. "Free" inhabitants correspond to the group usually referred to as *numpang* (though Rothenbuhler does not use this term), who were free of the obligation to pay land-rent and corvée. Rothenbuhler makes it clear that there was great variation even within the same Residency in the arrangements made for these groups.

Pekalongan

I. The *baturs* who do duty in Semarang or on the cruisers get one *jung* rice-field for their maintenance, but against that they have to supply:

1. 4 ten-cent pieces per year for a statement that they are freed from the payment of head-money.
2. a string of cotton thread for nothing or, if they don't have it, 3 ten-cent pieces.
3. towards the end of the fast month 4 ten-cent pieces called *pamalam* and *pariyoyo*, for the party which is celebrated then.
4. every 5 to 6 months one capon for nothing, or enough money to pay for one.
5. three and sometimes four times a year, 25 to 30 lengths of split bamboo for the making of fences.
6. three ten-cent pieces towards the buying of thatch.
7. the so-called *panajung* or *jung* money, being two ten-cent pieces for every *jung*.
8. 8 barrels of rice for each *jung* to be delivered to the Company, for which payment is made. Should someone not be able to supply his quota because of a bad harvest or whatever other reason, he has to pay the Regent half a ducat for each barrel.

Aristocracy and peasantry in the tides of world capitalism

    9. from each *jung* 4 bunches of paddy, none of which goes to the Regent, it only being used for the maintenance of the *ulu-ulus*, village officials in charge of irrigation. They all have their own district and are obliged to see that the water does not bank up but that it is shared out to everyone as is necessary.
   10. at the beginning of the new year a bottle of oil from each Umbul or Mantri who has it supplied in turn by the ordinary people.
   11. a lot of coconut on demand by the Regent, for nothing.
   12. also money contributions, should the Regent want to make something or have need of buffalo, or horses have to be bought for the *gladak*. Then each Mantri or Lurah has to contribute something and they, likewise, look to their underlings, not counting all the many other small items which cannot really be kept track of as they are not fixed but only occur under certain circumstances.

II. The *baturs* who have to work in the warehouse or supply firewood in the *dalĕm* of the Regent, each have one *jung* rice-field for their maintenance and have to supply:

    1. 8 barrels of rice to the Company.
    2. 12 *ongos* [swathes] of paddy called *punjung* [gift of honour to a superior] for nothing, or 60 bunches, of which each may not weigh less than 10 to 12 *kati*. This is for the Regent's horses and for delivery to Semarang.
    3. 4 more bunches of paddy for each *jung* for the maintenance of the *ulu-ulus*.
    4. 6 fowl and 6 ducks per year, for nothing.
    5. *grabak* or *cacah* money, amounting to 30 ten-cent pieces per year.
    6. a string of cotton thread or 3 ten-cent pieces per year.
    7. *panajung* or *jung* money, 2 ten-cent pieces yearly.
    8. 4 ten-cent pieces per year for the celebration of *puasa*.
    9. 3 ten-cent pieces per year for the buying of thatch.
   10. a few times a year, 25 to 30 lengths of split bamboo for the making of fences.
   11. as many coconuts, capons etc. as demanded and also some oil and other things at the start of the new year.

III. The *baturs* who are used for other duties here on the *paseban* e.g. the carrying of lances etc. do not enjoy more than half a *jung* rice field for their existence but have to pay the same taxes as the above, with the exception of the *grabag* and statement money and the supply of thread and paddy, fowl and ducks; they also only have to supply 4 barrels of rice and 1 ten-cent piece for *jung* money, or the half of the above.

IV. The *baturs* who work in the stables or gardens of the Regent or do other lesser work, have even less for their maintenance than those just mentioned, only a quarter of a *jung*, but on the other hand they are freed from everything those above are exempted from and from the supply of rice as well, and they only have to pay half a ten-cent piece for *jung* money.

V. The free inhabitants of the main *nagari*, or those who do not have rice-fields and are thus not subject to corvée, have to supply yearly:

1. *grabag* or *cacah* money, up to 30 ten-cent pieces.
2. 6 fowl and 6 ducks.
3. a string of cotton thread or 3 ten-cent pieces.
4. for the purchase of *atap* another 3 ten-cent pieces.
5. the so-called *wang paneser* or voluntary gift, amounting to 4 ten-cent pieces per year.

Rothenbuhler goes on to describe the "free" inhabitants of the *nagari* situated at a greater distance away who have to pay the same taxes as those just mentioned, except for the *atap* money from which they are exempted. He says however that the inhabitants of the mountains, where there are absolutely no rice-fields, have to be treated much more gently than those who live in the low-lands, as they are ready to leave at once for the slightest reason, going where they can just as easily live. They also have no shortage of bamboo or wood to build their houses. For this reason they only have to supply a contribution of 32 ten-cent pieces per year, for each one who owns some fruit trees and has laid out *gaga* fields, while all the others are completely exempt.

He also says that the free inhabitants, both in Pekalongan and in the *desas*, who are widows or still unmarried, both men and women, if living in their own house have to pay half the *grabag* money or 15 ten-cent pieces per year, along with 4 or 5 fowl and ducks, and sometimes half a string of thread as well or more according to circumstances, but are freed from all other taxes. When two unmarried men or women live together in one house, both having a share of it, they have to supply twice as much. But in the case of someone who only lives with someone else and does not have a share in the house, they are exempted from all taxes, even if they are married and have their husband or wife with them, as long as they are classified as *bujangs* who have no possessions but work for others to earn their living.

Rothenbuhler says also that apart from the *baturs* there is another kind of working people here, known by the name of *"orang di balakan"* ["people at the back"]. They inhabit the *desas* and are not employed directly in corvée for the Company or the Regent but are rented by the latter to private individuals, in which case the inhabitants no longer have anything to do with them excepting for the delivery of rice to the Company. For them, this was fixed at 10 barrels per *jung* on payment to the above-mentioned or his relatives, idem the Pepatihs Kliwons, Mantri etc. for maintenance, otherwise they would have no means of existence. Such inhabitants are obliged to do corvée for the owner, be it as stable-boy, pikeman or whatever.

Their taxes comprise:

1. *cacah* money or 30 ten-cent pieces per year.
2. a string of cotton thread.
3. 6 fowl and 6 ducks.
4. the *wang paneser* or 4 ten-cent pieces.
5. 4 bunches of paddy from each *jung* for the *ulu-ulus*.
6. 6 bunches padi for the Regent.
7. 10 barrels of rice for delivery to the Company on payment in the same manner as noted for the *baturs* doing work for the Company. Also some other articles and some money now and then when the owner of the *nagari* or the Regent needs something, e.g. a horse, a buffalo, a lot of pikes etc.

The Mantris and other heads are themselves exempt from these and other taxes, but in extraordinary cases, when the Regent has to have money, as after his appointment,[115] and in other situations as well, they are also given to understand that money is expected from them, each to give as much as he can spare, up to 40, 50 and 60 and more Spanish dollars each. This is a custom which takes place across Java, including the mountains. Rothenbuhler says that it cannot be seen as a really objectionable one as each gives as much as he wants and he wants to please as this is an old tradition respected by the Javans. They also know that a newly appointed Regent who has nothing of his own, which is usually the case, and who sometimes needs very large sums to repay the expenses incurred by his appointment, is obliged to act in this way, and sometimes even harder.

Wiradesa

In this Regency, says Rothenbuhler, the taxes are arranged quite differently than in Pekalongan, but they weigh no less heavily on the ordinary man. The *jungs* are much bigger in this district than in Pekalongan.

The taxes on a *batur* who has a *jung* rice-field, equivalent to those who work at Semarang and here, consist of:

1. the *wang grabag* or *cacah* money up to 30 ten-cent pieces.
2. a string of cotton thread or 3 ten-cent pieces.
3. the making up of another 4 strings of the same thread, for which they get the cotton.
4. a yearly tax on each house or an evaluation called *pacumplang*, up to 4 ten-cent pieces.
5. the *wang paneser*, or the so-called voluntary gift, up to 4 ten-cent pieces.
6. the *panajung* or *jung* money, at 8 ten-cent pieces the *jung*.
7. 12 barrels of rice from each *jung* yearly for delivery to the Company on payment. But if the harvest fails – which often happens as Wiradesa lies so flat that it floods very easily, and dries out as quickly – Rothenbuhler tells the owner it is enough to pay only 8 ten-cent pieces as his whole share, which the Regent pockets: otherwise, just like in Pekalongan, he has to pay half a ducat for each barrel which he is behind.
8. the *wang parolo*, or *solo* gift, introduced when the Regent had to go on a journey to the high country, and which since then has always been levied, amounting to 4 ten-cent pieces per year.
9. the Governor's gift being 4 ten-cent pieces.
10. 20 bunches of *padi cerowok* for the *ulu-ulus*.
11. 10 bunches of *"padi jujun"* [?] or fodder paddy for the Regent's horses.
12. for one family, a barrel of rice each year for the Regent.
13. the land council money, 7 farthings a year.
14. 5 farthings and a fowl per *jung* for the maintenance of people of standing, like delegates or the *mantri anoms*, who survey the pepper and coffee, when they pass through with their retinue and have to be fed and given lodgings everywhere.

15. lastly, these *baturs* also have to relinquish a quarter of their *jung* which is given to the Patih or Kliwon to see what further taxes or demands following the circumstances will be made, like bamboo, *atap*, coconuts, capons, money for buying buffalo, *gladaks*, horses, etc.

The other *baturs* of Wiradesa who are employed on the *paseban* on carrying duties and in the *dalĕm* of the Regent and for other small jobs, all have no more than a *bau* or a quarter *jung* each, and have to supply:
1. 2 strings of cotton thread or 6 ten-cent pieces.
2. the *wang pacumplang* or house estimation, 4 ten-cent pieces.
3. 5 bunches of *padi cerowok* for the *ulu-ulus*.
4. 2½ bunches of *padi jujun* or fodder *padi* and
5. 1½ barrels of rice of the Company.

but they are exempted from everything else, which is likewise the case regarding those *nagaris* where the inhabitants are not employed by the Company, but are hired out by the Regent or handed over to the Mantris and other heads for their maintenance. These people and the unmarried or *bujangs* are under the same regulations as those of Pekalongan.

The free inhabitants of the main *nagari* and *desas*, also had to pay quite heavy taxes, i.e.:
1. the *cacah* or *grabag* money up to 30 ten-cent pieces.
2. a string of cotton thread or 3 ten-cent pieces.
3. the making of another 4 equal strings of thread.
4. the *wang pacumplang* or house estimation of up to 4 ten-cent pieces.
5. the *wang paneser* or the voluntary gift of 4 ten-cent pieces.
6. the *solo* gift of up to 4 ten-cent pieces.
7. His Excellency's gift of 4 ten-cent pieces.
8. the land council money of 7 farthings.
9. a barrel of rice for every member of the household.
10. 4 fowl and 2 ducks per year.
11. at the passing through of people of standing or delegates, 5 farthings and one fowl.

Batang

Rothenbuhler says that although this Regency is very extensive it is not very well populated as it is, for the greater part, made up of waste lands. It can boast of very few good rice-fields with the result that the taxes in this district are not nearly as important as those in the first two, which have enough good rice-fields and where the people can easily dispose of the products which are left over. The Batang *nagaris* are usually too far away for the products to be transported and they can rarely dispose of their excess products in their neighbourhood, although near the main *nagari* there are some villages which are better off in this respect and which, therefore, also have to pay more tax. Nonetheless, these are but few in number, while the others are scattered here and there in the mountains and forests and usually have to live from their *gaga* fields and the cutting and sale of bamboo in their neighbourhood. As a result, it was quite impossible to make a decent survey of all of this, as there were only a few *desas* which could be compared in all respects with each other, most of them differing, due either to the greater or lesser fertility of the ground, the location and the kinds of products occurring there. However, in order to give some idea, he would give as examples three *negaris*, the first two being located far away in the mountains, towards the princes' lands, and the third on the lower ground not far from the main *nagari*.

A. The *desa* Kali Mangis, lying close to the Mancanagara lands. The *baturs* of this *desa* had to work in the Pekalongan warehouses and for that they enjoyed half a *jung* rice-field which was easily as much as three-quarters of a *jung* in Pekalongan, as the *jungs* there were much larger. But on the other hand they had to supply as well:

1. 4 barrels of rice to the Company yearly in payment, or by default, 10–12 ten-cent pieces for each barrel, after the harvest.
2. a *lurah* had to supply two barrels, while being exempt from all other taxes, so as not to give them any reason for complaint, as otherwise they were ready to move at the slightest incident to the nearby well-populated *nagaris* in the high country where the common man was in no way burdened as much as in the lands of the Company. It was impossible, says Rothenbuhler, to prevent this kind of movement.

B. The *desa*, Kali Balik, lying still farther away from Pekalongan, but also in the mountains and near the Mancanagara lands. This village also had rice-fields, which were divided up among the inhabitants so that each *batur* had ⅜ of a *jung*. As the *jungs* here were even larger than those in the former *desa*, that amounted easily to ¾ of a Pekalongan *jung*, for which enjoyment these inhabitants were obliged to work in Semarang and also to supply four barrels of rice for the Company (in the case of a *lurah* two barrels) annually.

In this and other *desas* nearby there were other *baturs* who only had a quarter *jung*, and they only supplied two barrels of rice yearly for the Company in payment. All these *baturs*, like those from Kali Mangis and for the same reason, were excused all further taxes.

The free inhabitants, in both these *desas*, and living in the area, also paid no taxes other than:

1. the *wang grabag* or *cacah* money, 20 ten-cent pieces.
2. 2 fowl.
3. 2 strings of cotton thread yearly. No more, otherwise they would certainly move to the princes' lands.

C. The *desa* Kali Pucang, situated near the main *nagari*. Along with a few other small *desas* it was specially designated for work on the *paseban* or *gladak* of Batang, for example, the transport of goods from one Regency to another.

The *baturs* of this *desa* had a quarter of a *jung* rice-field for their maintenance and, alongside the work they do, were obliged to supply each year:

1. 2.5 barrels of rice for the Company on payment.
2. 4 ten-cent pieces for the purchase of *atap*.
3. 2 strings of cotton thread, and various other contributions which were not fixed.

The free inhabitants in this and the other *desas* in the low-lands, as also those from the main *nagari*: paid:

1. 32 ten-cent pieces for *grabag* or *cacah* money.
2. 2 strings of cotton thread.
3. 2 fowl.
4. another fowl at the new year, and for a widower or unmarried person whatever they can, or as is noted sub Pekalongan.

The same arrangements applied to the other *desas*, as far as the local situation and other circumstances permitted. Some, who had no rice-fields, were exempt from paying all taxes except the *cacah* money and the supply of some bamboo which grew near their *nagaris*. The same also applied to those *nagaris* relinquished to the Mantris and other heads for their maintenance, although for the rest, the arrangements were the same as at Pekalongan.

The categories of taxation from Rothenbuhler's account:

1. The rice delivery to the Company (the Mataram *pajěg*), which was according to Boomgaard[116] generally a fixed amount of perhaps a third of the expected produce of the landholding.
2. The *panajung* or *jung* money, for the benefit of officials without salary lands (*lungguh*), which according to Boomgaard could be as much or more than the *pajěg*. Here, however, it is always listed as a small cash payment much less than the *grabag*.
3. The *grabag* or *cacah* money. According to Boomgaard this was a poll tax affecting all households, whereas the first two only applied to those in possession of arable lands. However, this does not appear to have been the case: if one looks at the five categories of inhabitant for tax purposes listed above sub Pekalongan, the first category paid no poll tax (they paid four ten-cent pieces a year for a statement of exemption) and neither did the third or fourth category. The "free inhabitants" paid half the usual amount (but those of Batang paid the full amount). In Wiradesa too not every category of worker paid in land was liable to *grabag*; and in Batang in two of the three villages used by Rothenbuhler the inhabitants were not liable to *grabag*.
4. *Wang petek*. Boomgaard says this is given as equivalent to *grabag* in some sources but in others is described as a tax levied proportionate to wealth, whereas *grabag* was the same for everyone. However, Rothenbuhler lists it as a tax which was levied by the Regent of Pekalongan from Javanese who were exempt from corvée. Furthermore, as noted above, *grabag* was not actually the same for everyone.
5. *Pacumplang*. According to Boomgaard, this was a house tax usually paid in cotton yarn. Here however it was paid in money (about one sixth of the usual amount for *grabag*), and was only levied in Wiradesa. However, Rothenbuhler does list another tax which consisted of a string of cotton thread or three ten-cent pieces annually.
6. Rothenbuhler also lists a large number of taxes in kind, again varying greatly from place to place and between one category of taxpayer and another: poultry, bamboo for fences, thatch, oil, coconuts; plus more rice for the upkeep of the village officials in

charge of irrigation, and rice as an annual gift of homage to the Regents.
7. Other money levies, such as for the upkeep of the *gladak*, for the hospitality offered to people of high rank passing through the district, for the celebrations at the end of the Fast, and for a New Year's gift to the Governor of the North-east Coast and his orderlies.
8. Rothenbuhler lists two more taxes not mentioned by Boomgaard i.e. the *wang paneser* or "so-called voluntary gift" as well as the *wang parolo* or *solo* gift made when the Regent had to make a trip to the high country – both of 4 ten-cent pieces. The taxes sub 7 and 8 were very unevenly levied.

Conclusion

It seems that the levying of taxes was much more complex and differentiated than Boomgaard's account suggests. This complexity and differentiation operated both geographically (certain regions were more lightly taxed because their inhabitants could more easily decamp to the territories under the central Javanese princes) and in terms of the complex format of taxpaying categories into which the working population was divided in any given locality. These categories not only divided the inhabitants into those who did and did not have rice fields, but also distinguished different groups within those who did have rice fields, on the basis of their different labour obligations. As with landholding, here too we find a complex and minutely distinguished hierarchy in Pekalongan society.

It is also clear from the way in which the taxes are specified that Pekalongan had a partly monetized economy although many taxes were still levied in kind, and Rothenbuhler claims that people preferred to receive land rather than money in payment for labour. From some of the information he gives, it seems that monetization may have gone further in the areas held by leaseholders than in the Regencies.

Old Pekalongan, New Pekalongan

The authors of the accounts of Banten and Priangan used for the first two sections of this chapter told us a little of local society and culture; Rothenbuhler confines himself purely to matters of accounting. Yet as a society and culture Pekalongan is no less interesting. In a travel account from 1865 Pekalongan is described as a real Javanese area, in contrast to the Pasisir areas to the east (the author considered Semarang very Arabicised, and the region from Surabaya eastward more Madurese than Javanese).[117] This "Javanese" character of Pekalongan is confirmed by the list of pastimes, including wayang, *macapatan*, and *sintren*, given in Vuldy's study.[118] In addition, Pekalongan occupies a special place in the geo-mythology of the Javanese world as one of the areas famous for being *wingit*, or spirit-haunted. Furthermore, its myths about those who have left the world of men for the world of ghosts tell us a little about attitudes to the social bond among those Javanese who were not members of the élite, and are thus never represented in the written sources, whether Dutch or Javanese.

The old Java: Javanese, free men, and ghosts

J.W. van Dapperen,[119] writing of the 1920s and 1930s remarked that belief in *siluman* (invisible beings or beings which appear at certain times and to certain people in their former but now discarded bodies) is very widespread in Pekalongan, both in the East and in the West. He describes the wood Si Rawung,[120] about 10 kilometres from Petarukan, formerly a large wood situated on a peninsula but subsequently, thanks to the great silting-up of the north coast (via the Comal river in this locality) only bordered by the sea on its north side. Part of the wood was converted to villages and 400 *bau* was made into a plot of land for a certain Mr Mackenzie. In this was a well-kept graveyard. When the trees on this land had to be felled the native population refused to do this work, and Christians and people from Cirebon had to be used. According to tradition, Sunan Geseng[121] had once lived here and had a *pesantren*: hence the place was called Si Geseng. In van Dapperen's time there were still some graves remaining (others had been washed away) and one of these was said to be that of Sunan Geseng himself. In the middle of the coconut gardens stood an old teak tree called Jati Songsong, which was said to be the *paseban* (audience-place) of the queen of the Java Sea, a place where many came to spend the night (*nyĕpi*). The whole area was believed to be the residence of innumerable ghosts, and it was also believed that the souls of dead pure-blooded Pemalangers (from the town of Pemalang in this area), nobility or commoners, went to Si Rawung, called Swarga or Kamaloka (Sanskrit terms for the abode of the Hindu gods). Before being allowed in they had to

Aristocracy and peasantry in the tides of world capitalism

undergo an interrogation and purification in the forecourt of Si Geseng. Nearby was a smaller place of reverence, called Si Ruwek or Si Kropak. On Kemis Wage and Jumat Kliwon [combinations of the five- and seven-day weeks recurring every 35 days] and on the great festivals, people came here from all over central Java in their hundreds. Those seeking riches made an offering of flowers at the *pesantren*. It was said that sometimes in the evening between 6 p.m. and 1 a.m. one could hear tambourines and gamelan instruments going out to sea in a great bustle, and this was said to be the queen of the Java Sea returning home after a visit to the mountains, accompanied by her host of followers. It was believed that those who saw her wearing a *parang rusak* kain and green *baju* and shaded by a red *songsong* were near their hour of death. [The Queen of the South Seas, Ratu Sagara Kidul or Nyai Lara Kidul, is still even today a figure of great presence on Java, although it seems surprising that this is also so on the north coast. At the period with which this book deals, the VOC establishment at Yogyakarta regularly paid for an offering to be made to her, to avoid misunderstandings in their relationship with the court.[122]] Another great *siluman* wood, called Si Loning, which had disappeared by van Dapperen's time, used to be nearby. The wood Si Roban near the Kuripan stop was another *siluman* wood where, for those who had eyes to see it, the kraton of Prabu Maharaja Trubiksa loomed up. People were mortally afraid to enter this wood, with stories told of people who had done so and never emerged, becoming *siluman*.

In another *siluman* story, that of a hamlet of Kalimusu village in district Bumiayu, a village official, the *kebayan*, Kaki Semprung, actually advised the villagers to choose the option of becoming *siluman* when they had the chance. The opportunity had opened for them as a result of a naughty boy making ash from an ants' nest, which proved to have the power to render people invisible. Kaki Semprung told them they should become *siluman* "in order to be free men" (*pradikan*) and no longer subject to rule (*ora kena reh maning*) – a striking example of the widespread concept that freedom was something unattainable except by those who were for some reason outside mainstream (as we should say) Javanese society. As we have seen in Rothenbuhler's account, the term "free men" (*pradikan, wong mardika*) was most often used to mean those who were exempt from either taxes, or more importantly labour services, or in some instances both, and were not among the landowners who formed the village core.[123]

The new Java: differentiation in ethnicity, ideology, and class

Pekalongan's experience in being drawn into the production of export crops was very different from that of Priangan. Whereas in Priangan coffee and the economic and social arrangements under which it was grown were well established under the Company and remained very much the same throughout the rest of the colonial period, Pekalongan, as part of the *pasisir* area, was only beginning to be a major focus of colonial enterprise in Rothenbuhler's time and was to undergo some major economic and social changes under the Cultivation System. The crops were different too: not coffee but first indigo and then sugar were important here. As we have seen, indigo was a recent introduction on the *pasisir*. It also imposed extremely heavy demands for peasant labour, as was apparent in the tables given by Rothenbuhler (see p. 329 ff. above) where the number of labourers the Company required for the indigo factories was larger than for any other category of labour.

There was widespread long-term peasant resistance to indigo growing: the peasantry had grown indigo as a valuable supplementary second crop but resisted pressure to develop it into a major year-round production occupying vast tracts of good farm land.[124] Villages whose *sawah* were allocated to indigo (and whole villages were simply assigned by colonial fiat) could not make enough to live: European sources concluded that the peasantry actually earned a derisory amount, insufficient to pay their taxes[125] let alone to feed them. Even in areas where indigo was not grown all year round, it took too much time away from rice and secondary crops: one Controleur estimated it took 176 days to grow plus 76 days of factory work.[126] *Herendiensten* – obligatory labour services – were also an issue: peasants fiercely insisted that these services, which still further consumed their time, should be commuted at the indigo manufacturer's expense.[127] Peasants fled the region, with one third of the households assigned to the Aschberg factory decamping, for example.[128] It was not that peasants were unwilling to engage in wage labour or market economy. Their opposition to the European manufacturers, and later on the Residency authorities who took over from the individual European planters, arose because the latter wanted too much indigo grown and were paying too little for it.[129] Indigo was a very unpopular crop all over Java, but geography and climate in Pekalongan seem to have made it a particularly precarious venture there. So strong was peasant feeling that in 1847 several hundred peasants by-passed the mediation of their "natural leaders" – which was "contrary to all custom and practice" – and attempted to confront the Governor-General, who was making a vice-regal tour of inspection.[130] Thus, Pekalongan peasants did not confine themselves to expressing the wish that they might become *siluman* in their search for freedom from oppression, and it is interesting that this radical consciousness had developed by the mid nineteenth century, seven decades earlier than the period the folk tales were collected.

The peasantry of Pekalongan had to support a three- or four-fold élite in their forced participation in indigo growing: European planters; Javanese Regents and the subordinate layers of the Javanese governing class; the Chinese money-lenders who financed the Regents, and to whom many were in debt; and the Dutch bureaucracy. Until the 1850s Pekalongan was the arena of a hard-fought struggle for profit between *priyayi* and Residency, and two Pekalongan Bupati were removed in 1847 and 1848.[131] A Dutch official wrote in 1830 that "anyone who is even a little acquainted with the native government knows that the chiefs, from the greatest to the smallest, have always extorted, still extort and will perhaps never stop extorting". On the other hand, a high Dutch official left for home with a fortune of three millions that he had made from indigo in Pekalongan Residency, apparently a still wealthier man than Rothenbuhler.[132]

After 1850, sugar became the major crop in Pekalongan. In contrast to indigo, it brought significant financial gain to the substantial peasants who formed the village government, while impoverishing other sections of the peasantry and freeing them for its workforce.

Again unlike Priangan, Pekalongan was a major centre of entrepreneurship, in which three communities, the Javanese, Arab, and Chinese, were involved in a network of interaction and rivalry. Under the category "foreign Asians" Rothenbuhler lists about 200 Buginese and other Indonesians, women and children included; and about 600 Chinese, not including women and children, in their own kampungs in Pekalongan, Batang, Wiradesa and Ulujami, and here and there in the desas. Their head, Tan Limko, leased the *shahbandarij* for which he paid Rd. 5925 per annum plus 4 *pikul* of cotton thread or, failing that, an extra Rd. 1000 payment.[133] Rothenbuhler makes no mention of the other foreign community for which Pekalongan was noted in the nineteenth century, that is, the Hadhramauti Arabs, many of them Sayyids. They seem to have migrated in the early nineteenth century, and became a high-status community with marriage ties not only with the local Pekalongan aristocracy but with central Javanese royalty.[134] One of their descendants was to become the famous Javanese painter, Raden Saleh.

Vuldy's assessment is essentially that three factors contributed to the formation of an élite of entrepreneurs in Pekalongan, namely the decline of the Javanese nobility, the industrialization of batik and the role of Islam as a network of communication and a rallying force. The first half of the nineteenth century was a critical time, when the nobility, reduced to the role of colonial tax collectors, sought a new type of legitimacy by allying themselves with newly-arrived Arabs. Both Arabs and Chinese financed the production of batik. The Chinese introduced a number of batik styles, in which the local nobility, heirs to refined kraton culture, also made a major contribution. The Dutch supplied thread and cloth, Javanese emigrating to other islands provided a market, and Pekalongan's coastal location enabled it to capitalize on the opportunities of the time.

Another nineteenth-century dynamic seems to have seen a shift in Pekalongan from a strongly Javanese to a more Islamic culture. Numerous Arabic texts were translated into Javanese, and there also appears to have been a sturdy Islamic ethos of honest toil that tended to devalue government service, if not to take a definitely negative attitude to colonial rule. Islam in Pekalongan seems to have been more socially radical than that of West Java. It produced sects with an edge of political and social critique, of which the best known is the Budiah movement led by Haji Rifangi. This was a puritanical and orthodox Muslim revivalist movement that called for a return to Koranic Islam and strongly criticised both Javanese customs considered contrary to Islam (such as *wayang* and *gamelan*) and the local élite, including both the religious functionaries and the Regents and their subordinates, who were stigmatised as sinful, ignorant, hypocritical and infidel. Those who served the kafir ruler were stigmatized as no better than dogs or pigs. Members of the movement withdrew from society at large (they did not take part in collective prayers at the mosque, nor use the *pengulu* for their marriages) into their own small communities. In this they resembled the later Saminists, whose ideology was Javanist where the Budiah were Islamic. Haji Rifangi's influence was at its height in the 1850s, and he was arrested in 1859 and exiled to Ambon – the well-nigh universal government response to a situation of this type.[135] The anti-colonial element in Pekalongan burst out even more strongly in the Revolution, when the *tiga-daerah* movement, a regional "social revolution" swept from power virtually the whole official hierarchy.[136]

As the century progressed, the growing Chinese community became more important commercially than the Arabs and Javanese. At the same time, proletarianization of the labour force seems to have developed quite rapidly. Piece-workers in the batik industry worked at home in its early period, but in the 1920s were increasingly forced to work in Chinese ateliers, many virtually enslaved. At the beginning of the twentieth century, batik entrepreneurs were prosperous and increasingly numerous, but the First World War, through its interruption of the import of raw materials and general economic effects, ended this prosperity. Vuldy notes the increased pressure of Chinese businessmen on the Javanese manufacturers, who were too feeble and ill-organised to resist it, leading to the racial troubles of 1931. The inter-war period, however, saw a growth in the production of cheap batik, destined principally for other islands and for export overseas, which was profitable for many Javanese small entrepreneurs. The number of people employed in the batik industry reached an all-time high on the eve of the Japanese occupation. This was also the time when the first cooperatives were set up by Javanese to free themselves of the Chinese monopoly in the supply of raw materials. According to Vuldy, commercial success, in combination with a certain organisational progress essentially provided by Islam, made possible the emergence of a Javanese middle class. The economic policies of the Sukarno government, especially in the import and distribution of cotton, favoured the batik industry and Pekalongan profited. Since then, however, conditions have been less favorable, due to the dominance of the market by *sablon* batik produced by ever-larger enterprises, which has left cooperatives and small entrepreneurs floundering. Population is now leaving the town.

Though Vuldy seems to perceive the emergence of a Javanese middle class after independence, Robison[137] sees the commodity industries of kretek, batik and textiles in the 1950s and 1960s very differently. He describes the transient success of a series of politically-connected licence-holders in the context of a continuing and serious real decline among indigenous producers, with the application of capital and technology shifting the bulk of manufacture into Chinese enterprises. Here we see an almost paradigmatic case of the relationsip between Islamicised *pribumi* entrepreneurs and their Chinese rivals: the very stuff that gave rise to Indonesia's first mass movement, Sarekat Islam, and continued to provide much of the dynamism of post-independence politics.

THE TIDES OF CAPITALISM: PEPPER, COFFEE AND TEA

The three regions dealt with here, therefore, had very different experiences of the encounter with the capitalist world-system as mediated by the VOC. Banten represents an early attempt from a strongly Islamic mercantile port society to catch the pepper tide of early capitalism. As both Braudel and Boxer[138] have noted, the pepper trade was of extreme importance in this period, with pepper the most profitable item of merchandise in the first half of the seventeenth century, before increasing demand for textiles caused these to overtake pepper and spices in purchases and sales by 1700. Banten however had lost this contest to the VOC, and with the relative decline in pepper's profitability the Company put its major resources into other products. Banten never recovered: ironically, the area that had been at the leading edge of a move towards a trade-base internationally-oriented, more "modern" economy and society became one of the most economically backward and socially conservative regions, the numerous ranks of the disaffected waiting sullenly for any chance to rebel.

World trade in the eighteenth century saw a phenomenal growth in the tea and coffee trades, which become more important than textiles, with the relative value of pepper and spices declining still further. In a sense, the shape of Priangan society was determined by both coffee and tea. The VOC put a massive effort into setting up the Priangan system for coffee, and this became even more important when by the late eighteenth century it was apparent that the Dutch had lost the battle for dominance in the tea trade to the English.[139] The contrast between the social effects of the introduction of coffee cultivation in Priangan and in Minangkabau is instructive: whereas in the latter society it had had a socially progressive effect and led to the undermining of the old royal dominance of society in favour of a new group of Islamic entrepreneurs,[140] in Priangan it led to an enormous strengthening of the old élite, who became neo-feudal grandees. The "traditional" nature of this society and the patron-client structures that underlay the Darul Islam movement after independence sprang from the VOC's policy of keeping the Priangan peasantry (by the use of force if necessary) in their native villages and under the jurisdiction of their local Regent.

In Pekalongan as in Priangan the labour demands on the peasantry for the forced cultivations and related work were huge, and we have seen just how much these increased (particularly, in this case, for the production of indigo) from the last decades of the eighteenth century, leading to what seems to the development of a sharpened class consciousness in the region's peasantry as evidenced by its protests against this forced labour. Rothenbuhler's report also gives evidence of a society with a very complex and minutely differentiated social and economic hierarchy, with each of the many groups having a particular and closely specified entitlement to land and consequent load of taxation in kind and in labour. His evidence suggests that socio-economic differentiation and differential taxation and corvée liabilities were even more complex and subject to local variations than Boomgaard has already suggested.[141]

In Pekalongan in the nineteenth century, alongside internal differentiation and developing class consciousness, a plural society was developing, encompassing Arab, Chinese and other populations, and eventually a conflict of interests between Islamic and Chinese entrepreneurs. In these developments and their political repercussions we see the birth of the new Indies.

In all three regions the authors of the reports note that population was fleeing, temporarily or permanently, to escape poverty or the burden of forced labour. This is also the case in reports on the Oosthoek, so that sometimes one asks where all these people were going. Rothenbuhler gives at least a partial answer in recording the magnetism of the neighbouring Princely Lands under the central Javanese rulers, which meant that villages adjoining these lands had to be given specially mild treatement. It may be that the apparent growth of population in the central Javanese lands[142] was not entirely natural growth, but had a major immigrant component. Population computation is further complicated by the fact that, as noted above, peasants who had left a region might return there when things improved.

Even in Pekalongan, the region where new opportunities are most in evidence, the peasantry did not display much evidence of response to market opportunities. It is common to hear explanations stressing the cultural factors that may have caused this difference between Javanese and, say, Minangkabau peasants, too often a sort of blame-the-victim approach. There is a simpler explanation, however: the peasantry was more than occupied in the dual task of fulfilling the requirements of the VOC and its successor government for unpaid labour – which in Pekalongan at least had increased four or five-fold over the last decade or two of the eighteenth century – and the struggle to grow their food. By the 1840s, it had become clear that the food production on Java was suffering badly, and production of compulsory crops like indigo not providing anything like the cash return to compensate for this. By this period too, as noted above, the traditional handicrafts of the peasantry had simply lost out to other, inescapable demands on the peasant's time.

Finally, the small sample here selected from the vast, vast corpus of VOC accounts is in itself instructive. Of course, these accounts construct an idealised reality (as idealised as that of Indonesian court texts, though the ideal itself is very different) that conceals the reality of incompetence, impotence and corruption for which the VOC at this period is famous. Of course, the precise specifications of produce did not translate so precisely and uniformly into deliveries, and there are some ringing silences about the "black" economy operated by such VOC potentates as the Delegate for Native Affairs. Yet it is remarkable that an institution in decline and disarray could still produce such comprehensive, dense, detailed accounting, and a tribute to the Dutch education system that lay behind its operations. Unfortunately these accounting techniques, like the technology of war, were just as useful for maintaining or instituting retrogressive social and economic arrangements as for progressive ones.

NOTES

1. Hildred Geertz, "Indonesian Cultures and Communities" in Ruth R, McVey ed., *Indonesia*, Yale University/HRAF Press 1963, pp. 24–96.
2. Michael Charles Williams, *Communism, Religion and Revolt in Banten*, Ohio University Monographs in International Studies, Southeast Asia series no. 86, 1990. p. 2.
3. Williams, *Communism*, p. 10.
4. Braudel, *Capitalism*, pp. 441–5.
5. Also known as Sultan Abu'l-Fath 'abdu'l-Fattah.

Aristocracy and peasantry in the tides of world capitalism

6 See Ann Kumar, *Surapati, Man and Legend: A Study of Three Babad Traditions*, Australian National University Centre of Oriental Studies Oriental Monograph Series no. 20, Leiden, E.J. Brill 1976, page 20.
7 "Bedenkingen over den staat van Bantam" door J.D.R.V.B. ("Bantam in 1786"), BKI new series no. I, 1856, pp. 106–170; and 309–357 ("Beschrijving van Bantam en de Lampongs"). There are overlaps between the two documents, and sometimes inconsistencies, e.g. in figures, between accounts of the same subject within the one manuscript, giving an impression of dizzying disorganization. I have therefore abandoned any intention of fidelity to the order of the original and drastically re-arranged de Rovere van Breugel's material, not even respecting the division between the two texts. Both contain a very large amount of descriptive material; the *Bedenkingen* also sets out a program for the improvement of the current state of affairs in Banten.
8 See pp. 339–41.
9 The Surasowan, later razed: only its outer pediment, opposite an archaeological museum commemorating Banten's past, can be seen today. The stones appear precisely cut and laid and there is very little sign of movement or disintegration.
10 Beschrijving (BS) 324–6.
11 BS 330.
12 Bedenkingen (BD) 151–64.
13 Boomgaard, *Children*, p. 19.
14 Boomgaard, *Children*, p. 19 and p. 57.
15 BD 111n. The old Amsterdam pound had 494 grams.
16 One *sangga* amounted to 5 *bos* of 13.5 *kati* according to some sources and 50 *kati* according to others: see *Encyclopaedie van Nederlandsch Indie* sub *Maten en Gewichten*.
17 BD 118–24.
18 BD 165.
19 See Remmelink, p. 131.
20 Waterloo on Yogyakarta in 1808, a report written for the Napoleonic Marshall and Governor General Daendels, which is to be found in *Reflections by several people on the cultivation of rice in Java, year 1806*, ARA.
21 BS 349–51 gives a list of over 20 varieties and asserts that 30–40 further varieties existed.
22 BS 331.
23 BS 333.
24 BS 332.
25 BS 333–4.
26 BS 336–7.
27 BS 170, 342–4; BD135–48.
28 BD136.
29 BD138.
30 The Banten pots of this period are quite famous, and can be seen in the Museum Nasional in Jakarta. There was also quite a significant import of Chinese, European, and Japanese ceramics into Banten in the 17th and 18th centuries. Specimens can be seen in the archaeological museum in Banten.

31 BS 351–6.
32 BS167.
33 BD 165–6.
34 BD 155–9.
35 BD 139–41, 150–3.
36 cf. J.W. Allen's position that in sixteenth century Europe, religion was actually a word for nationalism: see J.W. Allen, *A History of Political Thought in the Sixteenth Century*, Methuen (University Paperbacks) London 1960.
37 "De laatste investiture van eenen Bantamschen Sultan", *BKI* I 1856 pp. 363–98.
38 "Laafste inuestiture" p. 373.
39 The dictionary defines this as wine of the sort customarily drunk in the mornings.
40 "Laafste inuestiture" p. 375.
41 "Laafste inuestiture" p. 377.
42 "Laafste inuestiture" p. 380.
43 "Laafste inuestiture" p. 381.
44 "Laafste inuestiture" pp. 382–3.
45 "Laafste inuestiture" p. 387.
46 "Laafste inuestiture" p. 388.
47 "Laafste inuestiture" pp. 389–90.
48 "Laafste inuestiture" pp. 393–5.
49 "Laafste inuestiture" p. 364.
50 *sawah, gaga,* and *huma* (swidden): as well as being the only region of Java to practice the last, Banten also had the highest proportion of dry rice (*gaga*): see Williams, *Communism*, p. 15. Towards the end of the nineteenth century the cultivation of coconuts as a cash crop, with marketing in Chinese hands, became important: ibid. p. 29.
51 Quoted in Williams, *Communism*, p. 41. The apparent neglect of the fields and laziness of the population may have been due to the rock-hard, unworkable nature of the soil in the dry season: see ibid. p. 29.
52 See *Herinneringen van Pangeran Aria Achmad Djadiningrat*, Kolff, Amsterdam/Batavia c. 1936, pages 21–4, where the author describes his experiences as a boy in a Bantenese *pesantren*.
53 On this rebellion, see Sartono Kartodirdjo, *The Peasants' Revolt of Banten in 1888*, VKI 50, 1966.
54 On van Haren and his writings, see Ann Kumar, "Literary Approaches to Slavery and the Indies Enlightenment: van Hogendorp's Kraspoekol", *Indonesia* 43 (April 1987) p. 64.
55 See Heather Sutherland, "Notes on Java's Regent Families" Part I, *Indonesia* 16, (October 1973) pp. 113–147; p. 128.
56 Peter Boomgaard, "Buitenzorg in 1805", *Modern Asian Studies* 20/1 (1986) p. 36f.
57 Collection Nederburgh 366, ARA. Completed in Batavia on 23 November 1796.
58 It also mentions the regions Ciblagon, Cikalong and Cilingse, but does not deal with these in detail.
59 Boomgaard, *Children*, p. 27.

Aristocracy and peasantry in the tides of world capitalism

60 The manuscript gives the Dutch form *Noempangers*, and says that the original form was Manoempangers (i.e. *manumpang*).
61 *Bumi* means land or earth.
62 See Ch.3 p. 208 above.
63 ms. Rangong.
64 The author of the "Beschryving van het Koningryk Jaccatra", VBG 1 pp. 19–41 remarks on the extreme simplicity of the diet (steamed rice, with Spanish pepper and a little salt, or the leaves of a plant called "combran" which has a salty taste; someone who has dried fish, buffalo meat or cooked vegetables being considered a gourmet) of both the common people and the Regents. The latter however were distinguished by their velvet and gold-embroidered clothes, and by their "great palaces of bamboo or wood, which are called *dalems*".
65 "Beschryving van her Koningryk Jaccatra", p. 39.
66 ms. *pantong*.
67 I do not know of any musical instrument of this name. The harp is not prominent in the Javanese musical tradition, though there are representations of small harps on Old Javanese reliefs.
68 The Dutch rixdollar was the major unit of account at this period but in actual transactions in the Indies the Spanish dollar was the preferred coin. On their relative values in Europe and the Indies, see Ch. 2. n. 150 above.
69 As noted above, there were 48 *stuivers* per Rixdollar (2.50 guilders).
70 Although there was local variation, a *kati* was roughly equivalent to 0.6 kilos. See *Encyclopaedie van Nederlandsche Indie* sub *Maten en Gewichten*.
71 This whole passage on Cianjur was very difficult to follow and required interpretation.
72 The Java *duit*, unlike the Dutch coin after which it was named, was accounted at 4 (rather than 8) to the *stuiver*, and thus 320 to the Spanish real. See E. Netscher and J.A. van der Chijs, *De Munten van Nederlandsch Indie*, VBG 3½ (1864) p. 66.
73 The *College van Heemraden* ("polder board": the Dutch official called a *heemraad* was a sort of dike-reeve) was set up in 1664, and was responsible for the upkeep of roads, bridges, dikes and dams and other matters relating to the lands of the Batavian Environs (*Ommelanden*). It was abolished in 1809 in Daendels' administrative reforms: see *Encyclopaedie van Nederlandsch Indie*, 2nd edition vol. II, 's-Gravenhage, Nijhoff and Leiden, Brill, 1918 pp. 77–8.
74 A *caing* (old spelling *tjaing* or *tjaeng*) was made up of 40 *sangga* of 5 *gedeng* each (the *gedeng* consisted of two *pocong* of 5 *kati* each) but was not a fixed quantity, as is apparent by the very large difference here between the hill *caing* and that laid down by the *College van Heemraden* [see note 73 above] See *Encyclopaedie van Nederlandsche Indie* sub *Maten en Gewichten*.]
75 See note 15 above.
76 See note 73 above.
77 p. 294.
78 Boomgaard ("Buitenzorg", pp. 38–9) however notes that it became the custom for the Company to pay the planter directly when he delivered his harvest at the government warehouse.

79 P.J. Veth, *Java, Geographisch, Ethnologisch, Historisch*, Haarlem, Erven F. Bohn, 1875–1882 III pp. 252–4.
80 Heather Sutherland, "Notes on Java's Regent Families" Part I, *Indonesia* 16, (October 1973) p. 126.
81 Karl D. Jackson and Johannes Moeliono, "Participation in Rebellion: the Dar'ul Islam in West Java" in R. William Liddle, ed., *Political Participation in Modern Indonesia*, Yale University Southeast Asia Monograph Series no. 19, 1973, pp. 1257. Further on the Darul Islam movement see C. van Dijk, *Rebellion under the Banner of Islam*, VKI 94, The Hague, Nijhoff, 1981.
82 Nederburgh 396, ARA.
83 The reports written for Nederburgh are of very uneven quality – Umbgrove's 1795 report on Cirebon (Nederburgh 371, ARA), for instance, is largely a picturesque description of the landscape by someone who seems to have had no knowledge at all of local society.
84 On the Chinese ancestry of the Regents of Pekalongan, see Chapter 4 p. 227. There were family ties between the Regent families of Pekalongan and Batang: see Remmelink, *Pakubuwana II*, p. 39, p. 266.
85 Ned. 396. pp. 22–3.
86 Cf. P.B.R. Carey, *Babad Dipanagara: An Account of the Outbreak of the Java War (1825–30): The Surakarta court version of the Babad Dipanagara with translations into English and Indonesian Malay*, Malay Branch of the Royal Asiatic Society, Kuala Lumpur 1981, p. LXIX n. 196, where it is noted of a time several decades later that in the sparsely populated area of Nanggulon some *jungs* were 100 times the size of the ordinary government *jung* of 2,000 square roods, while others were much smaller.
87 Ned. 396 pp. 13–14.
88 Ned. 396 pp. 24–5.
89 Boomgaard, *Children*, p. 21. Se also Remmelink, *Pakubuwana II*, pp. 130–1 re the fortunes earned by Company officials – "certainly not . . . from their monthy salaries of about fifty-five rixdollars a month" at an earlier period.
90 See F.S. Gaastra, "De VOC in Azie, 1680–1795" in *Algemeene Geschiedenis der Nederlanden*, vol. 9 (1980) pp. 427–464, esp. Tabel 7.
91 Ned. 396 p. 27.
92 Ned. 396 pp. 28–9.
93 Ned. 396 pp. 32–4.
94 Ned. 396 pp. 29–31.
95 In the central Javanese principalities, the *gladak* was the place outside the north gate of the *alun-alun* where porters, draught horses and carts were stationed; in the colonial government's territory, it was one of the posts or halts along the major roads where coolies were assembled in readiness, and served also as an overnight station for military contingents passing through. It was also called *pradah*.
96 See Chantal Vuldy, *Pekalongan: Batik et Islam dans une ville du Nord de Java*, Etudes insulindiennes/Archipel 8, Editions de l'Ecole des Hautes Etudes en Sciences Sociales, Paris 1987, p. 66.

97 Roger Knight, "The Indigo Industry and the Organisation of Agricultural Production in Pekalongan Residency, North Java, 1800–1850", paper presented at the fourth national conference of the Asian Studies Association of Australian, Monash University, May 1982, p. 31.
98 Boomgaard, *Children*, p. 27.
99 And in addition 5 horses and 4 *prau mayang*.
100 And in addition 29 horses and 30 buffaloes.
101 *Lurah* is most commonly used for village heads, but here seems to mean one of the various levels of supervisors.
102 And in addition 4 "cruisers" and 4 *prau mayang*.
103 And in addition 3 horses and 1 *prau mayang*.
104 And in addition 12 yoke of buffaloes.
105 And in addition a cruiser and a *prau mayang* for the Karwelaan timber raft.
106 And in addition a *prau mayang*.
107 And in addition 7 horses.
108 And in addition 40 carts (*pĕḍati*).
109 And in addition 1 cruiser and 1 *prau mayang*.
110 The word used in the report in actually *kombuis*, which usually means a ship's galley.
111 Ned 396 pp. 10–16.
112 Robert van Niel, "Rights to Land in Java", in T. Ibrahim Alfian, H.J. Koesoenanto, Dharmono Hardjowidjono and Djoko Suryo, *Dari Babad dan Hikayat sampai Sejarah Kritis, Kumpulan Karangan dipersembahkan kepada Prof. Dr. Sartono Kartodirdjo*, Gajah Mada University Press 1987, pp. 120–153 (see p. 127f). However, van Niel says that the term *cacah kerja* (which is the Malay equivalent of the Javanese *cacah karya*) was a later usage foregrounding the household that worked the land rather than the land itself. See also Carey, *Babad Dipanagara* p. LXXII n. 232, where it is noted that in Jipang, which in the second decade of the 19th century had a declining population due to poor government and bandit raids (like much of the eastern *mancanagara*), a distinction was made between *cacah gĕsang* ("live" or "inhabited" *cacah*, and *cacah pĕjah*, "dead" or "uninhabited" *cacah*. This also supports the idea of *cacah* as usually being a numerator for land rather than people.
113 Boomgaard, *Children*, p. 61. However, the two terms were used synonymously in Japara, another north coast area.
114 Boomgaard, *Children*, p. 64.
115 At a Regent's investiture he was expected to provide food, drink and entertainment first for local Europeans, Chinese and *priyayi* at one reception, and then for the common people at another. Sutherland notes that those few Regents who had survived their early career without accumulating debts often fell once and for all into the hands of the moneylenders after meeting the investiture bills. She also notes the ingenuity of some Regents in exacting gifts and a variety of financial advantages from their subordinates and from the villagers under them: see Heather Sutherland, *The Making of a Bureaucratic Elite: The Colonial Transformation of the Javanese Priyayi*, Asian Studies Association of

Australia, Southeast Asia Publications Series no. 2, Heinemann, Singapore, 1979, pp. 22–3.
116 Boomgaard, *Children*, pp. 22–3.
117 Raden Mas Arya Purwalelana, *Lampah-lampahipun*, Batavia, Landsdrukkerij, 1865–6 pages 12–13, 42f and 176.
118 Vuldy, *Pekalongan* pp 230–40: *macapatan* is the singing of Javanese verse, *sintren* is a very Javanese folk ritual to bring the *widadari* from the moon.
119 J.W. van Dapperen, "Volkskunde van Java IV", *Djawa* 16/4–6 pp. 172–86.
120 This haunted forest was visited by a late 19th century traveller and his companion who saw a *siluman* there: see Ann Kumar, *The Diary of a Javanese Muslim: Religion, Politics and the Pesantren 1883–1886*, Faculty of Asian Studies Monographs, New Series no. 7, A.N.U., Canberra 1985, p. 21.
121 The local story about Sunan Geseng is quite different from that given by D.A. Rinkes, ("De Heiligen van Java III", TBG LIII 3–4, pp. 269–300). This local story identifies Sunan Geseng with Kontela or Konteya, the well-known heathen (Hindu) ruler of Cahyana, Purbalingga, who is connected with the legend of Gunung Lawet. This ruler converted to Islam and took the name Darmakusuma. Sech Maghribi told him to do *tapa* on the north coast and to spread Islam there while waiting for a light from Mecca which would shine in the west. Darmakusuma went to Si Rawung, taught there in the pesantren and waited for the light. This was a long time in coming and his heart burned with pain – hence the name Sunan Geseng, "the burning one". Eventually the light appeared and he followed it to Cirebon, where Sunan Gunung Jati had instituted the famous gathering of the *walis*. After some time he died in Cirebon and his corpse was brought back to Si Rawung.
122 See a report made by Matthijs Waterloo, First Resident at the Yogyakarta court, to Nicolaus Engelhard, Governor of the North-East Coast, included with the van Ysseldyk report in ARA, Nederburgh 389.
123 Other *siluman* stories include one about Jais, from Kali Suren in Pangebatan, on the boundary of Galuh Timur, who with his friends was invited to a wedding which proved to be a *siluman* festivity; and one from Tegal fishermen of the village of Bungku, where the *siluman* was a member of Dampu Awang's crew who took the form of a giant shark and inflicted an epidemic on the village. "Dampu Awang" probably refers here to Zheng He (old romanisation: Cheng Ho), the Ming admiral who in the early fifteenth century visited the north coast of Java and made such an impression as to become a mythologized cult-figure in Javanese (and Balinese, Kalimantan, Sumatran) legend, being identified, according to Pigeaud and de Graaf, with an older autochthonous sky god. He is usually portrayed however as the ultimate rich foreign trader: see H.J. de Graaf and Th.G. Th. Pigeaud ed. M.C.Ricklefs, *Chinese Muslims in Java in the 15th and 16th centuries: The Malay Annals of Semarang and Cerbon*, Monash Papers on Southeast Asia no. 12, Melbourne 1984, pp. 51–4 and 135–9. See also Pierre-Yves

Manguin, "The Merchant and the King: Political Myths of Southeast Asian Coastal Polities", *Indonesia* 52 (Oct. 1991) pp. 41–54.
124 Knight p. 17 gives as an example an area of 2000 *bau* under one planter, a truculent Scot.
125 One source states that peasants only earned less than a quarter of their *pajĕg* (see Knight p. 27; and in addition, the amount of *pajeg* was actually increased when padi land was assigned to export crops (Knight p. 29).
126 Knight p. 22.
127 Knight p. 24.
128 Knight p. 27.
129 Knight p. 34.
130 Knight p. 1.
131 Knight p. 11 and p. 18.
132 Knight p. 10 and p. 16.
133 Ned 396 pp. 21–3.
134 See Kumar, *Diary*, pp. 14f. on the relationship of the Pekalongan Arabs to the second Sultan of Yogyakarta and his entourage.
135 On the Budiah movement, see Sartono Kartodirdjo, *Protest Movements in Rural Java: A Study of Agrarian Unrest in the Nineteenth and early Twentieth Centuries*, Oxford/ Institute of Southeast Asian Studies Singapore, 1973, p. 118 ff.
136 See Anthony J.S. Reid, *Indonesian National Revolution 1945–50*, Longman, Studies in Contemporary Southeast Asia, Melbourne 1974, p. 64.
137 Richard Robison, *Indonesia: The Rise of Capital*, Asian Studies Association of Australia, Southeast Asia Publications Series no 13, Sydney etc. 1986, p. 57.
138 For Braudel see Ch. 1 above. See also C.R. Boxer, *The Dutch Seaborne Empire 1600–1800*, Hutchinson (History of Human Society series), London, 1965, p. 199.
139 Holden Furber, *Rival Empires of Trade in the Orient, 1600–1800*, University of Minnesota Press (Europe and the World in the Age of Expansion series), Minneapolis 1976, p. 255 remarks that coffee never recovered from the violent price fluctuations of the 1730s, which caused the Dutch to destroy trees and that throughout the 18th century Java coffee never succeeded in overcoming either the increased competition from West India coffee in Europe or the continuing preference for Mocha coffee in Asia and the Levant. Though a relatively steady earner of profits, coffee was never to play a role in the East India trade comparable to tea.
140 See Christine Dobbin, "Economic Change in Minangkabau as a Factor in the Rise of the Padri Movement, 1784–1830", *Indonesia* 23 (April 1977) pp. 1–38.
141 See above p. 346–7.
142 See above Ch. 1, p. 36.

Part Four

INTELLECTUAL TRANSFORMATIONS

6
New ways of seeing: ethnicity, history, religion, kingship, society

ETHNICITY: SELF AND OTHER THROUGH DUTCH, CHINESE AND JAVANESE EYES

As we saw in the last chapter, some areas of Java were ethnically more diverse as a result of their increasing incorporation into the world-system. Of course, foreigners had been coming to Java for as long as recorded history: indeed, for longer, as archaeological finds of Indian pottery from before the birth of Christ attest. But until the VOC period they had not held levers of power to any significant degree. How did the three principal races involved with political, economic, and social power view each other? This chapter deals first, briefly, with Dutch and Chinese views but is particularly concerned with a shift in the Javanese discourse towards a certain view of ethnicity.

The type of ethnography represented here is that familiar type of account which sets out to characterise racial characteristics and national character: something that in the European tradition is at least as old as Herodotus but probably reached its heyday in the high colonial period, with increased self-confidence and greater possibilities for travel for Europeans; and after decolonization gradually receded from high-literate culture to the realm of popular oral culture. In the case of Java, in sheer absolute volume, the Dutch have a clear dominance in laying down their opinion of others, which we can readily perceive in the number and bulk of their accounts. A very extensive compilation of this sort of Dutch material is presented in Boomgaard's *Children of the Colonial State*[1] It seems to me however quite indefensible to give a picture of the manners and mores of a colonized people by piling up account after account written by the colonial masters, most of which judge

Javanese realities by European ideals rather than European realities. Ethnographic material of this type had never been part of the Javanese intellectual tradition, which was universalist rather than particularist in approach, though a strong sense of Javanese ethnicity as the *ne plus ultra* of human socialization can be read between the lines, as it were. However, a Javanese text from about this time deals with the subject of the characteristic traits of the various races present in Java: the first words, to my knowledge in a discourse not previously found in Javanese writing. In addition, a Chinese account from the same period – prejudicial ethnographic characterisations being very much a time-honoured part of the Chinese literate tradition, as much as the European – made it possible to add a third perspective, presenting us with something like an ethnographic three-way mirror through which to try to grasp the same reality.

The Dutch account

The text used here is that of Stavorinus. In his first volume he gives the following description of the Javanese:[2] They are of middling size, and in general well-proportioned, of a light brown colour, with a broad forehead, and a flattish nose, which has a small curve downwards at the tip. Their hair is black, and is always kept smooth and shining with coconut oil. Their principal weapon is the kris. "Arrogant towards their inferiors, they are no less cringing with respect to their superiors, or whoever from whom they have any favour to expect." Their dress consists of a piece of cotton, which they wrap round the waist, and drawing it between the legs, fasten it behind. The only other item of clothing worn by the common people is a small cap, though "Those of more consideration, wear a wide Moorish coat of flowered cotton, or other stuff, and in general turbands, instead of the little caps." Any hair other than that on the head is carefully eradicated. The women are little better dressed, in a sarung which covers the bosom and hangs down to the knees. The hair of the head, which they wear very long, is turned up, and twisted round the head like a fillet, fastened with long bodkins of different sorts of wood, tortoiseshell, silver, or gold, according to the rank or wealth of the lady. This hairstyle, called a *conde*, is also in vogue among the Batavian ladies. It is often adorned with a variety of flowers.

Both men and women are very fond of bathing, especially in the morning. Children of both sexes go entirely naked until the age of eight or nine. Twelve or thirteen is the age of puberty.

The Javanese are polygamous, marrying as many wives as they can maintain, and taking their female slaves as concubines; the common people, however, cannot afford more than one wife. The women are more comely than the men, and are very fond of white men. They are jealous in the extreme, and know how to make a European who has been unfaithful to them repent of his incontinence through the administration of drugs which will disqualify him from any future adventures: Stavorinus says he has heard of too many instances of this to doubt the practice.

On architecture: "Their dwellings may, with greater propriety, be called huts, than houses." They are constructed of split bamboos, interlaced or matted, plaistered with clay, and covered with *atap*. The entrance is low, and without a door or shutter. The whole house usually consists of a single room in which the family and sometimes numerous poultry live together. The houses are sited in a shady place, or planted about with trees. "Such as possess more property, are provided with a little more comfort and convenience; but it is always in a wretched, paltry manner."

Their chief food is boiled rice and their drink water, though they have a little *arak* when they can get it. They are almost continually chewing betel, or *pinang*, and smoke a sort of tobacco, the so-called Java tobacco. They sometimes put opium into their pipes with the tobacco, in order to invigorate their spirits, but continual use of it is deadening.

They have no tables or chairs, sitting on the ground or on mats. They do not use knives, forks, or spoons, but eat with their fingers.

They have a kind of musical instrument "called gomgoms" which consists of a hollow iron bowl, and comes in various sizes and tones, "which do not make a disagreeable harmony, and are not unlike a set of bells."

They are very fond of cock-fighting, and though they be ever so poor would sooner dispose of all their other property than their game-cocks. They also play a kind of tennis, hitting the ball (about the size of a man's head, made of matted reeds, and hollow) with the feet, knees, or elbows, and are very dexterous in keeping it in motion.

Their manner of salutation consists in touching the forehead with the right hand, accompanied by a slight inclination of the body.

The Mohametan religion predominates over the whole island, except, it is said, for some "aboriginal idolatrous natives" over the mountains to the south.[3] Mosques are erected all over the island; and the people are "very particular about the tombs of their saints, and will suffer nothing unbecoming to be done upon or near them."

They have both male and female physicians, who have been known to effect very surprising cures by means of the medicinal and vulnerary herbs of the country. They have no knowledge of anatomy, and rely chiefly on friction of the affected part, first anointed with water mixed with ground wood or oil, with two fingers of the right hand.

For agriculture they use buffaloes rather than horses: though they have enough of the latter, they are of a diminutive size, while the buffaloes are very large, "bigger and heavier than our largest oxen." They are led by the nose; watered three time daily to cool themselves; and the female gives milk: "but it is little valued by the Europeans, on account of its acrimonious nature."

Yet in a chapter entitled *Importance of Java to the Dutch East-India Company: Reflections of the Conduct of the Company towards the Native Princes And towards their Javanese Subjects [&] Necessity of Reform in these Points*, Stavorinus introduces a different perspective on the characteristics of the Javanese. Though he has earlier[4] described Java as arguably the "most precious jewel in the diadem of our Company", Stavorinus' policy recommendations are a response to the assumption, which becomes explicit in the course of this brief chapter, that something or many things are very wrong here. He begins by recommending "cordial exertions to promote the cultivation of its highly fertile soil with industry and vigour, by ceasing to depress and impoverish the native by constant injustice and continual extortion, and by avoiding, in future, every species of war, which, by producing a still greater depopulation, would bring destruction to the Indians, and ruin to the Company" and goes on to describe the situation of the Javanese princes and the role they should play in the future. They are, he says, reluctant vassals of the Company, and so weakened by the depopulation of the country that should they manage to free themselves from this present bondage they would be obliged to submit to the first foreign power that wished to establish itself on the island. They should therefore be indulged in "matters of small moment" in order to secure their loyalty. But it is also necessary for the Company to secure the attachment of the common Javanese by preventing the shameful treatment and crying injustice which they experience at the hands of the Governor, Residents and Regents. Stavorinus begins this

New ways of seeing

chapter by remarking that "The Javanese are said to be of an indolent disposition, and that much pains must be taken to excite them to the performance of any labour." [echoing the opinion of the author of the report on Priangan in the previous chapter]. He goes on to propose that they should be allowed to keep that proportion of their property left after they have furnished to the Company the quantities and qualities required of their hands. At present, he says "The common Javanese are in an absolute state of slavery; they are no more masters of what little they seem to possess, than an unconditional slave, who, together with all he has, belongs to the master who has purchased him, his labour, and his posterity, for money. The common Javan, is not only obliged, at fixed periods, to deliver a certain quantity of the fruits of his industry to the Regent placed over him, in behalf of the Company, for whatever price the latter chooses to allow him, and that price, moreover, paid in goods, which are charged to him at ten times their real value [a practice which the conservative author of the report on the Priangan decided to downplay, but which is well attested by other witnesses]; but he likewise cannot consider what may remain to him as his own property, not being permitted to do with it what he may think fit, nor allowed to sell it to others, at a higher, or a lower rate; and he is, on the contrary, compelled to part with this also, as well as what was claimed of him in behalf of the Company, to the same petty tyrant, for himself, at an arbitrary, and frequently at an infamous price. The Regents experience, in their turn, though, perhaps, in a less iniquitous degree, the oppression of the Residents; whilst in the country of Jaccatra, the commissary for inland affairs [i.e. the Delegate for Native Affairs of the previous chapter] acts the same part, in a no less unjustifiable manner, under the immediate eye of the Governor General, towards the native Regents and common Javanese in that province."[5]. The chapter concludes with the statement that the explanation of the decrease in population should be seen in the operation of this oppression as well as in the effects of warfare, usually seen as the sole cause.

Following his policy recommendations and diagnosis of the evils of the present situation, Stavorinus repeats this theme of the root cause of Javanese indolence:

> "The inhabitants of Java possess, in common with all the rest of mankind, a natural and innate desire of having the free command and disposal of their own property; and, like others,

they would, to obtain this, submit to heavy labour, and be more industrious, in proportion as they had the more certain prospect of earning a property, and of security in the possession and enjoyment of it.

But now, deprived of the most distant prospect, and not encouraged by any hope of bettering their situation, they sit down sullenly contented, as it were, with the little that is left to them, by their despotic and avaricious masters; who, by this unwise, as well as unfeeling, conduct, extinguish every spark of industry, and plunge their subjects into the gloom of hopeless inactivity."

The proof that it is not the climate that causes indolence is the case of the Chinese on Java. These "open their variegated shops next to the dwellings of the Javanese, and till with laborious industry the neglected soil around the wretched habitation of the native." Their diligence and perseverance, surpassing that of many Europeans of the same station, can be attributed to the comparative freedom they enjoy in the retention and enhancement of their property.[6]

His further notes on food, dress, housing and household goods, law and religion may be omitted here.

Concerning the Indies Dutch, Stavorinus on one occasion attended at Semarang a party given by the Governor of the Northeast Coast for his little boy's birthday. Stavorinus comments:

"On the occasion of this festival, two of the elders of the church at Samarang, the official, and the lieutenant of the artillery, danced a reel, for the diversion of the company.

I only notice this circumstance to show that, in these parts, no such rigid discipline prevails, with respect to the conduct of elders of the church, and no such scandal is occasioned by their dancing in public, as at Groningen, although the parson was himself one of the spectators, and highly applauded the agility of their dancers, saying with Solomon, that there was a time to weep, and a time to laugh; a time to mourn, and a time to dance."[7]

This is one of many European accounts of Java that stress the hierarchical nature of Javanese society – a system which we have long accepted as the basis for military discipline but have increasingly come to see as foreign to civil society. In Java this distinction was not at all clearly made: as we shall see below the

New ways of seeing

word *bala*, or *wadya* for example, is one which means both soldier and subject of the king.

Stavorinus' account is predicated on the assumption that something is very wrong is Java, an assumption that is, to my knowledge, virtually universal in the European reports of this period. In addressing the problem, he sets out for us an early example of a theme that would come to prominence later, that is, a critique of social ills centring around insecurity of property, which was a central pillar of the reform proposals put forward by Dirk van Hogendorp, under the influence of Adam Smith, and by Raffles. Here we may note both the superiority of the European intellectual tradition at this period in its development of the idea that socio-economic structures influence human behaviour, which is not entirely due to inherent racial characteristics; and the fact that Stavorinus' analysis runs contrary to that of the author of the report on Priangan, who protests that the native is irredeemably lazy and must be forced to work (which was, of course, the only way to obtain his labour at the prices paid by the Company).

A third theme, very mildly adumbrated by Stavorinus but occuring frequently in other accounts, is the way in which the Dutch in the Indies were not like those in the homeland. The difference is attributed sometimes to the effect of intermarriage with women of mixed blood, sometimes to the effect of the sole purpose of life amongst the Indies Dutch being the pursuit of pecuniary gain, a point of view eloquently put by the famous liberal reformer Dirk van Hogendorp.[8] Non-Dutch observers (English, French, Germans) take the same line, which is pursued with particular vehemence and frankness by an observer named Selberg in the 1840s.[9] (One quotation may perhaps be provided as indicative: "Faith, friendship, and love are words which give rise only to a derisive smile among a great part of the Europeans who live here. A stay of short duration among them soon reveals the repulsive shadow-side of European civilization. Sensuality of all kinds unnerves, through the freedom obtaining in respect to sexual connections, the body. The enjoyment of strong drinks, the senseless misuse of which is reinforced by the silly belief that one must drink to live (*aut bibendum aut moriendum*), the foods excessively seasoned with hot spices, and the artificial sexual stimulation have dulled the feelings and attenuated the life-force. In this luxurious sensuality the last trace of the higher life is lost and the dominant pursuit is entirely directed towards money." and so on.[10] Selberg considered that only European vices and sins had been conferred upon the Javanese, and thought that in the field of medicine, his special interest, Javanese remedies were superior to European ones for the treatment of gastric complaints but Europeans were wholly ignorant of these[11]).

Stavorinus briefly mentions the extent to which patricentric Islamic law on inheritance was modified in favour of women in Java, again something which would be noted by other observers. Another of his remarks on Javanese women, that they are jealous in the extreme, and know how to make a European who has been unfaithful to them repent of his incontinence through the administration of drugs which will disqualify him from any future adventures is probably a reference to the practice of *guna-guna* which inspired a hysterical fear among some of the Indies Dutch well into the 20th century[12].

The Chinese account[13]

The exact date at which this account was written is puzzling: a preface by Le-Wei mentions meeting the author in 1798 after a gap of 20 years during which the latter had been abroad; another preface by Lew-He-Ching says the author went overseas and taught school in 1783; the author's preface is dated 1791; but in the text itself[14] there is a reference to the English being in power in 1814.

The author, Ong Tae Hae, arranges his material as follows: Section I is a description of various places: Batavia, Samarang, Pekalongan, Banten and the soil and manners of Java. Section II is an account of celebrated persons (Ong Sam Po [i.e. the famous Chinese admiral Zheng He[15]], fairies, priests, virtuous wives). Section III is an account of different nations – the Dutch, the English, the French, Manila men, Javanese, "Islams" (converted Chinese), Malays, Bugis, Balinese, Butonese, Papuans, natives of Ceram, Kering, Timor, and Pasir on Borneo, the Portuguese, Biajus or Dayaks, Bimanese, Bandanese, Ternatans, and the people of the Cape of Good Hope; also of the inhabitants of the islands to the west and north, including Mangalore, Ceylon, Cochin, and Bengal. Section IV deals with "Miscellaneous Matters", everything from the climate and Mecca to large numbers of curious animals such as iguanas, geckoes, flying fish, and rhinoceroses. Section V, "Other things worthy of observation" deals mostly with technical inventions: barometers, quadrants, ships, the balloon or celestial boat, telescopes, Javanese hanging rattan bridges, but also with medicine, secret societies, Dutch doctors, coins, and military tactics. Section VI deals with fruit and flowers, and Section VII with Manila and Formosa.

His account of Batavia begins with the statement that "all the foreigners have submitted" to the virtuous influence of "our government". He goes on to state however that the territory of Batavia originally belonged to the Javanese, "but the Dutch, having by stratagems and artifice got possession of the revenues, proceded to give orders and enact laws, until squatting down all along the seacoast, they have exacted duties, issued passports, guarded ingress and egress, put down robbers, and brought the natives under their entire control"[16] – something they have been able to do because they are deep-schemed and thoughtful. Ong gives an account of the Dutch and Javanese hierarchies, beginning with the Governor in the first case and the Susuhunan in the second.[17] Later in the work[18] he returns to the history and nature of Dutch domination in the following passage: "It is now about 1,800 years since the Dutch nation was established, and a little more than 200 years since they took possession of Batavia. At first they were driven thither by adverse winds, when seeing that the country was extensive, and adapted for the building of a city, they pretended to take shelter in Bantam bay, and sent in a humble petition, accompanied by large presents, intreating the Sultan of Bantam to allow them to borrow for a time a place on the sea-shore, where they might repair their vessels. It was not long, however, before they requested leave to erect a stockade, with the view of screening those who were within from those who remained without; on which occasion they increased the amount of their presents. The disposition of the Javanese is stupid and foolish, unsuspicious and uncalculating; being moreover desirous of European gold, Bantam speedily fell into the hands of foreigners, and Batavia soon followed. The Dutch then entered into a treaty with the Susuhunan or Emperor of Solo, engaging to pay him a certain amount of tribute annually; and thus all the territory along the coast came under the superintendance of the Dutch. They then erected forts and defences, and encroached more and more, as the silk-worms devour the leaves; until their military defences are now become very strict, having a guard-house, Jaga at every gate; while their sentinels keep incessant watch, night and day, never laying aside their weapons, so that the whole year round we never hear of thieves.

Intellectual Transformations

They have also established a poor-house, *Miskin* – for the reception and maintenance of sick and destitute persons. Whenever a person comes to die, who has no near relatives at hand, he sends for a notary who draws up a testament according to the desire of the sick person, which is as firm as iron and never departed from; this will is then delivered to the orphan chamber, Weeskamer – to be deposited there, until the relatives of the deceased come to claim the property, which is paid over with the annual interest; as well as the proceeds of the sale of houses or lands, slave-men or slave-women, and the account of all debts due to the estate, distinctly arranged, without confusion; the least failure in which would lead to the imprisonment of the parties.

There is also a Commissary[19] who is charged with the superintendance of all places in the interior: besides which they have a collector of customs, Shahbanda who takes care of all affairs relating to the port. There are also outer and inner magistrates or tomonggongs who regulate matters in the city and suburbs. The flowery Chinese, and every description of foreigners, have all got Captains placed over them, who are charged with the regulation of affairs belonging to their own countrymen, while great offences and capital crimes, are all given over to the Dutch to decide. The laws and regulations are carefully drawn up and rigidly executed, which is one cause of their perpetuity."

In Ong's account of the Chinese hierarchy, he begins with the statement "Our rich merchants and great traders, amass inexhaustible wealth, whereupon they give bribes to the Hollanders, and are elevated to the ranks of great Captain . . ." He notes the role of the Captains as legal arbiters, remarking "With respect to flagrant breaches of the law and great crimes, together with marriages and deaths, reference must invariably be made to the Hollanders. Those who journey by water and land, must all be provided with passports, to prevent their going and coming in an improper way; from this may be inferred how strict the Hollanders are in the execution of laws, and how minute in the levying of duties." In describing Chinese commerce he notes that formerly the Chinese were allowed to repatriate their profits in silver, but this was then forbidden by the Dutch, and profits had to be taken out in goods. However the English have now (1814) abolished the oppressive laws of the Dutch, and invited people to trade as formerly, so that merchants come from far and wide.

Ong also remarks that those who come from China are preferred as sons-in-law to those born in the country. He notes the large numbers of slaves kept and the strict distinction between master and servant ("when they wait upon their masters, they bend their knee"). In contrast, manners between members of the opposite sexes are characterized by extreme freeness ("some of them proceed so far as to go arm in arm, or to take one another round the waist; so little do they know of the decencies of public morals"); and in general "the pleasures of these western regions are enjoyed without knowing what sort of things politeness, rectitude, and shamefacedness are: thus extravagance is carried to its utmost length, and lusts gratified without restraint, just as inclination prompts."[20]

In his section on Banten,[21] Ong notes the chiefs' extreme fear of the Hollanders to whom they dare not show the least neglect, and the fact that when the Sultan dies his son cannot succeed without Dutch approval.

The Javanese,[22] according to Ong, are dull and stupid by nature, not understanding the use of reason, and thinking that the Hollanders reverence them, and therefore take the trouble to collect their revenues; they imagine also that the Hollanders respect them, and have therefore built them a fort, and personally act as their guards of honour. They are spread abroad along the north coast as far as Balambangan, and westwards to Johore, Palembang, Champa, and the Lampungs, and scores of other places. Though the Javanese number millions, and the Hollanders cannot muster one to their thousand, the latter are courageous and scheming, and have entrapped the Javanese by overawing them with majesty and alluring them with gain. The Javanese are pliant and fearful, and the distinction between superior and inferior is very strictly marked, as by the *sembah* [obeisance]. They cultivate their fields, reaping only one harvest per year.[23] Their rice is of a long grain and very soft, much superior to that of China. It is not ground by mill, but beaten with pestles in a wooden trough. Their fruits are finer in flavour than those of Canton and Fukien. Pineapples and watermelons, which are naturally heating, are here considered cooling against heat and noxious winds. Coarse vegetables are even dearer than fowls and ducks, and because grain is easily raised few people will bother with vegetables. They look upon wind as a demon, and on water as a medicine; all those who are exposed to the wind, and consequently get fevers, have only to bathe in the river to recover.

The concerns of each family are managed by women, and hence

parents prefer to have daughters, by whose marriage sons-in-law are brought into the family, while sons are lost to others. Their houses are like pavilions, open on all sides; they use neither chairs nor tables, but use mats to sit on. The floors of their rooms are all covered with these mats, and surrounded by tapestry; their beadsteads are not high, their mattresses are soft, and their pillows are piled up like a tower, six or seven stories high. They generally sit cross-legged, and squat down when they see a visitor, holding each other's hands by way of ceremony. They commonly esteem betel, and when a stranger arrives they present it as a mark of respect, in vessels which are made of gold and silver among the rich, and brass among the common people. They have brass spittoons as large as flower-pots. Men and women sit together without restriction or suspicion. They have no chopsticks but eat with their hands. Beef is considered a delicacy, but they do not touch pork or dog's flesh. The women's feet are not bound up, and they use no cosmetics or flowers in the hair. Their gowns have no collars and they wear petticoats instead of drawers. Men, on the contrary, have collars, wear flowers in their hair, and wear pantaloons instead of petticoats. Thus their customs appear to be the very opposite of the Chinese.

Women immediately after labour, and young children afflicted with the small-pox all bathe in the river. They also prick the pock with a needle till the matter comes out and suffer no ill effects from it. No matter how hot and sultry the weather, they never take off their clothes or fan themselves, but always sleep in close rooms, with curtains spread over them; the least exposure to the wind brings on sickness, so they use glass for doors and windows, since it keeps out the wind but lets in the light [needless to say, this can only have been a small minority].

The Dutch have deluded the Javanese into consuming opium until they became so weak and emaciated, so dispirited and exhausted, that they could no longer think of regaining their land or revenging their wrongs. "The Javanese, being originally a stupid and ignorant race, were readily overcome by this poison, and lost all care for themselves; but we Chinese, of the central flowery land, have also been deluded by them; for no sooner do we partake of this substance, than we lose all anxieties about our native land, have no further concern for father or mother, wife or children, and are plunged into unspeakable misery. At the same time Europeans forbid their people the use of this drug, and severely punish those who offend; how is it then that we Chinese, together with the Javanese, are so thoughtless as to fall into the snare! In this scheme of the Europeans they seem to have laid a foundation not to be rooted up for a myriad of years; having done which, they live at their ease, without dread of danger, while they give themselves up to the work of fleecing the people."

Ong also deals with the Europeans on Java. The Dutch receive the most extensive coverage, in two separate sections of the work.[24] They are described as inhabitants of the "north-west corner of the ocean". They have high[25] noses and red hair, white faces and grey eyes; they do not allow their beards to grow; their coats are clean and neat, with short bodies and narrow sleeves; while their gait is light and nimble. They say that their country is very cold, with frost and snow in October, when the leaves all fall from the trees. "Many of their people, they affirm, attain to 100 years of age; but the climate of Batavia is extremely hot, the leaves do not fall in Autumn, and bathing may be employed all the year round: thus the energies wasting away, people do not attain to great longevity; and fifty or sixty years are looked upon as the maximum. Those who are born in Batavia have not red hair, and their eyes are dark, which is perhaps to be ascribed to the climate."[26] Ong is not complimentary in his treatment of the Dutch character, as the following passage shows: "With respect to the Dutch, they are very much like the man who stopped his ears while stealing a bell.[27] Measuring them by the rules of reason, they scarcely possess one of the five cardinal virtues;[28] the great oppress the small, being overbearing and covetous, thus they have no benevolence; husbands and wives separate, with permission to marry again, and before a man is dead a month his widow is allowed to go to another, thus they have no rectitude; there is no distinction between superiors and inferiors, men and women are mingled together, thus they are without propriety; they are extravagant and self-indulgent in the extreme, and thus bring themselves to the grave, without speculating on leaving something to tranquillize and aid their posterity, thus they have no wisdom. Of the single quality of sincerity, however, they possess a little."

The English[29] also dwell in the north-west corner of the ocean, very near to the Dutch, whom they much resemble in person and dress; but their language and writing are different. The English nation is poor but powerful, and being situated at a most important point, frequently attacks the Dutch and French, with whom they share the sovereignty of Europe. English manufactures are very superior, while their swords and guns, and other implements, are the best in all countries to the north-west. Those who trade to Batavia all reside in factories, and submit to the regulations of the Dutch, who treat them well, and do not dare to quarrel with them. Of late they have made a new settlement at Malacca, but the regulations there are oppressive and unfriendly, so that the Chinese of the place have moved elsewhere. (Ong was also under the impression that the English were poor, without precious metals or a coinage of their own, because of the dominance of other European coins in the islands.[30])

The French[31] are also described as residing in the north-west corner of the ocean, very near the English and Dutch. Their appearance, apparel, and household furniture are all similar to those of the Dutch, but their language and literature are different. They are violent and boisterous by disposition. Their country is poor, and contains but few merchants, hence they seldom come to Batavia. Whenever the Dutch are insulted by the English they ask assistance from the French, because the kingdom of France is large and the population numerous, so that the English are somewhat afraid of them [perhaps a reference to the incorporation of the Netherlands into Napoleon's bid for European supremacy].

Ong also mentions the Portuguese[32] listed however among the Asian populations,[33] between Pasir on Borneo and the Biajus or Dayaks, as a Batavian population resembling the Dutch in their customs and language and employed mainly as clerks or soldiers. The Dutch do not allow them to rise in office, though they prefer the women, who are beautiful, as wives.

Ong was also impressed by European inventions, particularly the quadrant, which he describes in detail, and Western skill in military manoeuvres.[34] He comments that "pirates do not dare to approach European vessels. Looking at our Chinese junks from Amoy, slightly formed and fastened with straw, they seem merely like children's playthings; on this account they are frequently attacked by robbers."[35] In the making of "sky-rockets or bombs", the skill of the English is much superior.

He deals also with other Asian races such as the Malays[36] described as crafty and treacherous, and very much addicted to piracy, suddenly appearing and disappearing to the alarm of the Chinese. Their language is employed by the Dutch as a medium of intercourse with the Chinese and natives, as the mandarin dialect is in China.

New ways of seeing

A group he desribes as "the Islams"[37] are Chinese who have been abroad for several generation and have abandoned their native language, customs, and religion, becoming Javanese and calling themselves Sit-lam. They then refuse to eat pork, and have their own Captain appointed by the Dutch. Ong seems to have been under some significant misapprehensions about Islam, however, as can be seen from the following passage on Mecca:

> On the shores of the western sea, is the residence of the true Buddha: the hills are exteremely high, and the whole ground is replenished with yellow gold and beautiful gems; which are guarded by a hundred genii, so that the treasures cannot be taken away. The true cultivators of virtue may ascend to Mecca, and worship the real Buddha, when after several years' fasting they return, and receive the title of dukun or doctor; they can then bring down spirits, and subdue monsters, drive away noxious influences, and behead demons. These dukuns carry rosaries in their hands, and are very compassionate; so that all who see them acknowledge their virtue.

In structural terms, Ong's account is quite similar to Valentijn's (see Ch.1, p. 15f), dealing as it does with hierarchies, geography, curiosities, and national customs, with the natural addition of European technological and military advances. Like comparable European accounts, but unlike Javanese ones, Ong's spends some time in detailing politcal and institutional arrangements, not always accurately, as for instance his account of Batavia's submission to the Chinese government or his material on the Javanese rulers. In some respects, however, he displays a frankness and realism that we would not find in Dutch accounts, as in his explanation of the Chinese Captains owing their position to bribing the Dutch – a relationship that the latter prefer to represent in legal-bureaucratic terms. Despite his flowery language which suggests an "unscientific" attitude to us, who can fault his perception of the European expansion as having laid a foundation not to be rooted up for a myriad of years, having done which, they live at their ease, without dread of danger, while they give themselves up to the work of fleecing people?

Ong deals with a wide spectrum of ethnic groups. That he should describe the Dutch as strict in executing laws and minute in levying duties is quite a testimony from a Chinese, presumably accustomed to a highly regulatory mandarinate; equally striking is his comment on the stringency of the laws against unpermitted travel, part of the iron determination to fix the peasantry to the soil noted above, which was such a notable feature of the colony and which struck other Europeans even into the twentieth century. On the other hand, few accounts by other Europeans would be likely to single out the Dutch as notably immoral, and worse, lacking in frugality: a popular English jingle of the day ran

In matters of commerce the fault of the Dutch
Is giving too little and asking too much.

The preference among Chinese for China-born sons-in-law forms an interesting parallel with Dutch colonial practice as described by Taylor.[38] Again, his comments on the Chinese in Java parallel those made by Stavorinus and other Europeans on the decay of the races manners and morals in the tropics.

Like Stavorinus, Ong seems to have been aware of the importance accorded to women and the matrilocal marriage tradition of the Javanese family, in his case, by comparison with Chinese norms.

In two other respects, Ong's account of the situation accords with European accounts, that is, in the increasing prevalence of opium, a theme which recurs again and again in the sources used for this book; and in the prevalence of piracy, which as Trocki has shown,[39] was indeed highly prevalent among the Malays up until the founding of Singapore after which the English indignantly suppressed it, at least partially to protect the Chinese opium trade.[40]

Hawks, other birds, and buffaloes: Javanese ethnography and self criticism

1. NBS 89

The work discussed here is very short but very wide-ranging;[41] its Javanese author is anonymous. It is also undated, but its reference to the "French General", i.e. Daendels, and to the British, suggest that it was written some time after 1811. It deals briefly with five different subjects. These are:

1. Kingship (eight stanzas). The virtuous king (*ratu kang ambĕk sadu*) is benevolent and maintains justice (*paramarta nĕtĕpi ngadil*); loves his subordinates;[42] is overflowing with generosity; takes pity

on the poor; knows how to please the hearts of his ordinary subordinates, and forgives transgressions. In relationships with other states, he avoids warfare even where others are in the wrong, and prefers to restore the situation through talks. He has no desire to shed the blood of his soldiers. Such a king is like the ocean, which in its vast capacity can contain and hold good and evil. He cools all the people of his kingdom. He is called a king with an oceanic heart, or likened to a large tree, broad and dense, leafy and sheltering for his subordinates. This is the outstanding[43] king. The despicable (=nista) king, on the other hand, is like a dry waterless sea useless to fish or to traders; or like a large tree without sheltering leaves or useful fruit. He cannot look after his army, and will certainly come to ruin, with his state (negara) being taken by an outstanding king. If a king is not sufficiently conscientious, if he is not swift to cut through problems, if the dispensing of justice is awry, and truth is shamed, if he is confused and sluggish in his thoughts, and behind-hand in his affairs with nothing being settled, he will certainly be worsted, as one with a bad character and unable to look after the ordinary subordinates, with many people suffering difficulty. He is like the orok-orok flower, beautiful at a distance with its yellow colour, but without fragrance or use and tending only to make the house dirty.

2. Ten stanzas dealing with the desirable characteristics in Bupati, whom we have seen presented in the Dutch reports largely in the role of economic managers. Here however they are described as officers (punggawa) of the capital (praja) and the regional centres (manca praja), another reflection of the military rationale of the Javanese aristocracy before their absorption into the colonial bureaucracy. They should have good character, a fortunate disposition, be faithful to their ruler, be able to command their associates, accommodate and care for all their people, be skilled in all competences, earning themselves the title of outstanding officers (punggawa utama). Once again, the despicable – nista – Bupati is defined as possessing the opposite of these attributes. In choosing Bupati, kings should bear in mind the following guide: the man chosen should be like four things, a jewel, a woman, a kris and a bird. A man who is like a jewel is one of an elevated and limpid character, who will not bring bad habits into the state, who fears God, who can penetrate to the meaning of things, who is careful in what he does, who knows good and evil, who knows his enemies, understands the greatest invulnerability, and the joys and sorrows

of the soldiery. "Like a woman" means someone with a fortunate disposition, patient, understanding, forgiving of mistakes and errors, one who can raise up the state, and can defeat enemies. Someone like this is protected by God, all his wishes are fulfilled, he is the surrogate of the king, he is subtle and does not create divisions. "Like a kris" means sharp in understanding, one who can understand an allusion, who knows the wishes of his subordinates great and small, who comprehends the silence of enemies and the movements of friends, who can defeat opponents, who is sharp with respect to the regulations of the state, who is loved by his subordinates, who can read the mood of the army. "Like a bird" means one who is sharp in speech to his subordinates, who can rule great and small, whose speech is to the point, who can comfort the soldiers and farmers with sweet words. Also, a bird flies far, and knows all the tricks of his enemy and can therefore defeat him. Through men with these four qualities the king will be firmly established, and the state stable, enduring, prosperous, famous and victorious in battle.

3. Candrakirana and Panji, in that order (five stanzas). Panji is the eponymous hero of the most popular of all Javanese "romances", as it is usually called, Candrakirana his beloved and wife. The author describes Candrakirana (*sang rĕtna Condrakirana*, "the honourable jewel Condrakirana", "jewel" being an honorific appellation used for women of great distinction, normally wives of kings or kings-to-be), princess of Kediri from the state of Jenggala, as the most renowned of all women in Java today, of a beauty absolutely unequalled. None of the princesses or wives of knights in Surakarta or Yogyakarta can approach her in beauty, and she is famed in the whole world. Her husband Panji is, equally, incomparably handsome (the word for female beauty is *ayu*, the word for males used here is *pĕkik*). Together they are the subject of kidung[44] written to ease the hearts of those who are love-stricken. The two of them are still an example today, and when pregnant women reach the time when they have the *tingkĕban* [the seventh month ceremony], the *cĕngkir gaḍing* [young, small, yellow decorative coconut] is inscribed with the likeness of Panji and Candrakirana, holding hands, so that the child may be like unto Panji if it is a boy, and Candrakirana if it is a girl. [For European ethnographic material on this custom, see the Cornets de Groot account above p. 116]

4. The protocol of war (five stanzas, one short canto, in the metre

New ways of seeing

of Pangkur). This section begins with the letter of challenge that should be sent. It goes on to describe the ferocious appearance of the warrior who is about to go into battle, and its terrifying effect.

5. The remainder of the work, 45 stanzas in all divided into 5 cantos, deals with the foreigners who have come to Java. As will be seen, all these races are likened to particular birds (rather than to the wider spectrum of animals and birds found in Aesop's fables with which Westerners are more familiar). The use of birds as metaphors for individual or national character is very common in Java and can be seen also in the recent novel, *The Weaverbirds* (*Burung-burung Manyar*).[45] The first group are the Chinese: they are bald-headed, with a long twisted pigtail; their clothes flap around them so that they do not have the semblance of a warrior. They eat lean pork and green frogs. They have no more idea of polite manners (*tatakrami*) than an ape climbing a branch. When they lease the right to tax a village, they strip it of all its crops, even down to the coconut buds, even before the tax is due. They go to any length to claim their rights, and are equally insistent in demanding payment of tolls. If one wishes to compare the Chinese to a bird, it would be the *kuntul* (a white heron), which has its haunts in the rice-fields where it looks for its prey, swiftly following the small frogs with its eyes. There is no equal to the *kuntul* in finding food: if a fish should show itself briefly in a swamp or at the edge of a river, it is taken. Even though the *kuntul*'s appearance is unprepossessing, for its feet are too broad and long and its neck swells up and extends excessively, it is nevertheless very quick and adroit in chasing any small advantage.[46]

Next the "wong Koja" [Indian Muslims, especially traders from Gujerat] are described. They dress in the Arab fashion like santri, which is fitting because their hearts are white, and they do not think about money. If it happens that they have to ask a Javanese to repay a debt, they adjust to the Javanese way: it is the established custom of the Javanese to promise to repay in three days but not to do so before three months. The Kojas run here and there every day going around with their merchandise, never admitting fatigue, always cheerful and concentrating their attention solely on their possessions. They carry an umbrella on their travels, they look like oily fish [*kutuk gagajih*]; and there is a proverb to the effect that if you manage to make any profit by beating down a Koja you are very lucky. They are different from the Malays, that is the Encik, who dress like princes wearing head-dresses (*dĕstar*) in the Batavian style called *ngin-angin* ("winds"), with *bajus* like mixed-blood Encik, and white singlets [?*kotang*]. This is all fitting to people of presence and dignity; they enjoy the good things like *priyayi*, but when they are in their homes they heat up leftovers themselves, and their wives send them on errands to buy cakes, telling them not to be tardy. The bird that is like the Encik is the *ĕmprit*, which can be domesticated by small children, is fine and vigorous and gives itself airs, [but] is flown on a string every day. But if it is in the haunts of men, the *ĕmprit* destroys the rice.

At the beginning of the next canto, the author remarks "I was astonished to see men from overseas who were exceedingly black, called Sepehi [Sepoys], very brightly dressed in jackets of red cloth, with white trousers or short breeches, with a dark ornamental strip of interlocking triangles. Only their cap was like a *kĕnong* [a small *gamĕlan* gong], set awry on their heads." He goes on to say that their disposition was rather unruly and when they went into the villages to buy maize (*jagung*) they terrified the inhabitants so much that they closed their houses and would not sell to them. Then the government issued an order forbidding the Sepoys to enter the houses of the Javanese, to the relief of the latter. The bird that is like the Sepoys is the crow (*gagak*), which swarms in the trees, is exceedingly black, and makes a *gaok-gaok* noise which is like a cry of pain, touching those who hear it to the heart. It would be appropriate if it had a gentle peaceful nature, but it has been decreed that the crow should have a common nature, and even eat corpses; it has no shame as regards dirty things.

There is another type of soldier who came to Java during the time of the French general,[47] the Ambonese. They are not proper people, but very common and repulsive. Their clothing is not fine, their jackets being of coarse weave and dark, fitting only for freebooters and not government soldiers, not an awe-inspiring sight. The bird that is like the Ambonese is the *pĕking* [a sort of weaver bird], which is unappealing, grey-khaki and downy, not worth eating, since it is only as big as a *kemiri* nut. They make trouble among the bamboo leaves and rises up in a mass, spreading out, but are completely without wit or strength.

The last canto, of 14 stanzas, deals with the Europeans who have ruled Java: famous, outstanding warriors who have roamed the world conquering other lands, unrivalled as they are on the battlefield. First are the Dutch, from the land of the white-skinned. Their clothing strikes fear – the jacket rather long and wide, the chapeau beautiful with three protuding peaks, all beautifully uniform, without a single one of incorrect form. If they are already furious for battle, they are of high courage and none is afraid to die, their resolve is unshakeable. [But] their disposition is gentle and patient, their intention not immoral, they are clever, deliberate and cautious. They are skilled at polite conversation, and have no difficulty in pursuing their aims, as in the proverb to the effect that if one has a certain wish, one should only cease one's efforts when it is attained. They are like the goshawk that looks about attentively as it flies high in the firmament, looking attentively below at what will become its prey, patient and subtle; when it has taken careful aim it swoops swiftly on its prey and takes it into the sky to eat it where no-one can follow, leaving those [chickens] left behind looking around in perplexity, startled and envious. The chickens can do nothing as they are inferior in respect of distance, speed, and ability.

There are other Europeans, from France, whose clothing is astonishing, their jackets have gold leaf, the officers have embroidery in one colour. Their defect is their hat, which is wide and only folded twice, set cross-wise, not straight, on their heads.

Another lot of Europeans who have come are the English. Their jackets are too short, straight, and tight, and their *kuluk* are also tight, cylindrical and without folding.[48] This indicates that their clothes do not hamper them in action, but they are not roomy enough, just very straight ("like a jewel that is only shaped, like kapok-wood that is carved"). When they go to war their enemies are annihilated; they are like the falcon (*pĕksi alap-alap*), which flies high into the firmament; once it swoops down on its prey this rarely escapes, no matter how large it is. All the birds fly away into the air, much afraid of the falcon, that breaks through all obstacles and cuts through all hindrances [*ingkang malang-malang putung, kang rawe-rawe rantas*: one of the best known Javanese proverbs]. All evil-doers are swept away, those who persist in error are punished, the immoral are under attack. They are real men, their disposition is arrogant, they are not fickle or frivolous but careful in governing so that they bring about the prosperity of the state (*nĕgara*).

The author goes on to say that this is unlike the Javanese soldiers, who are always changing their clothes, at great expense, as they always like to imitate others, in the Dutch time the Dutch way, in the French season the French way, in the English season the English way. They are not steadfast or dashing; they turn and twist here and

Intellectual Transformations

there. It is characteristic of the Javanese always to be changing; it seems as if they are heroes but when they are sent into battle they are swept away like a dam by water; they run away without resistance. They are only seasonally brave: if they have been stripped bare apart from their pants, then they will resolve not to fear death, that is, if they have a good leader: the bravery of the Javanese is in following a leader. The Javanese are like buffaloes, excessively stupid. If they are not beaten and driven they won't do anything, and even if they are beaten they are still totally unconcerned. They can only be arrogant: if you want to pass them they fill up the road. At home they [Javanese, not buffaloes] are sad because they are being dunned for their debts.

Comment

This text is much more obviously foreign to those who come from the European literate tradition than is the Chinese account. In literary terms, it is in poetry, and highly metaphorical: a Bupati, for instance, should it is said be like a jewel, a woman, and a kris, while the different races are likened to one of the many birds from the rich world of Javanese nature, familiar alike to court and village. Other parts of the text draw on the equally rich but less universally accessible world of Javanese literature, as in the *nista, madya, utama,* classification. The account appears to lack the political-institutional focus of Stavorinus and Ong. And although both of these are in fact quite miscellaneous in their coverage, we are more inclined to see a lack of unity in the Javanese text. Yet it has its own logic. It begins with the central focus of all Javanese accounts of what we would call politics and society, i.e. with the king and his ministers. It goes on to Panji and his wife, the most exemplary and central of all princes and princesses, whose centrality also appears in Cornets de Groot's account of early nineteenth century Gresik, Ch. 3 above. And it goes on to problematise, to use an ugly contemporary word, the current situation of the Javanese *vis-à-vis* other races, and to explain it. In doing so it makes a radical innovation. As stated above, ethnography had not been part of the Javanese literate tradition, although there was an implicit assumption that Java and the Javanese are the normative centre of the world[49] – an assumption that seems very arrogant to us, who have generally made the same assumption about ourselves (as, too, have the Chinese). In this text we see the emergence of a negative ethnicity,

New ways of seeing

which is set off against the superior accomplishments of other races, a negativity that we will see again below in the *Wicara Kĕras*. Furthermore, the unknown author goes on to explain the situation of the Javanese as being due to the military superiority of Europeans (and the hopelessness of Javanese soldiers on this front), their moral superiority, and the inability of Javanese to handle money. Despite its lack of a sophisticated tradition of socioeconomic analysis and metaphorical presentation, this Javanese explanation actually canvasses the major emphases of Western scholars seeking to explain Asia's domination by the West from the time this first became apparent down to Braudel (see Ch. 1). It is this aspect of innovation, and of analysis of a contemporary problem – again not a feature of the Javanese literate tradition – that we miss if we are preoccupied with the literary, exotic, and naive aspects of this text. These are the first[50] stammering phrases of a theme that was to become dominant in the laments of Indonesian and Malay peoples for their historical fate. A much later Malay analysis of the Malay situation, quoted by Roff,[51] contains the following passage: "Intellectually, the Malays are poor in knowledge, in culture and in the general means of cultivating the mind. Their literature is poor and unelevating; their domestic surroundings from childhood are poor and seldom edifying; their outlook on life is poor and full of gloom; their religious life and practice is poor and far removed from the pure original teachings of the Prophet. In short, the Malays cut poor figures in every department of life." This is close to the position of the Javanese author.

What is remarkable about the Javanese account is that it agrees with the Chinese one that the Javanese are dull and stupid. Perhaps it is not surprising that neither of these accounts take Stavorinus's sophisticated line that the behaviour of the Javanese is conditioned by the oppressive and hopeless situation they live in, but it is remarkable that the Javanese account is the only one where the author does not take his own race as setting the norms of civilized human behaviour. (Though Stavorinus and Ong both comment unfavourably on the "colonials", this in fact indicates the degree to which they assume that the manners and morals of the home country are exemplary, and any deviation from them is necessarily a decline from the ideal.) He accords not only military but moral superiority to Europeans. In view of the ample pejorative comment on the manners and morals of the Indies Dutch provided by reformers and non-Dutch Europeans, the fact that the anonymous

Javanese author yet perceived behind this degeneracy a superior moral system, and a similar superiority in the English, is food for thought indeed.

In Java itself this addressing of a historical condition, the subjugation of the indigenous majority to foreign minorities, seems to fall into abeyance from this time until the rise of the Indonesian nationalist movement in the twentieth century. We do not find it in Dipanegara's mystic traditionalism, with his condemnation of the court's adoption of European ways, which in his account meant gambling and other forms of dissipation rather than the European virtues described by the author of NBS 89; nor in the didactic works of the nineteenth century Javanese rulers who were maintained by the colonial government, which largely return to the a-temporal, universalist, generalizing style of the past, and are silent on colonialism and ethnicity.

Strong words on the Javanese nation: the *Wicara Kěras* of Yasadipura II

There was a side to the Javanese courts that is not reflected at all in the guardswoman's diary used in Chapter Two, or in Dutch accounts. This is the life of the mind, the role of the court élite in preserving and extending the moral and philosophical heritage of Javanese civilization. Pakubuwana IV, who appears in the diary and in Dutch reports as an ambitious young player in a politico–military contest, had more to him than this: he was not only a considerable patron of but also a participant in this intellectual activity, being the author of the *Wulang-reh*, one of the best-known modern Javanese didactic works.[52] He was also a notable patron of music and wayang, part of a flowering of court arts that cannot be covered here. The Kasunanan over this period produced in addition two of the most famous of modern Javanese literati, the father and son Yasadipura I[53] and Yasadipura II, who are most known (if at all) in the West for their role in transmitting Java's great cultural heritage of Indic and Islamic works, particularly the former. It is the second Yasadipura with whom we are concerned here, not as transmitter of the past but as creator of something new: as author of two works that are very much of his times and one of which, particularly, addresses contemporary problems in a new way.

New ways of seeing

The lessons of history

"immense advances in both historical knowledge and interpretation ... are very largely the products of the West's contacts with South East Asia. Through these contacts western scholars became interested in South East Asian history, and South East Asians developed an awareness of their own history that they had never before experienced." (D.G.E. Hall, Introduction to *Historians of South East Asia*, 1961[54])

* * *

The works of Yasadipura analysed here do not share the celebratory, festive tone of the guardswoman's diary, which presents to us the aesthetic and martial glamour of an ancient court civilisation. By contrast, the first of these works, the *Wicara Kĕras*[55] has a rough, angry, even vituperative tone, and the second, the *Sasana Sunu*, is a moving, eloquent, austerely glittering, formally perfect summation of the moral fortitude necessary to be the finest type of Javanese *priyayi*.

The *Wicara Keras* is less formally perfect and gives the impression of pastiche. However, in this work Yasadipura departs in a significant and innovative way from the established ways of describing the world provided by the Javanese intellectual tradition. It is quite true that he would have known many Javanese works, the Babad, that relate Java's history, but they are overwhelmingly narrative in an epic style, and provide little analytical historiography. The *Wicara Kĕras* introduces a critical historiography, developing the general theme that the present age is a degenerate one. This conceptualisation of a degenerate present is something very familiar to students of Old Javanese literature; but we must pause to ask what was the Old Javanese concept of "the present" and what is Yasadipura's. The Old Javanese "present" is the Kaliyuga,[56] the last and worst of four immensely long ages that go to make up the huge cycle of Indic cosmic time. By contrast, Yasadipura's "present" is just his own lifetime, and it is contrasted to a "past" not counted in aeons but comprising mostly that part of his own century that was within living memory. It is within this short time-span that he sees the phenomenon of degeneracy, which is clearly a Javanese historical phenomenon and not a universal cosmic one. Unlike Old Javanese texts, he takes his good and bad

Intellectual Transformations

examples from specific historical figures, members of the Javanese élite whom the author himself knew, had known, or had heard of. For this reason the *Wicara Kĕras* is not just *of* its time, as the synthesis of the *Sasana Sunu* also is, but actually *addresses* its own time far more extensively and explicitly than the *Sasana Sunu*.

The evidence of degeneracy most frequently cited is that those who by virtue of their birth should be outstanding, are in fact only making large claims which they cannot fulfill.[57] There are those who claim to be the children of *paṇḍita* (sages, ascetes) but cannot stand hunger (*bĕtah lapa*: note the always positive connotations of going hungry and its importance for Javanese asceticism); those who claim to be the children of *pujangga* (literati) but cannot write; those who claim to be the children of *sujana* but are confused; those who claim to be the children of *ulama* but cannot *ngaji* (recite the sacred texts) which is like being of Chinese descent and without a pigtail; those who claim to be the children of *santri* but cannot recite the *kulhu* [the 112th chapter of the Quran, a very commonly used prayer]; those who claim to be of royal descent, and *should* be precise in their thinking; those who claim to be the children of *kaum* and cannot say the prayers. People like this are the result of a satanic conception[58] and are devils and traitors to their people (*sesetanan anjaili paḍa bangsa*). They are only brave with their own people (*mung wanine paḍa bangsa*); instead, they should be like Sultan Mangkubumi [the first ruler of the Sultanate of Yogyakarta, who reigned from 1755 until 1792), who performed *tapa* and was capable, who discussed things and did not maltreat people, and did not like to fight his fellow Javanese (*lamun aprang paḍa Jawa nora arsa*: here there seems to be some element of putting a better light on the heroes of the old days than we might think the evidence supports). People of the degenerate present should follow an example from the glorious past, even if this example were a "Buddhist" [i.e. an adherent of pre-Islamic Javanese religion], despite Yasadipura's exhortations to follow the example of the Prophet and uphold Islamic Law elsewhere in the *Sasana Sunu*.

Yasadipura passes heavy judgment on the Javanese as a whole. They are insufficiently united, the texture of their minds is rough, they like silly tricks and if praised and made much of readily put on airs; they are confused by flattery so that they do not know north from south, and forget that they are an Islamic people brave in battle (*lali bangsa paḍa Islam wani jurit*);[59] and thus they are being reduced to the rank of beggars.[60] Yasadipura's *eheu fugaces* seems

New ways of seeing

confirmed by Raffles' characterisation of the Javanese as "a quiet domestic people, little given to adventure, disinclined to foreign enterprises, not easily roused to violence or bloodshed, and little disposed to irregularities of any kind.[61] However, Raffles had his own reasons for portraying the Javanese as the sort of people who would give a new, English, colonial master, little trouble.

Much of the work consists of good and bad examples. Since many of these are, to the non-Javanese reader, unknown or unfamiliar, only those which may be better known will be cited here.[62]

Among the good examples is Surapati, from the "past age" (*pantěs-pantěse kaya ing nguni, Surapati rajeng Pasuruhan*), a brave and successful ruler contrasted to the stupid Rangga of Madiun of the present.[63] For those in the service of the king, the example given is the mythological Patih of Raja Arjuna Sasrabau, called Patih Suwanda. Yasadipura describes his prowess and courage in battle, as in his famous encounter with Prabu Rawana.[64]

Other good examples of Patihs are Sindureja, who took poison rather than wait to be dismissed,[65] and Raden Pringgalaya,[66] who when disgraced took poison rather than live on in shame. In connection with this example the author says: "It is our adat from the oldest times, that a *punggawa* who has been involved in a *pěrkara* [an intrigue or political manoeuvre bringing discredit] should prefer death to confinement". Concerning more recent Patihs, Yasadipura says that Danureja I of Yogya [Patih February 1755– August 1799] can be called one who was in the *utama* (outstanding) to *madya* (middling) range; in Surakarta Sindureja [Patih from around October 1782 to July 1784[67]] was again in the *madya* range, sometimes approaching *utama*, and was able to argue with the Dutch.[68]

Also praised are Adipati Jangrana of Surabaya and Cakraningrat of Madura, and Jayaningrat of Pekalongan.[69] The author says that if these three leaders had still been around the Chinese war would not have happened. But the ruler succumbed to the baneful influence of Tirtawiguna,[70] who ended up being exiled, tricked by the Company. And the three *punggawa* committed suicide by poison.[71] "Such was the character of the Bupati of yore, all placed their trust and confidence in the Supreme Soul, and generally thought nothing of death. Rarely were they not frank in speech; they could stand much humiliation but did not know disgrace" (*yeku amběking bupati nguni, pada kanděl kumanděl ing Suksma, lumrah tan etung patine, arang ingkang mbaludus, bětah wirang tan iděp isin*").

Other positive examples are: Tuměnggung Puspaněgara of Surakarta who rose from being a Balinese merchant,[72] and Arungbinang, who, when he fought on the side of the Dutch, could command the obedience of their warriors, who carried out all his orders unhesitatingly.[73] Also praised is Kudanawarsa,[74] the Mangkunegaran Bupati, who was faithful and brave and of beneficent character: he was indeed a knight and Mangkunegara's only companion, sharing with him hunger and suffering.

Canto II gives an account of the Pandawa-Korawa conflict of the Mahābhārata, the great theme of the wayang, and points out how the former group triumphed even though they were few and weak and poor, because they always remembered God and were patient and did not do evil and performed *tapa*. Canto VIII, verse 26 returns yet again to *tapa* and its relationship to social rank in an important passage. This deals with the difference between those of royal descent (*santana*) and the little people (*wong cilik*) in their spiritual power (*prabawa*). If one of the latter performs *tapa* for a year, it is not certain that he will acquire *walat*[75] because he is lacking in *prabawa* [spiritual force and authority, a difficult term to translate, but one often associated with those of royal birth] but one of royal birth will only have to do *tapa* for one moon because of his great *prabawa*. That is the proportion of their difference, a moon to a year. For a *santana* is not just of noble descent (*turasing andanawarih*), he is the fruit of *tapa*. In other words, in the Javanese moral world, unlike the Indic, *tapa* is hereditary, and explains the special qualities of those of royal blood, the *santana*. A rather striking story from one of the Surapati Babads nicely illustrates both the hereditary nature of the "cosmic credit" acquired through *tapa* and its connection with high rank: there was an ascete (*wong tapa*) whose particular form of *tapa* was to hang upside-down in a banyan tree (the insignia of royalty or vice-royalty in Javanese towns). His aim in doing this was to attain kingship, and the gods rewarded him. He became able to transmute himself into spirit, and thus entered into the mind of a queen, who became pregnant. She gave birth to a son of god-like radiance, who became the great Surapati.[76] Other similar stories abound in Babad literature.

Yasadipura says that *tapa* is an activity uniquely elevated, there is nothing in the universe to be compared to it; and the meaning of *tapa* is that our desires are curbed (*tapa iku pan luhur pribadi, mungguh lakune ing alam donya, tan ana onḍe-onḍene, těgěse tapa iku, barang karěp cinegah sami*). Good desires, such as carrying out *ibadah*

New ways of seeing

and reading the Koran, or *primbon* (instructional compendia), or stories from old times containing good examples, may be carried out. When one is performing *tapa* one must nullify all hindrances, cast aside all impurities, not fall into pride or boastfulness or the love of praise and admiration: otherwise your *tapa* will fail, and the dry mouth and empty stomach will be for nothing. Some further insight into the conception of *tapa* is given by the author's assertion that although a caterpillar is a lowly creature if it peroms *tapa* only for a month to the utmost of its mental capacity, finally its *tapa* is accepted by the Creator (Hyang Kang Murbeng Alam) and it becomes a pupa and eventually a butterfly, all the result of *tapa*. Sultan Agung, the great ruler of early seventeenth-century Mataram, is then adduced as a supreme example of *tapa*: no-one dared to step on his shadow, for if they did they would fall nerveless to the ground. He could attend Friday prayer at the Kabah without anyone knowing of it. Yasadipura says that to imitate him is too heavy a task: a lighter one is to follow the examples of Sinuhun Kapugĕran[77] and Sultan Mangkubumi [the first ruler of Yogyakarta]. The latter's *tapa* was at least equivalent to that of Mangkunegara [whom he joined in rebellion but later deserted, see above p. 54], but it was adulterated with excessive loquacity;[78] he was full of tricks and chicanery to serve his own ends, but he did not complain or ask for help, and he was by nature courageous enough to do battle. This recognition of Mangkunegara as the supreme example of the power of *tapa* seems to be maintained in his reputation in Surakarta today, where he is the only past ruler who is popularly known by a special cognomen, Pangeran Samber Nyawa, "the soul-striking Prince". Do not, Yasadipura goes on, be like Raden Wirameja who merely made a show of rebelling while not having the courage to fight a cat. [Wirameja or Wiratmeja, also known as Raden Mas Guntur, was a descendant of Sunan Amangkurat II and a son-in-law of Mangkunegara I. He led a rebellion in the Blora-Jipang area from August 1761, which ended when he was captured and killed by Surakarta forces in September 1762. Ricklefs[79] says that he was "one of the most important rebels of the 1760s" but the author of the *Wicara kĕras* obviously takes a different viewpoint.] Prowess on the battlefield is a very important type of *tapa*.[80]

From this one can see that what seems amorality to us (the apparently indifferent classing together of those who took very different stands, especially vis-à-vis the Dutch) is actually the product of a different morality: power and success *follow* virtue, i.e. *tapa*. Note also that the fruits of *tapa* are hereditary. This idea is also reflected in the description of someone as *wijiling tapa*, "the outcome of *tapa*", that is, a descendant of someone who performed great *tapa*, that is so often tagged onto those who achieve great things by the authors who celebrate their lives. Needless to say, this belief provides a powerful ideological underpinning for the position of the upper class as a whole as well as an explanation for the differing fortunes of those who make it up.

Comment

The *Wicara Kĕras* like the Mangkunegaran diary reveals the old Javanese ethos for the king and his servants: bravery on the battlefield, exemplified by the legendary Patih Suwanda, but also strongly reinforced by Islam (was this strong martial aspect of the Islamic tradition a continuity between past and present that facilitated conversion?), the ability to live in hunger and privation (*lara lapa*). Perhaps surprisingly, given the emphasis on loyalty to the ruler found elsewhere, Yasadipura clearly feels that rebellion is acceptable or justified if one does it whole-heartedly and succeeds: he praises the examples of Surapati, the ultimate succesful upstart, in origin a Balinese slave (though the Babad always solve the problem of explaining his success by providing him with a royal ancestry) and of Mangkubumi, who was also in origin a rebel, though of the blood royal. It seems that while *priyayi* are enjoined to glory in their service (they are described as *abdi*, servants, and *ngawula*, serving, is their highest good) and to be steadfast, loyal, careful, well-mannered and patient, there is a different morality envisaged for those whom we might designate as the real players in the historical game: the great warrior lords, Bupati and *punggawa*. If they are allowed to venture on risky and ambitious political manoeuvres they are also expected to pay a high price when these go wrong. One of the striking things about the *Wicara Kĕras* is its strong and repeated statements placing a positive value on suicide, with examples of those who followed this honourable path, and heaping scorn and vituperation on those of the degenerate present who were prepared to allow themselves to be imprisoned. It is far better to die than to live if you are not able to make good words already spoken (*ujar kang wis kawuwus*).

The concept of *tapa* is central to both the *Wicara Kĕras* and the

Sasana Sunu. Here however a new light is thrown on it, i.e. its hereditary nature, with a clear explanation of the relative periods of time those from different ranks need to carry it out to achieve their aim. It does not *exclusively* work in favour of those of high birth, however: everyone can make it if their effort is sufficiently large, whether the Balinese merchant or the caterpillar. One should not assume that this explanation of the basis of political power has entirely lost its force: I remember being told, in the early '80s, how Suharto as a young soldier had carried out *tapa*, walking or immersing himself in the river all night long, as an explanation of how he came to hold his present position.

The judgment passed in the quotation from Hall at the head of this section is, simply, absurd. The Javanese have for as long as writing existed remembered and recorded their history: and in particular the history of their kings and most of all those kings who were great founders and unifiers. Airlangga – who for a time managed to unite the whole Brantas valley region into a single realm, a feat that eluded his successors for centuries afterwards – and Agung, who in his unprecedented series of conquests of regional centres welded together the kingdom of Mataram, are the two pre-eminent examples. Most Babad historiography is an epic celebration of the military feats of rulers. Now, in Yasadipura, we find those "immense advances in interpretation" that Hall refers to as the beginnings of an analytical historiography. Yasadipura's analysis rests on a pessimistic interpretation; reminding one of Auden's characterisation of Clio as the Madonna of silences to whom we turn when we have lost control.[81]

Another new thing is the presence of a negative sense of ethnicity, as in NBS 89, above. Yasadipura says that the Javanese are insufficiently united, the texture of their minds is rough, they like silly tricks and if praised and made much of readily put on airs; they are confused by flattery so that they do not know north from south, and forget that they are an Islamic people brave in war; and thus they are being reduced to the rank of beggars.

The whole concept of "nation" or "people" seems to be in the process of emerging through a shift in concept of *bangsa*. Before this time (and even after it) *bangsa* was used as a classifier for any sort of classification of human beings or human-like beings. In the *Sasana sunu* (see below) it is used to contrast two types of people, those who do physical work (*bangsa badan*) and those who do mental work (*bangsa ati*). Elsewhere it is used to rank different levels of

Muslims along a scale of stages leading to spiritual enlightenment, with the ordinary people (*bangsa riya* or *riah*) at the bottom and those who have achieved union with Reality at the top.[82] It could also be used to distinguish jinns and devils (*bangsa jin, bangsa setan*) from human beings. Here however Yasadipura uses the word to denote the Javanese people or nation as a whole, and to assess them critically.

Yasadipura can therefore be said to work with some very well-established beliefs and to be the product of an old military society, but also to introduce radically new concepts of history. The capacity for innovation was undoubtedly there; but it was to be blighted by the intellectual famine of the nineteenth century as surely as the peasantry's efforts to engage with the opportunities of a market economy. In a colonial situation where the Javanese courts lacked the financial resources to revamp their old educational role and the colonial government had no intention of filling this gap, where people were not free to travel or to publish without censorship, where stringent measures were taken to silence Muslim thinkers and separate them from the "Javanist" leadership, no meaningful analysis of the nature of the Dutch-Javanese historical encounter was possible. In the late colonial period, far from the West encouraging a new interest in history, it placed it in two psychological categories, the repulsive and the dangerous. As far as the former is concerned, a famous Sumatran wrote:

> The glorious past of Indonesia is of course not presented ... It is said that Indonesia has no history and that there is only a Dutch history in Indonesia, which is officially called the Dutch East Indies. And it is suggested to Indonesian youth that the so-called "East Indies history" is a history of Dutch epics, which only magnifies the glory of the Dutch race ... the kernel of the so-called East Indies history with which Indonesian youth is taunted ... But on the other hand every opposition by the Indonesian princes and chiefs against the penetration of the whites is branded as rebellion and revolt. Thus, too, must Indonesian youth parrot its masters and call its own heroes, like Dipo Negoro, Toeankoe Imam, Tengkoe Oemar and many others, rebels, insurrectionists, and so on.

And then defiantly: "But yet they, too, were national heroes just as were William of Orange, William Tell, Mazzini, Garibaldi etc., to whom we owe reverence."[83] – with this last remark entering the

New ways of seeing

terrain of the dangerous, the affirmation and publication of highly-charged parallels between Dutch and Javanese or Indonesian historical aspirations. The fate of those who dared to do this is strikingly exemplified by the furore surrounding Suwardi Suryaningrat's sarcastic article "If I were a Dutchman" written around the celebrations of the Netherlands independence and published in 1913, the year its author was exiled for political subversion. It is not, then, under the benevolent guidance but against the opposition of the West that the development of a meaningful analytical historiography, begun in Yasadipura's time but dormant until decolonization in the wake of the Japanese Occupation,[84] has taken place.

A NEW SYNTHESIS FOR PERILOUS TIMES: THE *SASANA SUNU* OF YASADIPURA II[85]

This work, written, the author tells us, in his old age,[86] is the most difficult modern Javanese work I have ever had to interpret, in fact the most difficult thing I have ever read. There are several things that make for difficulty in Javanese works: the language has a rich variety of idiom; it has an extremely finely nuanced vocabulary whose distinctions are not accessible to us, let alone easily translatable; and as in other highly literary texts the language, within the formal constraints of verse (*tembang macapat*) is heavily reworked for literary effect at the expense of normal syntactic order and clarity. In the *Sasana Sunu* all these factors operate *a fortiori*, and it is a text that abounds in the different literary devices that in Old Javanese literature were known under the collective name of *alaṃkara*. Among these, *yamaka*, repetition/alliteration, often of a very complex and artificial type, seems to have been a continuing favourite with Javanese poets since Old Javanese times. Yasadipura II would have been very familiar with Old Javanese works that make heavy use of these literary devices, notably the Ramayana kakawin, which either he or his father Yasadipura I rendered into a modern Javanese version.[87] There is indeed an Old Javanese work, a short poem by Tanakung, that has virtually the same title as the Sasana Sunu. This is the *Putra Sâsana:* or *Suta Sâsana:*[88] which on inspection however turns out to be only a few pages long when transcribed and dealing for a major part with the filial relationship and that with one's teacher. Of course, one may speculate, its existence may have prompted Yasadipura to write the much

Intellectual Transformations

weightier and equally literary *Sasana Sunu*. But I do not wish to present the *Sasana Sunu* as essentially a derivative of the Old Javanese didactic tradition, even though this was part of Yasadipura's intellectual background. This tradition was heavily Platonic and universalistic, dealing in ideal-types (ideal king, ministers, and servants, usually) and making no reference to particular times, places, and situations. In the *Sasana Sunu*, by contrast, we do see a new shift in the discourse to address the author's time, place, and situation.

Apart from its literary elaboration, the *Sasana Sunu* belongs to that category of moral-philosophical text – a type not peculiar to the Javanese tradition – written with the assumption that its study would be a lengthy and demanding process. Later generations of Javanese concurred in that assumption, taking the *Sasana Sunu* as the central text for group study of Javanese philosophy. My in these terms over-hasty reading of it should therefore be regarded as provisional – and this is more than ritualised post-modern relativism.

One can, I think, gain a certain entrée or access to the text by comparing it to a manual written for the instruction of young men in a very strict, let us say Catholic, religious school a generation ago. Some of the injunctions, for instance the section on friendship (what type of people to have as friends, preceded by what sort of people *not* to have as friends) could almost have come from any religious tradition. The same could be said for the injunctions against drink and gambling. The whole, however, is peculiarly Javanese, and Javanese of a certain period. What makes it Javanese is the synthesis of Javanese, Indic, and Islamic elements, and what makes it of a certain time is that this synthesis would have been different in earlier times and would not "hold" for later ones – though the latter judgment must be considerably qualified by noting that the *Sasana Sunu* was recognised far into the twentieth century as *the* great guide for the Muslim Javanese, together with the Ramayana providing all that one needs to lead the good life.[89] So its particular synthesis held for much longer than one might have expected, considering the rise of more exclusivist forms of Javanese Islam in the nineteenth and twentieth centuries.

Apart from this synthetic quality, the other most obvious feature of the *Sasana Sunu* is its comprehensive ethos of self-denial and abnegation, of an asceticism of breath-taking austerity. It was written when its author was already old,[90] and some would say

New ways of seeing

disposed to be rather hard on the young. It concentrates on shaping the personal qualities of those, young *priyayi*, whom it instructs, again somewhat similar to the educational philosophies of the great boarding schools of the Western tradition (Protestant as well as Catholic). It deals extensively with these qualities. Less extensively, it presents a picture of Javanese society (though there is no Javanese equivalent of this word) and makes some comment on the nature of the times in which it was written. Both these things are, I think, innovations and interesting.

First, however, let me give an outline of the text so that its general shape and proportions can be seen. The title of the text, *Sasana Sunu*, is a combination of two words chosen for their alliteration as well as their meaning: *sasana* means teaching or moral instruction; and *sunu* is one of the Javanese words for a son or a number of sons. So in its title the text announces itself as a didactic work for the young males of the governing élite. However, *sasana* can also mean, *inter alia*, seat or throne, and it seems likely that this other layer of meaning – the teaching as throne and foundation for the young *priyayi* – and perhaps others again were in Yasadipura's mind when he composed this master-work. Here I will take up only a few of its aspects, viz. the text as a synthesis of Javanese, Indian, and Islamic ideas; as a vehicle for a highly-developed personal morality/ethos; as a view of Javanese society; and as a comment on the times.

Javanism and Islam: a new synthesis

The second canto states in the strongest terms that one must observe the Shariah, and condemns (stanza 21) those mystics (*ahlul hakekat*) who say that nothing is forbidden – a reference to the heterodox but nevertheless widespread Sufi belief, represented by the mystic al-Hallaj and his Javanese counterpart Seh Siti Jenar,[91] that for those who have reached the ultimate state of enlightenment (that of oneness with Reality, *hakekat*), the prescriptions and prohibitions laid down by the Law for ordinary mortals are no longer binding. This seems a very orthodox position, and when I was transcribing the text I was surprised by its saturation with Arabic words. It would be easy to go through the text picking out all these words and using them as evidence of the ascendancy achieved by Islam. In one sense this would be valid, and in parts of the text a strongly Islamic position is taken. Canto II, for instance,

Intellectual Transformations

advises the young men the text addresses to follow the *shariah*, to know *sunah, fardu, wajib, batal,* and *kharam*,[92] and the Five Pillars; and not to be *kafir, fasik,* or *musyrik,* i.e. infidels, heretics, or apostates. It admonishes them against laughing at people performing the *salat,* and saying *arak* is *halal,* which strikes the reader as perhaps a momentary descent from the elevated tone that distinguishes most of the text into the real world of youth.

However, one must also look at the way in which an Islamic concept is generally coupled with a Javanese one, and perhaps even more importantly at the whole context of both, formed by the framework of the topic under discussion in which they occur. So the Arabic word *adil* (just, justice), for example is always in a compound with the Sanskrit-derived compound *paramarta* ("in the highest degree") and Canto X verses 16–18 reads: "the lord of the multitude [i.e. the ruler] has been created the representative of God, and he will of a certainty be just towards all his people. The meaning of justice in the highest sense is precisely that he will forgive his servants, his care for them overflows" – in short, justice has been transformed into a much more royalist and paternalist concept of forgiveness and benevolence. Perhaps the best-known context of the word *adil* in Java is in the messianic concept of the Ratu Adil or Just King, where the bringing of justice is again linked with royalty. Again, the section on speech (Canto IX) begins with an injunction to avoid *tĕkabur/kibir* (overweening conceit), *ujub* (the desire to impress), *riya* (the desire for praise and prominence), *sumungah* (boastfulness), *duraka* (speaking ill of others) and *dora* (bad conduct, misbehaviour, lying[93]): the first three are from Arabic, the fourth Javanese, the fifth Sanskrit, the last again Javanese. The result of not taking care to follow this injunction will be a decline in one's rank – the word used is *darajat,* again from the Arabic, but wholly congruous with the Javanese sense of hierarchy. The concept of *tĕkabur* also occurs in the section on honour (*kurmat*) to guests, Canto VIII, which once again shows an Arabic word, *kurmat,* used to describe a very Javanese preoccupation with the outward insignia of rank[94] (but also, lest one be tempted into Orientalist stereotype, a very Dutch one, to judge from the huge amount of sumptuary regulations issued by the VOC government to regulate the display of pomp via gilded carriages etc. among its employees.[95]) Offering a hot drink (*wedang*) is described as the *adat* (another Arabic word) of all Javanese – and therefore, to judge from the attitude to Javanese *adat* displayed throughout the text,

New ways of seeing

something to be respected and never altered. The whole section on *kurmat* procedures is preoccupied with Javanese ideas of hierarchy (in age and in rank) for instance as it applies in the reception of guests, including the important point – perhaps a common pitfall for young *priyayi* – that messengers are entitled to the same marks of distinction as their masters would have received if present. The bad effect of a *faux pas* on this issue has already been seen from the Mangkunegaran diary account.[96]

The exemplary works which the author advises his young audience to read are again a synthesis: Canto III stanzas 3–4 advises reading (or to be exact singing/reciting) the *Nitipraja*, *Wulang Reh*, *Pranitisastra*, and Old Javanese *Ramayana*. The first and last are works from the Hindu-Javanese tradition. The *Wulang Reh* was written by Pakubuwana IV, the same Sunan whose political manoeuvres have been related in the first part of this chapter. Versions of the *Pranitisastra*, based on an Old-Javanese original (the *Nitisastra*) were written in 1798 by Yasadipura I and in 1808 by Yasadipura II himself.[97] In Canto V, the *Kisangsul Ambiya* [Lives of the Prophets: a Javanese version is attributed to Yasadipura [98]] and *Kitab Insan Kamil* [Book of the Perfect Man, i.e. a Life of Muhammad, of which there are numerous Javanese versions] are quoted as displaying the manifold ways in which the devil tempts mankind. In Canto VI, the examples of the Prophet (in eating little) and of Moses (in demonstrating the power of prayer) are coupled with an injunction to follow the Yudanagara: this is apparently a story centring on the characters Koja Jajahan and a king, but whose principal content is lessons on statecraft.[99] From the contexts in which it is cited in the *Sasana Sunu*, however, it would seem to have been used as a source of instruction on manners. Canto VII gives advice about sleeping towards the *kiblat*, and quotes the Kitab Insan Kamil which tells how Allah descends to earth in the last third of the night (from 1.30 to 3.00 a.m.), so that one should try to wake up at this time, apparently a widespread Muslim belief.

The commendation of restraint in food, drink, and sleeping, however, leads up to a eulogy of *tapa* (Canto VII verse 14), a Sanskrit borrowing in one sense but nevertheless perhaps the most enduringly Javanese of spiritual values. It reads:

> He who has great abilities, he who has supernatural power, and he who becomes a *priyayi*, all have their roots in *tapa*. Every great matter has its origins in *tapa*, which is followed by

403

happiness. Even if one is very able, and even if one becomes a *priyayi*, if this does not originate in *tapa* it is riches from the devil.

Even if the devil has the ability to confer supernatural power, the power one obtains from him lasts only a moment, and later one will be powerless against the wise and knowledgeable.

Tapa on its own can be translated as "penance" but is usually conceptualised in a compound as *tapa-brata*, penance through self-mortification and abstinence.[100] In Javanese works, *tapa* is frequently glossed as "death in life" (*mati ana sajroning ngurip*), and Canto I, stanza 10 introduces this concept, advising the young *priyayi* not to concern themselves about whether their life will be long or short: what should occupy their thoughts is to *live as if they were dead*. *Tapa* appears again in Canto XI (stanza 7f) in a hybrid with the Arabic *tobat*, repentance, in which the young *priyayi* are advised to prepare themselves for the fact that no-one remains in a high position forever and that they should meet this contingency with *tobat* and *tapa*, the most efficacious way to restore their rank.

Canto XI verses 17–19, dealing with the duties of a Mantri in the ruler's service, is particularly interesting for our understanding of Javanese civilisation at this period, as Yasadipura explicitly classifies the dual inheritance making up Java's religious tradition into a left and a right-hand branch. From the Left, a Mantri must know about Janaloka, Ngendraloka, and Guruloka, Sanskrit compounds meaning the Abode of Men, Abode of Indra, and Abode of [the god] Guru. The first being the place of humans, knowing about it means knowing the proper behaviour and activities of humans (*tatakramanipun, pakariyane ing manungsa*). Ngendraloka is where Batara Endra has his *kraton*, and knowing Ngendraloka means knowing the *tataning panĕmbahing dewa* (the proper arrangements for the veneration of the gods). The third, Guruloka, is the place of Batara Guru or Girinata, and knowing Guruloka means knowing the *sĕmbah mring Hyang Girinata* (the act of homage paid to Hyang Girinata). From the Right a Mantri must know about *sarengat, tarekat*, and *kakekat*, the three stages of enlightenment for a Muslim who takes the path of joining a mystic order (*tarekat*) in order to attain knowledge of the ultimate Reality (*kakekat* or *hakekat*, Arabic *ḥaqīqa*). So it seems that the parallel is that observance of the Islamic Law (*sarengat*) belongs to the province of humans, the path of the *tarekat* raises one to the world of the Gods,

New ways of seeing

and knowledge of ultimate Reality to that of the highest Godhead. [In the Javanese classificatory system, left is usually ranked higher than right: is Yasadipura making a point about the relative ranking of the Indic and Islamic heritages of the Javanese by assigning the Indic to the left-hand side?]

Canto XII, verses 22–32, counselling against an idolatrous deification or anthropomorphism of krisses, uses material from both the left- and right-hand traditions. The point made is that the power of krisses is only an external one (*wasiyat lair*) as is evident from the cases of Siyung Wanara of Pajajaran in the Babad story[101] and Aswatama and the magic weapon Cundamanik.[102] It is much better to have inner spiritual power (*wasiyat ati*), as in the case of Sunan Giri, the *wali* who when his state was attacked by the heathen forces of Majapait threw down the pen he was using, which thereupon changed into a kris that on its own put the Majapait army to flight.

Priyayi behaviour

The main concern of Yasadipura II in this work, to judge by the proportions of the text devoted to the different subjects, is to form certain definite personal habits and attitudes in the young *priyayi* he addresses. Much of the time he is dealing with prohibitions. Canto II deals with the concept of *ĕndĕm*, "intoxication". There are numerous different sorts of *ĕndĕm*, as follows. Firstly, strong drink is to be avoided because of its effect on behaviour, making the drinker over-confident and ill-mannered, turning his attention from God and his religion – and also because it means one destroys one's own body. Also reprehensible is excess preoccupation with fine clothes, thinking oneself as exquisite as Arjuna or Panji, a common fault with young people who do not realise that true beauty is of the heart; and also intoxication with pleasure and sleeping. Next comes intoxication by *hawa nafsu* (passion) which drives one to unreasonable anger with others for the slightest offence; and intoxication through desiring something beyond all reason. [The baneful effects of *hawa nafsu* are foregrounded in one of the works of the famous Malay intellectual Raja Ali Haji of Riau (c. 1809–c. 1870), which particularly castigates the qualities of contentiousness, arrogance, stubbornness, and the desire for self-aggrandisement.[103] It is interesting that whereas the Arabic word *nafsu* means something equivalent to "soul",[104] in Java its derivatives *nafsu* and in common

405

speech *něsu* have come to mean passion of an undesirable and baneful character, and in particular the passion of anger – yet another example of the dangers inherent in focussing on the Arabic word rather than on the Javanese concept that it expresses.]

In the same Canto, stanza 24 speaks out against opium: it is not the man that consumes opium, but opium that consumes the man (*dudu wong kang mangan apyun, apyun kang mangan janma*). It is an offence against the Shariah; however, it is permitted, according to the Kitab Sarahbayan,[105] to use a little opium in a fever medicine. Stanza 27 deals with gambling, also forbidden by the law, and together with opium-smoking the most usual reason that people take to crime. Stanza 28 advises against putting too much credence in the 30–*wuku* system,[106] which is used to predict the future life of a new-born baby in detail, since believing in what is predicted causes our perceptions to alter and we really seem to perceive that it has come about. On the other hand, the sciences of mysticism,[107] astronomy (*falak*) and astronomy (*nujum*) come from Arabia and the Prophet. Stanza 33 says that, according to a prohibition of the ancestors, the gamelan should not be used at the *mamantu* (wedding) ceremony, and in fact the gamelan is prohibited by our religion. However, it is allowed (according to established custom) at the *tětakan* or *khitanan* (circumcision) and at the *tingkěban* (7–month ritual for pregnant women) ceremonies and in fact, though rather ostentatious, is in common use, especially among the king's courtiers. If you are in this position, when the gamelan begins to play you should say a prayer to God and to the ancestors who have made the prohibition, asking their forgiveness and permission to listen to the gamelan; and six days or a week beforehand you should make an offering in a secluded spot asking for a sign that your request is granted.

Related to the concept of *ěnděm*, is that of *pakarěman*, which might perhaps be translated as "infatuation" or "attachment". These include love of wealth (*karěm dunya*), whose baneful consequences are illustrated in the story of the *kaum desa* (village orthoprax Muslim) Ki Nurngali,[108] a friendless man who tried to "dam up" his wealth, against the advice of the Panitisastra, and ended up by being killed for it. The fact that the person chosen to illustrate the dangers of not allowing wealth to flow freely is a village Muslim official is consonant with the frequent depiction in Javanese texts of *santri* as stingy.[109] The *Wicara kěras* also condemns love of money, which is only permissible if it is used to finance the state or the

New ways of seeing

army or given to the poor and deserving – here again regarding money as something that should not be "dammed up".

Canto V adds *sabeng wanadri* or *samodra* (making trips to the forest or sea), and *kasektin* (supernatural power) to the list of undesirable attachments As well as these numerous prohibitions, the text puts great emphasis on correctness in all areas of deportment – as for example in the following areas:

Clothing. This is dealt with in Canto III stanzas 6–25. Yasadipura begins by listing those batik patterns that should not be worn. This remains until the present day a major decision for a Javanese when dressing for a social occasion, and all sorts of calculations factoring in the social status of all those present, the nature of the occasion, etc. have to be considered.[110] Yasadipura gives the following general guidelines: batik of the style *tambal sukaduka* should not be worn, whereas *tambal kanoman* and *tambal miring* are quite acceptable.[111] You should not wear either a *kain* or a *sabuk* (cummerbund) of *lurik* of the *tuluh sela* pattern.[112] Acceptable colours in batik are green, yellow, violet (*wungu*) pinkish-red (*dadu*) and white, but blue-black (*wulung*) should not be worn (this is followed by a parenthetical comment that if your body is weak, do not keep a black horse). If you are strong, you may wear a *sabuk* of *cinḍe kěkělingan*,[113] but do not wear the pattern *solok; limar* and *gěḍog* you may wear as you wish.[114] And you must not dare to wear any of the patterns forbidden to all but royalty (*laranganing ratu*).[115] Do not wear batik of modern styles such as Baron Sakender or one that has pictures of people, which is semi-*haram,* or of living things: after all there is no lack of batik of *lung-lungan, cěplokan*, and *gogoḍongan* patterns.[116] If you are not wearing a *kělambi* (jacket), do not knot a handkerchief around your neck and keep it on when you pray – this is particularly forbidden. Your clothing must be appropriate to the occasion.

The rest of this section is devoted to a long and subtle discourse on the concept of *běsus*, a word which is which is difficult to translate but perhaps corresponds most closely to the English "smart". It is not a virtue, nor really a vice, being permissible up to a certain point. Those who carry it to excess will come to poverty, their livelihood (*rijěki*) will diminish as Mother Providence (*Mbok Rijěki*) will be alarmed at the sight of them. The degree of smartness should be adjusted to the occasion, with special outings requiring differentiation from everyday life: the *jingkěngan* (head-cloth) should be worn with *pĕnyon* and *monḍolan*.[117] For the sages smartness is only a "cover": they do not allow it to penetrate to the heart. If you do allow it to become internalised (*kang bĕsus anrus ing batin*, stanza 23) you will shut the door to good fortune and open the door to loss, distance yourself from prosperity and piety, draw close to all sorts of evil and sin, become greedy and self-seeking instead of grateful, hard and impatient instead of patient. The *ulama* dress themselves as if they were dressing a corpse.

Therefore, you should practice moderation in the quality of *bĕsus*.

Friendship. Canto V gives advice against making friends with those who are *boḍo* (brainless) or *tanpa budi* (ill-bred) or *tan rahayu* (malevolent, evil) or *tan bisa ing sastra* (illiterate) or *pasĕk* (heretics) or *drĕngki* (envious, ill-wishing) as well as positive recommendations about making friends with those who are *bĕrbudi* (well-bred), *wicaksana* (wise), *sujanma kang gĕḍe ngamalira / ngamal saleh* (good people who are pious and full of good works). On the other hand, as a friend one has a duty not to reveal other people's secrets, and to be steadfast (*mantĕp*) in friendship.

Eating. Canto VI gives detailed instructions for the etiquette to be followed here. Muhammad only ate once a day, at mid-day, and always said *bismillah* before and *alhamdulilah* after eating. In addition, one must follow the Yudanagara,[118] being polite and neat, sitting in the proper fashion, not with the feet out or the knees up, and not talking while eating. One should offer food politely to guests, and not urge them to talk; nor should one ever finish eating before they do. As a guest you must similarly be well-behaved and not criticise what you are offered either out loud or internally. This is reinforced by the story of Nabi Musa who while on a journey with the *ummat* prayed for food from heaven on condition that no-one should criticise it; when some did presume to say that there was one defect, in that there were plenty of side-dish but no fresh vegetables, it all disappeared into the heavens again. When your wife serves you food at home, do not wolf it down or criticise it if it is not to your taste – a few tactful words afterwards about what you like are enough. Don't regard cooking as a trivial matter – it is our link to life. Do not be gluttonous, or you will die young. Be moderate in everything. Carrying out *tapa* for the whole of your life brings many benefits. Do not get into the habit of having an early morning meal, this will darken your heart and dull your wits. If you

New ways of seeing

eat until you are sated, you will be irritable and sleepy, your sharpness of mind will be dulled. Eating to satiety is only appropriate for those who do heavy work such as lifting and ploughing – such people are described as *bangsa badan* (physical people) – not for *priyayi* who have to use their minds and hearts: they are the *bangsa ati* (spiritual people) (stanzas 28–9).

Sleeping, going out, staying in. Canto VII gives detailed prescriptions on these matters, laying down the proportion of the day it is right to spend sleeping (8 hours in total) and explaining how Allah descends in the last third of the night spanning 1.30 to 3.00 a.m., a Muslim belief, at which time one should, if possible, wake up. Earnest prayers (*salat kajat*) at *lingsir wěngi*[119] of *malěm Jumungah* [the eve of Friday] will be granted. Yasadipura points out the bad effects of sleeping when the sun is up, or taking too long an afternoon sleep except occasionally when one is very tired. The direction in which one should sleep is towards the west, the *kiblat*, like a dead man, and sleeping towards another direction has a baneful effect on one's livelihood, friendship, or health.

Two things may be noted here: the characteristic Javanese prizing of restraint and self-denial in all things, whether food, drink, or sleep, leading into the eulogy of the power of *tapa* quoted above; and secondly the rather drastic consequences that are said to follow from what appear to us to be only minor breaches of deportment. In the section on going out, for instance, the young *priyayi* are advised to say *bismillah* when they walk, and to bow their heads slightly so as to avoid glancing around: a man who glances around while walking will have his heart shredded to pieces; and when at home they should not stand arms akimbo in the doorway, for this will drive away good fortune. However, the strategy of frightening the young into conformity with reigning morals and manners seems to be practised at one time or another in most societies.

Receiving guests, Canto VIII: Standards of reception required for everyday acquaintances and for guests from afar differ: the former may be idle callers who disturb one's official work, the latter must be well received, even if you have to pawn your ceremonial lance to provide refreshments, for this is the *adat* of all Javanese. If you receive a visitor who is of superior rank, you must receive him with due ceremony and sit before him in the proper fashion, with bowed head and hands resting in your lap, speaking softly, and taking care not to appear above yourself. The old must be well received, but those who are old and wise must receive superior distinction. If a *fakir* comes and asks something from you, give it without delay if you have it – in this way you will not cut off God's mercy, for our livelihood has its origins with God. Envoys must be shown the same distinction and honour as their masters when they visit you. If you have to give a message to an envoy, make it as short as possible so that no confusion will arise.

Speech, Canto IX: As noted above, this section begins with an injunction to avoid *tĕkabur/kibir* (overweening conceit) *ujub* (the desire to impress), *riya* (the desire for praise and prominence), *sumungah* (boastfulness), *duraka* (speaking ill of others) and *dora* (lying). By speaking ill of others you add their sins to your own; by lying you darken your heart: it is as if your house was in darkness and you had no lamps to light it and guard your possessions. In addition, lying will make your rank (*darajat*) decline and you will sink to the most lowly station. Don't criticise people, don't speak without a reason, don't tell jokes or pointless or irreligious stories, or speak for the sake of speaking, don't be given to joking (*sĕsĕmbranan*) which will destroy the gracious and winning modesty and reserve (*kajatmikan*) you should have and also wipe out your store of *tapa brata*, causing a decline in your rank. Good-Fortune (*Ki Bĕgja*) will desert you and Ill-Luck (*Ki Cilaka*) be with you day and night.

Since speech is an activity involving other people of different kinds and conditions, Yasadipura goes on to give the young *priyayi* guidelines they should observe. When conversing in a large gathering do not be the first to speak and do not hasten to sum up if a consensus has been reached: this should be left to the most senior person. You must observe the Yudanagara.[120] Even when speaking with those whose rank is higher than yours, you must weigh their utterances so as to decide whether they come from the three evils (*hawa nĕpsu kalawan ĕblis*), from the angels or from Adam: what is inspired by the first three must be rejected, that which comes from the last two is equally good. Lastly, he gives advice on how to respond if your Lord (*gusti*) asks your opinion: answer according to your knowledge, and give examples. If your Lord should be of an opinion which will lead to his shame, it is your duty to prevent this happening: to be an accomplice in reprehensible

New ways of seeing

deeds is not true service, and those who think that it is do not truly love their Lord but are simply desirous of praise and vainglorious (*yen gustinira arsa / pikir ingkang nĕmpuh / sanadyan tumibeng nista / tumurunga milya anut anglabuhi / aywa mĕngĕng ing cipta / yeku dudu pasuwitan kaki / pan sayĕktining wong asuwita / ingkang mangkana pikire / pikir suwitan iku / wĕtune tan ngeman ing gusti / amung mburu aleman / anjurung kumlungkung).*

Perspectives on society

It should be said to begin with that the Sasana Sunu is *not* about "society" but about the moral formation of the elite: in this respect it resembles the old-fashioned generalist education of the English élite. Canto X, however, in laying down the proper behaviour for young *priyayi* as they receive appointments, does provide some insights on how society was perceived to be organised, and, to a lesser extent, on how it really operated. It begins by advising the young men not to complain if they are appointed to a low post such as a village *bĕkĕl*. [Court-based appanage holders left the administration of the populations assigned to them in the hands of local tax-collectors called *bĕkĕl* who gathered the land-rent (*pajĕg*) and some other taxes, of which they received a percentage. For the most part they were from the upper echelon of village society and on the lowest rung of the hierarchy of officials under the appanage system[121]] If that is their lot, they must master the requirements of the job, set out under the headings *saguna, satata*, and *satau. Saguna* means knowing all about the farmer's equipment: harrow, plough, sickle, crowbar, different types of axes and hoes, adzes and choppers, as well as about livestock. [This passage exhibits a new trend to a more empirical and pragmatic attitude to management, though far less than is exhibited in Vietnamese works of comparable period.[122]] Then they must work diligently in the fields, and not relax their efforts; when they have a good harvest they must surrender the correct amount to their superior as tax when it is due. If their land is taken away from them they must not resist and fight. [Carey notes that it was often the case that on the replacement of the appanage holder in the royal capital, an all too frequent occurrence, a new *bĕkĕl* would be appointed and it often happened that the current *bĕkĕl* would abscond with the cash advances from the cultivators or refuse point blank to make way for the new appointee. This was the most frequent cause of the numerous "village wars" (*prang desa*) which plagued the countryside of south-central Java at this time and which one Dutch traveller referred to as being almost a daily occurence in the years immediately preceding the Java war.[123] Yasadipura says that if the young men behave in this way they will be despised and cut off from the *priyayi* class. *Satata* means knowing the ways of the farmers, setting up a mosque close to water and providing the *santri* with rice-fields, and not taking any part of the *zakat* and *fitrah*.[124] [Participation by *priyayi* in the collection and particularly in determining the distribution of these religious contributions opened opportunities for misappropriation, and there were occasions when members of the *santri* community complained that officials had acted improperly in this way.[125]] They should also create a *kabayan*[126] who is strong and of good character.[127] They should build a fence around the village and be hospitable to visitors. *Satau* means maintaining the *adat* of the villages of the area[128] – and not setting up your own *adat*. They should not allow bad people to gather in their area; and govern the common people (lit. little people, *wong cilik*) in such a way that they know what they are doing. If there is a thief among them, forgive him, but if he does not stop his evil-doing drive him away so that he does not contaminate others. Set up a mosque and see that everyone goes there on Fridays [note the assumption in this passage that the rural areas to which the *priyayi* would be posted could be assumed not to have mosques]: if the population is strong in *ibadah* (observance of the rules of Islam) there will be few who fall into evils such as gambling and opium-smoking. Remember that poverty [i.e. from gambling and opium-smoking?] is the root of crime.

Yasadipura next lays down the right way to serve at the capital (*nagari*) for those who are appointed there. You must be diligent (*tabĕri*, a word that occurs frequently in this type of discussion). If you have not yet been granted rice-fields [as appanage lands], do not reveal your desire for them and reconcile yourself to living in the *pasewanan*.[129] Be humble in your dealings with your fellow *priyayi*, and be very attentive to the instructions of your superiors, outwardly and inwardly. Remember that your Lord (*gusti*) is the representative of God, and that he will be just to his subordinates (as noted above, the gloss given for "just" is forgiving, long-suffering, benevolent). Towards one's fellows in service one should not be too quick to criticise, and one should sincerely commiserate with them when they incur their master's anger: one day it may be

New ways of seeing

your turn, and your companions in service are like your brothers [in such a situation].

Yasadipura then deals with the rank-order of those to whom one owes the deepest respect (in Javanese, those who are *sinĕmbah*). First is the ruler; second your parents; third your parents-in-law; fourth your *guru*; and fifth your older brothers. Mantri must pay this respect to Tumenggungs, and Tumenggungs in turn to those of the blood royal (*santana*). With this last, unelaborated statement Yasadipura brings us up against one of the central principles of Javanese society: the concept that descent, or to use the old-fashioned term blood, was of central importance in the formation of a man, and that royal blood conferred a social rank higher than any other. The ruler's close relatives, the *santana*, rank above those who have risen to high rank, that of Mantri and Tumenggung, in the service of the ruler and the state. He justifies this reverence by reference to the *dalil*[130] which commands us to revere Allah and His Messenger, and those who have government over us. The canto ends with the instruction that when they become *priyayi* they must put to use four *budi*: those of the *priyayi*, *santri*, *sudagar* (merchants) and farmers (*tani*). *Budi* is an untranslatable, much-used, word meaning, in this instance, the best normative conduct of the four groups named, who may perhaps be compared to the "estates" of French society of the *ancien regime*. The *budi* of the *priyayi* is to maintain the proprieties and good forms of social intercourse, not to behave in a common way, to dress appropriately, to be rather frugal in respect to food, to be careful and precise, to treat other people's opinions nicely, to be able to get people to work together, not to be afraid of suffering a personal loss, to be intelligent and civilized in action and thought. The *budi* of the *santri* is to be pure and holy, to multiply the works of Allah and give thanks to Him. The *budi* of the farmer is to work long and hard at all sorts of work, heavy and light. He is never envious or given to talking about other people's affairs, never presumptuous or arrogant. He is steadfast (*mantĕp*, another concept on which great value is placed) and in earnest and stout-hearted about his work, not given to time-wasting and shirking. Finally the farmer is *tĕmĕn*, which can be translated as "sincere" or "honest" but has the interesting twist of being used of inferiors vis-à-vis their superiors.[131] Thus the young *priyayi* whom Yasadipura addresses should imitate the humble farmer in being *tĕmĕn* in their work for the ruler: it is inconceivable that the ruler should be asked to display the same quality towards them.[132] The *budi* of the merchant is to be calculating, economical and careful and treat his undertakings with respect. So the special task of the *priyayi* therefore is to combine the special code of his own estate, the purity of the *santri*, the earnest application of the farmer, and the careful calculation of the merchant.

Where Canto X dealt with the responsibilities of the lowly *bĕkĕl desa*, Canto XI deals with those of high officials, Mantri and Bupati, and the highest of all, the Patih. It repeats some of the injunctions of Canto X concerning diligence and taking care of the *sawah* provided as appanage land. The account given of a Mantri's duties is surprising: it advises him to follow the established *adat* and responsibilities associated with this position, but in setting these out concentrates exclusively on religious expertise, categorised into two divisions, the Left (the Hindu) and the Right (the Islamic), as explained above. The text then deals with the heavy responsibilities of state which fall on Bupati, and their need for ceaseless vigilance and self-denial in cutting through impenetrable problems, difficulties, and disagreements. They must be skilled at creating cooperation, at carrying decisions into practice, and keep the flow of work moving along so that things do not fall into stagnation. Once again, the necessity of being steadfast (*mantĕp*) is underlined. Serving the king is not like being a rich merchant who can pursue his own wealth and nothing else. In dealing with the position of Patih, Yasadipura uses the very common trope of the *kris* (the ruler) and its sheath (the Patih): the sheath must follow the shape of the *kris*, or they cannot work together; while if the *kris* fits well into its sheath, the state will be safe from all evils and the sharpness of the *kris* will not be in evidence. As well as having this special relationship with the ruler, the Patih must be skilled in regulating all the high offices of the state and maintaining justice: if a Patih destroys a good division of responsibility, this will lead to disaster in carrying out the ruler's orders. Yasadipura says he will not prolong his discussion of what a Patih should be, as there are many examples from the old days to be followed.

This section utilises many of the literary conventions and tropes that are common in moral treatises dealing with kings and their ministers, such as the *kris*-sheath trope, and the *nisṭa-madya-utama* (low-middling-outstanding) classification for evaluating men and their actions. Thus Seh Malayu, who began life as a robber but repented and became Sunan Bonang's pupil, eventually himself becoming a *wali* with the title Sunan Kalijaga, is an example of someone who began as "low" but was able to rise out of this state. It is interesting that Sunan Bonang, when Seh Malayu tried to rob him, saw that the evil-doer before him was actually the descendant of a good family – *trah wong aběcik* – a typically Javanese explanation of what it is that gives someone the potential to rise out of a low life.

Cantos XII–XIII deal with the question of what causes a decline in one's rank, and the flight of one's *wahyu*, the last a very important concept. The first cause of this given is taking food from the mouths of the poor (the *wong cilik*), who have so little and whose life is so hard. If one follows *hawaning ati* (the passions of the heart) instead of *wajib* (duty), this will certainly have a bad effect on your *wahyu*. Building an excessively large and fine house is another thing that can only cause a decline in your fortunes. Stories from both the Left (*pangiwa*) and the Right (*panĕngĕn*) traditions prove this: the strong and wealthy *danawa* [demons of the Mahābhārata stories depicted in *wayang*] and the Arabian kings who constructed palaces rivalling heaven all came to bad ends. If you do your work well you will get real praise from your Lord, whereas even if you have a fine house, if your work is behind-hand and full of mistakes you will certainly arouse his anger. Yasadipura lists the signs that a man's *wahyu* is about to leave him: if he is repeatedly warned not to do something, but nevertheless goes ahead and does it, or if he wrongs or mistreats someone despite attempts to restrain him. Here *wahyu* is described as being like the soul, very pure and, if one could see it, like a clear light, shining like the moon. "Small *wahyu*" (*wahyu alit*) is like a clear star. If it is asked to be party to a bad deed, it becomes disturbed and angry, and then appears dull and dirty. It will certainly flee elsewhere, since there is no lack of places for it to perch. It will seek a heart that is pure and wise, fortunate and sage, for there it will be cared for. To keep your *wahyu* is difficult, but becomes easier with practice. You must be watchful and mindful, remembering God and his commands, doing good in the world. You must reduce your eating and sleeping, in order to obtain rank. Be familiar with Javanese and Arabic literature. Know the Islamic Law, and the established *adat* and customs. Be steadfast without anxiety. Take direction from a teacher. Interestingly, stanzas 17–21 say that both the Left and the Right, i.e. the Hinduized and the Islamic traditions, can provide a good path for one: there is no evidence that Yasadipura felt that the Islamic tradition had actually superseded the Hinduized one, however valid this may have been in the past. Associate with those who may not be clever but are charitable to the poor and needy (*pěkir miskin*). Good deeds are a part of a shining *wahyu*, the sign of God's love.

This is the most extensive definition of the central concept of *wahyu* and those who have it provided by Yasadipura.[133] Kings are the principal vehicles of *wahyu* in Javanese literature. In a Javanese Babad dealing with the Chinese War that began in 1740, a story is told of how when Mangkunegara I was born the reigning kings's *wahyu* moved from him to Mangkunegara's mother, so that the baby was born with a special glow, and many interpreted this to mean that he would become a great leader in war.[134] This understanding of *wahyu* as a physical manifestation of light (a star, a ball of light) is also found as we have seen in the *Sasana Sunu*. Although the word is from the Arabic *wahyu* and means "revelation" it has become naturalised in Java to such an extent that there is a popular *wayang lakon* centring on the struggle between the Pandawas and Korawas for the *wahyu*, which underlines its association with legitimation and the right to power already suggested by the story about the birth of Mangkunegara I. As the concept is presented in Yadadipura's *Sasana Sunu*, it appears not as an exclusive attribute of prophets or the ruler but as a quality which all members of the élite can aspire to possess, and which has a sort of Indic, *karma*-like quality in that it is increased or decreased by good or bad deeds. In other words, the Javanese governing class has appropriated (not to say pirated) and redefined a term which in the rest of the Muslim world is identified with the Prophets (*nabi*) and above all with Muhammad and the revelations made to him by God and recorded in the Koran. They were not content to claim the lesser form of illumination (*ilham*) possessed by the *wali* (saints, friends of God), but put themselves into the category of the Prophets, so much nearer to God.[135]

The lessons of history again

In this largely a-historical treatment, the last ten stanzas of Canto XIII again introduce a historical perspective. This Canto describes the Kalisangara, the age of evil omens in which the author and his audience live, as worse than the Kali Yuga,[136] the last and most degenerate of the four Hindu cosmic eras. Interestingly, Yasadipura gives one mythological and two historical examples of the evils of the Kalisangara. The mythological one is the story of Aswatama

New ways of seeing

from the Mahābhārata; the historical ones are the Chinese War that began in 1740 in Batavia with the Chinese revolt against persecution and subsequently spread to the court of Mataram; and the revolt of Trunajaya. [Trunajaya's rebellion from the mid 1670s was the first serious threat to the kingdom of Mataram]. He creates a sense of impending disaster for the (un-named) Kingdom in his treatment of the Chinese War (stanzas 31–2), saying:

> My sons, be careful if there is a disturbance in another realm (*něgěri*)! As an example from the past, the beginning of the Chinese War [in 1740] was in Jakarta, whence it gradually spread eastwards, and then gave rise to an upheaval in the kingdom of Kartasura. Finally the whole kingdom was torn to pieces because we[137] were disunited. The leaders were at odds with one another, and so the common people were scattered without coming to rest. It has now become the custom of Javanese soldiers to be like a heap of rice straw, or a dyke of rice-straw, under attack by a large swift body of water. First it is carried away piece by piece and then [returning to the army] the whole of it is swept away without a backward glance at their Lord, like a broom that has lost its binding.

– echoing the theme of Javanese military incompetence that we have already seen in NBS 89 (see above, p. 387–8). In this, historical, rather than cosmic, contingency, there is great necessity for prayer, fasting, and sleepless vigilance, and for all the servants of the king to loyally carry out his orders and do their best to save the realm which has provided them shelter. They should not desert king and kingdom along with the evil opportunists who are finding opportunities for theft.

The second event referred to is an earlier one, what Yasadipura calls a disturbance within a single realm, Mataram.[138] As a result of quarrels among those who thought only of their own interests and forgot they were of common birth, the realm was split apart and the common people scattered, leading to the disaster of Trunajaya. In describing these two wars Yasadipura seems especially concerned to impress on his young audience the fate of the common people when the élite lose sight of their responsibilities in the pursuit of naked self-interest, another manifestation of his generations loss of virtue, a word which here encompasses not only the English "virtue" but also the Latin *virtus*.

Intellectual Transformations

* * *

The *Sasana Sunu* is a speaking testimony, of a very different kind to Cornets de Groot's account of Gresik, to the enormous density and complexity of Javanese socialisation. Cornets de Groot's account does not go beyond the "exterior" socialisation common to all Javanese over great expanses of space and time; the *Sasana Sunu* reveals the interior socialisation of the élite, the ruling virtues and beliefs which were meant to guide them and which they might or might not follow. This complex world of values, norms, and aesthetic preferences has so far been an almost entirely closed world to non-Javanese, represented only in schematic and over-simplified forms. In Java it is said of an unsocialised child that he or she is *durung jawa*, not yet Javanese, for a Javanese is a creation not of nature but of society, of an enormous investment of time and effort. Javaneseness implies a civilization, not just a set of genes. It must I think be clear that much of what Yasadipura has written here could have equally well been written (in fact, has many times been written) by moralists in the Judaeo-Christian tradition, or by Confucians: do not lie, take care what friends you make, don't take drugs, don't cheat on your taxes, don't take food out of the mouths of the poor, and so on. As for the more "particular", the more peculiarly Javanese, the *Sasana Sunu*, like the account of the Gresik pantheon, shows that three worlds, the Javanese, the Indic, and the Islamic, coexisted in Java, not vestigially but amply and richly in the consciousness of folk and élite. Yet the Indic and Islamic worlds are more dominant in the vocabulary and idiom than in the actual underlying concepts: in fact, the borrowed foreign vocabulary has very often been drastically bent to confer radically different ideas than those for which it was devised. Those whose attention is fixed on the word rather than the concept are doomed to form a quite erroneous impression of the values inherent in Javanese civilisation.

Three strongly Javanese ideals seem to stand out in the *Sasana Sunu*: a comprehensive practice of penance (*tapa*), the cultivation of death-in-life; an all-pervasive hierarchy marked in every detail of speech, dress, and deportment; and the supreme spiritual value of serving the king, the Lord. As far as this last is concerned, in Canto IV stanzas 35–9 Yasadipura says that carrying out your allotted tasks in the service of the King can be compared to prayer (performance of the five daily *salat*): your Lord is the true Kalifah – a sentiment that puts serving the ruler on a par with serving God.

New ways of seeing

This is far indeed from that attitude to rulers frequently found in Islam that the pious man should not associate with courts or serve kings, who are in mortal peril of their souls.[139] In such ideals, and in the distinctive pattern of moral and intellectual concepts through which the élite learned to apprehend their world, just as much as in the pattern of daily life and the life cycle described in the ethnographic material of Cornets de Groot, it was the Javanese world, that, velvet glove and iron hand, dominated the Indic and Islamic. The self-confidence on which this assured and subtle control depended was, however, certainly beginning to falter, as both the historical section in Canto XIII and the *Wicara Kĕras* reveal.

Nevertheless, despite the very significant innovations in Yasadipura's world-view that the historical challenges he clearly saw had precipitated, his prescription for dealing with these challenges remains a conservative one. He repeatedly recommends the imitation of examplary figures from the past and advises that Java's *adat* should be maintained, not changed, and that the young *priyayi* should not invent their own *adat*. (He is, however, aware that certain important parts of Javanese *adat*, such as the playing of the gamelan at some of the core ceremonies of Javanese life, are actually contrary to Islam.[140])

Yasadipura is also conservative in his strong support for the king-centric polity, where subjects seek salvation by serving (*ngawula*) their king, which is for them a religious observance. By contrast, in an Islamic work on kingship, the *Taj us-Salatin* – the Javanese version of which is attributed to Yasadipura I and which would therefore have been well known to Yasadipura II[141] – the king is depicted as *the servant of his subjects*, personally responsible on the day of judgment for any hardship or oppression his subjects suffer. If he does not serve them well, the pains of hell are his reward. In this text the examplary stories of good kings portray them as spending their nights going around their kingdom disguised in common clothes, finding out the sufferings of the least in the kingdom and carrying on their own shoulders sacks of food for the unfortunate.[142]

Thus Javanese kings retained their old position and acquired from Islam both confirmation of their martial role (as we have seen in the Mangkunegaran diary and in Yasadipura's identification of Islam with the martial virtues) and a new lustre in the shape of the light of prophecy (*wahyu*), by a rather audacious act of appropriation.

Intellectual Transformations

These works of Yasadipura II are still firmly set in the old world of Kingship and service by an élite with a special moral claim to their position of moral guardianship of the voiceless "little people", the world of *tapa*, *ngawula*, and *wahyu*. There is as yet no concept for society (*masyarakat*), though it may be argued that the idea is present in the *Sasana Sunu* in advance of the actual term. Nor do terms relating to new ideals of government by consultation (*musyawarah*) and consensus (*mupakat*) find a place in Yasadipura's analysis. Certainly, there is no sign of the concept of rights (*hak*) or of popular sovereignty (*kedaulatan rakyat*). Somewhere between the time of Yasadipura II and the present, Islam has helped to bring about a revolution in Indonesian social and political thought.

Yet, the achievements of this period are far from negligible. The materials discussed here have revealed an innovative spirit in the Javanese intellectual world, opening new topics: the relative position of the Javanese in relationship to other races; the nature of the lessons to be learnt from recent history and the moral renewal that was now required; the necessity of loyalty to the *bangsa*, now a focus of loyalty, formerly owed exclusively to the King; and what we would call "social engineering". Though this is only a beginning, it is a remarkable one in view of the extreme weight of the old intellectual tradition, which contained no place for this type of critical analysis of the present. Java's unwilled absorbtion into the world-system had given rise to a major Javanese re-thinking of their place in the world. This re-thinking broke through the old Platonic format of universal ideals for king, ministers, and servants to allow the emergence of a new view of a Hegelian world made up of differentiated and competing peoples caught in historical time and place.

NOTES

1 Boomgaard, *Children*, Ch.8.
2 John Splinter Stavorinus, Esq., trans. Samuel Hull Wilcocke, *Voyages to the East-Indies*, vol. 1 (*A Voyage to the Cape of Good Hope, Batavia, Bantam, and Bengal, with Observations on Those Parts, &c. in the years 1768–1771*), London (G.G. and J. Robinson) 1798, pp. 221–47.
3 Presumably the Badui of West Java.
4 Stavorinus p. 313.
5 Stavorinus pp. 365–6.
6 Stavorinus pp. 369–70
7 Stavorinus p. 144.

New ways of seeing

8 See further Ann Kumar, "Literary Approaches to Slavery and the Indies Enlightenment: van Hogendorp's Kraspoekol", *Indonesia* 43 (April 1987) pp. 49–52
9 E. Selberg, *Reis naar Java en bezoek op het eiland Madura*, n.d. n.p.
10 Selberg p. 83,
11 Selberg p. 104, pp. 85–6.
12 The best known literary treatment of this theme is Couperus' novel *De stille kracht* (the silent power).
13 Ong-Tae-Hae, *The Chinaman Abroad; An Account of the Malayan Archipelago, particularly of Java*, London, trans. W.H. Medhurst, 1850.
14 Ong, p. 20.
15 Old romanization Cheng Ho.
16 Ong, pp. 2–3.
17 The latter not very accurately, e.g. he writes that the other native chiefs all call themselves Sultan, and invariably acknowledge the Susuhunan as their liege lord, whereas Sultan is of course the title of the rulers of Yogyakarta, formal equals and actual rivals of the Susuhunans of Surakarta.
18 Ong, pp. 28–9.
19 Presumably our old friend the Delegate for Native Affairs again.
20 Ong, pp. 9–10.
21 I have omitted his descriptions of Semarang and Pekalongan.
22 Ong, pp. 15–19 and p. 32, which partly repeats what has been said on the previous pages but adds that the Javanese year consists of 12 months, reckoned from the appearance of the new moon, and that different places have different dialects and Javanese writing "resembles crawling worms".
23 This was indeed the case at this period. On the impediments (labour availability, unpredictability of the rains of the west monsoon to irrigate the second crop, and impossibility of growing two crops in less than 14–15 months with the inputs then available, see *Reflections by Several People*, answer to Qn.3 in first set of questions, ms. pp. 20–21).
24 Ong, p. 5 and pp. 28–30.
25 elsewhere (p. 3): long.
26 Ong, p. 30.
27 Medhurst's note: i.e. they hide their vices from themselves thinking they are also concealing them from others, with reference to a Chinese story about a man who stopped his ears while stealing a bell thinking that others would also be deaf to the sound by this action.
28 Medhurst's note: benevolence, righteousness, propriety, wisdom and truth.
29 Ong, p. 28, p. 30.
30 See his account of ducatoons, rupees, duits, Spanish silver dollars and other coins on p. 67.
31 Ong, pp. 30–1.
32 p. 37.
33 And said to be called "black demons" by the Chinese.
34 Ong, p. 68.
35 Ong, p. 60.

Intellectual Transformations

36 Ong, p. 33.
37 Ong, p. 33.
38 See Jean Gelman Taylor, *The Social World of Batavia: European and Eurasian in Dutch Asia*, Madison, Wis: University of Wisconsin Press, 1983.
39 Carl A. Trocki, *Prince of Pirates: The Temenggongs and the Development of Johor and Singapore 1784–1885*, Institute of Southeast Asian Studies/Singapore University Press, 1979.
40 See Buckley, *Anecdotal History of Old Times in Singapore*, p. 229.
41 NBS 89 = Mal 5057 / Cod.Or. 10.733 of the Leiden University Library collection. The language of this work was extremely difficult, not only for the author but even for someone with the encyclopaedic knowledge of Dr. Supomo Suryohudoyo, who provided generous assistance. What follows is therefore the best available interpretation, with some parts still not absolutely clear.
42 "Subordinates" is a translation of Javanese *wadya*, which means both soldiers and subjects of the king, a reflection of the military character of the Javanese state also seen in the use of military titles like Tumenggung for high officials.
43 Outstanding king = *ratu utama*. The three-fold Sanskrit classification *niṣṭa, madya, utama*, despicable, middling, and outstanding, is very frequently used in Javanese literature. It is found at least as early as the Nitisastra: see R. Ng. Dr. Poerbatjaraka, *Nītiçastra: Oud-Javaansche tekst met vertaling*, Bandung, A.C. Nix, 1933

It is also found in the Ślokantara (see *Ślokantara: an Old Javanese Didactic Text*, critically edited and annotated by Sharada Rani. [New Delhi] International Academy of Indian Culture, 1957.), p. 29, where verse 2 reads "the best money is that one earns oneself with hard work; middling is money received from one's father; despicable is money from one's mother, and most of all from one's wife". It is very likely found elsewhere in Old Javanese works.
44 *Kidung* are long poetic works written in indigenous Javanese (*těngahan*) metres, as opposed to those written in Indic metres, which are called *kakawin*. An English translation of a Panji *kidung* can be found in S.O. Robson ed. and trans., *Wangbang Wideya: A Javanese Panji Romance*, Bibliotheca Indonesica no. 6, KITLV, The Hague, Nijhoff, 1971.
45 Y.B. Mangunwijaya, trans. Thomas M. Hunter, *The Weaverbirds*, Lontar Jakarta 1991: see pp. 26–32, and 297f., where a number of different birds are characterised; p. 34, where Teto, the hero, is likened to a hawk though later to the weaverbird (*burung manyar*, which is the bird of a *wuku* signifying someone who sets out to do great things), described in the novel as a bird where the male builds a very elaborate nest and destroys it if it is not chosen by a female. See also pp. 285–6, where Atik the heroine likened to a fantail.
46 Pigeaud mentions a number of birds, storks and herons, that have a connection with the supernatural in Java and says this is particularly so with the *kuntul*: see Th. Pigeaud, "Alexander, Sakèndèr en Sénapati", *Djawa* 7, 1927, pp. 321–361 (p. 352).
47 i.e. Daendels.
48 There was of course a variety of British military attire at this as at other

New ways of seeing

periods, but the short tight jacket and cylindrical hat were common: see Lieut.-colonel John Luard, *A History of the Dress of the British Soldier, from the Earliest Period to the Present Time*, London, William Clowes and Sons, 1852, pp. 101 ff and Plates XXXII-IV. French military dress with the somewhat longer jackets and wide hats is seen in Plate XXXV.

49 An assumption implicit in the very language, where one says of a child who has not yet acquired manners and morals that he is *durung Jawa*, not yet Javanese.
50 That is to say, of course, the earliest that I know of. There may well be an earlier example from the vast unexplored corpus of Javanese literature.
51 William R. Roff, *The Origins of Malay Nationalism*, Yale University Press, New Haven and London, 1967, p. 161.
52 See C.F. Winter, *Javaansche Zamenspraken*, 5th printing, vol. 1, E.J. Brill, Leiden, 1911, p. 353.
53 On Yasadipura I, see S. Soebardi, *The Book of Cabolek: A Critical Edition with Introduction, Translation and Notes; A Contribution to the Study of the Javanese Mystical Tradition*, Bibliotheca Indonesica 10, The Hague, Nijhoff, 1975, p. 16ff.
54 Oxford University Press, Historical Writings on the Peoples of Asia series, p. 2.
55 The *Wicara Kĕras* has been published in various versions, e.g. *Sĕrat Wicara Kĕras* [in Javanese script] Tan Khoen Swie, Kediri, 1926. References here are to the Surakarta manuscript transcribed in A. Sarman, *Tinjauan Kitab Wicarakeras*, M.A. thesis, Gajah Mada University, Yogyakarta 1971.
56 The *yugas* are the four ages within the Mahāyuga. They are the Kṛta, Tretā, Dvāpara and Kali ages, of respectively 4,800, 3,600, 2,400 and 1,200 "years of the gods", each of which is equivalent to 360 human years. The Kaliyuga is said to have begun in 3102 B.C., believed to be the year of the Mahābhārata war.
57 Canto I verses 13–17.
58 *sayĕkti liniron bĕlis, duk ibune sacumbana lawan bapake nguni, setan kang amomori*.
59 Canto III, verse 22.
60 Canto III verses 21–5.
61 Thomas Stamford Raffles, *The History of Java*, vol. 1, London 1830, pp. 78–9.
62 Canto I verses 22–6.
63 Canto II verse 8. This is presumably a reference to the major rebel Pangeran Rangga (or Rongga), a descendant of the *wali* Sunan Kalijaga and therefore a figure to be reckoned with, who was active from the mid 1760s through to 1778. However, from Ricklefs' account it does not seem that he had any particular association with Madiun: see Ricklefs, *Mangkubumi*, p. 237f.
64 Canto VI verse 22. Suwanda, who seems to have been a very popular figure in court circles, is also immortalised as one of the famous "three examples", *Tripama*, in the poem of that name by Mangkunegara IV; the other two are Karna and Kumbakarna.
65 The title Sindureja was conferred on Patihs of Mataram (including, to confuse the picture further, Tirtawiguna, whom Yasadipura uses as a

Intellectual Transformations

bad example, when he was appointed Patih of the Left in 1743) and in both its successor states of Surakarta and Yogyakarta. At a guess the one meant by Yasadipura is Raden Adipati Sindureja (formerly Mangkuyuda of Kedu) who was appointed Patih of Surakarta around October 1782 and lasted less than two years before dying "apparently of natural causes": see Ricklefs, *Mangkubumi*, p. 266.

66 Canto VII, verses 20–3. Pringgalaya was appointed Patih of the Right on November 13 1743 at the same time as Tirtawiguna was appointed Patih of the Left. He died in 1755 but according to the Babad Gianti he was poisoned by his enemies rather than taking his own life: see Remmelink, *Emperor*, p. 202 and p. 252 and Ricklefs, *Mangkubumi*, p. 88.

67 See Ricklefs, *Mangkubumi*, p. 428.

68 Canto VII, verse 13ff.

69 Canto VIII, verse 1ff. These titles were hereditary in the ruling families of, respectively, Surabaya, Madura, and Pekalongan, which were three of the most politically weighty regions. The Cakraningrat who was a contemporary of Tirtawiguna (see following note) was Cakraningrat IV, and the Jayaningrat, Jayaningrat II: see Remmelink, passim. However, the Regents of Surabaya at the same period did not bear the title Jangrana.

70 Tirtawiguna was an influential courtier under Pakubuwana II. A man of low birth, he was successively secretary to the Sunan, *wĕdana gĕdong* and Patih of the left (there were at times two Patihs in the Javanese courts, representing the left-hand and right-hand branches of the symmetrically designed administrative corps). He was regarded by the Dutch as one of their more reliable allies at court and under the name Carik Bajra was also a Babad author. See Remmelink, passim.

71 This is also difficult to square with history: Cakraningrat IV was exiled in 1746, after he had risen in rebellion in protest against the VOC's parsimonious reward for his services in the Chinese War. His predecessor Cakraningrat III was stabbed to death aboard a ship in 1718 as a result of a misunderstanding (see further H.J. de Graaf, *Geschiedenis van Indonesië*, van Hoeve, 's-Gravenhage/Bandung, 1949, pp. 245–6 and 291–2).

72 I am not sure who is meant here: there were Regents of Batang who bore this title but they were of Chinese extraction, see Remmelink p. 266.

73 Canto VIII, verses 20–1. This is presumably Tumenggung Arungbinang, the powerful Wedana of Madiun who was as an old man banished by Pakubuwana III for extorting money from his subjects and involvement in court plots. After the intervention of a Dutch official who claimed that the accusations were not sufficiently proved he was allowed to return to court but died shortly afterwards: Ricklefs suggests this death like other timely deaths in Java "may not have been entirely above suspicion." (Ricklefs, *Mangkubumi*, p. 267).

74 Canto VIII, verse 23.

75 *Walat* is a personal spiritual force, acquired by exceptional men, that can strike down lesser mortals. It is especially associated with people of high rank, and one can be struck by *walat* for, for instance, towering above one's teacher, considered highly disrespectful of his superior

status. The *Wicara Kĕras* uses the example of a case where a certain aristocrat was killed by someone who was *not* affected by *walat* but actually raised in rank to underline a derogatory assessment of this particular aristocrat.

76 See Kumar, *Surapati*, p. 153. This story also illustrates the Javanese belief that a person's rank is obvious from his physical appearance, and that persons of royal or spiritually exalted status are distinguished by a radiance.
77 Presumably Pangeran Pugĕr, who after rebelling against Amangkurat III became Sunan in 1704 with the title Pakubuwana I.
78 *cucut*, which I have read as a variant of *cocot*, as in the expression *kakehan cocot*, to talk too much.
79 *Mangkubumi*, p. 123.
80 On the religious aspect of royal prowess on the battle-field see Robson, *Wangbang Wideya*, esp. p. 133.
81 From memory: I could not re-find this passage.
82 See published edition of the *Cĕnṭini*, Canto 215 stanza 10ff.: the *bangsa riah* are synonymous with the *ngam* (Arabic *'āmm*, ordinary, commonplace, general) or great majority of unlearned Muslims, followed by eight levels of *mukmin* (believers) in ascending order.
83 Mohammad Hatta, "Indonesia Free" in *Portrait of a Patriot, Selected Writings by Mohammad Hatta*, Mouton, The Hague, 1972, p. 210.
84 On developments at this time, see Mohammad Ali, "Historiographical Problems" in Soedjatmoko, Mohammad Ali, G.J. Resink and G.McT. Kahin. eds., *An Introduction to Indonesian Historiography*, Cornell Modern Indonesia Project, Ithaca, 1965, p. 1.
85 Verse numbers and references are based on the printed text, which is the edition published by the Departemen Pendidikan dan Kebudayaan for its Proyek Penerbitan Buku Sastra Indonesia dan Daerah, R.Ng. Yasadipura II, ed. Sudibjo Z.H., *Serat Sanasunu*, Jakarta 1980. Unfortunately, as is often the case in this otherwise valuable series of text editions, the manuscript on which it is based is not specified. The manuscript version transcribed by me is LOr 1806 from the Leiden University library Oriental collection: see Theodore G. Th. Pigeaud, *Literature of Java: Catalogue Raisonné of Javanese Manuscripts in the Library of the University of Leiden and Other Public Collections in the Netherlands*, vol. II, *Descriptive List of Javanese Manuscripts*, The Hague, Martinus Nijhoff, 1968, vol. II p. 85. This was clearly the same text as the printed one, though there were occasional differences in the number of stanzas per canto and variations in wording throughout. Of the two texts, the manuscript version had a greater number of corruptions.
86 Canto XII, stanza 41. The work was completed by 1819, the date of LOr 8564 (see Pigeaud, *Catalogue*, vol. II pp. 482–3).
87 Christiaan Hooykaas, *The Old Javanese Ramayana: an Exemplary Kakawin. as to Form and Content*, Akademie van Wetenschappen, Amsterdam, Afdeeling Letterkunde. Verhandelingen. Nieuwe reeks. Deel 65, no.1, Noord-Hollandsche Uitgevers Maatschappij, Amsterdam 1958.
88 Manuscript number CB (Collection Berg) 153 of the Leiden University Library: see Pigeaud, *Literature of Java*, vol. II, p. 786.

Intellectual Transformations

89 See R.M.Ng. Poerbatjaraka, *Kapustakan Djawi*, Djambatan, Jakarta 1957, p. 146.
90 See Canto XII stanza 37.
91 Both of whom were put to death for allegedly spreading heretical teachings. For a brief account of the theological and political rationale for al-Hallaj's condemnation and execution in 309 AH, see Duncan B. Macdonald, *Development of Muslim Theology, Jurisprudence and Constitutional Theory*, New York (Scribner) and London (Routledge), 1926, pp. 183–6. On the condemnation of Siti Jenar see Soebardi, *Book of Cabolek*, p. 35.
92 Muslim cannon law divides actions into five classes, i.e. obligatory, recommended, permitted/indifferent, disapproved, and forbidden. The terms *fard* and *wājib* are used for the first category, and *haram* for the last. *Sunna* is a term used for old custom or usage, which should be followed in preference to innovation (*bid'a*). See Macdonald, pp. 73–4. *Batal* is a term meaning legally void.
93 According to Gonda, *Sanskrit in Indonesia*, p. 392, this is probably from the Sanskrit *duracara*.
94 See Heather Sutherland, *The Making of a Bureaucratic Elite*, p. 36, on the type of *priyayi* who was known to be *gila hormat* [*hormat* being the Malay equivalent of *kurmat*], i.e. mad about the outward distinctions due to his rank.
95 These regulations can be found in J.A. van der Chijs, *Nederlandsch-Indisch plakaatboek, 1602–1811*, Landsdrvkkerij, Batavia, 1885–1900, 17 volumes, under the heading *Pragt en Praal* ("Pomp and Circumstance").
96 See above p. 79.
97 The first was a Kawi-miring version, the second a Kawi-jarwa: see Poerbatjaraka, *Kapustakan Djawi*, p. 148.
98 See Winter, *Zamenspraken*, p. 354.
99 See Pigeaud, *Catalogue vol. 1, Synopsis of Javanese Literature 900–1900 A.D.*, The Hague, Nijhoff, 1967, pp. 106–7.
100 See e.g Rani, *Slokantara*, section 25, where *tapa* and *brata* come at the top of the list of the Ten Best Things.
101 Siyung Wanara (later title, Arya Banyak Wide) was the son of a ruler of Pajajaran whose father attempted to put him to death as a baby because of the prediction of a holy-man whom the ruler had unrighteously murdered that the ruler's then unborn child would wreak revenge on him. Siyung wanara however survived and subsequently became a kris-smith of great supernatural power who imprisoned his father in an iron cage, becoming king of Pajajaran himself. The most accessible version of the Babad story is found in the Meinsma edition, W.L. Olthof, *Poenika Serat Babad Tanah Djawi Wiwit saking Nabi Adam doemoegi ing taoen 1647/Babad Tanah Djawi in Proza: Javaansche Geschiedenis*, M. Nijhoff, 's-Gravenhage, 1941, pp. 13–17.
102 The story of Aswatama (Sanskrit Aśwatthāmā) occurs in the Bharatayuda section of the Mahābhārata. In it, Aswatama seeks to defeat the God Kresna (Sanskrit Kṛṣṇa) and the Pandawa (Pāṇḍawa) brothers, who have come to take his magic jewel, by loosing the world-shaking fire-arrow Brahmaśirah. Kresna counters this weapon with

one of his own, the Śirśāntyani, and so Aswatama has to surrender his jewel and is punished with 1,000 years torment and disgrace for loosing this dreadful weapon: see S. Supomo, *Bhāratayuddha: an Old Javanese Poem and its Indian Sources*, New Delhi, International Academy of Indian Culture and Aditya Prakashan, 1993, Canto 51.

103 See Barbara Watson Andaya and Virginia Matheson, "Islamic Thought and Malay Tradition: the Writings of Raja Ali Haji of Riau (ca.1809–ca.1870) in Reid and Marr eds., *Perceptions*, pp. 108–128. The work in question is the *Kitab Pengetahuan Bahasa*, see p. 118.

104 It is used for the translation of this concept from the Greek philosophers: personal communication, Dr. A. Street.

105 Although the second part of the title of this book seems to be Arabic *bayān*, exposition or commentary, the compound *Sarahbayan* is not an Arabic construction. I am not sure which work is meant; one guess might be the *Bayān al-sirr* (see Kumar, *Diary*, p. 65) but this is a compendium relating to mysticism, and it seems more likely that some other exposition, relating to practice, is meant here.

106 See Chapter 3 above on the *wuku* system.

107 The term used is *iladuni*, presumably a contraction of '*ilm ladunī*, knowledge imparted directly by God through mystic intuition, a Sufi concept.

108 Canto III, stanza 32f.

109 See e.g. G.W.J. Drewes, *An Early Javanese Code of Muslim Ethics*, Bibliotheca Indonesica 18, The Hague, Martinus Nijhoff 1978, p. 37.

110 For an account of how such calculations are made in the present, see Justine Boow, *Symbol and Status in Javanese Batik*, Asian Studies Centre, Uni-versity of Western Australia Monograph Series no. 7, 1988, Ch. 5, p. 80ff.

111 *Tambal* are patchwork patterns. Patchwork garments seem to have had a sacral significance in some cases, as with the Anantakusuma jacket worn by rulers at accession and other ritual occasions, or in the patchwork robes of Tenggerese priests. On *tambal kanoman* and *tambal miring* see J.E. Jasper and Mas Pirngadie, *De Inlandsche Kunstnijverheid in Nederlandsch Indie*, vol. III, *De Batikkunst*, p. 143. I have been unable to find any information on the pattern *tambal sukaduka* ("joy and sorrow patchwork"), however. On the almost universal knowledge of batik patterns among the Javanese see Ponder, *Javanese Panorama*, pp. 138–9.

112 I have been unable to locate this *lurik* pattern.

113 i.e. Patola, an expensive silk double-ikat cloth from Gujerat in India, usually with a geometric pattern representing the compass, and thought to have special power.

114 Jasper and Pirngadie vol. II, *De weefkunst*, p. 261 list patterns of Indian *cindẹ* cloths, but do not list one called *solok*. *Limar* are patterns based on lozenge shapes (see Jasper and Pirngadie II pp. 233–4) and *gĕdog* is a type of *lurik* in which the patterns are based on two threads of different colours twisted together (see Jasper and Pirngadie II pp. 210 and 216).

115 See also above, the Mangkunegaran diary. According to K.R.T. Hardjonegoro (personal communication) there was a considerable increase in *larangan* from the time of Pakubuwana III on.

Intellectual Transformations

116 *Lung-lungan* are tendril patterns, *cĕplokan* stylized flower and fruit patterns, and *gogodongan* leaf patterns.
117 The correct way of wearing the headcloth for Javanese males relied on the use of a piece of turtle shell (in modern times, brass) called the *tusuk konde* to fix the bun or hair-knot (*mondolan.*). Since the word *pĕnyon* is derived from *pĕnyu*, turtle, it would appear to be a synonym for the *tusuk konde*.
118 See above p. 405–6.
119 *lingsir wĕngi* is one of the traditional Javanese divisions of the night, usually given as from midnight or 1 a.m. to 3 a.m., but sometimes as from 2.a.m. to 6 a.m.: see Chapter 3 p. 140f above.
120 See above p. 403.
121 See diagram in Carey, "Just King", p. 69.
122 See Alexander Woodside, "Political Theory and Economic Growth in Late Traditional Vietnam", in Reid, forthcoming (pp. 12–13).
123 Carey, *Just King*, p. 76
124 Paying *zakat* is one of the five pillars of the faith, and there are precise specifications about the types of property subject to *zakat* and the rate to be paid (see also Ch.3 above, p. 165–6). The *zakat* money is used for the poor, slaves, debtors, travellers, and those in the service of God. *Fitrah* ia a charitable contribution usually of about a *gantang* of rice made by every member of the mosque congregation at the end of the fasting month, for the purpose of allowing the poor to celebrate the great annual festival at the end of the fast. It is also known as *zakat badan* to distinguish it from the true *zakat* levied on property.
125 See e.g. Kumar, *Diary*, p. 44.
126 On the function of the *kabayan* in village government, see Ch.3, p. 172 above.
127 Here the printed text reads "who does not smoke opium" instead of "of good character".
128 Referred to as the *mancapat/mancalima*, four-sets and five-sets, since villages were traditionally conceptualized in groups of four, at the compass points, around a centre. This four-five compass classification is very old and is depicted in textile patterns, and correlated with colours and the five days of the market week.
129 The *pasewanan* is a *pĕndapa* (pavilion) in the palace forecourt, used for audiences. The implication is probably that one should be prepared to put in time at court, perhaps as a lowly *magang*.
130 A legal foundation, in this case one of the texts from the Koran or Hadith in which Mohammed exhorts his followers to obedience to him and to those in authority over them. An example is *surah* 4:59, which reads: "You who believe! Obey God, obey the Messenger [Muhammad], and those in authority among you!".
131 I owe this insight, among many others, to Dr. Supomo Suryohudoyo.
132 S.a. Soemarsaid Moertono, *State and Statecraft in Old Java: A Study of the Later Mataram Period, 16th to 19th Century*, Cornell Modern Indonesia Project Monograph Series, Ithaca, N.Y., 1963, p. 97.
133 Yasadipura also speaks of "*wahyu jali*", which is presumably from the

New ways of seeing

Arabic *jal*, evident, manifest, brilliant, from a base meaning to shine, to be brilliantly evident.

134 See Remmelink p. 218. See also A.L. Kumar, "The 'Suryengalagan Affair' of 1883 and its successors: born leaders in changed times", *BKI* 138/2-3 (1982), p. 364.
135 See Macdonald, *Muslim Theology*, p. 281.
136 Although the relationship of the Kalisangara and Kaliyuga is far from clear, verses 39-40 state that in the Kaliyuga the upper classes are well off, but in the Kalisangara all classes of society are wretched and powerless.
137 In the Javanese, the pronoun is implicit and could also be read as "they" instead of "we".
138 Here called Ngeksiganda, an allusive pun on the alternative form of its name, Matarum, which can be read fancifully as "fragrant eye" (= *ngeksi ganda*).
139 See also Kumar, *Diary*, p. 98.
140 I witnessed this same unease in a princess of the Mangkunegaran kraton who was both anxious that Javanese traditions such as the *bĕḍaya* and *srimpi* dances should not die out, and aware that they were in conflict with the demands of Islam.
141 See Winter, *Zamenspraken*, p. 352.
142 See the 7th chapter of this work, of which three editions are fairly accessible, i.e. Bukhari Al-Jauhari ed. Khalid Hussain, *Taj Us-Salatin*, Dewan Bahasa dan Pustaka, Kuala Lumpur, 1966; Jumsari Jusuf ed., *Tajussalatin*, Departemen Pendidikan dan Kebudayaan, Proyek Penerbitan Buku Bacaan dan Sastra Indonesia dan Daerah, Jakarta, 1979; and Bokhāri de Djohōre, ed. Aristide Marre, *Makōta Radja-Rādja, ou la Couronne des Rois*, Paris, 1878.

Conclusion:
The Legacy for Indonesia

Indonesia is not Java; yet Java contains Indonesia's major potential or major problem, depending on what can be done there. What was the significance of this period for the future Indonesia?

At the level of the state, the wars that ravaged Java from the late 1620s to the late 1770s had ended the sempiternal Javanese dream of political unity. Not only did the number of political units increase with the partition of Mataram and the division of Cirebon; the territorial integration earlier achieved by Mataram was reversed in the reign of Pakubuwana II and never regained. I have argued above[1] that the Javanese state should not be seen as a type of state – a "theatre state" – presenting an absolute contrast to an ideal-typic Western state, but simply as a patrimonial state with a pronounced military character. In the sources used here, we see the celebration of a military aristocracy/royalty – through the weekly tournaments at Surakarta or in Gresik, and in the martial dances and displays which figured prominently in the public ritual even of the cultivated *women* of the court, the *prajurit estri*. (By way of comparative perspective, it may be remembered that this military element was an important part of the political theatre of English royalty, until the last twenty years saw a change to the acting-out in television shows of a new "theatre of domesticity".) Even court music was used at court to underline the *prabawa*, the personal force and authority, of the great. The Babads too celebrate the prowess of the great military leaders; and Yasadipura II reproaches his generation of Javanese for forgetting that they are an Islamic people brave in war. In all these sources as well as in the guardswoman's diary of the Mangkunegaran court with its *santri* warriors, we see a martial Islam very different from the quietist, yogic form that Geertz has described as characteristically Javanese.[2]

Conclusion

Though the strongly martial character of the Javanese court was not introduced by Islam, it was confirmed and strengthened by a corresponding strand in the Muslim ethos, and this correspondence was probably one of the strongest factors facilitating conversion to Islam, trade networks and mysticism notwithstanding. One more great war would be fought in respect of this courtly military tradition, the Java War of 1825–30, led by a prince who despite his Islamic commitment had also drunk from the springs of Javanese aesthesticism. This would be followed by a period of economic and intellectual deprivation, and of such political impotence that Dutch histories of this period would not need to include a single Javanese name.

There was also another aspect of the court, its position of moral leadership, most highly and self-consciously developed among the *priyayi* in an ascetic, morally puritanical and intellectualizing – in contrast to the martial, amorous, and aesthetic style of the princes – behavioural code, whose finest statement is the *Sasana Sunu*. But both princes of the blood royal and the *priyayi* themselves are not in doubt about their relative rank, as we see in the remark about "weak *priyayi*" in the Mangkunegaran diary, and Yasadipura's very explicit formulation of one of the central principles of Javanese society: the concept that descent was of central importance in the formation of a man, and that royal blood conferred a social rank higher than any other. Thus the ruler's close relatives, the *santana*, rank above those who have risen to high official rank in the service of the ruler and state. The *priyayi*'s chief glory is in serving (*ngawula*) those who are where they are by virtue of their birth and their ability to live up to the more dangerous role assigned to them.

The Javanese state was, then, based upon a three-pronged claim to leadership: in the refined and civilised, the martial, and the moral. To these must be added its strong ideological link with the world of agriculture: just as the heart of the palace was the *pĕtanen* ("farmer's place", housing the rice deity and her consort), so also the ceremonial cooking of rice was one of the ruler's most sacred ritual tasks. But the effectiveness of this traditional leadership was now reduced by the political and economic splintering of the Javanese states.

Turning from the state to Javanese society, over much of the island we see a society that was not in comparative terms characterised by a tendency to centralisation in one or two

The legacy for Indonesia

dominant cities, but replicative, given to the hiving-off of villages by what Christie has called fission and the provincial replication of kratons. This meant that there was a relatively even spread of what we are accustomed to term "civilisation" "the great tradition" or "high culture" across Java, despite the lack of large urban nodes of the scale that historians in the West have equated with the development of civilised society. This tightly-knit and by pre-industrial standards remarkably all-of-a-piece social web was somehow integrated and "civilized", even in the provinces, and must have minimised the extent of cultural loss to society that we would normally expect with the phenomenon of the moving capital, frequently shifted as it was at change of reign or after military disasters. There is a greater consistency in the Javanese socio-cultural formation over both space and time, a Javanese commonality between capital and province, aristocrat and villager, that resides in the rituals of Javaneseness and shared systems of meaning, than we have hitherto recognised. The Javanese were formidably well socialised, compared, say, to Chinese society above the family level.

This is not to deny the reality of class and status differences: for this was, also, a profoundly hierarchical society, with extraordinarily careful and exact differentiation of rank both in the court and in the village, as is apparent both from the Javanese sources (the practice from the Mangkunegaran diary, the theory from the *Sasana sunu*) and from the European reports from the different regions of Java.

* * *

How did the VOC, a capitalist chartered company, impinge upon this society? What was the effect of the policies instituted by the "capitalist" VOC as it pursued its business?

Firstly, it extracted huge amounts of labour from Javanese society,[3] as the Cultivation System would afterwards, both in Priangan (exemplifying "old colonial" Java) and in Pekalongan, which was part of the more recently acquired *pasisir* region that was to become the birth-place of the Cultivation System. The retreat from rice cultivation noted in regions like Pekalongan and Gresik set the trend which would result in the famines of the 1840s. The enormous increase in labour demanded also had a great impact, as Boomgaard has convincingly shown,[4] on the disappearance of free

Conclusion

wage labour, and on the elimination (by about the 1840s) of the peasantry's ability to maintain money-making occupations like textile production and independent cash cropping in response to market opportunities. Nineteenth century colonial reports reveal a continuing emphasis on the question of how to extract more labour from the Javanese. Furthermore, by its use of the Bupati to extract resources by force (which involved an acceptance of the perks of both sides) the VOC and its successor state created a psychological situation which, though unquantifiable, clearly would have driven home the lesson to Javanese peasants that they had no right to their resources in labour and goods, which could be taken at any time. Their lives shaped by the VOC's response to the market filtered through the directives of their traditional rulers, Java's peasants became part of the world economy on the most demoralizing terms, unable even to see the path they were being dragged along, let alone to devise their own response to economic conditions.

Evidence from both ends of Java reveals the application, as far as was possible, of a policy of forcing fugitives from intolerable conditions back onto the land they had fled, in order that they should continue to labour there as required. Sources from all over Java amply testify to the peasantry's attempts to resist enchainment to the land and flee from the burdens imposed upon them. Some were more fortunate in their geographical location, like the Pekalongan peasants who lived close enough to the princely lands to flee across the border and could therefore be only lightly taxed by the Pekalongan authorities. On the individual level, however, the life-histories of these peasants are unrecorded in the writings of the literate, whether Dutch or Javanese; indeed their voices are muffled by the multiple layers of the élite in a plural society under a system usually referred to as "indirect rule". In their day to day lives the peasantry were dealt with by the élite without benefit of due process, and we lack even the police records that in other colonies reveal something of their lives. Yet the presence of the peasantry is not entirely dismissed in the records of the literate. They receive some acknowledgment, as in Yasadipura's injunction against the great moral sin of stealing from those who have so little. Their virtues – working long and hard at all sorts of work, heavy and light, stoutness of heart, steadfastness, sincerity, lack of presumption and arrogance – must be cultivated by the *priyayi* in Yasadipura's program of moral perfection: an intellectual counterpart of the architectural statement of the *pětanen*. Even the

The legacy for Indonesia

conservative author of the report on Priangan admits the central importance of the enormously hard labour required from the peasantry, an admission by no means universal among VOC officials. Their initiative is attested in the peasant response to textile production and cash cropping, despite the massive expropriation of their labour. Their desire to escape from "being ruled" is reflected in a ghostly fashion in the *siluman* stories of Pekalongan; and later, outside the period covered here, would be more directly manifest in the same region by peasants appealing over the heads of their "traditional leaders" to the Dutch colonial authorities who were evidently recognised as the ultimate authorities over the disastrous indigo-producing industry.

Secondly, by the period dealt with here – in fact by as early as the 1730s – the VOC had brought about massive ecological devastation, in particular, the deforestation of the coast and of the Batavian Environs (*Ommelanden*).

Thirdly, though it is depicted in colonial historiography as a centralising force in Javanese history, the VOC was in fact profoundly decentralising both politically, as noted above, *and* economically, by creating a number of élites (the VOC qua centralised company, VOC officials qua private entrepreneurs, the Bupati, and the Chinese), none of them strong enough economically and politically, even if they had had the will, to become an innovative capitalist class. (This is an island-wide view: these élites were not all equally strong in every area, nor was the relationship between them everywhere the same.) Though the dominant myth of colonial historiography is the unification of the Indies, this was not so much unification as agglomeration: not even, to twist Marx's famous metaphor, at the level of a sack of potatoes, but of quite disparate units to which any commonality was never imparted.

Looking at the dimension of regional variation, we can see from the reports of VOC officials that the Company created at least three Javas by its actions (not to speak of the howling wilderness in the Eastern Salient, the *Oosthoek*): it destroyed Banten's relatively highly capitalised mercantile economy, based on a politico-economic system in some ways more like the maritime Malay states than like the states of central Java; ironically, this area became the most backward in Java, the only one where swidden cultivation survived till modern times, and the most sullenly resentful of Dutch rule. It created a neo-feudal society in Priangan under the financially very succesful system of compulsory coffee cultivation,

Conclusion

which made the Bupati into great and absolute feudal lords (vis-à-vis those below them) in a fossilised society closed off to influences which would have questioned the status quo, as was to become apparent much later with decolonisation and the Darul Islam rebellion. And it created a new society on the *pasisir*: plural, differentiated, locus of more "modern" social and political movements. The *pasisir* had been in pre-colonial times a major centre of Javanese Islam, and of Chinese trade; the presence of the VOC tended to drive a wedge between these two, and out of this growing tension would arise the first mass movement of the Indies, Sarekat Islam. Later, under the VOC's heir the Cultivation System, the *pasisir* was also the locus of a developing class consciousness among the peasantry worst affected by the system of forced cultivation, such as the indigo growers of Pekalongan. The proletariat of the *pasisir* later played a central role in the growth of the Indies communist movement.

The evidence from these very different regions does not support either van Leur's assessment of the relatively negligible character of the VOC's impact on indigenous society,[5] or the picture – drawn by both conservative and Marxist theorists – of capitalism as tearing asunder a "traditional", i.e. backward, Asian society and paving the way for the new world. The first, van Leur's picture of a proudly autonomous Eastern civilization, following a "gradually ascending line . . . climbing through throughout the eighteenth century [and] into the nineteenth century"[6] is disproved by the striking unanimity of contemporary sources, Dutch and, most strongly, Javanese, that Java and the Javanese had declined from a populous and glorious past to a fairly wretched, less populous and prosperous, present, subject also to the unchecked depredations of pirates and "rabble". However unquantifiable this perception may be, the fact that it occurs across racial lines and across regions with such frequency commands some credence. Similarly van Leur's picture of two equal civilisations developing separately from each other[7] is destroyed by the evidence from all regions of Java of great economic and social transformation due to the European presence, and of new intellectual developments focussing precisely on the problems caused by the interaction of Javanese with Europeans and Chinese. Writing history that is centred on Indonesian society should not entail inventing a fictitious separateness and lack of historical agency for Europeans; and it is argued here that Europeans had a very significant historical agency, particularly in

The legacy for Indonesia

the application of modern techniques to politically, socially and economically regressive ends.

Van Leur's second hypothesis may be considered something of a straw man to attack after the work of Geertz and Reid, but the differing regional perspectives presented here provide new food for thought. The VOC's impact was very far from negligible and it did destroy much in the Javanese societies it impinged upon. But was it modernising in the way it reversed the progress made to a more capitalised economy in Banten, and enforced – or rather, created – a feudal socio-economic structure in Priangan, where the widespread, officially "illegal" practice of paying the peasant cultivator in kind represented a backward step in terms of monetization? Even the "new" Java on the *pasisir* relied on "traditional" economic arrangements (rule through the Bupati, tax-farming, and the extraction of goods and labour in place of money taxation, for example) that went back far into the Old Javanese period. If there is a parallel between VOC practice and that of the modern world, it is Mao's China that springs to mind, with its substitution of labour for capital, transformation of plenty into famine through the pursuit of implicitly "higher" interests of state, restrictions on freedom of travel, forcing of fugitives back on the land, and hostility to intellectual freedom and innovation. Thus the categories of capitalism and modernity seem to dissolve before our eyes as we view these practices, underlining how far the VOC in its later period (and its successor colonial government) actually were from idealtypic capitalism.

Fourthly, the VOC was also strikingly unable to provide minimal security on land or sea: time and again the sources speak of piracy, and "rabble", a situation which continued to exist in many regions of Java even up to the late nineteenth century. To the extent that it did maintain order, it relied on alliances with local Javanese bullyboys. The sources attest to an increase in social violence proportionate to the degree of VOC penetration, particularly striking in the region around Batavia and in Cirebon. There were revolts everywhere, both by "rabble" and by princes. The *pax neerlandica* was as illusory as colonial unification. P.J. Veth's *Java, Geographisch, Ethnologisch, Historisch*, which appeared in three volumes in 1875–1882,[8] the classic High Orientalist account of Java, describes the island as the nicely-tamed garden of the east, a tribute to the *pax neerlandica* written, in first person travelogue style, by someone who never visited the island. Comparing Veth's account with other

Conclusion

accounts of regions of Java is very instructive. In 1872 a Dutch tobacco planter named C.C.A. Amand wrote to the colonial government giving an account of conditions in Kediri. The description of this region by Veth[9] includes extensive descriptive material on the natural landscape ("the rich and charming variety of colours and tints, of forms and lines, the interchanging of land and water, of plains and mountains, of coasts and islands, of grey rocks and green sawahs, of houses and ships."). It also describes such man-made features as roads and bridges (and planned railways), houses (the fact that Veth had never visited Java does not prevent him from assuring us that the buildings around the *alun-alun* of Tulung Agung are nicely whitewashed and well maintained) and antiquities of interest to the traveller. There is, however, a virtual silence on the population of this landscape, apart from the following remarks: the Javanese workers responsible for building a bridge over the Kali Brantas, lacking as usual pride in their work, omitted to place the architect's name beside the date; Trenggalek is distinguished by a general abstinence from opium and consequent prosperity and freedom from crime, while in the rest of Kediri there are many opium-smokers; and Blitar has become more prosperous since it came under Dutch rule. The Javanese, in other words, appear on the few occasions they are mentioned as poor workers, people who are likely to fall into opium and crime, and passive recipients of colonial bounty. Amand's decription of the region gives a complete different picture of Kediri. He depicts it as actually ruled, in the very extensive layers of society not controlled by the colonial state, by competing bands of armed men whom we can call bandits or *jagos*, with whom the Javanese bureaucrats who formed the link between local society and colonial government maintained a regular working relationship. Furthermore, Amand claimed that this situation obtained not just in Kediri but in all of Java: and this as late as the 1870s! Henk Schulte Nordholt argues that this can be seen as a case of incomplete state-formation similar to that which allowed the rise of the Mafia in Sicily.[10] Here I argue that it was due to the political splintering of the Javanese states and the failure of the colonial state to provide an adequate replacement for the old kingdoms.

We also find in Dutch sources used in this book an acute awareness of the great changes that followed Chinese penetration, which is usually represented as socially baneful, involving illegal exploitation and leading to the corruption of the admirable, pristine

The legacy for Indonesia

simplicity of the Javanese and the growth of violence in society. Sometimes however it is seen as economically positive (in the sense that a Chinese leaseholder could "do more with", i.e. get more out of, a region than could a Javanese Regent). As Carey points out, the coastal areas of Java were significantly affected by Chinese penetration at an earlier period than was the case for central Java.[11] Even in central Java, however, it seems likely that the identification of the Chinese with the Dutch, and anti-Chinese prejudice, pre-dates the latter years of the Java War, which Carey views as the formative period for later anti-Chinese sentiment: we can already see this identification of Chinese and Dutch in the guardswoman's diary.[12] The anonymous author of NBS 89, within his metaphorical framework, identifies the Chinese with ruthless economic exploitation.

The tacit acceptance by Dutch officials of Chinese practices theoretically condemned as illegal leads on to the fifth point: though the Company introduced Western ideas of the inalienability of private rights to land and other property and though its history and that of the colonial state that succeeded it have been written in terms of a series of legal contracts concluded with native rulers, its actual practice was far from following these ideals and must have contributed to the marginal role of the Law in Indonesia today, compared with some other societies, and the widespread cynicism concerning the relationship between legal forms and reality. In addition, even within its limited sphere of operation the Law in late colonial Indonesia was unambiguously an instrument which the strong used against the weak (as in the one-sided enforcement of contracts between sugar plantations and Javanese peasant growers), in contrast to the European historical evolution in which the Law progressively enabled at least the middle class to emancipate themselves from arbitrary rule. For the peasantry, any sort of formal procedure, even a colonial one, only became part of their life at a very late period.[13] This too must have been a factor that has contributed to Indonesian attitudes.

In sum then, the policies of the VOC and its successor government were destructive and reactionary, and do not accord with our view of the extraordinary modernising push of Europe. This was due to a large extent to the place of the United Provinces in Europe at this period: having once been at the cutting edge of Europe's modernity in nation- and economy-building, they were now, as remarked in Chapter One, small, weak, and poor, lagging behind the major powers in politics and science.

Conclusion

On the other hand, it would be quite wrong to deny that the Dutch retained very significant advantages of European modernity, particularly the technology and techniques, such as those of accounting, reporting, and organisation. Paradoxically, these modern techniques were used to maintain reactionary regimes on Java. For the VOC and its successor state brought the techniques (material, organisational and intellectual) of modern Europe but not its spirit. This was a poisonous combination, which can be seen in a number of fields: economy, political structures, education – which, provided late and in small measure, stressed technical competence uninformed by any spirit of enquiry – and law. Van der Kroef in a curious but not unenlightening essay described the prevailing spirit of the Indies Dutch as not universalism but particularism.[14] Crudely put, this literally meant one law for you, another for me, applied to the different ethnic groups of the Indies. Even where a single group, such as the Javanese, was concerned, policy was to support the most reactionary sections of society, except for short periods of more liberal policies that were soon abandoned. In addition to their technical and organisational skills the Dutch like other Europeans were greatly advantaged by a more global or "aerial" overview of Java: the other characteristic of the hawk to which the author of NBS 89 likens Europeans. They were part of the first, slower but sure, Information Technology revolution. These two factors are part of the explanation of the question sometimes asked as to why the Javanese did not throw out the Dutch at the end of the eighteenth century, when they must have known their military weakness. Another part of the explanation relates to the political fragmentation of Java that was so far advanced by this time.

* * *

But not all was destruction and regression in these decades. First of all one cannot but be amazed at the capacity for survival of Javanese society, with all its socialisation and hierarchy, under stresses which one may well have expected to result in complete social disintegration. And Javanese court circles apparently still possessed, after a century of horrific warfare and disruption, the capacity for intellectual innovation, and exhibit an undoubted awareness of the seriousness of the challenge posed by the West: in the sources used here, there is no evidence of the Dutch being

The legacy for Indonesia

compared to the *punakawan* (clown figures) of *wayang*, with their bizarre and ridiculous (if supernaturally potent) elements.[15] On the contrary, the Dutch are taken very seriously, and their dominance is not seen to be due to supernatural or mythic factors. And ironically, the shock of these Europeans with their reactionary policies *did* have a modernising effect on intellectual life, involving, I have suggested, a rethinking of the world-view from a Platonic to a Hegelian format. These new ideas were not due to the fertilisation of Western ideas, in contrast to the influence of Dutch studies in Japan, just as the rise of analytical historiography was not prompted by any Western example but by an historical shock of great magnitude. This shock also led to the emergence of nationalism, the need to understand why Javanese could not compete militarily or economically with foreigners, and thus a shift to empiricism and more modern intellectual perspectives. There was a break in the old exclusively Platonic format of universal ideals and the emergence of a new view of the world as consisting of differentiated and competing peoples caught in history. As we have seen in Chapter 5, the author of the remarkable NBS 89 explains the situation of the Javanese as being due to the military superiority of Europeans (and the hopelessness of Javanese soldiers on this front), European moral superiority, and the inability of Javanese to handle money. Despite its lack of of a sophisticated traditon of socio-economic analysis and its, by conventional standards, fanciful metaphorical presentation, this explanation actually canvasses the major emphases of Western scholars seeking to explain Asia's domination by the West from the time this first became apparent down to Braudel. Evidently something of the strengths of "modern Europe", traditionally a source of pride for European scholars, were also visible to the Javanese behind the military and economic weakness of the Dutch.

The roots of nationalism are visible in the concept of *bangsa* in NBS 89 and in Yasadipura II's work, though in the writings of this period, as in Sukarno's later,[16] it is hard to distinguish between "nation" and "race". This still hazily defined nationalism had no institutional basis like the *pesantren* to carry it through the nineteenth century, and yet succeeded in establishing its dominance over the competing claims of Islam and Marxism in the twentieth when the conditions described by Anderson[17] for the emergence of a full-blown colonial nationalist movement eventually came about. Along with the rise of the concept of the nation went a concern for

Conclusion

its unity. Though I cannot agree that division of the polity had traditionally been regarded as "temporary and anomalous" (if "constantly recurring")[18] the Javanese undoubtedly remembered their great unifying kings – Siṇḍok, Airlangga, Kṛtanagara, Agung – above all others. But they also knew the fragility of these unifying endeavours, and the speed with which they might subsequently be undone. Now, some were evidently beginning to see political disunity as due not merely to the failure of kings, but as due to the failings of the Javanese as a whole. The Javanese, once the centre and pinnacle of their ethnic universe and the dominant military power of their region, were now beginning to assess themselves quite differently vis-à-vis other peoples.

At this period, there seems to be as yet no questioning of the centrality of the Ruler or call for radically different "political" arrangements. And yet, the redefinition of the term *bangsa* to describe a Javanese nation provides an alternative, and perhaps implicitly competing, focus vis-à-vis the "high centre" of the Ruler and his servants that the *Sasana Sunu* still takes as its chief subject; and a discourse on what we would call "social engineering" and "social responsibility" also seems to be emerging, not too long after the concept of the social causes of the behaviour of the individual was developed in Europe.

This still ill-defined focus on society was later carried foward and more sharply focussed by Islam. As we have seen, from at least the mid eighteenth century, Islam already offered anti-Dutch leadership in a way that was to be more spectacularly evident in the Java War. The sources used in this book reveal a perhaps surprising social presence of Islam across a wide range of social classes and geographical regions: though in addition, an equally surprising presence of "Javanism" and Indic elements on the "Islamic" north coast. Thus we have to revise our picture of a sharp cultural contrast between central Java and the *pasisir*, in favour of one where both Islamic and pre-Islamic civilisation were fully and richly present in court ritual, in the prescriptive socialisation of the Javanese, in the highly-developed intellectual synthesis laid down by Yasadipura II, and in the rich texture of provincial life. VOC officials regarded Islam as an enemy to be expelled from the political arena as far as possible. In areas where the VOC was strong, the *priyayi* were forced to abandon their role as the "secular arm" enforcing Islamic law and the paying of Islamic taxes as had once (even if imperfectly) been the case. Yet Islam was first to

The legacy for Indonesia

respond to the new possibilities of mass mobilisation of the twentieth century, providing not only organizational form but also intellectual and political innovation in its non-king-centric critique of the colonial situation: astonishingly, somewhere in the period between the *Sasana Sunu* and independence, Islam seems to have triumphed over the nineteenth century colonial persecution to bring about something like an intellectual revolution, introducing a whole swathe of new concepts relating to social organisation and the relationship of the individual to society. Society, *masyarakat*, replaces the focus on the king. The old concept of service (to the king, *ngawula*) is replaced by the concepts of consultation (*musyawarah*) and consensus (*mupakat*). The governing élite are no longer there by virtue of *tapa* leading to the bestowing of *wahyu*, but because of their function of representation (*perwakilan*) and representation not of kings or princes but of the common people – the *rakyat*, a concept that is also new, replacing the old *bala tani* (common soldiers and peasants, by extension subjects) of Yasadipura's time. The idea that service to the king is the supreme moral good of an individual's life, a central pillar of the "Javanist" philosophy, was thus radically challenged by Islam.

Finally, we see in this period the first faint signs of the rise of new forms of radicalism among the indigo-growers of Pekalongan who would in an unprecedented move by-pass their traditional leadership and appeal directly to colonial officialdom for redress of intolerable conditions.

To sum up, this was a period where policies, structures, and ideas were invented and implanted which took such hold that much of the future of Java and then of Indonesia was shaped by them. In the case of those that followed from VOC policies, it is easy to trace the continuity with and development of these policies and structures under the succeeding colonial government. With the new ideas from the Javanese side, in contrast, we seem to see only aborted beginnings, or beginnings that would not be built upon for a century and more. Though the VOC was really in no position to control intellectual developments, its successor the colonial state, through an all-pervading censorship and the withholding of any enlivening Western education, seems to bring about a withering of the new intellectual trends such as empiricism and critical self-examination.

It is far more likely, however, that these beginnings were indeed built upon, but in a way that is still invisible to us, since little has

Conclusion

been done to develop perspectives on nineteenth century history that go beyond those of the colonial government's reports. Even these reports, however, make it clear that new ideas were abroad, both among the peasantry and in the *pesantren* world, which gave birth not just to movements protesting the justice of colonial power structures[19] but – less obviously but of more long-term significance – to a whole new intellectual framework for viewing society. It is to be hoped that the historians of the future will recover this subterranean intellectual history, the underground emergence of an indigenous modernity not envisaged by the colonial government.[20]

So these were, then, profoundly ambiguous encounters with Europe. The Javanese, or some Javanese, did see superior qualities in Europeans, but Dutch policies revealed that the European format of technological advances in conjunction with political and social modernisation was one that could be broken apart, with the technology (material and organisational) just as useful in the support of a reactionary ramshackle empire. Hence a profound ambivalence among the descendants of these Javanese, and other Indonesians, to Western ways, and their suspicion of the relevance of ideals to practice. The oft-criticised brutally technological understanding of "moderen" in Indonesia should not be too hard to understand. And yet, I argue, the shock of military and economic defeat did lead to a profound transformation and renovation of the Javanese view of the world, whose subsequent history is yet to be told.

A sequel to these ambiguous political and intellectual encounters is now being played out. The two sides are larger, and more diffuse: instead of "Europe" (represented successively by the Dutch, French, English, and Dutch again) we have "the Western world", which includes America and Australia; instead of Java, we have Indonesia, now an independent nation of half a century. And there are other differences: for instance, whereas the Dutch generally did not assert that Indonesians should conform to European norms, today Western commentators from diverse countries are not slow to compare Indonesia unfavourably with the West. This is generally an ideal-typic, not to say idealised, "West", against which Indonesian political and other practice is measured. This intellectual sleight of hand can hardly be un-noticed in Indonesia.

But also new and important is a shift taking place within Western countries: the children of the West's prosperity are now dismantling or nullifying the once, in the period described in this book, "modern", and now "old" European intellectual and organisational

The legacy for Indonesia

techniques. The old quantificative, generalist empiricism, philosophically indefensible perhaps but rather strictly organised and replicated, is under attack from new super-critical theorists sponsoring pluralities of meanings, relativism, and intellectual play and *bricolage*. This new attitude to knowledge, in its more sophisticated forms, is perhaps more justifiable in meta-theoretical terms but it is very loosely organised and produces many strange and diverse hybrids On another front, the extreme specialisation of the unreconstructed empirical sciences is breaking down the broad overview of things so characteristic of the old Europe (that masterly, hawkish overview that the Javanese author saw as characteristically European), leading to a proliferation of the twigs and little attention to the tree of knowledge. It will be interesting to see whether the ex-colonies of Europe join in destroying the once-powerful, if philosophically rough-and-ready, tools of the "old" West, or whether they will still see some use in these discarded and despised implements and turn them to their own purposes. But that, as they say, is another story.

NOTES

1. See Chapter Two, p. 87f.
2. See his description of the *wali* and "culture hero" Sunan Kalijaga in *Islam Observed*, pp. 25–9.
3. See especially Ch.5 above.
4. Boomgaard, *Children*, p. 124.
5. Notably in his famous review article, "On the eighteenth century as a category in Indonesian history", republished in J.C. van Leur, *Indonesian Trade and Society: Essays in Asian Social and Economic History*, W. van Hoeve, The Hague/Bandung, 1955, pp. 268–289.
6. van Leur p. 283.
7. van Leur pp. 284–5.
8. It was reissued by the same publishers in a second edition of 4 volumes in 1896–1907, with substantial revisions by Joh. F. Snelleman and J.F. Niermeyer. References here are to the first edition.
9. Veth III pp. 731ff.
10. See Henk Schulte Nordholt, "De jago in de schaduw: misdaad en 'orde' in de koloniale staat op Java" *De Gids* 146, 1983, pp. 664–675.
11. See P.B.R. Carey, "Changing Javanese Perceptions of the Chinese Communities in central Java, 1755–1825", *Indonesia* 37 (April 1984), p. 41.
12. See ch. 4, p. 200.
13. Compared, say, to British India.
14. See Justus M. van der Kroef, *The Dialectic of Colonial Indonesian History*, C.P.J. van der Peet, Amsterdam 1963.

Conclusion

15 Ricklefs, *Mangkubumi*, pp. 26–30.
16 See for example Sukarno's 1927 article, "Towards the Brown Front" in *Under the Banner of Revolution*, vol.i, Publications Committee, Djakarta 1966, pp. 33–6.
17 Benedict Richard O'Gorman Anderson, *Imagined communities: reflections on the origin and spread of nationalism*. London: Verso, 1983 (revised and extended 2nd. edition, Verso 1991).
18 Ricklefs, *Mangkubumi*, p. 143.
19 See Kumar, *Diary*, Ch. II, esp. part iv.
20 By contrast, the nineteenth-century Javanese *priyayi* typically confined their literary activities – at least those that were published – to a-historical didactic texts avoiding ethnic, political, and religious problems, and anodyne travel accounts.

Bibliography

JAVANESE AND MALAY SOURCES

Manuscript

KITLV Or [Koninklijk Instituut voor Taal-, Land- en Volkenkunde Oriental ms.]. 1 No. 231.
NBS [Netherlands Bible Society] 89 = Mal 5057 / Cod. Or. 10.733 of the Leiden University Library collection: *Sasana Sunu* and didactic poem on kingship and statecraft.
LOr [Leiden Oriental manuscript] 1806, *Sana Sunu*.
LOr 8564, *Sana Sunu*, dated 1819 A.D.
CB [Collection Berg] 153 of the Leiden University Library, Old Javanese poems in Indic metres.
Surakarta manuscript of *Wicara Kĕras* transcribed in A. Sarman, *Tinjauan Kitab Wicarakeras*, M.A. thesis, Gajah Mada University, Yogyakarta 1971.

Published

Bokhāri de Djohōre, ed. Aristide Marre, *Makōta Radja-Rādja, ou la Couronne des Rois*, Paris, Maisonnerre 1878.
Bukhari Al-Jauhari ed. Khalid Hussain *Taj Us-Salatin*, Dewan Bahasa dan Pustaka, Kuala Lumpur 1966.
Jusuf, Jumsari ed., *Tajussalatin*, Departemen Pendidikan dan Kebudayaan, Proyek Penerbitan Buku Bacaan dan Sastra Indonesia dan Daerah, Jakarta 1979.
Mangunwijaya, Y.B. trans. Hunter, Thomas M. *The Weaverbirds*, Lontar Jakarta 1991.
Olthof, W.L. *Poenika Serat Babad Tanah Djawi Wiwit saking Nabi Adam doemoegi ing taoen 1647/Babad Tanah Djawi in Proza: Javaansche Geschiedenis*, M. Nijhoff, 's-Gravenhage, 1941.
Poerbatjaraka, R.Ng. Dr. *Niticastra: Oud-Javaansche tekst met vertaling*, Bandung, A.C. Nix, 1933.
Rani, Sharada, ed. and trans. *Ślokantara: an old Javanese didactic text*, [New Delhi] International Academy of Indian Culture, 1957.

Bibliography

Robson, S.O. ed. and trans. *Wangbang Wideya: A Javanese Panji Romance*, Bibliotheca Indonesica no. 6, KITLV, The Hague, Nijhoff, 1971.

Soebardi, S. *The Book of Cabolek: A Critical Edition with Introduction, Translation and Notes; A Contribution to the Study of the Javanese Mystical Tradition*, Bibliotheca Indonesica 10, The Hague, Nijhoff, 1975.

Sĕrat Wicara Kĕras [in Javanese script] Tan Khoen Swie, Kediri, 1926.

Winter, C.F. *Javaansche Zamenspraken*, 5th printing, vol. 1, E.J. Brill, Leiden 1911.

Yasadipura II, R.Ng. ed. Sudibjo Z.H. *Serat Sanasunu*, edition published by the Departemen Pendidikan dan Kebudayaan for its Proyek Penerbitan Buku Sastra Indonesia dan Daerah, Jakarta 1980.

WESTERN SOURCES

Archival

1. Algemeen Rijksarchief, The Hague

A. Reports of Governors of the North-East Coast for their Successors

Memorie van overdracht of van den Burgh for his successor Johannes Siberg, 1780 (Nederburgh Collection no. 381).

Memorie van overdracht of Johannes Siberg for his successor Jan Greeve, 18 September 1787 (Nederburgh Collection no. 382).

Memoie van overdracht of Jan Greeve for his successor P.G. van Overstraten, 1791 (Nederburgh Collection no. 384).

Memorie van overdracht of Pieter Gerard van Overstraten for his successor Johan Fredrik Baron van Reede tot de Parkeler, 1796 (Nederburgh Collection no. 386; s.a. van Alphen – Engelhard Collection 2nd section/ 1900, no. 191 and 192 [notes]).

Memorie van overdracht of Johan Fredrik Baron van Reede tot de Parkeler for his successor Nic. Engelhard, 1801 (van Alphen – Engelhard Collection nos. 191–2).

B. Nederburgh Collection

Nos. 309, 352, 365, 366 (Nederburgh's Consideratien over de Jacatrasche en Preanger Regentschappen en over de vraag of daeruit meerder verdelen voor de Comp. te trekken zijn dan thans geschied, 1796), 371, 389 (Korte schets van het Sulthans Hof op Java, by Wouter Hendrik van Ysseldijk, [also including a report made by Matthijs Waterloo, First Resident at the Yogyakarta court, to Nicolaus Engelhard, Governor of the North-East Coast 1793], 390, 395, and 396 (Pekalongan in 1798, by Rothenbuhler) Collection Nederburgh 396, ARA. Completed in Batavia on 23 November 1796.

C. Baud Collection

Nos. 993, 1021, and 1033.

D. *Collection Van Alphen – Engelhard*

2nd section, acquired 1900.
Nos. 78 (J. de Rovere van Breugel's report on Banten, 1787), 118 (P. Engelhard's journey through Java and the Preanger Regencies in May–August 1802), 169 (Siberg's journey to central Java and to Tegal and Pekalongan in 1781), 170 (report of Nierport, Gezaghebber of the Oosthoek, for his successor Barkeij in 1784). 171 (Siberg's diary of his journey to the Oosthoek in June–July 1784), 196 (Nicolaus Engelhard's journey from Semarang to Japara, Juana, Rembang, Madura and Banyuwangi and back, Sept.–Nov. 1802), 238 (Engelhard's journey from Semarang to Cirebon in 1806), 239 and 240 (reports by and for van den Berg, Solo and Jogjakarta 1806).

2nd section acquired 1916.
Nos. 74, 75, 80, 84, 97, 101–113, 117, 118, 149.
Mailrapporten 1890 no. 578; 1891 nos. 58, 320, 382, and 47; 1893 no. 197.

E. *Hoge Regering te Batavia*

Section XVI (Cirebon) nos. 999, 1000, and 1001.

F. *ARA First Section, Archives and collections of families and private persons*

Journals of several journeys through Java made by Abraham van Riebeck 1703–1713 (inventaris 1.10.45).

G. *Koloniaal Archief*

KA 3708, Vereenigde Ooost-Indische Compagnie Overgekomen Berichten [henceforth VOCOB] 1789, and KA 3754, VOCOB 1790, KA 3833, VOCOB 1792; also KA 3445, VOCOB 1784; KA 2802, VOCOB 1758; KA 3256, VOCOB 1773; KA 3859, VOCOB 1793.
Mailrapporten 1798 and 1801.

2. Koninklijk Instituut voor Taal-land- en volkenkunde, Leiden

Manuscript no. H [Hollands: Western language manuscript] 363, *Tractaten gesloten met de zelfbestuurders van Surakarta en Yogya Batavia 1755–1830.*

India Office

Mackenzie Private Collection nos. 2–10, 12, 13, 21, 24, 56, 74, 76, 79, 82 and 86.

Published

Abdullah bin Abdul Kadir, trans. A.H. Hill *The Hikayat Abdullah*, Oxford U.P., Kuala Lumpur and Singapore etc. 1970.
Abdurachman, Paramita R. *Cerbon*, Sinar Harapan, Jakarta 1982.
Ali, Mohammad "Historiographical Problems" in Soedjatmoko, Mohammad

Bibliography

Ali, Resink, G.J. and Kahin, G.McT. eds., *An Introduction to Indonesian Historiography*, Cornell Modern Indonesia Project, Ithaca 1965.

Allen, J.W. *A History of Political Thought in the Sixteenth Century*, Methuen (University Paperbacks) London 1960.

Altona, T. "Over den Oorsprong der Kalangs" TBG LXII (1923) pp. 515–547.

Andaya, Barbara Watson and Matheson, Virginia "Islamic Thought and Malay Tradition: the Writings of Raja Ali Haji of Riau (ca. 1809–ca. 1870) in Anthony Reid and David Marr eds., *Perceptions of the Past in Southeast Asia*, Heinemann (Asian Studies Association of Australia Southeast Asia Publications Series) Singapore 1979 pp. 108–128.

Andaya, Barbara Watson *To Live as Brothers: Southeast Sumatra in the Seventeenth and Eighteenth Centuries*, Honolulu, University of Hawaii Press, 1993.

Anderson, Benedict R.O'G. *Mythology and the Tolerance of the Javanese*, Cornell Modern Indonesia Project Monograph Series 1965.

Anderson, Benedict Richard O'Gorman *Imagined communities: reflections on the origin and spread of nationalism*. London: Verso, 1983 (revised and extended 2nd. edition Verso 1991).

Basso, Aldo P. *Coins, Medals and Tokens of the Philippines*, Menlo Park, Cal. Chenby, 1968.

Beeckman, Daniel, ed. Chin Yoon Fong *A Voyage to and from the Island of Borneo*, Dawsons of Pall Mall, Folkestone and London 1973.

Begin ende Voortgangh, van de Vereenighde Nederlantsche Geoctroyeerde Ooost-Indische Compagnie, vol. 1, *Historishe Verhael Vande Ryese gedaen inde Oost-Indien, met 15 Schepen voor Reeckeninghe vande vereenichde Gheoctroyeerde Oost-Indische Compagnie: Onder het beleydt van den Vroomen ende Manhaften Wybrandt van Waerwijck*, Amsterdam: n. p. [1644].

Behrend, T.E. "Kraton, Taman, Mesjid: A Brief Survey and Bibliographic Review of Islamic Antiquities in Java", *Indonesia Circle* 35, November 1984, pp. 29–55.

Behrend, T.E. "The Serat Cĕnṭini: A checklist of Manuscripts and Preliminary Ordering of Recensions", unpublished paper, A.N.U. 1986.

Behrend, T.E. *The Serat Jatiswara: Structure and Change in a Javanese Poem 1600–1930*, A.N.U. Ph.D. 1987.

Berg, L.W.C. van den "Het Mohammedaansche godsdienstonderwijs op Java en Madoera en de daarbij gebruikte Arabische boeken," *Tijdschrift voor Indsche taal-, land- en volkenkunde* 31 (1886) pp. 518–55.

—— *Inlandsche rangen en titels op Java en Madoera*, Landsdrukkerij, Batavia, 1887.

"Beschryving van her Koningryk Jaccara", VBG 1 pp. 19–41.

"Bijdrage tot de kennis der residentie Madioen", TNI 17/2 (1855) pp. 1–17.

"Bijdrage tot de kennis van de zeden en gewoonten der Javan" in TNI 1852, Part II, pp. 257–80, 346–67, 493–418, and 423–432 (the last pages being notes by Rouffaer); and TNI 1853 Part I, pp. 81–103.

Bleeker, P. "Statistisch-Ekonomische onderzoekingen en beschouwingen op koloniaal gebied", TNI second series 1/1 (1863) pp. 190–202.

—— "Nog iets over de vermeedering van Java's bevolking sedert 1785", TNI third series 3/2 (1869) pp. 488–90.

Blussé, Leonard *Strange Company: Chinese Settler, Mestizo Women and the Dutch in VOC Batavia*, VIKI 122, Foris Publications, Dordrecht, 1986.

Boomgaard, Peter "Buitenzorg in 1805", *Modern Asian Studies* 20/1 (1986) pp. 33–58.

—— *Children of the Colonial State: Population Growth and Economic Development in Java, 1795–1880*, Free University Press 1989.

—— "Java's Agricultural Production 1775–1875" in Maddison, Angus, and Prince, Gé eds *Economic Growth in Indonesia, 1820–1940*, VKI 137, Foris, Dordrecht, 1989.

Boow, Justine *Symbol and Status in Javanese Batik*, Asian Studies Centre, University of Western Australia Monograph Series no. 7, 1988.

"Het bouwen van Javaansche huizen", *Djawa* 4, 1924, pp. 105–117.

Boxer, C.R. *The Dutch Seaborne Empire 1600–1800*, Hutchinson (History of Human Society series), London, 1965.

Braudel, Fernand, trans. Kochan, Miriam *Capitalism and Material Life 1400–1800*, Weidenfeld and Nicolson, London 1967.

Brumund, J.F.G. "Het landbezit op Java", TNI 21/1 (1859) pp. 47–56 and 87–104.

Buckley, *An Anecdotal History of Old Times in Singapore: from the foundation of the settlement under the Honourable the East India Company, on February 6th, 1819 to the transfer to the Colonial Office as part of the colonial possessions of the Crown on April 1st, 1867*, University of Malaya Press, Kuala Lumpur, 1965.

Cannon, Garland *The Life and Mind of Oriental Jones: Sir William Jones, the Father of Modern Linguistics*, Cambridge U.P. 1990.

Carey, P.B.R. ed. *The Archive of Yogyakartha*, vol. 1: Documents relating to Politics and Internal Court Affairs, Oriental Documents III, British Academy Oriental Documents Committee, Oxford University Press.

—— *Babad Dipanagara: An Account of the Outbreak of the Java War (1825–30): The Surakarta court version of the Babad Dipanagara with translations into English and Indonesian Malay*, Malay Branch of the Royal Asiatic Society, Kuala Lumpur 1981.

—— "Changing Javanese Perceptions of the Chinese Communities in Central Java, 1755–1825", *Indonesia* 37 (April 1984).

—— "Waiting for the Just King: the Agrarian World of South-Central Java from Giyanti (1755) to the Java War (1825–30)", *Modern Asian Studies* 20/1 (1986) pp. 59–137.

Chalmers, Robert *A History of Currency in the British Colonies*, London, Eyre and Spottiswoode c. 1893.

Chaudhuri, K.N. *Trade and Civilisation in the Indian Ocean: An Economic History from the Rise of Islam to 1750*, Cambridge U.P. 1985.

"Cheribon in den goeden ouden tijd", TNI new series 8/2 (1979) pp. 161–218.

Chijs, J.A. van der *Nederlandsch-Indisch plakaatboek, 1602–1811*, 17 volumes, Landsdrukkerij, Batavia, 1885–1900.

Chirapat Prapandvidya, "The Sab Bāk Inscription: Evidence of an Early Vajrayana Buddhist Presence in Thailand", *Journal of the Siam Society* vol. 78, part 2, 1990, pp. 11–14.

Christie, Jan Wisseman "States Without Cities: Demographic Trends in Early Java", *Indonesia* 52 (Oct. 1991) pp. 23–40.

Couperus, Louis *De stille kracht: roman*, 13th edition, L.J. Veen, Hogeningen, 1974.

Bibliography

Craig, William D. *Coins of the World 1750–1850*, Racine, Wis., Whitman, 1966.
Crawfurd, John *A Descriptive Dictionary of the Indian Islands and Adjacent Countries*, Bradbury and Evans, London 1856.
Dapperen, J.W. van "Het Tegalsche Ruwat (Het Verlossen, bezweren van kwade invloeden)", *Djawa* 3, 1923, pp. 223–30.
—— "Volkskunde van Java IV", *Djawa* 16/4-6 pp. 172–86.
Dijk, C. van *Rebellion under the Banner of Islam*, VKI 94, Martinus Nijhoff, The Hague, 1981.
Dissel, J.A. van "Eenige bijgeloovigheden en gewoonten der Javanen", TNI third series 4/1 (1870) pp. 270–9.
Dobbin, Christine "Economic Change in Minangkabau as a Factor in the Rise of the Padri Movement, 1784–1830", *Indonesia* 23 (April 1977) pp. 1–38.
Drewes, G.W.J. *An Early Javanese Code of Muslim Ethics*, Bibliotheca Indonesica 18, The Hague, Martinus Nijhof, 1978.
Drijber, S.A. "Het Legioen van Mangkoe Negoro", *Indisch Miliair Tijdschrift*, 31, 7–12 (1910) pp. 306–11.
Eyck van Heslinga, E.S. van *Van compagnie naar koopvaardij: de scheepvaart-verbinding van de Bataafse Republiek met de kolonien in Azie 1795–1806*, Hollandse Historische Reeks 9, Amsterdam 1988.
Foucault, Michel *The Archaeology of Knowledge & The Discourse on Language*, trans. Sheridan Smith, A.M. Harper Torchbooks, New York 1972.
Furber, Holden *Rival Empires of Trade in the Orient, 1600–1800*, University of Minnesota Press (Europe and the World in the Age of Expansion series), Minneapolis 1976.
Gaastra, F.S. "De VOC in Azie, 1680–1795" in *Algemeene Geschiedenis der Nederlanden*, vol. 9 (1980) pp. 427–464.
Geertz, Clifford *Negara: The Theatre State in Nineteenth-Century Bali*, Princeton University Press 1980.
Geertz, Hildred "Indonesian Cultures and Communities" in Ruth R. McVey ed., *Indonesia*, Yale University/HRAF Press 1963.
"Het gemeenteleven op Java, in de inlandsche en de Europeesche maatschappij", TI 20/1 (1858) pp. 233–40.
Gericke, J.F.C. and Roorda, T. *Javaansch-Nederlandsch Handwoordenboek*, 2 vols. enlarged and amended by Vreede, A.C. and Gunning, J.G.H. Johannes Muller, Amsterdam and E.J. Brill, Leiden, 1901.
Gibb, H.A.R. and Kramers, J. eds. *Shorter Encyclopedia of Islam*, Ithaca: Cornell University Press 1957.
Gonda, J. *Sanskrit in Indoesia*, Sarasvati Vihar Series no. 28, International Academy of Indian Culture, Nagpur 1952.
Graaf, H.J. de *Geschiedenis van Indonesie*, van Hoeve, 's-Gravenhage/Bandung 1949.
—— "Titels en namen van Javaanse vorsten en grooten uit de 16e en 17e eeuw", BKI 109 (1952) pp. 62–82.
—— *De Vijf gezantschapreizen van Rijklof van Goens naar her hof van Mataram 1648–1654*, Martinus Nijhoff for the Linschoten-Vereeniging, 's-Gravenhage.
Graaf, H.J. de and Pigeaud, Th.G. Th. ed. Ricklefs, M.C. *Chinese Muslims in Java in the 15th and 16th centuries: The Malay Annals of Semarang and Cerbon*, Monash Papers of southeast Asia no. 12, Melbourne 1984.

Groneman, J. *De garĕbĕg's te Ngajogyakarta*, Martinus Nijhoff, The Hague 1895.

Guillot, Claude " Les Kalang de Java: rouliers et prêteurs d'argent", in Lombard, D. and Aubin, J. eds. *Marchands et hommes d'affaires asiatiques*. Paris, ed. EHESS 1988, pp. 267–77.

Haan, F.C. de "Naar Midden Sumatra in 1684", *Tijdschrift voor Indische taal, land, en volkenkunde* 39 (1897), pp. 340–53.

—— *Oud Batavia: gedenkboek uitgegeven door het Bataviaasch Genootschap van Kunsten en Wetenschappen naar aanleiding van het driehonderdjarig bestaan der stad in 1919*, 2 vols, G. Kolff, Batavia 1922.

—— *Priangan: de Preanger-Regentschappen onder het Nederlandsch bestuur tot 1811*, 4 vols., Bataviaasch Genootschap van Kunsten en Wetenschappen 1910–12.

Hageman, J. Jcz. "De Adipatti van Bezoeki op Java, 1811–1818 Historisch onderzoek", TNI second series 3/1 (1865) pp. 444–452.

—— "Geschied- en aardrijkskundig overzigt van Java, op het einde der achttiende eeuw, TBG IX, 1860, pp. 261–419.

—— "Namen de gewestelijke Europesche Gezaghebbers, enz., op Java en Madura", TBG XIII (1864) pp. 227–265.

Hall, D.G.E. ed. *Historians of South East Asia*, Historical Writings on the Peoples of Asia vol. 2, University of London, School of Oriental and African Studies, London, 1961.

Hardjodibroto, R. Soemantri "De wijzingen der gebruiken en gewoonten aan het Solosche hof", *Djawa* 11, 1931, pp. 159–170.

Harris, John, ed. *Navigantium atque Itinerantium Bibliotheca*, London: Bennet, 1705.

Hatta, Mohammad "Indonesia Free" in *Portrait of a Patriot, Selected Writings by Mohammad Hatta*, Mouton, The Hague, 1972.

Hefner, Robert W. *Hindu Javanese: Tengger Tradition and Islam*, Princeton U.P. 1985.

Herinneringen van Pangeran Aria Achmad Djadiningrat, Kolff, Amsterdam/ Batavia c. 1936.

Hoadley, Mason Claude *Javanese Procedural Law, A History of the Cirebon-Priangan "Jaksa" College, 1706–1735*, Cornell University PhD, University Microfilms 1975.

Hoevell, W.R. van "Onderzoek naar de oorzakken van het onderschied in voorkomen, kleeding, zeden en gewoonten, taal en karakter tusschen de Soendanezen en eigenlijke Javanen", TNI 4/2 (1842) pp. 132–69.

Hogendorp, C.S.W. de *Coup d'Oeil sur L'île de Java et Les Autres Possessions Néerlandaises*, C.J. de Mat, Bruxelles 1830.

Hooykaas, Christiaan *The Old Javanese Ramayana: an Exemplary Kakawin, as to Form and Content*, Akademie van Wetenschappen, Amsterdam, Afdeeling Letterkunde. Verhandelinen. Nieuwe reeks. Deel 65, no. 1, Noord-Holland Uitgevers Maatschappij, Amsterdam 1958.

Hopkins Terence K. and Wallerstein, Immanuel *Processes of the World-System*, vol. 3, *Political Economy of the World-System Annuals*, Sage Publications, Beverly Hills/London, 1980.

Houtsma, M.Th., Wensinck, A.J. et al., *The Encyclopedia of Islam*, Leiden, London: Brill/Luzac, 1934.

Bibliography

Hughes, Thomas Patrick *A Dictionary of Islam, being a Cyclopaedia of the Doctrines, Rites, Ceremonies and Customs, together with the Technical and Theological Terms of the Muhammadan Religion*, London, W.H. Allen n.d. (originally written c. 1886).

Inggris, "Het roewatanfeest in de desa Karangdjati in Bagelen", *Djawa* 3, 1923, pp. 45–50.

Jackson, Karl D. and Moeliono, Johannes "Participation in Rebellion: the Dar'ul Islam in West Java" in Liddle, R. William ed., *Political Participation in Modern Indonesia*, Yale University Southeast Asia Monograph Series no. 19, 1973.

Jasper, J.E. "Tengger en de Tenngereezen", *Djawa* 6 (1926) pp. 185–92 and 7 (1927) pp. 23–37, 217–237 and 291–304.

Jasper, J.E. and Pirngadie Mas *De Inlandsche Kunstnijverheid in Nederlandsch Indie*.

Jay, Robert R. *Javanese Villagers: Social Relations in Rural Modjokuto*, MIT Press 1969.

Jessup, Helen *Court Arts of Indonesia*, Asia Society Galleries in association with H.M. Abrams, c. 1990.

Jonge, J.K.J. de *De Opkomst van het Nederlandsch Gezag in Ooost-Indie*, Martinus Nijhoff, The Hague 1878.

Jorg, C.J.A. *Porcelain and the Dutch China Trade*, The Hague, Martinus Nijhoff, The Hague, 1982.

Kartodirdjo, Sartono *Protest Movements in Rural Java: A Study of Agrarian Unrest in the Nineteenth and Early Twentieth Centuries*, Oxford/Institute of Southeast Asian Studies Singapore, 1973.

Kartodirdjo, Sartono *The Peasants' Revolt of Banten in 1888*, VKI 50, 1966.

Kern, R.A. "Djakat Anak", BKI 103 (1946) pp. 547–553.

Ketjen, E. *Bijdrage tot de geschiedenis der Kalangs op Java"*, TBG XXVII (1883) pp. 185–200.

Knebel, J. "A Propos d'armes et d'autres objets désignés par les Javanais sous les norms de Kyai, Njai, Poen et Si, Kuämpiehan et Kasiat. Croyances populaires et traditions", TBG xl (1898) pp. 239–286.

—— "De Kalang-legende volgens Tegalsche lezing", TBG xxvii (1894) pp. 489–515.

Knight, Roger "The Indigo Industry and the Organisation of Agricultural Prodution in Pekalongan Residency, North Java, 1800–1850", paper presented at the fourth national conference of the Asian Studies Association of Australian, Monash University, May 1982.

Koentjaraningrat *Javanese Culture*, Institute of Southeast Asian Studies, Singapore, O.U.P. 1989.

Koesoemo Joedo, P.A. "Het Javaansche Voorerf", *Djawa* 4, 1924, pp. 147–8.

Koloniale Verslag, 's-Gravenhage, Departement van Kolonien, 1868–1923.

Kraemer, H. "Het Instituut voor de Javaansche Taal te Soerakarta: Bijdrage tot de geschiedenis van de studië van het Javaansch" *Djawa* 12/6 (Dec. 1932) pp. 261–5.

Kroef, Justus M. van der *The Dialectic of Colonial Indonesian History*, C.P.J. van der Peet, Amsterdam 1963.

Kromodjojo Adinegoro, R.A.A. "Begraafplaatsen der Oude Bupatien van Grisee voor, tijdens en na Compagnies Tijd", *Djawa* 5, 1925, pp. 253–7.

Kumar, Ann *Diary of a Javanese Muslim: Religion, Politics and the Pesantren*

Java and Modern Europe

1883–1886, Faculty of Asian Studies Monographs, New Series no. 7, Australian National University, Canberra 1985.

—— "Javanese Court Society and Politics in the Late Eighteenth Century: the record of a Lady Soldier: Part II: Political Developments: the Courts and the Company 1784–1791", *Indonesia* 30 (October 1980), pp. 67–111.

—— "Javanese Historiography in and out of the Colonial Period" in Reid, Anthony and Marr, David eds, *Perception of the Past in Southeast Asia*, Asian Studies Association of Australia Southeast Asia Publications Series no. 4, Heinemann 1979, pp. 187–206.

—— "Literary Approaches to Slavery and the Indies Enlightenment: Van Hogendorp's Kraspoekol", *Indonesia* 43 (April 1987) pp. 43–65.

—— *Surapati, Man and Legend: A Study of Three Babad Traditions*, Australian National University Centre of Oriental Monograph Series no. 20, Leiden, E.J. Brill 1976.

—— "The 'Suryengalagan Affair' of 1883 and its Successors: Born Leaders in Changed Times" *BKI* 138/2-3 (1982).

—— "A Swedish View of Batavia in 1783–4: Hornstedt's Letters", *Archipel* 37 (1989) pp. 247–82.

Kunst, Jaap *Music in Java: Its History, Its Theory, and Its Technique*, The Hague, Nijhoff, Third Edition, 1973.

Kussendrager, R.J.L. *Verzameling van oudheden en derzelver fabelachtige verhalen in de Residentie Passaroeang met een geographische beschrijving dier residentie en eene kaart*, P.N. Dupain, Rotterdam 1843.

"De laatste investiture van eenen Bantamschen Sulan", BKII 1856 pp. 363–98.

Leur, J.C. van *Indonesian Trade and Society: Essays in Asian Social and Economic History*, W. van Hoeve, The Hague/Bandung, 1955.

Lieberman, Victor "Some Thoughts on Mainland-Archipelagic Patterns during the "Last Stand of the Indigenous States", c. 1750–1850", in Reid, *Last Stand*.

Louw, P.J.F. and de Klerck, E.S. *De Java-Oorlog van 1825–30*, 6 vols., The Hague: Nijhoff, 1894–1909.

Louw, P.J.F. *De Derde Javaansche Successie Oorlog* (Batavia: Albrecht Rusche, 1889).

Luard Lieut.-colonel John *A History of the Dress of the British Soldier, from the Earlies Period to the Present Time*, London, William Clowes and Sons, 1852.

Macdonald, Duncan B. *Development of Muslim Theology, Jurisprudence and Constitutional Theory*, New York (Scribner) and London (Routledge) 1926.

Maddison, Angus "Dutch Income in and from Indonesia, 1700–1938" in Maddison, Angus and Prince, Gé *Economic Growth in Indonesia, 1820–1940*, VKI 137, Foris, Dordrecht 1989, pp. 15–41.

Manguin, Pierre-Yves "The Merchant and the King: Political Myths of Southeast Asian Coastal Polities", *Indonesia* 52, Oct. 91, pp. 41–54.

Mangunwijaya, Y.B. trans. Hunter, Thomas M. *The Weaverbirds*, Jakarta, Lontar 1991.

Markham, Albert Hastings ed., *The Voyages and Works of John Davis*, London, Hakluyt Society, 1889.

Maurenbrecher, E.W. "Sintren en Lais in Cheribon", *Djawa* 20 (1940) pp. 119–21.

Bibliography

Meinsma, J.J. "Over de tijdrekenning bij de Tenggerezen", BKI 27 (1878) pp. 131–150.
McCusker, John J. *Money and Exchange in Europe and America 1600–1775: A Handbook*, Williamsburg, Va., University of Carolina Press 1978.
Moertono, Soemarsaid *State and Statecraft in Old Java: A Study of the Later Mataram Period, 16th to 19th Century*, Cornell Modern Indonesia Project Monograph Series, Ithaca, N.Y. 1963.
Mook, H.J. van "Koeṭa Geḍe", *Koloniaal Tijdschrift*, 15 (1926), pp. 353–400.
Nagtegaal, Luc *Rijdende op een Hollandse Tijger: De noordkust van Java en de VOC 1680–1743*, Proefschrfift, Rijksuniversiteit te Utrecht, 1988.
Nes, J.F.W., van "De Chinezen op Java", TNI 13/1 (1851) pp. 238–53.
Netscher, E. and van der Chijs, J.A. *De Munten van Nederlandsch Indie*, VBG 31/2 Batavia, Lange 1864.
Niel, Robert van "Rights to Land in Java", in Alfian, T. Ibrahim. Koesoenanto, H.J., Hardjowidjono, Dharmono and Suryo, Djoko *Dari Babad dan Hikayat sampai Sejarah Kritis, Kumpulan Karangan dipersembahkan kepada Prof. Dr. Sartono Kartodirdjo*, Gajah Mada University Press 1987, pp. 120–153.
Niemann, G.K. "Over het geloof aan gelukkige en ongelukkige tijden", BKI 17 (1890) pp. 133–141.
Ong-Tae-Hae trans. W.H. Medhurst *The Chinaman Abroad; An Account of the Malayan Archipelago, particularly of Java*, London, 1850.
Oxford University Press, Historical Writings on the Peoples of Asia series.
Paulus, J., et al., eds. *Encyclopaedie van Nederlandsch Oost-Indië*, 2nd ed., 8 vols., Leiden, E.J. Brill, 's-Gravenhage, Martinus Nijhoff, 1917–1939.
Peacock, James L. *Rites of Modernization: Symbolic and Social Aspects of Indonesian Proletarian Drama*, University of Chicago Press 1968.
Perron-de Roos, E. "Correspondentie van Dirk van Hogendorp met zijn broeder Gijsbert Karel", BKI 102 (1943) pp. 125–273.
Pigeaud, Th. "Alexander, Sakèndèr en Sénapati", *Djawa* 7, 1927, pp. 321.
—— *Java in the Fourteenth Century*, KITLV Translation Series 4/4, The Hague, Martinus Nijhoff 1962, vol. IV.
—— *Javanese volksvertoningen: bijdrage tot de beschrijving van land en volk*, Batavia, Volkslectuur, 1938.
—— *Literature of Java: Catalogue Raisonné of Javanese Manuscripts in the Library of the University of Leiden and Other Public Collections in the Netherlands*, vol. II, *Descriptive List of Javanese Manuscripts*, The Hague, Martinus Nijhoff, 1968.
—— *De Serat Tjabolang en de Serat Tjentini: Inhoiudsopgaven*, Verhandeling van het Koninklijk Instituut LXXII/2, Bandoeng, A.C. Nix, 1933.
Poerbatjaraka, R.M.Ng. Voorhoeve, P. and Hooykaas, C. *Indonesische Handscrhiften*, Bandung, Nix, 1950.
—— *Kapustakan Djawi*, Jakarta, Djambatan, 1957.
—— Nītiçastra: Oud-Javaansch tekst met vertaling, Bandung, A.C. Nix, 1933.
Ponder, H.W. *Javanese Panoroma: A Further Account of the World's Richest Island with Some Intimate Pictures of Life Among the People of its Lesser Known Regions*, London, Seeley Service n.d.

Purwalelana, Raden Mas Arya *Lampah-lampahipun*, Lands-drukkerji, Batavia 1865-6.
Raffles, Thomas Stamford *The History of Java*, 2 vols., Oxford in Asia Historical Reprints, Oxford University Press, Kuala Lumpur/London/New York 1965. [reprint of 1817 edition]
Ras, J.J. *Hikajat Bandjar: A Study in Malay Historiography*, Bibliotheca Indonesia (KITLV), The Hague, Nijhoff, 1968.
Realia: Register op de Generale Resolutien van het Kasteel Batavia 1632–1805, The Hague, Martinus Nijhoff, 1886.
—— ed., *The Last Stand of Asian Autonomies: Responses to Modernity in the Diverse States of Southeast Asia and Korea*, Basingstoke, Macmilla, forthcoming 1997.
—— "A New Phase of Commercial Expansion in Southeast Asia, 1760–1850" (p. 3) in Reid, *Last Stand*.
Reid, Anthony J.S. *Indonesian National Revolution 1945–50*, Longman, Studies in Contemporary Southeast Asia, Melbourne 1974.
—— *The Last Stand of Asian Autonomies: Responses to Modernity in the Diverse States of Southeast Asia and Korea*, Basingstoke, Macmillan, forthcoming 1997.
Reinwardt, C.G.C. ed. de Vriese, W.H. *Reis naar het oostelijk gedeelte van den Indischen Achipel in het jaar 1821*, Frederik Muller, Amsterdam 1858.
Remmelink, W.G.J. *Emperor Pakubuwana II, Priyayi and Company, and the Chinese War*, Proefschrift, Leiden 1990.
Reynolds, Clark G. *History and the Sea: Essays on Maritime Strategies*, University of California Press 1989.
Ricklefs, M.C. *A History of Modern Indonesia: c. 1300 to the present*, Macmillan Asian Histories Series, London 1981.
—— *Jogjakarta under Sultan Mangkubumi 1749–1792: A History of the Division of Java*, London Oriental Series no. 30 (School of Oriental and African Studies), Oxford University Press 1974.
—— *Modern Javanese Historical Tradition: A Study of an Original Kartasura Chronicle and Related Materials*, SOAS, London 1978.
—— "Some Statistical Evidence on Javanese Social, Economic and Demographic History in the Later Seventeenth and Eighteenth Centuries", *Modern Asian Studies*, 20/1 (1986).
—— *War, Culture and Economy in Java 1677–1726: Asian and European Imperialism in the Early Kartasura Period*, ASAA Southeast Asia publications series no. 2, Sydney, Allen and Unwin 1993.
—— and Voorhoeve, P. *Indonesian Manuscripts in Great Britain*, Oxford University Press, London 1977.
Rinkes, D.A. "De Heiligen van Java III", TBG LIII 3/4, pp. 269–300.
Robison, Richard *Indonesia: The Rise of Capital*, Asian Studies Association of Australia, Southeast Asia Publications Series no. 13, Sydney etc. 1986.
Roff, William R. *The Origins of Malay Nationalism*, New Haven and London, Yale University Press, 1967.
Ronkel, Ph.S. van 'Aangeteekeningen over Islam en folklore in Westen en Midden-Java', BKI 101 (1942) pp. 311–339.
—— *De roman van Amir Hamza*, E.J. Brill, Leiden 1895.
Roo de la Faille, P. de "Uit de Oude Preanger", BKI 100 (1941) pp. 415–24.

Bibliography

Rouffaer, G.P. "Vorstenlanden", *Adatrechbundels*, 134 's-Gravenhage, Martinus Nijhoff (1931).

Rovere van Breugel, J. de "Bedenkingen van den staat van Bantam", BKI, new series, I (1856) pp. 110–169.

—— "Beschrijving van Bantam en de Lampongs", BKI, new series, I (1856) pp. 309–362.

Sakurai, Yumio "Abandoned Villages in the Red River Delta in the 18th and Early 19th Century" in Reid, *Last Stand*.

Schafer, Edward H. *The Vermilion Bird: Tang Images of the South*, Berkeley and L.A., California U.P. 1967.

Schrieke, B.J.O. *Indonesian Sociological Studies*, vol. 2 and 3 of Selected Studies on Indonesia by Dutch Scholars published for the Royal Tropical Institute, Amsterdam, W. van Hoeve, The Hague and Bandung 1955 and 1957.

Schulte Nordholt, Henk "De jago in de schaduw: misdaad en 'orde' in de koloniale staat op Java" *De Gids* 146, 1983, pp. 664–675.

Selberg, E. *Reis naar Java en bezoek op het eiland Madura*, n.d. n.p.

Seltman, Friedrich *Die Kalang: Ein Volksgruppe auf Java und ihre Stamm-Mythe: Ein Beitrag zur Kulturgeschichte Javas*, Stuttgart, Franz Steiner, 1987.

Sieraden en lichaamsversiering uit Indonesia, Volkenkundig Museum Nusantara, Delft 1984.

Snouck Hurgronje, C., trans. O'Sullivan, A.W.S. *The Achehnese*, 2 vols., Leyden, E.J. Brill, 1906.

—— ed. Wensinck, A.J. *Verspreide Geschriften*, 6 vols., Bonn and Leipzig, Kurt Schroeder, 1923–7.

Soehari, S. "Pinggir", *Djawa* 9 (1929) Parts 4–5, pp. 160–8.

Stapel, F.W. *Corpus diplomaticum Neerlando-Indicum*, BKI 96 (1938) and vol. 5, vol. 6, The Hague, Martinus Nijhoff, 1955.

Stavorinus, John Splinter Esq., trans. Samuel Hull Wilcocke, *Voyages to the East-Indies*, vol. 1 (*A Voyage to the Cape of Good Hope, Batavia, Bantam, and Bengal, with Observations on Those Parts, etc. in the years 1768–1771*), London, G.G. and J. Robinson, 1798.

Stern, Philippe *L'art du Champa (ancien Annam) et son evolution*, Toulouse, Les Frères Douladoure, 1942.

Sukarno "Towards the Brown Front" in *Under the Banner of Revolution*, vol. i, Publications Committee Djakarta 1966, pp. 33–6.

Sutherland, Heather "Notes on Java's Regent Families" Part I, *Indonesia* 16, (October 1973) pp. 113–147.

Sutherland, Heather A. and Bree, David S. "Quantitative and Qualitative Approaches to the Study of Indonesian Trade: The Case of Makassar" in Alfian, T. Ibrahim Koesoenanto, H.J., Hardjowidjono, Dharmono and Suryo, Djoko *Dari Babad dan Hikayat sampai Sejarah Kritis, Kumpulan Karangan dipersembahkan kepada Prof. Dr. Sartono Kartodirdjo*, Gajah Mada University Press 1987, pp. 369–408.

Sutherland, Heather, *The Making of a Bureaucratic Elite: The Colonial Transformation of the Javanese Priyayi*, Asian Studies Association of Australia, Southeast Asia Publications Series no. 2, Singapore, Heinemann, 1979.

Taylor, Jean Gelman *The Social World of Batavia: European and Eurasian in Dutch Asia*, Madison, Wis., University of Wisconsin Press 1983.
Temple, R.C. ed. *The Travels of Peter Mundy 1608–1667*, 5 vols. Cambridge, Haklyut Society, 1907–1936.
Tirtakoesoema, S. "Tumplek Punjen", *Djawa* 19 (1939) pp. 89–93.
"De toestand van Bagelen in 1830", TNI 20/2 (1858) pp. 65–84.
Trimingham, J. Spencer *The Sufi Orders in Islam*, Oxford, Clarendon Press, 1971.
Trocki, Carl A. "Chinese Pioneering in Eighteenth Century Southeast Asia" in Reid, *Last Stand*.
—— *Prince of Pirates: The Temenggongs and the Development of Johor and Singapore 1784–1885*, Institute of Southeast Asian Studies/Singapore University Press 1979.
Valentijn, François, *Oud en Nieuw Ooost Indien, vervattende een naauwkeurige en uitvoerige verhandelinge van Nederlands mogentheyd in die gewesten, benevens een wydlustige beschryving der Moluccos, Amboina, Banda, Timor, en Solor, Java, en alle de eylanden onder dezelve landbestieringen vehoorende; het Nederlands Comptoir op Suratte, en de levens der Groote Mogols; als ook een keurlyke verhandeling van 't wezentlykste, dat men behoort te weten van Choromandel, Pegu, Arracan, Bengale, Mocha, Persien, Malacca, Sumatra, Ceylon, Malabar, Celebes of Macasser, China, Japan, Tayouan of Formosa, Tonkin, Cambodia, Siam, Borneo, Bali, Kaap der Goede Hoop en Mauritius.* 5 vols., 1724–1726.
Veth, P.J. *Java, Geographisch, Ethnologisch, Historisch*, Haarlem, Erven F. Bohn, 1875–1882.
"Vorstenlanden: Gegevens betreffende bestuur en rechtspraak in het prinsdom Mangkoenagaran (1867–1913)," *Adatrechtbundels*, 25 (1926) 's-Gravenhage, Martinus Nijhoff, pp. 70–104.
"Vorstenlanden: Gegevens," *Adatrechtbundels*, 25 (1926), pp. 75–76 and 91–92).
Vuldy, Chantal *Pekalongan: Batik et Islam dans une ville du Nord de Java*, Etudes insulindiennes/Archipel 8, Editions de l'Ecole des Hautes Etudes en Sciences Sociales, Paris 1987.
Wallerstein, Immanuel *The capitalist world-economy*, Cambridge University Press/Editions de la Maison des Sciences de l'Homme, Paris.
—— *The Modern World System: Capitalist Agriculture and the Origins of the World Economy in the 16th Century*, Studies in Social Discontinuity, Academic Press, New York/London 1974.
Wertheim, W.F. *Indonesian Society in Transition*, W. van Hoeve, The Hague, 1964.
Williams, Michael Charles *Communism, Religion and Revolt in Banten*, Ohio University Monographs in International Studies, Southeast Asia series no. 86, 1990.
Winter, C.F. "Instellingen, gewoonten en gebruiken der Javanen te Soerakarta," TNI 5, (1843) pp. 459–86, 546–613 and 690–744.
Winter, C.F. Sr. "Javaansche overleveringen", BKI LV (1903) pp. 403–441.
Winter, [C.F.] "Oorsprong van het zoogenoemde Kalang-volk", TNI 2/2 (1839) pp. 578–88.
Winter, J.W. "Beknopte beschrijving van het hof Soerakarta in 1824," BKI 54 (1902), pp. 15–172.
Woodside, Alexander "Political Theory and Economic Growth in Late Traditional Vietnam" in Reid, *Last Stand*.

Bibliography

Yusuf, Achmad "Pasren dalam rumah adat Jawa", Jakarta Museum 1982.

Zerubavel, Eviatar *The Seven Day Circle: The History and Meaning of the Week*, University of Chicago Press 1989 (original edition, The Free Press 1985).

Zwart, Ir.W. "De Kalangs als houtkappers in dienst der Compagnie" TBG LXXIX (1939) pp. 252–261.

Index

Abul Nazar Muhamad, Sultan 262–3
Abu'l-Fath 'abdu'l-Fattah *see*
  Ageng, Sultan
Aceh 29, 49
Adiarsa 234, 294, 297, 303–4, 308, 313
Adikusuma, Tumenggung Rangga
  303
Adilangu 225
Adinagara, Mas Tumenggung 226
agar-agar, Lampungs 276
Ageng, Sultan 240, 258–9, 285
agriculture: irrigation 246, 253; cash
  crops 198; corvée obligations 174,
  197, 239, 281, 287, 329–32, 341;
  Cultivation System 251–2, 284,
  321, 350, 432, 435; Madura 216;
  post 1795 growth 249–50; rites
  121–2; slash-and-burn 258;
  village hierarchy 173; *see also*
  individual crop
Agung, Sultan 29, 178, 395, 397
Airlangga 397
Aji Saka 179
Aji, Sultan 259
alcohol: *arak* 95, 224–5, 244; Islam
  99; *Sasana Sunu* 405
Amand, C.C.A. 437
Amangkurat I 232
Ambonese 386
Amidjaja, Sastra 125–6, 127
Andaya, Barbara 28
Anderson, Benedict Richard
  O'Gorman 440
Anom, Sultan 231

Antaboga 156
Arabs: cultural influence 176–7;
  Pekalongan 352
arak 95, 224–5, 244
aristocracy: and VOC 194; Banten
  262–5, 284–5; blood 431; Islam
  441–2; peasants 433; protocol 79;
  Sasana Sunu 401–10; *see also*
  Regents
Arjanagara, Tumenggung 215
Arjuna 114–15, 160
Arungbinang, Tumenggung 394,
  424
Asiatic Council 25–6
Astradinata, Kyai Aria 263
Aswatama 405, 416–17, 426–7

Babad Tanah Jawi 144, 147, 158, 159
Balambangan 35, 178, 207–8, 209,
  210–13
Balambangan War 210, 212
Bali: Balambangan 35; calendar 156;
  Javanese influence 27, 28;
  Pangeran Patih 254
Balinese, Nusa Baron 208
bamboo, Banten 275
Bandung 235; coffee 293, 295, 302;
  cotton thread 297; indigo 296;
  Regent 305, 307
Bangil 213
Bangkalan 206, 216, 218
bango tulak cloth 132–3
Banten 258–85; Chinese account 377;
  Dutch effect on 434; Javanese

Index

culture 4; pepper 271–3; *sĕlir* 62; Valentijn's survey 16; VOC acquisition 34; VOC tributes 240–1
Banyumas 68–9, 70
Banyuwangi 206, 207, 210–11
Basa Endara 145
Batang 226–7, 322; corvée labour 329, 330–1; piracy 204; population 327–8; Regent's income 325–6, 327; taxation 344–6
Batara Angsoar 148
Batara Basuki 153
Batara Bayu 149
Batara Bisma 154
Batara Bok Werang 152
Batara Brama 140, 151
Batara Candra 149
Batara Endra 404
Batara Gana 150
Batara Guru 140, 145, 146–7, 159, 160, 404
Batara Indra 151
Batara Kala 119–20, 140, 151, 160
Batara Kresna 160
Batara Maharsi 149
Batara Sakri 153, 156
Batara Sambu 150
Batara Siwa 153
Batara Tantra 152
Batara Termuru 145
Batara Wisnu 140, 146, 152
Batari Durga 154
Batavia: *arak* 224–5; China tea trade 24–5; Chinese settlers 32, 41, 193, 199–201, 375–6; modern state 13; new markets post 1795 248–9; timber shipping 197; tin 25; trade prices 198–9; VOC conquest 29; VOC Office 232–40; VOC policy 193
Batavian Environs 232, 238–40, 244–5
Batavian Republic 25
batik 352, 353, 407, 427
Batara Guru, Dewi Uma 160
Batulayang 235; coffee 293, 295, 303; cotton thread 297; Regent 305, 307, 312
baturs, taxation 338–40, 342–3, 344–5
Baud, J.C. 201–2

Bawean 219
Beaulieu, Augustin de 49
Behrend, T.E. 130
Besuki 206, 207, 209
bincilan 131–3
"bird people" 287
birds' nests, Lampungs 276, 278
birth, ceremonies 112, 182
birthdays 57, 96–7, 131, 182–3
Blussé, L. 12, 32
Bogor *see* Buitenzorg
Boja Nagara 271
Bonang, Sunan 414–15
Boomgaard, Peter 207, 251, 264; *batur* 338; deforestation 246; ethnography 267–8; monetization 318; taxation 346, 347
Boxer, C.R. 354
Bratanagara, Tumenggung 215
Braudel, F. 8, 9–13, 14, 29, 258, 354
Brebes 230
Buddhism, calendar 141–2
Budiah movement 352–3
buffaloes, Banten 275
Buginese 260, 351
Buitenzorg 236–7, 292–3, 297–8, 312
Buminata, Pangeran 55, 82
Bumis 288, 297
Bupatis *see* Regents
Burgh, Governor J.R. van den 68, 195, 198–9, 212–13, 219, 226

Cabolang, Ki 90–3
cacah 69, 254, 287, 336, 361
Cakradiningrat, Raden Tumenggung 217–18
Cakradiningrat IV 216
Cakradiningrat VII, Panembahan Adipati 218
Cakranagara, Raden Tumenggung Panji (Raden Haji Sigaar) 230
Cakraningrat III, Tumenggung 424
Cakraningrat IV, Tumenggung 393, 424
calendar 131–3, 139–58
Candrakirana 384
Candranegara, Tumenggung 215
cardamom 250, 298
Carey, Peter 169, 241–2, 438

Cengkalsewu 222–3
Ceringin 274
Chaudhuri, K.N. 1, 7, 22–3
childbirth 116, 132
children: betrothal 268; clothing 369; exorcisms 118–19; *kuncung* (forelock of hair) 186; rites of passage 112–13
China: British trade 24; demography 8–9; monetarization 12, 37; technology 10; towns 12, 13; US trade 25
Chinese settlers: Banten 261, 273, 278, 281; Batavia 32, 41, 193, 199–201, 375–6; Buitenzorg 237; Captains 381; Cirebon 34–5, 231–2; Dutch view 372, 437–8; Eastern Salient 208; entrepreneurs 199–201, 209; ethnography 374–82; Javanese account 385; leaseholders 206, 209; money 198; opium 278; Pekalongan 322, 351, 353; private trade 250; rice trade 31; sailors 197; Semarang 224; taxation 201; Ulujami 228–9; VOC policy 30
Chinese War (1740) 32–3, 54, 416, 417
Christie, Jan Wisseman 180
Cianjur 236; coffee 292–3, 298, 301–2; products 297–8; Regent's accounts 304–5, 306–7, 312, 313, 317
Ciasem 234, 294, 297, 304, 308, 312
Cininga 231
circumcision 63, 112–13, 115, 136, 176, 183, 186
Cirebon: cardamom 298; coffee 244; Priangan 233; report 196; revolts 34–5; Valentijn's survey 16; VOC acquisition 30; VOC tributes 231–2
Citra Wati *see* Dewi Sri
Citrasuma, Tumenggung 221
clothing: *awisan* 108; *badong* 101; Banten 266–7; Chinese account 378; Dutch account 368; of Imam 162; pregnancy 116; Priangan 291; restrictions 108; *Sasana Sunu* 407–8, 427–8; tourneys 134
cock fighting 78–9
coconut oil 246, 274

coconuts 358
Coen, J.P. 237
coffee 244; Balambangan 35; Banten 273; Cianjur 298; importance 354, 363; introduction 31; payment system 299–301, 314–16; Priangan 288–9, 292–6, 299–304, 309–10, 354–5; price 309–10; problems with cultivation 250; production figures 244, 249; VOC policy 248
Compagnie des Indes Orientales 22
concubines 49, 62–3, 99; *see also sĕlir*
coral, Banten 275
Cornets de Groot, A.D. 111–18, 121–77, 182, 202, 418
corvée labour 174, 197, 239; Banten 281; Pekalongan 329–32, 341; Priangan 287
cotton 242, 245, 251, 256; Banten 274–5; Batulayang 305; Pekalongan 323–4; Priangan 288, 296–8; production figures 250
Cramer, C.H. 272–3
creation myths 157
crime, punishment 78, 107–8
cubeb 230, 245, 255
Cultivation System 251–2, 284, 321, 350, 432, 435
curcuma, Priangan 299

Daendels, – 76, 259
damar, Lampungs 277
dance 64–7, 97–8, 101–2, 136–7
Danureja, Patih 228
Danureja I, Patih 393
Dapperen, J.W. van 119–20, 348
Dasa Muka 160
Dasa Rata 160
death 116–17; auspicious days 131; Banten 270; graveyards 126; Islam 176; Tenggerese ritual 179
debts, Javanese custom 385
deforestation 10, 31, 41, 220, 246
Delegate for Native Affairs: behaviour to peasants 371; corruption 315; income 308–9; moneylending 316, 317; Regents' debts with 313–14

Index

Demak 31, 199, 225
Dersa Nala 160
Dewa Ditia Kawaca 160
Dewa Sadana 122
Dewas 159
Dewi Bandan Dari 160
Dewi Basa Endari 145, 160
Dewi Budru Bumi 160
Dewi Dara (Dewi Sinta) 145
Dewi Dari (Dewi Landep) 145
Dewi Gangga Wati 160
Dewi Gannggi Hara 160
Dewi Indra Narum 160
Dewi Kumalaram 160
Dewi Landep 145–6
Dewi Lasmadari 160
Dewi Naga Gini 160
Dewi Naga Wati 160
Dewi Prawi 160
Dewi Rauwati 160
Dewi Sekandi 146
Dewi Sekar Taji 116
Dewi Srengeni Wati 160
Dewi Sri 121, 122, 128–31, 140, 145–6, 155, 160
Dewi Srinadi 160
Dewi Tara 160
Dewi Tari 160
Dewi Uma 160
Dewi Wantnu Hara 160
Dewi Wiratna 160
Dipati, Pangeran *see* Mangkunegara I
Diradamet 66, 102
divination 147–58, 163
divorce 115, 170, 269
Djaka Sudana 121
Dutch: behaviour 373–4; Chinese account of 379, 381–2; ethnography 367–74; Javanese account 386–7, 389–90, 439–40; Javanese language 201–2; present giving 87; view of history 398; *see also* Vereenigde Oost-Indische Compagnie

earthquakes, divination 163
East India Company (British) 22, 23, 25
East India Company (Dutch) *see* Vereenigde Oost-Indische Compagnie
Eastern Salient 35, 205–6, 207–19
education 169, 175–6, 181
Eka Laya 160
Engelhard, Governor Nicolaus 35–6, 196, 250
English: Chinese account 379–80; Javanese account 387; Javanese language 201–2; Lampungs 241; opium trade 382; pepper 272; trade deregulation 376; *see also* East India Company
ethnicity 178–80, 224, 367–99
exorcism 118–21

fasting 162, 186
First World War, Pekalongan 353
fishing, Banten 276
food: Banten 266; Chinese account 377; Dutch view 369; fasting 162, 186; Priangan 359; religious meals 166–7; *Sasana Sunu* 408–9
Foucault, M. 14–15
Fourth Anglo-Dutch War (1780-1784) 17, 24, 25, 197
France, Napoleonic Wars 18–19
French settlers 380, 387
funeral rites 117
furniture 266, 369, 378

Gagar Mayang 160
Gajah Mati 178, 179
Galuh 231
gambling 239
games 134–6, 137–8, 369
gamelan 97, 101, 109, 185; Islam 406, 419; tourney 134, 135; types 138–9; weddings 113, 188–190
Garebeg Besar 59, 98
Garendi, Raden Mas 54
Gatut Kaca 160
Gebang 231
Gede, Aria Rangga 301
Geertz, Clifford 28, 87–8
Geertz, Hildred 258
Geseng, Sunan 348
ghosts 348–9

463

Giri, Sunan 91
Glonggong 222
gods 159–61; exorcism 120–1; Tenggerese 184; *wuku* calendar 147–56, 186
Goens, Rijklof van 48–9
gold-dust, Lampungs 276–7
Goldbach, Arnold 207
Governors of North-East Coast: *Memorieen* 195; 205–231
Graaf, H.J. de 36
Great Britain: monetarization 37; Napoleonic Wars 18; smuggling 24; thalassocracy 39; *see also* East India Company; English
Greeve, Governor Jan 52–3, 78, 195, 196; coffee 244; Mangkunegara I 86–7, 99, 101; Pakubuwana IV's marriage 108
Gresik 4, 111–177, 207, 214–15
Grinding 237, 304, 306
griya agĕng, offering 132
Guntur, Raden Mas (Wirameja) 395
Gunung Kidul 70

Haan, F. de 38
Hageman, J. Jcz. 217, 237
Hall, D.G.E. 391, 397
Hamzah b. 'Abd al-Muṭṭalib 49, 95
Han Boey Ko 209
Han Hin Song 208
Han Tjampit 209
Haren, Onno Zwier van 285
Hartsinck, Andries 86
harvest, taxation 175
Heekeren, J.H. van 283
Hendradi 160
hierarchies 372–3, 413
Hinduism: calendar 142–3; cultural influence 177; exorcism 120–1; gods 159–61; Kalangs 180; Tenggerese 179; tradition 415–16; *wuku* calendar 158
Hogendorp, Dirk van 40, 195–6, 207, 221, 373
Hopkins, T.K. 36–7
houses 369; Banten 261–2, 265–6; construction 127–8; division 124–6;

kratons 53; *pasren* 127, 128–31; positions 123–4

Ijen, Mt. 35
Imhoff, Governor-General von 33
India: demography 8, 9; monetarization 12; towns 12, 13
Indian Muslims 385–6
Indic tradition 418
indigo 251; Banten 273; Batulayang 305; forced labour 197; introduction 31; Mangkunegara I 76; Pekalongan 324, 350–1; Priangan 288, 296–8, 309–10; production figures 246, 250; unpopularity 350–1, 356
Indonesia 430; Chinese trade 24; circumcision 183; Western view 443–4
Indrajit 160
Indramayu 231
Inggris 118–19
irrigation 246, 253
Islam 369–70; alcohol 99; auspicious days 131; Banten 262–3, 270–1, 285; calendar 144; Chinese account 381; Chinese War 32–3; *ḍikir* 97; fasting 186; food 408–9; Gresik 161–7; Javanese gods 161; and kingship 396, 419, 442; Mangkunegara I 57–60; military element 430–1; monetarization 11–12; Pekalongan 352; priests 163–7; prophets 60, 98; rites of passage 176; *Sasana Sunu* 400–5; Shi'ism 167; slaves 178; technology 10, 11; Tenggerese 179; times of the day 141; urbanization 13
ivory, Lampungs 277, 278
Iyang Kuwera 154

Jabung Kala 156
jaguran 135
Jakarta: *see* Batavia
jakat 164–6
Jakatra, Valentijn's survey 16
Jakatra Lands 237–40, 298
Jambi 28
Jampang, coffee 301–2

Index

Jangrana, Adipati 393
Japan: demography 9; monetarization 12; towns 13
Japara 205, 206, 221
Jasper, J.E. 141, 184
Jati Ngarang 133
Java War (1825-30) 1, 200, 431, 441
Javanese language 201–2
Javanese Wars of Succession 29–30
Jay, Robert R. 121–2
Jayadiningrat, Raden Adipati 228
Jayadirana, Tumenggung 214
Jayadirja, Tumenggung 215
Jayadiwirya, Tumenggung 228
Jayanagara, Tumenggung 212
Jayanegara, Tumenggung 229
Jayaningrat, Patih 84–6
Jayaningrat I, Tumenggung 227–8
Jayaningrat II, Tumenggung 228, 393, 424
Jayavarman II 27
Jayengrana, Tumenggung 228
Jones, Sir William ("Oriental") 181
jung 104, 322–3, 336–7
Juwana 223

kacang 232, 247
Kaduwang 70
Kaki Among 120–1, 132
Kalangs 178, 178–80, 254, 323
Kali Yuga 416–17
Kalisangara 416–17
Kaliwungu 226
Kama 160
Kampung Baru 236
kapok, Banten 275
Karangjati, exorcisms 119
Kartayuda, Aria 304
kaum 97
kayu soga, Banten 274
Kediri 169, 437
Kendal 226
Kertanegara 213
kingship: Islam 402, 419, 442; Javanese view 382–3, 394, 396; military element 430–1; *Sasana Sunu* 414
Klatak 212
Knight, Roger 328

Koentjaraningrat 119
Korea, demography 9
kraton: fire 53, 96; Mangkunegara I 53–7; *pasren* 130–1
Krawang 234; coffee 294, 303; cotton thread 297; Regent's accounts 306, 308, 312, 313
Kroef, Justus M. van der 439
Kudanawarsa 394
Kudus 221–2
Kuning, Sunan 54
Kusuma, Pangeran Raja 263

labour 31, 196–8; corvée 174, 197, 239, 281, 287, 329–32, 341; migration 355; peasant attitude 311–12; Pekalongan 329–32, 341; Priangan 288; recompense 332–6; VOC demands 432–4
lais 160–1
Lamajang 207, 212
Lamongan 167, 168, 207, 214, 215
Lampungs: Banten 240, 241; cotton 274; English 241, 272; opium 278; pepper 271, 272; products 276–7; religion 270; salt 275
land: classification 124–6; corvée obligations 197; Sultan of Banten 281–2; taxation 69–72, 104, 175
Landep 160
language 111, 201–2
Lasem 220
laws, Banten 269–70
Leijden, J.C. 202
Leur, J.C. van 435
Lieberman, Victor 201
Limbangan 231
Ling-ling Mendana 159
literature 89–93, 399–400
logging, production figures 246
loro blonyo 129–30
ludruk 185

Macan Putih 35–6, 42
Madati 160
Madiun 102, 169
Madura 216–18; emigration 168, 208; Governors 205; green *kacang* 247; Valentijn's survey 17; VOC

465

acquisition 30; VOC office 206; *see also* Bangkalan
Maha Yakti 148
Mahamarti 132
Majapait 27–8, 131–3
Major Cĕnṯini 88–9, 110, 121
Makassarese, Semarang 225
Malang (Supit Urang) 207, 212–13
Malays: artillery 11; Banten 260; Chinese account 380; Javanese account 385–6; piracy 380, 382; Semarang 224, 225
Malaysia: circumcision 183; Javanese influence 27–8
mancanagara 69–71, 77
Mandarese 272, 278
Mangkubumi, Sultan of Yogyakarta 82, 396; Javanese view 392; Mangkunegara I 54–6, 102; marriage 108; surrender 34; *tapa* 395
Mangkukusuma, Raden Tumenggung 222
Mangkunegara I, Pangeran Adipati 34, 47–88; birthday 96–7; Chinese 200; household 61–7; *kraton* 53–7; Kudanawarsa 394; Mangkubumi 102; money 68–77; presents 86–8; *tapa* 395; *wahyu* 416
Mangkunegara, Pangeran Arya 53
Mangkunegara V 107
Mangkunegara VI 107
"Mangkunegaran Legion" 76
Mangkurat II 29, 30
mangsa 142
Mangunwijaya, Y.B. 130
marriage: ages 183; Banten 268–9; concubines 62, 99; customs 113–15, 136; harvest festival 121; infidelity 170; Kalangs 178–9; and *kuncung* 186; matrilocal tradition 377–8, 382; *paningsĕt* 106–7, 192; permission 174; Pinggir 178–9; polygamy 115, 369; ritual 176; royal 77–8; VOC policy 283; wedding procession 188–90
Marxism, Banten 285
Mas Said *see* Mangkunegara I
Mataram 241–2; Babad Tanah Jawi 158; Eastern Salient 207; female guard 47, 48–9; Giri 91; influence in Asia 28; Javanese Wars of Succession 29–30; Mangkubumi 56; Mangkunegara I 53–88; partition 34; power 40–1; rebellion 417; unification of Java 29; Valentijn's survey 16; VOC 29–31
Mataram, Pangeran Surya 77
Matesih 70
Maurenbrecher, E.W. 160
Mayang Sari 159
medicine 370, 374
Megatsari, Raden Tumenggung Aria 222
Megatsari, Tumenggung 222
Meirop, Lieutenant Pieter 210
Melayukusuma 207
Menak 49–50, 95, 98
Mengwi, Balambangan 35
migration 288–9, 355, 433
military forces: arms 10–11; fear of military service 208; female guard 47–53; Governor of Java 203; Mangkunegara I 63–4, 71; navy 197, 202–4, 216; Pekalongan 330–2; priests 64, 101; rulers 430; salaries 73; taxation 71; VOC levies 197, 330–2; wage bills 75
Minangkabau, coffee 354
monetarization 11–12, 37; Banten 280; Pekalongan 347; Priangan 318; VOC effect on 436
money: Chinese 198; goods in kind equivalents 69; inflation 37, 243; Javanese systems 73–4; Priangan 359; shortage 198–9; Spanish 103–4, 106
morality 169–70
"Multatuli" 285
Mundy, Peter 49
music 99, 101, 109, 369; dance 136–7; instruments 186; *see also* gamelan
mythology 159–61

nabi 60, 98
Nabi Kilir 98
Nagagini 156

Index

nagara agung 69–71, 77
Nagtegaal, Luc 30
Nakula 160
names, childhood 112
Napoleon 18–19
Natadiningrat, Raden Tumenggung 226
Natakusuma, Adipati 228
Natakusuma, Pangeran 216
Natapraja, Raden Tumenggung Aria 222
nationalism 440
navy: Eastern Salient 216; VOC 202–4
Nawang Kain 160
Nawang Sih 160
Nawang Wulan 121, 133, 159–60, 179
Nederburgh, S.C. 196, 286–21
Netherlands: economic development 20–1; growth 23; revolution 21; technology 9; thalassocracy 39; towns 13
Ngantang 212–13
Ngenis Kyai Ageng 60
Niel, Robert van 337
Nini Among 120–1, 132
Nini Lodaya 120
Nini Sentani 120
Nini Towong game 161
Nitidiningrat, Adipati 212
Nordholt, Henk Schulte 437
North-East coast 205–231
Numpangs 288–9, 297, 338
Nurcahya 159
Nusa Baron 207, 208, 212
Nyai Lara Kidul *see* Queen of the South Seas

officials 170–2, 172–3, 187
Ong Tae Hae 374–82
Oosthoek *see* Eastern Salient
opium 201, 239; Bandung 305; Banten 268, 278; British trade 24; Chinese 232, 378–9; Gresik 170; Priangan 291; *Sasana Sunu* 406
Orang Dagang 268
Overstraten, Pieter Gerard van 195–6, 200, 201, 202–3; Bangkalan 218; Banyuwangi 211; Besuki 209; Cengkalsewu 222–3; census 205; cotton 245; indigo 246; Kendal 226; Lamongan 215; Malang 213; military forces 203; rice 243; Semarang 224; Sumenep 217; Tuban 220

Padmanagara, Pangeran 63
Pagaden 234, 294, 297, 312
Pajang 98
Pajangkungan 220
Pakubuwana I, Sunan 30, 216, 232
Pakubuwana II, Sunan 33–4, 54, 216, 241
Pakubuwana III, Sunan 34, 55, 68, 78, 424
Pakubuwana IV, Sunan: arts 390; Chinese 200; court life 79–86; Mangkunegara I 57, 87; marriage 78; Wulang Reh 403
Palembang, Javanese influence 28
Palm, W. A. 36, 42–3, 219
Palo 220
Pamalang 229–30
Pamanukan 234, 294, 297, 312, 313
Pamarden 68, 69, 70
Pamekasan 217–18
Panarukan 206, 207, 209
Panca Resmi 149
Panca Sila 2
pandang, Banten 274
Pandeglang 258
paningsĕt 106–7, 113, 192
Panjer 68, 69, 70
Panji 177, 384
Parakanmuncang 235; coffee 293, 295, 303, 310; cotton thread 297; indigo 296; jurisdiction 287; Regent's accounts 305, 307, 312
pasisir: culture 177; Dutch effect on 435
pasren 127, 128–31
Pasuruhan 208, 212
Pati 222
Patih, Pangeran 254
Peace of Amiens 25
Pekalongan 226–9, 321–54; corvée labour 329–32; migration 433; radicalism 442; Regent's income

467

324–5, 327; rice 432; VOC offices 205, 206
penance *see tapa*
Penatayuda, Adipati Singasari 303
pepper: Banten 258, 263, 264, 271–3, 279, 280, 354; effect on rice cultivation 28; forced labour 197; Lampungs 276; Mangkunegara I 76; Priangan 296, 309–10; problems with cultivation 250; production figures 245, 250
Perang Cina *see* Chinese War
petroleum 246
Petruk 146
Pigeaud, Dr. Th. G. Th. 89, 93
pinang, Banten 273
Pinggir 178
piracy 11, 202–5, 278–9, 280, 380, 382, 436
polygamy 115
Ponder, H.W. 114–15
Ponorogo 102
population: Asia 8–9; Balambangan 35, 207–8; Banten 240, 260, 281; Batang 327–8; Cornets de Groot 167–8; decrease 371; growth 34; North-East coast 205; Pekalongan 327–8; Valentijn's survey 16; Wiradesa 327–8
Porong 212
pottery, Banten 275, 357
Praba Sini 160
Prabalingga (Banger) 207, 209, 217
Prabu Dasa Muka 160
Prajurit Balambangan 178
prajurit estri corps 47–53, 430
Prang Wadana, Pangeran *see* Mangkunegara I
Prawiradingrat, Tumenggung 211
Preanger lands *see* Priangan
pregnancy 116, 384
presents: Bupatis 174–5; Mangkunegara I 86–8; marriage 113, 114
Priangan 285–321; coffee 244, 249, 292–6, 299–304, 354–5; Dutch effect on 434–5; smallpox 169; VOC acquisition 30; VOC tributes 232–6

priests: divorce 170; Islam 162, 163–7; soldiers 64, 101; upkeep 175
Princely Lands 241–2
Princeneiland 276
Pringgalaya, Raden 393, 424
priyayi see aristocracy
pucuk, Banten 274
Puger 211, 212
Pulau Panjang 260–1
Purbanagara, Pangeran *see* Suryakusuma
Purbaya, Pangeran 80–1, 84–6, 109

Queen of the South Seas (Nyai Lara/Loro Kidul, Ratu Sagara Kidal) 120, 185, 349

Raffles, Thomas Stamford 111, 133, 140–1, 143, 201, 373, 393
Rangga, Pangeran 423
ranks of office 170–3, 187
Ratih 160
rattan 275, 276
Ratu Sagara Kidul *see* Queen of the South Seas
Ratu Sarifa 34
Reede tot de Parkeler, John Fredrik Baron van 196, 199, 200, 203, 224
Regents: and VOC 194; annual journey to Semarang 174–5; birth of a child 112; Chinese entrepreneurs 199–200; conflict with VOC officials 351; debts 341–2, 361; Dutch effect on 435; Eastern Salient 207; Javanese view 383–4; marriage 113, 114; military forces 203–4; officials 170–2; Pakubuwana I 31; payment system 299–301; residence 123–4; *Sasana Sunu* 414; taxation 70, 174; tourney 134, 135; VOC jurisdiction 33–4; VOC labour demands 31; VOC offices 206; VOC policy 313; *waringin* trees 123
Reid, A.J.S. 23, 250
Reksapraja, Tumenggung 221
Rembang 205, 206, 219–21
Remmelink, W.G.J. 33, 42

Index

Residents: local knowledge 196; reports 3; taxation 72
resistance, Eastern Salient 207
Reynolds, Clark G. 39
rice: Banten 274, 284; Chinese entrepreneurs 199; division of labour 121–2; efficiency of cultivation 27; goddesses 160; harvest 121, 290; maintenance 289–90; measures 183; offerings 132; overall production 243–4; Pekalongan 322–3, 432; Prabalingga 209; Priangan 291–2; taxation 72; types of cultivation 358
Ricklefs, M.C. 31, 32, 34, 36, 75, 156–7
Rifangi, Haji 352–3
Rijck, Commandant Adriaan van 179, 212
rites of passage 112–17, 176
Robison, Richard 353–4
Roff, William R. 423
ronggeng 136, 185
Rothenbuhler, Frederik Jacob 207, 228, 250–1, 321–54
Rouffaer, G.P. 68, 69–70, 109
Rovere van Breugel, Jonkheer Jan de 259–85

Sadana, Kajang 155
Sadana, *pasren* 130
Sadewa 160
sailors, VOC levy 197, 204
salt production 247
saltpetre production 247
Saluwat, Raden Mas 63
sandalwood, Banten 274
Sang Hyang Tunggal 159
Sang Hyang Wenang 159
Sang Marmarti 132
Sang Yang Arsi Narada 145, 146–7
Sang Yang Giri Nata *see* Batara Guru
santri, soldiers 64, 101
santri lalana 89–93
Sarekat Islam 435
Sasana Sunu 397–8, 399–419
Schophofft, Hendrik 207

science 14–15, 181–2
Secadiwirya 219
Segala Erang 231
Seh Malayu 414–15
Selastri 160
Selberg, E. 373–4
sělir 62–3, 64–5, 99
Semar 146
Semarang 223–5; annual journey of the Bupatis 174–5; cardamom 298; corvée labour 330, 331, 332; garrisons 203; survey 202; VOC acquisition 30; VOC offices 205, 206
Sena 160
sěntong těngah see pasren
Serang 258
Si Rawung 348–9
Siberg, Johannes 195, 199–200, 213, 229, 245
sickness 116–17, 159, 168–9, 187, 370, 374
Sidayu 114, 167, 168, 207, 214, 215
siluman (ghosts) 348–9, 362
Sindureja, Raden Adipati 393, 424
Singasari, Ingabei Panji 222
Singasari, Pangeran 54
Sinta *see* Dewi Sri
sintren 160–1, 186
Siti Jenar, Seh 401
Siyung Wanara 405, 426
slavery: Balambangan 207; Banten 269, 282; Chinese account 377; Islam 178; pirates 279; *sělir* 62; western abolition 19
smallpox 169, 236, 282, 329, 378
smuggling 217; Balambangan 35; Banten 278–9, 280; Bawean 219; gold-dust 277; opium 278; tea 24–5
Snouck Hurgronje, C. 162, 183
Soehari, S. 178
soldiers *see* military forces
Sri *see* Dewi Sri
states, creation 21–2
Stavorinus, John Splinter 368–74
Subali, Raja 160
Sufism 401
sugar 244–5; Banten 273; Batavian Environs 239; Chinese settlers 32;

469

Pekalongan 324, 351; production increase 249; VOC policy 248
Suharto, President, *tapa* 397
Sukapura 231
Sukarno 440
Sukasih 160
sulphur 35, 247, 250, 277
Sumadiwirya, Tumenggung 226
Sumanagara, Tumenggung 226
Sumanegara, Regent of Pekalongan 228
Sumatra, VOC 29
Sumawikrama, Tumenggung 223
Sumbadra 115
Sumedang 235; coffee 293, 294, 295, 303, 310; cotton thread 297; indigo 296; jurisdiction 287; Regent 286, 305, 307, 312, 313
Sumenep 202, 216–17
Sunda Strait 260
Sundanese 230, 231
Supit Urang *see* Malang
Supiyah, Raden Ayu 77
Supraba 160
Suraadiwija, Tumenggung 213
Suraadiwikrama, Rangga 211
Surabaya 207, 214–15
Suradiningrat, Raden Tumenggung of Kudus 222
Suradiningrat, Regent of Demak 222
Suradiningrat, Tumenggung of Sidayu 215
Suradipura, Tumenggung 220
Surakarta: foundation 13; Islam 202; Mangkunegara I 47–88, 54, 55–6; military post 242; society 77–88; Sunan's lands 241
Suramenggala, Pangeran 273
Suranagara, Tumenggung 303
Surapati 30, 396
Surengrana, Aria 303–4
Surianatakusuma, Adipati 303
Suryakusuma, Raden (later Pangeran) 77, 86–7
Suryamerjaya 86–7
Suryaningrat, Suwardi 399
Sutadilaga, Aria 304
Suwanda, Patih 393

Suwarti 160
Suwiskar 160

taledek 185
Tampa Uni (Dewi Srinadi) 160
Tan Jok 228
Tan Lekko 228
tandak 136–7
Tangerang 237–8, 304, 306, 308, 312
tapa 159, 394–7, 403–4, 408, 442
Tapa, Kyai 34, 240
taxation: Banten 281–2; Batang 344–6; Batavian Environs 239–40; Chinese 201; Chinese entrepreneurs 200; corruption 77; Gresik 174; Islam 164–6; land 69–72, 201; Pekalongan 327, 337–42; tax-collectors 411–12; Wiradesa 342–3
tea 24–5, 354
technology 9–11, 14, 181
Tegal 119, 205, 206, 230
temples: Banten 270; childbirth 116; marriage 113; position 123; prayers 161–2
Tengger, times of the day 141
Tenggerese 179, 180
textiles 245; *bango tulak* cloth 132–3; Banten 274–5; batik 352, 353, 407, 427; *see also* cotton
Teylingen, Th. van 230
thalassocracies 39
theatre, *ludruk* 185
"theatre state" 87–8
Thousand Islands 260
Tilutama 160
timber: deforestation 10, 31, 41, 220, 246; Pekalongan 324; VOC corruption 31; wood-fleets 204
times of day 139–42
tin, Batavia 25
Tirtakusuma, Raden 223
Tirtawiguna 393, 424
tobacco 247, 251, 292
tooth filing 113, 166, 176
tourneys 134–5
towns 12–15
transport: coffee 294–6; rice 243–4

Index

travel: tolls 200; VOC control 198, 382
Trenggalek 87
tripang, Lampungs 276
Tritra Gatra 154
Trocki, Carl A. 422
Trunajaya 417
Tuban 220–1
Tulang Bawang 271, 272, 276–7
Tunjung Biru 160

Ulujami 228–9, 323, 332
Umar Maya 98
Umbgrove, J.L. 196, 230, 231
United States of America 25
urbanization 12–15

vaccinations 169, 236, 282
Valentijn, François 15–17, 38, 49
Vereenigde Oost-Indische Compagnie (VOC): administrative divisions 205–42; Ageng 258–9; autocracy 193; Balambangan 35; Banten 34, 258–60; Batavia 29, 193; Chinese settlers 30, 32–3, 200–1; Cirebon 34–5, 231–2; decentralisation 434; decline 23–4; early military encounters 29–31; Eastern Salient 207–19; evolution 22, 23; governor reports 194–6; Japara Office 221–3; labour demands 31, 197, 356, 432–4; Mangkunegara I 54–6, 68, 71, 76; matchmaking 108; migration policy 288–9; military forces 202–4; Pakubuwana IV 79–86; payment system 299–301, 314–16; Pekalongan Office 226–9; policy changes 248, 249; policy on Regents 313; presents 86–7; Priangan 285–6; private trade 24; profits 41, 200; protocol 79; Rembang Office 219–21; Semarang Head Office 223–9; State takeover 25; sumptuary regulation 79, 402; tea 24–5; Tegal Office 229–31; total produce 242–8; tribute 204–5
Veth, P.J. 436–7
village government 172–3

villages: Banten 265–6; Pekalongan 328; ranks and titles 172–3; tax-collectors 411–12; taxation 69
VOC *see* Vereenigde Oost-Indische Compagnie
Vorstenlanden 241–2, 243
Vriese, W.H. de 42

wahyu 415–16, 428–9, 442
walat 394, 424–5
wali 60, 98
Wallerstein 20–2, 36–7
Wanayasa 294, 297
Wardati 160
warfare, technology 10–11
waringin trees 122–3
Warsiki 160
Warwijk, Admiral Wybrandt van 49
Watu Gunung 136, 144–7, 157, 177
wayang 102, 135, 136–8, 184, 440
weapons: Banten 267–8; Mangkunegara I 63–4; technology 9–10
weeks: *bincilan* 131–2; *wuku* calendar 157–8
weights and measures: *amet* 105; *bau* 104; *cacah* 69, 254, 287, 336, 361; *gantang* 183; *jung* 104, 322–3, 336–7; *koyan* 41
Wertheim, W.F. 193
Wicara Kĕras 390–99, 406–7, 419
Widadaris 145–6, 159–60
Wikkerman, Johan Cezar van 211
windu cycle 143–4
Winter, C.F. Sr 111
Wiradesa 228, 322, 326–8, 329, 331–2, 342–3
Wiraguna, Tumenggung 210
Wirameja, Raden 395
Wiranatakusuma, Adipati 302
Wirasaba 86–7
Wiratanudatar, Adipati 301
Wiryakusuma, Kyai Aria 273
Wiryanagara, Tumenggung 227
Wisesa 159
women: circumcision 63; clothing 267; concubines 62–3, 99; cotton spinning 245; court diarists 52–3; divorce 115; inheritance 374;

471

marriage customs 113–15; *prajurit estri* corps 47–53, 430; pregnancy 116, 384; rice cultivation 121–2
wuku calendar 144–58, 179, 185–6, 406
Württemberg, Hartoch van 203, 224

Yang Asmara 149
Yang Kama Jaya 150
Yang Luratna 151
Yang Maha Dewa 148
Yang Singa Jalma 155
Yang Yama Dipati 147
Yasadipura I 390, 403, 419

Yasadipura II 390–420, 433, 441
Yogyakarta: Chinese leaseholders 201; creation of Sultanate 34, 56; female guard 48; forced labour 197; foundation 13; Mangkunegara I 102; Sultan's lands 241; taxation 77
Ysseldijk, Wouter Hendrik van 201
Yusuf, Achmad 129–30
Yusup 112, 113, 114

zakat 412, 428
Zerubavel, Eviatar 157
Zheng He 362